Public
Budgeting
and
Finance

Readings in Theory and Practice

Public Budgeting and Finance

Readings in Theory and Practice

EDITED BY

Robert T. Golembiewski

UNIVERSITY OF GEORGIA

F. E. PEACOCK PUBLISHERS, INC., ITASCA, ILLINOIS

TABLE OF CONTENTS

PREFACE

It is a useful administrative truism that where one sits often determines what one sees and how one reacts. Thus it was for me. I had long been concerned with the lack of useful teaching materials in Public Administration. Rather than doing much about this basic need, I indulged my own long-run romance with theoretical and applied behavioral analysis relevant to organizations. As Academic Director of the MPA Program at the University of Georgia for the last several years, however, the lack of teaching materials became of far more immediate concern. At U. of G. we are attempting to provide up-to-date training—what I fancy as the training of "professional generalists" with broad *and* deep competencies—and we are providing that training for students at the University center and throughout the state. We see ourselves concerned not only with quality training, but also with training in large numbers. The ready availability of teaching materials is vital to achieving such ambitions.

Public Budgeting and Finance is one of several attempts to provide teaching materials for our use and, hopefully, for the use of others. There seems no question that the need exists. Consider only a single point. Derived from the same motivation as the present collection, a comprehensive set of readings suitable for graduate and undergraduate courses in Public Administration has already appeared.[1] The wide acceptance of that publication reinforces three beliefs underlying this volume. First, I feel Public Administration as an area of specialization gives every indication of rising beyond its "topping-out" point reached after World War II. Second, I feel that unparalleled demands for professional training in Public Administration will be increasingly made on those of us in our nation's colleges and universities. My friend, Dean Stephen Bailey of Syracuse, foresees at least a ten-fold multiplier at work; I agree with his prediction. Third, I feel that conveniently available teaching materials can serve as a valuable catalyst for the present ferment affecting research and teaching in the arts and sciences of public management.

At least two other aids to teaching in Public Administration will appear. A reader in public personnel is still some time off. However, *Perspectives on Public Management: Cases and Learning Designs* will be published about the same time as the present volume.[2]

---

[1]Robert T. Golembiewski, Frank Gibson, and Geoffrey Y. Cornog, eds., *Public Administration: Readings in Institutions, Processes, and Behavior,* Chicago: Rand McNally & Company, 1966.

[2]Robert T. Golembiewski, ed., *Perspectives on Public Management: Cases and Learning Designs,* Itasca, Ill.: F. E. Peacock Publishers, Inc., 1968.

Such an effort patently rests on diverse research and publishing talents. It is at once humbling and challenging to attempt to give some pattern to the products of these many talents. I have tried to act as a cutter and setter of gems in this case, selecting among the richness of voluminous literatures and striving to bring out the particular features of individual pieces by providing appropriate settings.

However successful my efforts at craftmanship, meeting the present challenge was at least eased for me in several senses. Thus I took advantage of early conversations with my colleagues, Drs. Frank Gibson and Ira Sharkansky, in developing the general format and coverage of the volume. In addition, Mrs. Sigrid Saunders was an invaluable aid in giving tangible order and form to my editorial decisions. Carol Holcomb, Lane Howell, and Mrs. Jennie Rogers provided the massive clerical and typing skills necessary for any such effort. The efforts of Philip Rosenberg also deserve note.

Robert T. Golembiewski

Athens, Georgia
June 30, 1967

CHAPTER I

SOME CONCEPTUAL CONTEXTS OF

PUBLIC BUDGETING AND

FINANCE:

WHAT?   HOW WELL?   BY WHOM?

Public budgeting and finance patently encompass a broad range of diverse phenomena, but that breadth and diversity can only be suggested here. However inadequate it must be, we cannot avoid the attempt here to indicate in conceptual terms some of what is meant by the term "public finance and budgeting." Three focal questions preoccupy this attempt: What is it? How well are we able to do what is required? and Who should do it? The perspective here is intentionally broad. Subsequent chapters will add much detail.

The "what" of public budgeting and finance here is given some initial content by two pieces that focus on the possible uses of financial data. The contributions, respectively, are drawn from Stedry and Simon and his associates. In turn, the two contributions add conceptual meaning to "budgeting" and microscopically detail the uses of financial data.

Andrew C. Stedry's "Budgets: Definition and Scope" provides some important variations on the theme of budgets as an instrument of control as well as a plan of action. Stedry's discussion of "standards" and "standard costs" also is useful, for to "plan" and "control" require some estimate of how much of which resources are required for specific objectives. Thus budgets require commitment to some total figure as well as to its component standards. "Standards" or "standard costs" imply what is to be demanded in work for some sum of dollars. For example, a department in a university may have a large budget for salaries, but if the faculty-student ratio is high also, this implies a standard that many professors may find unattractive even though their salaries are quite pleasing. Directly, budgeting and finance must motivate individuals to strive to meet a total budget as well as induce them to accept its component standards.

Despite their brevity, the excerpts from Stedry establish that the "what" of public budgeting and finance encompasses many phenomena at the heart of the management of men and the coordination of cooperative behavior. Only a little interpretation makes the matter clear. Thus the "plan" aspects of budgeting and finance require that their processes must lean toward the future, and embody and reflect some sense of things as they might be improved or as they would be at their best. The "plan," however, cannot command total attention. The "control" aspects imply that the processes of public budgeting and finance also must rest upon a strong sense of things as they are, or as they might be at their worst. Avoiding the worst, while attempting to permit the best, this is a human challenge of heroic dimensions. Just that challenge rests very near the central phenomena of public budgeting and finance.

Despite their value, the comments from Stedry certainly do not even begin to suggest the manifold characteristics of the "what" of public budgeting and finance. Simon and his associates provide some of the additional conceptual detail in an excerpt on "Management Uses of Figures" from their book Centralization vs. Decentralization in Organizing the Controller's Department. Basically, they argue that three types of questions must be considered by any comprehensive program of the "internal reporting" of financial data. According to Simon, these three types of questions are: (1) Score-Card Questions, that is, questions such as "Am I doing well or badly?"; (2) Attention-Directing Questions, that is, those such as "What problems should I look into?"; and (3) Problem-Solving Questions, that is, questions such as "Of the several ways of doing the job, which is the best?". Patently, these questions relate to both the planning and control aspects of financial reporting stressed by Stedry.

In their own way, the three types of questions isolated by Simon and his collaborators sharply imply the centrality of the phenomena associated with public budgeting and finance. This point will be illustrated only. Thus Score-Card Questions patently must play a crucial role in every organization. That is, organizations have as their basic purpose the effective utilization of collective resources. "Are we doing well or badly?" consequently must be of central organizational concern. Providing appropriate answers to Score-Card Questions is, however, not only a central need. Perhaps more important, the processes of providing those answers are very delicate ones indeed. Directly, budgeting and finance personnel could easily come to be seen as punitive because of their basic and traditional role. They provide answers to Score-Card Questions; and they provide those answers to top management to control those at lower levels.

Hence the dual importance of giving extensive and successful attention to Attention-Directing Questions and Problem-Solving Questions. Two factors suffice to develop the point. First, answers to these two types of questions can be helpful at many levels of organization. In providing such answers, and particularly in providing them directly to lower levels of organization, finance and

2

budgeting officials can help compensate for the punitiveness inherent in some of their other activities such as providing answers to Score-Card Questions. Second, financial and budgeting officials apparently are less active in seeking answers to the latter two types of questions, and particularly to Problem-Solving Questions. No doubt the traditional concern with Score-Card Questions helps explain this inactivity, for his traditional concern implies that the internal financial reporters would be less equipped and motivated to handle such questions. In addition, answering Problem-Solving Questions requires working closely with officials at all levels, while budgeting and finance personnel typically identify more closely with top management. Finally, officials at various management levels who had been disciplined via answers to Score-Card Questions would be reticent to accept or ask for help. That is, to ask for or to accept help potentially risks providing "inside information" to budgeting and finance officials which in turn may be used against the manager.

The main thrust of the excerpts from Simon may be brought to a firm point. The three types of questions involving financial data highlight the breadth and diversity of public budgeting and finance. That significance extends from providing data about the effectiveness of performance all the way to providing these yardstick data in helpful and humane ways.

Given the scope of the phenomena relevant to public budgeting and finance, their underlying theory and its associated arts provide little comfort. Aaron Wildavsky's "Political Implications of Budgetary Reform" makes both points effectively. Thus Wildavsky notes that the insistent and long-standing demands for "better budgeting" involve far more than technical tinkering. The proposed reforms, he notes, "inevitably contain important implications for the political system, that is for the 'who gets what' of governmental decisions." At the same time, Wildavsky notes that significance must be paired with humility concerning our present ability to design a budget system adequate to distribute the appropriate "whats" to the proper "whos." Thus he concludes of the "normative theory of budgeting" that "we know very little about it." Even greater humility is in order about our capability to change the political system so that it will support the budget system of grand design.

Some of the major theoretical difficulties facing public budgeting and finance may be summarized. Directly, complaints about the budgetary processes face a task of incredible complexity. That is, changes in those processes rest significantly upon changes in the underlying political system of which existing budget practices are but one reflection. Wildavsky illustrates the point well by noting some of the roadblocks facing "orthodox recommendations" for change such as those of Arthur Smithies. These recommendations argue for a comprehensive review of the budget by a single person or by some small, cohesive group. Our political institutions, however, tend to generate many centers of power, which are often hostile to the orthodox recommendations.

Given major theoretical difficulties of coping with the phenomena of public budgeting and finance, control over public expenditures becomes an issue of enormous significance. That issue cannot be accorded just treatment in this volume—indeed, not in a dozen volumes of the present size—but two useful perspectives on control over public expenditures can be provided economically. William Jump, a reknowned finance officer in the Department of Agriculture, provides one line of insight in hearings before the House Appropriations Committee. Basically, Jump emphasizes certain inherent administrative features that limit the probability of padding or overstaffing. Overhead controls by financial officials in positions such as his have their place, he explains. Eagle-eyed legislators can also make a major impact. But the most powerful forces toward efficient use of public funds inhere in the program drives of government executives. The active official has so many good ideas for programs, that he must necessarily utilize men and money wisely. If anything, understaffing will be the crucial problem, for resources typically will be inadequate to do all of what the eager program official would like to have done. Moreover, the program official must justify his own demands for whatever resources are available in often-pointed competition with other program executives about who is likely to get the most mileage out of any funds. Thus part of the control over public expenditures comes from the individuals charged with spending them. This is a happy outcome indeed.

The tough-minded reader might be impressed only in part by Jump's thesis. Even if all program executives are as eager as Jump implies, his argument still applies only to spending whatever is made available. The control of the level of expenditures, of how much should be made available, is at least as important a matter. This implies no criticism of Jump, for control of the level of expenditures sorely challenges anyone's analysis. In his own way, indeed, Jump reflects the difficulty of controlling the level of expenditures. Thus he clearly notes his respect for the strong tendency of program executives to resist anyone—even Jump—who "meddles" with their budgets! In short, attempting to control the level of expenditures hits Administrative Man where he hurts. Financial decisions influence not only the size of programs which he supports, but also help determine whether an organization is "dying" or "on the move," with implications extending from doing today's job badly all the way to ineffective recruiting that implies long-run failure. The influence of decisions about the level of expenditures extends from what an agency can be today all the way to what it will be in the future.

However, if Parkinson's jaunty argument has even a very approximate validity,[1] concern about the level of expenditures is more or less pointless. Expenditures will rise as fast as income does, goes the central core of Parkinson's argument, and public expenditures may rise even faster than income. The point may be put otherwise. What goes up in this case, in sum, is not likely to come down. Wars encourage sharp rises in the level of public expenditures, and peacetime never quite seems capable of reversing the trend toward massive spending. Expenditures still chase after income, even if they do not surpass it.

---

[1]C. Northcote Parkinson, *The Law and the Profits*, Boston: Houghton Mifflin Co., 1960, especially pp. 5–18, 150–53, and 218–22.

Individuals become accustomed to large public outlays, and perhaps to the inevitable wastefulness associated with warfare.

In contrast to Jump, Parkinson is a determined skeptic. Two Parkinsonian "laws" underlay his skepticism: (1) work expands to fill the time available; and (2) one multiplies subordinates but not superiors. Parkinson does acknowledge boundary conditions that can bring up short the reinforcing inevitabilities that balloon public expenditures, but he sees these boundary conditions only as "danger points" that presage "international disaster." His boundary conditions offer little hope this side of calamity, simply, as he intends.

Observers of more serious mien than Parkinson also have addressed themselves to the control over public expenditures. The reference is to those making "orthodox recommendations" for budgetary change. They reflect a noteworthy sameness. Thus orthodox commentators consider both the efficient use of what monies are made available and the level of total expenditures. Generally, moreover, these observers are optimistic that something meaningful can be done at both levels. Indeed, the orthodox observers also are pretty much agreed about what should be done and who should do it. Basically, orthodox opinion prescribes comprehensive budgetary control through the person of the President or, more realistically, through the institution of the presidency. Or to put the matter otherwise, orthodox opinion gives less attention to the constitutional sharing of powers by Congress, the President, and the courts than it does to comprehensive central control from a single source. Similarly, orthodox opinion devotes less attention to the values of diversity than to the ideal of central direction.

The Report of the President's Committee on Administrative Management presents one version of the orthodox solution of control over public expenditures in the excerpts reprinted in this chapter. Though the Report has its numerous predecessors and successors, its sense and its spirit must be considered the most influential statement of how our problems of budgeting and finance should be coped with at the highest level of responsibility. Without question, then, the Report is an important factor shaping the conceptual contexts of public budgeting and finance. Hence it is fittingly reprinted as the concluding selection of this first section introducing some major conceptual emphases in public budgeting and finance.

The Report of the President's Committee is dated in many details, of course, but it is as current as today in its main thrust. That is, the Report's basic purpose is the same one which motivates the overwhelming bulk of thought about public budgetary practice: to assure that the Chief Executive can "fulfill the responsibility of his office under the Constitution," which operationally means in the orthodox opinion that "he must possess undivided executive powers and adequate means with which to exercise them."

BUDGETS: DEFINITION AND SCOPE

ANDREW C. STEDRY

In an attempt to eradicate, or at least mitigate, some of the ambiguity which will result from the particular usage of the term "budget" in this thesis, it is necessary to relate it to the definitions in common use. The most comprehensive use of the term is exemplified by the following definition of "budget" by Eric Kohler as:[1]

1. A financial plan serving as a pattern for and a control over future operations;
2. hence, any estimate of future costs;
3. a systematic plan for the utilization of man power, material or other resources.

Implicit in Kohler's definition is the existence of a multiplicity of purposes for which budgets are constructed.

Two major functions are, however, immediately discernible. First, a budget may serve as a *plan*, indicating requirements of certain factors (e.g., cash, productive capacity) at some future date which serves the function of providing information for subsequent decisions and possibly guiding them. Second, a budget may serve as a *control*, containing criteria of cost or performance which will be compared with actual data on operations, thus facilitating evaluations and possibly encouraging or even enforcing some measure of efficiency.

As may be already apparent, these separate functions (i.e., planning and controlling) need not be mutually exclusive nor, in practice, is it unusual for both to be represented in a single document. That these functions are (rightly or wrongly) fused is aptly indicated by the following description of "production planning and control" by MacDonald:[2]

... one of the essential steps in the preparation of the production budget is the translation of sales estimates into specific production plans. While this activity is primarily the responsibility of the production executive, usually exercised through the head of planning or a production control

---

Article is from Andrew C. Stedry, *Budget Control and Cost Behavior*, pp. 3–12, © 1960. Reprinted by permission of Prentice-Hall, Inc., Englewood Cliffs, New Jersey, and the author.

[1]E. L. Kohler, *A Dictionary for Accountants*, Englewood Cliffs, N.J.: Prentice-Hall, Inc., 1956, p. 67.

[2]J. H. MacDonald, *Practical Budget Procedure*, Englewood Cliffs, N.J.: Prentice-Hall, Inc., 1939, p. 101.

department, it is so fundamental to practical budgetary control that it is essential that the budget executive at least be familiar with the essential features of it.

There is certainly no doubt indicated in MacDonald's remarks about the advisability, or even necessity, of interlacing the planning and control functions to the point where they become indistinguishable. A question might be raised, however, as to whether the interrelationship described can, in fact, be achieved with only one set of budgeted figures—a set which would need to serve both planning and control functions at various tiers (and over various persons) in an organization. Consider, for instance, the impact of the following remark as quoted by two other authors:[3] "A good plan (e.g., a budget or sales forecast) does not necessarily yield a good control." Also, "Good planning data and good control data are not necessarily the same."[4] Therefore, it is evident that there is some room for disagreement as well as some need for clarification in these areas, planning and control.

In order to clarify this distinction, reference will be made to sales budgets where it is usual for distinctions of this kind to be recognized in the literature,[5] possibly because widespread divergencies between plans and actual operations are more frequent than in, say, production or financial budgeting. One type of sales budget (frequently termed a "quota") is designed specifically as a control device. Its aims are to effect the motivation and guide the judgment of the salesmen by comparison of budgeted and actual performance. This comparison may be (and sometimes is) re-enforced by connection with various rewards and penalties. On the other hand, the tie between these quotas and the planning of output is often extremely loose. The planned output is often based on "estimated" or "expected" sales, and the relations of these expectations to the quotas suggests an assumption that at least some of the quotas will not be achieved.[6] A question arises as to why the "quota" concept is generally not carried over into other areas of budgeting—e.g., production—as a control device. As far as may be discerned, the reasoning is somewhat as follows: the budget must serve as a coordination device. Hence production must be planned so that the needs emanating from "expected sales" will be met along with other criteria, such as the size or fluctuations in inventory, that are regarded as prudent. The assumption which is made in practice (or at least in descriptions of practice) is that the figures to be used for control purposes and the estimate of needs

---

[3] A. Charnes and W. W. Cooper, "Optimization in New Item Production," Third Annual George Washington University—ONR Logistic Conference, January, 1952.

[4] *Ibid.*

[5] *See,* for example, J. B. Heckert, *Business Budgeting and Control,* chap. xi, New York: The Ronald Press Company, 1946.

[6] A third figure is sometimes apparent. A sales "forecast" emanating from the sales department may be adjusted downward (to compensate for anticipated optimistic bias) to obtain the sales expectation.

(i.e., the production plan) are the same.[7] It is an hypothesis of this thesis that the equality of the figures used for the control and planning budgets need not be assumed, but that its desirability is a testable proposition. Or, in other words, does some figure other than the planned amount, when used in the control budget, produce a performance which is actually closer to the planned amount?

The questions which arise regarding the disparity of plans and controls indicate that the "budget process" is actually not a homogeneous mechanism but rather a collection of processes with a variety of aims and procedures of application. . . .

BUDGETS: STANDARDS AND STANDARD COSTS

In order to convey the applicability of the treatment of "budgets" in this paper to control systems using "standards" and "standard costs" as elements of control, the similarity of these various elements will now be discussed. It will first be desirable to examine "standards" and "standard costs" to provide a framework for the discussion of similarities and differences.

Both "standards" and "standard costs" are so intimately related that the one is generally included with the other in any description of cost or profit control mechanisms. It is thus necessary, in order to maintain contact with the main body of accounting literature, to explain the context in which they (i.e., "standards" and "standard costs") will be used in this thesis.

In order to introduce these concepts as they will be used here, the definitions of Eric Kohler will be cited. He defines a *standard* as, "A desired attainment; a performance goal; a model."[8] It will be noted that Kohler views a standard as something to be striven for, and that although various types of schemes are used to set standards, the basic correspondence between

---

[7]This assumption is typified by some remarks of W. Rautenstrauch, and R. Villers, *Budgetary Control*, New York: Funk and Wagnalls Company, 1950. They state:

> The *yearly production budget* is not equal to the sales forecast, nor to the sales forecast less inventory on hand but to *sales forecasts plus (or minus) the increase (or reduction) of inventory required to bring the actual inventory to the level of budgeted inventory* (p. 114).

This budget is the only one which they propose for control purposes. Note that the distinction between what the budget *is not* and what it *is* is only one which (algebraically) assures that the estimates provide for a continuing enterprise. The possibility that estimated need and the need as stated in the control budget may not agree is not considered. It should be noted in this connection that Professors Rautenstrauch and Villers are industrial engineers. Their views, however, do not differ from those indicated in the citation of MacDonald, *op. cit.*, an executive, nor markedly from those of Heckert, *op. cit.*, chap. xviii, an accountant, on the subject of production budgets.

[8]Kohler, *op. cit.*, p. 389.

standard and goal remains unaltered. Standards are frequently encountered in such specific contexts as "standard time," "standard material usage," etc. In contrast to standard, Kohler defines *standard cost* as, "A forecast or predetermination of what costs should be under projected conditions, serving as a basis for cost control, and as a measure of productive efficiency when ultimately compared with actual costs."[9]

Even with the fairly explicit definitions of Kohler, the problems of classification are not always straightforward. For example, items such as "standard labor costs" and "standard material costs" can be classified as "standard costs" and passed by without further discussion, since an absence of ambiguity in these classifications is usually assumed. But what about "standard overhead expense" and like items? Are these a "standard," or a "standard cost"? It is evident that there is some difference in the dimensions, at least as far as control is concerned. Whereas goals or levels used for control which are expressed in units other than dollars are necessarily classed as standards (or budgets, as will be explained later), those which are expressed in dollar terms are frequently classed as standard costs, but not invariably.

In practice, moreover, a "standard time" (expressed in hours) for a particular operation extended by a "standard rate" (cost per hour) for a worker employed on the operation is usually termed a "standard labor cost" for the operation. Any two out of the three figures in this case may serve as the basis for control; the particular pair chosen is a matter of convenience. Conceptually, there is little difference between controlling input or output

---

[9]*Ibid.* It should be noted that there are several types of standard costs in common use. Since these distinctions are not of prime interest here they will be discussed only briefly. A first classification may be made into two types: *basic standards* and *current standards*. The basic standard is essentially an index number. It is not used for control purposes, other than to exhibit a trend, and frequently is an old standard or actual cost as of a given date, etc. On the other hand, current standards represent the type used in the ordinary context of standards for cost control. These may be set in a variety of ways and may be further subdivided on this basis into two classifications: estimates and standards. Both are expected to relate to current and future production and "the difference between the two is even conceptually a matter of degree. Estimated costs are the looser of the two." (A paraphrase of W. W. Cooper, "Historical and Alternative Costs: A Study of Some Relations between the Economic Theory of the Firm and the Accounting Control of Operations," Doctoral Dissertation, Columbia University, 1950, chap. v, pp. 18–19.)

Additional distinctions, often made, are *ideal* (or *perfection*) *standards* and *attainable standards*. These are both current standards, but the attainable standards are assumed to be able to be obtained under conditions of a reasonable degree of efficiency and effort. They may be either estimates based on past performance or *engineering standards*. The engineering standards are set by time study for labor cost or similar devices for other types of cost. These, too, are in reality estimates, since the standards are often subject to negotiation and there exists no reliable scientific basis upon which to justify an assumption of precision. So-called ideal standards are generally engineering standards, intended to describe the cost that could be attained under "optimum" efficiency. These are the closest to the concept of optimal cost in economic terms, but generally speaking each standard is set individually so that the factor interactions assumed in economic theory are not considered.

in physical units as opposed to dollar terms, although they may require different procedures.[10]

From the above comments it may be inferred that the choice of a common denominator—a *numéraire*—is in reality fairly arbitrary, and hence the terms "standard" and "standard cost" can be used more or less interchangeably, at least in a theoretical document of this kind.

Another issue which requires clarification involves the difference between budgets and standards. The distinctions made in the literature vary considerably from author to author so that a concise summary is difficult to achieve. A view which is widely held, however, is that the difference is one of scope. This viewpoint is exemplified in the following remarks of S. Henrici.[11]

> ... Budgets are customarily set for all departments in the company, from sales to manufacturing. But standards are frequently set only for the manufacturing divisions and can, indeed, be confined to controllable costs in a limited number of cost centers ...

Similar statements may be found in Lang, McFarland, and Schiff[12], and Heckert[13], who consider scope the essential difference. Henrici, however, considers scope only one of the distinctions, and not the primary one. He states:

> The first distinction between standards and budgets is one of purpose. Budgets are statements of expected [sic] cost ... Standards on the other hand, do not necessarily show what costs may be expected to be [sic] but

---

[10]Problems exist, of course, which may definitely indicate preference of one type of unit or the other. In the case of nondivisable joint costs, for example, dollar figures may be misleading. On the other hand, in the control of operations which involve large-scale aggregations of items with a multiplicity of physical units, dollar amounts may provide the only practicable solution.

[11]S. B. Henrici, *Standard Costs for Manufacturing*, New York: McGraw-Hill Book Company, 1947, p. 232. A quotation from this same author, to be given shortly, indicates, however, that issues of purpose may also be used to distinguish between "budgeted" and "standard" cost.

[12]Cf., for example, T. Lang, W. B. McFarland, and M. Schiff (*Cost Accounting* New York: The Ronald Press Company, 1953), who state, "Control implies the desired objectives through the measurement of results, especially through comparative reports" (p. 435). Keller, *op. cit.*, likewise appears to overestimate the role of the accounting function. He notes:

> The first requisite for the control of material costs is organization, with responsibilities clearly established for all phases of the control problems. The accountant is the keystone in such an organization, for control will be no better than the accounting records and data which are established (p. 158).

Both of these authors depend upon the efficiency of their reporting schemes for control. It would seem, however, as though the best reporting scheme would be totally impotent as a control if there were no mechanism for translating reports into action. A *reductio ad absurdum* is sufficient to demonstrate the fallacy in both statements. If both supervisors and budgeted personnel were to ignore all reports—a possibility not excluded by the authors' statements—they would be valueless, regardless of how "good" they were as reports.

[13]Heckert, *op. cit.*

rather what they might be if certain highly desirable performances are attained . . .[14]

On the other hand, I. Wayne Keller proposes a distinction which might well be considered dictated by (in the linguistic sense) "common usage." He writes:[15]

> . . . for control purposes the terms "standard" or "standard cost" are applied to the measurement and control of the costs of direct material, direct labor, and scrap [sic]. Expense is controlled through expense "budgets" rather than expense "standards."

It is apparent from the foregoing conflicting distinctions that no common denominator exists upon which to base a single, well-defined criterion of separation between standards (including standard costs) and budgets. The situation is perhaps best explained by the following statement of the National Association of Accountants' (formerly N.A.C.A.) report, "A Re-Examination of Standard Costs." In relating standard costs to the "scientific management" movement, they note.[16]

> Historically, standard costs as we now know them and business budgeting developed at about the same time, but in the earlier years their development was largely separate. Standard costs developed in the factory while budgeting was applied first to the financial aspect of business. Later on it was realized [sic] that both were merely applications of the same management philosophy and that they were complementary parts of a complete programme of cost control.

This view, which minimizes the difference between budgets and standards, would seem to be most sensible in light of the profusion of conflicting statements which may be found. It also seems, however, that planning and forecasting budgets might properly be differentiated from standards, although standards are frequently used in the determination of the plans and forecasts.

On the other hand, a control budget, as defined *supra*, carries with it the connotation of a "goal" or "desired attainment" which is noted in Kohler's definition of standard. It may thus be seen that "budgeted performance" and "standard performance" differ only in name if they are both goals or desired attainments.

Agreement among writers is more or less general only in the matter of the difference in scope exhibited by budgets and standards. It would not be contrary to this consensus if some distinction were made; e.g., a budget is a goal on a large scale, a standard a goal on a smaller scale. But even this

---

[14]*Ibid.* It should be noted that this distinction is not consistent with the definition of Kohler, *supra*, which is used in this paper. (Henrici lists two other distinctions which also depend upon a definition of budget at variance with Kohler's.)

[15]I. W. Keller, *Management Accounting for Profit Control*, New York: McGraw-Hill Book Company, Inc., 1957, p. 97.

[16]National Association of Accountants (formerly National Association of Cost Accountants), "A Re-Examination of Standard Costs," Reprinted from *N.A.C.A. Bulletin*, Vol. 29, No. 11, Sec. 3, Research Series No. 11 (February 1, 1948), p. 438.

distinction would appear to be artificial from the standpoint of classification by function since both a budget and a standard may, in this context, serve the same purpose.

In any case, in this thesis, the meaning of budget (as a control device) will be interpreted as a goal or desired attainment, and the foregoing discussion and quotations used should suffice to justify, to a first approximation, why findings from a study of "budgets" should also be applicable to "standards" or "standard costs" as one or the other (or all three) are used as part of a cost control system.

HOW A BUDGET CONTROLS

In the preceding sections of this chapter, it was noted that there is a control aspect of budgeting that is distinguishable, in some sense, from either planning or forecasting. Assume for the moment that this distinction is valid and can be sufficiently well demarcated; let it then be assumed that a mechanism has been created for the sole purpose of producing and administering a control budget. A question may then be asked as to just what the budget control system and the budget documents (which are an integral part of the system) should consist of in order to insure that the cost or performance elements budgeted are in fact being controlled.

It would seem reasonable that in order to insure some form of control, the process by which control is exercised should be analyzed. In other words, assurance of control would seem to require some answer to the question, "Just how do budgets control?" This issue is rarely addressed in the budgeting literature except by implication and by reference to "experience," "practice," and intuitive appeals that are more or less plausible (when stated).

A more than usually lucid treatment is presented by Henrici. He notes:[17]

> The difference in a given period between actual cost and standard cost, known as the "variance," tells management to what extent costs can be controlled. The variance itself is not a control, for costs are not controlled by compiling statistics about them. The control consists of the steps that management takes to regulate or limit costs. And the effectiveness of these steps is gauged by the degree to which actual costs approach standard; in other words, by the size of the variance.

An important feature to be noted in Henrici's remarks is the absence of the commonly held assumption that the means of reporting and controlling are the same.[18] A second unusual feature is the concept of an approach to standard as a criterion of effectiveness. It should be noted in this regard that Henrici's definition of standard involves a concept not far removed from the "technological optimum" of economics. He considers

---

[17]Henrici, *op. cit.*, p. 154.

[18]Lang *et al*, *op. cit.*

12

standards as emphasizing "what *should* be" and having a "primary purpose of establishing a 'sea level,' so to speak, from which to measure cost altitudes."[19] However, standards are frequently set by a criterion which is at best awkwardly paraphrased somewhat as follows: "Standards should be set so that they are 'attainable but not too loose'."[20] If standards are interpreted in terms of this latter criterion, an "approach to standard" implies little more than an approach to a level of performance which was a priori assumed to be approachable, or perhaps more important, capable of betterment.

Returning to the problem of how this approach to standard is to be effected, Henrici's mechanism can be largely considered a search for cause. He assumes that, "Behind every variation from standard cost there is a reason in operating conditions—and very often an apparently good reason."[21] The size and trend of the variances direct supervisory attention to certain phases of activity and the causes of an unfavorable variance are ascertained. These causes are generally assumed to be remediable or nonremediable; "corrective action" is taken in the former case, whereas the latter is dismissed or excused in one form or another.

What has been described above is the essence of so-called "principle of exceptions" or "management by exception." It should be noted that a step has been taken in this thesis in the development of systematic search techniques for the finding and correcting of "remediable causes" of higher costs (or alternatively, lost profit) including the determination of priorities in the order of search. This work is described in Chapter 5. However, the process of "following up" unfavorable variances would seem to be only part of the gain which might be achieved from a system of budgets or standards.

The process of investigation per se places the burden of proof upon management to discover the cause of variances. This is partially transferred to the manager or department head within whose jurisdiction the unfavorable variance occurred; e.g., a report of explanation is required of him so that he must hunt for causes, or at least reasons, to enter in such a report.

---

[19]Henrici, *op. cit.*, p. 5. But note, however, that there is, within these broad directives, a problem of measurement of standards. Even in the area in which the most extensive work on standards has been performed—the calculation of standard time—the issues are not clear-cut. J. G. March, and H. A. Simon (*Organizations*, New York: John Wiley & Sons, Inc., 1958) point out that:

> ... Often it is unclear whether standard times reflect "average time using average skill and average effort," "minimum time" or "average time over a series of trials by individuals randomly selected from a pool of industrial workers" (p. 16).

It is thus apparent that, even with the best of intentions, a standard can be misleading.

[20]*See* R. H. Robnett, T. M. Hill, and J. A. Becket, *Accounting, A Management Approach*, p. 431, Homewood, Ill.: Richard D. Irwin, Inc., 1954; Lang *et al*, *op. cit.*, chap. xvi, especially p. 320; and Heckert, *op. cit.*, p. 171, for only a few instances of the application of this criterion.

[21]Henrici, *op. cit.*, p. 154.

Often such reports are used to initiate or justify a requested change which, if granted or acceded to by "higher" management, will allow the department head to eliminate or reduce the reported causes of trouble. Alternatively, the report may focus on the existence of some "uncontrollable factor." In principle it may show inefficiency as one root of the difficulty, but here psychological (or economically rational) factors are likely to enter to cloud or obscure matters so that recourse must generally be had to other sources; e.g., bolstering of the controls by independent (internal) auditors, special studies, etc. Here again variations in report content as well as differing sources of information are utilized to achieve (or to attempt to achieve) "control."

Consider once more the problem of control as it depends on the motivation (or other psychological and organizational) factors as they affect the person who "causes costs to happen" in the first instance. The process of consideration may well commence with the setting or changing of a standard. The setting of the standard is not sufficient of itself to assure or even invite compliance. The problem of directing activity toward a goal is one of "motivation;" a problem which is ignored, by and large, in the cost accounting and budgeting, except insofar as it deals with issues such as understanding (or the lack thereof) of accounting reports by others. However, as the psychologist Ruch points out, motivation is an integral part of goal-striving activity:[22]

> In any activity there are certain internal conditions or forces *without which there would be no activity* [italics supplied]. These internal conditions [motives] serve to direct the organism toward certain *goals*, regardless of whether these goals are, at the time, present in the organism.

This viewpoint (i.e., when there is no motivation there is no activity) is fundamental to much of psychology. To bring the matter somewhat closer to this thesis, it would appear that Ruch implies that a budget or goal, even if externally imposed, must receive some internal recognition if it is to be at all effective. The following quotation from H. J. Leavitt may be utilized to develop this line of thinking more fully. Professor Leavitt notes:[23]

> No matter how much power a changer may possess, no matter how "superior" he may be, it is the changee who controls the final change decision. It is the employee, even the lowest paid one, who ultimately decides whether to show up for work or not.

It may be perceived from the foregoing remarks that a major area for investigation of the means of budget control involves the relationship between motivations and budgets and standards considered as goals.

.   .   .   .

---

[22]F. Ruch, *Psychology and Life*, Chicago: Scott, Foresman and Company, 4th ed., 1953, p. 105.

[23]H. J. Leavitt, *Managerial Psychology: An Introduction to Individuals, Pairs, and Groups in Organization*, Chicago: The University of Chicago Press, 1958, p. 132.

MANAGEMENT USES OF FIGURES

Herbert Simon, George Kozmetsky, Harold Guetzkow and Gordon Tyndall

In the seven companies studied, accounting information is used at various executive levels to answer three different kinds of questions:

Score-card questions: "Am I doing well or badly?"
Attention-directing questions: "What problems should I look into?"
Problem-solving questions: "Of the several ways of doing the job, which is the best?"

The organizational problems of providing effective service to management in the score-card and attention-directing areas were usually quite different from those of providing services in the area of special studies. Different sets of operating executives are generally involved in the two areas; and the kinds of data and analyses used may be quite different. Because of these differences, a controller's department which is well organized to provide the one type of service, may or may not be well organized to provide the other.

SCORE-CARD AND ATTENTION-DIRECTING USES

In a factory the total departmental variance from standard or from budget would be an example of an item of score-card significance and use for the supervisor of the department concerned.

To the factory manager, the cost variances of individual departments would be attention-directing items—they would be one of the pieces of information which would direct his attention to departments requiring more careful review.

Acceptance of standards and the constructive use of accounting data for score-card and attention-directing purposes requires that the operating executives have confidence in the standards and in the performance reports that go to their superiors. In all cases, a close and direct relationship between accounting personnel and operating personnel appeared to be the most important factor in producing this confidence. This relationship needed to be close in the standards-setting procedure so that the operating man might have an opportunity to negotiate a standard which he could regard as a reasonable and attainable forecast of his operations. The relationship needed to be close in the reporting process so that the operating man might have help in interpreting his variances, and might have a part in developing

---

Article is from *Centralization vs. Decentralization in Organizing the Controller's Department,* New York: Controllership Foundation, Inc., 1954, pp. 2–4, 22–24, 26–27, 28–30, and 32–33. Reprinted with permission of authors and publisher.

the explanations of off-standard performance that were presented to his superior. Hence, for effective attention-directing service, *it is essential for the controller's department to develop direct and active channels of communication with the operating executives at those points in the organization where operations are being measured.*

PROBLEM-SOLVING USES

When data are used for problem-solving purposes—to choose among alternative processes, to decide whether to buy new equipment, to help in policy decisions—a special study is usually required. This commonly draws upon engineering estimates and industrial engineering standards as well as accounting information and usually means going back into the basic records of the accounting system.

There are two principal ways in which accounting data may come into the problem-solving process:

Executives may turn to the regular accounting and statistical reports for help.

The controller's department may make special studies for particular problems.

In which of these directions does the greatest promise lie for improving this aspect of controllership service? In the direction of more elaborate periodic reports or in strengthening the special studies services? This study indicates that *further development of staff and facilities for special studies is a more promising direction of progress than elaboration of periodic accounting reports.*

In one company, an annual calculation is made for each factory of the ratio of profit earned by that factory to investment in factory facilities. For the plant manager this has a *score-card* value. If he earns a high percentage of profit, or if his profit goes up from one year to the next, he is likely to feel that he is doing a good job. If the profit is low or goes down, he is likely to be encouraged to additional effort. In some cases, the use of the accounting results as the basis for a supervisory bonus emphasizes the score-card function. Note that in these cases, the accounting figures act as a stimulus, but do not help the manager decide what can or should be done.

This very same figure, the factory's rate of return on investment, is used by top management in this company as an *attention director*. Those factories which consistently turn up with low or declining profit percentages are regarded as trouble spots requiring special attention from the company executives. In those factories where the rate of return is regarded as satisfactory, the manager is left rather free to run his own show. For the company management, therefore, the return figure is more than a score-card record. It also directs attention to operating units which need special analysis and review. Thus, the same item of information may be an attention director for one executive but primarily a score card for others, or it may have both score-card and attention-directing utility for the same person.

For example, take a factory general foreman or department head. His job consists in considerable part in "pushing" the work. He generally spends a large part of his time on the factory floor where he can actually observe the work being performed. He is concerned with seeing that jobs are filled, but that superfluous men are not on the payroll; that emergencies are met quickly and effectively, and delays minimized; that short-run, day-to-day problems of all sorts are handled promptly. His direct face-to-face contact with his subordinates and their work gives him many sources of information about what is going on, and he regards accounting information as only a supplement—and, in many instances, a not too important one—to the other sources. Accounting data are useful to him mainly in giving him a score card, summarizing for longer periods his day-to-day impressions. They also are useful in directing his attention to matters that are not visible and tangible—say, the rate of consumption of expendable tools, or of operating supplies.

In most of the companies, any appropriation for major new equipment has to be justified by an economy study or savings statement. This is an example of the "problem-solving" uses of accounting data. These uses go beyond the case where out-of-line accounting figures call attention to a problem or show in what area the problem lies. In problem-solving uses, the actual accounting data are inserted in the equation, so to speak, in order to solve the problem. Apart from plant and equipment studies, the most common examples of the problem-solving use of accounting data are in the comparison of profitability of product lines as a basis for a selective selling program, and the use of accounting data to forecast working capital requirements.

At higher levels of management the problem-solving uses of accounting data appear more commonly. For the vice president for manufacturing there are policy problems—developing and putting into production new products, plant location decisions, installation of new equipment and replacement of old, make-or-buy decisions, and so on. In many of these areas of decision, accounting data are used for problem-solving purposes. Sometimes they apparently are not used where they *could* be. They are used in preparation of special analyses or studies usually prepared by the executive's own assistants or by "staff" departments.[1] An equipment study, for example, would be most often made by the industrial engineering department. Sometimes, special studies are assigned to the controller's department and, even more frequently, that department is called on by other special-study units to supply the accounting data or dollar statistics

---

[1]As is well known, "staff" is a slippery word that is perhaps best avoided altogether. In this publication the term is used simply as a shorthand way of referring to all the departments of a company other than manufacturing, sales, and engineering; and to all the departments of a factory other than the manufacturing and maintenance departments.

needed for an analysis. Hence, the extent to which accounting data are used for problem-solving purposes depends very much on the kinds of staff assistance available to the vice president and on how much he is accustomed to use them.

Another concern of the manufacturing vice president is the evaluation and development of men. He needs to learn how his subordinates are doing, their strengths and their weaknesses. Moreover, the vice president has far less opportunity than the factory department head to observe his subordinates on the job. Hence, he is more dependent on reports as a basis for evaluating their progress and problems. He often uses accounting data and reports of internal auditors as a score card for his subordinates, and as a means of directing his attention to the areas where he needs to apply pressure or raise questions.

Observations made on this survey indicate that the score-card and attention-directing uses are apt to be more frequent than the problem-solving uses at all levels of management. First-line supervisors tend to use such data primarily as a fill-in on aspects of the work that they cannot appraise from actual contact. At higher levels, the data are used as a means of judging subordinates and as an independent check on what is happening at the operating level. Problem-solving uses of accounting data occur primarily in administrative units (staff units) for making analyses or special studies, for use by general management.

SCORE-CARD AND ATTENTION-DIRECTING USES OF DATA

It has been pointed out that no sharp line can be drawn between the score-card and the attention-directing uses of accounting data. What is a score card for the factory manager may be an attention director for the vice president for manufacturing; what is a score card for the regional sales manager may be an attention director for the general sales manager.

Illustrations of Score-Card and Attention-Directing Uses of Data

Here are some typical interview replies that illustrate the relation of the two uses:

A general sales manager was asked:
"How do you tell when your regional managers are doing a good job?"
"The main things are the sales figures. Then, we've got to watch their expenses. Let's look at our weekly summary statistics. I see that the sales of X product are low compared to the quota. I go back to the regional report and see that New England is the low region, also which of the sales branches in the region are low. Then I know to whom to write a letter to follow it up."
One of the regional sales managers in the same company was asked:
"How do you tell when you are doing a good job?" He replied: "I have a sales quota and an expense budget. I try to operate my region so that I

will meet the quota or surpass it; and at the same time, I try to do the job in the most economical manner."

. . . .

Attention Directing and the "Principle of Exceptions"

The use of accounting data to call attention to problems is closely related to what is usually called "the principle of exceptions." For this procedure to work, the operating man must accept the validity of the standards for determining what is "out of line." Moreover, effective attention-directing uses of accounting data imply that it is through such data that problems are called to the attention of operating executives or general management.

Persons interviewed consistently reported that, in many instances where the production and sales executives *might* have had their attention directed to problems by accounting data, they had already learned of the problems from other sources before the accounting reports appeared. For example, delays due to equipment breakdown or material shortages are almost immediately brought to the attention of the foreman and usually the department head. If the problem is a serious one, the news travels upward rapidly, even to vice presidential and presidential levels. On these matters, accounting reports usually provide the supervisors with history but not with news.

On the other hand, in the course of his daily work even a first-line supervisor may find it difficult to learn that a particular machine logs excessive down-time because of mechanical failure. Here, a monthly summary of machine down-time with notation as to causes can be a valuable attention-directing report.

Interview data show conclusively that supervisors up to factory department heads use accounting reports for attention-directing purposes largely in areas that are not easily visible in the course of day-to-day supervision. The following comment of a factory department head is typical:

> "Every day when I go out through the departments, I know the standard number of men who should be working on each operation. If I see more than the standard number working on a job, I check up to see why the extra people are there." "Couldn't you get that from the daily variance report?" "Yes, but I'd have to wait two days."

Operating supervisors were seldom able to cite other types of examples of the attention-directing services of the accounting system. On other items—direct labor, material usage, yield—the common reaction was: "We know all about that before the accounting reports come."

The following conclusions validly generalize survey information about attention-directing uses of accounting data by supervisors and executives who have direct contact with the factory floor or the sales market.

A large part of an operating executive's knowledge about his operation comes by direct observation and informal reports. These reports are frequently verbal and come to him through the regular supervisory channels. Accounting reports are only one, and not always the most important, of his sources of information, although they may be of considerable use in confirming his observations.

The operating executive has special needs for periodic accounting reports on items that are not "visible" from direct, day-to-day supervision. In manufacturing, machine performance and consumption of operating supplies are examples of such items.

For executives further removed from actual operations, the greatest significance of attention-directing accounting data lies in the information they transmit independently of operating supervisors. The existence of this independent source and channel of information has important consequences for the relations between executives at lower and higher levels.

. . . .

THE ROLE OF STANDARDS[2]

When accounting data are used for score-card or for attention-directing purposes, a comparison of the actual data with some kind of standard or norm is always involved. This need not be a deliberately designed and established standard of the sort involved in a standard cost system, but may be any figure that is regarded as a "normal," "expected," "reasonable," or "satisfactory" value for the figure in question.

If an operating department head has become accustomed to "red" variances of $50,000 a month measured against the standard cost of his operation, then he is likely to regard a month in which his "red" variance is only $25,000 as a good one, even though the performance is still below standard. Similarly, a considerable number of executives were encountered whose real concern was not how they were making out with reference to the accounting standard, but how well they were doing in relation to historical records of past performance, or comparison with other plants in the same company.

Acceptance of Standards

Interview results show that a particular figure does not operate as a norm, in either a score-card or attention-directing sense, simply because the controller's department calls it a standard. It operates as a norm only to the extent that the executives and supervisors, whose activity it measures, accept it as a fair and attainable yardstick of their performance. Generally, operating executives were inclined to accept a standard to the extent that they were satisfied that the data were *accurately recorded*, that the standard level

---

[2]Findings with respect to standards are in close agreement with other previous studies. *See* especially: John D. Glover and Fritz J. Roethlisberger, "Human Reactions to Standards and Controls," chap. viii in *Controllership in Modern Management*, T. F. Bradshaw and C. C. Hull (eds.), Chicago: Richard D. Irwin, Inc., 1949; and Chris Argyris, *The Impact of Budgets on People*, New York: Controllership Foundation, Inc., 1952.

was *reasonably attainable*, and that the variables it measured were *controllable* by them. When there were doubts as to the accuracy of recording or classification of data, when the factors causing variances were thought to be beyond their own control, the executives simply did not believe that the standard validly measured their performance. Then they were influenced by it only to the extent that they were forced to think about the reactions of their superiors.

The degree of acceptance of standards was not the same, of course, in all the factories visited, nor even among different departments in the same factory. Some of the reasons for this are technical, and these will be discussed in the following paragraphs. In addition to the technical reasons, the length of time a cost system has been in operation has an important bearing on the validity and acceptability of standards. In all the companies studied, several years were required after the installation of a cost system before it was "shaken down" and a reasonably acceptable system of cost determinants arrived at. The same thing was observed in a case where a new processing department had recently been introduced in a factory which had a long-established cost system in its other departments.

It is not necessary to report on the degree to which standards were accepted in these various factories. As already mentioned, the range in level of acceptance was great. It is important, however, to learn what conditions have to be met so that accounting standards have a constructive influence upon operations, and how these conditions can be brought about through proper organizational relationships between the controller's department and the operating departments. For these reasons, the objections to existing accounting standards will be examined in some detail.

Two kinds of objections to standards were most frequently encountered. Some were criticisms of oversimplified determinants that failed to account for important external factors causing variability in costs. Thus, in several cases a cost that was only incurred during one season of the year received the same budget allowance per unit of output throughout the year. The fact that monthly variances in these cases were virtually meaningless tended to discredit the accounting standards and reports based on them.

In many instances the nature of the manufacturing operation practically precludes the establishment of adequate budget determinants. One problem frequently encountered is variation in the quality of raw materials. Food processing companies have continual difficulties of this kind, but similar troubles are found in other concerns. In companies like Westinghouse, where a standard cost often has to be estimated on each order, the task of arriving at acceptable and accepted standards is equally difficult.[3]

---

[3]These problems, of course, go beyond the controller's department to the other departments, like industrial engineering, that establish the physical determinants of standards. Nevertheless, even when the controller's responsibility is limited to "dollarizing" physical standards established by other departments, the variances appear on accounting reports and the accounting personnel are the ones principally criticized for unacceptable standards.

The recalculation of indirect costs was the second major source of distrust of accounting standards—and this on two scores. Almost all operating men stated their dislike at having on their statements items they did not regard as within their control. The objections were particularly strong when the items were not shown at standard, but caused variances on the statements.

Moreover, in the case of indirect items that were admitted to be partially controllable—maintenance expenditures, for example—doubts were frequently expressed as to the accuracy of the charges. In almost all companies there was a widespread belief (not entirely without foundation) that maintenance foremen inflated their time estimates to absorb idle time. As a matter of fact, at least one maintenance department head stated that he did just that: "Suppose the charges don't balance—there's $1,000 unallocated. Well, we know in X department they have some rough edges, so we shove that charge off on them." When clerical errors occur in charging supplies and maintenance to the proper accounts, they also feed this distrust.

In addition, there were frequent objections to the "lumpiness" of indirect charges. "You go along for months with favorable variances and then one month you'll take a licking." This sometimes led to the uneconomical ordering of small quantities of supplies, and pressure was often felt (and, fortunately, frequently resisted) to postpone necessary maintenance: "The machine was still not fixed and we were running out of our budget expense, but I didn't stop. They came around afterwards and said, 'You're way over your budget.' I said, 'Look out there. The machine is running, isn't it? Isn't that what the boss wants?' "

But a department head in another factory said, "I will sometimes pull back on some repairs when I think I can get along without them, especially toward the end of the month." Finally, supervisors could not always predict which month's budget would be charged with an expenditure. "When they throw charges in, they don't throw them in until the end of the month. I think I'm going along pretty well and then—bang—they hit me with some charges."

Reactions to Unacceptable Standards

Now, what occurs when an operating executive is placed in a situation where he fundamentally mistrusts the standards for any of the reasons discussed above, but where his superiors hold him responsible for unfavorable variances and expect explanations from him? There were frequent opportunities to observe how operating men reacted to such situations. The answer was always the same. When the operating man is placed in the position of justifying his performance in terms of a standard that he doesn't regard as fair he has two choices: to change the performance, or to change the measurement of it. And since he regards the measurement of his performance as unfair, he almost inevitably chooses the second alternative. The following two comments are typical of many made during the interviews:

"If you find a variance that's way out, it's either a poor budget or it's not set up properly."

"My boss comes around and asks me about my variance once in a while. This is often a good opportunity to point out things which are wrong with the accounting reports. If I say the standards are off, he should go back and see why the standards are off."

The first reaction of a supervisor who is confronted with an unfavorable variance in an account is to suspect that something has been charged to the account which should not have been charged. Hence, in a situation where the cost accounting is not completely trusted, a great deal of energy of accounting and operating personnel goes into discussion and debate about the correctness of the charges.

The second reaction of the operating man is to look for uncontrollable external circumstances that can explain the unfavorable variance. Thus, in the case of the seasonal item mentioned before, the operating man explains his unfavorable variances by pointing out that they will be balanced by favorable variances the next summer.

Distrust of standards coupled with pressure to eliminate variances leads to preoccupation with "wooden money" savings—to use a term that was current in one factory. When attention is directed by accounting data to an uneconomical operating practice and the practice is corrected, this leads to a real saving for the company that will ultimately be reflected in profits. When the concern with variances is centered on detecting wrong charges and getting these shifted to the proper account, only "wooden money" is saved and company profits are not increased. Here are typical reports by operating men of their use of accounting data to produce "wooden money" savings:

"The foreman keeps a running total of what he has spent. When the report comes back from accounting, he checks his total. It is important to analyze the charges slip by slip. We find that saves us five to six thousand dollars a month on incorrect charges by accounting or some other department."

"There's a good example of another reason why I think these reports are good. If I hadn't had that report, I would never have known this was charged against me."

In the interviews, the relative amount of emphasis on "wooden money" savings proved to be a sensitive index of distrust of standards. In situations where confidence in standards was lowest, the examples given by respondents of their use of accounting data almost all involved reclassification of charges, and not instances where accounting showed opportunities for improving operations.

POLITICAL IMPLICATIONS OF BUDGETARY REFORM

Aaron Wildavsky

A large part of the literature on budgeting in the United States is concerned with reform. The goals of the proposed reforms are couched in similar language—economy, efficiency, improvement, or just better budgeting. The President, the Congress and its committees, administrative agencies, even the interested citizenry are all to gain by some change in the way the budget is formulated, presented, or evaluated. There is little or no realization among the reformers, however, that any effective change in budgetary relationships must necessarily alter the outcomes of the budgetary process. Otherwise, why bother? Far from being a neutral matter of "better budgeting," proposed reforms inevitably contain important implications for the political system, that is for the "who gets what" of governmental decisions. What are some of the major political implications of budgetary reform and where should we look to increase our knowledge about how the budget is made? We begin with the noblest vision of reform: the development of a normative theory of budgeting that would provide the basis for allocating funds among competing activities.

A NORMATIVE THEORY OF BUDGETING?

In 1940, in what is still the best discussion of the subject, V. O. Key lamented "The Lack of a Budgetary Theory." He called for a theory which would help answer the basic question of budgeting on the expenditure side: "On what basis shall it be decided to allocate X dollars to Activity A instead of Activity B?"[1] Although several attempts have been made to meet this challenge,[2] not one has come close to succeeding. No progress has been made

Article is from *Public Administration Review*, Vol. 21 (Autumn, 1961), pp. 183–90. Reprinted with permission of author and publisher.

This research was begun on a Ford Foundation Grant for Research in Public Affairs awarded through Oberlin College which made it possible for the author and a student, Judd Kessler, to interview some fifty officials involved in budgeting in Washington, D.C. Further work is continuing under a grant from Resources for the Future. I would like to thank these organizations for their support. I am also grateful to V. O. Key, Jr., Charles Lindblom, Nelson Polsby, and Allan Schick, for their useful criticisms. I would welcome comments from students and practitioners interested in studying the budgetary process.

[1]V. O. Key, Jr., "The Lack of a Budgetary Theory," *American Political Science Review*, Vol. 34 (December, 1940), pp. 1137–44.

[2]Verne B. Lewis, "Toward a Theory of Budgeting," *Public Administration Review*, Vol. 12 (Winter, 1952), pp. 42–54, "Symposium on Budgetary Theory," *Public Administration Review*, Vol. 10 (Spring, 1954), pp. 20–31; Arthur Smithies, *The Budgetary Process in the United States*, New York: McGraw-Hill Book Co., 1955.

for the excellent reason that the task, as posed, is impossible to fulfill.[3] The search for an unrealizable goal indicates serious weaknesses in prevailing conceptions of the budget.

If a normative theory of budgeting is to be more than an academic exercise, it must actually guide the making of governmental decisions. The items of expenditures which are passed by Congress, enacted into law, and spent must in large measure conform to the theory if it is to have any practical effect. This is tantamount to prescribing that virtually all the activities of government be carried on according to the theory. For whatever the government does must be paid for from public funds; it is difficult to think of any policy which can be carried out without money.

The budget is the life-blood of the government, the financial reflection of what the government does or intends to do. A theory which contains criteria for determining what ought to be in the budget is nothing less than a theory stating what the government ought to do. If we substitute the words "what the government ought to do" for the words "ought to be in the budget," it becomes clear that a normative theory of budgeting would be a comprehensive and specific political theory detailing what the government's activities ought to be at a particular time. A normative theory of budgeting, therefore, is utopian in the fullest sense of that word; its accomplishment and acceptance would mean the end of conflict over the government's role in society.

By suppressing dissent, totalitarian regimes enforce their normative theory of budgeting on others. Presumably, we reject this solution to the problem of conflict in society and insist on democratic procedures. How then arrive at a theory of budgeting which is something more than one man's preferences?

The crucial aspect of budgeting is whose preferences are to prevail in disputes about which activities are to be carried on and to what degree, in the light of limited resources. The problem is not only "how shall budgetary benefits be maximized?" as if it made no difference who received them, but also "who shall receive budgetary benefits and how much?" One may purport to solve the problem of budgeting by proposing a normative theory (or a welfare function or a hierarchy of values) which specifies a method for maximizing returns for budgetary expenditures. In the absence of ability to impose a set of preferred policies on others, however, this solution breaks down. It amounts to no more than saying that if you can persuade others to agree with you, then you will have achieved agreement. Or it begs the question of what kind of policies will be fed into the scheme by assuming that these are agreed upon. Yet we hardly need argue that a state of universal agreement has not yet arisen.

---

[3]Key, in fact, shies away from the implications of his question and indicates keen awareness of the political problems involved. But the question has been posed by subsequent authors largely in the terms in which he framed it.

25

Another way of avoiding the problem of budgeting is to treat society as a single organism with a consistent set of desires and a life of its own, much as a single consumer might be assumed to have a stable demand and indifference schedule. Instead of revenue being raised and the budget being spent by and for many individuals who may have their own preferences and feelings, as is surely the case, these processes are treated, in effect, as if a single individual were the only one concerned. This approach avoids the central problems of social conflict, of somehow aggregating different preferences so that a decision may emerge. How can we compare the worth of expenditures for irrigation to certain farmers with the worth of widening a highway to motorists and the desirability of aiding old people to pay medical bills as against the degree of safety provided by an expanded defense program?

The process we have developed for dealing with interpersonal comparisons in Government is not economic but political. Conflicts are resolved (under agreed upon rules) by translating different preferences through the political system into units called votes or into types of authority like a veto power. There need not be (and there is not) full agreement on goals or the preferential weights to be accorded to different goals. Congressmen directly threaten, compromise, and trade favors in regard to policies in which values are implicitly weighted, and then agree to register the results according to the rules for tallying votes.

The burden of calculation is enormously reduced for three primary reasons: first, only the small number of alternatives which are politically feasible at any one time are considered; second, these policies in a democracy typically differ only in small increments from previous policies on which there is a store of relevant information; and, third, each participant may ordinarily assume that he need consider only his preferences and those of his powerful opponents since the American political system works to assure that every significant interest has representation at some key point. Since only a relatively few interest groups contend on any given issue and no single item is considered in conjunction with all others (because budgets are made in bits and pieces), a huge and confusing array of interests are not activated all at once.

In the American context, a typical result is that bargaining takes place among many dispersed centers of influence and that favors are swapped as in the case of log-rolling public works appropriations. Since there is no one group of men who can necessarily impose their preferences upon others within the American political system, special coalitions are formed to support or oppose specific policies. Support is sought in this system of fragmented power at numerous centers of influence—Congressional committees, the Congressional leadership, the President, the Budget Bureau, interdepartmental committees, departments, bureaus, private groups, and so on. Nowhere does a single authority have power to determine what is going to be in the budget.

THE POLITICS IN BUDGET REFORM

The seeming irrationalities[4] of a political system which does not provide for even formal consideration of the budget as a whole (except by the President who cannot control the final result) has led to many attacks and proposals for reform. The tradition of reform in America is a noble one, not easily to be denied. But in this case it is doomed to failure because it is aimed at the wrong target. If the present budgetary process is rightly or wrongly deemed unsatisfactory, then one must alter in some respect the political system of which the budget is but an expression. It makes no sense to speak as if one could make drastic changes in budgeting without also altering the distribution of influence. But this task is inevitably so formidable (though the reformers are not directly conscious of it) that most adversaries prefer to speak of changing the budgetary process, as if by some subtle alchemy the irrefractible political element could be transformed into a more malleable substance.

The reader who objects to being taken thus far only to be told the obvious truth that the budget is inextricably linked to the political system would have a just complaint if the implications of this remark were truly recognized in the literature on budgeting. But this is not so. One implication is that by far the most significant way of influencing the budget is to introduce basic political changes (or to wait for secular changes like the growing industrialization of the South). Provide the President with more powers enabling him to control the votes of his party in Congress; enable a small group of Congressmen to command a majority of votes on all occasions so that they can push their program through. Then you will have exerted a profound influence on the content of the budget.

A second implication is that no significant change can be made in the budgetary process without affecting the political process. There would be no point in tinkering with the budgetary machinery if, at the end, the pattern of budgetary decisions was precisely the same as before. On the contrary, reform has little justification unless it results in different kinds of decisions and, when and if this has been accomplished, the play of political forces has necessarily been altered. Enabling some political forces to gain at the expense of others requires the explicit introduction and defense of value premises which are ordinarily missing from proposals for budgetary reform.

Since the budget represents conflicts over whose preferences shall prevail, the third implication is that one cannot speak of "better budgeting" without considering who benefits and who loses or demonstrating that no one loses. Just as the supposedly objective criterion of "efficiency" has been

---

[4]*See* Charles E. Lindblom, "The Science of 'Muddling' Through," *Public Administration Review* (Spring, 1959), pp. 79–88, for a description and criticism of the comprehensive method. *See* also his "Decision-Making in Taxation and Expenditure," in National Bureau of Economic Research, *Public Finances: Needs, Sources, and Utilization,* Princeton, N.J.: Princeton University Press, 1961, pp. 295–327, and his "Policy Analysis," *American Economic Review,* Vol. 48 (June, 1958), pp. 298–312.

shown to have normative implications,[5] so a "better budget" may well be a cloak for hidden policy preferences. To propose that the President be given an item veto, for example, means an attempt to increase the influence of the particular interests which gain superior access to the Chief Executive rather than, say, to the Congress. Only if one eliminates the element of conflict over expenditures, can it be assumed that a reform which enables an official to do a better job from his point of view is simply "good" without considering the policy implications for others.

Arthur Smithies may stand as a typical proponent of a typical reform. Identifying rationality with a comprehensive overview of the budget by a single person or group, Smithies despairs of the fragmented approach taken by Congress and proposes a remedy. He suggests that a Joint (Congressional) Budget Policy committee be formed and empowered to consider all proposals for revenue and expenditure in a single package and that their decisions be made binding by a concurrent resolution. And he presents his reform as a moderate proposal to improve the rationality of the budget process.[6] If the proposed Joint Committee were unable to secure the passage of its recommendations, as would surely be the case, it would have gone to enormous trouble without accomplishing anything but a public revelation of futility. The impotence of the Joint Committee on the Legislative Budget,[7] the breakdown of the single Congressional attempt to develop a comprehensive legislative budget,[8] and the failure of Congressional attempts to control the Council of Economic Advisers[9] and the Budget Bureau,[10] all stem from the same cause. There is no cohesive group in Congress capable of using these devices to affect decision making by imposing its preferences on a majority of Congressmen. Smithies' budgetary reform presupposes a completely differ-

[5]Dwight Waldo, *The Administrative State*, New York: Ronald Press, 1948; Herbert A. Simon, "The Criterion of Efficiency," in *Administrative Behavior*, 2nd ed., The Macmillan Company, 1957, pp. 172–97.

[6]Smithies, *op. cit.*, pp. 192–93ff.

[7]Avery Leiserson, "Coordination of the Federal Budgetary and Appropriations Procedures Under the Legislative Reorganization Act of 1946," *National Tax Journal* (June, 1948), pp. 118–26.

[8]Robert Ash Wallace, "Congressional Control of the Budget," *Midwest Journal of Political Science*, Vol. 3 (May, 1959), pp. 160–62; Dalmas H. Nelson, "The Omnibus Appropriations Act of 1950," *Journal of Politics*, Vol. 15 (May, 1953), pp. 274–88; Representative John Phillips, "The Hadacol of the Budget Makers," *National Tax Journal*, Vol. 4 (September, 1951), pp. 255–68.

[9]Roy Blough, "The Role of the Economist in Federal Policy-Making," *University of Illinois Bulletin*, Vol. 51 (November, 1953); Lester Seligman, "Presidential Leadership: The Inner Circle and Institutionalization," *Journal of Politics*, Vol. 18 (August, 1956), pp. 410–26; Edwin G. Nourse, *Economics in the Public Service: Administrative Aspects of the Employment Act*, New York: Harcourt Brace, 1953; Ronald C. Hood, "Reorganizing the Council of Economic Advisors," *Political Science Quarterly*, Vol. 69 (September, 1954), pp. 413–37.

[10]Fritz Morstein Marx, "The Bureau of the Budget: Its Evolution and Present Role II," *American Political Science Review*, Vol. 39 (October, 1945), pp. 363–98; Richard Neustadt, "The Presidency and Legislation: The Growth of Central Clearance," *Ibid.*, Vol. 48 (September, 1954), pp. 631–71; Seligman, *op. cit.*

ent political system from the one which exists in the United States. To be sure, there is a name for a committee which imposes its will on the legislature and tolerates no rival committees—it is called a Cabinet on the British model. In the guise of a procedural change in the preparation of the budget by Congress, Smithies is actually proposing a revolutionary move which would mean the virtual introduction of the British Parliamentary system if it were successful.

Smithies (pp. 188–225) suggests that his proposals would be helpful to the President. But the membership of the Joint Committee would be made up largely of conservatives from safe districts who are not dependent on the President, who come from a different constituency than he does, but with whom he must deal in order to get any money for his programs. Should the Joint Committee ever be able to command a two-thirds vote of the Congress, it could virtually ignore the President in matters of domestic policy and run the executive branch so that it is accountable only to them.

I do not mean to disparage in any way the important problem of efficiency, of finding ways to maximize budgetary benefits given a specified distribution of shares. In principle, there seems to be no reason why policy machinery could not be so arranged as to alter the ratio of inputs to outputs without changing the distribution of shares. One can imagine situations in which everyone benefits or where the losses suffered in one respect are made up by greater gains elsewhere. There may be cases where such losses as do exist are not felt by the participants and they may be happy to make changes which increase their felt benefits. The inevitable lack of full information and the disinclination of participants to utilize their political resources to the fullest extent undoubtedly leave broad areas of inertia and inattention open for change. Thus, the "slack" in the system may leave considerable room for ingenuity and innovation in such areas as benefit cost analysis and the comparability and interrelatedness of public works without running into outstanding political difficulties or involving large changes in the system. Most practical budgeting may take place in a twilight zone between politics and efficiency. Without presenting a final opinion on this matter, it does seem to me that the problem of distributing shares has either been neglected entirely or has been confused with the problem of efficiency to the detriment of both concerns. The statements in this paper should be understood to refer only to the question of determining shares in the budget.

WHAT DO WE KNOW ABOUT BUDGETING?

The overriding concern of the literature on budgeting with normative theory and reform has tended to obscure the fact that we know very little about it. Aside from the now classical articles on Congressional oversight of administration by Arthur MacMahon,[11] an excellent study of internal

---

[11] Arthur McMahon, "Congressional Oversight of Administration," *Political Science Quarterly*, Vol. 58 (June, September, 1943), pp. 161–90, 380–414.

budgetary procedures in the Army by Frederick C. Mosher,[12] and an interesting case history by Kathryn S. Arnow,[13] there is virtually nothing of substance about how or why budgetary decisions are actually made. Of course, the general literature on decision making in national government provides some valuable propositions, but it is not keyed-in to the budgetary process. Yet the opportunities for developing and testing important propositions about budgetary decisions are extraordinarily good and I would like to suggest a few of the many possible approaches here.

How do various agencies decide how much to ask for? Most agencies cannot simply ask for everything they would like to have. If they continually ask for much more than they can get, their opinions are automatically discounted and they risk a loss of confidence by the Bureau of the Budget and Appropriations subcommittees which damages the prospects of their highest priority items. The agencies cannot even ask for all that they are authorized to spend because their authorizations commonly run way ahead of any realistic expectation of achievement. At the same time, they do not wish to sell themselves short. The result is that the men who make this choice (an official title is no certain guide to whom they are) seek signals from the environment—supporting interests, their own personnel, current events, last year's actions, attitudes of Congressmen, and so on—to arrive at a composite estimate of "what will go." A combination of interviews, case studies, and direct observation should enable the researcher to determine what these signals are, to construct propositions accounting for the agencies budgetary position, and to generally recreate the environment out of which these choices come.

Once having decided what they would like to get, how do agencies go about trying to achieve their objectives? Today, we do not even have a preliminary list of the most common strategies used by participants in trying to influence budgetary outcomes. Again, the techniques listed above should bring the necessary data to light.

Perhaps a few examples will demonstrate the importance of understanding budgetary strategies. There are times when an agency wishes to cut its own budget because it has lost faith in a program, for internal disciplinary reasons, or because it would like to use the money elsewhere. If the agency is particularly well endowed with effective clientele groups, however, it may not only fail in this purpose but may actually see the appropriation increased as this threat mobilizes the affected interests. One budget officer informed me that he tried to convince the Budget Bureau to undertake two projects which the agency did not want but which several influential Congressmen felt strongly about. Otherwise, the official argued, the Congressmen would secure their desires by offering additional projects to their colleagues. The Budget

---

[12]Frederick C. Mosher, *Program Budgeting: Theory and Practice*, with Particular Reference to the U.S. Department of the Army, Public Administrative Service, 1954.

[13]*The Department of Commerce Field Offices*, Inter-University Case Series No. 21, University: University of Alabama Press, 1954.

Bureau turned him down and the result was nine unwanted projects instead of two.

The appearance of a budget may take on considerable importance, a circumstance which is often neglected by proponents of program budgeting. Suppose that an agency has strong clientele backing for individual projects. It is likely to gain by presenting them separately so that any cut may be readily identified and support easily mobilized. Lumping a large number of items together may facilitate cuts on an across-the-board basis. Items lacking support, on the other hand, may do better by being placed in large categories so that it is more difficult to single them out for deeper slashes.

We might also inquire (through questionnaires, interviews, direct observation, documentary research) about the participants' perceptions of their roles and the reciprocal expectations they have about the behavior of others. In speaking to officials concerned with budgeting I was impressed with how often the behavior they described was predicated on a belief about what others would do, how they would react in turn, how a third participant would react to this result and so on. Budgetary items are commonly adjusted on the basis of mutual expectations or on a single participant's notion of the role he is expected to play. I strongly suspect, on the basis of some interviewing, that if we studied conceptions of role prevalent on the House Appropriations Committee, their transmittal to new members and staff, and the consequent resistance of members to seeing party as relevant to choice, we would understand a great deal more about the characteristic behavior of many members as budget cutters.

My interviews suggest that the administrator's perception of Congressional knowledge and motivation helps determine the kind of relationships he seeks to establish. The administrator who feels that the members of his appropriations subcommittees are not too well informed on specifics and that they evaluate the agency's program on the basis of feedback from constituents, stresses the role of supporting interests in maintaining good relations with Congressmen. He may not feel the need to be too careful with his estimates. The administrator who believes that the Congressmen are well informed and fairly autonomous is likely to stress personal relationships and demonstrations of good work as well as clientele support. Priority in research should be given to study of these perceptions and the ways in which they determine behavior.

Another approach would be to locate and segregate classes of administrative officials who are found by observation to have or not to have the confidence of the appropriations committees and to seek to explain the differences. For if there is any one thing which participants in budgeting are likely to stress, it is the importance of maintaining relations of confidence and they are highly conscious of what this requires. Since it appears from preliminary investigation that the difference is not accounted for by the popularity of the agency or its programs, it is possible that applications of some gross psychological and skill categories would reveal interesting results.

Many participants in budgeting (in the agencies, Congress, the Budget Bureau) speak of somehow having arrived at a total figure which represents an agency's or an activity's "fair share" of the budget. The fact that a fair share concept exists may go a long way toward explaining the degree of informal coordination that exists among the participants in budgeting. Investigation of how these figures are arrived at and communicated would help us understand how notions of limits (ceilings and floors) enter into budgetary decisions. A minimum effort in this direction would require the compilation of appropriations histories of various agencies and programs rather than just individual case histories which concentrate on some specific event or moment in time. Investigation of the Tennessee Valley Authority's experience in securing electric power appropriations, over a twenty-five-year period, for example, reveals patterns and presents explanatory possibilities which would not otherwise be available.[14]

By its very nature the budgetary process presents excellent opportunities for the use of quantitative data although these must be used with great caution and with special attention to their theoretical relevance. Richard Fenno has collected figures on thirty-seven bureaus dealing with domestic policies from 1947 to 1958 from their initial estimates to decisions by the Budget Bureau, appropriations committees in both houses, conference committees, and floor action. Using these figures he expects to go beyond the usual facile generalizations that the House cuts and the Senate raises bureau estimates, to the much more interesting question of determining the conditions under which the patterns that do exist actually obtain.[15] Although such data do not by any means tell the whole story, they can be used to check generalizations about patterns of floor action or conference committee action which would not otherwise be possible.

After giving the matter considerable thought, I have decided that it would not be fruitful to devise a measure which would ostensibly give an objective rank ordering of bureaus and departments according to their degree of success in securing appropriations. The first measure which might be used would be to compare an agency's initial requests with its actual appropriations. The difficulty here is that agency estimates are not merely a measure of their desire but also include a guess as to what they can reasonably expect to get. The agency which succeeds in getting most of what it desires, therefore, may be the one which is best at figuring out what it is likely to get. A better measure, perhaps, would be an agency's record in securing appropriations calculated as percentages above or below previous years' appropriations. But this standard also leads to serious problems. There are fortuitous events—sputnik, a drought, advances in scientific knowledge—which are

---

[14]*See* Aaron B. Wildavsky, "TVA and Power Politics," *American Political Science Review*, Vol. 55 (September, 1961), pp. 576–90.

[15]From a research proposal kindly lent me by Richard Fenno. *See* also his excellent paper, "The House Appropriations Committee as a Political System: The Problem of Integration," delivered at the 1961 meeting of the American Political Science Association.

beyond the control of an agency but which may have a vital bearing on its success in getting appropriations. Indeed, some "affluent agencies" like the National Institutes of Health may find that there is little they can do to stop vast amounts of money from coming in; they may not even be able to cut their own budgets when they want to do so. Furthermore, agencies generally carry on a wide variety of programs and the total figures may hide the fact that some are doing very well and others quite poorly. Thus it would be necessary to validate the measure by an intensive study of each agency's appropriations history and this would appear to make the original computation unnecessary.

The purpose of this suggested research, much of which the author intends to pursue, is to formulate empirically valid propositions which will be useful in constructing theories (general explanations) accounting for the operation and outcomes of the budgetary process. A theory of influence would describe the power relationships among the participants, explain why some are more successful than others in achieving their budgetary goals, state the conditions under which various strategies are or are not efficacious, and in this way account for the pattern of budgetary decisions.

With such a theory, it would become possible to specify the advantages which some participants gain under the existing system, to predict the consequences of contemplated changes on the distribution of influence, and to anticipate sources of opposition. Possibly, those desiring change might then suggest a strategy to overcome the expected resistance. But they would not, in their scholarly role, accuse their opponents of irrationality in not wishing to have their throats cut.

It would also be desirable to construct a theory of budgetary calculation by specifying the series of related factors (including influence relationships) which affect the choice of competing alternatives by the decision makers. This kind of theory would describe how problems arise, how they are broken down, how information is fed into the system, how the participants are related to one another, and how a semblance of coordination is achieved. The kinds of calculations which actually guide the making of decisions would be emphasized. One would like to know, for example, whether long-range planning really exists or is merely engaged in for form's sake while decisions are really based on short-run indices like reactions to last year's appropriation requests. If changes in procedure lead to different kinds of calculations, one would like to be able to predict what the impact on decisions was likely to be.

THE GOALS OF KNOWLEDGE AND REFORM

Concentration on developing at least the rudiments of a descriptive theory is not meant to discourage concern with normative theory and reform. On the contrary, it is worthwhile studying budgeting from both standpoints. Surely, it is not asking too much to suggest that a lot of reform

33

be preceded by a little knowledge. The point is that until we develop more adequate descriptive theory about budgeting, until we know something about the "existential situation" in which the participants find themselves under our political system, proposals for major reform must be based on woefully inadequate understanding. A proposal which alters established relationships, which does not permit an agency to show certain programs in the most favorable light, which does not tell influential Congressmen what they want to know, which changes prevailing expectations about the behavior of key participants, or which leads to different calculations of an agency's fair share, would have many consequences no one is even able to guess at today. Of course, small, incremental changes proceeding in a pragmatic fashion of trial and error could proceed as before without benefit of theory; but this is not the kind of change with which the literature on budgeting is generally concerned.

Perhaps the "study of budgeting" is just another expression for the "study of politics"; yet one cannot study everything at once, and the vantage point offered by concentration on budgetary decisions offers a useful and much neglected perspective from which to analyze the making of policy. The opportunities for comparison are ample, the outcomes are specific and quantifiable, and a dynamic quality is assured by virtue of the comparative ease with which one can study the development of budgetary items over a period of years.

DEPARTMENTAL BUDGETARY PROCEDURE
WILLIAM JUMP

MR. DIRKSEN. Mr. Jump, for the record, I wonder if you could give me a brief statement of your own budgetary procedure within the Department itself, that is to say, the mechanics for setting up the budget, and then I would like to have you continue from that point on and give me a statement concerning your presentation to the Budget Bureau.

MR. JUMP. What we do, briefly, Mr. Dirksen, is to call for estimates to be submitted by all of the bureaus and offices, usually during the month of June. During the war, by reason of numerous shifts in the war situation, our policy determination, our procedure, and our normal time scheduling, all have been disrupted and have had to be adjusted from month to month and week to week, as wartime changes required.

In general, however, our procedure is to ask the bureaus to submit their original estimates bearing in mind existing policy, as defined by legislation, departmental administrative policy and program plans, the continuing need for economy, and the need for coordinating as far as possible at the bureau level the various programs and interrelationships involved, before they submit their estimates to the Department. It is our feeling that we ought to get as much program coordination as possible at the bureau, or operational level, first.

Normally those are the principal injunctions that we give in asking for the first, or original bureau estimates, but it has been a long time since we had a normal year. During the war years we have had, each year, to formulate a pretty careful and informative statement of internal departmental policy governing the considerations that the bureaus particularly ought to have in mind in the preparation of their estimates. In other words, a guide, you might say, in the preparation of their estimates; but by and large in normal times we start out on the theory that while every bureau and program head ought to, and is expected, in formulating his original estimates, to have fully in mind probable overall budgetary limitations and economy in public expenditures, nevertheless the Department ought to give each bureau a chance to express its ideas of what is necessary or desirable in the particular field of activity in which they operate.

The idea is that the people who are in charge of the program agencies, and therefore closest to the actual needs in each field, ought to have an opportunity, at least annually, to submit estimates that reflect the changes

---

Article is from *Hearings before the Subcommittee of the Committee on Appropriations*, U.S. House of Representatives, 2nd session, on the Agriculture Department Appropriation Bill for 1947, Washington, D. C.: U.S. Government Printing Office, 1946, pp. 69–81.

they think should be made to assure adequate public service in the particular fields with which they are charged. That is one way you can be sure, from year to year, of determining the extent to which the various bureaus have a constructive approach to the overall job of the bureau and a carefully planned program, based on adequate self-analysis and program appraisal with respect to current public needs, public reactions, and other factors having an important bearing on their work. If, on the other hand, you get the original estimates on a basis that is too strictly inhibited to start with, such as, for example, a requirement that the overall estimate made must come below a certain amount, or some similar stricture, you will never see, in any systematic, concrete, or carefully developed form, the plans which the head of program may have in mind; you will not get any such plan, when you get the estimate. In normal times, therefore, we conceive it to be proper and advisable to get in the original estimates from the bureaus on this basis in the first instance and then for the Department to give them adequate and competent consideration, and to make such revisions as may be necessary, in the light of many overall considerations, including of course overall budgetary policy, insofar as the Department can apply the latter.

Mr. DIRKSEN. Do those estimates come to you?

Mr. JUMP. Yes, they come to our office. We study them carefully and make certain digests and analysis of them, and at this first phase we end up with a certain set of overall statements not too unlike those we bring here to the committee, except perhaps somewhat more in detail. We then submit these to the Secretary personally so that he can have a bird's-eye view of the recommendations submitted by the bureaus and we go over them with him in a somewhat general fashion, in order to have a broad policy determination made by the Secretary to govern our approach to the departmental budget preparation.

Mr. DIRKSEN. May I ask whether the bureau chiefs make a personal presentation to you?

Mr. JUMP. Not right at this time; that comes later, as a very important part of the process. As I said, after the original bureau estimates come to us we have a conference with the Secretary, to ascertain overall, broad policy determinations and establish a general framework on which we will base such revision as may be necessary of the bureau estimates to bring them into complete harmony with the overall departmental objectives and requirements and to bring the aggregate sum involved down to a figure that will more nearly reflect our interpretation of the budgetary or fiscal situation. At the same time, we get the Secretary to indicate whom he would like to have, from the general staff, to work with us in the detailed consideration of the estimates for that particular year. While at this stage we actually work on a committee basis, we have avoided setting up an organic budget committee in the Department over the years, because of the tendency of such committees to become frozen, the tendency of the membership to get frozen, whereas, from year to year or period to period the basic considerations chiefly involved in building an agricultural budget are quite different, and a committee designed for one period might not be useful in a later year or period and might not be in sufficiently close touch with the policy of the Secretary currently in office. While we do not have a formal committee, we have always recognized that the nature and extent of the functions and programs of the Department of Agriculture are such that the budget formulation has to be done by a highly collaborative process that will provide for application to consideration of the estimates of legislative requirements, current policy, program planning, administrative management, budget techniques and so on, at one and the same time. So, we ascertain from the Secretary personally, each year, whom he would like to have work with us on the budget from his general staff. At various times we have had the Under Secretary or the Assistant Secretary, sometimes both of them, but usually one or more of the assistants to the Secretary are designated by the Secretary in this informal way to work with our staff on the estimates. It has to be someone who can put in considerable time, day after day, for a period of weeks, because, as this committee so well knows, it is a big job to go over all of these items. This year Mr. Minor was designated by the Secretary to work with us all the way through on the 1947 budget. In addition, we work closely with such officers as the Agricultural Research Administrator, the Solicitor, the Director of Personnel, the Director of Information, and other assistants to the Secretary and other general officers, where their fields of activity may be especially involved.

In the first conference we hold with the Secretary, and before we have our sessions with the various bureaus, we try to develop a general policy directive to guide our consideration in formulating the type of budget to be submitted to the Bureau of the Budget. Usually that directive is very general at this stage, since the hundreds of individual items and projects have not yet been examined in detail. The preliminary policy conference may be brief or it may last for an hour or two. Then we go back and begin work on the estimates in detail. At the beginning, our own staff and the person or persons designated by the Secretary usually spend 3 or 4 days in studying the various requests the bureaus have submitted, looking at the totals involved, the relationships which seem to require especial coordination, either intra- or inter-departmental in character, and other general factors. In addition to the general officers the Secretary has designated to work on the budget, this group usually will include Mr. Roberts, my principal assistant who specializes on the budget side of our work, Mr. Wheeler, the Chief of our Division of Estimates and Allotments, and, as budget examiners, several of our staff assistants who by assignment specialize in handling budgetary, financial, and program matters for our office with respect to particular agencies or programs of the Department. For example, I have one such staff assistant, Mr. Lynch, who is our staff assistant for the Farm Security Administration, the Farm Credit Administration, and the Rural Electrification Administration. He keeps in as close touch as possible with those agencies throughout the year, on a day-to-day basis, and is very familiar with all important program developments in those agencies which have financial or budgetary implications, and it seems that most of them do have such implications. We do not have a large staff of these men. It ranges from three to six, dependent upon our finances and ability to find suitable people for such assignments. They are difficult jobs to fill. These staff assistants go through the estimates in detail and by reason of their familiarity with particular programs they raise a great many points that need to be explored in detail with the bureaus.

Then, keeping in mind our general policy understanding, and trying to be as fair and as objective and as intelligent as we can be, we set up a general framework, quite tentative in nature, as the rough outline of the overall budget, bureau by bureau. But still we make no final decisions until after we have a separate conference—they are really hearings, pretty much the same as you have here, but we prefer internally to call them conferences—with each of the bureau chiefs and their principal assistants and can go into the items with them in some detail. At this stage we spend several hours, about like you do here, going over the estimates of each bureau but in the meantime our staff assistants and the members of the Division of Estimates and Allotments have been having a great many individual informal meetings and conferences with the proper people in the bureaus, in an effort to bring about a better understanding on our part, clear up doubtful points, and so on. This we have found to be a very valuable part of the process.

In the course of the conferences with the bureau chiefs, we usually, though not always, have to tell them that the estimates have to be reduced in a material way for the Department as a whole, because frequently the amount which the bureau is asking for is rather tremendous. This is not a reflection on the desirability of the items they submit, the needs they reflect, or of the soundness of their proposals. Rather, it is just a fiscal fact, and we have to distill out of these estimates a budget that will be within the fiscal boundaries that a Secretary of Agriculture may deem it practicable to submit as his recommendation to the President. Sometimes we lay out the whole departmental budget before a bureau chief so that he himself can see the necessity for a material revision. As a rule, it is necessary to revise the bureau estimates materially at this stage. The departmental group usually sets a tentative total figure to be attained by each bureau in the revision but, and this is very important, in making the revision we generally depend in the first instance, to a very large degree, upon the bureau or program head to exercise his best judgment as to how this may most wisely be done. We reserve for the Department, the Secretary, let us say, the right to review and to differ, but we ask the bureau head first to submit a digest in which he lists the increases and decreases that he originally asked for, with a new, additional column, labeled "revised departmental estimate" in which he presents a breakdown reflecting the judgment of the bureau in case a stipulated sum has to be cut off of the original total of the estimates.

This shows us how the bureau would revise the estimates to come within a new tentative ceiling that the departmental group has established. We have, in effect in the meeting, verbally given the bureau heads a tentative ceiling that is as fair as we can make it, taking into account the agricultural situation, the need for the various items as stated in the estimates which the bureaus have submitted, any laws recently passed by the Congress, like the new extension law, for example, or any other new factors that our experience and observation indicate need especially to be considered in a given year. The important thing here is that we have been able to depend upon the bureau to designate the relative importance of the various items as seen from the standpoint of their own judgment, which is highly valuable, since they are the ones most familiar with their own fields and the problems and needs involved. The Government has invested considerable money in the existence of these bureaus and their program leaders. We try to realize on this investment by utilizing their advice and judgment all the way through the process.

They come back with their revision on this basis. Sometimes they appeal when they are not satisfied that an effective budget can be formulated on the basis of the tentative ceiling. If they do, we try to work things out on a basis that will be reasonable, all factors considered. After we get in the revised bureau proposals we restudy them rather carefully. If we believe the adjustments made are sound, that as between bureaus they will provide a balanced and coordinated program, and so on, we submit them to the Secretary with a recommendation for approval. This is usually done by personal contact with the Secretary, so we can respond to any questions he may desire to raise as he looks at the original and revised proposal for each bureau. If the Secretary approves the revised setup, we then notify the bureau and they put the estimates in final form on that basis. Sometimes the Secretary will make a change or two, based on his personal judgment. Sometimes these changes are based on special questions we raise for his personal consideration. If such changes are made, we reflect those in the notice we give the bureau at this stage. If, when the bureau submits its digest revising its original estimates and upon restudy by the departmental group, there are proposals which seem, for any reason, to be inadvisable, or tend to unbalance some program that involves, for example, one or more of the other bureaus, or that seems not in full accord with some general policy plan or objective, then we will have a further conference with the bureau, and by a process of discussion and negotiation we usually work out a final settlement on what seems to be the best basis taking all circumstances into account.

In submitting the revised breakdowns of the estimates, to bring them within a new aggregate total, the bureau heads know that they have the right to appeal directly to the Secretary, if they deem that appropriate, and they understand that such an appeal is not in any way resented by the group that is revising the overall budget. In many years we do not have any appeals. In certain years we may get one or two. I think that is about as many as we have ever had. When that occurs we go into the whole thing again and, if possible, make adjustments that will comprise a workable setup.

At our conference with the bureau head, and before he makes the revision of his estimates, we discuss all of the expenditure items in such detail as may be needed. This discussion is quite substantive in nature. We keep in mind our mission to serve the farmer and the Nation, and our obligation to do that in the best and most economical manner possible with the funds provided or to be requested. We know, and our bureaus know, that the public has a right to expect a full dollar value, and more if possible, for every dollar we spend, and that it is our obligation to plan and manage our work on that basis. We go into legislative, public, industry, or similar consideration, any questions of functional duplication, overlapping, interbureau or other relationships involved, questions of policy, matters of program coordination, and any other points involving economy in expenditures, etc., that the detailed examination of the estimates or our day-to-day contact during the year has indicated ought to be considered in connection with the estimates.

There are two variations of the procedure I have been describing by which we consider the original bureau estimates. One is that in a case where only one or two items are involved we usually arrive at a direct final settlement with the bureau which does not depend upon the procedure I have been sketching, where a revised digest to meet a new ceiling is the principal instrument for decision.

The other is, that in certain cases, where major agricultural policy or some other especially complex issue is involved, instead of a straight revised estimate to come within a new total, we may ask the bureau, in the course of our departmental conference with them, to submit a new summary, in a form we have evolved over the years, that will show in five comparable columns, first, what is being done in the current year; second, the variations originally proposed by the bureau, and third, fourth, and fifth, the variations which the judgment of the bureau would dictate if the estimates had to be revised on the basis of 75, 50, and 25 percent, respectively, of the budget as originally proposed. In the instances where this method is used, we explain the main issues involved to the Secretary, give him the recommendation of the departmental group, state the pros and cons, and get the Secretary to make a selection, you might say, between the alternatives. On occasion, we will have the head of the bureau present at a session of this type with the Secretary, but that has not been the general rule. It is a session like you have here, in the committee, when you make your committee determinations and the Department is not present, for obvious reasons.

To summarize, in all of this part of the departmental process, three important principles are observed: As competent an overall objective, departmental analysis, review, and evaluation of the bureau estimates as we can provide; maximum utilization of the first-hand knowledge, judgment and responsibility of the bureau and program people; and final decision by the

Secretary of Agriculture, since the estimates process is a program-planning and program-building process of paramount importance.

When the departmental decisions have been made the estimates are put in the form required by the Bureau of the Budget and sent to that Bureau with a letter of transmittal from the Secretary. We start in June. They are sent to the Budget Bureau September 15.

MR. DIRKSEN. May I ask you a question at that point?

MR. JUMP. Yes.

MR. DIRKSEN. Are you equipped with investigators and examiners to check into the operations of the bureaus in Washington to determine whether it is possible to eliminate some personnel in the office; and my second question is whether you are equipped with people to go into the field to check their operations there?

MR. JUMP. The answer to that question is both yes and no. We have a few people and we do some of that but not on the scale that I think you may have in mind. We have a small staff of about four men now serving as staff assistants or budget examiners. We should have a larger staff of this type. But we have had some reductions in funds as well as difficulties in recruiting suitable people.

The four staff assistants that I have mentioned are not attached to any division of the office. They operate all the way across the office, internally, but they specialize upon certain bureaus or programs as assigned to them, like the one I mentioned who specializes with respect to the Farm Security, Farm Credit, and Rural Electrification Administrations. We divide the major programs of the Department so that each one of these men is responsible for keeping in touch from day to day with the affairs of that program that may involve financial or budgetary implications. But we are not equipped and do not attempt to do from the central organization of the Department an intensive job of management control. In view of the size and nature of the Department of Agriculture programs it would take a very large staff to do that. Of course, we check and examine all specific estimates that are submitted but I take it you have in mind a more continuous process.

In addition to this staff of program assistants in the Office of Budget and Finance we have a small division known as the Division of Fiscal Management, which engages in various kinds of management survey and similar operations such as work simplification, improvement of procedures, and so on. For example, these people are interested in eliminating and simplifying forms, simplifying procedures, improving the handling of operating details, eliminating waste, and so on; the things that typically are done by units of that sort in the Government. For example, they are now making a study of administrative expenses of various types.

In addition to that the Office of Personnel has a Division of Organization and Personnel Management which also does some work of the type you mention. The two Management Divisions, the one in the Office of Personnel and the one in the Office of Budget and Finance, work in very close

41

cooperation and handle a number of things on a joint basis. For instance, together, they implement the leadership of the continuing Management Improvement and Manpower Utilization Program which the Department has under way and which I outlined at last year's hearings.

The Office of Plant and Operations also has certain responsibilities in the survey and improvement field that relate to housing, better utilization of space, the handling of the mails and files, the elimination of dead files, and so forth. In other words, each of these staff offices is responsible for stimulation of effort in management improvement throughout the Department, for some checking and for leadership in their own field. They are all brought together for coordination and cooperation through an administrative council, and through conferences of key management representatives for each bureau. A certain amount of survey work is done but we do not now have what you might refer to as a separate bureau of efficiency, such as you had back in the old days when there was an independent Bureau of Efficiency with a staff of people who were constantly going out on specific jobs and checking into Government operations, trying to effect improvements. A good deal of that is being done, but on a more cooperative basis with the operating agencies.

There is another philosophy that has to be taken into account with respect to that, and that is that when people come in from organizations outside of their own departments and offices, with outside investigators, empowered to simplify procedures, or to effect changes in organization or operations, they are met by a natural antagonism, that springs up on the part of the people who are held responsible for program results, against someone who drops in to tell them how they should run their programs. Sometimes the great value that lies in introducing a fresh, outside viewpoint, is lost, in part at least, by this well-known human reaction.

So that during the past several years we have engaged in quite an effort to get the bureaus within each of these major programs affected, to themselves set up and equip themselves with a staff that will be able to do more and more of the kind of work that you speak of at the bureau level, and as the Department itself has tended to evolve into about 10 major organizations, instead of having 35 or so individual bureaus, a great deal can be done at the operating level. For instance, the Production and Marketing Administration which Secretary Anderson has established, has within its own organization a very good management organization. They are aware of all of the problems peculiar to the organization; the people know them and see them from day to day, and then plans and recommendations receive an acceptance that would be difficult for outsiders to get.

MR. DIRKSEN. Of course, Mr. Jump, I will say at that point if it is left to the bureaus, with their self-interest, the probability is you will not get the results that you would like.

MR. JUMP. That is quite right. I was going to make that point before I got through. You can't afford to put all the eggs in the one basket, but I do not want to overlook the importance of these units operating right in the bureaus. Since I have observed a tendency for the value of this home-grown variety of self-improvement to be overlooked in favor of outside experts who may be better but who come and go and sometimes do not get such a good acceptance from the responsible program operators. In addition to the efforts of the departments, staff offices, and the bureaus themselves we have a somewhat loosely knit organization, which consists of people all over the Department who are working, in many different ways, on all kinds of management and operational improvement work, in all of the bureaus. This is the Department of Agriculture Organization and Procedure Conference. It elects its chairman, and brings together all the people engaged in different kinds of work, for joint consideration of ways and means to improve the Department's methods of operation.

To get to your point, I agree fully that we cannot afford to leave this kind of function solely with the idea that it is all going to be worked out properly; we have got to go beyond that. And I can assure you that in our administrative processes, in our personnel processes, and in our budget and fiscal processes, the operation, the examination, and the controls are not left completely with the bureaus.

We are working at it from the departmental level all the time, but the point is, I think we would have to stop short of saying that we are fully equipped, either as to money or as to people, to meet the kind of intensive departmental examination and control that is inferred by your question, that is, to give a real intensive management supervision in reference to the Department at large. We expect our bureaus to do a lot of that, and they are functioning that way.

Mr. Reid, do you have any comment you wish to make concerning the idea that is under consideration?

Mr. Reid. No; I think you have made a very full statement.

Mr. Dirksen. Mr. Jump, I have one other question. Would it be fair to assume that after your conference with the Secretary and you have established what you think of as overall ceilings for the estimates, whether you are asked to reshuffle the various amounts as necessary within those ceilings?

Mr. Jump. Yes; but we do not stop there. The bureaus may go back to the departmental committee, the informal budget committee that I described, where we have spent many hours going over the reports furnished by the bureaus. And in the course of the hearings, or the conferences with the bureau, we do a great deal just like you do here, even more so, of this type of adjustment.

BUDGET BUREAU CONSIDERATION

After our departmental estimates go over to the Bureau of the Budget, that Bureau has its hearings, and the staff of the Budget Bureau goes into the details of expenditure in a most intensive way. They go into the

43

expenditure details more intensively than I think this committee or any other committee will ever get the time to do. You do not have the time to do it in your committee hearings; you cannot spend as much time as they do on these detailed expenditure matters. And of course, I do not believe this is a type of examination you can make by just coming to a hearing, either in the Department, or those held by the Bureau of the Budget or Congress. You cannot depend upon that alone. It is a continuing process; an everyday problem. There are items that come up every day, items in our office, and I am sure in the Office of Personnel, and in Mr. Thatcher's office, where we are able to refer, or redirect or modify a course of action and lay the groundwork for administrative action either currently or when the next estimates are compiled.

GENERAL DISCUSSION OF PERSONNEL ESTIMATES

MR. DIRKSEN. I have one other question in connection with the proposals in the 1947 budget. Have any of the bureau chiefs submitted any recommendation for the reduction of personnel?

MR. JUMP. Oh, yes. In these estimates, which are before you for 1947, we have reductions involving about 400 man-years in Washington personnel. Mr. Roberts has tables by bureaus showing the reduction of around 400 man-years. There are both decreases and increases in personnel in the field service, the net increase being contingent upon the action taken by Congress on the program increases that are submitted in the Budget estimates.

MR. DIRKSEN. But these were decreases that were effectuated as a result of pressures of your office on the bureau chiefs?

MR. JUMP. Not necessarily. This matter of reduction of force, according to my observation, is more a matter of dollars than any other factor; personnel is based almost solely on the amount of. money allowed. The measure of the program authorized is expressed in dollars in the Budget grants. It takes a certain amount of personnel to accomplish that authorized program objective. If the program is modified the dollars are modified, up or down, and in the case of an ordinary type of program the personnel required likewise fluctuates, up or down. I have been unable to understand the amount of energy that is being required to be used by the Departments, and the Bureau of the Budget, and the amount of dependence which the Congress apparently has placed on the recently instituted personnel ceiling procedure, because it is so easy to control Government personnel, and every other expenditure factor, by the basic decision to grant, withhold or modify the appropriation. That is the basic thing which settles, or ought to settle, the question of how much personnel you are going to need or be allowed to have. To supplement that with an elaborate additional process such as is now in effect for quarterly personnel ceilings seems superfluous.

I have observed this and similar matters over the years in the Department of Agriculture, and there are two things that are important in addition to all procedures and other factors that apply: One is, in general, our personnel in the Department of Agriculture has a very salutary attitude toward the spending of other people's money.

Because the Department has had a tremendous turnover in personnel in the last 10 or 15 years, we have worked hard to see that the new personnel which comes into the Department understands that we are spending public, or other people's money and that this requires greater care than if we were spending our own money. When we find that someone in the Department does not seem to carry through on this basis we are disappointed, and we do not like it.

MR. JUMP. And to continue—we want them all to be exposed to the idea that when they are spending government money it is the people's money, the money of the taxpayers of this country, and there is a certain attitude of care and prudence and caution that you are obligated to carry out with respect to that if you are going to stay in business as a public official. I would put the acceptance of that idea and the performance under it—the way it has sunk into the minds and being of the people in the Department of Agriculture—against any group in the country. Of course, we make some mistakes; we have our slips; we do not succeed 100 percent. We are always embarrassed when we do have someone who makes a slip, and it would be contrary to human nature to expect us not to have a slip of some kind in a thing of this character. But in general I am inclined to place a great deal of dependence and reliance upon the attitude which I have described, because I believe it is a basic requirement for economical operation of a public activity. I believe it is something which has had a great deal to do with the splendid record which those in the Department of Agriculture have made in carrying out the great programs which the Department has carried out, in all of their ramifications, over the years. That is the first point, the matter of attitudes held by public employees. In my judgment, it is a basic thing.

Second, in the Department of Agriculture I have observed this: That there is what amounts to a natural law that is working all the time on such matters as these estimates and on how money is spent, that is more of a guaranty against overstaffing and similar offenses than anything that budget experts or anybody else might do, and that is that the people who make up our program leaders—and this is not new to you, because you know so many of these people—have got so many things that they see that ought to be done within the range of authorized activity in their respective fields and that they urgently desire to do in order to get more effective program accomplishment and that are needed in the public interest but that they are unable to do at any given period. You run over in your minds the people you know in such departments as the Soil Conservation Service, the Forest Service, and other similar groups, all of them have things that need to be done in their authorized field of work, things that ought to be done now—and they feel that very strongly—something which is in the interest of the public they serve. People who have this kind of interest in their program simply do not use 25 employees where 20 would suffice. They do not propose an allotment of $25,000 for a job that can be done for $20,000. To do so makes it impossible to utilize men and money for another part of the job they have been authorized to do. In budget making they will come in and say, "We would like to have $75,000 to do a certain thing." They will make a full explanation in writing, giving the breakdown in great detail. We will all talk it over in considerable detail.

Should it develop that the aggregate total, of which this would be only one increment, thereafter has to be reduced, they do not come back and say, "If we can not have $75,000 we can not do anything." They do not ordinarily come back and say that they must have the $75,000 or nothing. They will come back and cut it down to $60,000 or $40,000. In some instances they may eliminate it altogether, but that would be as a last resort. In the revising of these budgets I have noticed a very definite tendency on the part of our personnel toward starting out the doing of one of these things on the basis which really means underfinancing of that particular idea rather than to ask for the entire matter of money required, having it refused, and having the thing obliterated completely. It is a tendency to try to start rendering some service with $20,000 which should not be started unless you have $50,000 in sight. My point is, in the urge to get things done whatever money is available is likely to be allotted in such a way that there may be underfinancing of a great many individual items rather than overfinancing or overstaffing of a few items with the others thrown out the window. This is a natural principle that I see working and while we cannot afford to base a budget on this idea by any means, yet that is the picture and a philosophical trend that I have seen running through the various programs down there at the Department for many, many years, and I think it is something which is going to, in all probability, continue in the years to come, because it reflects how these folks feel about the work in which they are engaged.

Mr. TARVER. Mr. Cannon, do you have any questions?

Mr. CANNON. Yes; I do have a few questions at this point. As you say, Mr. Jump, it is very easy to control the number of personnel by controlling the amount of money that is appropriated. Do you feel that that is the better way to do that?

Mr. JUMP. I certainly do feel that. To my mind, there is nothing superior to the dollar in controlling Government expenditures. I know it does not quite meet the situation, because you will continue to get letters about the number of Government personnel, travel of Government employees, and so on, but the real way to control expenditures is to control appropriations. If you do not have the money, naturally, you cannot operate. We would like to have the decisions made by the Congress, by giving us the money for what Congress wants us to do, what programs Congress wants carried out and the amount for each, and depend upon us to do it properly. If Congress issues the money to us by way of appropriation for us to do a job, and we do not perform it properly, then we would be subject to criticism and we would expect it. If the money is not appropriated the job could not be done and there would be no criticism on that score. We feel that Congress can best indicate its will by appropriating money for the programs it wants carried out and withholding appropriations for those not wanted.

Mr. DIRKSEN. Mr. Chairman, may I ask a question at this point?

Mr. TARVER. Have you finished, Mr. Cannon?

Mr. CANNON. Yes. I just wanted to ask a question at this time on that point.

Mr. DIRKSEN. I just have one question here, really. Is this not another way of saying, or would it not be a better way to say it that it would be better to operate one function or project adequately than to be operating two or three or perhaps even three or four inadequately from the standpoint of funds, which would mean, coincidentally, inadequate personnel, material, and so forth?

Mr. JUMP. I think that is quite true.

Mr. TARVER. Mr. Cannon, do you have any further questions along the line of our present inquiry?

Mr. CANNON. The head of each one of these different activities engaged in field work is sincerely convinced of the importance of his work, and the advantage of spending additional funds and having additional personnel, and any of them, if the money was provided would double his force and double his activity in the way that he would consider advantageous for that particular operation; is that not so?

Mr. JUMP. That is quite so. And frequently, I might add as a further point, in the way that Congress would consider to be advantageous in the public interest, also, if it were clear that the money could be spared for such purposes.

Mr. CANNON. But the unfortunate thing is that Congress cannot spend money on all of these different kinds of things to the extent that they would like to have it spent; that is, that these various heads of these activities would like to have it spent, and I might add, perhaps as the Congress itself might like to have it spent, and the question arises as to whether or not it is something which will be spent advantageously. Congress must allocate funds in such manner as to come within necessary budgetary limits. You say that almost invariably all of these research agents are met with resentment on the part of the activities that are being investigated?

Mr. JUMP. No, sir; Mr. Cannon, I did not mean to give you that impression—not resentment. As a matter of fact, we have had excellent cooperation, I think, all the way down the line.

Mr. CANNON. I quite distinctly remember the use of the word "resentment." We can have the reporter read that part of your testimony back if you think it would assist you in answering the question.

Mr. JUMP. If I used the word "resentment" I used in inadvisedly, and I should have chosen another word. As a matter of fact, as I said before, we have had excellent cooperation. Perhaps I can get at it better by telling you what I had in mind. What I was trying to say, Mr. Cannon, is that efforts to set up one great big management-survey organization in the department, certainly in a department like the Department of Agriculture, and then to turn it loose on all of these bureaus, I do not believe would be advantageous. I would rather see, if we had but the one choice, to strengthen from within three or four segments of the Department, strengthen their own organization for management and improved operations generally. Let me give you an illustration or so. If you take the triple A for purposes of study, I know a great many people would be surprised to learn that the triple A has been one of the most interested and most cooperative organizations in the matter of developing effective management-improvement operations. I say "surprised" because most people probably do not expect that a farm-program organization like triple A, with all of its county committees, and so forth, would be much interested in operational simplification and improvement. However, the whole triple A organization, Washington and field, is intensely interested in such improvements. They have, for instance, eliminated 57 forms that were being used by farmers all over the country, millions and millions of copies, trying to simplify and make their own program more workable and more economical to operate. They have an intensive improvement under way, with everyone cooperating. Since it is cooperative and pretty largely home grown in nature, it has the full sympathy and understanding of the people in the triple A itself. On the other hand, if we were to bring into that organization people from the outside to devise methods for operating the program they would feel that they, the triple A, were being superseded by experts, whereas they are the people who are responsible for getting results, and on the other hand, for any bad results which might accrue from making a misstep they would feel that the program was one with which they were the most intimately acquainted, and that they knew the program, and were responsible for it, and they would be very careful in anything they did in connection with that program.

It is not a question of antagonism, as we commonly use the term; it is more largely a lack of faith in outside people who would be connected with such a matter because they would feel that they did not have the knowledge of the department, the interest in the department, and certainly that they did not have the responsibility in that particular branch or division for the carrying out of its program, and they might feel that any suggestions which they might make might be more reckless and not as well considered as they would be otherwise. This does not mean there is no place for the outside surveyor or investigator because each approach is needed. I am just mentioning some of the limitations if we depended too much on any central staff.

Let me say this further: I am not satisfied with our present situation. I do not think anybody is. Certainly, we ought to have better and stronger implementation at the department levels. I just do not think we ought to go all the way off the level ground of sensible operation, and fail to take full advantage of the ideas of the program people themselves, who bring out new ideas, people in whom they have faith, and who are properly equipped to give such ideas. I think that those are things which should be considered most carefully.

FISCAL MANAGEMENT

PRESIDENT'S COMMITTEE ON
ADMINISTRATIVE MANAGEMENT

Sound fiscal management is a prime requisite of good administration. The responsibility of the Executive for the preparation of a fiscal program in the form of a budget for submission to the Congress and for the direction and control of expenditures under the appropriation acts must be carried on faithfully, effectively, and under clear-cut authority. To establish strict accountability of the Executive Branch for the faithful execution of the laws enacted by the Congress, there must be an independent audit of financial transactions by an independent officer reporting directly to the Congress and who does not exercise any executive authority.

From the standpoint of overall control the system of fiscal management of the Government now has four major defects, namely, (1) the inadequate staffing of the Bureau of the Budget; (2) the vesting in the Office of the Comptroller General, which is not responsible to the President, of the settlement of claims, the final determination concerning the uses of appropriations, and the prescribing of administrative accounting systems; (3) the absence of a truly independent and prompt audit of the financial transactions of the Government, whereby the Congress may hold the Executive Branch strictly accountable; and (4) the failure to devise and install a modern system of accounts and records.

Our recommendations for improvement of the fiscal administration of the Government are designed to correct these major faults, to return executive functions to the Executive Branch, and to make it accountable to the Congress.

Before taking up these recommendations in detail, we may review briefly the division of authority and responsibility between the Congress and the Executive Branch for the determination and execution of fiscal policies. The general theory underlying the Constitution is that the Congress shall be responsible for the determination and approval of the fiscal policies of the Nation and that the Executive shall be responsible for their faithful execution. The right of the legislative body to control the purse was a well-established principle prior to the American Revolution and was incorporated in the Constitution. The Congress, as representative of the people, enacts the laws; the duty of executing them is placed by the Constitution upon the President.

This division of authority under our constitutional system was well stated by President Wilson in a message to the Congress on May 13, 1920.

Article is from the Committee's *Report*, Washington, D.C.: U.S. Government Printing Office, 1937, pp. 15–24.

The Congress and the Executive should function within their respective spheres. Otherwise efficient and responsible management will be impossible and progress impeded by wasteful forces of disorganization and obstruction. The Congress has the power and the right to grant or deny an appropriation, or to enact or refuse to enact a law; but once an appropriation is made or a law is passed, the appropriation should be administered or the law executed by the executive branch of the Government. In no other way can the Government be efficiently managed and responsibility definitely fixed.

The Congress enacts the necessary revenue laws, authorizes activities which require the expenditure of public funds, and makes the appropriations. But the trust residing in the Congress does not end with the enactment of appropriation measures; its responsibility requires also that it possess suitable means with which to hold the Executive accountable for the faithful and effective execution of revenue and appropriation laws. Likewise the responsibility of the Executive Branch can be established only if it is given undivided executive powers. If the Chief Executive is to fulfill the responsibility of his office under the Constitution, he must possess undivided executive powers and adequate means with which to exercise them.

A. BUDGETING AND ADMINISTRATIVE CONTROL

The creation in 1921 of the Bureau of the Budget was a major step in the direction of effective administrative management in the Federal Government. It placed upon the President responsibility for the preparation of a comprehensive annual budget and recognized the need for executive discretion and leadership in preparing and submitting to the Congress a program of revenue and expenditure. At the same time it provided the President with one of the primary instruments needed for effective overall management of the executive establishment. The Director at the head of the Bureau is appointed by the President and, though within the Department of the Treasury, reports directly to the President. Through him the President can review and control the effectiveness of governmental agencies.

Purpose of the Budget System

It is the purpose of the budget system to provide in financial terms for planning, information, and control. Through the budget the spending agencies are required to translate their work programs in advance into fiscal terms, so that each activity may be brought into balance and proportion with all other activities, and with the revenues and resources of the Government, and in harmony with long-range and general economic policies. The budget not only serves as the basis of information for the Congress and the public with regard to the past work and future plans of the Administration, but also as the means of control of the general policy of the Government by the Legislative Branch and of the details of administration by the Executive. The Bureau of the Budget was therefore set up as the right arm of the

President for the central fiscal management of the vast administrative machine and to enable him to submit regularly to the Congress a complete report on past activities and a future program for advance approval by the Legislative Branch.

In addition to its duties in the preparation of the annual budget, the Bureau of the Budget was given administrative research functions of outstanding importance. It was charged with the responsibility of making a continuous study of the organization, operation, and efficiency of the Executive Branch of the Government. Through its control over budgeting the Bureau is in a key position to detect weaknesses in the organization and functioning of the various departments and agencies and is the appropriate agency continuously to investigate administrative problems and to make recommendations to the President and the departments in the interest of economy and efficiency.

Substantial progress has been achieved through the Bureau of the Budget during its 15 years of operation. A spotlight has been thrown on national fiscal problems. The Executive has been placed in a better position to plan and control the fiscal program, for which he is held responsible in the public mind. It has been possible to scrutinize departmental needs in detail, and the departments have been assisted in improving their budgetary practices. The Congress has been presented not only with a more intelligible picture of the Nation's finances and financial problems but with a clear comparison between estimates and actual expenditures for the particular governmental activities. Substantial advances in improving governmental operation and in coordinating activities have been effected through the agency of the Bureau. Its staff has aided the President in the performance of many difficult administrative duties. The technical phases of budget making have been constantly improved and refined.

At no time, however, has the Bureau of the Budget achieved or even approximated its maximum possible usefulness and effectiveness as an instrument of administrative management. Because of its small operating appropriation, the Bureau has failed to develop an adequate staff of the highest attainable competence. Such a staff is necessary if it is to cope with the problems raised by a rapid growth in the magnitude and complexity of governmental organization and expenditures. It has not perfected its own organization and methods as a directing and controlling agency of the President. Rather, the Bureau has emphasized the task of preparing the Budget to the distinct disadvantage of its important complementary functions. It has only partially developed supervision over the execution of the Budget by the spending agencies.

The administrative research functions placed upon the Bureau are practically undeveloped; it is in this respect that the Bureau has missed its greatest opportunity. The Budget and Accounting Act of 1921 specifically authorized the Bureau to make detailed studies of the administrative departments and establishments for the purpose of advising the President intelligently as to changes that should be made in their organization and methods, in the grouping of services, and in the appropriations for various activities. The Bureau of Efficiency was abolished by an act of Congress, approved March 3, 1933, mainly on the grounds that it duplicated work that the law required the Bureau of the Budget to do. Its records and files were transferred to the Bureau of the Budget, but adequate provisions for carrying on its work are still to be made. Research in administrative organization has been negligible. Recommendations for reorganization have been conspicuously absent.

Staffing of the Bureau of the Budget

One obtains a vivid realization of the inadequate staff of the Bureau of the Budget from the fact that its appropriation for the current fiscal year (ending June 30, 1937) amounted to only $187,000—a sum considerably less than is spent by a single finance and accounting division of some of the great Government departments, and less than 3 percent of the amount required to audit the expenditures. It has a total personnel of only 45, and aside from the statutory positions of Director and Assistant Director, has only two positions compensated in excess of $6,000 per annum. Only $18,700 was provided for "research, surveys, and assistance." Yet this small staff is charged with preparing a budget of billions and with aiding the President in the exercise of his vast responsibility for the overall management of the huge and intricate Federal administrative machine.

If the Bureau of the Budget is to be developed into a serviceable tool for administrative management to aid the President in the exercise of overall control, it needs greater resources and better techniques. If continuing power is given the President to transfer and consolidate executive establishments, he will need adequate information, based on analyses of the greatest competence, as a guide to action. The Bureau of the Budget is the logical staff agency for the performance of this service. It should be given appropriations and a staff commensurate with the magnitude of the assignment. A relatively small sum invested in strengthening the Bureau of the Budget as a staff agency of the President will yield enormous returns in the increased efficiency of Government operation. It is with this in mind that recommendations regarding the Bureau of the Budget are presented.

The Director of the Bureau of the Budget is one of the few Government officers in a position to advise the President from an overall, as opposed to a bureau or departmental, point of view. He should therefore be relieved to the greatest possible extent from the minor details of administration. He should be released for duties of maximum importance to the President and freed so that he may attend important conferences of Cabinet officers and planning groups, where programs are being considered that may eventually result in appropriation requests or in changes in governmental organization or procedure. In accordance with suggestions made elsewhere in this report, the salary of the Director should be increased. It should be possible for the

President to select a Director from the career service, though he should continue, of course, to have the right to appoint a man of his own choosing.

The position of Assistant Director of the Bureau of the Budget should be filled under civil-service rules, preferably by promotion from the career service. It should be a high permanent post to which career men should be encouraged to aspire. Continuity in office is important if the Assistant Director is to have the necessary background from which to advise a new Director concerning the techniques of budget making and the intricacies of Government machinery and if he is to be skilled in the execution of policies and programs. Breadth of experience, depth of knowledge, and broad vision are needed in this office; these can be obtained only through intensive training and long experience in the Government itself. The Assistant Director should maintain the ordinary contacts with the administrative and budget officers of the departments as well as with the heads of other overall management agencies such as the civil-service establishment. He should direct the activities of the several divisions of the Bureau of the Budget and in every possible way should assume responsibilities that would leave the Director free to concern himself with matters of major policy and program.

If the Bureau of the Budget is to perform effectively its functions of fiscal and overall management it must be staffed with an adequate personnel. Division chiefs of high competence should be appointed from the career service. It should continue to have a career man as administrative assistant to attend to the institutional needs of the Bureau, such as personnel, appropriations, organization, financial records, and general services. The Director should have the authority to appoint a number of special assistants from inside or outside the service for special assignments and to retain consultants from business and the professions on a temporary basis for investigations or conferences in technical fields. The right to transfer or detail personnel from other Government agencies is of particular importance to the Bureau of the Budget and this should be authorized. For long-term periods the Bureau should reimburse the departments from which the personnel are borrowed. In turn, the Bureau should be permitted to accept reimbursement from Government agencies when it undertakes studies of organization and procedure at their request.

Activities of the Bureau: Estimates

The preparation and execution of the Budget are essentially executive tasks. The Bureau of the Budget as a managerial agency of the President should therefore be made responsible for the execution, as well as the formulation, of the budget as a national fiscal plan. The task of scrutinizing and passing upon departmental estimates and of exercising some measure of continuing direction over the execution of the budget should be assigned to a special division in the Bureau. The highly important task of budgeting requires a staff of unusual competence, breadth of vision, keen insight into governmental problems, and long acquaintance with the work of the Government. Only a staff having these qualifications can be of assistance to the President, the Congress, and the departments in the preparation and consideration of a budget. Well-considered and informed central direction of budgeting is essential; arbitrary, uninformed, and undiscriminating decisions must be avoided.

The staff in charge of budget estimates must keep in constant touch with the entire administrative machine for the purpose of developing and executing both short-term and long-term fiscal plans. Through this staff the President may exercise effective control over the formulation and execution of fiscal plans and policies and may review carefully and wisely the departmental estimates. In this manner fiscal planning may assume its proper relationship to the economic and social planning for which the Nation holds the President responsible.

Administrative Research and Other Managerial Activities

The President needs a research agency to investigate the broad problems involved in the administrative management of the Government—problems of administrative organization, finance, coordination, procedures and methods of work, and the many technical aspects of management. The function of investigation and research into administrative problems should be developed as an aid to overall executive management.

Economy and efficiency in government require constant investigation and reorganization of the administrative structure. It is a mistake to assume that the Government can be reorganized once and for all. Continuous study of the administrative organization of the huge Federal machine is necessary; new activities are constantly emerging and old activities are constantly changing, increasing, decreasing, or disappearing. Unless there is a special agency equipped to investigate problems of organization, new activities are set up without careful attention to where they should be located and what kind of organization is required. This results in costly mistakes and confusion. On the other hand, when the need for certain governmental activities declines or disappears, unless there is a special agency constantly studying the organizational requirements, adjustments are made late or not at all.

A division of administrative research in the Bureau of the Budget is the logical place to develop these functions which were authorized in the act of 1921. It should stimulate the continuous study of organization, methods, and procedures at the departmental or bureau level by the departments and bureaus themselves. It should engage in such studies on its own initiative where necessary, but should follow the policy of aiding and encouraging the departments to study their own organizational and procedural problems. It should endeavor to develop principles of organization that have general applicability and to act as a clearing house and consultation center for administrative research carried on in the departments. It should not undertake studies in fields in which other agencies of the Government are more competent or for which they are better equipped. Above all, persons engaged in administrative research should be freed from detailed routine duties involved in handling budget estimates.

The administrative research activities should be concentrated in a separate division of the Bureau of the Budget. It should be headed by a permanent chief possessing in unusual degree imagination, vision, creativeness, and analytical insight, as well as intimate acquaintanceship with both the practices of government and the principles of public administration. The research division must be staffed with persons of unusually high competence. Important research assignments upon administrative problems can be carried out successfully only by highly trained and experienced persons familiar with the organization and techniques of public administration. Flexible staff arrangements are necessary to permit the use of specialists drawn from the Government and from business for temporary periods.

A division of information should be established to serve as a central clearing house for the correlation and coordination of the administrative policies of the several departments in the operation of their own informational services, and to perform related duties. The United States Information Service might well be transferred to this division. It might also develop into a service which would supervise and foster regional associations of executive officers of the Government and other activities for coordination of the field services. The Director of the Bureau has been authorized by law to approve the use of printing and binding appropriations for the periodicals and journals published by Government agencies; the chief of the division of information could assist him in carrying out this duty.

The President has turned to the Bureau of the Budget for assistance in carrying out a number of important executive duties placed upon him. By reason of its close contact with the operating departments and with the President as a managerial agency, the Bureau is better able to perform these activities than are other administrative units.

One of the most important of these activities is the preparation, consideration, and clearance of Executive orders. Executive orders have been used since the early days of the Government, and, with the great increase in size and complexity of the governmental machine, have been utilized to an ever-increasing extent. They are particularly necessary in periods of emergency when there is rapid change in governmental policies and organization. Executive direction and control of national administration would be impossible without the use of this device. The activity of the Bureau of the Budget as a clearing agency in the issuance and amendment of Executive orders should be continued and strengthened by the development of a more adequate and expert staff. It should be equipped to aid the President in the consideration of administrative problems and to draft the necessary Executive orders.

Wider use could be made of Executive orders to establish uniform codes regulating management throughout the Government. These codes might well cover such matters as budgetary and other financial practices and controls, personnel, supplies, coordination, and other matters related to general organization and management. Such regulations should be promulgated after careful consideration by the departments. They could be arranged in suitable codes and would be of material assistance in guiding administrative officers.

Departmental regulations governing internal organization and management might also be cleared with the Bureau of the Budget. The purpose would not be formal approval or disapproval, but to give to the departments such assistance as the experts of the Bureau might be able to render and to enable the Bureau to inform the President upon any matters which should be brought to his attention. This clearance would result in the establishment of a greater degree of uniformity in the departmental management practices in matters in which uniformity is desirable. It would provide a desirable pooling of the experience of the several departments in many management activities. The Bureau of the Budget should be equipped to assist the departments, at their request, in preparing regulations relating to their internal management.

Another important activity of the Bureau of the Budget as a staff aid to the President is in connection with proposed legislation arising within the executive departments and establishments. In addition to his position as the head of the Executive Branch, the President is charged by the Constitution with important legislative duties, including the duty to advise the Congress "from time to time" of such "Measures as he shall judge necessary and expedient." As Chief Executive he may require "the principal Officer in each of the executive Departments" to give him an "Opinion, in writing, * * * upon any subject relating to the Duties of their respective Offices." Though the final authority for all legislative acts rests with the Congress and the President, it is the duty of the executive departments to supply the Congress with information and advice concerning the laws which they administer.

Inasmuch as a large part of all legislation is concerned with the structure and functioning of administrative departments and · the creation and modification of administrative powers, the Congress is entitled, in the consideration of such legislation, to have from the administrative departments the benefit of their experience and special knowledge. All legislation recommended by the Executive Branch of the Government should be carefully considered before presentation to the Congress. The administrative, financial, legal, international, and other effects and implications of all such proposals should be thoroughly examined and the proposed legislation should be carefully drafted. Conflicts and differences between administrative departments concerning proposed legislation, whether of major policies or details, should, so far as possible, be adjusted before such bills are presented to the Congress. Though the ultimate decision in all such conflicts rests with the Congress, its work is hindered by differences between departments. These ordinarily should be adjusted within the Executive Branch of the Government in accordance with the constitutional concept of a single, and not a plural, Executive.

During recent years the Bureau of the Budget has functioned as an agency for the President in the clearance of the fiscal aspects of legislative measures proposed by the executive departments. This clearance is of value to the Congress and to the departments and is essential to the exercise of the authority and responsibility of the President. It should be applied to all legislation proposed by the executive departments and agencies and should not be limited to fiscal considerations. The Bureau of the Budget could well take over the present duties of the National Emergency Council in this respect.

To aid the President in carrying out this responsibility the Bureau of the Budget should develop a staff equipped to act as a clearance agency on all aspects of proposed legislation and to provide the departments with expert and technical assistance. This would enable the Administration to prepare more expertly proposed legislative measures and to insure that ill-considered measures are not submitted to the Congress.

Recommendations

Our recommendations regarding budgeting and administrative control may be briefly summarized as follows:

1. The Director of the Bureau of the Budget should be relieved from routine duties and thus enabled to devote himself to problems of fiscal policy and planning. Provision should be made for an adequate permanent staff of the highest competence, implemented by special assistants on assignments from the operating agencies and by temporary consultants and specialists recruited from business and industry for special assignments.

2. The execution, as well as the preparation, of the budget should be supervised by the Bureau of the Budget and should be closely correlated with fiscal programs and plans.

3. The administrative research function of the Bureau of the Budget should be adequately developed to aid the President in his duties as head of the executive establishment. The Bureau should carry on constructive studies in public administration for the constant improvement of Government organization and procedure and should also stimulate continuous study of these problems by departments and bureaus.

4. The information function of the Bureau of the Budget should be developed and improved. The United States Information Service should be transferred to it, as should other appropriate activities in the coordination of the field services of the Government.

5. The Bureau of the Budget should serve in various ways as an agency of the President. Improvement should be made in its facilities for the clearance of Executive orders and the establishment of uniform codes of management in the Government. It should assist the departments in their regulations governing internal organization. It could render important service to the President and to the Congress in coordinating and clearing legislative recommendations which originate in the Executive Branch.

B. DIRECTION AND CONTROL OF ACCOUNTING AND EXPENDITURES

A second important phase of fiscal management is the direction and control of expenditures through the system of accounting. The present accounting system of the Government is badly scattered and presents a rather incongruous mixture of antique and modern practices. Essential parts of the system are now found in the Treasury Department, divided among three or four important Treasury units, in the General Accounting Office, and in the various operating bureaus, departments, and establishments. At the same time, the warrant procedure that dates back to Alexander Hamilton's day pursues its plodding way alongside the latest machine bookkeeping. Financial reporting from the various accounts is far from being systematized, is generally lacking in telling information for administrative purposes, and is often delayed beyond the point of any practical value.

Although the Budget and Accounting Act of 1921 had as one of its main objects the improvement of the Government's accounting system, very little of real and lasting value has as yet resulted. The Comptroller General was vested with authority under this act to prescribe a system of administrative appropriation and fund accounting in the several departments and establishments. Fifteen years have since elapsed, and still no comprehensive and adequate system of general accounts has been developed by the Comptroller General's office.

The authority which the Comptroller General has exercised over departmental accounting procedures has, in many cases, improved the accounts in the departments and establishments. But these procedures have continually stressed the bringing of accounting information into the General Accounting Office, with little consideration for the informational needs of the Bureau of the Budget, of the Treasury Department, and ultimately of the President. The tendency, therefore, has been to deprive the Executive of adequate accounting machinery, or even authority to develop this important instrument of financial direction. Because of the lack of interest in administration little effort has been made, for example, toward the development of unit or cost accounts. It is very doubtful if the Congress intended that the accounting provision of the 1921 Act should work in this way. Certainly it is inconsistent with Executive responsibility and efficient administration.

The time is ripe for a return to the basic notion that served as the groundwork for the original accounting system of the Government. There should now be installed in the Treasury Department a modern system of general accounting and reporting that would produce accurate information quickly and easily concerning expenditure obligations, appropriation and allotment balances, revenue estimates and accruals, and actual collections, as well as cash disbursements and receipts. Not only should the accounting methods be standardized throughout the governmental agencies, but there should be a complete revamping of the accounting procedure which would enable the Treasury Department to secure reliable information at a moment's notice on the status of all revenues and expenditures of the Government. There is abundant evidence that these accounting improvements are greatly needed, and that they can now be properly made.

Current Control of Expenditures

Through the accounting system current control over expenditures is exercised. This function is often confused with the function of audit. Current control involves final decisions as to proposed expenditures and the availability of funds. An audit is an examination and verification of the accounts after transactions are completed in order to discover and report to the legislative body any unauthorized, illegal, or irregular expenditures, any financial practices that are unsound, and whether the administration has faithfully discharged its responsibility.

A true audit can be conducted only by other officers than those charged with the making of decisions upon expenditures. No public officer should be authorized to audit his own accounts or financial acts and decisions. The maximum safeguard is provided when the auditor is entirely independent of the administration and exercises no executive authority. The control of expenditures is essentially an executive function, whereas the audit of such expenditures should be independent of executive authority or direction.

Although the title of the Budget and Accounting Act indicates that the principal purpose was to provide a budget system and "an independent audit of public accounts," the distinction between "control" and "audit" was confused in the act. It placed certain control functions, as well as the auditing function, in the Office of the Comptroller General, who was thus made both a "comptroller" and an "auditor." This has created an undesirable and anomalous situation: As an auditor the Comptroller General properly performs his function without the direction of any executive officer; but as a comptroller, exercising the executive authority to determine the uses of appropriations, to settle accounts and claims, and to prescribe administrative accounting systems—functions which are universally recognized as executive in character—he is improperly removed from any executive direction and responsibility.

Furthermore, the Comptroller General, as a comptroller, determines in advance the legality of expenditures and issues rules and regulations which govern the administrative procedures and practices of the executive establishments; later, as an auditor, he reviews and audits the action taken under his own previous decisions. The more the Comptroller General exercises control over expenditures through advance decisions, approval of contracts, preaudits, and otherwise, the less competent he becomes to audit them. This system results in divided authority and responsibility for the proper expenditure of public funds and the accounting therefore; it deprives the President of essential power needed to discharge his major executive responsibility. Equally important, it deprives the Congress of a really independent audit and review of the fiscal affairs of the Government by an official who has no voice in administrative determinations, which audit is necessary to hold the Administration accountable.

The removal from the Executive of the final authority to determine the uses of appropriations, conditions of employment, the letting of contracts, and the control over administrative decisions, as well as the prescribing of accounting procedures and the vesting of such authority in an officer independent of direct responsibility to the President for his acts, is clearly in violation of the constitutional principle of the division of authority between the Legislative and Executive Branches of the Government. It is contrary to article II, section 3, of the Constitution, which provides that the President "shall take Care that the Laws be faithfully executed."

In the recent case of *Springer* v. *Philippine Islands* (277 U.S. 189), which involved an attempt to vest executive powers in a legislative body, the Supreme Court declared:

> Legislative power, as distinguished from executive power, is the authority to make laws, but not to enforce them or appoint the agents charged with the duty of such enforcement. The latter are executive functions.

The settlement of accounts and the supervision of administrative accounting systems are executive functions; under the Constitution they belong to the Executive Branch of the Government. The audit, by the same reasoning, should operate under legislative direction. The Comptroller General today straddles both positions.

Prior to the adoption of the Budget and Accounting Act of 1921, accounts and claims were settled by the auditors, all of whom were Treasury officials, and the accounting procedures were prescribed by the Comptroller of the Treasury. Strictly speaking, there was no independent audit. When the Congress adopted legislation providing for a National Budget system in 1921, it also provided for an independent auditing office. The hearings on the act, as well as the language of the act itself, indicate clearly that the purpose in creating an independent auditing office was to enable the Congress to secure adequate and full information upon the finances of the Government. Members of the special committees of the House and the Senate complained that the auditors and the Comptroller of the Treasury, being a part of the administration and subject to removal, would not come before congressional committees and criticize the existing financial practices.

Major attention at that time was focused upon the provisions of the act relating to the creation of a National Budget; the far-reaching implications involved in placing the accounting and controlling authority in an auditing officer independent of the Executive were not clearly realized. There was, however, no lack of warning on this point. During the hearings on the act, in 1919, a number of outstanding witnesses who advocated the creation of an independent auditor stated that he should be charged with the sole task of auditing expenditures after they were made and reporting the results of the audit to the Congress. These witnesses expressed grave doubt as to the wisdom of giving to this independent auditing officer the controlling function as well, for this they regarded as unquestionably executive in character. Among those who called attention to this important distinction were men like former Governor Frank O. Lowden of Illinois, Senator Carter Glass (then Secretary of the Treasury), President Frank J. Goodnow of the Johns Hopkins University, President Nicholas Murray Butler of Columbia University, Mr. John T. Pratt, President of the National Budget Committee, Mr. Henry L. Stimson, later Secretary of State, and Dr. Frederick A. Cleveland.

At various times in the hearings, members of both the House and the Senate committees expressed their own doubts concerning the wisdom of granting controlling and accounting authority to an independent auditor. But the final act transferred to the Comptroller General all the powers formerly exercised by the auditors and by the Comptroller of the Treasury.

Results of Independent Control

The results of placing executive powers of control in an independent auditing office may be reviewed briefly. Before 1921, when the head of a department questioned a ruling of the Comptroller of the Treasury, or when the President requested it, the ruling was referred to the Attorney General for a legal opinion. Since 1921 this practice has been discontinued. An impasse has resulted. The first Comptroller General of the United States consistently refused to submit any disputed question to the Attorney General or to modify any of his rulings in conformance with the opinions of the Attorney General. It is significant that the Attorney General has been sustained repeatedly when the issues were taken to courts of law.

Both the Attorney General and the Comptroller General are directed by the Congress to render opinions or decisions interpreting the meaning of congressional acts. Executive officers customarily turn to the Attorney General when there is any question about the authority or the legality of an action which they are contemplating. The present conflict of authority between these two officers leads to a great deal of uncertainty, delay, and expense, and at times reaches almost to the point of administrative paralysis. Speed, decision, vigor, and common sense in the conduct of national affairs have been subordinated to technical rulings on doubtful questions.

The virtual discontinuance of the practice of referring disputed rulings to the Attorney General for an opinion upon legal issues results in the Comptroller General interpreting his own jurisdiction and the scope of his authority through his own rulings. This is an extraordinary principle, clearly contrary to our political institutions and constitutional theory.

Before 1921 there was comparatively little complaint that the rulings of the Comptroller of the Treasury, precursor of the Comptroller General, encroached upon administrative discretion. This was probably because the

Comptroller of the Treasury was a part of the administration itself, even though he had semi-independent status, and because of the practice of referring disputed questions to the Attorney General. From 1921 on, however, the Comptroller General, through numerous rulings, has carried his authority into areas which are clearly in the realm of executive decision. Any volume of the published rulings of the Comptroller General affords a wide variety of examples of this invasion of administrative responsibility. Many of his rulings go far beyond the terms of any statute.

Rulings by an independent auditing officer in the realm of executive action and methods, even when they seem wise and salutary, have a profoundly harmful effect. They dissipate executive responsibility and precipitate executive uncertainty. Many of the rulings of the Comptroller General, though issued in the belief that they are in the interest of strict legality, undoubtedly impede the work of the departments and add to their operating costs. Administrative officers have found it necessary to go not merely to their superior officers for the approval of plans but also to the office of Comptroller General for the approval of legality, form, and procedure. This division of authority destroys responsibility and produces delays and uncertainty. It has become increasingly difficult, and at times simply impossible, for the Government to manage its business with dispatch, with efficiency, and with economic sagacity.

An effective continuing executive control over the administration of the Government to insure economy, legality, and expedition is impossible so long as such wide authority over plans, forms, and procedures is exercised by the General Accounting Office. The Comptroller General has also extended his authority into administrative matters by the expansion of the preaudit (i.e., audit before payment), by the increased use of advance decisions, and by his rulings, all of which have constantly brought more and more administrative questions to him for final determination. The operating plans of the administration are greatly affected, and sometimes controlled, by his rulings. Fiscal practices are to a large extent governed by his decisions. These are areas of control that are customarily entrusted to executive officers, both in Government and in private business administration.

Numerous delays in administration are inevitable under the current procedures and routines of the General Accounting Office. Every voucher must be examined and passed upon in a single office at the seat of the Government. Final settlements are delayed from a period of 3 months to as long as 3 years after the original transaction has been consummated. Of what value to the Congress or to the administration is an audit which is not completed until after 3 years? Executive officers are unable to obtain accurate current reports on the financial status of their own departments or bureaus. The delay in the audit has also created much uncertainty as to the authority of executive officers, with consequent delay in administrative action. Delays are often expensive. Promptness is essential to vigorous, decisive, and efficient public administration.

Audit of Expenditures

The General Accounting Office has failed to achieve an independent audit of national expenditures. It has not supplied the Congress with the comprehensive information concerning the financial administration of the Government which an audit should render. The Budget and Accounting Act provides that the Comptroller General shall report to the Congress the results of his audit and his investigations into the financial transactions of the Government and states that he "shall specifically report to Congress every expenditure or contract made by any department or establishment in any year in violation of law." Except in a few isolated cases the Comptroller General has not carried out this provision of the act. He has rarely called attention to unwise expenditures or unsound fiscal practices. Since the present arrangement delays the final settlement of accounts, in some cases for as long as 3 years, it is impossible for the Comptroller General even to complete his audit of any fiscal year in time for it to be of any material value to the Congress.

The fundamental reason why the Comptroller General has failed to provide the Congress with a complete, detailed, and critical audit of the fiscal accounts of the Government, however, is the anomalous and inconsistent position of his office.

The results of the vesting of important executive authority in the Comptroller General, an independent officer, who is not responsible to the Chief Executive, nor, in fact, to the Congress or to the courts, are serious. Effective and responsible management of the executive departments is impossible as long as this unsound and unconstitutional division of executive authority continues. At the same time, the Congress is unable to secure a truly independent audit, which is essential if it is to hold the administration to a strict accountability.

Recommendations

Our recommendations regarding the direction and control of accounting and expenditures are as follows:

1. For the purpose of providing the Chief Executive with the essential vehicles for current financial management and administrative control, the authority to prescribe and supervise accounting systems, forms, and procedures in the Federal establishments should be transferred to and vested in the Secretary of the Treasury. This recommendation is not new. In 1932 President Hoover recommended to the Congress that the power to prescribe accounting systems be transferred to the Executive Branch, stating:

> It is not, however, a proper function of an establishment created primarily for the purpose of auditing Government accounts to make the necessary studies and to develop and prescribe accounting systems involving the entire field of Government accounting. Neither is it a proper function of such an establishment to prescribe the procedure for nor to determine the effectiveness of the administrative examination of

accounts. Accounting is an essential element of effective administration, and it should be developed with the primary objective of serving this purpose.

In 1934 a special committee of the United States Chamber of Commerce on Federal expenditures, headed by Mr. Matthew S. Sloan, recommended that all accounting activities be removed from the Comptroller General and placed in a General Accounting Office directly responsible to the President. This committee stated in its report:

> Since the Comptroller General is not under Executive control, as he reports to Congress and is responsible only to that body, the Executive is deprived of one of the most essential means of establishing effective supervision over expenditures, namely, a satisfactory accounting system directly under Executive control. Moreover, the Comptroller General is now in the anomalous position of auditing his own accounting.
> The Committee is convinced that accounting should be segregated from auditing, and that accounting should be centralized in an agency under the control of the President. Such a system would provide the administration with machinery necessary to establish control over expenditures and also afford Congress an independent agency for checking the fiscal operations of the administration.

2. For the purpose of fixing responsibility for the fiscal management of the Government establishment on the Chief Executive in conformity with the constitutional principle that the President "shall take Care that the Laws be faithfully executed," claims and demands by the Government of the United States or against it and accounts in which the Government of the United States is concerned, either as debtor or as creditor, should be settled and adjusted in the Treasury Department.

3. To avoid conflict and dispute between the Secretary of the Treasury and the departments as to the jurisdiction of the Secretary to settle public accounts, which conflicts and disputes have so marred the relationship between the Comptroller General and the departments in the past, and to make it impossible for the Secretary of the Treasury to usurp any of the powers vested in the heads of departments by the Congress, the Attorney General should be authorized to render opinions on such questions of jurisdiction (but not on the merits of the case) upon the request of the head of the department or upon the request of the Secretary of the Treasury, and the opinion of the Attorney General on such questions of jurisdiction should be final and binding.

4. In order to conform to the limitations in the functions remaining within the jurisdiction of the Comptroller General, the titles of the Comptroller General and the Assistant Comptroller General should be changed to Auditor General and Assistant Auditor General, respectively, and the name of the General Accounting Office should be changed to the General Auditing Office.

5. The Auditor General should be authorized and required to assign representatives of his office to such stations in the District of Columbia and

the field as will enable them currently to audit the accounts of the account-able officers, and they should be required to certify forthwith such exceptions as may be taken to the transactions involved (a) to the officer whose account is involved; (b) to the Auditor General; and (c) to the Secretary of the Treasury.

The auditing work would thus proceed in a decentralized manner independent of, but practically simultaneous with, disbursement. Duplication of effort and delays due to centralization in Washington could be reduced to a minimum. It would not be necessary for the Treasury Department to duplicate the field audit of the General Auditing Office. Exceptions would be promptly reported to the Treasury. Prompt, efficient service could be afforded in the scrutiny of questioned vouchers and in the review of accounts of disbursing officers.

6. In the event of the failure of the Secretary of the Treasury and the Auditor General to reach an agreement with respect to any exception reported by representatives of the Auditor General concerning any expenditure, it should be the duty of the Auditor General to report such exception to the Congress through such committees or joint committees as the Congress may choose to designate.

CHAPTER II

SOME ASPECTS OF THE

INSTITUTIONAL CONTEXTS OF

PUBLIC FINANCE AND BUDGETING:

SHARED POWERS, MULTIPLE ACCESS,

AND COMPLEX DYNAMICS

An old European peasant saying has it that the wise man puts all his eggs in one basket, and he watches that basket. Given due attention and strength or lack of thieves, that man can conveniently protect all his eggs. If his attention wavers or his strength is inadequate, however, all of the eggs may be lost in one fell-swoop The underlying strategy thus minimizes the risk of a small loss. Alas, the strategy also maximizes the risk of a total loss.

The men who helped shape our political institutions followed an opposed strategy. They advised, in sum, that we distribute our political eggs among several baskets. The negative root-belief is that the electorate cannot be expected to be either eternally vigilant or broadly informed. The positive root-belief is that the interests of the electorate can, will, and should be engaged in enough significant cases to make their impact felt.

The working accommodation in America has been the despair of doctrinaire thinkers, having as it does dual goals: the control of necessary (but dangerous) political elites; and the control of vital (but lethargic) mass electorates. Native cunning, therefore, called for political institutions set against one another so that some degree of mutual surveillance was built into the system without rigidifying it. As a result our political eggs are scattered, with dual expectations, in several institutional baskets. Thus the chances are increased that no faction can steal all our political eggs. Relatedly, any really ambitious egg-snatchers are more likely to receive the multidirectional attention that sooner or later will motivate the electorate to turn the rascals out. The underlying strategy minimizes the chance of maximum loss, and is prepared to absorb smaller losses as a major cost.

How American political institutions put their eggs in several baskets may be suggested via the late Mort Grodzins' image of a layer cake. Grodzins described the "vertical" sharing of power in our federal system between the central government, the states, and local governments as the several multicolored strata of a political layer cake. The differing widths of the various strata of the cake reflect the differing power of the several levels of government in various issue-areas. The analogy permits multiple comparisons with life. The thickness of the several strata in a layer cake vary widely from point to point, for example, just as the power of various levels of government varies in various areas. Further, the several strata of a layer cake subtly blend into one another in some places, while they stand boldly distinct at others. Just so is power usually shared, although at times one level or another may exercise a virtual monopoly. Grodzins' image can be extended to the "horizontal" sharing of powers at the federal level between the legislative, executive, and judicial branches. This horizontal sharing of powers is commonly referred to as the "separation of powers" plus "checks and balances." The analogy also applies to state and local governments in much the same ways.

Putting our political eggs in several baskets has had profound effects on public finance and budgeting. Indeed, perhaps the central issue of all public administration today concerns the basic redefinition of the scope of the powers of the various levels of governments. The "perhaps" requires emphasis, for the point oozes controversy. Thus the scope of power has been a recurring problem, and observers may differ widely about whether the issue is as central today as it was (for example) during the 1860's. Some will argue, beyond this point, that the present pattern of shared powers prevents creative adaptations to new conditions. Others thank their lucky stars for countervailing governmental powers, "vertically" and "horizontally," such sharing being in their eyes the major preventative against making public policy a vehicle for drastic social experimentation.

Three articles reprinted below carry the burden of illustrating the impact of the sharing of powers on public budgeting and finance, with initial emphasis on the "horizontal" sharing. First, Frederick J. Lawton's "Legislative-Executive Relationships in Budgeting as Viewed by the Executive" incisively analyzes the various institutional features that reinforce the growing impact of the presidency on the budgeting and financial processes. Because of where he sits and the nature of the interests he represents, the President has seen his office become institutionalized as a presidency of some 2,000 immediate aids, including the vital Bureau of the Budget. Prior to World War II, roughly, the President had only a handful of immediate aids. The influence of the presidency on budgeting and finance has burgeoned correspondingly, if limits on that influence are still great. Thus it is a mistake to think of this massive presidency as a unity, for its several members have been known to speak in diverse tongues, both formally and informally. Nor have executive agencies always accepted presidential direction without question. Also, the power of congressional committees and subcommittees is legendary, presidency or no. Qualifications and all, the trend-line for the presidency is up, very sharply.

In sum, the presidency does permit the focusing of great and growing resources and prestige to influence budgeting and financial decisions. Illustratively, the Bureau of the Budget occasionally has used the ultimate presidential weapon, the power to "impound" funds whose expenditures Congress had authorized. The presidency's power of impounding—an "implied power" at best—is a super item–veto. That is, the executive can in effect use it to negate total bills or individual items of both legislative authorization and appropriation, and without the possibility of his action being formally overridden by the legislature as is the case with his constitutional power of veto. Of course, use of impounding by the executive runs the risk of stirring-up countermeasures by the legislature. Less ultimately, the Bureau's influence over allotments for spending by executive agencies also reflects the substantial power of the presidency.

The implied growing relative disadvantage of Congress in affecting spending decisions receives detailed attention in "Congress's Fiscal Role Is Object of Growing Concern." The article is organized around the several stages of the complex congressional budgetary procedure. At each of these stages, the selection emphasizes how legislative institutions, practices, and history are such as to reduce the ability of Congress to provide comprehensive financial control. Thus the very existence of two houses of Congress—with different terms, constituencies, personalities, and styles of decision making—generates powerful centrifugal forces that fragment legislative consideration and oversight of financial matters, for good or ill. The detailed catalog reinforces the validity of Lawton's observation in the preceding piece that legislative-executive relations are not simply a "direct and inevitable outgrowth of the separation of powers." In massive reinforcement, Congress and its electoral system "fosters localism" (in Lawton's terms) and provides multiple points of access for diverse organized interests who seek to get their concept of public or private advantage embodied in legal principle or in actual practice. These "organized interests" include both executive agencies and multifarious associations representing industries, the professions, veterans, and so on.

Granted that Congress may be characterized as relatively "diffuse" and the presidency as relatively "focused" in making budget and financial decisions, one need not make the value judgment that the legislature must be or can be only a mirror image of the institutionalized presidency. Maintaining a certain substantial difference between the Congress and the presidency, of course, is consistent with the practice of keeping our political eggs in several baskets. The orthodox expert opinion does not take this point of view, however. That opinion tends toward the mirror-image role for Congress, toward "executive leadership" over "disciplined political parties." This is the "put all your eggs in one basket" approach. Both strategies have their patent costs, and it is perhaps the guiding genius of our institutions that we can peacefully maintain the two strategies in confusing and ever-changing sets of balances in various issue-areas at different times. That we tolerate complexity while safeguarding personal freedom and while supplying an unparalleled prosperity to increasingly larger segments of our population is the despair of dogmatic thinkers. Perhaps our "mixed" institutions do not, overall, do as well as they might. But neither are they likely to do as poorly as more "pure" institutions might.

The "satisficing" character of congressional institutions receives more microscopic support from Ira Sharkansky's "An Appropriations Subcommittee and Its Client Agencies." The Fogarty Subcommittee gets Sharkansky's attention. That creature of Congress patently had a life-style of its own, and it had substantial autonomy in determining the "how" and the "what" of its oversight activities. In this simple statement inheres enormous potential for sensitive supervision of agencies whose programs are known intimately, and perhaps even compassionately. Oppositely, however, the same statement also contains the seeds of mischievous localism and disregard of overall policy. Congressional history contains many examples of both kinds, and of much between the two extremes.

Getting the best of all legislative worlds has proved challenging. The rub is that a determined effort to eliminate congressional localism also threatens sensitive and intimate oversight. No trade-offs are pure gain, consequently, and managing the balance of overall policy versus local initiative and adaptability poses a continuing challenge.

The vertical sharing of powers—between federal, state, and local jurisdictions—raises similar issues about interpenetration and the locus of control. In general the working solutions are similar to those in the case of the horizontal sharing of powers. Morton Grodzins' "The Bundle of Governmental Services" establishes the interpenetration of local/federal spheres. Directly, Casa Grande dramatically reflects the image of a very complex layer cake indeed. Its bundle of services, for example, diversely involves federal/local officials. In some cases, services are provided completely outside the context of local government by state or federal agents. In other cases, local jurisdictions are the sole or prime providers of services and of the resources they require. In between, complex varieties of sharing exist.

Given this complex interpenetration of levels of government, three related questions assume massive proportions: Who will exercise control? What will be controlled? and How will controls be exercised? Working solutions cover a wide range. Sometimes firm and relatively unflinching federal attempts to control are observed. More typically, local governments are given only the variously specific outlines of policy limits. Perhaps the dominant pattern is one of a complex sharing of controls, in keeping with the prevailing shared responsibilities for running an effective program. The root-issue, in any case, involves developing some relatively effective and relatively acceptable mix of centralization/decentralization.

Not all observers are satisfied with today's solutions of the "who," "what," and "how" of exercising control. Harold M. Groves addresses himself to the complex issue of the nature and locus of public control, for example, with the purpose of arguing a particular point of view. His "Centralized Versus Decentralized Finance" argues that existing institutional arrangements do not encourage decentralizing financial authority to local jurisdictions. He makes the usual point for putting our eggs in fewer baskets, if not necessarily in one basket. Thus some jurisdictions are so numerous, e.g., school districts, that in many cases they are too small to economically support a desirable array of services. Many requests for "local control," if honored, will in actuality or by intention consequently result in reducing the level of public expenditures, and/or the quality of services. This illustrates the heart of Groves's argument.

Not that the issue is a black/white one for Groves. He notes the values inherent in numerous local jurisdictions, for example. Thus numerous school districts provide opportunities for actual experience by many citizens in control over the complexities of their own governance. Again, there is a crucial rub. Achieving the value of local involvement may compromise achieving the value of educational enrichment. And if education is less effective, so also will people be less equipped to take good advantage of the opportunities for local involvement.

Although cries against "power-hungry central officials" are common at all levels of government, Groves continues, numerous harsh realities concerning "factions" or "interests" argue for a considerable centralization of authority. Consider an obvious case, Groves's charge that local governments in many cases are characterized by a "civil service infested with patronage and with the inferior talent that must be expected at highly inadequate salary scales." Realistically, the reason may be that some constellation of local interests like a "courthouse gang" finds it convenient to preserve such a state of affairs despite the long-run costs. Centralizing a certain amount of authority in such cases may be the sine qua non of getting effective action on a program. Any "power-hungry central bureaucrats" would be certain to note such a necessity. And even administrators with strong preferences for decentralizing authority could either give up on their program or attempt to force necessary changes at the local level.

Indeed, less obviously, authority is often centralized because local officials want it that way. Thus local officials may lack the necessary skills or knowledge to act authoritatively with confidence. Local officials also often can use central authorities to insulate themselves from demanding local interests or individuals who have no real claim but to whom the official does not feel he can safely say: "No." Thus the local official can have his cake and eat it too. "Now you know I would like to help you," the official might explain. "But headquarters really has my hands tied in this case. Sorry." Of course, the official's hands also may be tied in ways he does not appreciate. But many are the cases in which the local official is thankful that central authorities took some of the heat off him.

Rufus Browning's "Innovative and Non-Innovative Decision Processes in Government Budgeting" illustrates some of the more complex senses in which "interests" are a significant factor in helping shape the institutional contexts within which issues of public finance and budgeting must be resolved. The primitive view—and sometimes the appropriate one—sees the capitol domes of our various seats of government as giant nipples around which the interests crowd to wax fat on the milk of public monies. Commonly, a more sophisticated and subtle view is appropriate, for the interests give to the commonweal as well as take from it. The interests can induce creative activism by government agencies on programs that are broadly necessary. They can also tie public agencies to serving a narrow clientele that might better be left to wither away. Maximizing the former and minimizing the latter constitute the dual challenges facing public budgeting and finance.

There is no easy cataloging of Browning's contribution, but patently he does not trace any straight-line relations between the interests and budgetary decisions. Thus one public agency he studied was submissive and docile. Yet a second agency attempted to create interests it could live with while it strived to creatively manage those interests that confronted it. Why agencies differ in responding to interests cannot be answered simply. Thus agency traditions will influence whether interests are toadied to or respected, whether their every whim is served or whether some creative amalgam is attempted between what clients want or could use and what an agency feels it can and should provide. Whether the agency contains many "professionals" or whether it is staffed by "nonprofessionals" also will be an important factor in helping determine the response to interests.

If the "organized interests" are crucial to understanding decisions about public finance and budgeting, there also is ample room for the "unorganized masses" to influence policy. Thus, occasionally, public interest will be deeply stirred by some event or cause. Then public officials are well-advised to take respectful notice. In addition, broad public opinion must support any long-run program. Manipulation and restricting information may suffice to protect administrators and politicians in the short-run, but at least in the long-run our institutions cannot remain inconsistent with deeply-held public attitudes. Eva Mueller's "Public Attitudes Toward Fiscal Programs" presents a method and some results relating to this crucial opinional undergirding of our political institutions and the fiscal programs they produce. The data reported by Mueller are dated, of course, but they reflect a prevailing agreement with both federal programs and with the taxing arrangements then in effect to finance them.

LEGISLATIVE-EXECUTIVE RELATIONSHIPS IN BUDGETING AS VIEWED BY THE EXECUTIVE

FREDERICK J. LAWTON

As most of you know, it happens that my vantage point has been on the executive side. You have to bear that fact in mind in considering my line of reasoning. Yet I myself would like to forget any particular angle and keep before me only what I know to be the requirements of effective government. These requirements are of great urgency at a time when the United States has assumed vast responsibilities not only for the welfare and security of the American people but also for the survival of freedom throughout the world.

I shall discuss first some of the controlling factors in legislative-executive relationships. Then I shall outline the budget process in the context of these relationships. Finally, I shall deal briefly with some of the more recent proposals for strengthening Congress in its budgetary operations.

The problem of legislative-executive relationships is frequently seen as the direct and inevitable outgrowth of the separation of powers. It is true that the system of divided powers as written into the Constitution in categorical language has no counterpart in any other political system. Nowhere can one observe as sharp a distinction as is established by the Constitution in giving the legislative power to Congress and the executive power to the President as the embodiment of a coequal branch of government.

Still it is easy to see that the separation of powers would be something quite different if it did not operate on the basis of an electoral system which fosters localism and pressure groups. The separation of powers would be something quite different if it operated under the influence of a party system which developed solidarities around general programs for governmental action—equally meaningful for the membership of Congress and the President. In other words, those who simply lay the complications of legislative-executive relationships to the separation of powers see only part of the picture. The other part—and the larger part—comes to light in those factors of law and usage that explain the difficulty experienced by Congress in attempting to function as a unified and self-directed institution.

To be sure, we have learned from experience that the most productive type of society is the kind of diversified society which exists in our country. A diversified society must reflect its divisions in the composition of the national legislature. If it were otherwise, it would be hard to see how representation

---

Article is from *The Influences of Social, Scientific, and Economic Trends on Government Administration*, Washington, D.C.: The Graduate School, U.S. Department of Agriculture, 1960, pp. 38–49.

could be attained in a democratic manner. What is important for my purpose here, however, is to suggest that the splintering effects of interest representation in Congress run counter to the practical maxim that the business of governing makes necessary a unified structure.

In this matter, the executive branch, under the Constitution, is more satisfactorily organized. For reasons persuasive in their own day—and increasingly persuasive in our time—the Founding Fathers insisted upon unified direction of the executive business of the nation under a single Chief Executive. This arrangement has provided the executive branch with considerable capacity for compounding different interests into a working formula for the pursuit of the common good. Congress, on the other hand, has for the most part remained without suitable machinery for initiating and enforcing broadly balanced programs for the attainment of national goals.

In the light of these considerations, it becomes very plain that legislative-executive relationships will continue to be molded by the stubborn realities of Congressional-Presidential government. The natural pulls and strains that run through a society of autonomous interest groupings will normally keep Congress and the President on different tracks. The basic reason, as I have tried to indicate, does not lie simply in the division of legislative and executive power. It lies in differences of political perspectives, which in turn are influenced by interest relationships. The political perspective of Congress is affected closely by the perspectives of its individual members, who have their political roots in their district. The President's perspective is necessarily national—not local.

It follows that those who have prescriptions for the improvement of legislative-executive relationships should first give appropriate attention to the controlling facts in the constitutional situation. Only by assessing these facts with calm objectivity can we discover the points where it would be practicable to attempt modifications in the existing arrangements in order to increase the effectiveness of our public management.

Against this background the tested value of the national budget system stands out in a doubly impressive way. Here, in the annual formulation of a comprehensive work plan for the Federal Government, a bridge has been erected between the legislative and the executive branches. A means of cooperation was found thirty years ago by the congressional architects of the Budget and Accounting Act which, as a basic governmental procedure, has been effective in a continuing way. Under this procedure, with the groundwork done in large measure on the executive side, Congress provided itself with a practical basis for instructing the departments annually about the programs to be carried out and the scale of individual activities.

Development of the budget process has introduced significant refinements into congressional control over the executive branch. Legislation, of necessity, confers responsibilities and grants authorizations to departments in quite general language. If an agency is directed to perform defined functions under law, it would still have wide discretion in determining how much or how little should be done in the performance of each individual function. Budgeting is like a mechanism for pumping fuel into the engines of government. It reserves for Congress the full opportunity for saying, on a year-to-year basis, in what scope and at what rates of progress departments should carry out their statutory assignments.

Budgeting is a bridge between the legislative and the executive branches also because it provides a method of reaching decisions of policy and administration in an orderly and informed way. Under the Budget and Accounting Act, the President was charged with the task of placing before Congress each year a complete budget as the plan of work for the whole Government. It was recognized clearly that the President alone had the constitutional standing to give a proposed budget the support of political responsibility. It was also recognized that he alone, as Chief Executive, was in a position to make available to Congress all the detailed technical information at his disposal throughout the executive branch. Congress, in turn, thus gained a stronger foundation for critical examination and final approval of the budget proposed by the President.

The importance of the Budget and Accounting Act as a milestone of responsible management has been pointed out frequently. Perhaps it is useful here to stress what I would like to call the constitutional significance of this legislation. Its constitutional significance lies in the achievement of a durable procedure for cooperation between the legislative and the executive branches. This bond of cooperation is of ever increasing consequence because the budget has emerged as the key document which controls the conduct of the entire business of the Federal Government.

The budget process as a procedure for cooperation between the legislative and the executive branches gains its strength from three basic elements. As I see it, the first of these, though sometimes pushed into the background, is the mutual appreciation by both branches of the need for approaching the budget as a joint effort. Only when there is acceptance of the cooperative implications of budgeting can one expect the greatest benefit from the budget process. A second element is the full utilization of the President's responsibility as constitutional head of the executive branch for the budget he submits to Congress. The largest returns accrue to Congress when it helps to keep the exercise of the President's responsibility unimpeded. The third necessary element of the procedure is free flow of budgetary information from the executive branch to Congress.

When I emphasize the value to Congress of the President's direct responsibility for the budget I do not mean to suggest that the President would or should ignore the interests of his principal advisers—the heads of the executive agencies. In actual fact, as many of you know, the preparation of the budget in the executive branch is a large-scale and intensive operation which, at various points in the sequence of stages, brings into play the judgments of a large number of responsible operating officials. This is both good and inescapable. One reason for wide participation in budgetary decisions is the obvious fact that budget-making for the entire Government is too big a job to be done by any agency singly, even when that agency is charged with explicit statutory responsibilities in the field, as is the Bureau of the Budget.

No less important is the fact that the President would hardly want to speak for the executive branch without being sure that he has tapped all the counsel available to him in his official family. In order to come forth with a well-considered budget, the President must place much reliance not only on the factual information but also on the evaluative judgments contributed by experienced and politically sensitive administrators. Consultation is essentially a way of give-and-take. In other words, although even the soundest advice is never automatically compelling upon the one charged with making the decision, nevertheless under normal circumstances he will not find it easy to brush aside thoughtful advice once it has been supplied.

Moreover, as a knowing observer once put it, department heads, whether or not possessed of political ambition, may be conscious of standing in a competitive position to the President. They may show little solidarity with him on issues affecting their own agencies. It is clear, therefore, that the budget submitted by the President could fall apart in Congress if strong subordinates undertake to convey their opposition.

When the President presents Congress with his budget, he therefore submits a document that rests on many vital agreements. But he must retain and defend the integrity of decisions that result from his more inclusive field of vision. There is reasonable assurance in the operation of the budget process that the various special points of view within the executive branch find recognition, yet they cannot be allowed to run roughshod over the more general points of view typical of the level of the President.

In brief, the pressure within the executive branch for specialized functional objectives—as in the promotion of business, labor, or agriculture and in a host of similar fields—is met by a strong counterpressure in support of general solutions based on coordination. But reconciliation of positions is accomplished not by command but by a meeting of minds. It is not to be assumed, of course, that the end product is perfect. It is important that the end product come as close as possible to representing a general executive position, by and large accepted by all concerned.

One thing that is not understood widely is the degree to which the budget process, in compounding executive positions, at the same time brings to the fore the attitudes of interest groups and the tendencies likely to emerge in Congress. One reason is that the President is naturally anxious to come forth with a budget that would appeal to public opinion as well as to most of those who exercise influence in the political arena. As Chief Executive interested in carrying out the Government's program, the President is obviously more concerned with a practical work plan than with a propaganda document.

In addition, of course, the individual departments in most instances have quite close relations with particular clienteles and individual committees or leading figures in Congress. As a result, internal consultation within the executive branch about the President's budget has also external aspects. Such consultation casts light not only on departmental preferences but also on the political scene, especially the trends of thought prevailing in Congress.

What this means is that the President, when making his final decisions on the budget, has the advantage of many different strands of information. He acts on the results of examination carried on in the first instance within the different departments, and subsequently on a broader scale by the Bureau of the Budget. All of this serves to relate governmental programs and performance to the needs of the next fiscal year. But the President also has before him a picture of the positions taken by interest groups and congressional committees, and of the currents of public opinion and general congressional sentiment as well. In this respect, the Bureau of the Budget will regard itself responsible for bringing to the notice of the President any congressional expressions of general budgetary policy, especially the views of the Appropriations Committees and other congressional committees having across-the-board responsibilities, like those of the Budget Bureau itself.

True enough, there will always be occasions when the President feels duty-bound to press for the recognition of issues on which members of Congress may have a neutral or even a negative attitude. To draw the attention of Congress to these issues—including issues that do not enjoy universal popularity—is one of the burdens of statesmanship. It is at the same time an essential feature of Congressional-Presidential government. On the other hand, in order to foster the general interest as he sees it, the President needs to give thought to what support is likely to emerge for his proposals within the legislative branch.

As a staff agency of the President, the Bureau of the Budget exerts no direct influence in the legislative handling of the budget. Its indirect influence is confined to what it contributes toward a satisfactory presentation to Congress of information helpful particularly to the Appropriations Committees. One thing, however, should be remembered. The budget as submitted expresses the President's policy recommendations. The Budget Bureau is not meant to have a policy position of its own. Nor could the Bureau be expected, in view of its staff character, to depart from the policy positions of the President. What the Bureau is intended to do—and what it is reasonably well equipped to do—is to serve as a dependable source of interpretive as well as factual information.

Only in a secondary respect does the Budget Bureau move outside its information role, and then only upon congressional demand. For example, the Bureau may be given specific authorizations under appropriation language to take care of certain minor budgetary problems, like approval of transfer of funds. On the basis of general law, the Bureau has the additional duty to report promptly on instances of departmental use of funds that would lead to deficiencies. Sometimes Congress has charged the Bureau with the task of determining reductions all across the executive map to meet a figure set by Congress in acting upon the President's budget. This, however, is a rather rare arrangement.

There are different ways in which the Budget Bureau provides Congress with information. In the first place, in accordance with the Budget and Accounting Act itself, the Bureau must furnish such information as is called for by any of the committees of Congress concerned with finance, whether revenue or appropriations. These requests fluctuate in numbers, and are usually more frequent during the period when the President's budget is in preparation and when things are being gotten ready for the hearings held by the Appropriations Committees.

Another customary form of making available to Congress the budgetary information of the executive branch is through testimony by the Director or other officials of the Budget Bureau. As you will recall, the explanation of detailed budgetary requests before the Appropriations Committees is offered generally by the individual agencies. Testimony by officials of the Budget Bureau usually centers upon matters of general significance for the executive branch as a whole or upon amplification of information previously supplied in the testimony of officials of individual agencies.

As may be expected, there are usually discussions between Appropriations Committee staff and staff of the Budget Bureau. These discussions, however, look to particular problems and respect the separate institutional responsibilities of the two branches under the Budget and Accounting Act. Special reports asked for by congressional committees are another avenue of information transmitted from the Budget Bureau. Occasional details of Bureau staff to congressional committees and a considerable variety of informal staff contacts are further illustrations of the exchange of knowledge.

But in this whole picture I wish to refer especially to the Budget Bureau's role as the President's legislative clearing house. Under the legislative clearance procedure—established by the President at the suggestion of the Chairman of the House Appropriations Committee as early as 1921—both congressional committees and executive agencies use the Budget Bureau to find out whether a specific legislative proposal is in accord with the program of the President. This procedure has the significance of a signal system by letting congressional committees and individual members of Congress know what the position of the executive branch is with respect to particular legislative proposals.

As I indicated earlier, the importance of the budget process as a method of regularized cooperation between the legislative and the executive branches should always be appreciated anew because it might otherwise too readily be taken for granted. I do not mind adding that in the protracted discussion of ways of improving legislative-executive relationships in the field of budgeting there is often too much of an implication of presumably serious deficiencies yet to be overcome. It would be better to begin with a thoughtful appraisal of the structure of relationships that has developed between the two branches since the adoption of the Budget and Accounting Act, and specifically during the past decade or so, in order to figure fruitfully what might be done further.

It is in this light that I should like to touch briefly upon the innocent panacea that has been suggested off and on throughout the years—the idea of an "independent" Budget Bureau. It is not too clear just how such independence could be guaranteed and what results might flow from it. It is obvious to me that this whole concept falls outside the frame of our Congressional-Presidential system of government, because true independence of an agency that made fundamental financial determinations binding on all other agencies would actually amount to political irresponsibility. There is implied in the concept of an independent Budget Bureau a bureaucratic supremacy exercised by a body of experts who would impose their infallible judgment on all concerned. If the experience of the last three decades has made clear anything, it has borne out the wisdom of the congressional builders of the budget system in embedding the budget process in the structure of constitutional responsibility.

Another suggestion that has been made at times is for a congressional Budget Bureau. This might mean a transfer of the existing Budget Bureau to Congress. If it meant that, the proposal would entail grave weakness by bringing about three highly undesirable consequences. The first would be the divorce of budget preparation and budget administration from the judgment of the Chief Executive about what activities and what funds are needed for the effective conduct of the Government's business. The second would be the destruction of the intimacy of the Budget Bureau's contacts with the wealth of detailed information now available to it within the operating services. The third would be the elimination in the budget process of that focal point for nationwide perspective and coordination which we possess in the Presidency. If, on the other hand, the idea of a congressional Budget Bureau rather meant an agency to serve as the congressional counterpart to the Budget Bureau as we have it now, the matter would reduce itself to a question of congressional staffing, especially of the Appropriations Committees. Such staffing, of course, must not lead to the result of having the same job done twice at different places.

Both of these ideas—that of an "independent" Budget Bureau and that of a congressional budget agency—have proved alluring to those who see a simple remedy to the tremendous increase in the size and scope of the budget during recent years. No one would deny that this development has produced entirely new and challenging problems for Congress. Forty years ago, the Federal Government's expenditures were less than 700 million dollars or about two and one-half percent of our total national income. With such a level of Government, problems presented by spending, borrowing, or debt management were of a lesser order. Today the economic and social implications of fiscal policy are of far-reaching importance to all of us. In a fiscal year, for example, when the Government takes more than 25 percent of our national income, the budget is certainly one of the most significant factors in the economic and social life of the nation.

I always have been impressed by the knowledge and understanding which so many members of Congress, particularly those on the Appropriations Committees, apply to the countless budgetary issues coming before them. Yet I feel that in approaching the budget, there is a tendency to get immersed in the complexity of the detail without first considering the broader determinations which have generally dictated the size and scope of the budget.

As I have suggested on previous occasions, the problem is a twofold one. First, there is the need for identifying and agreeing in Congress on the kind and amount of information that is required to evaluate both the budget as a whole and its thousands of component parts. And second, there is the need for providing within the Congress itself the kind of arrangements to insure the best use of this information.

With respect to the first part of the problem, I believe that there is a general misconception about the kind of information necessary to test the validity of the budget. The size and emphasis of the President's budget is not governed by a multitude of unrelated decisions on individual items and activities. The major determinant in any budget is whether a given activity should be conducted at all, and if so at what level. All decisions on individual activities must be made in the light of broader factors—primarily the expenditure and revenue outlook, the international scene, economic conditions, and provisions of existing law.

These are the kinds of questions the President faces again and again in the preparation of the budget. Long before detailed estimates are prepared by the agencies, the basic decisions have been reached which, together with mandatory expenditures under existing law, control the broad outlines of the forthcoming budget. A forecast of changed economic conditions in relation to requirements of existing law, for example, may change the expenditure needs for veterans programs by more than $1 billion. The same assumption applied to other programs, such as public assistance grants, can also add or subtract hundreds of millions in the Federal Government's expenditures.

Certainly Congress, for its scrutiny of the budget, should have all the information that is needed to view independently and with full understanding the budgetary needs of the Government. I am inclined to think, however, that this is not simply a matter of increasing the quantity of information to be placed before Congress. Instead of being a matter of quantity, it is first a matter of the relevance of information. That is to say, instead of knowing more about the lesser detail of individual budgetary proposals, Congress might want to know more about those matters, issues, and problems that govern the budget in its main elements and as a whole.

I think that Congress, particularly in recent years, has made progress in obtaining from the executive branch much of the information that is essential to an appraisal of the Government's fiscal requirements. There has been, however, considerable debate within Congress over the question of the best organization and procedure to permit an adequate review of the information now available to it.

Three major types of congressional action affect the budget—authorizations, appropriations, and taxation measures. The authorizing bills are handled by the substantive committees. The appropriations are considered by the two Appropriations Committees. And taxation bills come before the Committee on Ways and Means in the House and the Committee on Finance in the Senate. Nowhere, however, does Congress pull the whole picture together.

To repair this situation is the motivation behind the idea of a Joint Committee on the Budget. In its more recent form, the proposal—going beyond the Legislative Reorganization Act of 1964—would provide an investigative committee with staff to do for the Appropriations Committees the work which the Joint Committee on Internal Revenue Taxation now does for the House Committee on Ways and Means and the Senate Committee on Finance. This would add to the facilities already at the disposal of the Appropriations Committees. While a joint staff might save overlapping and duplication between the two houses, I believe that the proposal would be successful only if the Appropriations Committees themselves came to the conclusion that they want a joint staff and will use it. Actually, there is sharp division on this point.

My own criticism of the proposal from the standpoint of equipping Congress with a method of evaluating fiscal requirements is that the projected role of the joint committee rests heavily on the expenditure side of the budget. It touches only very lightly on the two equally significant aspects of budgetary consideration—revenue requirements and authorizing legislation. The revenue side of the budget must be considered in relation to the expenditure side. Still more important, however, is the review of the fiscal effects—especially the effects upon subsequent budgets—of authorizing legislation, which is introduced and considered in every session of Congress. Such analysis is at present beyond the purview of the Appropriations Committees or any other single committee in either house.

Another idea is that of a single annual appropriation bill, as a sort of logical counterpart to the fiscal integration achieved in the budget submitted by the President. A more sweeping proposal, discussed at some length in recent years, would make a number of changes in existing budgetary practices and procedures. (1) It would enact into law as a statement of congressional policy the objective to balance the budget and provide for a reduction of the national debt under conditions of high employment, production, and purchasing power. (2) It would require that the annual economic reports of the President or the economic reviews of the Council of Economic Advisers set forth a four-year estimate of desirable levels of governmental expenditures and receipts. (3) It would give the President the item veto, exercised by most governors. (4) It would require that budget estimates transmitted to Congress be based on a consolidated cash statement. (5) It would require a separation in the budget of investment-type expenditures from operating expenditures and, in addition, four-year estimates of investment-type expenditures in appropriate detail. (6) It would provide for appropriations for major nonmilitary investment-type programs to be available for four years.

In the matter of a statutory "freeze" of fiscal policy, it might be questionable whether such policy can or should always be based on only one or two major objectives. In time of war, for example, whether hot or cold, even though production and employment are high, it may be impossible to balance the budget without such drastic tax increases that incentives to needed war production are impaired. Similarly, a statement of major objectives of fiscal policy should probably also take into account the need to meet essential levels of public service and to provide a balanced and equitable tax system.

As for four-year projections of desirable levels of expenditures and receipts related to the gross national product, our experience in the Bureau of the Budget indicates that long-range estimates are an important and necessary step in developing better guides for fiscal policy. Many problems remain to be solved, however, before the present exploratory work reaches a stage which would warrant the establishment of a statutory requirement.

The increasing recognition by both the public and Congress of the usefulness of consolidated cash totals has contributed to a better understanding of the economic significance of fiscal policy. While therefore greater emphasis upon this approach to budget presentation is desirable, some limitations should perhaps be pointed out. Even in measuring the economic impact of the Government's financial operations, presentation on a consolidated cash basis goes only part way. It does not, for example, differentiate between those expenditures or receipts which have immediate or pronounced effects on the economy and those which have not. Moreoever, since fiscal policy cannot be based exclusively on economic considerations, more than one type of budgetary presentation is necessary as a guide for policy decisions.

There is no single "all-purpose" classification or presentation of budgetary facts which will meet all the needs of Congress, the President, and the operating agencies.

With respect to a separation of operating expenditures from capital and other investment expenditures, the Budget Bureau has long recognized the need for a budget classification which would identify expenditures of an investment or similar character. A special analysis published for the first time in the budget for 1951 was presented as an experimental effort to provide a tentative new classification of expenditures according to the duration and nature of benefits flowing from them. Improved data have since then become part of the budget document. One of the major problems is, of course, the definition of investment and similar expenditures.

Four-year availability of appropriations for investment programs may both encourage advance planning and allow the executive branch greater flexibility in timing expenditures for these programs in the light of changing economic conditions. Orderly planning of advance commitments for such investment programs is one of the most difficult but most important objectives to achieve.

The most important and most controversial of the proposals for budgetary reform is the item veto. There have been differences of opinion as to whether a constitutional amendment would be required to give the President this power or whether legislative action would be sufficient. The need for the item veto is increased in case Congress makes use of the so-called omnibus appropriation bill, as it did in 1950. A single appropriation bill magnifies the problem of legislative riders on appropriation acts. The experience in 1950 with the consolidated appropriation bill strengthens my belief that a single bill is fertile ground for the inclusion of legislative riders, despite restrictions in the Senate and House rules relating to legislation in appropriation bills. Practically speaking, therefore, it would be better first to provide for the item veto before action is taken to consolidate appropriations into one bill. Unfortunately, the probabilities of successful legal attacks upon the item veto when this is based simply on legislative rules seem somewhat greater with respect to riders than with respect to appropriation amounts.

So much for some indication of the nature of proposals advanced in recent years to strengthen further the legislative-executive relationships which have developed in such remarkable consistency under the Budget and Accounting Act. As I conclude, I seem to end up with these principal points:

First, only a utopian would imagine that the underlying factors of Congressional-Presidential government would yield to mere procedural elaborations of the budget process. A significant improvement in legislative-executive relationships must cut more deeply. Here the critical question is how Congress itself looks upon the way it is organized internally for asserting its institutional identity and unity.

Second, there is nevertheless wide agreement that room exists for procedural perfections in the present state of legislative-executive operations in regard to the budget. In fact, in matters of management nothing should ever be regarded as the last word on how a thing is to be done. Complacency in this matter is a dangerous narcotic. But I am far from sure that each proposal for improvement brought forth during these past years has been examined with sufficient care in all of its implications. Nor do I feel that it would always be to the benefit of good government to enact proposals into inflexible statutory requirements when cautious experimentation appears a more fruitful course. Above all, the mental reservations toward many of these proposals expressed in the Appropriations Committees certainly deserve respectful attention.

Third, it might be well for me to refer in this context to the pioneering activities of the joint accounting project, which was undertaken with strong congressional support by the General Accounting Office, the Treasury Department, and the Bureau of the Budget. What we need perhaps is some such joint project to explore with care the field I have discussed here, with continuing participation of the Appropriations Committees or also other committees of Congress. No one could know what would be the outcome. But it might help to clear the air.

And fourth, in whatever is done we should be a little closer to earth than we have been so often of late and firmly reject the implication that this or that innovation will in itself produce telling economies. The reckless overselling of ideas is one of the less satisfying aspects of the political process. When it comes to significant economies, no device and no mechanism can automatically do the trick. This is a matter of unwavering determination of priorities, and the resistance to such priorities is spread all over the political landscape.

CONGRESS'S FISCAL ROLE IS OBJECT OF GROWING CONCERN

CONGRESSIONAL QUARTERLY

One of the important continuing problems facing public officials and legislators is the financial management of the Federal Government. During the last 30 years, and particularly since World War II, it has become increasingly difficult to plan Government expenditures and revenues and to assess these plans intelligently.

With proposed federal expenditures in the fiscal 1964 administrative budget on the threshold of $100 billion, many legislators are concerned that the budget process engaged in by Congress does not provide them with adequate control over the Government's financial activities. Similar concern during the last decade has prompted attempts to create new procedures for budgetary management.

Although financial management problems of the Government has been subject to voluminous research, encompassing many sophisticated and some esoteric explanations and proposals, the following discussion is limited to the more prominent Congressional problems in handling huge spending programs and some of the attempts and proposals to solve these problems.

BACKGROUND

Congress has always considered one of its principal sources of power to be its authority to provide the executive agencies of Government with money to perform their functions. This power of the purse has provided Congress a form of control over programs and policies of the executive branch.

Throughout the nation's history, control of the appropriations process has been a responsibility of Congress. By the 1920s, the Government's financial activities were sufficiently large and complex that new devices were created by Congress to control them. ... Since the 1920s, many observers believe, the increase in the Government's activities has far exceeded the ability of Congress to manage the spending required to finance these activities. Reform attempts in the late 1940s were not successful.

The common complaint heard from Congressmen today is that the budget process is incomprehensible or, at best, largely uncontrollable. The result has been a frustration—for the average taxpayer who wants to know where his dollars are going and for the average Congressman who is expected to understand the Government's spending plans and vote intelligently on them.

Article is from "Congress's Fiscal Role Is Object of Growing Concern," *Congressional Quarterly*, Part I of 2 Parts, Washington, D.C.: Congressional Quarterly, Inc. (June 7, 1963), pp. 886–91. Used with permission of publisher.

Discussion of budgetary reforms is most common following some event, remark or proposal that relates to major increases in spending. A financial official high in the Executive Branch took note of this recently by observing: "They (Congressmen) hope that in tinkering with the process they might find a magic answer to the basic problem." This problem, in the view of the official, is that Congressmen seem determined to favor economy while voting for programs that require spending. There are many Senators and Representatives, however, who consider reforms more than "tinkering with the process."

Sen. John L. McClellan (D., Ark.), the chief advocate of a long-standing proposal to create a Joint Congressional Budget Committee (*see* below), recently said: "Although we are now operating in an era of annual expenditure budgets of $100 billion, the procedures used by the Congress in carrying out these vital responsibilities are fundamentally no different than those used 20, 30 or 40 years ago. In other words, the methods and procedures which we now use in the appropriations process are simply inadequate to meet present-day needs."

THE BUDGETARY PROCESS

The immensely complex budgetary process begins in the various agencies of the executive branch as estimates are made of the funds needed to carry out Government programs. All of the estimates are brought together by the Budget Bureau (which is part of the President's Executive Office) and coordinated with Presidential policies and anticipated revenues.

The President presents his budget to Congress in January. The estimates and requests that it contains are for the fiscal year which will begin the following July 1 (fiscal years run from July 1 to June 30).

To better prepare Congress to handle the complex budget, it has been suggested that the key members or staff personnel of the Appropriations Committees be brought in during planning by the Executive Branch, perhaps during the latter stages of Budget Bureau consideration. Exactly how this could be accomplished, considering the traditional separation of the two governmental branches, has never been made clear. An official of the Budget Bureau has indicated that it would be unrealistic to attempt to bring legislators into the budget-process before the actual document was completed and sent to Congress. (A proposal to change the fiscal year and consider appropriations separately from regular legislation is discussed below.)

Congress Grants Spending Authority

The expenditure of money by a Government agency is the last of three main steps: Congress first *authorizes* a program or activity for which funds will be needed and sets a ceiling on what these funds will be. Secondly, Congress *appropriates* the money, that is, authorizes its expenditure; this amount often is lower than the maximum amount specified in the authorization. Thirdly, the agency in the Government branch *spends* the money.[1]

The authority for executive agencies to spend federal funds can be granted only by Congress. The Constitution states: "No money shall be drawn from the Treasury, but in consequence of appropriations made by law." The House of Representatives has required since 1837 that appropriations must have been previously authorized by law. Once funds have been appropriated or otherwise authorized, their expenditure is under the control of the departments and agencies of the Executive Branch.

Limits to Congressional Control

The distinction between Congress granting agencies the authority to spend funds and the agencies actually spending the funds usually is lost in the public debate about Government spending. Congressmen realize, however, that their control over annual outlays is relatively limited and that their real power to influence spending is through action on new requests for authority to obligate (in effect, spend) funds. House Appropriations Committee Chairman Clarence Cannon (D., Mo.) recently said that the "grant of authority to obligate (i.e., the appropriations bill) is the significant point of decision in the appropriations process."

In agencies with normally fixed and consistent year-to-year expenses, the distinction is generally unimportant. But in the case of agencies with large and long-range procurement programs, such as a defense weapons system, appropriations must be authorized in sufficient size to assure contractors that payment will be made in future years as the project moves toward completion. This is particularly true of the defense program, which accounts for a major portion of the federal budget. Thus the proposed expenditures for any given fiscal year may have been appropriated in large part by previous Congresses and be outside the control of the Congress to which the budget was submitted.

In the proposed fiscal 1964 budget, Congress will be able to vote on only approximately $44.7 billion of the anticipated total spending of $98.8 billion, Cannon said. The remainder is from obligational authority approved in previous years.

---

[1] Budgetary terms defined: Definitions of the three key terms used in the accompanying discussion of the procedure by which Government agencies spend money follow: *Authorization Bill.* Authorizes a program, specifies its general aim and conduct, and puts a ceiling on the monies that can be used to finance it. Usually enacted before appropriation bill is passed; *Appropriation Bill.* Grants the actual monies approved by the authorizations bills, but not necessarily to the total permissible under the authorization bill. Normally an appropriation bill originates in the House and is not acted on until its authorization measure is enacted; *Expenditures.* The actual spending of money as distinguished from the appropriation of it. Expenditures are made by the disbursing officers of the Administration; appropriations are made only by Congress. The two are rarely identical in any fiscal year; expenditures may represent money appropriated one, two or more years previously.

Nevertheless, Congressmen at one time or another vote on a large portion of the Government's spending plans, even though these plans may be spread over many years. But even the power to vote on appropriations—and presumably, therefore, to influence spending—is circumscribed, primarily by certain "fixed" obligations that recur year after year. The best known of these expenses are benefit payments to veterans ($5.5 billion in fiscal 1964) and interest on the public debt ($10.1 billion in fiscal 1964).

Expenditure control also is circumscribed by "backdoor" spending. The term includes a variety of devices by which agencies enter into financial obligations over which Congress has limited or no control. Sharp Congressional disapproval of these devices has limited their use since 1961. The most recent example of action to limit "backdoor" financing was in House passage May 3 of a bill to extend the life of the Export-Import Bank of Washington, a federal lending agency. . . .

The lack of year-to-year control over actual Government expenditures has produced criticism that the basic system of separating appropriations and expenditures is wrong and should be changed to place the budget on a completely annual basis; an appropriation voted by Congress would have to be obligated and spent in the same year. However, long-range procurement or development projects would still require some sort of commitment to contractors for periods longer than one year, thus in effect, informally obligating Government funds.

In cases where Congress currently requires that funds must be obligated (but not necessarily spent) within the fiscal year (or they revert to the Treasury), some agencies are placed under a time squeeze which creates major administrative problems. This squeeze results (1) because the appropriations are often not passed until September or October (instead of by July 1) and (2) because there are limits in the bill on the amount of the appropriation which can be obligated in the last month or two of the fiscal year (to discourage last-minute spending by agencies which find a surplus at year's end). The eight or nine months remaining in the fiscal year are often not enough time to implement new programs (hire new personnel, acquire equipment, make adjustments for reductions in budget requests, etc.).

CONGRESSIONAL PROCEDURE

The Congressional procedure which leads to the expenditure of funds is another—and more frequent—subject of criticism. It is a four-step process: the substantive legislative committees of each chamber of Congress consider the proposed programs, most of which will later require granting of funds by the Appropriations Committees of each chamber.

The Labor and Education Committees, for example, would consider proposals for federal school aid and the Foreign Relations and Affairs Committees would consider foreign aid. These Committees prepare the legislation providing the dimensions of a particular program; usually they authorize the maximum amount that may be spent for it. The very nature of legislative committee action will have a pronounced effect on the appropriations made later.

A frequent criticism of the Congressional budget process is that no method exists to regularly and systematically reconcile authorizing legislation with budgetary considerations. Dual memberships for Senators on some legislative committees and Appropriations subcommittees, however, has to some extent lessened the problem in that chamber. No similar situation exists in the House.

Importance of Subcommittees

Although the President's budget is sent to Congress at the beginning of each session in massively detailed form, it is seldom debated or considered as a whole. The detailed business of studying the budget proposals and preparing the legislation for appropriations is done piecemeal in the subcommittees of the Appropriations Committees. Consideration of the budget begins in the House, which has assumed for itself the prerogative of originating money bills in keeping with its right—specified in the Constitution—to originate revenue-raising measures. (See box.)

House-Senate Feud

Many Senators have disputed the exclusive right of the House on money matters. In 1962, this dispute produced a Senate-House stalemate that delayed enactment of money bills well into the summer. The dispute centered on whether the Senate could (1) originate its own appropriations bills and (2) add to House-passed appropriations bills funds for items either not previously considered by the House or considered and rejected.

The dispute, which started as a spat on the physical location of conference committee meetings, became increasingly farcical as it continued on into the summer and fall with two octogenarian members of Congress as the central antagonists: 83-year-old Rep. Clarence Cannon (D., Mo.), chairman of the House Appropriations Committee, and 84-year-old Sen. Carl Hayden (D., Ariz.), chairman of the Senate Appropriations Committee. The feud held up final action on appropriation bills for three months until a temporary accord, reached in July, broke the stalemate. Late in the session, however, a Senate-House disagreement over agricultural research funds resulted in a three-week deadlock on the agriculture appropriations bill. This disagreement finally was resolved, but only after a bitter exchange between the Senate and House.

Further bitterness resulted when Cannon Oct. 12 blocked action on the first fiscal 1963 supplemental appropriation bill, charging the Senate had added "unwarranted sums" to the measure. In retaliation, the Senate Oct. 13 adopted a resolution asserting its "coequal power" with the House to originate appropriations bills.

Although the 1962 dispute was very serious and may well be repeated in the future, long-time students of Congress point out that the two houses have been arguing throughout their entire existence over which one has the right to originate appropriation bills. Considering the arguments of tradition and precedent that have been marshalled on both sides, observers doubt that any permanent solution to the dispute will be reached. (See 1962 Almanac, p. 144, for details on the 1962 Senate-House feud.)

The work on the budget in the House is divided among the 14 specialized subcommittees of the 50-member Appropriations Committee, such as defense, foreign operations, public works and so on. Generally, the members of these subcommittees become quite knowledgeable and often expert on their particular area. Critics of this system say the only people who really understand the complex budget are the subcommittee members. In addition, the average Congressman or the interested citizen can comprehend the proposals contained in the budget only by reading the House subcommittee hearings (held in closed session), which cover many thousands of pages. Because only the handful of House subcommittee members (ranging from 5 to 12) have complete grasp of the contents of specific parts of the budget, they—and particularly the subcommittee chairman—wield tremendous influence over what programs and activities will be undertaken.

The normally professional and competent but nevertheless parochial approach of each subcommittee towards its particular area is another factor contributing to Congress' inability to consider the President's budget in its entirety and maintain effective control over the Government's total expenditures.

Hearings Duplication

During the course of what are acknowledged to be detailed hearings, the House Appropriations subcommittees gather considerable information from Executive Branch officials who manage the program under discussion. One of the criticisms of the Congressional procedure in general is the excessive time consumed by repetitious testimony on one subject by executive officials before companion committees of the Senate and House.

It has been suggested that the time and energies of Congressmen and top Government officials could be conserved if the Appropriations subcommittees (and most of the substantive legislative committees, too) were to hold joint hearings. The primary objection that has been made to this suggestion is that the 13 Senate Appropriations subcommittees often act as courts of appeal for agencies whose budgets have been reduced by the House.

Policy Aspects Neglected

One official in the executive branch acknowledged that the House subcommittees carefully study the budget, but he said that an overall concern for policy cannot be undertaken in the Appropriations Committees. He said there should be greater concern for policy consideration during the authorizing process in the substantive legislative committees. Another critic has said that Congress often prefers to ignore difficult policy aspects by immersing itself in a sea of detail.

To bring some additional emphasis on policy into the budget process in Congress, it has been suggested by Arthur Smithies in his book, *The Budgetary Process in the United States*, that the Appropriations Committees hold preliminary general hearings on the budget with testimony from the Budget Director and the heads of executive departments. The Committees then would provide guidelines for their subcommittees. The Committee chairmen and ranking minority members would keep in touch with subcommittees as work progressed and hold full-Committee discussions if necessary.

Smithies suggested that programs be considered and appropriations be made in broad terms "to permit unified consideration of the budget and to permit flexible administration in the executive branch." Congress, he said, should require that the President's budget be submitted in March rather than January; the actual document should include less detail than is currently provided. In combination with stricter full-Committee control, these changes would work to minimize the "divisive influences" that currently tend to fragmentize the appropriations process. He also urged that subcommittee reports indicate the relation between new appropriations and expenditures previously authorized and expected to occur in the future. He also urged that appropriations be recommended and enacted in an omnibus appropriations act, subject to Presidential "item" veto of legislative riders. (*See* below for discussion of Congress' one attempt at omnibus appropriations.)

Human Problem in the House

One of the major obstacles to adoption of any of these reforms is simply the resistance to change that naturally pervades a vast and complex existing system. Within the Congressional system, however, many observers believe the key obstacle to be the chairmen of the House appropriations subcommittees. The very considerable power of these individuals resulting from their control of particular parts of the budget inevitably has made most of them reluctant to accept changes that would limit their authority. And it is a characteristic of most reform proposals that they would tend to diminish subcommittee power. One Congressman has put this problem somewhat more bluntly: "Men who run those House Appropriations subcommittees have devoted their careers to relatively restricted specialties. It is the one opportunity they have to excel, to dominate the House. That day when they stand in the well of the House and manage a complicated money bill through, as the outstanding expert on the subject, is their day in the sun each year. It is something they look forward to, and will not easily relinquish."...

POSTWAR REFORM ATTEMPTS

Congress has made a few post-World War II attempts at reforming its budgetary procedures:

Legislative Budget. In the Legislative Reorganization Act of 1946, Congress attempted to assert new and meaningful control over the budget process through the creation of a legislative budget. After three unsuccessful attempts to use this device, it was abandoned as an unqualified failure.

The legislative budget's main feature was the establishment of a maximum amount to be appropriated each year. The House Ways and Means and Appropriations Committees and the Senate Finance and Appropriations Committees were to meet jointly at the beginning of each session and prepare a legislative budget which would include estimated total revenue receipts and expenditures for the coming fiscal year. This was to be in addition to the President's annual budget estimates which Congress would receive before the legislative budget was prepared. The legislative budget had to be finished by February 15. The budget report of the four Congressional Committees was to be accompanied by a concurrent resolution adopting the budget and fixing the maximum amount to be appropriated in the coming fiscal year. Congress could not appropriate more than estimated receipts unless it included in the concurrent resolution wording that increased the public debt by the amount of the excess appropriations.

Attempts to implement the legislative budget in 1947, 1948 and 1949 failed or were ineffective. In 1947, both houses adopted a concurrent resolution but the Senate added amendments. Conferees could not agree on dividing an expected surplus between tax reduction and debt retirement. In 1948, both houses adopted the same legislative budget, but Congress appropriated $6 billion more than the ceiling in the resolution. In 1949, the process broke down entirely when the deadline for a budget was moved from February 15 to May 1. By that date, 11 appropriation bills had passed the House and 9 had passed the Senate; the legislative budget was never produced.

One of the principal reasons the legislative budget failed was the inability of the four Committees to make accurate estimates of spending so early in the session and before individual agency requests were considered in detail. In addition, the joint committee was said to be inadequately staffed and, with more than 100 members, much too unwieldy for effective operation. The budget ceilings—as indicated by the 1948 experience—did not prove to be binding. Another reason for the failure was simply Congress' practice of passing appropriation bills separately without strict control on total outlays.

Expenditure Analysis. Another section of the 1946 Act relating to fiscal controls never was implemented. It directed the Comptroller General (and the General Accounting Office, which he heads) to analyze expenditures of executive agencies which he thought would help Congress decide if appropriations were being properly used. However, Congress has never made an appropriation enabling the GAO to make such analyses although funds have been requested on a number of occasions.

Omnibus Appropriations. Failure of the legislative budget prompted a serious effort in Congress in 1950 to combine the numerous separate appropriations bills into one omnibus measure. The traditional practice in Congress of acting on a series of individual appropriation bills over several months made it difficult to restrain total spending effectively. In 1950, the House

91

Appropriations Committee agreed to try the omnibus approach on a trial basis. The bill was approved by Congress about two months earlier than the last of the separate measures in 1949. In addition, the omnibus bill was about $2.3 billion less than the President's budget requests. The omnibus approach was praised by many observers and organizations. It was particularly warmly received by persons or groups seeking reductions in federal spending. House Appropriations Committee Chairman Cannon said: "The single appropriation bill offers the most practical and efficient method of handling the annual budget ..."

However, in spite of Cannon's support, the Committee in January 1951 voted 31 to 18 to return to the traditional method of handling appropriation bills separately. Following the vote, Cannon charged that "every predatory lobbyist, every pressure group seeking to get its hands into the U.S. Treasury, every bureaucrat seeking to extend his empire downtown is opposed to the consolidated bill. ..."

The Senate in 1953 voted to make another attempt at an omnibus bill and to place limitations on various forms of spending, but the proposal was not acted upon in the House. Similar proposals were introduced in the Senate in succeeding Congresses but were not acted upon.

The idea of a single bill was attractive to many persons because it presented an overall view of how much money Congress was permitting the various governmental agencies to spend. Consideration of a grand total presumably would make it easier for conservatives to press their case for fiscal retrenchment. Proponents also argued that the process was more orderly and more informative to members of Congress. They said that the budget was processed more carefully and that fewer amendments were proposed or accepted in Committee than before.

Opponents said that the omnibus approach actually required more time during consideration and that members of Congress were less likely to vote against the one big bill than against several smaller bills regardless of how much waste was in either type. They said that there was greater opportunity for reducing expenditures under the traditional method of appropriations. They also said the bill was more confusing and did not show overall expenditures because supplemental and deficiency items were not included.

Balanced Budget. Another device that has been proposed to control federal spending is the mandatory balanced budget. This proposal has taken various forms; generally it would require the President to submit a balanced budget or to include with an unbalanced budget recommendations on the least objectionable reductions to bring it into balance. Resolutions have been introduced in both houses on various occasions requiring the President to cut his budget by a certain percentage or to limit spending in the coming fiscal year to a certain maximum amount. The steady increase in spending and the many budget deficits since World War II have indicated that Congress has not considered this approach to be an effective fiscal control. It has been argued that even if Congress were to adopt some of these proposals, they would not be effective because Congressmen would continue to vote for increased appropriations.

Separate Budget Session. Another proposal that has never gone far in Congress is to consider regular legislation and appropriations measures separately during two legislative sessions. In previous Congresses, Sen. Warren G. Magnuson (D., Wash.) has sponsored legislation to establish two annual sessions. No action has occurred. On April 9, 1963, he introduced another bill (S 1301) for this purpose.

S 1301 would provide for a regular session beginning in January to consider regular legislation. Normally, fiscal legislation would not be considered at this session. A second and entirely separate session would begin on the second Monday of November and extend through Dec. 31. The appropriations measures would be considered during this session. S 1301 would establish the calendar year as the Government's fiscal year. The President would have to submit his budget by July 15 to allow time for discussion prior to formal Congressional consideration in the November-December session.

In addition, the annual budget would have to contain two items not currently required by law: (1) the amount of proposed appropriations and expenditures which are reimbursable to the Treasury and (2) a report on the total capital assets of the Government and their value at the end of the last fiscal year.

Supporters of the proposal say that two sessions would provide better organization and would permit Congressmen to concentrate their full attention on the important appropriations matters. Although S 1301 does not require the first session to end until the second one is scheduled to begin, if a summer recess were possible, advocates say, Congressmen would be able to talk with their constituents about the President's proposed budget which would be available by July 15.

Presidential Commission. Republican members of the Joint Economic Committee in March 1963 requested President Kennedy to appoint a Presidential Advisory Commission on Federal Expenditures "as an essential step to controlling the rapidly rising level of federal spending." The Commission would study and make recommendations on a variety of subjects including the federal budgeting and appropriations process, federal spending priorities, existing federal activities "which could be better performed" by the private sector of the economy or at the state and local level, and other areas. At a press conference April 3, President Kennedy expressed no interest in the idea.

JOINT COMMITTEE ON THE BUDGET

The only significant fiscal reform that Congress has had under consideration in recent years is the creation of a Joint Committee on the

Budget. This proposal, which has been before Congress throughout the last decade, has passed the Senate six times: in the 82nd, 83rd, 84th, 85th and 87th Congresses and the current session. It has never passed the House. Sen. McClellan, the chief sponsor of the proposal on Jan. 25, 1963, again introduced a bill (S 537) to establish a Joint Committee. The bill, with the co-sponsorship of 77 Senators, was passed May 20 by a voice vote. There has been no indication that the House is more receptive than in past years. (Somewhat similar or related proposals have been introduced in the House.)

S 537 would create a Joint Committee composed of 14 members, 7 from each of the Senate and House Appropriations Committees. Its essential function, however, would be providing a professional and nonpartisan staff of fiscal experts. This permanent staff would make continuing budgetary studies of proposed and existing programs. S 537 authorizes the Committee "to inform itself on all matters relating to the annual budget" of the Federal Government. This broad grant of authority would permit the Committee—through its staff—to provide Congress with a variety of information to assist legislators in making appropriations decisions. The Committee also could make suggestions to improve Governmental efficiency and economy. At the beginning of each session, the Committee would report to the Appropriations Committees the total estimated costs of all previously authorized programs including the cost in the current, ensuing and future fiscal years.

The underlying assumption of the Joint Committee proposal is the belief of many Congressmen that they do not have sufficient knowledge about the Government's financial activities to vote intelligently on requests for appropriations. As political science professor John S. Saloma, of the Massachusetts Institute of Technology, said in testifying for the Committee: "The problem is not so much one of insufficient information as it is one of too much undigested information. ... (The Committee) is, in essence, another alternative, another approach, to the unsolved problem of placing meaningful fiscal information at the disposal of Congress." Another witness, U.S. Comptroller General Joseph Campbell, said the Committee "would provide a means for bringing together for the Congress the results of work being performed throughout the Government on budget and other financial matters, and for an independent appraisal of such results by a joint committee of the Congress."

Objections Raised. For all the arguments in favor of a Joint Committee, several important objections have been raised to the proposal. Most basic is the question of whether or not Congress should attempt a more detailed study of budgetary programs and proposals. This criticism implies that Congress will not attain any more satisfactory control over Government spending by an even more minutely detailed examination of the budget than currently exists. Rather, this argument says, the need is for a more general approach to the budget, more consideration of broad policy matters; it implies less detailed expertise and more general understanding of the budget. In addition, the argument implies that because of the scope of the budget and the time required to prepare it, the budget process is not particularly suited to the detailed study of proposed purchases and activities that is currently attempted. Advocates of this position argue that attention to detail should come in budgetary review of activities already undertaken. Such an approach also would require greater use of statistical methods of estimation during Congressional consideration of budget proposals and less dependence on what one critic has called "cost information (composed of) an agglomeration of detail."

In addition to the general criticism that the Joint Committee idea is simply the wrong approach, there have been specific objections to the proposal itself. Although supporters of the Joint Committee idea argue that Congressmen need more professional staff assistance to understand the budget, it is true that the Appropriations Committees of both houses have the authority to hire whatever staff they feel is necessary. The chairman of the House Committee, Clarence Cannon, has always preferred to borrow investigators from other Government agencies to supplement the permanent Committee staff.

Another objection raised against the Joint Committee is that its membership, under S 537, would include only members from the Appropriations Committees. It has been suggested that members from certain other committees, particularly the revenue and oversight committees, also be included.

The Joint Committee proposal has also been criticized because it would have the authority to make comments and recommendations as to the effect of basic legislation on general economy and efficiency. Comments of this nature might not be well received by substantive legislative committees, particularly ones which are uncommonly sensitive about divisions of authority in Congress. As one Congressman put it: "Imagine the reaction of the legislative committees to continuing free advice on various subjects from appropriations members."

Lastly, the Joint Committee has been criticized as a duplication of existing effort. It is argued that the Committee would be another layer on an already too stratified organization. In its sweeping charge of authority to examine the budget proposals, the President's State of the Union and Economic messages, overall revenue estimates and changes in economic conditions, it would necessarily be infringing on the responsibilities of existing and competent committees, including Appropriations, Ways and Means, Finance, Joint Internal Revenue, Joint Economic and Government Operations. The Committee's supporters, however, rejoin that although certain duplication would occur, the new group often would be drawing on the knowledge of these other groups, gathering information not otherwise available and, most importantly, providing a Congressional focal point for all the information.

Joint Policy Committee. In his book on the budgetary process, Smithies argues for the creation of a Joint Budget Policy Committee of 18 members including the chairmen and ranking minority members of the following

Committees: Appropriations, House Ways and Means, Senate Finance and Joint Economic. There would be six members from Congress at large. The leadership of both political parties would be "strongly" represented.

Smithies said this Committee would "consider the fiscal policies embodied in the President's budget and Economic Report and ... provide a fiscal policy framework for the work of the Appropriations Committees and revenue committees." Before Congress passed appropriations measures, which would be in an omnibus bill, the Joint Committee would include its budget policy findings in a concurrent resolution for adoption by both houses. He also said that the Appropriation Committees' reports on the omnibus bill should show that appropriations and expenditures conform to the budget policy adopted in the concurrent resolution.

Smithies said the Joint Committee "should act on an informal, advisory and consultative basis rather than attempt to give specific instructions to the financial committees. ... The main business of the Joint Committee would be to introduce fiscal policy—consideration of the economic impact of the budget—into Congressional procedures. ... It should attempt to harmonize the work of the revenue committees and the Appropriations Committees."

AN APPROPRIATIONS SUBCOMMITTEE AND ITS CLIENT AGENCIES: A COMPARATIVE STUDY OF SUPERVISION AND CONTROL

IRA SHARKANSKY

This paper presents an effort to adapt techniques of content analysis and measurement to the study of relations between a House appropriations subcommittee and the agencies whose budget estimates it reviews. Since Arthur Macmahon's pioneering work on the topic observers have depended on interviews and impressionistic readings of the published record for their evidence.[1] They have identified a variety of attitudes on the part of the committee members, ranging from the obsequious to the pugnacious. And they have noted various techniques of committee control and agency compliance or evasion. They have also expressed varying opinions about the efficacy and utility of congressional oversight.

The existing literature leaves at least one question partially unanswered: how does the subcommittee divide its supervisory and control efforts among the agencies within its jurisdiction? This study deals with this question, and illustrates a method that may have wider application in the systematic study of legislative-executive relations. Limitations of my own confine it to a sample consisting of a single subcommittee—headed by Congressman Fogarty (D., R.I.)—four agencies under its jurisdiction, and a span of budget years from 1949 to 1963.[2]

SUBJECTS

Experience with an earlier study identified the Fogarty Subcommittee as a body that shows a high regard for compiling a "complete public

---

Article is from *American Political Science Review*, Vol. 59 (September, 1965), pp. 622–28. Used with permission of author and publisher.

[1] Arthur W. Macmahon, "Congressional Oversight of Administration: The Power of the Purse," *Political Science Quarterly*, Vol. 58 (June and September, 1943), pp. 161–90; 380–414. *See* also Warner Schilling, "The Politics of National Defense: Fiscal 1950," in Schilling *et al.*, *Strategy, Politics and Defense Budgets*, New York: Columbia University Press, 1962, pp. 1–266; Edward Banfield, "Congress and the Budget: A Planner's Criticism," *American Political Science Review*, Vol. 43 (December, 1949), pp. 1217–28; Elias Huzar, *The Purse and the Sword*, Ithaca, N.Y.: Cornell University Press, 1950; Seymour Scher, "Conditions for Legislative Control," *Journal of Politics*, Vol. 25 (August, 1963), pp. 526–51; Aaron Wildavsky, *The Politics of the Budgetary Process*, Boston: Little, Brown and Company, 1964; Richard Fenno, "The House Appropriations Committee," *American Political Science Review*, Vol. 56 (June, 1962), pp. 310–24.

[2] Calendar years 1948 to 1962. A given budget (or fiscal) year (e.g., 1963) begins for the subcommittee with the opening of hearings in the early months of calendar 1962. Dates in this study are in terms of budget years.

record" about its annual review of agency budget requests. Although the subcommittee members do not rely solely on the hearings for their information about agency operations, they try to collect for the record all the information they consider pertinent to their budget decisions.[3] In this way, they say, they hope to make it relatively easy for other congressmen and interested members of the public to evaluate the subcommittee's budget recommendations. Much of the information the members elicit at the formal hearings they have already reviewed independently. Moreover, the members also show some genuine dependence on the annual hearings as a source of information. Subcommittee and agency staff aids report that members generally confine their administrative-oversight activities to the period of the hearings. Between the passage of one appropriations act and the next year's hearings there is little direct contact between subcommittee members and agency officials. The subcommittee staff maintains contact with the agencies during the year, but much of this is in preparation for the formal hearings. Because most of the data for this study come from the published record, the "records orientation" of the Fogarty Subcommittee was an important factor in its selection.

The Fogarty Subcommittee has a reputation for being generous in granting funds to the agencies within its jurisdiction,[4] but this may not bias the relationships with the agencies that are the subject of this study. There is no necessary connnection between generosity in appropriations, and a posture of laxity or severity in the subcommittee's supervision and control over agency operations. Also, a comparison of Fogarty subcommittee members with other members of the Appropriations Committee over the 1949-63 period indicates that the subcommittee members are not atypical in two respects that might affect their supervisory and control efforts. Their *skills* for the tasks of supervision and control—as measured by their pre-congressional occupations and length of service both in congress and on the Appropriations Committee—and their *positions on political issues*—as measured by their voting record on the *New Republic's* index of domestic liberalism[5]—score much the same as those for the Appropriations Committee as a whole.[6]

---

[3]For a member's comment to this effect, see House Appropriations Subcommittee on the Departments of Labor and Health, Education and Welfare, *Departments of Labor and Health, Education and Welfare Appropriations for 1959: Hearings*, 85 Cong. 2 sess., Washington, D.C.: U.S. Government Printing Office, p. 201.

[4]Wildavsky, *op. cit.*, p. 87.

[5]*See* Donald R. Matthews, *U.S. Senators and Their World*, Chapel Hill: University of North Carolina Press, 1960, pp. 276–78.

[6]On the basis of pre-congressional occupations, the members of the Fogarty subcommittee appear somewhat less able, on the average, to deal with complex technical and political matters than other members of the Appropriations Committee. During the 1949–63 period, only 70 percent of the subcommittee members came from occupations that would suggest a high level of relevant skills (i.e., law and other professions, journalism and politics), while 81 percent of all Committee members came from these fields. The difference in skill-potential disappears, however, if long experience in Congress or on the Appropria-

The four agencies that provided the sample for this study are the Children's Bureau (CB), the Office of Education (OE), the Food and Drug Administration (FDA) and Howard University (HU). These agencies have remained within one administrative unit (at first, the Federal Security Agency, then the Department of Health, Education and Welfare) over the 1949-63 period, and they represent various phases of HEW activity. CB and OE are disseminators of grants-in-aid, concerned with health and welfare, and education respectively. FDA is a regulatory agency concerned with health. HU is one of the units in the Department that has special status as a "Federally Aided Corporation." The sample agencies also differ greatly in the amounts of their recent appropriations requests, in increases in requests over the past decade, and in demonstrations of independence toward the supervisory and control efforts of the subcommittee.[7] Each of these characteristics may have an impact on subcommittee-agency relationships.

The sample agencies are entirely civilian. Secrecy was not a significant obstacle to an observer's reliance on published records, as it might be in the case of agencies involved with military or international activities.

MEASUREMENTS

This study relies almost exclusively on an analysis of subcommittee hearings, subcommittee *Reports* and agency budgets. Interviews served only a secondary role, as a means for clarifying and checking relationships perceived in the published records. Some distinct benefits derive from such a heavy reliance on published materials. The raw data are widely available in federal depository libraries for any student who wishes to test the findings on the same data, or on similar data about the behavior of other actors. Furthermore, problems of rapport between interviewer and informant do not bias the data collection. Although faulty schemes of classification may bias the use of published records, the basic materials remain unmarred, and the student can reclassify them as he proceeds.

---

tions Committee can make up for an unimpressive occupational background. Subcommittee members have had more experience in both areas: 78 percent of them in the 1949–63 period entered Congress before 1950, while only 63 percent of all Appropriations Committee members entered so early; and 60 percent of the subcommittee members joined the Appropriations Committee before 1950, in comparison to only 51 percent of the entire committee.

During the period of the study, subcommittee members voted in accord with the *New Republic's* conception of domestic liberalism 48 percent of the time, while the full committee voted that way 42 percent of the time.

[7] In the last year of the study's time span, the agencies' requests were: OE, $598 million; CB, $80 million; FDA, $28 million; HU, $13 million. Over the period 1951–63, the percentage increases in budget requests were: OE, 2120; FDA, 565; CB, 335; HU, 280. A comparative study of the agencies' budget strategies *vis à vis* the subcommittee revealed that OE was generally the most aggressive toward the subcommittee, HU was generally least aggressive, while CB and FDA fell in the middle range. *See* Ira Sharkansky, "Four Agencies and an Appropriations Subcommittee: A Comparative Study of Budget Strategies," *Midwest Journal of Political Science* (forthcoming).

The primary task in analyzing quantitatively the contents of published documents is their reduction to units that "make sense" as valid indicators of certain behaviorial traits. This may be a formidable task. The records relevant to the present study include monetary data, workload data, prose statements, questions and answers. No single codification could meet all the analytical needs. The literature on content analysis provides some guidance in the development of techniques, but it contains little beyond some general principles, and highly specialized operations useful only in a limited number of problem areas. Since one of the cardinal principles states that the nature of the research problem and the available data are crucial in determining the techniques that are fruitful and feasible, a great deal is left to the inventiveness of the student.[8]

The concept of "administrative oversight" has many facets and it is necessary to devise measures that will accommodate its components. Subcommittee supervision may vary in the *attention* paid to agency operations, in the *thoroughness* of supervision and in its *incisiveness*. Variations may also be observed in the efforts of subcommittee members to make *independent investigations* of agencies—as opposed to inquiries that rely on the cooperation or cues of agency officials. Among types of formal control efforts— publicly recorded—subcommittee adjustments of appropriations may be distinguished from the directives written into committee *Reports*. Measures can be defined that indicate the variation in each of these factors shown by subcommittee behavior *vis à vis* particular agencies. The product of the analysis accordingly will be a profile of overt administrative oversight, showing the relative severity of supervisory and control efforts directed at each agency.

(1) A count of individual questions directed at witnesses from each agency provides a gross measure of the *attention* the subcommittee members devote to the affairs of each agency. A "question" is defined here as a unit of discourse that includes one inquiry. At times, a sentence ending in a question mark may include several inquiries. In making this analysis, each distinct inquiry was regarded as a separate question. Also, some statements not followed by a question mark were so defined when they seemed to be treated as such by the participants in the hearing, e.g., when they elicited a reply from a witness, or when a following statement indicated they were meant to be inquiries. The score for each agency in Table 1 represents the mean number of questions asked by subcommittee members during hearings in the odd years from 1949 to 1963.

(2) The proportion of agency activities covered by subcommittee questioning provides a measure of the *thoroughness* with which the subcom-

---

[8]*See* Bernard Berelson, *Content Analysis in Communications Research*, Glencoe, Ill.: The Free Press, 1952; Robert C. North, *Content Analysis*, Evanston, Ill.: Northwestern University Press, 1963; Harold Lasswell (ed.), *Language of Politics*, New York: George Stewart Press, 1949; and Ithiel de Sola Poole (ed.), *Trends in Content Analysis*, Urbana: University of Illinois Press, 1959.

mittee supervises each agency. Making this measure operational involved two complex tasks: (a) defining the field of activities encompassed by each agency; and (b) defining a level of questioning that is "minimum coverage" of an activity.

The *Annual Reports* of the agencies, budget statements read at the opening of each year's hearings and *New York Times* articles about the agencies provided a list of their activities. A preliminary effort to code the members' questions into their subject-matter categories resulted in a redefinition of this list. It became evident that some closely related categories could be combined, while some additional categories were necessary to accommodate distinctions in the minds of legislators and administrators.[9]

Plainly, Congressmen cannot question thoroughly every agency activity during each year's hearings. In measuring "coverage," therefore, it is necessary to use a double standard that considers an item to be covered if it receives either frequent attention at a fairly low level of intensity, or less frequent attention at a higher level of intensity.[10]

While coding the questions, it became evident that individual inquiries may have a latent, as well as a manifest content.[11] That is, the context of some questions suggests that they might have several meanings to either the interrogator or the respondent. Congressmen frequently leave qualifying nouns or adjectives out of their verbiage, making it necessary to infer their referents from the surrounding context. Questions that could refer to several items accordingly were coded into as many categories as their contents— manifest and latent—seemed to require. This appeared safer than attempting the doubtful procedure of deciding what was "uppermost" in the minds of the actors.

(3) The frequency with which subcommittee members ask agency witnesses to justify their activities, and the frequency with which they ask about the cost of agency operations provide two crude measures of the relative *incisiveness* with which the members supervise agencies. Each of these question-types are probes. Justification questions call on agency officials to go beneath the surface to explain the need or utility of specific budget requests, while cost questions impose the discipline of calculation on administrators. The data in Table 1 represent the percentage of questions asked in odd years 1949-63 that were "justification questions" and "cost questions."

---

[9]For a list of the categories used, *see* Ira Sharkansky, "Four Agencies and an Appropriations Subcommittee: A Comparative Study of Budget Relations," (Ph.D. dissertation, University of Wisconsin, 1964, chap. iii).

[10]This study defines an item as "covered" if it received mention in 5 percent of the questions directed at the agency over the odd years 1949–63, or in at least 10 percent of the questions in one year's hearings. Admittedly, "coverage" of an activity is a rough measure of thoroughness. It does not mean that the subcommittee members give their attention to every issue and ramification related to an item.

[11]*See* Alexander L. George, "Quantitative and Qualitative Approaches to Content Analysis," in Ithiel de Sola Poole (ed.), *op. cit.*, pp. 7–32.

TABLE 1
AGENCY SCORES ON MEASURES OF SUBCOMMITTEE SUPERVISION AND CONTROL

MEASURE	AGENCY SCORE			
	OE	CB	FDA	HU
1. *Subcommittee attention:* Mean number of questions asked each agency, odd years 1949–63	321	159	123	104
2. *Subcommittee thoroughness:* Percentage of items receiving "minimum coverage," odd years 1949–63	45	58	57	64
3. *Subcommittee incisiveness:* a. Percentage of questions asking witnesses to justify activities, odd years 1949–63	39	29	37	22
b. Percentage of questions asking witnesses about cost, odd years 1949–63	21	24	18	44
4. *Independence of supervision:* a. Difference between mean percentage of questions about items highlighted in cues and the mean percentage of questions about all agency activities, 1951, 1957, 1963.	+3	+6	+8	+10
b. Ratio of questions asked department to questions asked agency, 1961, 1963	1:4	1:6	1:8	1:9
5. *Control over expenditures:* Median difference between original agency requests and subcommittee recommendations, 1959–63 (in millions)	—$31	—$1	—$9	—$5
6. *Control via Committee Report:* Number of directives about agency affairs in Committee *Reports* of 1951, 1957, 1961	17	5	2	9

(4) Two measures provide indices of the relative *independence* with which the subcommittee supervises each agency: (a) the frequency with which members avoid a reliance on agency cues while fashioning questions at the annual hearings; and (b) the frequency of questioning about agency affairs directed at witnesses outside the agency itself. The significance of an inquiry into the subcommittee's independence derives from the realization that members are hard pressed for time and staff assistance to be used for administrative oversight. Because of this, they frequently rely on the agencies themselves to provide cues about the items worthy of questioning. The items that tend to attract members' attention are those highlighted in agency budget documents, and in the opening statements read by the lead-off agency witness. By questioning an item that is expensive, or that has changed markedly in cost from the previous budget, or one that is featured in an oral statement,[12] subcommittee members can feel they are examining something that is "important" in some sense. An index of subcommittee nonreliance on agency cues to items worthy of questioning should stand as an indication of

---

[12]Agency officials as well as subcommittee members perceive these as cues that will elicit Congressional questioning. Agency budget officers write the opening statements for the hearings, knowing that these are the final communications legislators will receive before questioning agency witnesses. And they know that large items, or items showing a marked change from the previous budget tend to attract attention. One of the considerations in requesting funds for an activity is, "How will it look?" If a request might appear out of place, it may be postponed in part, or divided into smaller pieces and distributed among inconspicuous budget headings. *See* Wildavsky, *op. cit.*, chap. iii.

the members' independence in going beyond a superficial examination of the agency's presentation. In order to construct this index, it was first necessary to list the activities given prominence in the agency presentations.[13] The difference between the mean percentage of questions referring to the items highlighted in agency statements or budgets, and the mean percentage of questions asked about all activities was then computed. The greater the incidence of questions directed at items emphasized in the agency's presentations, the less is the subcommittee's independence.[14]

TABLE 2

AGENCY RANKINGS ON MEASURES OF SUBCOMMITTEE SUPERVISION AND CONTROL

MEASURE	AGENCY RANKING			
	OE	CB	FDA	HU
1. Subcommittee attention	1	2	3	4
2. Subcommittee thoroughness	4	2.5	2.5	1
3. Subcommittee incisiveness				
a. Justification questions	1	3	2	4
b. Cost questions	3	2	4	1
4. Independence of supervision				
a. Nonreliance on agency cues	1	2	3	4
b. Questioning nonagency sources	1	2	3	4
5. Control over expenditures	1	4	2	3
6. Control via Committee *Reports*	1	3	4	2
Mean ranking	1.6	2.6	2.9	2.9

An index of the subcommittee's attention to nonagency sources of information about agency affairs gives another indication of the legislators' independence in going beyond a superficial examination of the agency's presentation. While it is not practical to measure the subcommittee's attention to each nonagency source of information, it is possible to gauge the relative attention to nonagency witnesses who testify at the annual hearings. These include the Department Secretary and his aides, interest group spokesmen and other congressmen not members of the subcommittee. The

---

[13]This study considers an item to be emphasized in the opening hearing statement of an agency if it is mentioned in at least 10 percent of the statement's lines. An item is of "large absolute magnitude" if it is at least 20 percent of the agency's total request. An item has shown "significant change" if it has shown an absolute increase or decrease of $200,000 since the last budget, or a percentage change amounting to 10 percent of the total change in the agency's budget.

[14]For example, suppose that the items emphasized in the budgets and statements of each of two agencies received mention in a mean 10 percent of the subcommittee's questions, and that in the case of one agency, all its activities—both those emphasized and unemphasized—received mention in a mean 5 percent of the questions. The index of subcommittee nonreliance would then be 10 minus 5, or 5. If in the second agency's case all activities received mention in a mean 8 percent of the subcommittee's questions, the index of subcommittee nonreliance would be 10 minus 8, or 2. The congressmen would be showing less reliance on the cues of the second agency. The data for this analysis came from the hearings of 1951, 1957 and 1963, chosen because they fall near the beginning, middle and end of the period studied.

best available measure of subcommittee attention to outside sources of information is the ratio of questions about each agency directed at the Department Secretary and his aides, to the questions directed at the agency witnesses during the same year's hearings. This measure is suitable because subcommittee members have an opportunity to question the Secretary and his staff at length about each agency. In contrast, the members have little opportunity to question interest group spokesmen, or nonsubcommittee congressmen about the agencies that attract few or none of these witnesses.[15]

(5) A comparison of each agency's request for funds, and the appropriation recommended by the subcommittee provides a measure of the legislators' attempts to impose controls over agency operations by means of adjusting the level of expenditures. In this study, the measure is defined by the median difference between the agency's request and the subcommittee's decision over the years 1959–63.[16]

(6) The subcommittee includes in its *Reports* directives about each agency's operations. A count of these provides a measure of control efforts by means of verbal instructions. The *Reports* used for this analysis are those written in 1951, 1957 and 1963.[17]

Table 1 provides the raw scores for each agency on the measures covered in the foregoing discussion. Table 2 provides the rankings for each agency on the various measures. In each case, the top rank of (1) indicates that an agency has been the subject of the most severe supervisory or control efforts.

Table 1 demonstrates the substantial differences in severity that mark the supervision and control efforts of subcommittee members toward agencies within their jurisdiction. However, Table 2 suggests that the subcommittee is not consistent in the degree of severity it maintains with respect to each agency. For instance, the Office of Education tends to receive a generally

---

[15]Because the Department Secretary and agency officials share an identity with the Administration, it might be said that the Secretary and his staff are not sufficiently independent of the agencies to be considered "nonagency" sources of information. Yet there are significant budget disputes between agency and departmental personnel. Department officials report in formal hearings and in interviews that agencies typically demand more funds than the department can allow them. From the agency view, the department is a brake against desirable expansion. Over the 1959–63 period, the department budget office reduced the requests of our sample agencies by $290.8 million, or 11 percent of the agencies' original requests. In the hearings, departmental witnesses have been critical of agency operations. In contrast, none of the interest groups or nonsubcommittee congressmen testifying in the odd years 1951–63 criticized agency operations. They either supported agency requests, or urged the replacement of budget cuts made by the department Budget Office or the Bureau of the Budget. The data for the analysis of subcommittee questioning of nonagency witnesses came from the hearings of 1961 and 1963, chosen because it has only been in recent years that the legislators have paid significant attention to nonagency witnesses.

[16]It was only in these years that information about the agencies' original budget request to the Department Budget Office was included in the hearings record.

[17]These years were chosen because they fall near the beginning, middle and end of the research span.

more severe treatment than the others dealt with—as defined by the mean rankings—but this is the only distinction among the agencies that is prominent across several measures. Somewhat less prominent is the finding that the Children's Bureau is treated more severely than the Food and Drug Administration and Howard University.

The Office of Education may receive greater attention than the others because its budget is substantially greater and has increased more rapidly. Or, the attention paid to OE may come as a result of its record of being more adventurous than the others in its disregard for subcommittee directives. A comparative study of agency behavior established that OE, among those covered, was most likely to evade questions asked by subcommittee members at the hearings, and most likely to disobey specific prohibitions that Committee *Reports* and appropriations acts imposed on policy. The subcommittee devoted a secondary level of supervisory and control efforts toward CB, and this agency scored second to OE in budget magnitude and aggressiveness *vis à vis* the subcommittee.[18]

The greater attention shown to OE and CB may not represent a conscious decision by the subcommittee members, so much as a subtle attraction to the affairs of agencies that are more prominent than others in the public eye. Just as the legislators are most likely to question items that are salient in the agencies' budgets or their witnesses' statements, so they may gravitate without design to more severe supervisory and control efforts for prominent agencies that spend much money and receive much political attention. My comparative study of agency activities demonstrated that more interest groups and nonsubcommittee congressmen testify on behalf of OE than the other sample agencies, and that budget statements of the Department Secretary and the President devote more space to OE activities than to those of other units. CB was in second place on each of these measures. An analysis of representative news media might also reveal that they pay more attention to the affairs of OE and CB than to the others.[19]

Another finding indicated by Table 2 is that each of the sample agencies receives the brunt of rather severe supervision on some dimension of subcommittee activity. The Children's Bureau scores second highest in the average number of questions and cost questioning; the Food and Drug Administration scores second highest in justification questioning, and Howard University scores highest in the proportion of items covered by questioning, and in cost questioning. This may suggest that subcommittee members try to probe all agencies in at least some respect. They may be "fishing" for instances of errant administrative behavior, or trying to put the fear of discovery into the minds of any administrators who might contemplate a deviation from subcommittee wishes.

[18]Sharkansky, "Four Agencies and an Appropriations Subcommittee: A Comparative Study of Budget Strategies," *op. cit.*

[19]*Ibid.*

CONCLUSIONS

This study provides some systematically collected data about the behavior of an appropriations subcommittee in its dealings with four agencies. Evidently, the legislators vary their oversight activity among agencies. They devote more than the average amount of supervisory and control efforts to the agencies that spend the most money, whose requests have increased the most rapidly, and whose behavior toward the subcommittee has deviated most frequently from subcommittee desires. In a sense, they allocate their time and staff assistance to agencies most "in need" of supervision and control. If disproportionate attention to this type of agency is typical of legislative-executive budget relations, then it may be said that the legislators maximize their resources for oversight.

Beyond these specific conclusions, the study has shown the practicality of using content analysis of appropriations hearings to devise indexes of Committee behavior—crude indexes, to be sure, but sufficient to support objective rankings along various measures of attitudes and activities.

THE BUNDLE OF GOVERNMENTAL SERVICES
MORTON GRODZINS

Casa Grande, Arizona, sits athwart one of two principal highways that run through the hot country from Phoenix to Tucson. Casa Grande was for many years nothing but a desert stop-off. Deep wells and irrigation have brought long-staple cotton to the Salt River Valley, and farming, wherever water is available, is intensive and profitable. The town is a shopping and marketing center for Pinal County, and to some degree a dormitory for the adjacent farm areas. Its population of 1,545 in 1940 almost tripled by 1950 when the census showed 4,181 residents. In 1958, according to unofficial estimates, Casa Grande with a population approaching 9,000 had become even larger than the county seat of Coolidge.

The bundle of governmental services delivered to the citizens of Casa Grande is a considerable one. Some of these services are not carried on by the city government at all, and for others, local officials have only peripheral responsibilities.

Public welfare activities in Arizona, for example, are administered by the counties under state supervision, and no item for welfare appears in the Casa Grande city budget. The case load within the city limits is nevertheless considerable: in the winter of 1958 some 300 residents of the city were receiving welfare aid, not counting recipients of child welfare services. By far the largest fraction of those receiving aid were under programs defined by national legislation and partially paid for with federal funds. For example, there were 159 persons in Casa Grande receiving old age assistance and 97 benefited from aid under the program for dependent children. A substantial, if uncertain, number of Casa Grande residents received Old Age and Survivors Insurance payments, a program wholly administered by the federal government.

In a similar fashion public health services for the residents of the city are largely carried on through programs of county, state, and federal governments. The city has a small item in its budget for health and sanitation activities, the local government's activity in this "local" field being largely confined to milk inspection and to sanitation control in restaurants and other places handling food. The county public health office operates a diverse program. Federal funds in 1958 were being utilized for the treatment of tuberculosis, for the investigation and control of venereal diseases, and for the reimbursement of nurses under the maternal and child care program. Polio vaccine provided at no cost by the United States Public Health Service was available. Federal aid was responsible for a contemplated

---

Article is from *The American System*, Chicago: Rand McNally & Company, 1966, pp. 156–71. Used with permission of publisher.

study of mental health. County and state officers were also at this time planning a county health center; they were confident that 30 percent of the cost of the building would be paid by the federal government under the Hill-Burton Act. These are but samples of the national government's role in activities carried out in the city of Casa Grande by officers of Pinal County under the supervision of, and with funds partially supplied by, the State of Arizona.

Federal-state collaboration supplies citizens of Casa Grande with unemployment insurance and employment placement services. The local office of the Arizona Employment Security Commission is a particularly busy place because of the seasonal nature of a large fraction of Casa Grande's employment needs. Standards of compensation, financing, and administration are regulated by the intricate system of federal-state law and administration.

Education in Casa Grande is not a responsibility of city officers. Separate districts for the high school and elementary schools are maintained, each with its own elected governing board and taxing power. Schools operate under the customary state legal and administrative standards. Arizona schools receive state financial aid to a degree roughly parallel to the national average. In 1957–58 the Casa Grande schools collected slightly more than 60 percent of their total revenues from local taxes, the remainder ($400,000) coming from state and county aid calculated on a per capita basis.

Federal contributions to the schools were peripheral but considerable. All schools participated in the federally sponsored free lunch and milk program. The high school received funds under the Smith-Hughes Act for special classes in vocational agriculture and homemaking. A portion of the salary of four teachers, out of a total of 36, was paid from this federal contribution. Direct supervision of these teachers was given by state officers who themselves were paid with federal funds and worked by federal standards. Several teachers have received summer training fellowships from the National Science Foundation. Technical aids to all parts of the schools come from publications of the United States Office of Education and the Department of Agriculture.

The proximity of Indian reservations to Casa Grande provided a relatively unusual point of national contact for the schools. Indian children for the most part attended reservation grammar schools, but in 1958 almost 10 percent of the high school students were reservation residents. The Bureau of Indian Affairs compensated the school on a per-student per-day basis.

Finally, the Casa Grande schools have benefited materially from the distribution of federal surplus property. The State Department of Public Instruction operated an office to facilitate the flow of federal surplus materials to local schools. This flow in the past has on occasion been too active, and several criminal indictments were at one time returned against some Arizona local school administrators who were acquiring federal surplus equipment in large quantities, including such items as B-27 bombers, and trading it to private businessmen, not always for the exclusive benefit of the schools. Casa Grande was not touched by this scandal, and the schools have received at virtually no cost an impressive quantity of surplus materials. These include for the high school such items as a truck; radios for classrooms; tools for the automobile mechanics and woodworking classes; and stoves, refrigerators, dishes, and dishwashers for the lunchroom. Surplus goods utilized by the school range from scrap paper to an outmoded Link Trainer for airplane pilots and several dismantled aircraft.

The Casa Grande Community Hospital, like the schools, is operated by a special local government. The hospital was the product of several acts of intergovernmental collaboration, initiated by a civic group and abetted by senatorial "casework." The local Lions Club was concerned with the community's need for a modern hospital facility, but little progress was made until a new city attorney for Casa Grande drafted a law, readily passed by the Arizona legislature as a state statute, which authorized creation of special hospital districts that could issue bonds and, under certain circumstances, levy taxes. The statute also provided that a certification of need had to be issued by the State Department of Health before the local district could be formed. Once initiated through this typical process of private-local-state collaboration, the Casa Grande Community Hospital soon received federal assistance. A grant of approximately $30,000 was made to the hospital by the Department of Health, Education, and Welfare under the Hill-Burton Act. These funds were used primarily for supplies and equipment. In addition, city officials succeeded in having an unused federal hospital, constructed during the depression by the Rural Resettlement Administration, declared surplus and given to the new community hospital. The surplus facility was then completely razed, and the new Casa Grande Community Hospital was able to salvage a substantial amount of building materials as well as a large number of beds, carts, stretchers, sickroom supplies, and other equipment.

A full quota of federally engineered local governments for agricultural purposes existed in Pinal County, providing important services to Casa Grande citizens. The County Agricultural Conservation and Stabilization Committee, whose offices were in the city, was responsible for administration of the soil bank (which provided payments to farmers for not growing certain crops and using the land set aside for rebuilding its fertility); the cotton marketing quota (which guaranteed cotton prices under a program limiting production); and the conservation practices program (which provided grants and loans for soil conservation). There were some 1,000 farms in the county of which more than 800 participated in one or more of the ASC programs. Perhaps 10 percent of the farmowners—estimates run from 50 to 100 of the participating farmers—were residents of Casa Grande itself. The funds distributed through ASC programs represented the largest single expenditure by any government within the county, and of course had the most profound effect on the economy of the city.

The Soil Conservation Service operating its characteristic local government, the Farmer's Home Administration, the Federal Land Bank, and the Agricultural Extension Service also provided significant services to the residents of the city, both directly and indirectly. For example, the Extension Service (whose offices incidentally were in the Casa Grande City Hall) operated a program in home economics administered through homemakers' clubs: three of the ten clubs in the county were in Casa Grande. Work with 4-H clubs also spilled over into the city, and the agent estimated that of the 560 farmers in the county who participated in technical meetings and demonstration programs, approximately 100 were city residents. A state program operating with funds supplied by the federal, state, and county governments (concerted through the University of Arizona), the extension service reflected more than the mixture of governments. It also illustrated, through the range of its activities and the clientele it served, the disappearing frontier between farm and city life. Finally, its sponsorship underscored the thin line separating public and private activities: as in other states, agricultural extension services of Pinal County were sponsored by the County Farm Bureau, a private organization.

The list of services, supplied by governments other than the government of Casa Grande, having direct and immediate local impact cannot be a complete one. The statute books are fat, and the vagaries of classification could spin the list out unendingly. The regulatory functions have so far been ignored. They were largely functions of the federal government and the state, alone or in combination, and included inspections for industrial safety and the purity of food and drugs, regulation of labor relations, licensing of the professions and vocations, examination of banks and the provision of deposit insurance. One important service, that of delivering the mail, had its purely federal administrative apparatus leavened by political influence of the states and localities. Finally, one function also touching the whole population, that of selective service, was operated jointly by the federal government and the state, making use of a state-appointed board of local citizens.

The services of government described thus far are carried on within the boundaries, and directly affect the residents, of Casa Grande. They can be considered local services of government, but they are not carried out by what is normally considered "the" local government, the municipality of Casa Grande. Indeed, these are services for which the municipality has little or no responsibility; they are the responsibility of the federal and state governments, the county, the school districts, and the several species of federally sponsored local governments for agriculture.

The streets of Casa Grande provide an avenue of approach to functions in which city officials have a more direct responsibility. The main street of the city is a federally aided state highway; it was constructed and maintained by the state highway department, utilizing standards of the federal government and paid for in part with federal funds. In an earlier

110

period the federal government's Works Progress Administration was responsible for a good share of all the paving done on the city's own streets. Now this is a state-local activity. The city spent more on its street program (some $55,000 in 1957) than for any other single function. By far the largest fraction of this money, almost $46,000, was collected by the state in automobile and gasoline taxes and returned to the city. Very few controls were exercised by state officers over expenditures for city streets. But technical standards for street construction, made available by both the state and federal governments, were an indispensable guide for the city's construction and maintenance program.

Police activities loom second largest in the city's budget. What has already been described as the national police system operated effectively in Casa Grande. The most notable objects in the office of the Chief of Police were a diploma signifying his graduation from the FBI's National Police Academy and an autographed photograph of J. Edgar Hoover. Contacts between field agents of the FBI, headquartered at Phoenix, and the local police department were frequent and cordial; an office in the city hall, also used occasionally by the state's game warden, was made available to the FBI representative during his weekly visits. FBI laboratory facilities in Washington, D.C., were utilized by the local police as a matter of course on difficult cases. Casa Grande police have also worked closely with the Narcotics and Alcoholic Control divisions of the Treasury Department. Training schools established throughout the state by the Arizona Chiefs of Police Association were for the most part staffed by FBI instructors. A special federal-local linkage in police work resulted from the city's southwestern location and the need of nearby farms for inexpensive seasonal labor supplied from Mexico. Control over the use of aliens in farm work was partially vested in the United States Border Patrol. An office of the Border Patrol was maintained in the Casa Grande City Hall, close to the local Chief of Police. The officers were friends, as well as close collaborators, although the patrol's duties only infrequently demanded services from local police.

One connection leads to another, and the Border Patrol's work in Casa Grande often led to the use of the city jail for federal prisoners who were awaiting transportation to other places. This was the source of a small city income and a larger city pride. When the jail was rebuilt and enlarged in 1957, city officers called upon the U.S. Bureau of Prisons for assistance. Consultations were held even before the blueprint stage, and a specialist from Washington, D.C., visited the city several times during actual construction. So it was that persons suspected of crimes against the laws of Arizona were lodged in the Casa Grande city jail, which was constructed under the *de facto* supervision of the federal Bureau of Prisons.

Federal-local collaboration was demonstrated daily in the local administration of justice. Arizona police magistrates were appointed to their part-time duties by city councils. (Casa Grande's magistrate sold insurance as

111

his principal occupation.) Jurisdiction of the courts was limited to the most minor offenses; traffic violations, vagrancy, and the like. Yet the federal government's impact on this most local of local courts was felt in a number of ways. For one thing the magistrate did everything within his power to assist the Border Patrol. If the Patrol suspected that a drunk or vagrant was an alien who had entered the country illegally, the magistrate would try to keep him in jail long enough for reports to come from Washington. A person who ordinarily would have been fined or given a suspended sentence was, at the request of the Border Patrol, kept the maximum period in jail. A similar service was performed for the local chief if he suspected that a person before the magistrate's court was wanted in other jurisdictions for more serious crimes. Finally, in cases where records from the FBI were already available on a person brought before his court, the magistrate found this information controlling. "When a man tells me that he has never been in trouble before but when the police department then gives me a record sheet from the FBI showing convictions in ten states running back for 20 years, then I know I have a person in front of me who deserves all the punishment I can give him."

The first city planning in Casa Grande was made possible by federal grants. These grants were administered by the Community Facilities Service of the General Services Administration under Public Law 352 of the 81st Congress. No local matching was required, and the city received $19,200 in all. Plans were made for a citywide drainage system and for sanitary sewers, curbs, gutters, and sidewalks for substantial portions of the city—improvements that were of the first importance to the rapidly growing community.

Two side effects were also significant. For one thing, the planning grants provided the first occasion on which city officials worked with the private engineering firm, Jones and Gore, a company that subsequently became the city's principal agent in negotiations with federal agencies. Jones and Gore was responsible for calling to the attention of city officials the availability of the planning grants. It undertook the work of soliciting a grant for the city on the understanding that no fee would be paid if the grant were not received and the subsequent planning not approved. The entire negotiation with the federal agency, aided by the city officers and by Arizona's United States senators, was carried on by the private firm. In subsequent years, the same firm played a similar role in the city's efforts to take advantage of other federal grants.

A second by-product of the planning grants was unexpected and the source of one of the few points of friction between the city and the federal government. The grants provided for repayment without interest to the federal government of the money advanced "when the construction of the public works planned with the aid of the government's advance is undertaken or started." This proved to be a point of embarrassment for the city when it wanted to construct a drainage system covering only a part of the city. The federal advance for the street drainage plans had amounted to $8,000.

Federal officials insisted that the total advance (rather than a fraction proportional to the construction contemplated) be repaid. Casa Grande officials in turn insisted that they were unable to repay the entire $8,000. The loggerhead had the effect of postponing construction of even the partial drainage system. So the federal planning grant, designed to encourage public works, in this case had the opposite effect. City officers were still somewhat wrathful concerning this point in 1958, but they were confident that federal rules would soon be changed to conform to their own more "reasonable" position.

Public health measures, although principally in the domain of federal-state-county services, do not completely escape the attention of city officers. Dysentery and infant diarrhea are particularly serious problems in the desert community, and the infant death rate has been a high one historically. To combat one important source of these difficulties, the city was aided, from 1950 through 1953, by a team of specialists from the United States Public Health Service (working through state and county health offices). The federal team made studies of the number and sources of flies, supplied spray trucks and insecticides, and began a systematic program to control flies in the city. Instructions for continuing this work were given by federal specialists to city workers, and the city has maintained the spraying program with what it believes to be considerable success.

One source of flies difficult to control was the city's raw sewage, which was dumped untreated in an open field at the outskirts of the city. This disposal system created health hazards and constituted, moreover, a considerable odoriferous nuisance. A better method of sewage disposal became one of Casa Grande's most pressing needs, especially if it wished to continue to grow. The federal government met this need, first, through a grant of $107,000 for the construction of a modern sewage disposal system; and, second, through a loan of $250,000 to enable the city to pay its share of the costs.

Application for the grant was formally made through the Arizona Department of Health, but city officials and their representatives carried out direct negotiations in 1956 and 1957 with the United States Public Health Service. City representatives in this matter included not only the engineering firm, Jones and Gore, but also a group of bond attorneys, and an investment securities company. Legislation limited the outright federal grant for the sewage disposal system to one-third of the total cost, and it was necessary for the city to raise an additional $250,000. A bond issue was clearly necessary, but private sources for the loan were not available at a reasonable interest rate. Consequently the city called upon still another federal department, the Housing and Home Finance Agency, which authorized the city to obtain the needed loan from that agency. The first bonds were ready to be issued when a private bonding house indicated its willingness to assume the lender's role at the already fixed rate of interest. The bonds were accordingly sold to the private company and the loan authorization was never utilized, cutting off this Casa Grande-federal contact. But it had well served its purpose. The interest rate paid on the bonds by the city would undoubtedly have been higher if federal loan funds had not been available.

The sewage disposal plant, made possible by federal grants and federal loans facilities, was under construction during the winter of 1958. But it was not the federal government's most valuable capital contribution to Casa Grande. City officials believed that in the long run even greater returns would come to the community from an airfield and a mountain park, the first an outright gift from the federal government, the second a virtual gift.

The airfield had been constructed on public lands during the war as a training facility and auxiliary landing area, and was declared surplus after the war by the Department of Defense. Casa Grande's interest in acquiring the field began in 1954 when the local Chamber of Commerce, in a report to the city council, urged the desirability of city ownership. Almost three years of negotiations were necessary before the field was transferred, the biggest stumbling block being the need for all other federal agencies to certify that the facility was not needed by them. Senators Hayden and Goldwater were active on behalf of Casa Grande at every step of the process. The facility is an impressive one, a complete square mile of perfectly flat table land. Land of this sort in the vicinity of Casa Grande was being sold in 1958 for building lots at approximately $1,000 an acre. Since the airport consisted of exactly 640 acres, city officers believed that in placing a valuation of $500,000 on it they were being conservative.

Improvements were needed on the airport when it was acquired. Its facilities consisted only of four paved runways. Even before the transfer of the airport title, city officials (again assisted by Jones and Gore) applied to the Federal Civil Aeronautics Administration for funds to improve the field. Aid was asked for the construction of an administration building, a water system, telephone and power lines, and runway lights. The original application had to be scaled down because of lack of funds available to the CAA, but the federal agency did give the city $5,000 of the $8,000 needed to bring water to the field. With the advice of the CAA district engineer, the city in 1958 resubmitted plans for additional improvement grants. City officers, confident that at least $30,000 in CAA funds would ultimately be made available for the airport, contemplated an investment of some $19,000 from the city's own funds. They considered this a good investment in a "$549,000 piece of useful property," especially since some of the airport land could be leased for industrial purposes. Once improvements have been completed, the field is expected to be completely self-supporting.[1]

---

[1]Acceptance of the airfield as a gift involved Casa Grande in a continuing federal relationship. The federal government, for example, retained the right to make use of the landing strips, subject to regulations of the CAA, and during periods of national emergency to take (but pay for) exclusive use of the field. The contract deed imposed the obligation on the city to maintain the field at all times. It cannot grant exclusive rights to the field or exclusive franchises (except for the sale of gasoline and oil) to service and sales agencies. Furthermore, the use of the field and its facilities cannot be limited "on the grounds of race, creed or color."

A parcel of federal land, even larger than the airfield, was being transferred in 1958 to Casa Grande. It consisted of no fewer than 1,400 acres and was named the Casa Grande Mountain Park. The land itself was less valuable than the airfield, being in a mountainous area, but the city assumed no financial obligation whatsoever in acquiring the park. The parkland was being acquired from the Bureau of Land Management of the Department of the Interior under federal statutes by which surplus portions of the public domain may be sold to public bodies for recreational purposes. The sale price was nominal—some three cents an acre—and the actual cash payments were assumed by the local Rotary Club which initiated the project. The Rotary also paid for initial improvements of the land. City officials believed the park would be of inestimable value in the years ahead. Senators Hayden and Goldwater again gave active aid to both city officials and Rotary Club members as negotiations for the land transfer were carried on.

Housing in Casa Grande has been affected by a number of federal programs. In 1946 a federal public housing agency built 20 low-cost housing units in the city, primarily for veterans. This project was given to the city in 1950, and in 1958 the units were still being rented. A more significant federal-local relationship in housing was a less direct one. The largest fraction of home construction in the area was financed by loans from the Federal Housing Authority and the Veterans' Administration. Under the FHA program individual loans were not approved unless an entire site met federal standards. The city supplied information regularly to the FHA on new subdivision sites, certifying to the width of streets, and to the provision of sewers, water, and other amenities. Further, the FHA would not approve building loans in unzoned subdivisions, and consequently the city had to bring up to date, and in some cases to alter, zoning requirements. The pressure on the city council to provide this kind of zoning—as well as to build streets and sewers—came from local builders and not from the federal agency. But the latter's demands were freely cited by the builders as compelling reasons for taking action, and the city council did what was demanded because the builders were important members of the community and because the city badly needed new housing. Thus FHA policies led to an extension and updating of zoning and in some cases to the annexation of new areas in order to bring them under the city's zoning authority. A final federal-local contact with respect to housing resulted from the appointment of the city building inspector as inspector for the FHA and for the VA. The local official received extra compensation for these services. In his capacity as a local officer, he inspected each new home five times during the construction period. The VA required four inspections. In this case he discharged his local and federal duties simultaneously. For the FHA, additional site inspections were required.

Officials of Casa Grande, in common with local leaders throughout the country, participated in federal civil defense programs. Two Casa Grande officers, their expenses paid by the federal government, have attended civil

115

defense training courses. Federal funds have furnished visual aid equipment for the training of local citizens in civil defense work. Local leaders in 1958 were completing a disaster relief plan under the supervision of federal and state officials. At that time, Casa Grande, unlike many other cities, had not taken advantage of the civil defense contributions program which made possible the acquisition of two-way radios for police and fire departments. The city officials were well informed about what was available to them under this program, however, and their plans included making application for this equipment.

This extensive list of programs involving many governments is not an exhaustive one. The federal contribution to the bundle of services in Casa Grande includes a considerable miscellany. The larger and better equipped of the city's two fire trucks was purchased at exceedingly low cost from the surplus property division of the federal General Services Administration. A principal building in the city was the National Guard Armory, used not only for training purposes but also as a facility for dances and other civic events. A rent-free office in the City Hall was provided the local officer of the Treasury Department's Bureau of Internal Revenue. The National Park Service maintained the Casa Grande Indian Ruins, a national monument closer to Coolidge than to Casa Grande, but which Casa Grande officials believed could be an important tourist attraction provided the Park Service did a more energetic job of publicizing and maintaining the ruins. Cordial relationships were maintained with officers of the nearby Gila, Pima, and Papago Indian Reservations. The city was an official weather reporting station for the United States Weather Bureau, supplying information twice daily to a central station in Phoenix. Similarly, the city provided a monthly report to the Department of Labor on building in progress. A brass plaque on the older portion of the City Hall, long forgotten by even the inhabitants of the offices, made known the fact that this focal point for the many activities of many governments was, appropriately enough, constructed in 1936 with federal funds through the Works Progress Administration.

Table 1 summarizes the responsibilities of the various governments for services provided the citizens of Casa Grande. The table attempts to take account only of formal spheres of authority, and if informal lines of influence were charted there would be many more indications of shared functions. The distinction between important and unimportant responsibilities is, of course, not an exact one. Judgments on this score were made after on-the-spot observations and after consultation with appropriate officials. Other observers might in some cases have judged differently: for example, they might not have given the Casa Grande city government a major role in civil defense. Yet the chart can be taken as a generally accurate map of which governments do what within the borders of Casa Grande. What does this sort of mapping reveal?

First, it is notable how many and how important are the functions provided to the local citizens by governments other than the municipality. Of

TABLE 1

THE BUNDLE OF GOVERNMENTAL SERVICES PROVIDED THE
RESIDENTS OF CASA GRANDE, ARIZONA, 1958

Service	City of Casa Grande	Special District	County of Pinal	Special Local Government Engineered by U.S.	State of Arizona	United States
1. Activities for which city government has little or no responsibility.[a]						
Agricultural conservation and stabilization				**	*	**
Agricultural extension			**		**	**
Bank examination and deposit insurance					**	**
Education		**	**		**	*
Employment security					**	**
Farmers Home Administration				*		**
Hospital		**			*	**
Industrial safety					**	*
Inspection of boilers, weights and measures; other commercial inspection	*				**	
Inspection of food and drugs	*		**		**	**
Labor relations					**	**
National Guard					**	**
Postal service						**
Professional licensing and examinations					**	*
Public health	*		**		**	**
Public welfare			**		**	**
Selective Service				**	**	**
Soil Conservation Service			*	**	*	**
2. Activities for which city government has important responsibilities.[b]					*	**
Airport	**				*	**
City planning	**				*	**
Civil Defense	**				**	**
Courts	**		**		**	*
Fire protection	**				*	
Garbage disposal	**				*	
Library	**					**
Parks	**				**	**
Police	**		**			
Recreation	**				*	**
Sewage and sanitation	**				**	**
Streets and highways	**	*			**	**
Zoning and housing	**				*	**

[a]This section of the table is abbreviated and is meant only to be illustrative.
[b]All lines in the official city budget are included in this section of the table.
**Major role.
*Minor role.

the range of services in the top half of the table, the city formally participates in only two, public health and inspection of commercial establishments, and in these only to a relatively minor degree.

Second, the activities for which Casa Grande has no formal responsibility are nevertheless shared functions. Only two federal activities—the postal service and the loans of the Farmers Home Administration—do not involve the state and *some* local government, or both. In even these two cases, state-local influence is not inconsiderable.[2] One state function, inspection of boilers and weights and measures, does not involve the federal government, but this is more the result of the classification scheme than of any real separation of functions: the federal government is heavily involved in the closely related and overlapping functions of providing for industrial safety and the purity of food and drugs.

Third, still focusing attention on the top portion of the table, in those functions which are not the responsibility of the city of Casa Grande, other local governments have important roles. These include the county, the special governments for education and for the hospital, and the federally sponsored or stimulated local governments in the large-spending agricultural programs and in Selective Service.

Fourth, without discounting the importance of the nonmunicipal local governments in the functions listed in Part 1 of the table, it can be said that the county is assigned its functions largely as an administrative arm of the state, and that the local governments for agricultural programs and for Selective Service are created specifically to administer federal programs. It is therefore obvious that, with the important exceptions of education and the hospital, the top half of the table represents a range of functions in which the federal and state governments take the leading role in providing services to the local community.

Fifth, the activities in which Casa Grande plays an important role (Part 2 of the table) are also activities to which the federal government makes a major contribution. No function of the municipality, as recorded in its own budget, is omitted from this listing. With only three exceptions, the budgeted local functions are also federal functions. And again the exceptions result largely from accidents of the classificatory scheme. Without doing violence to common sense, for example, it could be said that the federal government has markedly influenced garbage disposal in Casa Grande through its aid in the fly control program and the sewage system. No direct federal participation was noted in recreation. Yet the federal government's virtual gift of the Mountain Park is probably the most important single factor in the future of the city's recreation program. Since recreation is carried as an item separate from parks in the city budget, however, it is shown in the table as not including a federal linkage. Finally, the city library has so far not profited from federal contributions. But the library is eligible for assistance under the federal Library Services Act and undoubtedly will take advantage of the program in the relatively near future.

---

[2]The Farmers Home Administration does not make loans directly but guarantees the payment of loans made by private local banks; services to farmers who make loans involve the local representative of the Farmers Home Administration in a multitude of ties with local and state officers.

In sum, then, the federal government supplies more services to the citizens of Casa Grande without the participation of the city of Casa Grande than the city provides without the participation of the federal government. Local services are not exclusively or principally the province of local governments. All governments in the American system provide local services. And the characteristic means of providing any given service is through the collaboration of several governments.

CENTRALIZED VERSUS DECENTRALIZED FINANCE

Harold M. Groves

It is an accepted rule that the Government should not perform functions that can as well be performed privately and that the Federal Government should not perform functions that can as well be performed by State and local governments. Unfortunately this doesn't help very much in making decisions as to whether functions should be assumed by the Federal Government or left to the States.

PRESUMPTION FAVORING DECENTRALIZED FINANCE

The presumption in favor of State and local government is based on the faith that decentralization is an important constituent of democracy. This faith is particularly plausible insofar as it applies the rule that matters which are solely or perhaps mainly of concern to a particular area should be left to the people of that area for decision. This interest in local autonomy carries the title "Home Rule" and it is guarded as jealously (and as frequently violated) as the similar right of the private individual to mind his own business when it does not conflict with that of somebody else.

Beyond this interest in home rule there are values in local government that are lost when responsibilities are assumed by central governments. One of these is participation—government by the people. The private citizen undoubtedly finds opportunities to participate in government at the local level which cannot be duplicated at the national level. At the city hall or State Capitol any public-spirited citizen can reach his alderman or legislator in person and he can appear to express his views at a public hearing. An ordinary "dirt farmer" can do all of this and get home in time to milk the cows. It may be prohibitively expensive for him to go to Washington and, anyway, he would need an elaborate organization to make much impression there. Rated by degree of participation, most democratic government is that by popular assembly or referendum where representatives can be dispensed with entirely. Next best is representative government in a small enough circle so that the ordinary citizen without undue sacrifice can make himself heard and felt.

Local government also offers to many an opportunity to participate in government in positions of responsibility. There are thousands of people

Article is from H. M. Groves, "Centralized Versus Decentralized Finance," *Federal Expenditure Policies for Economic Growth and Stability,* Joint Economic Committee, Congress of the United States, Washington, D.C.: U.S. Government Printing Office, November 5, 1957, pp. 188–94.

whose career as a representative of the people is and will be confined to membership on the school boards of our some 65,000 school districts. This is not only of some value in itself—it is a training school and a testing ground from which the upper echelons of government recruit talent.

Local governments also serve as experiment stations in which new ideas may be tried out without the risk and expense (to say nothing of the inertia) that would be involved if the experiments were national in scale.

These positive values of local government are reinforced by the negative aspects of far-flung centralized bureaucracy. Distrust of such is deeply rooted among Americans, especially those who lean toward an anti-monopoly philosophy. Central government is not only big; it is also single; it possesses unique coercive powers; and it offers no alternatives to its customers. Like all large monopolistic organizations it suffers the inefficiencies that rise from inadequate knowledge at the center of what is really needed at the periphery.

Of course, it can be argued plausibly that some central sharing in the financial support of local functions is quite different from Federal assumption of sole responsibility and control in these areas. It is argued that in communities with limited resources, grants-in-aid may increase local independence by freeing some of their limited funds for services of their own choosing. But this new freedom is like that of a son who earns part of his support and gets the remainder in a regular (but not guaranteed) allowance from his benevolent parents. He is not really fully free and responsible until he subsists on his own income supplied by himself.

THE CASE FOR CENTRALIZED FINANCE

All of the above is widely appreciated in this country. But there is another side of the picture that offers persuasive support for a degree of centralized responsibility at least greater than that which prevailed in the 1920's.

Slow Progress and Undemocratic Procedures in State Government

The States and municipalities (particularly the former) would be in a stronger position as candidates for more responsibilities if they had (or would) put their own house in order. Following the Commission on Intergovernmental Relations one can list the areas that need attention as follows:

1. There are antiquated representation systems that underrepresent large and recently developed centers of population in one or both legislative bodies. What becomes of the democratic principle when a majority in the legislature can be elected by a quarter of the eligible voters and when A's vote counts for 10 times as much as B's? Some of this might be defended on the dubious ground of area representation; most defense is the obvious rationalization of a special interest. Some progress in reapportionment is being made continuously but it is not

enough to offset population changes now going on; thus on balance the problem is a growing one. Some effort has been exerted to devise machinery that can cope with vested interests in this area but it has been successful in only a few States.

2. There are antiquated constitutions providing for weak executives, too many elected officers, too infrequent legislative sessions and budgets, and too limited financial powers.

3. There are still many cases of civil service infested with patronage and with the inferior talent that must be expected at highly inadequate salary scales.

4. There is the record of neglect in dealing with the metropolitan problem regarded by many critics as the No. 1 domestic issue. This is the problem which has resulted from the recent vast movement of population into some 168 metropolitan areas and out of their centers to their peripheries. If these areas had governments coterminus with their functions they would still be hard pressed with such matters as strangulating traffic, decadent sections, crowded schools, delinquent gangs, and of course excessive tax rates. Usually added to all this is an antiquated political geography with many units of government, some of them poaching on their neighbors. One district may have a factory and another the workers. These problems will not yield except to great courage and imagination at the State level. Not too much of this kind of leadership has developed.

Regressive Taxation

The States and municipalities have on the whole a regressive tax system based at the local level on the general property tax and at the State level on the retail sales tax. The Musgrave studies[1] have indicated that in State and local taxes the poorest bracket of taxpayers ($0 to $2,000 net income) pay almost half again as much per thousand dollars of net income as the well-to-do (over $10,000 net income). Moreover, there is ground for the view that the trend is toward more regressivity. Eleven States have enacted sales taxes since World War II and no States have enacted new net income taxes. This means that a vote for decentralizing the financial responsibility for a function is a vote for regressive as against progressive taxation. This is not a matter of equity alone; it also involves economics. It is the progressiveness of the tax system that gives it much of its built-in flexibility—its propensity to produce automatic surpluses and deficits to meet the needs of compensatory budgeting.

Those who favor decentralization should logically be in the front rank of the crusaders for better and more aggressive State and local government. Actually this is often not the case and it leads to the conclusion that these people are probably more interested in less government, less total taxes, and less taxes for themselves than in decentralization as such.

[1]Richard A. Musgrave, "Incidence of the Tax Structure and Its Effects on Consumption," *Federal Tax Policy for Economic Growth and Stability*, Joint Committee on the Economic Report, 84 Cong., 1 sess., Washington, D.C.: U.S. Government Printing Office, 1955, pp. 96–113.

Interstate Competition

The States and municipalities are in a relatively weak financial position because they are amenable to interterritorial competition to a far greater degree than the Federal Government.

The proposition that Federal aid involves only the collection of revenue that might have been raised locally, the sending of this revenue to a distant capital, from whence it is returned with some part missing, is at most a half-truth. The full truth would add that if the central government (for better or for worse) did not support this function and raise the tax for it, the function probably would not be supported at all and the tax for it would not be raised. The competitive factor, among others, also provides a rationale for distributing aid to strong districts as well as weak ones.

The degree to which taxation influences industrial location and the degree to which competition influences State and local decisions concerning taxation are matters long in dispute. It is evident that State and local governments are not completely captive and that the deductibility of State and local taxes on Federal income-tax returns gives them some protection. State and local government under the pressure of earlier public works postponement and increased population have been expanding their outlays for public services with some aggressiveness. It is true also that no empirical study has ever established the alleged fact that areas with high taxes or relatively progressive tax systems have suffered in industrial development. But anyone who observes legislative bodies cannot doubt that the pressure is real and important. It is nonetheless real because a lot of it is mainly fear psychology.

The degree of interterritorial competition is probably increasing. A perusal of newspapers and magazines indicates that the "booster spirit" is everywhere going strong. It takes the form of advertising, developmental corporations, subsidies, tax exemption, and a "favorable tax climate." Concerning the latter, one former director of a State division of industrial development observed:[2]

> In an era of industrial mobility, no State can stand alone in its adherence to a tax structure strongly oriented to the "ability to pay" theory. Continued adherence to this theory, in the face of defections by contiguous or "competitive States" will have the certain long-range effect of decreasing the rate of personal-income growth and denying improved employment opportunity to the very persons supposedly benefited by the application of this theory.

Interdependence

The trend of the times is toward more interdependence. This thesis can be supported by the impressive evidence concerning migration, travel,

---

[2]Robert D. Siff, "Some Pertinent Points on Industrial Development Policies," *Tax Policy*, Vol. 24, Nos. 2–3, Princeton, N.J.: Tax Institute, Princeton University Press, 1957, p. 11.

and interterritorial exchange of all sorts. This interdependence means that the people of Podunk, N.Y., have some equity in the maintenance of public standards in Podunk, N. Mex., and vice versa. It is characteristic of the satisfaction of human wants through government that the benefits derived from government outlay are largely indirect and frequently extraterritorial.

The growth of interdependence is particularly relevant with regard to education. Educational standards may seem at first to be of concern mainly to pupils and parents or at most the citizens of the community in which the youth are reared. But what becomes of this conclusion when we confront the statistics of migration and observe how many now being educated in one community turn up eventually as workers and citizens of another?

Interdependence means that the interest in many matters formerly of strictly local concern is now a divided one. The degree of interest for parties involved is difficult to discern and to implement. Our Federal aid system is one means by which a partnership of interest is combined with a partnership of financial responsibility and control. The control issue is the most sensitive one; the Kestnbaum Commission surveyed this area with great care and although it recommended some changes in detail, it is fair to say that on the whole it found the controls conservative and salutary. They have encouraged such State improvements as merit-system civil service and State highway departments.

The General Level of Public Expenditures

It is apparent that one's reaction to the question of Federal versus State financial responsibilities is conditioned considerably by his reaction to public expenditures as such. If he thinks they are too high he will probably favor decentralization. The States and municipalities for reasons previously cited will not spend as freely as does the Federal Government with its far superior taxing power. The proper level of overall public expenditures is the subject for other panels. Here it may be said that proponents of liberal government spending have these points on their side:

As the economy advances and per capita income increases, free income (above biological necessities) increases still faster. This free income is subject to a degree of discretion not true of the hard core of necessities. It is everywhere devoted in large measure to services where the Government competes with private disposition most effectively. Some of the ugliest aspects of the American way of life, such as slums, crowded schools, youth delinquency, and mental illness are in the area where government programs are most effective. The wastes of government are regrettable but they probably are minor compared with those of private consumption which in the United States are legendary. The typical American consumer thinks nothing of driving a station wagon across town to mail a letter. Governments are sometimes extravagant but they also frequently are niggardly. The case I know best is the Internal Revenue Service which in the opinion of many critics has always been substantially undermanned. Under present conditions

124

the belief that the acceleration of private expenditures as against government expenditures necessarily results in the healthiest society is not tenable.

CENTRALIZATION AND ECONOMIC CONTROL

One would be insensitive to the wave of the present if he did not attempt to relate our problem to that of controlling inflation. For the maintenance of at least the present Federal role in the overall expenditure picture it can be said, looking at the long run, that Federal expenditures and taxes are more amenable to control than those of the States; that the government's large role in the economy is what makes compensatory controls effective and that this role would diminish if the Federal Government relinquished a large area to the States; that it is the predominantly progressive overall tax system that affords built-in flexibility and that this is maintained only by the Federal Government's role. On the other hand controllability is no good if it isn't used; this seems to indicate a reduction in Federal expenditures now that inflation is our gravest problem; if the States do not take up the slack, so much the better. Those who cherish Federal expenditures for their nonfiscal or institutional objectives have the obligation to offer some remedy for inflation other than reduced public expenditures.

Of course, what would really now aid the States would be an acceleration of economic growth, an end to inflation, a loosening of tight money (which interferes with their borrowing), and a continuance of Federal spending at least insofar as it supports the States. This program sounds a little like the politician's platform of a soldiers' bonus, reduced taxes, and a balanced budget. But we have not exhausted the field when we have accepted a high level of public expenditures and rejected tighter money as remedies for inflation. Simplest but not the most popular remedy is to plug loopholes in existing taxes and thus add to the Federal budget surplus. Obviously cutting taxes and letting expenditures ride is a perverse answer. Perhaps we should look for something new as an inflation control; for example, decelerated depreciation, a tax on bank loans, and a sales tax on industrial equipment have been suggested. A graduated overall expenditure tax to supplement the income tax would be a promising instrument of control if it could be administered.

On the other hand, if as alleged and as seems probable, our present inflation problem is due in large part to cost-push causes; that is, to monopolistic pressure (business and labor) upon the price level, then we surely have to look for something new in inflation controls. The nearest thing to a fertile suggestion that has so far come to our attention is that of Sumner Slichter to disallow wage increases (for a time) as corporate income-tax deductions. Alternatively we might levy a special payroll excise tax in much the same way and to the same effect. These proposals involve the administrative problem of separating wage increases from payroll additions due to expansion; and they throw all the bonus of monopolistic pricing on labor. It would be more logical to levy a special sales tax on the receipts from price increases; but in only a few cases are commodities sufficiently standardized to separate genuine price increases from changes due to innovation in product. To all of these possibilities the objection will be made that they constitute government tampering with the free market. But here the ready answer is that it is the absence of a free market that creates our problem to begin with.

At any rate it seems inadvisable to reorder our intergovernmental fiscal relations as a remedy for inflation. That some Federal expenditures can and should be cut is conceded, but most of them (from our point of view) are inelastic in the downward direction. And in some areas expenditures should be increased.

This is not to say that nothing should be done about inflation. The author will not attempt here to arbitrate among the several suggestions listed above, but he does wish to leave the thought that the time is ripe for the exercise of some further ingenuity with regard to the inflation problem.

QUANTITATIVE PICTURE OF FEDERAL-STATE FINANCE

We may turn now before drawing a conclusion to the quantitative picture and ask what it shows regarding the alleged encroachment of the Federal Government on the States. Over the long view, the relative position of State and local governments in total expenditures has undoubtedly dropped sharply. In 1927 State and local expenditures were nearly three-quarters of the total (73.1 percent); in 1940 they were still more than half (52.8 percent); and in 1956 a little more than one-third (33.6 percent). The 1956 proportion is the same as that of 1948, indicating no postwar trend. Much of the recent alleged aggrandizement of the Federal Government has been for military items; if they are abstracted from the picture, Federal, State, and local outlays are not far from equal. This was also true during the late 1930's when the military proportion of the Federal budget was much less. As to Federal aid, since 1940 it has increased more rapidly than State and local expenditure but less rapidly than total expenditure. Over the longer pull, however (comparing the present Federal position with that of the late twenties), the Federal role by any standard has increased quite substantially. The expansion occurred during the thirties and included, of course, the important area of social security.

Comparing the United States with other countries as to centralization one finds such data as the following (the figures indicate the ratio of local taxes to total taxes 1947-53):[3]

United Kingdom	8	Italy	18
France	13	Switzerland	51
Germany	14	Canada	26
Sweden	25		

[3]Economic Commission for Europe, (Research and Planning Division), "Changes in the Structure of Taxation in Europe," *Economic Bulletin for Europe*, Vol. 2, No. 3, Geneva, 1951, p. 59; Canadian Tax Foundation, *The National Finances, 1954-55*, Toronto, p. 10.

In conclusion and to indicate a personal position on our problem, the author finds himself in general agreement (as to the matters discussed in this paper) with the Kestnbaum Commission's report which may be summarized as follows: The Federal system on the whole was found to be in healthy condition; the values of local autonomy are real and important and always need stressing; these values may be overbalanced by the great advantages of national or joint action in particular areas changing with time; it behooves the States deploring Federal encroachment to put their own houses in order. The States and municipalities are still finding plenty of scope for such vision, energy and ingenuity as they are able to summon. The Federal system in this country has preserved a degree of local autonomy unsurpassed at least by that of any of the world's great powers.

The pragmatic and sensible solution of Federal problems is not likely to lie in loyalty to any slogan but in the balanced weighing of values in the case of each new issue as it arises.

INNOVATIVE AND NONINNOVATIVE DECISION PROCESSES IN GOVERNMENT BUDGETING

RUFUS P. BROWNING

GROSS DIFFERENCES IN THE BUDGET PERFORMANCE OF THE WELFARE AND LABOR DEPARTMENTS

The Department of Welfare, including other functions as well as the corrections and mental health programs discussed here, is one of the largest state agencies. It is known as innovative and progressive and aggressive; it has a reputation for knowing what it wants and getting it; it has expanded very rapidly since 1945. We may separate for illustrative purposes the mental health and corrections institutions from the central administrative apparatus of the Department of Welfare—central executive and staff operations, and line employees such as probation and parole officers working out of field offices which are not attached to institutions. In 1945, the Department of Labor and this Administration appropriation of the Department of Welfare were about equal (Table 1). (Labor has no institutions.) But in the time it took Labor to double in expenditures, to the biennium ended July, 1963, Welfare Administration multiplied its expenditures by 10 and the Institutions almost quintupled. (The disparity is actually even greater than these figures indicate since they do not include huge building programs for correctional and mental institutions.)

TABLE 1

BUDGET PERFORMANCE OF THE WELFARE AND LABOR
DEPARTMENTS SINCE 1945

	Department of Labor	Department of Welfare Administration	Institutions
Expenditures in 1945–47 ($000,000)........	1.1	1.3	10.4
Expenditures in 1961–63 ($000,000)........	2.2	13.2	48.5
Change in employment financed by state taxes, 1945–63......................	182–167 (−7%)	1790–5608 (+213%)	
Agency requests: Average biennial % increase requested.....................	16%	58%	27%
Growth: Average % increase in biennial expenditures.........................	11	40	24
Average % cut from requests............	4	9	2

Labor has gradually *lost* authorizations for personnel positions via the legislative expedient of eliminating positions which happened to be vacant at

Article is adapted from a paper prepared for delivery at the 1963 Annual Meeting of the American Political Science Association, New York City, September 4–7, 1963. Used with permission of author.

budget time, so that Labor's state-financed personnel have declined in number while Welfare's have more than trebled. Welfare has consistently asked for much more than Labor—since 1945, Welfare, has twice requested biennial increases of 150% for administration—and consistently received much more, even though the percentage cut from Welfare Administration requests has been substantially larger than the cut from Labor requests.

It is not surprising that the Department of Labor has had a reputation of weak leadership in its field, a reputation for not wanting much and not getting what it does want. Labor has been almost stable in the size and scope of its programs, while Welfare has revolutionized existing programs and added many new ones. Why this tremendous growth in one agency and its policies, so little growth in the other? Why was Welfare so innovative, spewing forth a flood of new policy proposals, and Labor so noninnovative?

PUBLIC GOALS OF PUBLIC AGENCIES

Public goals are not the same thing as decision rules used to select specific policies. Public goals may remain stable for years while agency policies and decision rules for selecting policies undergo rapid change; or policies and rules may hold steady as the agency revises its public version of what it is doing and wants to do. Nevertheless, once we understand that we cannot expect to find the origins of every agency decision in its public goals, it is useful to look at them because they tell us something both about how the agency rationalizes its activities to itself, and how it persuades others to support it. Rationalizations are often associated with specific aspirations, and the persuasiveness of public goals is one important aspect of an agency's ability to attain its aspirations.

The statements of purpose which preface the budget requests of the Welfare and Labor Departments are strikingly different in tone. The Department's request opens with a perfunctory reference to "administering laws in the fields of ... ", and so on. Welfare's opening statement, in contrast, reads as follows: "The purposes of this department are to promote an integrated social welfare program which conserves human resources by providing just and humane services to ... the mentally ill and retarded; by preventing dependency, mental illness, delinquency, crime and other social maladjustments; ... and by providing for the rehabilitation of juvenile delinquents and adult criminal offenders." The Department of Welfare is explicitly not just administering the laws—it is promoting a program.

Although Welfare's requests are included in the regular executive budget along with those of other agencies, the Department has a large enough staff that it is able to prepare its own version of its requests and the justifications for them. For the present biennium, this amounts to a book of more than 400 pages with many tables and single-spaced text, more than 80% of it devoted to mental health, corrections, and central executive requests. There is persuasive material throughout the document, but the

129

opening letter of submission by the director of the department contains a particularly strong and broad statement of Welfare's public goals.

Discussing those parts of the budget which provide "for the extension and intensification of services," he asserts that the object is "to do a better job of rehabilitation and treatment ... by reaching more of the people requiring these services earlier and with a more intensive effort." Then comes a tie-in to potent social, moral, economic, and political objectives—"By so doing, we can reduce human suffering and waste and look forward to fiscal economy in the long run by shortening the span of dependency and the length of time in need of institutional care." Extension, intensification, do a better job, reach more of the people earlier, more intensive effort, reduce suffering, look forward to economy, shorten dependency and institutional care—every phase evokes the department's orientation toward the future, toward objectives it is moving to attain. This is the esprit of the department. And the objectives invoked are about as persuasive as they can be.

Among the specific requests for program improvements justified under these objectives are an additional half million dollars in state aids to communities to increase the number of community mental health clinics from 20 to 24 over two years; $400,000 for a new day care program for the mentally ill; $2 million to improve treatment programs at county mental hospitals; $300,000 for state mental health planning and promotion of community services; $1.4 million for clinical and ward staff in three state mental hospitals, partly to intensify treatment; $800,000 for treatment and ward care staff at colonies for the retarded, partly to intensify rehabilitation for release to community living; $500,000 for increased administrative and service workloads in support of these increased treatment programs; $130,000 for outpatient and day hospital programs; $150,000 for research on mental retardation; $230,000 to improve educational and recreational programs at correctional institutions; $200,000 for administrative and clerical support of correctional security and rehabilitation programs; and others.

In short, the Welfare Department has developed methods of generating (a) specific policy proposals, (b) persuasive justifications for them. These are problems which dominate the budget process for an agency that wants to go somewhere, cannot depend as a matter of course on powerful support from a favored group, and must cultivate broad support among diverse publics. (As they say in the department, prisons don't have alumni associations.) Whether or not an agency is successful in developing persuasive justifications, however, its anticipations of how the governor and particularly in this case the legislature will react to its proposals, and the effect of these anticipations on the agency's requests, are matters of interest. We need to specify, then, processes: (1) for generating and choosing among policies which meet the agency's aspirations; (2) for eliminating or modifying requests which may get the agency into trouble; and (3) for insuring satisfactory levels of support for the remaining requests. The second of these processes refers to political penalties for making certain requests. For some agencies and agency heads, simple rejection of requests may be painful enough to prevent its making the request in the first place, but usually some other penalties are involved—public criticism, insult, and ridicule (public at least to one's colleagues and subordinates), loss of support for other requests, and loss of confidence from others with damage to future requests and to career chances.

Logically, the second process—changing proposals preferred internally so as to avoid unwanted consequences of explicit requests—is a subset of the first process. Agency aspirations include satisfactory standards for political consequences of making requests as well as standards for agency operations. It is useful to distinguish between avoidance aspirations and attainment aspirations, however, because quite different kinds of events affect them. Avoidance concerns may be strongly influenced by legislative action and offer therefore a means of legislative control, even when an agency gets its policy and budget proposals from outside the legislature. Obviously, the third process, agency procedures for insuring support, is also strongly affected by anticipations of legislative behavior, but there is quite a difference between anticipations which cut off certain requests altogether thus preventing them from becoming policy, and anticipations which cause agencies to work extra hard to elicit support.

SOURCES OF POLICY INNOVATIONS AND AGENCY COMMUNICATION WITH THEM

New policies do not fall out of thin air. Departments of government do not usually work out their problems in isolation. Legislators, clientele and other organized interests, corporate sellers of goods and services, researchers and consultants in academic life, and many others may be interested in the agency's policies, dissatisfied with existing policies, and more or less active in proposing new ones. If outside sources actively sell their policies, the innovative agency need only be a willing receptor. On the other hand, if outside sources generate alternatives but do not actively sell them, then the agency must make some positive effort to find them. The vigor of outside sources of new policies, the extent to which these sources sell their policies to the agency, and the extent to which the agency searches on its own for policy innovations are crucial variables affecting the direction and rate of agency innovation. It is of course possible, even likely, that various sources of policies will come up with similar solutions to similar problems. Nevertheless, that others support similar policies may be a strong reinforcement to an agency, both in deciding what it wants to do and in justifying what it decides upon.

In other words, innovation in a particular agency is likely to be more a social than an intellectual process, to depend more on communication and persuasion than on problem-solving. This is certainly true of the innovative Welfare Department, which is not so much an original thinker as a diligent searcher and vigorous organizer.

131

Intra-agency Promotion of Search for Innovations

The Welfare Department promotes active search for new policies at all levels. Divisions, institutions, departments within institutions are urged to ask for what they feel they need. They are persuaded to re-evaluate their objectives and progress toward them, and to develop coherent, justifiable programs. The department encourages new programs, accepts substantial portions of them, supports them vigorously before the legislature, and gets large parts of what it wants. It gets enough so that subunits are able to solve the problems of the moment—that is, to reach their most urgent objectives—and move on to new ones. The result of this happy sequence is that subunit as well as departmental goals rise rapidly and continuously. Subunits are generally enthusiastic about their progress and put much effort into searching for improved programs and more persuasive justifications.

Numerous comments from institutional administrators testify to the importance of departmental encouragement and of the legislative support which follows:

> "The department has always backed us up on everything we think we need. We have great confidence in their support. In fact, they are very grateful if we have ideas."
> "The state through the legislature and the department has subscribed to the program as expressed in its goals and has been willing to financially support the achievement of the goals. ... We have had excellent financial support of all aspects of the program. ... We were not restricted in any of our plans."

. . . .

In contrast, new budget requests from subunits of the Labor Department have usually been discouraged and almost always rejected in the past. A consequence of this was that some divisional administrators lost enthusiasm for making requests and attempting to justify them:

> "I have been conditioned by the attitude of the commissioners, I would play my cards thinking, 'Would he kill this or not.' "
> "I've been around here long enough to think we can't get anything."
> "Our request measures up to what we think we can get."
> "I was in charge of preparing requests for additional personnel. It was discouraging because there was no support from the director. If you can't get support from your own director, you can't expect to get it any place else."
> "We've had three decades of conservatism."

The difference is obvious. Over the years requests by Labor subunits adjusted almost to coincide with the constraint imposed by stable expectations. In the Welfare Department, expectations learned from past experience, of how the department and the legislature will treat budget requests, are not stable; they rise, and aspirations rise with them.

In turn, agency search for policy innovations is a direct function of aspiration levels. In the Welfare Department, where aspirations are high, where many problems are perceived and put up for solution, search is intensive. In the Labor Department, problems which call for solutions through budget requests are dimly perceived, poorly specified and left unsolved; aspirations (in the sense of criteria for selecting particular budget requests) are modest; and search is minimal. No goals means no problems means no search.

An extremely important group of sources of new policies—we will note shortly how important they are—are represented in the communications, in the literature and meetings, of a number of professions. Psychologists, psychiatrists, hospital administrators, nurses, social workers, criminologists, lawyers, engineers, economists, and others who specialize in one or another of Labor and Welfare's policy areas, produce policy recommendations and information about consequences of particular alternatives, in reports on what similar agencies elsewhere are doing and in reports of professional research. This material does not sell itself to agencies—they must search for it, dig it out for themselves. Even trivial gestures in this direction, such as reading three or four professional journals regularly, may take a surprising amount of initiative and effort (as we well know). More intensive search activity, for example sending large numbers of employees to professional conferences, is expensive as well; it uses resources which may be scarce and better applied to direct agency operations, and it uses them for a purpose which is particularly open to legislative attack.

Constraints on the resources as well as on the aspirations of the Labor Department limit sharply the search it undertakes among its professions, relative to Welfare's search for innovation among *its* professions. We can make some easy though potentially misleading and perhaps even somewhat inaccurate quantitative comparisons. The Labor Department now receives 11 professional journals, plus 5 proceedings of annual meetings. The Welfare Department, *in its central offices alone*, not including any of the institutions (where many more people are employed but the percentage of professionals is lower), has 128 subscriptions to a total of 105 journals. With respect to trips to out-of-state professional meetings at state expense, the Labor Department sent its employees on a total of 9 trips to 5 different meetings in fiscal 1961-62. The Welfare Department in calendar 1962 sent its personnel on 281 trips to 91 different out-of-state professional conferences; and these figures are from an incomplete listing of such trips. In addition, Welfare officials participated in at least 10 business meetings out of state not connected with a particular profession; and sent at least 20 people to 10 institutions or agencies in its field in other states, to find out about particular programs developed at these places. As one would expect, Welfare Department officials are much more conscious of professional standards than their Labor counterparts, and they are generally more aware of what similar agencies elsewhere are doing. Labor has much less well developed standards and, with some exceptions, knows little of what goes on in other states.

(These comparisons may be misleading because they reflect opportunities for fruitful search and the vigor of the relevant profession as well as the agency's propensity for search. One might assert that Labor does not search for innovations among its professions because they do not produce them. Lacking comprehensive knowledge of other states' labor departments and of the literature of Labor's policy areas, I cannot disprove this hypothesis. A fair test would compare several agencies in the same policy field and therefore the same search opportunities rather than agencies in different fields. For instance, we would expect to find some variation among state mental health agencies in search activity, and a direct connection between these variations and agency budget requests.)

Passive Receptivity to Local Demands and Changing Technology

Explicit encouragement of innovation in the Welfare Department, and a budget process which consistently grants the department and its subunits substantial portions of what they want, incline them to be more receptive to demands for innovations as well as to search actively for them. Since it is easy to make requests, it is not difficult to respond favorably to other people's needs. Employees and clientele are encouraged to state their needs, and the institution is in a position to try to satisfy them.

Since every new request must be justified in writing in the Welfare Department, it might seem that local requests like those noted above would be troublesome for the institution. Actually, it always seems possible to tie them to a justification acceptable enough to indicate sincerity if not to prove need. Furthermore, many local demands genuinely satisfy departmental objectives; or to put it differently, some objectives are shared by the institutions and departmental executives. It is also true, however, that some of these are objectives that would not be attended to on the initiative of the department; if no request is made, the relevant objective is not acted upon or is taken care of in some different way. So even if we point out a large area of shared goals between the institutions and divisional and departmental executives, we must admit that many items get into the budget only because some subunit far down in the department or some outside source requested them, and institutional officials were willing to buck them up the line. The fact that the director of the Welfare Department agrees to include in his budget requests to the governor and the legislature a particular locally inspired request from an institution by no means indicates that the department would have taken care of the felt need which produced the request. Requests of local origin focus attention on objectives which would otherwise be neglected.

There are three basic departmental decisions on institutional budget requests. Some are rejected by the department. A second group, at the other extreme, are proposals which represent the department's highest priority goals. These are items the department will get into its budget by hook or by crook. If the institution directors concerned are willing and eager to put them into their requests, fine. If not, they may be persuaded or cajoled or instructed to include them. Or the central divisional offices may make a request themselves and assign the new personnel to the institutions. The third main set of decisions consists of acceptances of budget requests not inspired by the department. In the Welfare Department, because of its policy of encouraging innovation, because of its willingness to delegate responsibility to subunits, and because criteria for rejection and criteria for top priority requests leave such a large open area between them, this set of acceptances is relatively large. If the department's leadership was not itself so demanding, the zone of acceptance would be considerably larger. In an agency like the Labor Department, where constraints imposed by expectations of legislative behavior are much more limiting, the zone of acceptance is small. The size of this zone of acceptance and the ability of agency subunits to fill it up with local solutions to local problems may very substantially affect the allocation of budget increases.

In addition to employees and clientele, industrial firms comprise an important source of innovations to which the Welfare Department is likely to be more receptive than many other agencies, certainly more so than the Labor Department. Differences in the physical plant of the two departments are obvious. Ancient chairs, battle-scarred wooden desks and filing cabinets, and 10 to 15-year-old typewriters are much more common in Labor than in Welfare. Machine dictation has long been *de rigueur* in the Welfare Department, but most of the Labor Department's inspectors still write out their reports in longhand.

Potential budget items proposed to the Welfare Department by firms partly overlap with innovations communicated through professional channels. A pharmaceutical house selling tranquilizers to mental hospitals may be able to reinforce its advertising with articles in professional journals or statements by professional groups, and with favorable reports of experience elsewhere with its product. But many firms selling products not so closely related to professional activities rely on a sales force or on catalogues to communicate with the appropriate agency subunit. Since firms are mainly interested in selling things rather than services to the Department's institutions, most of the impact of innovation by firms falls on budget requests for repair, maintenance, and capital items. Thus, 13 wooden ladders of varying lengths are replaced by higher-cost magnesium ladders. (One hopes that the new ladders will be more durable than the old, and that they will make workers more productive and safer, as well as making their work easier.) A 12″ garden tractor is replaced by a 24″ one. A new cushion stuffer is justified on the grounds that the old one is outdated. Brush, broom, and dustpan are replaced by a shop vacuum cleaner. Muscle is replaced by a telescopic lift. Standard teaching equipment and methods are replaced by tape recorders, film and filmstrip projectors, television sets, and duplicating machines. A concrete cutting saw replaces some applications of air hammers, while a special machine for drilling through walls replaces them for that purpose. Automatic sprinkler systems are installed. A $400 paint mixer replaces hand mixing.

I would not imply that these are unprofitable changes—I have not tried to evaluate them. The point is rather that changes in technology, largely executed by business firms, change both standards and costs of living for government agencies, as they do for everyone else. Outlays for products subject to innovative effort by firms often run over 20% of an agency's budget. Major construction, which I have not examined but which has experienced rapid innovation and increase in cost, is sometimes a large proportion of an agency's operating budget. In short, technological changes and consequent requests by government employees for facilities which become standard in the skilled trades or in firms may account for a substantial portion of the total increment requested. Although acceptance of these changes may be justified on various grounds—increased productivity, for example, or on grounds that modern facilities are a necessary side payment to skilled employees—we may at least note that technological changes are likely to promote some agency subgoals more than others. The subgoals "Maintain a satisfactory physical plant" and "Make prisoners literate and skillful" both belong to the objective, "Rehabilitate criminals." Buying a concrete saw promotes the first of these subgoals; buying six weeks of skilled instruction at the same price does more for the second. Such a comparison is almost never made, to be sure. Repair, maintenance, and minor capital improvements are evaluated according to one set of criteria; expansion of the educational program, by other criteria. This flow of new products and the efforts of firms to sell them have the greatest impact on activities which involve new facilities rather than new personnel—a particularly significant point in view of the reluctance of some legislative bodies to grant increases in personnel, even while they permit facilities to improve. (The suggestion that some agency subgoals are promoted more than others because of the sales activities of business firms needs to be confirmed by further research, however—it may be that the only agencies which are able consistently to improve their physical plant are those which are generally wealthy.)

The cumulative effect of the local demands of clientele, and employees, and of changing technology and persistent sales efforts by firms, is probably great. The readiness of agencies to accept alternatives proposed by these sources is a most important variable and one we often take for granted. It is true that these sources of innovation are fragmented. The changes they induce come in bits and pieces rather than in neat packages gift-wrapped in idealistic prose. But dozens of small alterations in an institution's staff, equipment, procedures, and buildings may have pervasive effects on recruitment, turnover, work performance, and clientele attitudes and behavior. Precisely how important these effects are remains to be established.

In this discussion of agency receptivity to local requests and to product innovations by firms, we have scarcely mentioned the Labor Department. The rate at which items from these sources enter Labor's budget requests is lower than for the Welfare Department. *Some* of this difference is due to differences in the rate at which local requests are made to the Labor Department and to differences in the volume of product innovations relevant to the department's functions. But the rate at which clientele and employees make demands on the Labor Department is itself a function, over the long run, of the department's receptivity to them; and in the one area in which Labor and Welfare are directly comparable (purchase of office equipment), Labor is much less willing than Welfare to request new products or new models of old products. As I noted above, the differences between the agencies in condition of physical plant are obvious. Furthermore, some kinds of office equipment are far from neutral tools. Dictating rather than handwriting reports may free substantial time for inspection. Automated record-keeping can alert an agency to problems that otherwise might escape its attention, and data made accessible can bolster requests weakened by the absence of supporting information.

Like the contrast between Welfare and Labor in rate of active search for innovations, the difference in receptivity seems to be a result of the adjustment of agency aspirations to its expectations of legislative treatment. An agency subunit which has trouble attaining its own main objectives is not likely to accept responsibility for meeting the local demands of others. And when potential requestors know in advance that requests are futile, they will not make them. (This does not mean that no demands impinge on the Labor Department, and it does not mean that the department never accedes to such demands—only that *local* demands by employees and clientele—in their unorganized state—are rarely made and rarely accepted.)

In addition to this damper on requests, there may be other differences in the relationships of the two departments to their immediate clientele which reduce the flow of requests. These differences are summarized in the difference between service and regulation—between doing something for people that they most urgently want, and doing something that recipients regard as against their interests. Welfare's clientele consists largely of the former, hence it is not surprising that the department receives from this source requests for expansion of services. But there is no reason for the firms which are inspected and regulated by the Labor Department to be interested in expanding its activities.

This difference should not be overdrawn, however, since an agency's relationship to its clientele is in part a creature of its own making. The Labor Department has beneficiaries of its operations—the employees of companies inspected for compliance with safety and with wages and hours regulations, and employees involved in workmen's compensation cases—but this clientele probably perceives the relation between its own objectives and the Labor Department's activities a good deal less clearly than Welfare clientele perceives the relevance of the operation of the state mental hospitals, for example. The Welfare Department's performance has shown its diverse clientele what it can do for them. As the department plays a larger, more active, more effective role in corrections and mental health programs, people's attention focuses increasingly on it. Labor's activities may have lacked both effectiveness and drama. Consequently, a public that might be interested in its programs, individuals who might stimulate the department to innovation by requesting solutions to local problems, is relatively apathetic and detached.

In sum, day-to-day experiences with clientele in the working lives of subunits, and innovations sold by firms, may bring specific problems and specific budget requests to the attention of lower-level employees and supervisors and administrators. The perception of events as problems to which solutions via the budget are appropriate, and the acceptance of specific demands, are subject to constraints which arise from the concern of agencies to avoid consequences of making certain kinds of requests before the chief executive and the legislature. These constraints result in lowered receptivity to local demands and local problems, cutting off and eventually attenuating these sources of innovation. Or the constraints sharply limit agency adoption of changing technology, with sometimes pervasive effects.

We have examined bits-and-pieces innovation. This kind of change lacks the title on the door—the connection to broad social objectives *follows* the decision. Pattern there may be to these innovations; of plan, there is little. For "policy" writ large, we must look to other sources.

Professions as Sources of Innovations in Policy

The main sources of new policies for the innovative, rapidly growing Welfare Department are neither local clientele demands nor shifting technology. They are the members of several professions, usually working in a nonindustrial context—in universities, in private nonprofit welfare institutions, and in government agencies in the corrections and mental health field in other states, in the federal government, and in other countries. The largest part of the Welfare Department's budget increase requests for program improvement goes for policies the department has taken over from these sources. These requests are also related most immediately to the public objectives of the department; they involve changes in the way the department handles its principal clientele, inmates of institutions and others under Welfare's supervision and care outside of the hospitals and prisons.

On previous pages I explained the public goals of the Welfare Department: reducing human misery and saving money in the long run. Then I listed some requested program improvements which were justified under these objectives—programs to enable the state mental health system to rely increasingly on county hospitals, local clinics, day care, and out-patient facilities, and to increase professional staffing for treatment and rehabilitation at all the institutions. We cannot hope to explain the choice of this set of means, or instrumental subgoals, by pointing to the public goals. There is nothing in the public goals to account for specific shifts in emphasis over a period of years, so we must go behind public goals to observe the sources of these requests, and then specify the rules with which the department picks and chooses among available alternatives.

We have already looked at how the Welfare Department dips continuously and eagerly into the stream of professional communications in search of policies. Perhaps it should not surprise us to find every one of the department's requests for new programs for the present biennium in the professional literature. I have yet to complete a systematic, comprehensive analysis of this literature, but even a casual inspection of a few journals and books in the mental health field, for example, reveals that they appear again and again in the form of recommendations or as reports on what is being done in some particular agency.

Furthermore, each of the mental health programs now being expanded or newly requested by the Welfare Department seems to have been around for a good long time. In 1937, a Citizens' Committee on Public Welfare in this state composed of both professionals and lay people, issued a lengthy report with many recommendations. Some of these recommendations have long since been attained; others were rejected or ignored or became irrelevant. But among the recommendations ... were these: that programs for early diagnosis and treatment be established to prevent institutionalization; that a state-supported mental hygiene program operate in the counties, including psychiatric services; that the state adopt the American Psychiatric Association's minimum standards for the operation of mental hospitals; that individual treatment with expanded professional staff supplant mass custody in mental hospitals; that the county asylums be transformed into hospitals for diagnosis and treatment; that medical and field work staff be increased at the colonies for the retarded to intensify rehabilitation and to permit the return of more inmates to their homes; that the state expand diagnosis, treatment, and training at correctional institutions in academic, vocational, moral and civic, dental, psychiatric, medical, and recreational areas. Some of these proposals are identical to ones now being pushed in the Welfare Department budget; others are worked out in only somewhat less detail.

In the postwar period, the journal *Mental Hospitals*, a publication of the American Psychiatric Association, reports monthly on similar proposals in other states and other countries. The June, 1950, issue holds up Virginia's "Duke Report" as a model; it recommends expanded use of local mental health clinics. At about this time, too, one begins to find a significant new kind of article on mental hospitals, reporting on recommendations that have become working programs. One state reports that pressure on its mental hospitals is relieved by new clinics which see as many patients as are admitted to the hospitals. A city opens a 42-bed psychiatric unit in its hospital to develop treatment facilities at the local level. A state passes legislation to allow mentally ill patients to be kept in a local hospital for ninety days. Reports from mental hospitals all over the country testify to the effects of changes in professional staffing, in treatment programs, and in admission and discharge policies: one hospital reports an 80% increase in direct discharge rates over a 3-year period; another announces a 34% increase in patient turnover in 2 years, a 28% decrease in returns.

What this means, for one thing, is that for any single agency in the mental health field, there is very little new under the sun. Even the policy innovations of this Welfare Department, which considers itself one of the leading such agencies in the country, up at the top with California and New York, have usually been proposed repeatedly and tried out elsewhere. They are drawn from the recommendations and experience of a broad range of agencies in many places, not just from the few wealthy ones—money is essential to put new ideas into effect on a broad scale, but it is not so necessary, in large quantities, for the processes of thinking and organizing which produce an idea and try it out. I am told that the department even picks up many useful ideas from agencies and institutions which are not otherwise outstanding.

The people who devise new methods in this field are professionals. They undergo long formal training in their professions, they are committed to professional aspirations, they take pride in their standing as professionals. When they do something new, when they show results that other professionals might be interested in, they are eager to publish a description or to talk about it at a meeting. Other professionals anxious to avoid being stick-in-the-muds, to avoid loss of professional status, and to do as good a job as possible, rush to inspect and adopt policies their colleagues are putting into effect.

This intensive professional activity constitutes a crucial difference between Welfare and Labor. Some professional associations specialize in areas of interest to the Labor Department, but they are much fewer in number, much less active in holding meetings and in publishing research and discussions of current problems and current solutions, and much less directly concerned with public policy than the groups with which Welfare regularly communicates. Professions in the mental health and corrections fields are more vigorous in producing and selling costly public policy innovations than those in the fields of industrial safety, workmen's compensation, apprentice training, and wage and hour regulation.

The key words here are "costly" and "public." With regard to costs, many policy changes proposed by professionals in Labor's policy areas do not involve governmental expenditures—for example, increases in the minimum wage do not necessarily require additional inspectors. Some additional educational and inspectional effort will be required for a time, but this can be and has been accomplished with existing staff. Policy innovations in corrections and mental health, on the other hand, tend to come in very expensive packages, involving massive and relatively high-salaried additions to professional staff and construction of new buildings. In short, professionals in the Labor field appear to have foregone objectives that require large budget requests—a constraint on aspirations which does not characterize the professions of social work, psychiatry, psychology, mental hospital administration, correctional administration and criminology.[1]

In addition to this difference in cost and therefore in budgetary impact of innovations proposed by professionals in the respective policy areas, there is a striking difference in orientation and content which is partly related to cost. Most of the professional journals to which the Labor Department subscribes address themselves to private industry rather than to public agencies. Officials of such organizations as the National Safety Council and the National Fire Protection Association are mainly heads of safety programs in manufacturing companies. Their journals are devoted to articles on safety devices, safety programs, and safety hazards and their cures in industry. This helps safety inspectors of the Labor Department keep up to date on new aspects of safety technology, but it doesn't help the department develop new programs for itself. What innovation there is in professions in Labor's policy area is directed toward the policies of firms rather than of governments. In contrast, the professions to which the Welfare Department belongs and listens operate almost entirely in areas where there is no distinction between public and private interest—for example, in the development of treatments for childhood schizophrenia—or in areas in which public agencies clearly dominate the field of operations, as in admission and discharge policies of large mental hospitals, the coordination of diverse facilities to meet the needs of a broad public, or almost the entire delinquency, crime, and corrections field.

In addition to setting objectives for future attainment, professions in the Welfare field, again in contrast to those in the Labor field, do a great deal to set standards for workloads of professional employees. These standards have two major effects. In the first place, as workloads (in this case, mainly institutional populations) change, very sizable budget increases will be requested if the agency has a clear conception of how many employees of various kinds it wants for a given workload, keeps careful data on workload, and always adjusts requests to maintain workload standards. About 40% of the Welfare Department's requested increase for the current biennium is identified in the budget as workload change, as contrasted to only 12% for program change.[2] The financial impact of workload standards closely adhered to can be large.

---

[1] One might argue that Labor's policies are inherently less budget-dependent than Welfare's, that innovations in Labor's policies naturally involve less additional expenditure than Welfare's. I do not think this is so, however. For one thing, Welfare initiates many policy changes other than those which appear in the budget; they are probably more innovative than Labor in this respect as well as in the budget. Secondly, anyone with a little imagination and a familiarity with public policies could easily think up a number of quite expensive policy innovations in the Labor field, or less expensive policies (in public tax funds) in the mental health field. Hence, I regard the avoidance of costly policies as a limitation on aspirations.

[2] This figure underestimates the actual cost in the present biennium of new programs, however, since an additional substantial amount goes to pay for operation over the entire present biennium of programs which were approved by previous legislatures but only operated in part of the previous biennium. The 12% figure for new programs also does not reflect the full future cost of new programs initiated in the present biennium.

Secondly, sticking closely to explicit workload standards is a pre-requisite to the solution of current problems. Suppose you institute an intensified treatment program at a mental hospital. If the population in the hospital stays the same but time-consuming admissions work increases, you will lose ground in your attempt to intensify treatment—*unless* you perceive that part of your workload is changing, *and* insist that admissions rates are just as valid as the traditional, accepted population figures, *and* make the appropriate request to take care of the workload increase. Furthermore, failure to solve current problems will detract from your ability to handle future ones, and it will even prevent some future problems from being evoked at all, since it is commonplace that solutions to problems evoke new problems.

The professions which stand behind the Welfare Department are constantly pushing target workload standards. The department uses the standards to specify desirable staffing patterns and to justify its requests. It is acutely conscious of changes in the nature and quantity of its work. In the Labor Department, largely unaided by its professions, such changes go unnoticed, or if noticed, are poorly defined in terms of the public objectives of the agency. The Department is authorized by statute to set standards for frequency of safety inspection in factories, for example, but has not done so. Since there is no precise and persuasively justified workload standard, increases in workload do not trigger requests for more personnel.

In sum, by generating policy alternatives and setting standards, professions may have an immense impact on an agency's ability to maintain and raise its aspirations; therefore on its budget; therefore on public policies realized through the budget. For the Welfare Department, professions are far and away the most important sources of policy alternatives. And if professions in the Welfare field play as large a role as I think they do in developing innovations in public policy and putting them into effect, then problem-evoking and problem-solving in the professions are central to the policy-making process.

"Political" Sources of Policy Innovations

Where do familiar public figures in our political landscape fit into this survey of sources of innovation—the elected chief executive, the legislative body, the organized interest group? For the most part, they do not fit at all. They are not customarily sources of new policies for either the Department of Welfare or the Department of Labor. One minor program in the Welfare Department was requested of it by the previous governor, but it is a small operation, not closely related to other major programs, and not even financed out of the department's budget. Furthermore, the program was suggested by the department itself in response to a request from the governor for ideas in an area of interest to him.

As for the legislature, both agencies report some contacts of the constituent case type, the legislator checking up on delay in a workmen's

142

compensation case or on a constituent's problems in getting his mentally deficient child into a state institution. The legislature is not a source of policy innovations for these agencies.

Other than the professionals in and out of state employ, there are few organized special interest groups in the corrections and mental health fields in this state. They support the Welfare Department's programs, but they mainly support the department's proposals rather than generate ones of their own, at least in recent years. . . .

AGENCY CONTROL OF PUBLIC POLICY

If the legislature tightly controlled the Welfare Department, none of the preceding would be very important. In fact, as we have noted, the department gets almost all of what it wants, if not this year, then next. The legislature and the governor largely acquiesce, apparently satisfied that the department's requests are worth paying increasingly large amounts for.

Why? An economist friend suggested to me that Welfare got more than Labor in the budget because it *should*. I agree that it should, but this begs the question of *why* we—and the governor and the legislature—think this way. It is, after all, not obvious on the face of it that preventing fatal and disabling accidents in industry is a less noble goal than helping the mentally ill out of their trouble. But we have been persuaded by a good many highly persuasive people, especially since the end of World War II, that we and our governments should and can do something about mental illness. In a flood of articles and books, scholarly and otherwise, in novels and in movies, we have observed the misery of the great asylums and witnessed the hope of individual treatment and recovery. Has anyone been persuading us of the need for government programs for industrial safety?

Governors and legislators share this experience with us, but they are exposed to additional persuasion as well. Almost all of the Welfare Department's budget tactics may be lumped together under the category of direct persuasion. The department works to persuade them of three things. It intones moral imperatives that most people would find very difficult to oppose. Then it lays out a budget which is in effect a plan, with much detailed persuasive material thrown in. This establishes a convincing link between the high-flying objectives and the dollar requests. The department's third persuasive thrust is to establish that the Welfare Department is expert and efficient, the ideal agency to entrust with the programs requested. This is accomplished mainly by showing very detailed knowledge of departmental policies and operations: "We do well in obtaining support because we always try to know about everything that is going on. If we don't, we can't make an interpretation of the program (to the appropriations committee, for instance). . . . Our purpose is to be on top of everything."

And there we have the answer to the question—Why do governor and legislature acquiesce in Welfare's requests? They have been persuaded to.

143

Professionals in the corrections and mental health fields have been persuading them for years, and home-grown professional public executives capped it off. The department has continuously raised the aspirations of the governors and legislatures it has served "under." The Welfare Department, backed by assorted professions and by the efforts of like agencies elsewhere, dominates policy initiation almost completely. It experiences some delay but only rare vetoes by the governor or legislature, so that little control is exercised over it via the anticipated reactions route. The Welfare Department largely controls state government policy in corrections and mental health, constrained by its professional ideology more than by legislative oversight or by executive leadership. Now, I am not saying that this is *bad*. I will sing no sad song of legislative impotence. My point is that we should know who's running the show, and we should know why they run it the way they do.

It is understandable why a really well-managed persuasive effort by an agency should be so successful. Legislators come to their jobs with relatively little knowledge of specific policies, and without well developed, thoroughly rationalized criteria for evaluating requests. A large portion of their communications, written and oral, about any particular program request is likely to emanate from the agency responsible for it. The agency supplies to the legislator a set of ready-made criteria for evaluating its own requests; if these justifications are well prepared, and if there is no strongly expressed counter-position, the legislator will find it easy to adopt them as his own. As one state legislator wrote a few years ago in *Mental Hospitals:*

> "Legislators seek supporting data to be sure that something is not being put over on them. Yet in many instances they are unable to interpret the material when it is presented because of the occupational terminology and the statistical approach. Consequently they dare not assume the responsibility for making large increases or large reductions in the budget requests. This is true, session after session and the legislators vote—reluctantly in many cases—to approve all or most of the items submitted to them. ... The result is that the growth and development of mental health programs rests for the most part on state executives."[3]

Many of the Welfare Department decision procedures that we have discussed—procedures for search, use of other agencies as reference group standards, rules for accepting proposals from various sources—are highly stable, changing only in response to some problem that they are not able to solve. The department's political tactics in the budget process are equally stable. Since the department enjoys great success, there is no reason to change them. These standard rules for persuasion specify the framework of public goals to which all requests will be tied and the persuasive activities that the department will perform. In general, almost all requests for new programs or for substantial numbers of a particular kind of personnel must

---

[3] J. R. Hall, Jr., State Senator of Oklahoma, "How the Mental Hospital Budget Looks to the Legislator," *Mental Hospitals*, Vol. 8, No. 6, p. 14.

be justifiable in terms of the objectives of rehabilitation and treatment. The pressure from the top level of the department for consistent justifications in these terms is so strong that requests from institutions presented for other reasons than these are sometimes left in the budget unchanged but with the justification entirely rewritten to emphasize rehabilitation and treatment.

Patterns of persuasive activities are equally stable. Department officials are always willing to speak to groups about the agency and its programs. The ... follow a routine in getting to know the legislators at each session. Introducing a new bill is accompanied by certain standard influencing activity. There is very little calculation in all of this, mainly the skillful execution of a well-adapted set of standard operations. As with other kinds of agency procedures and policies, there is some learning of budgetary procedures from professional sources and practices of other agencies. Techniques of program budgeting and workload measurement, which can be used to increase the persuasiveness of budget requests, are increasingly put into practice by the Welfare Department.

The Labor Department offers an interesting contrast. Moving in recent months to request new programs, the department has few standard procedures for budget tactics, and none that have been shown to be successful. There is a good deal more search, experimentation, and learning of new tactics here than in the Welfare Department. In the event of some success with these new procedures, they will quickly become standard, presumably.

PUBLIC ATTITUDES TOWARD FISCAL PROGRAMS

Eva Mueller

Insights into people's attitudes toward fiscal programs are needed both by policy-makers and fiscal theorists. Although popular preferences cannot be regarded as a mandate to policy-makers, information on how people feel and what they want should be available and should have some bearing on policy decisions.

Personal interview surveys can throw light on the citizen's attitudes toward various government spending programs, the level of taxation, and budget deficits. More important, surveys can give us some understanding of the nature of people's fiscal preferences—their origin, congruence, and stability.

Theoretical work on the problem of budget determination by economists quite properly has emphasized such criteria as fiscal soundness, economic stability, economic growth, and income redistribution. At the same time it is agreed that, in addition to promoting these ends, fiscal policy should be governed by a welfare criterion. The maximum-welfare principle of budget determination requires that marginal outlays be allocated between private and public goods and between alternative government programs in accordance with consumer preferences.[1] If this principle is to advance the discussion of budget determination, it is necessary (1) to search for methods which can reveal people's preferences for public services, and (2) to gain some understanding of the nature of these preferences. This paper is directed toward both of these problems.

Section I will discuss the potentialities and limitations of sample surveys in measuring attitudes toward fiscal programs, based on data collected by the Survey Research Center of The University of Michigan on an experimental basis. Some comparisons will be made with voting systems. In Section II a brief account of major empirical findings to date will be presented. Section III will be concerned with the congruence and stability of

This study was made possible by a grant from the Rockefeller Foundation to the Survey Research Center of The University of Michigan for theoretical analysis of economic survey data. The author also wishes to express her gratitude to Dr. George Katona who contributed valuable suggestions at all stages of this study and to Wallace Wilson for his participation in the analysis.

Article is from *The Quarterly Journal of Economics*, Vol. 87, Cambridge, Mass.: Harvard University Press, Copyright, 1963 (May, 1963), p. 210–24, 226–32, by the President and Fellows of Harvard College.

[1]More precisely, the maximum-welfare principle of budget determination as formulated by Pigou and Dalton requires, first, that resources should be allocated among different public uses so as to equalize the marginal return of satisfaction for each type of outlay; second, it requires that public expenditures be pushed to the point where the utility of the marginal expenditure dollar equals the utility of the marginal tax dollar. For further discussion *see* Richard A. Musgrave, *The Theory of Public Finance*, New York: McGraw-Hill Book Co., 1959, pp. 110–15.

fiscal preferences. It will be demonstrated that certain aspects of the preference system for public goods and services are not clearly crystallized in the consumer's mind; hence these attitudes have elements of inconsistency and may change easily under the impact of new information or new circumstances. In Section IV some of the determinants of attitudes toward fiscal programs will be explored. Particular interest centers around the role of considerations of direct personal benefit in shaping attitudes.

I. SAMPLE SURVEYS AS A TOOL FOR MEASURING ATTITUDES TOWARD FISCAL POLICIES

Attitudes toward government spending programs, taxes and deficits are a complex matter. Moreover, answers to survey questions may be influenced by the wording of the questions. Therefore, the answer to a single question (such as is sometimes posed in public opinion polls) is likely to be misleading. For example, people might be asked—"Do you think the federal government is spending about the right amount on improving our roads, or should it spend more, or less?" By itself the distribution of answers to this inquiry is difficult to interpret. However, if corresponding questions were asked also about school construction and slum clearance, one would be in a position to draw conclusions such as this: more people see a need for additional spending on school construction than see a need for more spending on highways. In other words, one can make valid comparisons between answers to parallel questions relating to different expenditures or taxes. Second, one can compare the answers by different subgroups of the population to the same question. By this procedure it might be learned that people in one section of the country feel a greater need for road improvement than people in another section, or that people with college training are more likely to favor outlays for schools than people with less education. Third, one can make comparisons over time of answers to identical questions. If more people favor an increase in defense spending now than some time ago, we are entitled to infer that concern about national security has intensified. Fourth, one may measure an attitude by asking not one but a series of questions on the same topic; the results would show to what extent and how answers are influenced by the context in which the attitude is explored.

Personal interview surveys can be conducted so as to allow people to explain their opinions fully in their own words. For instance, some people may explain that they are opposed to greater outlays on roads because they generally favor economy in government; others may be against greater outlays on roads because they own no car; still others may feel that the existing roads are good and not too overcrowded; still others may oppose spending on roads because they believe that additional defense spending is more urgent. The frequency of various reasons for holding an opinion is a crucial piece of information for the policy-maker who wants to obtain a full understanding of popular preferences.

147

Finally, surveys can yield information on functional relationships between variables. For example, they can show whether people who favor higher government spending also favor higher taxes; or they can tell us how strongly preferences for various fiscal policy alternatives are related to political party identification.

Voting systems designed to reveal public preferences toward fiscal programs have been discussed extensively in the public finance literature.[2] It would appear that a well-designed personal interview survey with a representative sample of the population could provide a more adequate picture of people's attitudes and preferences than a popular referendum in which the total electorate could register their opinions in the voting booth. The drawback of any voting system is that it is impossible in the context of an election to ask people to respond to a lengthy series of carefully interrelated questions; nor is it possible to call for anything but "yes" or "no" answers (at most, one might get people to assign varying numbers of points to a series of alternatives). Of course, sample surveys are subject to sampling errors; but, it takes a probability sample of only 2000 cases to keep the sampling error below 4 percentage points. Inadequate questions may bring about reporting errors of much more serious magnitude.

Yet there is one danger in public opinion surveys which may be present to a lesser extent in a popular referendum. People may be asked in a survey to judge various policies, when they have little knowledge or conviction about the issues involved. An *ad hoc* answer may then be given which does not reflect any clearly formulated attitudes or preferences. Prior to an election, the issues involved usually are discussed by public figures, in the mass media and by the candidates, so that the level of information and preparation may be higher than in the case of an unexpected interview. However, it is clear that many people have little knowledge and no opinion even about proposals, for instance regarding bond issues, that appear on the ballot.[3] This raises the question of the existence of preferences and their stability, which will be dealt with in Section III. We turn first to an examination of the nature of current attitudes.

II. SOME SURVEY FINDINGS

The data on consumer attitudes toward government expenditures, the level of taxation, and deficits were collected as part of three surveys conducted in 1960 and 1961. The three surveys were concerned primarily

---

[2]*Ibid.*, Chap. vi, pp. 116–35.

[3]In 1958–59, a heated controversy took place in the state of Michigan regarding the imposition of an income tax. The problem was extensively discussed in the mass media and by public figures from the governor to business and labor leaders. Nevertheless a survey conducted in Detroit in early 1959 showed that 18 percent of all adults could not say whether a sales or an income tax would be better for Michigan, and a considerably larger proportion had no definite opinion on the relative fairness of income, sales and property taxes. *See* Elisabeth J. L. David, "Public Preferences and the Tax Structure: An Examination of Factors Related to State and Local Tax Preferences" (Ph.D. thesis, University of Michigan, 1961).

with other economic problems, and the questions on attitudes toward federal fiscal policies were added for exploratory purposes. In each survey a nationwide cross-section of households were selected for interview. In complete families the husband was designated as respondent in half the cases, the wife in the other half (the choice was made by a random procedure); in families where the head was not married, the head was automatically the respondent.

TABLE 1
NUMBER OF PROGRAMS FOR WHICH PEOPLE FAVOR SPENDING MORE OR LESS THAN NOW

Number of Programs	(1) More Spending Favored in General[1] (%)	(2) Less Spending Favored[1] (%)	(3) More Spending Favored Even if Taxes Had to be Raised[2] (%)
None	6	39	14
One	7	22	36
Two	9	16	19
Three	12	10	11
Four	15	6	8
Five	14	3	4
Six	12	1	3
Seven	8	1	2
Eight or more	15	1	2
Not ascertained	1	1	1
Total	100	100	100
Number of cases	2256	2256	956

[1]Question asked in June and November, 1961.
[2]Question asked only in November, 1961.
The questions were: "The government spends money on many things. On this card is a list of some of the things on which the government spends money. How about ... (specific program) ... do you think the government should be spending more money, less money, or about the same amount?" (The question was repeated for each program.) "You said the government should spend more money on ... (name items) ... ; if the government had to raise taxes to finance the additional expenditures, then for which of these things would you favor spending more money?"

The finding which emerges most clearly from the survey data is that a large majority of the American people have favorable attitudes toward a number of major government expenditure programs. These attitudes are closely connected with the widely held belief that the federal government has great capabilities for influencing the level of economic activity and for bringing about the proper functioning of the economy.[4] The inquiry began by handing respondents a card showing a list of eleven "things on which the government spends money."[5] For each category of expenditure respondents were asked to indicate whether in their opinion the government should spend more money than now, less money than now, or about the same amount. The first column of Table I shows that only 6 percent of the people interviewed did not think that any of the government programs enumerated should be

---

[4]This point is treated more fully and documented by George Katona, *The Powerful Consumer*, New York: McGraw-Hill Book Co., 1960, pp. 174–75 and 231–32.

[5]The specific items on the card are listed in Table 2 below. Three items were dropped from the list after the first round of data collection and three others added, as indicated in Table 2.

enlarged. Sixteen percent checked the answer "more" only once or twice, about half checked it three to six times, and a fourth checked it seven times or more. The table also shows (column 2) that 39 percent did not advocate the reduction of any government program, and about the same proportion would like to see one or two programs cut back. Very few people checked the answer—"less should be spent"—for more than three of the eleven items listed on the card. These distributions of answers clearly point to widespread support for many government programs.

At the same time attitudes toward individual programs differ sharply. In Table 2 programs are listed in order of the frequency with which the answer "spend more" was checked. Over half of the people interviewed expressed the opinion that more money than now should be spent for (1) help to older people, (2) help for needy people, (3) education, (4) slum clearance and city improvement, and (5) hospitals and medical care. Only a small percentage feel that less money should be spent on any of these programs. There were four other programs—public works, defense, support for small business, and highway construction—to which between one-third and one-half

TABLE 2

ATTITUDES TOWARD GOVERNMENT PROGRAMS

Program	Government Should Spend . . .					
	More (%)	Less (%)	Same (%)	No Opinion (%)	Total (%)	More Even if Taxes Had to be Raised[2] (%)
Help for older people.........	70	3	23	4	100	34
Help for needy people........	60	7	28	5	100	26
Education..................	60	7	25	8	100	41
Slum clearance, city improvement[1].............	55	9	24	12	100	[3]
Hospital and medical care....	54	9	28	9	100	25
Public works[1]..............	48	11	31	10	100	[3]
Defense, rearmament[2]........	47	6	34	13	100	30
Support for small business[1]....	37	11	31	21	100	[3]
Highway construction........	36	10	45	9	100	13
Unemployment benefits......	29	14	45	12	100	10
Parks, recreational facilities...	27	15	48	10	100	7
Space exploration[2]...........	26	32	28	14	100	14
Support for agriculture.......	20	26	34	20	100	6
Help to other countries[2]......	7	53	28	12	100	2

[1]Question asked only in June, 1961.
[2]Question asked only in November, 1961.
[3]Not available.
For questions: see Table 1.

of those interviewed would like to see more funds allocated. Finally there were a number of programs which received support in the sense that the proportion who said that the government should spend more money than now was greater than the proportion who said that the government should spend less. There are only three programs for which the answer "spend less" was more frequent than the answer "spend more."

It appears from Table 2 that a rank ordering of public preferences can be achieved by survey methods. We are justified in concluding, for example, that additional aid to older people or to education would meet with more widespread public approval than additional outlays on parks and recreational facilities or aid to the unemployed. However, some caution in interpretation is necessary. Many people may respond to these survey questions on the basis of the values which they see in the programs and possibly on the basis of feelings about present adequacy. Few are in a position to judge whether better services might not be provided from present outlays or whether additional funds could indeed be utilized to good advantage (for example, in the case of space exploration).

The questions analyzed so far were posed without reference to methods of financing. In order to see whether people were prepared to pay for the many increases in spending for which they indicated their support, a further question was asked. After respondents had expressed their attitudes toward each government program, the interviewer summarized the programs checked "spend more" and asked: "You said the government should spend more money on . . . ; if the government had to raise taxes to finance the additional expenditures, then for which of these things would you favor spending more money?" In other words, people were asked to reconsider their previously stated preferences. It was suggested to them that they may not have thought of the necessity of raising taxes to finance the additional expenditures; and they were asked whether in this case they would still stick to their previous opinion. The third column of Table 1 shows that many people revised their opinions in response to the new question. They listed considerably fewer government programs on which they favored additional spending, but they still expressed a desire for the expansion of a number of government services. Half of the people said they would be willing to pay more taxes for two or more expanded programs, while only 14 percent were unwilling to pay higher taxes for any government programs.[6] Yet there is no single program so popular that a majority would be prepared to pay higher taxes for it.

The rank ordering of programs is not changed greatly if extent of support is judged by the proportion of the people who are willing to pay more taxes for each program. Education heads the list according to this second ranking, with 41 percent favoring greater outlays for education, even if these additional outlays would require tax increases. Help for older people ranks second in this list, followed by defense, help for needy people, and expenditures for hospitals and medical care. The proportion who, when reminded of taxes adhered to their original opinion that more should be spent, is highest for education and defense; it is particularly low for support to agriculture,

---

[6]The question was asked in what appeared to be an unbiased and understandable form; yet alternative wordings were possible. One might have referred specifically to the respondent's tax bill ("your taxes"). The actual wording of the question was meant to imply increases for all taxpayers. Again, one might have asked *first* what programs people would be willing to pay higher taxes for, and *second* which programs should be undertaken, if free funds were available. How such changes in the question would have affected the level of positive responses cannot be predicted without further experimentation; it is unlikely that they would have significantly altered the rank ordering of the various programs.

parks and recreation facilities, aid to the unemployed, and highway construction.

The choice posed by this line of questioning is, of course, not sufficient. There are two alternative means by which stepped-up government programs might be financed: deficit spending and reductions in less preferred government activities. People's attitudes toward budget deficits and taxes may be clarified by considering this broader range of alternatives.

There is no evidence that the *existing* federal debt causes great concern or uneasiness. In the fall of 1961 only about half of the people interviewed knew that deficits were being incurred, and a substantial proportion of those who were aware of federal deficits were unable to answer a question about possible effects of deficits on business conditions. The small group who did have an opinion consisted of 8 percent who saw favorable effects (more money being spent, more income and employment), 10 percent who argued that there is no effect, and 15 percent who saw unfavorable effects. Unfavorable effects cited were, in addition to feelings of insecurity and fiscal unsoundness, the possibility that taxes would have to be raised or that inflation would ensue.

Predominantly negative attitudes toward deficits were expressed, however, when the advisability of *additional* deficits came under discussion. In the fall of 1961, in order to raise the problem of new sources of funds, people were asked—"If the cold war with Russia should cost us *more* money during the next few years, do you think the government should raise taxes, or spend less on other things, or go further into debt?" The alternative of going further into debt was almost unanimously rejected, as Table 3 indicates. Most people probably could not support their antipathy to growing deficits by acceptable economic arguments. The tradition that the government budget should be balanced may have some relation to the maxim that one's private budget should be balanced. It is a belief which appears to be so well established that it is not contingent on economic circumstances.

TABLE 3

Opinions about Three Methods of Financing Additional Cold War Costs
(November, 1961)

Method of Financing	All Families (%)	Family Income				
		Under $3000 (%)	$3000–4999 (%)	$5000–7499 (%)	$7500–9999 (%)	$10,000 and over (%)
Raise taxes.................	29	21	31	35	36	29
Spend less on other things....	62	62	62	60	60	68
Go further into debt.........	4	3	3	4	9	6
Depends; uncertain; not ascertained	11	18	9	7	6	9
Total...................	1	1	1	1	1	1
Number of cases............	956	246	197	256	106	106

¹Columns add to more than 100 percent since some few respondents suggested a combination of methods.

The question was: "If the cold war with Russia should cost us more money during the next few years, do you think the government should raise taxes or spend less on other things, or go further into debt?"

Debt *reduction* is favored by many people, but it clearly has less priority in most people's minds than the expansion of a number of government programs. In connection with taxes we shall discuss "habituation," i.e., getting accustomed to a level of taxes which, when first reached, seem "too high." There is no specific empirical evidence that habituation also occurs in connection with the national debt; but such an inference would probably be quite safe. In November, 1960 and in June, 1961, people were asked—"Some people say that there will be some disarmament and therefore our government will spend *less* on arms and defense. Suppose this is the case, what would you say should be done with the money saved?" Table 4 shows that only 14 percent of the people interviewed (and 22 percent of those with incomes over $10,000) spontaneously suggested debt reduction; an even smaller proportion suggested tax cuts, while about half answered that the government should then spend more on other programs, particularly public welfare programs, public construction programs, and education.[7]

TABLE 4

ALTERNATIVE USES OF DEFENSE SAVINGS SPONTANEOUSLY MENTIONED

(November, 1960 and May–June, 1961)

		Family Income				
Alternative Uses	All Families (%)	Under $3000 (%)	$3000– 4999 (%)	$5000– 7499 (%)	$7500– 9999 (%)	$10,000 and over (%)
Reduce government debt.....	14	11	13	13	18	22
Reduce income taxes........	10	6	9	12	14	20
Public welfare programs......	20	27	23	17	15	14
Education (other than school building).................	13	10	12	15	17	17
Build schools, highways, etc...	10	7	12	11	11	11
Increase financial help to other countries................	3	1	2	3	3	3
Other......................	15	10	18	16	18	21
Uncertain.................	15	24	13	13	8	6
Not ascertained............	13	14	12	14	12	9
Total...................	1	1	1	1	1	1
Number of cases............	2690	677	569	684	306	343

[1]Adds to more than 100 percent because respondents were allowed more than one mention.

The question was: "Some people say that there will be some disarmament and our government will spend less on arms and defense. Suppose this is the case, what would you say should be done with the money saved?"

[7]It may be pointed out here that the majority of respondents paid little heed to the introductory sentence regarding disarmament. People answered in terms of their preferences between various fiscal alternatives, rather than in terms of a program particularly suited to replace spending on arms and defense. Nevertheless, one clear conclusion regarding the disarmament problem can be drawn from our data: If disarmament should become possible, there are a number of major government spending programs which many people would like to see stepped up in place of defense spending. The fear that the government, in order to maintain full employment, might have to undertake projects little valued by the public is without foundation. This problem has been discussed by Emile Benoit in *Economic Impacts of Disarmament*, U.S. Arms Control and Disarmament Agency Publication 2, Washington, D.C.: U.S. Government Printing Office, 1962, and in "The Propensity to Reduce the National Debt out of Defense Savings," *American Economic Review*, Vol. 51 (May, 1961), pp. 455–59, with some reference to Survey Research Center data.

Spontaneous answers to a nonsuggestive question usually bring forth those matters which are salient to the respondent. Nevertheless some alternatives, such as debt reduction, may have been overlooked. Therefore the inquiry about possible uses of defense savings was carried further by suggesting five specific possibilities and asking people to rank these in order of preference. The five choices were: (1) increase financial help to other countries, (2) reduce government debt, (3) reduce income taxes, (4) build schools, highways, and the like, (5) step up public welfare programs—to help needy people in the United States. Table 5 shows for each alternative the proportion of people who ranked it first, second, third, etc. It appears that over half of the people interviewed ranked the two domestic expenditure programs—public welfare spending and public construction—first and second. Reduction in taxes and in the public debt were typically ranked third and fourth, while foreign aid tended to be the least preferred use of the money. A substantial minority—about one in four—put debt reduction ahead of expenditure programs *and* tax reduction, but many more assigned a relatively low priority to debt reduction.

One may conclude from the admittedly limited data regarding attitudes toward the public debt that the status quo is accepted by the majority of people without serious misgivings. A desire to see the debt reduced is present but is not very meaningful, since the desire for additional government programs seems to be stronger. On the other hand, any departure from the status quo in the direction of a significant increase in public debt is disliked and evokes fears of financial irresponsibility.

Attitudes toward taxes also seem to be characterized by a widespread acceptance of the status quo, that is, acceptance of prevailing levels of taxation. But, while in the case of the debt any dissatisfaction takes the form of a feeling that it should be reduced, in the case of taxes there is diversity of opinion: a sizable minority believes that it might be advisable to step up taxes; and another sizable minority is eager to have taxes reduced.

Table 1 above clearly points to some willingness to accept *tax increases*. It shows that half of the people interviewed said that they were prepared to pay additional taxes in order to make possible larger outlays on two or more government programs. Later in the interview, it may be recalled, people were asked to choose between three alternative methods of financing additional cold war expenditures—raising taxes, spending less on other things, or going further into debt. Given these alternatives, about 30 percent clearly expressed themselves in favor of higher taxes (Table 3). This then is a group which seems to be willing to pay additional taxes, at least for a program which they view as being important.

Regarding *tax reductions*, people first were asked a nonsuggestive question which they had to answer in their own words: In case a reduction in defense spending should become feasible, what should be done with the money saved? Only 10 percent replied spontaneously—"reduce taxes"—in this context, as Table 4 indicates. Many more people mentioned alternative spending programs. Table 5 shows that when people were asked specifically to rank five alternative uses of defense savings, some who had not thought of tax reduction previously ranked it as their first or second choice. In all, 37 percent ranked tax reduction first or second, and only a slightly smaller proportion ranked it fourth or fifth.

The finding that most Americans feel no pronounced dissatisfaction with the prevailing level of taxation may be explained in part by "habitua-

TABLE 5

ATTITUDES TOWARD ALTERNATIVE USES OF DEFENSE SAVINGS

(November 1960 and May–June 1961)

Ranking	Public Welfare Programs (%)	Build Schools, Highways and the Like (%)	Reduce Government Debt (%)	Reduce Income Taxes (%)	Increase Financial Help to Other Countries (%)
All Families (Number of cases = 2700)					
Ranked as first choice.....	30	23	24	16	3
Ranked as second choice...	22	31	15	21	5
Ranked as third choice....	19	24	16	24	9
Ranked as fourth choice...	17	13	29	22	11
Ranked as fifth choice.....	5	2	8	11	60
Not ascertained.........	7	7	8	6	12
Total...............	100	100	100	100	100
Income under $3000 (Number of cases = 677)					
Ranked as first or second choice...............	64	52	29	32	5
Ranked as third choice....	14	23	15	27	7
Ranked as fourth or fifth choice...............	12	13	41	27	70
Not ascertained.........	10	12	15	14	18
Total...............	100	100	100	100	100
Income $3000–7499 (Number of cases = 1253)					
Ranked as first or second choice...............	54	56	38	38	8
Ranked as third choice....	20	23	18	24	9
Ranked as fourth or fifth choice...............	20	15	37	32	74
Not ascertained.........	6	6	7	6	9
Total...............	100	100	100	100	100
Income over $7500 (Number of cases = 649)					
Ranked as first or second choice...............	41	53	51	39	9
Ranked as third choice....	23	25	14	20	11
Ranked as fourth or fifth choice...............	29	16	30	35	71
Not ascertained.........	7	6	5	6	9
Total...............	100	100	100	100	100

The questions were: "Some people say that there will be some disarmament and therefore our government will spend less on arms and defense. Suppose this is the case, what would you say should be done with the money saved?" "Here are some suggestions that have been made. Please tell me which use of the money appears best to you, which is second best, third, etc." (A card listing the five alternatives was shown to the respondent.)

155

tion."[8] Survey Research Center studies have shown repeatedly that visible advances in the cost of living are strongly resented, when they first occur. Many people know about them, and this knowledge adversely affects their willingness to buy. Later consumers become accustomed to the new price level, and after a year or two the original resentment diminishes.[9] Data on attitudes toward taxes collected in June, 1951 suggest that tax increases also are resented at first, but then are gradually accepted. It may be recalled that Congress enacted a tax increase in September, 1950. Although this increase was occasioned by war, 40 percent of the people were of the opinion in June, 1951 that taxes should be reduced, and another 40 percent argued that *no* further increases should be made. Most significantly, about 60 percent explained spontaneously in 1951 that "taxes already are high." This figure stands in sharp contrast to the 20 percent who gave a similar response in 1961. Habituation to prevailing tax rates was undoubtedly facilitated by rising real income.

Acceptance of current tax levels may also be explained by the fact that most people are not social innovators, nor do they feel that they understand fiscal problems. Hence the majority of Americans do not formulate ideas as to how the level of taxation, much less the system of taxation, might be altered. Of course, strong dissatisfaction would lead people to visualize alternative levels of taxation and to express a preference for something other than the status quo. Because of habituation, dissatisfaction is unlikely to persist, however, except under extreme circumstances.

One important implication of the findings presented is lack of congruence in people's thinking about fiscal programs.[10] Although there is strong support for the extension of a number of government programs, only a minority of the people interviewed would like to see taxes raised, and hardly anyone would like to see these expenditures financed by deficits.[11] One explanation might be that each citizen would prefer to have some government programs reduced in order to allow greater scope for others which interest him. This explanation is contradicted by the finding (Table 2) that for only three out of fourteen major government programs is there a sizable group of people who advocate a reduction in spending, while for the

---

[8]It does not follow from this finding that a tax reduction would have no favorable psychological effects. More recent Survey Research Center studies on attitudes toward tax reduction will appear in the book, *The 1962 Survey of Consumer Finances*, Survey Research Center, Institute for Social Research, Ann Arbor: University of Michigan, 1963.

[9]For further detail *see* George Katona and Eva Mueller, "Consumer Attitudes and Demand, 1950–52," *op. cit.*, pp. 16–26; and Eva Mueller, "Consumer Reactions to Inflation," *Quarterly Journal of Economics*, Vol. 73 (May, 1959).

[10]The term "congruence" is used in this paper to denote harmony among attitudes. It is looser than the term "consistency," which is used where the answer to one question strictly predetermines the logical answer to another question.

[11]Favorable attitudes toward additional expenditures also have been found to coexist with dislike of additional taxes in Germany and Sweden. *See* Günter Schmölders, *Das Irrationale in der Öffentlichen Finanzwertschaft*, Hamburg: Rowohlt, 1960.

remaining eleven programs the group favoring increased spending is much larger than the group favoring cutbacks.

An alternative explanation is consistent with our findings and with recent psychological research. Although there is considerable evidence that people strive to avoid dissonance or incongruence (by problem solving behavior or suppression), dissonance may be tolerable when the conflicting desires or beliefs are peripheral to the person's psychological field. In the case of fiscal policies, the average citizen does not have to make decisions through which his conflicting preferences are confronted. He may not even think about (or discuss) fiscal problems enough to be bothered by lack of congruence. Hence in that area he may remain unaware of contradictions, look the other way, or just hope that more knowledgeable people in government will make the right decision for him.

By contrast, if a consumer wants a new TV set *and* a new washing machine and he can afford only one of these without drawing on his savings (which he dislikes), he is in a crossroad situation. He must deliberate until he arrives at a decision as to which course of action he prefers. Thus, while we have reason to assume that preference functions for alternative uses of private funds (including the savings alternative) have some firmness and consistency, our findings raise doubt whether the corresponding concept of a preference function for alternative fiscal policies is fruitful. We shall pursue this problem further in the next two sections by examining the congruence and stability of fiscal preferences and their origin.

III. THE CONGRUENCE AND STABILITY OF FISCAL PREFERENCES

Attitudes toward fiscal programs undoubtedly vary in stability. At the one extreme there are attitudes which are long-standing stereotypes, firmly rooted in people's thinking and seldom consciously re-examined. The conviction that deficits are bad is probably of that kind. At the other extreme may be fleeting notions which also have not been carefully thought through, being of little salience at the moment. In between are many attitudes which are rational in the sense that they are based on some degree of deliberation. These attitudes are related to values, perceptions and group belongings, but can be modified by environmental changes and new information. Their stability and congruence depends in part on external conditions, in part on the extent to which they are integrated into the central attitude structures of the individual.[12]

Besides the contradiction between attitudes toward spending and attitudes toward means of financing already discussed, ... findings appear in

---

[12]The distinction between habitual ways of thinking and genuine decisions is treated by George Katona, *Psychological Analysis of Economic Behavior*, New York: McGraw-Hill Book Co., 1951, chap. iv.

the survey which suggest that some fiscal policy attitudes are not very certain or firm. ...

. . . .

[For example,] evidence of inconsistency and instability was obtained from a set of re-interviews in the fall of 1960 with respondents first interviewed prior to the 1956 election.[13] Respondents were presented with a number of statements in 1956 and asked to express their agreement or disagreement. These same people were presented with the identical statements four years later and were asked to react to them once more. Thus it is possible to determine what proportion took the same position at both times and what proportion took a different position after four years. The statements related to a variety of topics: isolationism, the overseas stationing of American troops in peace time, a full employment guarantee by the government, the proper sphere of government vs. private business, racial equality in housing and employment, and school desegregation. Also included were three statements concerning government expenditure programs:

> If cities and towns around the country need help to build more schools, the government in Washington ought to give them the money they need.
> The United States should give economic help to poorer countries of the world even if those countries can't pay for it.
> The government ought to help people get doctors and hospital care at low cost.

Table 8 shows people's reactions to the three fiscal policy statements in 1956 and 1960. The overall change in attitudes over the four year period was relatively small, with medical aid and foreign assistance showing some increase in popular support and school construction showing some decline in response to environmental changes over the four year period. Yet many more individuals shifted position that would have been necessary to bring about the overall change. That is, some people shifted from approval to disapproval, others moved in the opposite direction.[14] At the bottom of Table 8 are shown the rank order correlation coefficients between the first and second response, using a five-point scale ranging from "strong approval" to "strong disapproval."[15] For all three fiscal issues the rank order correlation coefficients are quite low. However, reactions to the other political issues posed yielded rank order correlation coefficients within the same range. Attitudes toward

---

[13]These data were collected as part of a continuing program of election studies directed by Angus Campbell, Philip E. Converse, Warren E. Miller, and Donald E. Stokes, *The American Voter*, New York: John Wiley & Sons, Inc., 1960.

[14]For a more general analysis of the problem of response instability, *see* George Katona, "Changes in Consumer Expectations and Their Origin," *The Quality and Economic Significance of Anticipations Data*, a Conference of the Universities-National Bureau of Economic Research, Princeton, N.J.: Princeton University Press, 1960, pp. 53–82.

[15]The coefficient is the tau-beta due to Maurice Kendall (*Rank Correlation Methods*, London: Charles Griffin, 1948), applicable to a table with unlimited numbers of ties, and hence useful for bivariate distributions with ordered categories. I am indebted for this analysis to Dr. Philip Converse.

TABLE 8

RESPONDENT'S REACTIONS TO VARIOUS POLICY ISSUES (1956 AND 1960)

Reaction	The Government Ought to Help People Get Doctors and Hospital Care at Low Cost		The United States Should Give Economic Help to Poorer Countries even if Those Countries Can't Pay for It[1]		If Cities and Towns Need Help to Build More Schools, the Government in Washington Ought to Give Them the Money They Need	
	1956 (%)	1960 (%)	1956 (%)	1960 (%)	1956 (%)	1960 (%)
Agree strongly	40	46	21	29	49	38
Agree, but not strongly	15	12	22	23	19	18
Not sure; depends	20	22	32	28	18	20
Disagree, but not strongly	8	6	10	6	5	8
Disagree strongly	17	14	15	13	9	15
Not ascertained	2	2	2	1	2	1
Total	100	100	100	100	100	100
Number of cases	1358	1358	1358	1358	1358	1358
Rank order correlation coefficient between 1956 and 1960 response	r = 0.45		r = 0.25		r = 0.34	

[1] The substantial level of agreement with this statement is not inconsistent with the unfavorable showing of foreign aid in Table 2. Here we see that many people agree that the United States should give *some* foreign assistance. Table 2 indicates that very few people favor *more* spending on foreign aid.

[2] Less than half of 1 percent.

159

school desegregation together with medical care were most stable (rank order correlation coefficients of 0.45), while attitudes toward foreign economic aid were least stable (0.25). The other issues are clustered in the interval from 0.25 to 0.37.

It may be inferred that many citizens find it difficult to appraise the wisdom of major foreign and domestic policies. Because of the complexities involved, people often do not seem to come to a clear conclusion as to what stand they should take. Instability and incongruence of expressed attitudes are the logical consequence of such uncertainty. Attitudes toward fiscal policies do not differ from attitudes toward other difficult political and social policy problems in this respect.

IV. GROUP DIFFERENCES IN ATTITUDES TOWARD FISCAL POLICIES

This section will examine group differences in attitudes toward fiscal policies with the aim of throwing some light on the problem of attitude formation. We shall first attempt to distinguish between those groups which are more or less likely to benefit by a given policy in order to see how far considerations of direct personal benefit govern attitudes. We shall also examine the relation of attitudes toward fiscal programs to income, education, age, and political party affiliation. Finally, we shall relate the need felt for more government services to the need felt for major consumer goods and services.

TABLE 9

NUMBER OF PROGRAMS FOR WHICH PEOPLE FAVOR SPENDING
MORE THAN NOW (1961)

	Family Income			
Number of Programs	Under $3000 (%)	$3000–7500 (%)	$7500–10,000 (%)	$10,000 and over (%)
	More spending favored in general			
None............................	8	5	4	7
One or two....................	17	14	18	16
Three or four.................	23	28	29	32
Five or six....................	28	26	27	25
Seven or more................	23	26	21	19
Not ascertained..............	1	1	1	1
Total......................	100	100	100	100
	More spending favored even if taxes had to be raised[1]			
None............................	18	13	9	15
One............................	33	35	40	37
Two............................	25	19	15	12
Three or four.................	12	20	20	24
Five or more.................	8	12	14	11
Not ascertained..............	4	1	2	1
Total......................	100	100	100	100

[1]Question asked only in November, 1961. For questions, *see* Table 1.

Beginning with income group comparisons, the data show that it is *not* true, as is sometimes supposed, that upper income groups are less favorably disposed toward the extension of government programs than lower income groups. The number of programs for which people would like to see the government spend more money is almost identical in all major income groups; the same is true of the number of programs for which people are willing to pay higher taxes (Table 9). The answer "spend less" does occur, however, slightly more frequently among upper than among lower income groups.

While the desire for extended government services is pronounced in all income groups, Table 10 shows that there are distinct differences in the kinds of services which are desired. In Table 10 a summary measure is used which shows the proportion who want more spent on a particular program minus the proportion who want less spent. Positive index values indicate that the proportion favoring expansion of a particular program exceeds the proportion favoring reduction; negative figures indicate the opposite. For example, if 40 percent want to see a particular program enlarged, 50 percent want no change, and 10 percent want a reduction, the index value is 30 (40 minus 10). All income groups strongly support more aid for older people and more aid for education. In addition, certain programs which are of direct benefit primarily to lower income groups are more widely advocated among those with smaller incomes than among the well-to-do. Aid to the needy, aid for the unemployed, hospital and medical care, and public works fall into that category. By contrast, aid to small business and highway construction receive widest support in the upper income groups. In all, considerations of direct personal benefit seem to have some influence on attitudes toward fiscal programs; yet it is clear that other considerations are at work also and may even be more decisive.

TABLE 10
INDEXES OF ATTITUDES TOWARD GOVERNMENT PROGRAMS (1961)

Program	Index Values of Attitudes toward Spending[1] Family Income		
	Under $3000	$3000–7500	$7500 and over
Education........................	43	59	53
Help for older people............	68	67	64
Slum clearance[2].................	42	52	37
Hospital and medical care........	54	45	33
Unemployment benefits..........	26	17	−2
Help for needy people............	63	51	39
Support for agriculture..........	8	−3	−27
Public works[2]..................	44	38	24
Help to other countries[3]........	−38	−46	−51
Defense[3].......................	35	42	45
Space exploration[3]..............	−18	−2	5
Highway construction............	18	28	27
Parks...........................	1	17	11
Support for small business[2]......	20	27	30

[1]Index value represents percent advocating increased spending minus percent advocating decreased spending; "no change" answers are disregarded.
[2]Question asked only in May–June, 1961.
[3]Question asked only in November, 1961.
For question, *see* Table 1.

161

The role of immediate self-interest can be tested by a number of additional comparisons. The index values shown in Table 11 are computed as in Table 10. The self-interest principle would suggest, for example, that people who are repeatedly unemployed would favor larger unemployment insurance benefits, while those who are never unemployed would favor no increase or even a decrease, or that expenditures to help older people would be increasingly favored with advancing age.

TABLE 11

ATTITUDES TOWARD SPENDING IN RELATION TO SELF-INTEREST

Type of Expenditure	Index Values of Attitudes toward Spending[1]		
Unemployment benefits..........	Repeatedly unemployed 60	Seldom unemployed 33	Never unemployed 15
Help for older people.............	Under 35 years old 57	35–54 70	55–64 66	65 years old and over 69
Support for agriculture...........	Farmers 9		Other occupations −8
Education.....................	Under 45: no children 64	Children under 18 in family 58	Over 45: no children 41
Highway construction............	Own no car 14	One car 28	Two or more cars 28
Slum clearance and city improvement..................	Central cities 48	Suburban areas 54	Adjacent areas 43	Rural areas 35

[1]Index value represents percent advocating increased spending minus percent advocating decreased spending; "no change" answers are disregarded.

Except in the case of unemployment compensation, these comparisons confirm the idea that direct personal benefit offers only a partial explanation of attitudes toward fiscal programs. In the case of unemployment compensation, closer knowledge and a different understanding of the problems among the unemployed may account for some of the observed differences, not merely self-interest. Regarding the other programs, many people expressed themselves in favor of greater expenditures from which they were not likely to reap direct personal benefit. They seemed to realize that the benefit of most government programs should be assessed from the point of view of the national welfare as a whole.[16] National benefit, in contrast to personal benefit,

---

[16]The distinction in the public finance literature between individual benefit and collective benefit has been criticized by Gerhard Colm, "The Theory of Public Expenditures," *Essays in Public Finance and Fiscal Policy*, New York: Oxford University Press, 1955, pp. 27–43. Our data suggest that even the individual citizen often does not make such a differentiation. Hence the notion that individual benefit can serve as a criterion for taxation appears artificial. *See,* however, Musgrave, *op. cit.*, pp. 87–88.

is difficult to assess. Looking at this broader frame of reference, many people might feel incapable of judging which course of action the government should pursue. Such feelings of ignorance or inability to choose between alternative possibilities must result in uncertainty or vacillation, and hence may account for some instability and inconsistency in attitudes toward fiscal programs.

If this interpretation of the data is correct, there should be greater congruence of attitudes among the upper income and better educated groups than among the lower income and less educated. The data confirm this inference in the sense that they show the upper income and better educated groups to be somewhat *more* willing to pay taxes (presumably to finance the government programs which they advocate) than other groups. The proportion of people who ranked tax reduction first or second, when asked to consider alternative uses of free public funds, was about the same in all income groups (Table 5). But a direct inquiry whether taxes should be raised in 1951 and an inquiry whether they should be lowered in 1956 both indicated that lower income groups are more eager for tax reduction than are the well-to-do. Questions about the advisability of tax reductions asked in 1961 and 1962 show that in both years opposition to tax cuts was more frequent among upper than among lower income groups, although the differences between income groups were greater in 1961 than in 1962. If the data on attitudes toward tax reductions are classified by education, it appears that willingness to pay taxes also rises with education. Indeed the income differences in attitudes toward taxes may to some extent reflect educational differences. The finding that upper income groups have somewhat more favorable attitudes toward taxes than lower income groups stands in sharp contrast to the frequently expressed opinion that the well-to-do, who pay much larger amounts of taxes, are more resentful of the tax burden than those in the lower income brackets. ...

.   .   .   .

CHAPTER III

SOME ECONOMIC POLICY CONTEXTS OF

PUBLIC FINANCE AND BUDGETING:

A BASIC FRAMEWORK AND SPECIFIC ISSUES

At their hearts, public finance and budgeting imply basic economic questions of who should and does get which scarce resources. To these central concerns this section turns. The present approach will have two main features. Thus the initial selection will present a basic framework for exploring the economic contexts of public finance and budgeting. Six subsequent selections will attempt to come to more detailed grips with a number of specific economic issues.

Walter W. Heller's "Economics and the Applied Theory of Public Expenditures" provides the general framework for this section's survey of economic issues with which public finance and budgeting must cope. Heller notes that the economic sciences and arts are still far removed from providing precise guidelines for public spending, and in so doing he articulates a dominant theme of the selections which follow. At the same time, Heller provides a progress report on the help that economic analysis can reasonably provide. In doing so, Heller stresses a second major theme of this section.

Heller's specific approach to outlining the incomplete but real contributions of economics to public budgeting and finance may be sketched. Heller focuses on the various economic functions of government; he indicates the tangled difficulties of attempting to use governmental controls or budgetary action where free-market dynamics cannot or should not determine outcomes; and he gives attention to the selection of alternative means for the effective performance of government functions or activities. Through it all, the themes of usefulness/incompleteness of economic analysis appear prominently.

Heller's qualified optimism about the usefulness of economic tools of analysis gets ample support from the mixed record of success of coping with the major components of "public expenditure theory." The following paragraphs will raise a number of these component issues, and they will introduce a corresponding number of pieces reprinted below. Each of these selections summarizes both specific problems and specific progress in putting economic analysis in the effective service of executive and legislative officials.

1. What is the "federal budget"? As Colm and Wagner detail in "Some Observations on the Budget Concept," no simple answer exists at either descriptive or prescriptive levels. Thus the "federal budget" is not a very specific notion, and conceptual variations of what it is and what it should be also differ significantly. In addition, Colm and Wagner emphasize the several senses in which the yearly "budget" presented by the President to Congress has, like Topsy, more or less "just growed." Finally, the authors sketch several recommendations for budgetary change that are required to meet several distinct if overlapping uses of budgeting processes and products. Financial data may be put to these three uses, that is:

a. Program analysis, e.g., for monitoring the current status and for programming future states of Program A;

b. Financial analysis, e.g., for determining whether debt management/cash flow policies are adequate to support some total mix of public goods and services; and

c. Economic analysis, e.g., for attempting to manage the various types of "inflation" by fiscal policies and public spending.

2. What rules should guide budgeting practices? The classical budgetary rule, perhaps, holds that: You certainly cannot spend more than you take in during (for example) a year, and you cannot spend very much more than you take in during the short run. This "balanced budget rule," as Colm and Young argue in their "In Search of a New Budget Rule," can be at once reasonable and have serious consequences. For example, attempts to balance the public budget when the economy is faltering may only deepen the downswing. In fact, such economies might paradoxically result in larger deficits (income minus spending) than policies less concerned with balanced budgets each year. Whatever the case, our deep national commitment expressed in the "full employment" legislation of 1946 sharply underscores the conclusion of Colm and Young that the "balanced budget rule" has serious inadequacies. "No budget rule can be accepted," they note "which is not compatible with a policy designed to support balanced economic expansion and stabilization."

If the liabilities of the "balanced budget rule" seem clear enough, Colm and Young are tentative about a specific replacement. Thus a second rule, a balanced budget over some more or less extended cycle, is analyzed critically. The authors devote even closer attention to an alternative budget rule which presumes the existence of valid and reliable tools for sophisticated economic analysis. If nothing else, Colm and Young demonstrate that those sanguine days are gone forever when persons in authority could support the simple "balanced budget rule" without serious reservations. The new age of working through and testing a rule and analytical techniques more congenial to "full employment" has been well begun, but only begun.

3. Must government spending always be too little and/or too late? Even given an appropriate budget rule, the timing of government spending as a vehicle

165

for economic stabilization still remains a central concern. Given the often-substantial lead-time between the decision to spend and actual significant public outlays, a family of arguments against government attempts at stabilization-by-spending gain force. These anti-spending arguments apply particularly where relatively full employment exists, where large numbers of employables are in the armed services, or where public spending requires skills that are already in short supply. Timing is crucial under any conditions, however. Thus public spending might come too late to keep the economy from "cooling down." More seriously, gearing-up for public spending might be completed just as the economy somehow recovered and a flood of growing confidence triggered private spending that had been deferred by economic warning signs. In such a case, increased public spending could "overheat" the economy and contribute to an inflationary spiral.

Murray L. Weidenbaum's "The Timing of the Economic Impact of Government Spending" presents valuable insights about safeguards against worst–coming–to–worst on timing the economic impact of public spending. He identifies four stages of the spending process:

a. The sequence of events leading to and including legislative authorization of appropriations;
b. The period during which contracts are placed;
c. The complex processes of gearing-up for production in private sectors of the economy; and
d. The completion of the processes leading to payments in private sectors of the economy.

In sum, Weidenbaum argues that government spending has a multiplier associated with it that has a variable impact on private consumption and investment at all stages of the spending process. That is, public spending need not always be too little and too late. Spending can have at least some impact almost as soon as the formal announcement is made.

Weidenbaum's analysis, however, rests on a crucial assumption—an underlying confidence in public decisions. If that confidence is lacking, less sanguine effects than Weidenbaum stresses are probable. Hence the pressure is really on for accuracy in economic analysis. As spending announcements have an impact, conversely announcing and then cancelling contracts for public spending as conditions change is a very poor tactic.

4. What are the dimensions of the public sector? Even if we are assured about timing and an applicable budget rule, further, any public spending must be concerned with crucial issues about the content of the public/private sectors. Many observers—like John Kenneth Galbraith—have noted that we spend too much on automobile tail fins and too little on education. He advises shifting resources in such cases from spending in the private sector to the support of the public sector. Galbraith's emphasis can be juxtaposed with that of an earlier selection. Colin and Young, that is, were concerned with a ceiling for public budgets in their search for a budgeting rule. Galbraith is interested in raising the "floor" of public spending by enlarging our working definition of acceptable uses of public monies.

166

Henry C. Wallich's "Public versus Private: Could Galbraith Be Wrong?" looks at the scope of the public sector, and sets sail against the prevailing current of opinion in the literature. *Wallich reviews Galbraith's position, and urges that bloated working definitions of the public sector can significantly endanger individual freedom. As Wallich recognizes, the issue is a profoundly difficult one, for too-zealous reservation of matters to the private sphere also could threaten individual freedom and some necessary things might never get done. Wallich's prime concern is that too much may be done, with consequent danger to individual freedom in the haste to right social wrongs and more widely distribute the benefits of prosperity.*

5. What is the history of spending in the public sector? The issues raised by Wallich are illuminated by a review of the history of spending in the public sector. Patently, that is, some kinds of public spending could reduce individual freedom. Expenditures for concentration camps, as an extreme example, clearly would have that effect. Other public spending—as for defense—might be largely necessary to preserve individual freedom.

As usual, the issues are more complex than they appear on the surface. Francis M. Bator helps develop major aspects of this complexity in the selection "Some Quantitative History." As Bator notes, merely "to add up all the money paid out each year by public agencies . . . is not a very revealing exercise." To do so would be to add apples and oranges. Thus Bator distinguishes two types of expenditures: "nonexhaustive" and "exhaustive." The former is spending that redistributes income or assets. In a direct sense, consequently, "nonexhaustive" spending does not absorb economic output. In contrast, such spending consists of "transfer payments" like unemployment compensation, old-age and retirement benefits, and so on. "Exhaustive" expenditures do absorb goods and services, oppositely. They are a measure of the public claims on output that is thus unavailable for private consumption or investment.

The two types of spending raise different challenges to individual freedom. Thus nonexhaustive spending essentially requires a redistribution of income, with important implications for the individual freedom (however that is defined) of all parties. Assume that some citizens contribute more and others receive more than the average contribution. The former citizens might complain that their freedom has been restricted by the provision of unequal contributions, which was enacted because of the lobbying of the officials in charge of the program. If the transfer payments have no "strings" attached to them, however, those individuals receiving more than they contributed may have their lives and freedom enhanced. Individual freedom faces at least two derivative challenges. The difficult decision, first, concerns the point at which the felt-deprivation of the former people is so great as to require ceasing or postponing further need-gratification of the latter people. There is no substantive rule for such a decision. Rather, our basic rule is procedural. When "enough" resistance is generated through our existing institutions and procedures, then the redistributing has tended to stop. To go further might endanger the "moving consensus" among the "over-payers" on which our relatively-peaceful political life in part depends; to stop short of "enough" resistance is to lose an

167

opportunity to increase the commitment of the "over-receivers" to their society. In any case, second, both parties would have to develop controls to help assure the responsibility and responsiveness of the public officials monitoring the program, a challenge that is always with us.

What the resultant impact on individual freedom would be in either case above, however, is problematic. Perhaps that is the wisdom of our traditionally lesser concern with the kinds of decisions made. Rather, our concern is more with the processes used to make decisions and with the resulting consensus about the decisions.

Exhaustive expenditures imply other, perhaps more serious, challenges for individual freedom. For example, they reduce the total pool of goods and services available to private consumers and investors during an economic boom, and thus may contribute to inflation. And once made, the objects of exhaustive expenditures also tend to remain under the direct control of the "public sector." These two examples suggest a broad challenge to individual freedom.

Bator provides valuable data on the distribution of public spending of both kinds in various areas. These data should enlighten discussions of the impact on individual freedom of spending in the public sector. The sharp increase over time in nonexhaustive vs. exhaustive expenditures, for example, has a significant place in any discussion about the growing size of our public budgets.

6. Who gets the benefits of public spending? Even if a broad-based consensus does support some program of public spending such as social security, it is not always clear who gets what at whose relative expense. The programs commonly are that complicated. Elizabeth Deran illustrates the point deftly. Thus some have argued that social security taxes are "regressive," that they "soak the poor." Others have argued that the taxes are "progressive" and oppositely "soak the rich." Deran summarizes the available evidence and finds support for both of the positions. In the process, she illustrates the complexity of the issues implied by transfer payments and income redistribution.

There may be a conscious motivation underlying Deran's analysis of who gets what in social security, in addition. Deran's piece implies the success with which public officials work both sides of many policy streets. It is easy to denigrate giving the impressions of simultaneously "soaking the rich" and "soaking the poor," but just such actual, if sometimes devious, give-and-take often is necessary to preserve and perhaps enhance the "moving consensus" on which our political institutions rest.

7. How are choices to be made from among desirable programs on which public monies could be spent? A brief review of the six emphases above generates still another basic question for public expenditure theory. If a budget rule is accepted, a ceiling on public expenditures may be defined, and their timing made easier. A working definition of the "public sector" involves determining the minimum level of public services that are considered tolerable, as well as indicating the particular beneficiaries of those services. However, still another class of choices must be made: given that every desirable program cannot be supported at once, which specific ones should be supported?

This seventh question will be postponed for now. Chapter VIII presents a number of selections that are helpful in working toward sharpening criteria for selectivity. That chapter focuses on a number of techniques which will facilitate making choices between alternative policies and programs. Gene H. Fisher's "The Role of Cost Utility Analysis in Program Budgeting" reprinted in Chapter VIII, for example, presents an approach to selectivity via a specific technique of economic analysis. Fisher's implied conclusion serves as a useful generalization: Available techniques or approaches always significantly influence what our policy can be and sometimes predetermine what it will be.

ECONOMICS AND THE APPLIED THEORY
OF PUBLIC EXPENDITURES

WALTER W. HELLER

What does the economist have to offer a perplexed public and its policymaking representatives on the theory of Government functions as they affect the budget? The cynic's offhand answer, "not much," may be close to the mark if one demands definitive rules of thumb for determining the precise scope of Government functions and level of Government expenditures. But if, instead, the demand is for economic guidelines to aid the budgetary decisionmaker (1) in blending rationally the service, stabilization, and income-transfer functions of Government, (2) in identifying those deficiencies in the private-market mechanism which call for Government budgetary action or, more broadly, those activities where Government use or control of resources promises greater returns than private use or control, and (3) in selecting the most efficient means of carrying out Government functions and activities (whether by Government production, contracts with private producers, transfer payments, loans, guaranties, tax concessions, and so forth)—if this is the nature of the demands on him, the economist is prepared to make a modest offering now and to work along lines that promise a greater contribution in the future.

In a sense, this paper is a progress report designed to show where the economist can already offer some useful counsel, to indicate some of the lines along which promising work is being done, and to suggest certain limitations or constraints within which the economic criteria for dividing resources between public and private use must be applied.

As a first step in the search for economic guideposts, we need to disentangle, classify, and define the basic objectives and functions of Government that shape its budgetary decisions. Fortunately, Prof. Richard A. Musgrave has developed a conceptual framework for this task in his "multiple theory of budget determination."[1]

The component functions of the budget as he brings them into focus are: (1) the service, or want-satisfying, function: to provide for the satisfaction of those individual wants which the market mechanism cannot satisfy effectively (e.g., education and conservation) or is incapable of satisfying (e.g., defense and justice); (2) the income-transfer or distributional

---

Article is from *Federal Expenditure Policy for Economic Growth and Stability*, Washington, D.C., U.S. Government Printing Office, 1957. Prepared for the use of the Joint Economic Committee.

[1]*See*, for example, "A Multiple Theory of Budget Determination," *Finanzarchiv*, Vol. 13, No. 3, 1957, pp. 333–43, and the relevant chapters of his treatise, *The Theory of Public Finance*, New York: McGraw-Hill Book Co., 1959.

function: to make those corrections in the existing income distribution (by size, by occupational groups, by geographical area, etc.) which society desires; and (3) the stabilization function: to join with monetary policy and other measures to raise or lower the level of aggregate demand so as to maintain full employment and avoid inflation. The first function is of dominant interest [here] and the succeeding sections of the paper return to it. But several general implications of the Musgrave system as a whole deserve attention before turning to specifics.

Musgrave's formulation helps unclutter our thinking on the component parts of the budget decision. It drives home the significant point that our decisions on how much and what kind of want-satisfying services to provide by Government budgets need not be tied to our demands on the budget for correction of either the existing patterns of income distribution or the level of aggregate demand. If we prefer, we can have a small budget for services (financed by taxes levied on the benefit principle) combined with a big budget for redistributive transfers of income (financed by taxes levied on the ability principle), or vice versa; and either combination can be coupled with either a deficit to stimulate demand and employment or a surplus to reduce demand and check inflation. In this respect, it is reminiscent of Samuelson's "daring doctrine" that by appropriate fiscal-monetary policy "a community can have full employment, can at the same time have the rate of capital formation it wants, and can accomplish all this compatibly with the degree of income-redistributing taxation it ethically desires."[2] Musgrave, in turn, points the way to achieving any combination of Government services, income redistribution, and economic redistribution, and economic stability we set our sights on.

So far, so good. The waters, though deep, are clear and relatively still. They get somewhat muddied and troubled when we move from the clear-cut want-satisfying programs (subject to the benefit principle) and clear-cut distributive programs (subject to the ability principle) into dual-purpose programs, transfers-in-kind in the form of subsidized housing, medical care, vocational education, and so forth. For here we are no longer furnishing services that the majority has voted to meet its own needs (including both selfishly motivated needs like defense and police protection and socially motivated needs like foreign aid) via Government, but are in effect requiring the minority to accept services which they might or might not have bought had they been handed an equivalent amount of cash. Perhaps they would have preferred to spend it on wine, women, and song, but the majority is apparently saying, "No, we know what's best for you." Can this be justified?

It may be digressing to do so, but let us consider for a moment the provision of free vocational education as a case in point. It might be argued that vocational training results in a direct increase in earning power of the

---

[2]Paul A. Samuelson, "The New Look in Tax and Fiscal Policy," in *Federal Tax Policy for Economic Growth and Stability*, Joint Committee on the Economic Report, Washington, D.C.: U.S. Government Printing Office, November 9, 1955, p. 234.

171

trainee (since employers will be willing to pay him higher wages) and that it should therefore be left in private hands or, if furnished publicly, should be financed under the market principle (by direct charges to the recipient of the service) rather than the budget principle (provided free of charge and financed by general taxation).[3] In terms of the service budget alone, the foregoing conclusion is probably right. But bringing in the redistributive motive puts subsidized vocational training in a different light. The voting majority may feel that income transferred in this form constitutes a more efficient and desirable form of transfer than a direct cash transfer. It insures that the transferred economic power won't be squandered in foolish and dissolute ways. It approaches reduction of economic inequality through greater equality of opportunity. In the process, it strengthens the economy's productive capacity.

The new welfare economics may protest that this is a form of tyranny of the majority of the voters over the minority, that each individual is his own best judge of his welfare. Since the equivalent cash payment would have been spent differently, it is said to be a violation of consumer sovereignty. But it is also quite possible that the recipient of the transfer in kind will vote with the majority to have this kind of program rather than a direct cash payment. The individual may accept and welcome the discipline in such an arrangement which overcomes his own self-deplored lack of willpower (a lack which is not restricted to children, aged persons, and imbeciles). How many of us would "prefer" to spend our time quite differently than we do if left to our own devices, yet are willing to accept, or even welcome, the tyranny of a deadline as a condition of participating in a desirable project? Seen in this light, the transfer in kind may interfere more with license than with freedom of consumer choice. I do not mean to dismiss the "tyranny" argument, but its force is certainly softened by the kind of consideration just examined. It may be further softened if we accept the proposition that the responsibility of the voters' representatives goes beyond a mere recording of individual preferences to leadership and education designed to redirect individual preferences along lines which a social consensus deems more constructive.

Even beyond this, the transfer in kind may actually have a large service component, i.e., secondary benefits which accrue to others than the direct recipient of the service.[4] For example, low-income housing may confer

---

[3]For a discussion of these principles *see* Gerhard Colm, *Essays in Public Finance and Fiscal Policy*, New York: Oxford University Press, 1955, pp. 8–11.

[4]To the extent that the income transfer motive is the sole or dominant motive for keeping certain services on the public budget (or at least causing us to supply them on the budget principle rather than the market principle), a rise in average family income and a decline in inequality will eventually bring us to a point where programs such as vocational education and low-cost housing should be moved off of the Government budget and into the market economy. This point is undoubtedly much more distant for some programs than others. Also, I do not mean to suggest that the main impact of economic growth and prosperity is to reduce Government expenditures. Both in the case of intermediate public goods (such as roads), the demand for which typically moves in accord with private goods, and in the case of "end item" services (such as better education and recreation), the

indirect benefits on high-income people in surrounding areas for which they are willing to pay a considerable price. Subsidized housing projects may replace unsightly slums, arrest urban blight which threatens to encroach on better neighborhoods, and reduce fire and police protection costs. To this extent, taxes on high-income people to subsidize low-cost housing may in large part be a payment for the indirect benefits they receive rather than a transfer payment. Clearly identifying and separating the service elements from the redistributive element in this manner suggests that the wants of third-party beneficiaries are being satisfied by using the direct recipient of subsidized housing, medical care, education and the like as the instrument, willing or unwilling, for this purpose.

This formulation may also shed new light on the theory of progressive taxation. Musgrave suggests that high-income people may be willing to pay proportionately more for a given government service than low-income people (i.e., the income elasticity of demand for the service is greater than unity), even in the case of government services like defense and justice which by their nature must be consumed in equal amounts by all persons. Add to this consideration the important indirect stake which the upper income groups have in subsidized programs for the lower income groups (i.e., programs not equally consumed by all). The direct beneficiary may put a low value on the service and a high value on money, while the indirect beneficiary (who gets secondary benefits in protection from epidemics, in arresting of urban blight, in a more stable body politic and labor force, and so forth) may put a relatively high value on the service and a low value on money. The tax policy result: progressive taxation on the benefit principle.

Given a framework for straight thinking about budget functions, the economist is brought face to face with two questions that come closer to the central problem of the proper sphere of Government activity. First, where competitive bidding via the pricing mechanism is inapplicable, how are the preferences of voters for governmental services to be revealed, measured, and appropriately financed? Second, waiving the question of measurement of preferences, where would the line between public and private control over resources be drawn if economic efficiency were the only criterion to be implied?

On the first question, insofar as it relates to individual preferences for public goods, economists have agreed on the nature and difficulty of the problem, have made some intriguing suggestions as to its solution, and have concluded that it is next to insoluble. The key difficulty is that the voting process, unlike the pricing process, does not force the consumer of public goods to show his hand. The essence of preference measurement is the showing of how much of one good or service the consumer is willing to forego

---

demand for which increases with higher standards of living, economic growth and prosperity mean higher rather than lower demands for Government services. (*See* Gerhard Colm, "Comments on Samuelson's Theory of Public Finance," *The Review of Economics and Statistics*, Vol. 38 (November, 1956), p. 410.)

as the price of acquiring another. But the amount of a public good or service (say, of defense, police protection, or schooling) available to the voter is independent of the amount he pays in taxes or the intensity of his demand for it.[5] Unless and until we devise a reliable and reasonably accurate method of detecting specific voter preferences in some detail, our definition of the proper sphere of government activity will have to rely chiefly on the informed judgment and perception of those whom we vote into legislative and executive office.[6]

This being the case, the economist's task is to contribute what he can to this informed judgment and perception. In effect, the economist's job becomes one of telling the voters and their representatives what their preferences as to governmental activities would be if they were guided by the principle of economic efficiency. In doing so, the economist is not proposing that decisions as to what kinds of activities should be assigned to government—what wants should be satisfied and resources should be redirected through government action—should be made on economic grounds alone. He is fully aware that values such as those of political and economic freedom play a vital role in these decisions. But he can perform the valuable service of identifying those deficiencies in the market mechanism and those inherent economic characteristics of government which make it economically advantageous to have certain services provided by government rather than by private initiative. In other words he can show where government intervention in resource allocation and use promises a greater return per unit of input than untrammeled private use.

The economist recognizes, of course, that there are areas in which he is necessarily mute, or at least should not speak unless spoken to. These are the areas of pure public goods, whose benefits are clearly indivisible and nonmarketable, and no amount of economic wisdom can determine the appropriate levels of output and expenditure.[7] In the realm of defense, for

---

[5]For an illuminating exploration of ways and means to get at a more valid and clear-cut expression of voter preferences for government services, *see* the pioneering work by Howard R. Bowen, *Toward Social Economy*, New York: Holt, Rinehart & Winston, Inc., 1948, especially chap. xviii, "Collective Choice." In this chapter Bowen explores both voting and polling techniques for ascertaining those individual tastes and preferences which cannot find expression in, or be measured by, the market mechanism.

[6]Insofar as voter wants in the public sphere go beyond individualistic preferences to general welfare choices (as Colm, in his article commenting on Samuelson's theory, argues that they not only do, but should), the problem changes form, but the desirability of sharper definition of voter preferences remains undiminished.

[7]No attempt is made here to define a public good. Samuelson (in "The Pure Theory of Public Expenditures," *The Review of Economics and Statistics*, Vol. 36 (November, 1954), p. 387) has defined "collective consumption goods" as those in which one individual's consumption of the good leads to no diminution of any other individual's consumption of that good. McKenna would broaden the definition to include as public goods all those that provide "benefit simultaneously and automatically to more than one member of society." It would seem that while the former definition leaves out many goods provided under the budget principle, McKenna's embraces quite a number provided under the market principle.

example, one successful Russian earth satellite or intercontinental ballistic missile will (and should), outweigh 10,000 economists in determining the appropriate level of expenditures. At most, the economist stands ready to offer analysis and judgments as to the critical levels of defense expenditures beyond which they threaten serious inflation in the absence of drastic tax action or curtailment of civilian programs, or, given that action, threaten impairment of producer incentives and essential civilian programs.

A much more fruitful activity for the economist is to demonstrate the economic advantage offered by government intervention, budgetary and otherwise, in those intermediate service areas where benefits are at least partially divisible and marketable. A number of economists have made useful contributions on this front.[8] In what situations does economic logic point to government intervention to correct the market mechanism's allocation of resources in the interests of greater efficiency in their use?

1. Where there are important third-party benefits (usually known as neighborhood effects, external effects, or externalities) which accrue to others than the direct beneficiary of the service as in the case of education, disease prevention, police and fire protection, the market price and demand schedules underestimate the marginal and total social benefits provided by the service in question. By and large, the direct beneficiaries are the only ones who enter the private market as buyers, with the result that the services would be undervalued, underpriced, and underproduced unless Government entered the transaction. Government is the instrument for representing the third-party beneficiaries and correcting the deficiency of the market place (though this is not to deny that private religious and philanthropic organizations, for example, also represent third-party beneficiaries and operate on budget rather than market principles).

2. Just as there may be indirect benefits not reflected in market demand, there may be indirect costs inflicted on society which do not enter the private producer's costs and therefore do not influence market supply. Classic examples are the costs of smog, water pollution, denuding of forests, and the like. In these areas, private output will exceed the optimum level unless government corrects the situation either by regulation or by a combination of expenditure and charge-backs to the private producers involved.

3. Where a service is best provided, for technical reasons, as a monopoly (e.g., postal service, electricity, railroad transportation), the Government is expected to step in either by regulation or operation to avoid costly duplication and improve the quality of service. Ideally, its function would also be to guide prices toward levels consistent with optimum output. Involved here is the problem of the decreasing cost industry, where efficient plant size is so large relative to total demand

---

[8]*See,* for example, O. H. Brownlee and E. D. Allen, "The Role of Government Expenditure," *Economics of Public Finance,* 2nd ed., chap. x, Englewood Cliffs, N.J.: Prentice-Hall, Inc., 1954. *See* also Max F. Millikan, "Objectives for Economic Policy in a Democracy" (especially pp. 62–68), and Robert Dahl and Charles E. Lindblom, "Variation in Public Expenditure," both in *Income Stabilization for a Developing Democracy,* Max F. Millikan, ed., New Haven, Conn.: Yale University Press, 1953.

175

that average cost decreases as output increases, and the market solution of the output and price problem will not result in best use of the productive assets. To push production to a point representing an ideal use of resources may require, if not Government operation, a subsidy financed out of tax revenues.

4. Government may enjoy some advantages in production or distribution which make it an inherently more efficient producer of certain services. Here, the classic case is highways, streets, and sidewalks. By providing them free to all comers, Government effects substantial savings in costs of distribution since it does not have to meter the service and charge a price for each specific use. In this category we might also fit projects, such as the initial development of atomic energy, which involve such great risks and huge accumulations of capital that the private market does not have the financial tools to cope with them.

ALTERNATIVE MEANS OF CARRYING OUT GOVERNMENT FUNCTIONS

Given the decisions as to the appropriate sphere of Government activity (on the basis not merely of considerations of greatest economic gain but also of value preferences), there remains the problem of choice among alternative methods to implement these decisions, to achieve given aims and satisfy expressed public wants. This choice will affect the budget in different ways. It may increase expenditures, decrease revenues, establish contingent liabilities, or perhaps have no effect on the budget at all (except for a small amount of administrative expenses involved in the supervisory and regulatory activities). Since the operational question is not merely what functions and activities Government should carry out, but what budgetary principles and expenditure levels these lead to, the problem of implementation must be included in any applied theory of public expenditures.

Here, the economist's role is to determine the most efficient method of providing the service or otherwise influencing resource allocation. He is concerned with minimizing costs, i.e., achieving the stated objective with a minimum expenditure of resources. Needless to say, other considerations will also influence the selection among alternative means, as even a brief consideration of the types of choices involved in the implementation process will make clear.

What are these choices? Take first the case of direct satisfaction of individuals' public wants. Should the Government produce the desired public goods or obtain them from private industry by purchase or contract? To accomplish redistributive ends, should the Government provide transfers in cash or transfers in kind?[9] Should Government rely on public production of

---

[9] One involves so-called resource-using (also called factor-purchase or exhaustive) Government expenditures, i.e., payments in exchange for current goods and services rendered, with direct control of resources remaining in public hands. The other involves transfer payments, i.e., payments made without any provision of current goods and services in return, with direct control over resources passing into private hands.

educational services, or should it consider private production combined with earmarked transfers of purchasing power to parents? Thus far, the choices all involve direct budgetary expenditures, the level of which differs, at least marginally, depending on the relative efficiency of the method chosen. But in making his choice, the policymaker must consider not merely the direct costs of providing the service but whether one method involves more or less disturbance of private market incentives and patterns of production than another, whether it involves more or less interference with individual freedom (which is largely a function of the extent of Government expenditures and intervention but certainly in part also a function of the form of that intervention), and so on.

Another set of choices may take the item off of the expenditure side of the budget entirely, or leave it there only contingently. Should such subsidies as those to promote oil and gas exploration, stimulate foreign investment, expand the merchant marine, promote low-cost housing, and increase the flow of strategic minerals take the form of (1) outright subsidies or above-market-price purchase programs, (2) Government loan programs, (3) Government guarantees, or (4) tax concessions? The choice will clearly involve quite different impacts on Government expenditures.

In many of these cases, the economist can be helpful with his efficiency criterion. But one would be naive to think that efficiency alone dictates the choice. The economist may show that a direct subsidy could stimulate a given amount of private direct investment abroad or a given amount of exploration for oil and gas, with a much smaller cost to the budget than is implicitly required in the tax concession method of achieving the same end. Yet, the costlier tax concession method may be preferred for two simple reasons: (1) It is virtually self-administering, involving no administrative hierarchy to substitute its authority for relatively free private decisions, and (2) It does not involve an increase in the expenditure side of the budget, a fact which has certain attractions to the Executive and Congress.

As yet, no clear boundary lines have been drawn among the various forms of Government intervention to mark off those that properly belong within the scope of public expenditure theory. But this illustrative review of the various choices makes clear that some forms of Government activity which are not reflected in expenditures at all (tax concessions) or only contingently (guarantees) are an integral part of such expenditure theory. In fact, there may be stronger case for embracing these in expenditure theory than many Government activities which require budgetary outlays but are conducted on the pricing principle, i.e., Government enterprise activities.

Economists are conducting some provocative inquiries into questions of alternative methods of carrying out Government programs in areas where the answers had heretofore been taken for granted. For example, the transfer of schooling to a private production and Government transfer payment basis has been urged by Professor Milton Friedman as a more efficient means of

177

providing the desired service.[10] Professor O. H. Brownlee is currently probing further into this question, as well as the possibilities of transferring other publicly produced services into the sphere of private production.[11] Once fairly conclusive findings are devised as to the methods most likely to minimize costs, there remains the vital task of blending these findings with the nonmonetary values that would be gained or lost in the process of transferring from public to private production.

SOME CONSTRAINTS ON THE APPLICATION OF SPECIFIC ECONOMIC CRITERIA

Repeatedly in this discussion, the note has been sounded that, in determining the level of Government activity, the policymaker cannot live by economics alone. More particularly, we need to guard against setting up our economic guides solely in terms of those considerations which lend themselves to sharp economic analysis and definition. In other words, the role of both economic and noneconomic constraints must be given full weight.

The former include a host of considerations relating particularly to economic motivation in Government versus private undertakings. Government may, for example, have a decided edge in the efficiency of distribution or be able to achieve a better balancing of social costs and social benefits in a variety of fields. Yet, there may be important offsets to these economic advantages in terms of (1) bureaucracy, (2) lack of the profit criterion to gage the results of Government activities, and (3) undesigned or unintended (presumably adverse) economic effects of taxation.[12]

The latter factor, in particular the fact that tax financing of public services involves breaking the link between an individual's cost of a given service and his benefit from it, may involve important offsets to economic advantages otherwise gained by Government expenditure. Thus far, to be sure, no dire consequences of the disincentive effects of taxation have been firmly proved, but changes in the form of private economic activity to minimize taxes are certainly a cost that must be weighed when netting out the balance of economic advantage in Government versus private performance of services.

---

[10]See Milton Friedman, "The Role of Government in Education," in *Economics and The Public Interest*, Robert A. Solo, ed., New Brunswick, N.J.: Rutgers University Press, 1955, pp. 123–44. In his prescription, Friedman would, of course, have Government regulate the private schools to the extent of insuring that they meet certain minimum standards in their programs and facilities.

[11]O. H. Brownlee, "Prices vs. Taxes," pp. 134–39, in Edmund S. Phelps (ed.), *Private Wants and Public Needs*, New York: W. W. Norton & Company, Inc., 1965.

[12]These less sharply defined economic effects have to be balanced, of course, against comparable and perhaps offsetting drawbacks in the market mechanism. For an exploration of some of these factors, both in the private and the public sphere, *see* Robert A. Dahl and Charles E. Lindblom, *Politics, Economics, and Welfare*, New York: Harper & Row, Publishers, 1953, especially part V. *See* also C. Lowell Harriss, "Government Spending: Issues of Theory and Practices," *Public Finance*, Vol. 12 (1957), pp. 7–19.

Beyond the economic factors, one encounters an even more basic and less manageable constraint, namely that of freedom of choice. Thus, it is quite conceivable that following the kinds of economic criteria discussed earlier in the paper would take us considerably farther in the direction of Government spending and control over resource allocation than we would wish to go in terms of possible impairment of economic and political freedom. This consideration enters importantly not merely in decisions as to the proper range of Government activity but also in choosing among alternative methods of providing Government services.

This is not to imply that all value considerations run counter to the expansion of the Government sector of our economy. Such expansion may serve a number of social values, such as greater equality of income and opportunity, a more acceptable social environment, and so on.[13]

To get all of these considerations into the decision-making equation on private versus public provision of a particular service, or on the choice among alternative forms of providing the service, requires a wisdom which goes well beyond the field of economics. Perhaps this explains why so few economists enter politics.

---

[13]This type of consideration is examined in William Vickrey, "An Exchange of Questions between Economics and Philosophy," in *Goals of Economic Life*, ed. by A. Dudley Ward, New York: Harper & Row, Publishers, 1953, pp. 148–77. *See* also Max F. Millikan, *op. cit.*

SOME OBSERVATIONS ON THE BUDGET CONCEPT

Gerhard Colm and Peter Wagner

During recent years official and nonofficial statements have emphasized the existence of a number of valid concepts of the Budget and the public has become familiar with, and has been greatly confused by, the various computations of the Administrative Budget, the Consolidated Cash Budget, the National Income Budget, to say nothing of references to a possible Capital Budget and an Accrual Budget.

The use of various budget concepts is justified by the fact that the budget serves different purposes. We may distinguish (1) program analysis, (2) financial analysis, and (3) economic analysis. For these purposes there is need for (1) a program budget, (2) a statement showing cash receipts and payments with consequent changes in the national debt, and (3) the Federal sector in the National Economic Accounts or National Economic Budget. The present Administrative Budget performs none of these functions satisfactorily.

While there is justification for the use of different budget concepts for different purposes, we need one budget concept which can be the basis for decisions within the Executive Branch and by Congress concerning the government programs. This basic concept should be the Program Budget. However, the decision-makers, and the public for appraising the actions by the decision-makers, need certain supplementary information. We regard the cash concept and the Federal sector in the National Economic Accounts or National Economic Budget as providing such essential information for the decision-makers and for an appraisal of the significance of government action by the general public.

Therefore, perhaps the most important task is to transform the present Administrative Budget into a true Program Budget. It is fully realized that the transformation of the Administrative Budget into a true Program Budget would involve substantial modifications; the present structure of that Budget—with some items on a cash and others on an accrual basis, and incorporating many other incongruities—has come about solely as a matter of historical accident, and has no logic to recommend it. To become a true Program Budget, the annual aspect of the Administrative Budget must be de-emphasized. Much more emphasis should be placed on

---

Article is from *Review of Economics and Statistics*, Vol. 65, No. 2, Cambridge, Mass.: Harvard University Press, Copyright, 1963, pp. 122–26, by the President and Fellows of Harvard College. Used with permission of publisher and authors.

functional aspects and a clear distinction must be made between programs involving only current expenditures, and others that may take many years to be completed. The Defense Department is moving in this direction under the guidance of Secretary McNamara and Assistant Secretary Hitch. A budget for each program would begin with the total cost of the program until completion, and then would annualize a portion of such cost in accordance with the anticipated schedule of progress of such a program. It is quite unrealistic, in many cases, to show the first year's figures of a specific program, as these may only amount to a fraction of what will ultimately be spent. The NASA program or multi-purpose dam construction are examples in this category.

With respect to the longer-range programs, the Program Budget would primarily give the estimated costs of the program as a whole and only as a secondary estimate a proposed phasing of the expenditures over a number of years. Any estimate of income and expenditures for any particular year must be based on such estimated phasing of the longer-range programs. What is referred to as the Administrative Budget is an estimate of year-by-year receipts and expenditures. Such estimates are based on the authority to incur obligations under existing and proposed programs. However, in translating the programs into yearly expenditures, no clear concept either of cash expenditures or of accruals is used. There are also internal transfers from one fund to another which are not eliminated so that what is called the Administrative Budget does not give a clear picture of all yearly expenditures, either under the cash or the accrual concept.

For purposes of financial planning, particular debt management, it is necessary to use a cash concept and eliminate all intra-fund transactions. Only such a consolidated cash statement permits conclusions with respect to the increase in the government debt either held by the public or by government agencies or government controlled funds. This leads to the first supplementary statement, namely the Consolidated Cash Account. This should take the place of the summary statement which is now given in the Budget document and which is often referred to as the Administrative Budget.[1] However, it should clearly distinguish between those transactions which lead to a change in the government debt held by the public in general (which would include the debt held by the Federal Reserve System and private banks) and the changes in the debt held by government agencies, government corporations, and government trusts.

For appraising the impact of the government operations on the economy in a particular year, another auxiliary statement is needed. For this purpose, a modified version of the Federal sector in the National Income Account is most useful. The word "modified" is used deliberately because the Federal sector of the National Income Account is deficient in one important

---

[1]This article was written before the publication of the 1964 Federal Budget. We are pleased to note that the new Budget incorporates this suggestion to a considerable extent.

respect—it does not include the impact on the economy made by government loans and loan repayments with the exception of price support loans made by the Commodity Credit Corporation. This is a serious shortcoming if we want to measure the Federal Government's influence on the economy. The impact of all Federal transactions, including both loans and expenditures, should be analyzed by their effect on the flow of income and employment. It is not intended to criticize the way the Commerce Department has developed these National Income Accounts. They were not originally designed to furnish guidance in the areas of Federal Finance; and given their original concepts, the loan figures were correctly left out of the Federal sector of the Department of Commerce statement since they appear in another category of their National Income figures. However, if we wish to use the Federal sector account as a guide in the future, the loan transactions of the Federal Government, separating those involving existing assets, must be included.

There is one other aspect that deserves mention in this connection. The economic impact of Federal Loan Insurance and guarantee activities should be stated in a supplement to the modified National Income Account. The economic impact of these programs may be of substantial importance even though they are reflected only with negligible amounts in budget expenditures. All these activities should be readily visible when reviewing the total impact of the government's activities in any one year. In general, it must be left to the user of the information to decide what part of the loans would be extended even if there were no Federal insurance or guarantee. However, insurance operations of such bodies as the FDIC and the FSLIC could be excluded for this purpose.

This modified type of National Income Account is preferred because it is (for the most part, though not entirely) on an accrual rather than on a collection and payments basis, and thus particularly useful in the type of economic analysis which uses the "Nation's Economic Budget" as a framework.

While showing expenditures on an accrual basis is useful for appraising the impact of government actions on the economy, this cannot be a perfect means of measurement. Thus, for example, even the accrual concept as used by the Department of Commerce is deficient in respect to awards for military hardware. In many cases the decisive influence of such awards on the nation's economic activity is initiated by the issue of authorization or the issue of a letter of intent. Thus, supplementary information should be provided which indicates the orders placed and similar facts with an immediate impact on the economy.

The accrual concept of expenditures is superior to the cash concept for measuring the Federal Government's impact on the economy. However, it does not follow that the accrual concept should also be used for the decision-making of Congress. The Hoover Commission had proposed such a shift in order to give Congress more immediate control over Government transactions. Congress had felt frustrated so often because appropriation actions which affect the authority to incur obligations would have little impact on the cash expenditures of the ensuing year, but would have only an impact on the cash expenditures of two or three years later. This led to the idea that appropriations should be based on the accruals, meaning on the work to be undertaken during the ensuing year. Public Law 84–863 provides some step in the direction of an accrual type budget for appropriation purposes. We doubt the desirability of such a development. A shift to accrual basis appropriations would deprive the Federal Government of much-needed flexibility with respect to the longer-range programs. Any change should be in the direction of providing greater flexibility rather than in extending such a restrictive appropriation base in the execution of longer-range government programs.

The proposed Program Budget, in itself, would shift the emphasis for at least a part of the Budget from the short-run to the longer-run aspect. In addition, the informational Federal sector of the nation's Economic Budget should give guidance for policies in support of longer-term growth and stability. For these reasons, it is suggested that complete economic budgets for the nation should be drawn up and presented to Congress for the year under consideration, for the preceding several years, and for a number of years ahead. In addition, a longer-term projection of the national economy ten years hence should be included, and a "flashback" of the position ten years ago would also be useful. While the responsibility for the presentation of the National Income Accounts for the past and current years should remain with the Department of Commerce, projections for National Economic Budgets for future years should be under the responsibility of the Council of Economic Advisers. Such a complete economic budget would include the figures for Federal receipts and expenditures each year. This requires parallel projections of Federal Budgets with the corresponding economic projections. The pricing of future government programs should be the responsibility of the Bureau of the Budget, while projections for resource allocation should be the province of the Council of Economic Advisers.

Concerning future projections of the nation's economy, Congress and the nation can make more meaningful decisions when they can visualize the consequences of these decisions in terms of their impact on future years. Annual budgets should never be viewed in isolation, although this practice did little harm at a time when the Federal sector was of little account in the evaluation of the American economy as a whole. Today when Federal receipts from and payments to the public account for 20-25 percent of our GNP, the trend of such government receipts and expenditures forms an important determinant shaping the course of the economy in future years. Knowledge of the Budget outlook covering a number of years ahead is essential when policy decisions based on budget considerations are being made.

It is most important that long-term outlook projections should be based on a reasonable estimate of economic growth rather than on prediction.

183

Similarly, National Economic Budget projections should be developed in accordance with freely published assumptions rather than as forecasts.

Today, budget estimates of revenues and expenditures pretend to be forecasts, but are really only estimates based on certain assumptions. This is inevitable because departmental estimates have to be prepared for a period up to two years ahead. The present practice has had unfortunate results, evidenced by the wide discrepancies between budget estimates and the actual out-turns. It is also subject to political pressures in the formulation of the underlying assumptions. For example, the temptation to show a balanced budget may have the result of forecasting unduly optimistic economic developments for the preparation of the revenue estimates.

This dilemma could be avoided if the preparation of Federal Budget estimates were based on clearly defined assumptions of a reasonable rate of economic growth. Of course, it is recognized that in practice there would often be deviations from the projected path. The President can deal with these in his Budget Message and the Economic Report which are finalized only shortly before publication. At the same time he could couple this with specific proposals for getting the economy back on the pattern of reasonable economic growth.

The introduction of a separate Capital Budget seems inadvisable. However, all capital expenditure items should be enumerated separately, and should be prominently featured. In this respect, the 1963 Budget tabulation on pp. 25-27 of the Federal Budget Document represents a great advance. More prominence might be given to the capital expenditure content of each budget, and capital expenditures for each agency should be mentioned separately and prominently.

Proponents of the Capital Budget concept maintain that it could be used to justify budget deficits up to the amount spent on such capital items, since even business firms do not find it "unsound" to go into debt for the acquisition of capital assets. However, there is a great deal of difference between business and government accounting. Also, it is felt that the existence of such a separate Capital Budget might distort Federal expenditures in ways that may not always be most desirable. It may well result in a preference for expenditures on physical assets rather than greater spending for intangibles such as health and education. A more convincing case for the introduction of Capital Budgets could be made if we could gradually evolve a concept of capital expenditures which would include both physical assets and investment in human capital as two types of investments in economic growth.

A case can be made for the introduction of Capital Budgets for such agencies as the Post Office where the existence of a chronic perpetual deficit may unduly inhibit the approval of substantial capital expenditure items which would improve efficiency. Also, in the case of FHA, FNMA, and other agencies which are required to operate programs on a self-substaining basis, the separate financing of capital expenditure by means of bonds with redemption dates in alignment with the rate of depreciation of these assets may well be considered, provided their financial operations are geared into the Treasury program for debt management and the general economic situation. The point to be made here is that scope for the useful adoption of capital budgeting in the Federal Government is considerably more limited than proponents of the idea allow, and that, with the exceptions mentioned above, no real economic purpose would be served by the introduction of a separate Capital Budget. However, it would be highly useful if projects could have separate classifications for investment in physical assets and in human capital, but would regard all such expenditures as investments in economic growth.

More education concerning the merits of the proposed Program Budget as well as the two supplementary statements is necessary, not only as regards Congress, but also—and ultimately perhaps even more important—in order to create a better informed public opinion. It is essential that Congress and the general public have a clear idea of the different functions of each of these concepts. Public and Congressional approval of the necessary changes will come more quickly if the various figures shown as Budget out-turns, depending on which of the three concepts has been employed, could be reconciled without too much strain in a similar manner to the process involved when the average citizen reconciles his bank statement at the end of each month.

It is felt that the adoption of these improvements would put us in a much better position to make economic policy decisions on the basis of economic and fiscal data, and would facilitate a more efficient allocation of our resources. Businessmen could make their investment decisions with the full knowledge of government programs for a number of years ahead while economists could make their recommendations with a greater degree of confidence and such recommendations would gain a greater measure of Congressional and public acceptance.

IN SEARCH OF A NEW BUDGET RULE

GERHARD COLM AND
MARILYN YOUNG

The Balanced Budget Role

The search for a new budget rule is predicated on the conviction that the balanced budget rule is not suitable for guiding public policy. Simple as this rule appears, it is meaningless unless it is said what budget ought to be balanced—the conventional budget, the consolidated cash budget, or a budget of current expenditures. Furthermore, there is hardly anybody today who would advocate that a budget should be balanced each year, irrespective of economic circumstances. *It is generally recognized that an attempt to balance the budget under adverse economic conditions may not only aggravate the situation, but may even lead to larger budget deficits than would result from a budget policy designed to support an expansion of markets. No budget rule can be accepted which is not compatible with a policy designed to support balanced economic expansion and stabilization.*

The balanced budget rule is not only deficient from an economic point of view but, also, it has little relevance for the attainment of economy and efficiency in government. It makes little sense if the drive for economy in government is pursued intensively only when a deficit exists or threatens to develop. To the extent that there is extravagance in government, reductions in expenditures should be made, irrespective of whether there happens to be a surplus or a deficit in the budget. It should not be assumed that maximum efficiency has necessarily been achieved when the budget is balanced.

Curtailing important programs such as the national security programs for the purpose of balancing the budget makes again, for different reasons, no sense. Such curtailments must be made on grounds of foreign and military policy, and the world situation. The fact that there happens to be an "X" billion dollar deficit in the budget, does not prove that an "X" billion dollar curtailment in national security programs is the best course of action. *Evaluating the necessity and merits of various programs, and searching for real waste and inefficiency in government operations, are more difficult than an appeal to the balanced budget rule, but the latter cannot be substituted for the former.*

With respect to the method of financing needed programs, whether by taxes or borrowing, it makes more sense to refer to the need for a balanced economy than to the need for a balanced budget. Must we then substitute

Article is from National Planning Association, *The Federal Budget and the National Economy*, Washington, D.C.: The Association, March, 1955, pp. 41–67. Used with permission of publisher and the authors.

the balanced economy rule for the balanced budget rule? Skeptics may say that, by accepting this formula, we would not be substituting a new rule for an outmoded one, but would be abandoning budget rules altogether. Those who have little confidence in economic analysis fear that the balanced economy argument would often be used to rationalize an expenditure, tax, or borrowing policy which might be politically expedient. They insist that the traditional budget rule, in spite of its defects, has one advantage: Once one has agreed which budget is to be balanced, the rule is definite and does not permit argument about its interpretation. This is true, but it is equally true that the balanced budget rule cannot be reconciled with the economic necessities of fiscal policy. Is there any way out of this dilemma? Is it possible to devise a guide for budget policy which establishes some rule of budget policy, and yet avoids the rigidity of the balanced budget rule?

Balancing the Budget over the Cycle

One suggested modification of the balanced budget rule has been the idea that the budget need not be balanced in any one year, but should be balanced over the period of the business cycle, which would include both years of business slack and years of prosperity. The deficit incurred during the bad years would be offset by a surplus during the good years.

This rule presupposes a regularity and foreknowledge of the cycle which actually does not exist. It also presupposes that over the long run a rise in the public debt would not be needed in support of economic growth. While it is possible that during certain periods private expansion and absorption of credit may be adequate for the support of continuing growth, it is equally possible that at times expansion will require that the public debt grow along with the level of total activities. If under such circumstances a budget surplus were enforced in order to repay the debt incurred during a previous recession, the expansion might be brought quickly to a halt.

The rule of balancing the budget over the cycle appears neither feasible nor, as a general rule, desirable. It should be added, however, that recognizing the possibility that the national debt may increase over the cycle does not imply any complacency about a rising national debt *burden*. A rising absolute amount of debt may mean a declining debt burden, if the national income rises more steeply than the interest service on the debt.

Balancing the Consolidated Cash Budget

A step toward loosening up the rigid budget rule is taken when the consolidated cash budget is considered as a guide for budget policy rather than the conventional budget.

The government's financing must be done with broad economic considerations in mind, and the budget statement which is used to guide the government's financial policy should be that which comes nearest to taking account of all government transactions, irrespective of the organizational, administrative, or legal form in which they are conducted. The consolidated

187

cash statement comes much closer to meeting this objective than the conventional budget.

Under prevailing conditions, if the Federal budget, measured in the conventional manner, is balanced, about $4 billion more is collected from the public than is disbursed to the public. The consolidated cash budget can therefore be balanced with about $4 billion less revenue than the conventional budget.

Nevertheless, it cannot be said that a balanced consolidated cash budget means that the government contributes as much to the flow of funds through the economy as it absorbs, or that the government is "neutral," causing neither inflation nor deflation. *For instance, a very large balanced budget is probably more inflationary, or less deflationary, than a smaller balanced budget.* The type of expenditures and the type of taxes, in addition to their amounts, also play a role. Besides, neither the consolidated cash budget, nor any other budget statement, really reflects all government operations.

None of the budget statements reflect government guarantees of private credit, though these guarantees may have much the same economic impact as government outlays. For instance, residential construction financed under an FHA or VA guarantee, which would not appear in the budget, might have much the same economic effects as residential construction financed through outright VA loans, which would appear in the budget. And the economic impact of a lease-purchase agreement for the construction of post offices, the cost of which would be spread in the budget over a period of years, might be similar to that of outright Federal construction of post offices, in which case the full cost would appear in the budget at the time of construction.[1] It should be noted that although the economic effects would be similar in these cases, they would not be precisely the same for there might be different effects on the private credit market.[2] Therefore, even a balanced budget does not mean that government operations are neutral with respect to the economy.

But should the government's budget policy be neutral? *Does not budget policy belong to the instruments which the government, in accord with the Employment Act, should use for promoting economic growth and stability?*

The budget policy which should be pursued depends to a large extent on the effectiveness of other government policy measures which are not, or not fully, reflected in the budget (e.g., credit policy, guarantees, wage and

---

[1]In the case of a lease-purchase agreement, the total government outlays would be greater than they would be in the case of outright government construction.

[2]Subsidies granted in the form of tax privileges (e.g., provisions for accelerated depreciation) provide another example of governmental transactions which affect the economy, but are not visible in the budget. Though subsidies in the form of payments are included among budget expenditures, tax subsidies are reflected only indirectly in reduced revenue. If the subsidies shown in the budget are added up, the result will always be incomplete. Tax subsidies are different from loan guarantees, however, in that tax subsidies do affect the budget surplus or deficit—even though the amount of their effects is unknown.

price policies, and foreign trade policies). Nevertheless, these nonbudgetary policies of the government are not so effective that the government could rely exclusively on them for accomplishing the purposes of supporting steady economic expansion.

Balancing the Budget under Conditions of High Employment

Another approach to the problem of modifying the balanced budget rule was suggested by H. Christian Sonne and Beardsley Ruml in the NPA pamphlet, *Fiscal and Monetary Policy*, published in 1944. They recommended that "tax revenues should balance expenditures at some agreed level of high employment and high production, and should provide for the amortization of the national debt when employment and production exceed those levels; but not before." A footnote qualified the term "balance" by saying that "a budget may be balanced in a financial sense, and still be very much unbalanced in an economic sense."

The idea that taxes should be adequate to meet expenditures under conditions of full employment found many supporters, among them the Committee for Economic Development. This rule requires that for the ensuing year expenditures and revenues should be estimated under the *assumption* that economic activity in the ensuing year will be on a high level. Government expenditure programs and tax measures should be so formulated that the budget thus computed will be at least balanced or, preferably, show a moderate surplus. If booming economic conditions should carry economic activity above what is regarded as a "high" level, tax yields and budget surplus would be higher than estimated. If economic activity should remain below that level, the tax yield would be lower too, and some expenditures (e.g., for unemployment compensation) would rise. Thus, without any change in legislation, a deficit would occur.

Only in case of a truly severe depression should this "built-in" flexibility be supported by a reduction in tax rates and the adoption of *additional* expenditure (e.g., public works) programs. If, under conditions other than a severe depression, additional expenditures should be adopted, additional tax measures would also be needed in order to satisfy the rule. Or if tax rates should be reduced, expenditures should be curtailed correspondingly, so that the budget would remain in balance or yield a moderate surplus under conditions of high employment.

This proposal has several advantages, namely:

1. The rule relates additional expenditures to the need for additional taxes, and tax reductions to curtailments in expenditures. Thereby it serves the requirements of budget discipline.
2. The rule permits deficits when a slack develops in the economy, thereby avoiding the harmful effects of a perverse budget balancing policy which would, in a recession, raise tax rates or curtail expenditure programs, and thereby aggravate the economic difficulties.
3. The rule does not require changes in expenditure programs or revenue legislation based on economic analysis and forecasting (except in

case of severe inflation or depression). Once set for a particular year, expenditure programs and tax rates would not be changed for stabilization purposes, since the variation in tax yields and outlays would occur automatically. It should be mentioned, however, that new projections would be needed yearly for the full employment levels of production, incomes, profits, sales, etc., so that expenditure programs and tax rates could be reset. In a growing economy with a growing tax base, the rule implies that either government expenditures should grow proportionately with the growth of the economy or that tax rates should be gradually reduced.

Compared with these advantages the rule has also several limitations:

1. The rule assumes that a balanced budget or a moderate budget surplus under conditions of high employment is always in accord with the economic requirements of maintaining full employment.

This basic economic assumption can be questioned on the following grounds. During some periods it might be desirable that the government run not only a balanced budget or a small surplus but a very substantial surplus. This could be true, for instance, in case of a boom with inflationary tendencies. On the other hand, there can also be envisaged situations in which individuals, under conditions of high employment, might desire to save more than the amount of private capital which business wished to invest over and above the funds derived through internal business saving. The rule of balancing the budget under conditions of high employment assumes that, under full employment, the amount which private individuals and corporations will desire to save will be no greater than the amount of funds needed for financing private investment. While this may be the case sometimes, there is no assurance that it will always be the case. Many economists believe that there is more reason to expect that, with rising income, over the long run the desire to save may exceed the desire to invest. In any case, the rule is based on an unproven economic assumption.

2. The rule assumes that in case of an economic contraction (short of an emergency) the deficits created automatically by the built-in flexibility of revenues and expenditures will be sufficient to support recovery to the full employment level. What the rule really accomplishes is that it avoids a "perverse" fiscal policy. However, to give positive support to recovery, a reduction in tax rates (not only a drop in yield), and an increase in expenditure programs (not only a rise in expenditures under existing programs), may be needed. Even in the relatively mild recession of 1954, the government found it necessary to reinforce the effects of built-in stabilization by a tax reduction.

3. The rule provides for positive measures of tax reduction or additional expenditure programs only in case of a severe depression. It abandons the notion that fiscal policy measures may be most effective when adopted before a severe depression has developed. Its main dependence on the automatic stabilizers makes it necessary to sacrifice the notion of preventive fiscal action. Policies designed to counteract a depression in the early stages would have to depend on other measures, such as credit and monetary policies.

The rule of balancing the budget (or aiming at a moderate budget surplus) *under conditions of high employment represents a great improvement over the traditional rule of balancing the budget under all conditions.* Its greatest advantage is that it does not necessitate adoption of economically harmful fiscal measures, as would result from adhering strictly to an annually balanced budget in case of economic fluctuations. *The rule fails, however, if fiscal and budget policies are considered as necessary instruments of an active stabilization policy.* Is it possible to further refine the budget rule to make it still more responsive to economic requirements, and yet to maintain some kind of budget discipline?

Balancing the Budget of Current Expenditures

A less restrictive budget policy could be obtained if the balanced budget rule—in the traditional or improved form—should be applied only to the budget of current expenditures. This would permit financing outlays for public investments by borrowing without violating the rule of balancing the budget of current expenditures.[3]

This would have the following advantages:

1. The further modification of the balanced budget rule would permit some government borrowing even under conditions of full employment. If the opinion is correct that in a period of rising income the desire to save may tend to exceed business's needs for outside funds, then this modification would move in the direction of supporting a better balanced economy. If, under certain circumstances, government borrowing for financing of capital outlays should have an inflationary effect, it could be counteracted by a restrictive credit policy on the part of the central bank.

2. This modified rule would also give some leeway for a more active stabilization policy in case of an economic contraction. It would permit stepping up of government investment programs without adoption of additional tax measures.

Thus, this policy would give a somewhat greater scope to an active stabilization policy, designed either to maintain or to restore full employment. On the other hand, this modified balanced budget rule still has certain limitations and possible disadvantages:

1. The rule permits borrowing under conditions of full employment of a maximum amount equal to certain outlays of the government. *However, there seems to be no reason to assume that the amount of borrowing which is required for supporting balanced economic growth should always or even generally happen to be identical with government outlays for specified capital investments.* Furthermore, the significance of this modification depends in part on the definition of capital outlays which is used. And whatever definition is used, if capital outlays are excluded from the current budget, it would become necessary to include in the current budget allowances either for the amortization of loans issued for the financing of the capital outlays, or depreciation allowances for those assets which are taken out of

---

[3]*See* Beardsley Ruml, *A Budget Reform Program*, 1953, and *Budget Reform—Round Two*, 1953.

the current budget.[4] This would somewhat diminish the difference between balancing the total budget and balancing the budget of current expenditures.

2. The proposal exempts capital outlays of a specified nature from the prescription that additional expenditure programs should be financed by additional tax measures. This exemption might introduce a bias into the budget process. The government might be more willing to adopt additional capital programs than other programs, regardless of the respective merits of the programs under consideration. For instance, there might result a tendency to favor large road construction programs as against aids to education irrespective of the relative urgency of the programs.

3. The fact that the rule would permit stepping up of investment programs in a contraction might lead to the freer use of this device, rather than of tax reduction, for combatting a recession—again irrespective of the relative merits of the two policies.

These merits and shortcomings would be more or less common to any form of a policy of meeting current expenditures by tax revenue and capital outlays by borrowing. Proponents of this rule, however, often make the further proposal that capital outlays, should, so far as possible, be administered by government corporations (or authorities), and that these corporations should place their own bonds on the market. Furthermore, these corporations should be entirely "taken out of the budget."[5] Although the question of independent financing of government corporations is only indirectly related to the matter of choosing an appropriate rule for budget policy, some of the ramifications of such a technique may be mentioned here.

Government corporations (or authorities) have proved to be useful instruments for quasi-commercial operations. The corporate form permits more flexible methods of management and budgeting than the departmental organization. It is another question as to whether government corporations should or should not place their own bonds on the market. Good experiences have been had with the revenue bonds of toll road authorities, which sometimes were more attractive to investors than the bonds of the states under whose jurisdiction those authorities operate. In the case of the Federal government, the situation would, however, be quite different. Bonds issued by government corporations without government guarantee would, in all probability, have to carry a higher rate of interest than bonds issued by the Treasury. It should be carefully considered whether outside financing of these public ventures has such advantages that it is worth paying the

---

[4]Inclusion of an amortization allowance in the current budget may be the most natural procedure, if the capital outlays are financed by issues of government corporations, and if the amortization period is in some reasonable relationship to the expected period of useful life of the assets.

[5]It should be mentioned here that, according to established practice, the budget expenditures total includes gross expenditures of general and special funds and the net expenditures of corporations wholly owned by the government, regardless of source of financing. Therefore, self-financing of government corporations in itself would not change the budget total.

additional costs. Furthermore, if very large issues are expected for financing Federal capital outlays, for instance, for a road construction program, their effect on the capital market should be considered.

In general, the government has the responsibility for choosing those methods of financing for public purposes which are most conducive to the maintenance of a high level of employment and production. This may require, under certain circumstances, government financing by short- or middle-term bonds, in order to leave the long-term market for private financing, for instance for housing mortgages. If government corporations should be entirely independent in their financing, they might wish to issue long-term bonds irrespective of general economic considerations.

We have already had the problem of coordinating Treasury and Federal Reserve policies. *If a number of government corporations should independently determine the terms for very large issues, the chance of obtaining a unified Federal economic and financial policy might be further impaired.*

During the 1930's, a number of government corporations had the right to float their own issues. The Treasury was given a sort of veto power. This arrangement did not work satisfactorily, and the Treasury bought most of the bonds issued by the corporations. Subsequently, the issue of such bonds was severely restricted. The government corporations received their advances from the Treasury. The financing of the capital outlays of these government corporations thus became part of the whole financial program of the Treasury. Whatever method of financing government undertakings should be used in the future, it should not reduce but should rather enhance the ability of the government to influence the capital market in the interest of economic stabilization. *Therefore, in case of large-scale financing by government corporations, adequate provision should be made to assure a method of financing which would not work at cross purposes with the objectives of Federal credit policy.*

The separate financing of government corporations has the special appeal that it would demonstrate the independence of capital investments from the budget. It suggests a "business-like" approach. The complete separation of these outlays from the budget, and from Treasury financing, would demonstrate to the public that there is in principle no difference between the floating of a loan for financing a self-supporting road system and the financing of private enterprise. If one believes that it will be in the interest of desirable economic expansion to promote a large amount of investments of this character, it may well be that acceptance by the Congress and the public can be won more easily if they are organized and financed as separate undertakings. This may be a wise policy for obtaining a desirable result with the least resistance.

Before accepting this policy as the only solution available, it should be asked whether there might not be a more direct way in which budget policy could be formulated so as to contribute to economic growth and balance. *However, even if some other formulation of a guide for budget policy should be found and adopted, government outlays for the various projects and functions*

193

should be so classified as to show, at least for information purposes, outlays for capital assets of various characters as distinct from current expenditures for the administration of the various government functions. Such a classification of expenditures can be adopted without taking capital outlays out of the budget and without using the amount of capital outlays as the sole criterion for determining the permissible amount of borrowing.

AN ALTERNATIVE ECONOMIC GUIDE
FOR A BUDGET POLICY

Main reliance on built-in stabilizers in budget policy is advocated most strongly by those who distrust our ability to guide fiscal policy by economic analysis and believe that monetary policy can be used as the main positive tool for promoting stability and expansion. Indeed, the history of economic analysis presents many examples of failure in diagnosis and even more of failure in prognosis. If one is resigned to the futility of a fiscal policy which takes economic analysis into account, some such automatic rule as we have discussed in the preceding chapter is probably the best solution.

If one has a more sanguine opinion of the possibilities of economic analysis, it is possible to envisage a budget rule under which economic analysis would be one of the guideposts for fiscal policy. Not only the immediate but also the longer range economic outlook would be taken into consideration. The experience with longer range or middle-range projections is not discouraging. Certainly more work needs to be done to improve the methods and sources for these projections. Also, they should be revised at least annually. Experience suggests that longer range full employment projections are more reliable than short-run economic forecasts.

In this chapter we spell out one way in which this type of rule might be carried out in practice. One of the main purposes of the proposal is that it would establish an organic relationship between the Economic Report and the Budget Message of the President.

Since there is no getting around the fact that the U.S. economy and the budget of the Federal government to a large extent mutually condition each other, it should be of interest to explore the feasibility of a budget policy guide which consciously is so designed that the fiscal policy of the government might be compatible with, and contribute to, an expanding economy of sustained high employment and stable prices. As a prerequisite for such a guide, it would be necessary that the estimates of budget receipts and expenditures be so presented that they could be viewed in the perspective of the major economic facts and prospects. Only in this manner would it be possible for budget policy to take economic requirements into consideration.

In order to avoid any vagueness, the following sections will spell out a possible procedure. This should be considered, however, more as an illustration than as a specific proposal and recommendation. The same objective could be reached in a number of ways.

194

Economic Analysis as a Guide to Fiscal Policy

As part of a procedure for implementing a budget rule based on economic analysis, the President might include in each Economic Report a projection of potential production under full employment covering a number of years. Also included would be projections of the amounts of goods and services which would probably be absorbed by consumer purchases, business investments, and government programs if existing tax and spending plans of the government and existing attitudes of business, labor, and consumers were to continue. This analysis would show whether markets were likely to fall below potential production, or whether purchases were likely to exceed potential supply (at existing prices). If economic imbalances were indicated, alternative computations would be prepared showing various possible changes in private attitudes and public policies which could bring effective demand and potential demand, and costs and prices, more nearly into balance. Use of such alternative projections would be only a logical refinement of methods developed under the Employment Act of 1946. The feasibility of projections of this kind has been demonstrated by the work of various government agencies, including the Joint Committee on the Economic Report, and private organizations, especially the National Planning Association.

It is a moot question whether the art of projecting national economic accounts, and the familiarity of the public with this tool of analysis, have advanced far enough to give it a formal place in official documents. It is a fact, however, that national economic projections have been widely used for internal policy consideration in government agencies. Some government officials have expressed the opinion that it would not be prudent to publish such projections in state documents—that they should be regarded as work sheets for use only by technicians. If published, such maximum employment projections would be mistaken for forecasts. However, it might be argued on the other side that, as far as we know, the projections of the Joint Committee Staff and the National Planning Association have not led to such misinterpretations. Many business firms are using economic projections regularly for providing a frame of reference for investment budgeting and other purposes of business management. Accordingly, the technique can no longer be regarded as merely experimental. Furthermore, it is difficult to see how the public can learn to appreciate these modern tools of economic analysis if it is not familiarized with them. It is immaterial whether these projections should be included as an integral part of the President's Economic Report, or whether the text of the Report should show only the main results of the projections— with details given in an appendix.

Based on alternative computations and on any other evidence which he deems pertinent, the President would recommend in the Economic Report a variety of economic policy measures, including changes in government programs and tax policies. This would be in line with the provisions of the Employment Act. The proposal would go beyond the provisions of the

195

Employment Act only in that the President would be specifically required to formulate his program in a longer run perspective.

Parallel to the economic projections in the Economic Report, there would also be presented a corresponding "budget outlook" in the Budget Message. The budget outlook would present projections of Federal expenditures and revenues over the same number of years covered by the economic projections. The budget outlook, like the projections in the Economic Report, would be based on a full employment assumption. By including economic projections and budget projections for the same number of years in the Economic Report and the Budget Message respectively, the interrelation between economic analysis and fiscal policy would be clearly demonstrated.

In order to show the importance of the recommended changes in the President's program, the budget estimates would be computed first under the assumption that existing policies would be continued, and second, under the assumption that the President's recommendations would be adopted. Presumably, the latter estimates would be consistent with the promotion of a balanced and expanding high level economy; they would fit into the economic full employment projections. Of course, not all recommendations for changes in expenditure or revenue policies would be motivated by the need to support balanced economic growth. Expenditure programs would be recommended primarily on their own merits. However, the method of financing—that is, the amount of taxation and borrowing or debt redemption—would be determined primarily in line with long-range economic considerations. Estimates for the first two years, the current and the ensuing year, would be presented in considerable detail; estimates for a number of additional years would be presented in a tentative and less detailed manner. The estimates would use the consolidated cash basis and would be accompanied by a statement of expected changes in government assets and liabilities covering the same period as the budget outlook.

The budget outlook would show for each year and the period as a whole a balanced cash budget, an excess of receipts, or an excess of expenditures, depending on the appraisal of the factors supporting or hindering balanced economic growth. Among the factors to be considered in determining the budget would also be the expected effectiveness of other economic policies, such as credit policy, tariff policy, etc.

Expenditures and revenues would be estimated on the assumption of approximately full employment and production. In this respect, the budget guide would work in the same manner as the rule previously described. The only difference is that the President would not necessarily set expenditures and revenues so that they would be balanced or show a moderate surplus at the high employment level. Depending on the long-range economic analysis, expenditures and revenues might be set at levels which imply either a budget surplus or a deficit. Exactly as in the case of the previously discussed rule, the expenditures and revenues would be permitted to fluctuate in response to changes in economic conditions. Assume, for example, that expenditures and

196

revenues were set so that the budget would show an excess of outlays of $5 billion under conditions of maximum employment. Then in case of an inflationary rise of incomes this deficit would automatically be diminished or transformed into a surplus. In the case of unemployment the deficit would automatically become larger. If, however, the President deemed it desirable that expenditure programs or tax rates be changed in order to support economic expansion and stability, it would be his responsibility to make the appropriate recommendations to Congress. Any recommendation for changes in expenditure programs that require congressional action or tax legislation, would be presented in an Economic Report demonstrating the necessity for these changes. *In other words, the effect of the built-in stabilizers would be re-enforced by affirmative measures if and when such changes in policy appear necessary—and not only when a severe depression has occurred.*

If the long-term budget outlook showed an excess of expenditures over receipts, the President would have to present an appraisal of the significance of this fact both in economic and financial terms. The computation in the Economic Report would show why financing some portion of government outlays by borrowing appeared necessary for promoting balanced economic growth. The statement of changes in assets and liabilities in the budget would show the effect of the expected deficit on the financial position of the government.

In addition, there might be a computation which would show the effect of borrowing on future tax requirements. Most government programs—except those for national security—have (or should have) a direct or indirect favorable effect on productivity and future output and income. Therefore, they are likely to contribute to an expansion of the future tax base and tax yields. Except in the case of national emergencies, the rise in tax yields which results from an expanding economy should be more than adequate to finance any increase in debt service which might take place. *In other words, borrowing, except under emergency conditions, should not necessitate an increase in tax rates for meeting a rising interest burden.* While this rule may be regarded as setting an upper limit to borrowing, it should by no means be assumed that borrowing up to that limit is always economically justified.

Reconciliation of Economic Policy and Political Strategy

This procedure would assure that an excess of expenditures would not be recommended simply because the sum of all desirable expenditure programs happened to exceed politically acceptable taxes. If there were an excess of expenditures shown in the budget, it would have to be justified by the analyses and computations presented in the Economic Report. Let us assume that the Economic Report indicated a need for a $5 billion excess of cash outlays for a specific year (assuming, for instance, $65 billion of expenditures and $60 billion of revenue). Let us further assume that in the process of congressional deliberation on the budget it turned out to be desirable to add a further $2 billion expenditure program. Then there should also be a $2 billion addition to revenues, either through an increase in tax rates or the imposition of new taxes. Conversely, if, subsequent to the determination of the over-all budget, a proposal should be made to reduce tax rates, it should be combined with a proposal to reduce expenditures.

Thus this procedure would be compatible with the principle that an addition to expenditures should be financed by additional tax measures, and that reduction in taxes should be related to a curtailment of expenditures. But in this case additions or reductions would be related to an economically and financially justified frame of reference. Depending on the requirements of balanced economic growth, the base to which additions and reductions were related might be a balanced budget, a budget with an excess of revenues, or one with an excess of payments. *It seems to us that we could have budget discipline with a balanced budget, a budget surplus, or a budget deficit.* Budget discipline then means that claims for additional expenditures would not lead to unsound financial policy, "sound" policy being defined as a policy in accord with the requirements of balanced economic growth.

There may be those who fear that the economic and financial analysis would be used only for rationalizing a politically expedient budget deficit. We can only answer that no system can work without some degree of intellectual integrity on the part of the people who are entrusted with the operation of the system. And it should be emphasized that this whole procedure is predicated on the belief that economic analysis can at least give us usable working hypotheses.

Increasing Budget Flexibility

Budget estimates, particularly of receipts, are often based on continuation of the level of economic activity prevailing at the time the estimates are made. This assumption seems to involve the least commitment. It is almost inconceivable that the President would predict a downswing extending 18 months ahead, since thereby he would admit failure in the efforts toward full employment to which the government is committed under the Employment Act. On the other hand, he is subject to criticism of unjustified optimism when he predicts a rise in the level of economic activity and expected tax receipts.[6]

This dilemma would be avoided if the budget projections were regularly based on a full employment *assumption* of the character discussed in the previous section. It would have to be made clear, however, beyond any doubt, that these estimates were not forecasts but were based on assumptions. In

---

[6]The President's budget estimates for fiscal year 1956 are based on the expectation that the level of economic activity will increase. The Budget Message of January 17, 1955, states that "[if present tax rates are extended and if] employment and production increase as currently anticipated, we can expect budget receipts to rise 1 billion dollars over 1955, to a total of 60 billion dollars in the fiscal year 1956."

In a statement to the press, the Secretary of the Treasury stated that the receipts estimates are based on the assumption that personal income will increase from $286.6 billion in calendar year 1954 to $298.5 billion in calendar year 1955, and that corporate profits will increase from $36.0 billion in 1954 to $38.5 billion in 1955. It should be noted that these are economic forecasts and not full employment projections.

order to drive home the hypothetical character of the budget estimates, it might be wise, at least occasionally, to include in the text of the budget hypothetical estimates which would show the effect which an economic downturn would have on revenue and expenditures.

In a budget based on a full employment assumption it would be desirable that there should be a contingency appropriation for expenditure programs which would rise even in case of a mild slack—for instance, the administration of unemployment compensation. However, allowances which would be needed only in case of an economic slack might be kept in reserve and the funds released by the Budget Bureau only in case of need. Only in case of a threatening or actual depression should it be necessary for the President to request of Congress supplemental appropriations.

A further method for introducing some budget flexibility for an anticyclical policy would be the setting up of two appropriation procedures, one for operating expenditures, and one for nonroutine programs which are suitable for anticyclical variation. Operating expenditures are usually authorized by yearly appropriations which lapse if unobligated at the end of the year unless specifically reappropriated. Nonroutine programs, at the present time, are sometimes appropriated for on the same yearly basis, sometimes on the basis of several years, and sometimes with the stipulation that the funds appropriated are "to remain available until expended." *It would be desirable if appropriations for all nonroutine programs could remain available until expended.* These programs would presumably include most public works and other capital outlays. The criterion for including a project in this category would be the ease with which it could be deferred or initiated earlier than originally planned, or stepped up or slowed down. In short, these would be programs especially suitable for cyclical variations.

Congress might appropriate each year funds for a number of projects which would under normal conditions be carried out over a period of several years. The executive could be authorized to step up or slow down these projects within the limits of the appropriation as an instrument of an anticyclical policy. In the Federal six-year program for public works, there already exists a starting point for the development of such a long-range program of nonroutine expenditures. This procedure may have some advantages compared with the proposal of building up a substantial shelf of public works.[7]

It is doubtful that it would be desirable or feasible to delegate to the executive the authority to change tax rates as an anticyclical device. However, it would be desirable if a simplified legislative procedure for anticyclical changes in tax rates could be worked out.

---

[7]Completely aside from economic considerations, but rather as a means of expediting the government's business, an experiment might be made in appropriating funds on a biennial basis for some of the routine activities of government. State governments often make biennial appropriations in routine fields and thus spare themselves annual repetitions of the full budget process.

Legislative Establishment of Guides for Budget Policy

It could be said that no legislative implementation would be needed for putting the foregoing procedure into effect. The President, under the Budget and Accounting Act as amended, is free to submit the budget in any way he chooses. Also, there is no limitation put on the number of years for which the President may submit budget estimates and recommendations. Finally, the Act does not prescribe the conditions under which the President should recommend an increase or decrease in taxes. Therefore, everything discussed in the preceding section could be adopted by the Chief Executive without any change in legislation. Nevertheless, it might be desirable to adopt some of the guides for setting up the budget by amendment of the Budget and Accounting Act. Such an amendment would dramatize for the country as a whole the desirability of these guidelines. They would be more widely understood and accepted if they were seen to represent not only the President's choice but also the will of Congress. Any such amendment would have to be written, however, in a way that would not freeze into legislation technical details which would deprive the Executive of the flexibility which might be needed in case of unforeseen circumstances.

Process of Congressional Consideration of the Budget

It would be desirable to improve the method by which Congress gives consideration to the budget transmitted by the President.

The unsuccessful experiment with a legislative budget, which was mentioned above, grew out of the desire for the creation of one body which could look at the budget as a whole before the various appropriation committees began their specific work.[8] A number of reasons have been mentioned for the failure of this unhappy legislative experiment. One of the reasons for this failure may have been the fact that this experiment was made at a time when there was a great deal of conflict between the legislature and the executive. However, it is to be expected that such periods of strain between the legislative and the executive arms of the government will occasionally occur. Also, the Joint Committee on the Legislative Budget was much too large to be workable. It consisted of the full membership of the Appropriation Committees of both Houses and of the Ways and Means Committee and the Senate Finance Committee. Finally, the legislative budget was concerned with setting ceilings for expenditures for the ensuing year, whereas the expenditures for the ensuing year are actually largely determined by the legislation and appropriations of previous years.

From this experience the following conclusions could be drawn: First, the committee concerned with the budget should be a small but very powerful one; second, this committee should concern itself less with expenditures for the next year than with basic legislation and appropriations which will affect expenditures over a number of years.

---

[8]*See* the discussion of George B. Galloway in *The Legislative Process in Congress,* New York: Thomas Y. Crowell Co., 1953, pp. 123 ff.

As one possibility, the function of examining the economic aspects of the budget as a whole might be assigned to the Joint Committee on the Economic Report. This committee cannot fulfill the functions which were given to it under the Employment Act of 1946 without consideration of the economic aspects of the budget. It must concern itself with the overall aspects of fiscal policy anyway. It has the advantages of being small (14 members) and of having an efficient staff experienced in fiscal analysis. If it were given this additional function, it might be renamed "The Joint Committee on Economic and Fiscal Policy."

Here we will not go into the question of the desirability of change in the composition of this Joint Committee. However, it may well be contended that a committee which is designed to give advice to the various legislative committees of Congress and to Congress as a whole should include the leadership of the two parties as well as individual members of the Senate and the House who, because of their own predilections, are particularly interested in serving on a committee concerned with economic and fiscal matters. If this committee should be given the duty of contemplating and reporting on both economic policy and budget financing as a whole, it would become one of the most important congressional committees.

If, by amendment to the Budget and Accounting Act, the President should be obliged to submit a budget outlook in the form in which it has been described above, then the Joint Committee might have the function of examining this budget outlook and of preparing a report of its own appraising the estimates and recommendations included in it. On the basis of this appraisal, the Joint Committee would prepare a report on the economic outlook and on the approximate levels of budget expenditures over a five-year period, and state what part of these expenditures should, if possible, be financed by taxation and what part by borrowing. *The Committee would be concerned with expenditure, revenue, and debt programs only to the extent that they are related to economic growth and stability.* The recommendations of the Joint Committee would then be considered by the appropriate legislative committees and the Congress as a whole.[9]

---

[9] A similar proposal was made by the Committee for Economic Development in a statement on *Control of Federal Government Expenditures*, January, 1955. The CED proposal differs from the proposal made by the National Planning Association in a Joint Statement of December, 1954 in that the CED proposes that the economic aspects of the budget be considered by a Joint Budget Policy Conference which "would include several members of the Congressional leadership and majority and minority representatives from the appropriations and revenue committees and the Joint Committee on the Economic Report."

We believe that such a Joint Budget Policy Conference would suffer from difficulties similar to those encountered by the Joint Committee on the Budget (established in accordance with the Legislative Reorganization Act of 1946). We think it would be more advantageous to have this function performed by the same group which has developed teamwork in the examination of the President's Economic Report. It would be up to them to bring their findings to the attention of the appropriate committees dealing with expenditures, revenue, and debt management.

We notice that in a dissenting footnote to the CED statement, Mr. J. D. Zellerbach, with the concurrence of Fred Lazarus, Jr., subscribed to the same position which was recommended in the NPA Joint Statement.

In several other countries, motions which add to the budget once it is formulated must be accompanied by motions proposing the way in which the additional expenditures are to be financed. Correspondingly, a motion which proposes a tax reduction must be accompanied by a motion proposing a corresponding reduction in expenditures or increase in borrowing. One might consider whether a rule of this kind would be useful and feasible under the conditions of the American congressional scene. In itself the rule would not mean very much. No rule could deprive Congress of the right of voting additional expenditures or curtailing taxes if the majority of Congress sees fit to do so, and if the President does not veto the proposal or cannot have his veto sustained. Nevertheless, such a rule would at least force every Senator or Representative who proposes additional expenditures or tax reductions to explain how they would fit into the long-range budget outlook as recommended by Congress, and what additional measures they might necessitate. It would emphasize what we have called the need for budget discipline.

It is certain this idea of combining the examination of fiscal and economic policies in one Joint Committee might meet serious objections. One important task would be that of establishing a workable relationship between the Joint Committee on the one hand, and the various committees concerned with appropriations, tax legislation and credit policies on the other. Another question relates to the ability of the technicians in the executive and legislative branches to prepare the meaningful economic projections and budget outlook estimates which the procedure requires. These considerations make it unlikely that an early adoption of this procedure will be possible. Nevertheless, it may be worthwhile to contemplate something which may appear as an ideal procedure even though, at best, only a step-by-step adoption appears feasible. However, at least a gradual movement in this direction seems to be desirable in order to assure that a fiscal policy be developed which makes its fullest contribution to economic growth and stability.

THE TIMING OF THE ECONOMIC IMPACT OF GOVERNMENT SPENDING

Murray L. Weidenbaum

The economic impact of a government spending program may occur at the time the disbursements are made or, depending on the nature of the program and the state of the economy, during earlier stages of the governmental spending process. This study indicates the possible effect on economic activity of each major stage of the process.

EFFECTS OF AN INCREASE IN GOVERNMENT SPENDING: THE SIMPLE CASE

Four phases of the federal spending process are highlighted: (1) enactment of appropriations, (2) placement of government contracts with the private sector, (3) production in the private sector, and (4) delivery to and payment by the public sector. A number of initial assumptions are made so that the effects on the economy arising directly from an increase in government spending can be readily examined. More complicated situations are dealt with subsequently.

An increase in government spending is assumed which consists entirely of expenditures for goods and services currently produced in the private sector of the economy. These expenditures are financed by borrowing idle funds. It is also assumed that there are sufficient idle resources and mobility in the economy to produce the goods and services without new fixed business investment or price or wage increases and without displacing any private demand. Also postulated is the availability of adequate financing for the government contractors. This increase in government spending generates no indirect effects on consumer or business expectations nor any changes in other government programs.

Phase I. Appropriation of Funds

The President transmits to the Congress an appropriation request which it enacts after due deliberation. Under the assumed conditions, there is no immediate effect on the economy as measured by any indicators of economic activity, such as GNP or the index of industrial production, or any of the lead series, such as the volume of new orders. Neither is there yet any change registered in any of the measures of government spending.[1] This stage may take one to two quarters of a year, on the average.

Article is from *National Tax Journal*, Vol. 12 (March, 1959), pp. 79–85. Used with permission of publisher and author.

[1]The series on budget expenditures, cash payment, and government purchases all measure essentially the payment stage of the spending process (Phase IV).

Phase II. Placement of Contracts

The government agency to which the appropriation is made places contracts with business firms in the private sector of the economy. The following are some of the events that would flow from the receipt by a manufacturer of a government order for items used by the government as well as by private industry.

He finds that he cannot fill the new order out of existing inventory or even from existing production lines. The additional volume of production can be obtained through more intensive utilization of existing capacity, requiring increases in inventories and working capital. On the basis of the company's past performance and the government order, the contractor obtains approval from his bank for a working-capital loan. The contractor begins to place orders for materials, to hire additional workers, and to subcontract parts of the order to other firms.

The first effect on economic activity will now be taking place. As deliveries begin to be made on raw materials and wages are earned by the first of the newly-hired workers who are tooling-up, the contractor will be drawing upon his loan authorization and making small amounts of payments to the various factors of production. An increase will be registered in the outstanding loans of the commercial banks and in the total money supply. Also, an increase will occur in gross private domestic investment, the component of GNP which contains the inventory accumulation resulting from the increased amounts of goods in process.

The economic activity represented by contract placements is not reflected in any of the generally used measures of government spending. These contracts are included, but not identified separately, in the reports by the Department of Commerce on new orders received by business firms. That the placement of government orders ("obligations incurred" by the federal agencies) is the phase of the government spending process which energizes private production on government account has been noted by a number of observers:

> The initial stimulus to production is provided by government contracts for procurement.[2]
> ... it is the placing of a contract, or its anticipation, which leads industry to plan its acquisition of materials and labor and to schedule its production ...[3]
> ... A change in the tempo of Government ordering is not immediately reflected in expenditures.

---

[2]Melvin Anshen and Francis D. Wormuth, *Private Enterprise and Public Policy.* New York: The Macmillan Company, 1954, p. 530.

[3]John Perry Miller, *Pricing of Military Procurement.* New Haven: Yale University Press, 1949, pp. 24–25.

204

But business is affected at once. When the flow of orders accelerates, the wheels of industry turn faster. When it decreases, output and employment drop.[4]

It is in the stimulus of productive activity rather than in the minor amounts of initial "make-ready" production that the contract-placement stage exercises an important effect on economic activity.

Phase III. Production of Goods

As quantity production gets under way on the government order, payments are made by the government contractor for wages to the employees engaged in the work, materials delivered, and the interest due on the working-capital loan. He will also be accruing profits on the order.[5] The costs incurred by the contractor during the entire production period should total the amount of the order. These outlays of government contractors are not reflected in government purchases of goods and services nor in any other government-expenditures series at the time they are made. They will currently show up in GNP—in the change in inventory segment of gross private domestic investment—to the extent they are not met by private inventory decumulation elsewhere. The amount of production on government orders remaining in business inventories during a given period cannot be identified in the available statistics and, hence, the amount of production carried on in the private sector on government account cannot be measured. Only a general idea can be obtained from series on contracts placed and deliveries made.

On the income side, increases will be registered in compensation of employees, corporate profits, rental income and, depending on the legal status of the contractor and subcontractors, earnings of unincorporated enterprises. Increases in consumer expenditures also occur as a result of these income payments. The exact amount of this secondary contribution to the increase of total output would depend on the marginal propensity to consume.

This stage may last from one quarter up to two years or more depending on the production time involved.

Phase IV. Payments for Goods

During Phase IV the contractors deliver to the government the goods which they have produced during Phase III. Following inspection, payment

---

[4]Murray G. Lee, *The Effects of Treasury Operations*. New York: American Bankers Association, 1955, p. 9.

[5]"It is ... a generally accepted accounting procedure to accrue revenues under certain types of contracts and thereby recognize profits, on the basis of partial performance. ... Particularly where the performance of a contract requires a substantial period of time from inception to completion. ..." American Institute of Accountants, *Restatement and Revision of Accounting Research Bulletins*, 1953, p. 95.

is made by the government. Several economic effects of this activity can be discerned.

The delivery of the equipment shows up as a decline in business inventories and, hence, in gross private domestic investment. It also is recorded as a government purchase of goods and services. These two movements tend to cancel each other out with no net effect on GNP. The government purchases do not represent payments to the factors of production but are more in the nature of intersectoral transfers—reimbursements to the government contractor for his outlays during the previous period.

Following the payment by the government, the contractor repays the working-capital loan. These actions reduce the amount of private credit, reduce the government's cash balances, and increase the cash position of the firm doing business with the government. The contractor can now disburse dividends, or set aside funds for tax payments, future expansions, or merely an improved cash position.

This is the period during which the government purchase shows up as a budget expenditure and a cash payment to the public.

Table 1 illustrates the relationship through time between the four major stages of the federal spending process and aggregate economic activity, based on a change in a federal spending program of 50.

Given the simplifying assumptions which have been made, the following is the sequence in which the various stages of the governmental spending process ordinarily enter into the movements of total economic activity.

1. The enactment of an appropriation indicates the size of a government spending program (for the period for which the funds are appropriated), but is not reflected in any measure of current economy activity.

2. The placing of government contracts and orders with the private sector gives rise to the beginning of production, and, hence, furnishes a measure of the early (and potential) impact of government spending (i.e., procurement) on the economy.

3. The actual production in the private sector on government account shows up in GNP as additions to business inventories. This is the stage when government contractors make disbursements for wages and materials. Because of the deficiencies in our knowledge, we cannot measure the magnitude of the private production on government account. Increases in consumer spending also occur during this period as a result of the payments to factors.

4. The completion of production of the goods and services ordered results in deliveries from the private sector to the government. This is the stage where the government spending program shows up as government purchases. With the simultaneous decline in private inventories of a corresponding amount, no net effect on GNP occurs during this period. However, this is the point at which the government generally makes its expenditures for the goods and services delivered to it—when this activity is recorded as a budget expenditure and a cash payment.

TABLE 1
ILLUSTRATIVE IMPACT OF THE MAJOR STAGES
OF THE GOVERNMENT SPENDING PROCESS

Stage	Inventory Accumulation	Government Purchases	All Other	GNP
Authorization..........	....	....	....	....
Contract placement*.....	+ 5	....	....	+ 5
Production.............	+45	.....	....	+45
Payment...............	− 50	+50	....	....

*Includes tooling-up expenses incurred prior to quantity production getting underway.
Notes: 1. Amounts shown are changes from the levels obtaining in period "O." 2. Only direct and primary effects are shown. Fluctuations likely to arise from other causes are not shown here or in subsequent amplifications.

RELAXING THE SIMPLIFYING ASSUMPTIONS

Some of the effects on the economy of the various phases of the governmental spending process may be examined under more complicated circumstances than in the previous section.

Anticipatory Effects

The government's act of embarking on a large new program can have a positive expectation effect on consumers and business under certain circumstances. Such was the case in the early stages of the Korean mobilization program when memories of World War II price rises and shortages set off a wave of private ordering and buying in advance of government purchasing.

Table 2 shows, in an idealized fashion, how favorable expectations resulting from the government embarking upon a new spending program (of 50) can be superimposed on the direct effects of such a program. The subsequent developments are similar to those in Table 1, except that the "second round" effect on consumer spending is specifically indicated here.

The anticipatory effect of government spending is too diffuse and elusive to be measurable. We simply do not know what the actions of businessmen and consumers in a given period would have been in the absence of the anticipatory effect of government activity.

TABLE 2
A NEW GOVERNMENT SPENDING PROGRAM
GIVING RISE TO FAVORABLE EXPECTATIONS

Stage	Consumer Expenditures	Inventory Accumulation	Government Purchases	All Other	GNP
Authorization.......	+10	+10	....	....	+20
Contract placement..	....	+ 5	....	....	+ 5
Production........	+35	+45	....	....	+80
Payment..........	+ 5	− 50	+50	....	+ 5

Availability of Resources

Unutilized capacity may not always be present. Substantial amounts of new investment may be necessary before production commences. In this

207

case, the production by private business includes additions to private plant and equipment needed to produce the government-ordered goods as well as actual production on the goods destined for government use. Table 3 shows the operation of these two different types of production activities arising from government orders.

TABLE 3
GOVERNMENT SPENDING REQUIRING PRIVATE INVESTMENT

Stage	Consumer Expenditures	Fixed Investment	Inventory Accumulation	Government Purchases	GNP
Authorization.......	....	....	....	....	....
Contract placement..	....	....	+ 5	....	+ 5
Investment.........	....	+10	....	....	+10
Production.........	+35	....	+45	....	+80
Payment...........	+10	....	−50	+50	+10

Under a situation of relatively full utilization of resources, the letting of additional government contracts may simply result in accumulations of backlogs. Placing contracts by the government would not immediately energize private production. Attempts by the government to bid away resources from private uses could result in rises in prices. There would not be any real increase in the production of the economy, except that resulting from changes in the product mix. Where the government resorts to material controls and allocation systems, the backlogs may accumulate in the private sector rather than in the work on government contracts. There would be no effect on the aggregate level of economic activity during any part of the government spending program. The authorization of the new spending program could not give rise to any changes in consumer and business outlays (resulting from changes in expectations) nor could the contract letting lead to any expansion in the volume of production. As a result, when production of the government-ordered goods is completed, there would be an increase in government purchases and an equivalent decline in consumer expenditure and/or business fixed investment, depending on which private demands were displaced.

Financing Private Production

It was assumed earlier that the government contractor can obtain financing and thus, once facilities and materials are available, can effectively carry on government-ordered production. It has been observed that the need for short- or long-term borrowing to finance current operations becomes much greater when a contractor embarks upon the performance of government contracts:

> Capital borrowings in the performance of Government contracts are frequently made necessary because of common delays in obtaining payment such as the slow processing of invoices, delays encountered in obtaining definitive contractual instruments authorizing payment, Government revisions of delivery schedules which delay or stretch out

deliveries over a longer period, thereby prolonging investments in inventories, and other Government action ...[6]

Both fiscal and monetary tools can affect private finance. In the absence of governmental assistance, there may be substantial financial as well as technological limits to large-scale expansion of production on government orders. As can be seen by the large array of governmental devices designed to ease the financing problems of government contractors and by the performance of the American economy during wartime, these financial limitations have generally not been controlling.

Financing the Government Expenditures

It was assumed earlier that the government payments to contractors would be financed by borrowing idle funds. Obviously, other financial techniques could alter the expansive effect of government purchases, but these matters are better treated as separate monetary and fiscal policy issues.

Changes in Rates and Levels of Government Spending

"Follow-on" orders—those which extend and maintain existing production—tend to result in continued stability rather than any net increment in total demand. Table 4 assumes that "follow-on" orders are placed which maintain the level of private production achieved with the original orders. The levels achieved during period 4 (when payment is made on the first series of contracts) are merely maintained in period 5 and beyond.

TABLE 4

ILLUSTRATION OF ACHIEVING A HIGHER LEVEL OF GOVERNMENT SPENDING

Stage	Consumer Expenditures	Inventory Accumulation	Government Purchases	GNP
Period 1 Authorization of program A	+10	+ 5	....	+ 15
Period 2 Contracts for program A	....	+ 5	....	+ 5
Authorization of program B	+10	+ 5	....	+ 15
Period 3 Production—A	+35	+45	....	
Contracts—B	....	+ 5	....	+100
Authorization—C	+10	+ 5	....	
Period 4 Payment—A	+10	−50	+50	
Production—B	+35	+45	....	+110
Contracts—C	....	+ 5	....	
Authorization—D	+10	+ 5	....	
Period 5, etc. Payment—B	+10	−50	+50	
Production—C	+35	+45	....	+110
Contracts—D	....	+ 5	....	
Authorization—E	+10	+ 5	....	

[6]National Security Industrial Association, *Report to Commission on Organization of the Executive Branch of the Government Regarding Military Procurement*, Washington, D.C., 1954, p. 57.

It should be noted there that the permanency of the change in the amount of government procurement is important. Where businessmen and consumers believe that an increase in government spending will be lasting, they may react, particularly in investment decisions, far more fully than if they regard such increases as merely transitory.

SUMMARY

The magnitude of changes in the various phases of the Federal spending process can have important economic effects under many circumstances; an awareness of these surrounding circumstances is essential to an adequate analysis of these changes in government spending patterns.

The very act of announcing and authorizing a new or increased spending program—the granting of new obligational authority—can sometimes give rise, by affecting expectations, to positive or even negative changes in business and consumer spending in advance of the actual letting of contracts or disbursement of government funds.

The act of placing contracts and incurring other obligations may not always signal the onset of production. The needed production facilities may not be readily available or backlogs of orders may first have to be worked off. Also additional working capital may be required. On the other hand, the government order may be filled out of inventory and no effect on economic activity would take place until some time later.

In addition to the direct effects of the government expenditure there will be the accompanying effects of the financing of this outlay. These are questions of monetary and fiscal policy primarily.

Although all of these complications may modify the effect on the economy of a program of government procurement from private industry, the basic relationships generally hold: The primary effect on productive activity (to the extent there is any) occurs in advance of the actual government expenditures. Under most of the circumstances that have been examined, the placing of orders induces (either immediately or after a delay) production on government account and such production remains in the private sector and does not show up as government expenditures until it is completed and the goods involved delivered to the public sector.

PUBLIC VERSUS PRIVATE:
COULD GALBRAITH BE WRONG?

Henry C. Wallich

In addition to free advice about growth, the nation has received helpful suggestions of another sort, in a rather opposite vein. It has been argued that we have all the production we need and to spare, but that too much of our growth has gone into private consumption, too little into public. We are said to be wasting our substance on trivia while allowing urgent public needs to go uncared for. This view does not complain of inadequate growth. But it sees us riding in tail-finned, oversized automobiles through cities that are becoming slums, finds our children sitting glued to the latest TV models but lacking schools where they can learn to read properly, and generally charges us with putting private profligacy ahead of public provision.

The general doctrine that in the United States public needs tend to be underfinanced in relation to private I first heard many years ago from my old teacher Alvin Hansen. It has always seemed to me to possess a measure of appeal. Throughout this book, I have been at pains to argue that with rising wealth and industrialized living, the need for public services advances, and probably faster than living standards. In part this reflects simply the familiar fact that the demand for services tends to expand faster than the demand for goods. In part, the social conditions of modern life are also accountable for the growing need for government services. Private business is learning to meet many of these new needs—for instance in the field of insurance. It is not inconceivable that some day we shall become rich enough to be able to indulge increasingly a preference for privately supplied services. But at present, and as far ahead as one can see, the trend seems the other way. I would footnote this reference by observing that to recognize a rising trend in the need for public services and to claim that at present we have too little of them, are two different things. The more than doubling of federal and also of state and local expenditures since 1950 should drive home that distinction.

The thesis that public services are neglected and private consumption inflated with trivia has found its most eloquent interpretation in *The Affluent Society* by John Kenneth Galbraith, to whom we were previously indebted for important insights into the workings of American capitalism. Galbraith argues that this imbalance is nourished by advertising, which creates artificial wants. He sees it further accentuated by an obsession with

---

Article is from Edmund S. Phelps (ed.), *Private Wants and Public Needs*, New York: W. W. Norton, 1965, pp. 42–54. The essay is from *Harper's Magazine*, Vol. 223 (October, 1961) and from *The Cost of Freedom* by Henry C. Wallich, copyright © 1960 by the author. Used with permission of Harper and Row, Publishers and the author.

production, which keeps us from realizing that our problems are not those of want, but of affluence. The imbalance is epitomized by our supposed tendency to limit public expenditures to what is strictly essential, while we apply no such criterion to private expenditures.

TOO MANY TRIVIA?

One may reasonably argue that Galbraith exaggerates the distorting influence of advertising. That would not alter the basic assumption on which his thesis rests—the assumption that there are better wants and worse wants. Scientific detachment notwithstanding, I find it extraordinarily difficult to disagree with this proposition. To rate an attendance at the opera and a visit to an (inexpensive) nightclub as equivalents, because the market puts a similar price on them, goes against my grain. So does the equation of a dollar's worth of education and a dollar's worth of chromium on an automobile. And a plausible case would probably be made, on the basis of the evolution of the species, that opera and education do represent more advanced forms of consumption.

But what consequences, if any, should be drawn from such judgment? It is one thing to be irritated by certain manifestations of our contemporary civilization—the gadgets, the chrome, the tail fins and the activities that go with them. It is quite another—and something of a *non sequitur*—to conclude from this that the only alternative to foolish private spending is public spending. Better private spending is just as much of a possibility.

And does this judgment yield a basis for trying to discourage the growth of the less "good" expenditures? In a free society, we obviously want to move with the utmost circumspection. It is worth remembering that even Thorstein Veblen, who went to some extreme in deriding the "leisure class" and its "conspicuous consumption," did not take an altogether negative view of all conspicuous waste. In *The Theory of the Leisure Class* he said, "No class of society, not even the most abjectly poor, foregoes all customary conspicuous consumption. ... There is no class and no country that has yielded so abjectly before the pressure of physical want as to deny themselves all gratification of this higher or spiritual need."

For fair appraisal of the case against trivia, we would also want to know the approximate size of the bill that is being incurred for various frills and frivolities. Gadgets in cars and homes have drawn the special ire of the critics. It is interesting to note, therefore, that expenditures for all kinds of durable consumer goods, including automobiles, run about 14 percent of personal consumption. The greater part of this, presumably, goes for the essential parts of fairly essential equipment. What is left for ornaments and gadgets does not loom impressively large. After all, not all the income in this country is spent by people for whom life begins at $25,000. The median family income is $5,600. Would the critics of the affluent society want to live on much less than that?

Whatever our private feelings about the gadgetry in our life, we probably do well not to stress them too hard. It is only too easy for some members of a community to work themselves into a fit of righteousness and to feel tempted to help the rest regulate their existence. In an extreme form, and not very long ago, this happened in the United States with the introduction of prohibition. Some of us may lean toward special taxation of luxuries, but surely no one wants sumptuary legislation banishing from our show windows and homes the offending contrivances. A new puritanism directed against wasteful consumption, however understandable, would make no great contribution to an economy that requires incentive goods to activate competition and free markets. Neither would it be compatible with the freedom that we value.

ENDS AND MEANS

It is the positive side of the case—the asserted need for more public services—that must chiefly concern us. My contention here will be that to talk in terms of "public vs. private" is to confuse the issue. More than that, it is to confuse means and ends. The choice between public and private money is primarily a choice of means. The sensible approach for those who are dissatisfied with some of the ends to which private money is being spent, is to specify first what other ends are important and why. Having determined the ends, the next step is to look to the means. That is the order in which I propose to proceed here.

The critics are right in pointing out that new material needs have been carried to the fore by social and economic evolution—even though they mislabel them as public needs. In the good old days, when this was still a nation of farmers, most people had no serious retirement worries, there was no industrial unemployment problem, good jobs could be had without a college degree, most diseases were still incurable—in short, social security, education, and health care found primitive and natural solutions within the family and among the resources of the neighborhood. Today, these solutions are neither adequate nor usually even possible.

Mounting wealth and advancing technology have brought within reach the means of meeting these needs. We can afford to live better in every way—more creature comforts, more leisure, more attention to matters of the mind and spirit. At the same time we can take better care of retirement, of unemployment, of illness, of education, of the possibilities opened by research, than ever before.

There are indeed new needs. The citizen-taxpayer has his choice of meeting them, as well as all his other needs, in one of two ways. He can buy the goods or services he wants privately, for cash or credit. Or he can buy them from the government, for taxes.

The nation as a whole pays taxes to buy public services as it pays grocery bills to buy groceries. The tax burden may be heavier for some individuals than for others. But the nation as a whole has no more reason to complain about the "burden" of taxes than about the "burden" of grocery bills—and no more reason to hope for relief.

Of the two stores, the private store today still is much the bigger. The public store is smaller, but it is growing faster.

Each store has some exclusive items. The private store sells most of the necessities and all of the luxuries of life, and in most of these has no competition from the government side. The public store has some specialties of its own: defense, public order and justice, and numerous local services that the private organization has not found profitable. But there is a wide range of items featured by both stores: provision for old age, health services education, housing, development of natural resources.

THE NEW NEEDS

The bulk of the new needs are in this competitive area. The fashionable notion is to claim them all for the public store and to label them public needs. The statistics say otherwise. They say in fact two things: First, the supply of this group of goods and services has expanded very rapidly in recent years; and second, they are being offered, in varying degrees, both by the private and the public suppliers. Let us run down the list.

Provision for Old Age Is Predominantly Private. The average American family, realizing that while old age may be a burden, it is the only known way to achieve a long life, takes care of the matter in three ways: (1) by private individual savings—home ownership, savings deposits, securities; (2) by private collective savings—life insurance, corporate pension funds; and (3) by public collective savings through social security. Statisticians report that the two collective forms are advancing faster than the individual. The increases far exceed the rise in the Gross National Product of almost 80 percent (in current prices) over the past ten years; they do not indicate either that these needs are neglected or that they are necessarily public in character.

Education: The Bulk of It Is Public; but a Good Part, Particularly of Higher Education, Is Private. Total expenditures for all education have advanced in the last ten years from $9.3 billion to $24.6 billion ($19.3 billion of it public). Education's share in the national income has advanced from 3.8 percent to 5.8 percent. The silly story that we spend more on advertising than on education is a canard, though with its gross of over $10 billion, advertising does take a lot of money.

Health Expenditures Are Still Mainly Private. At considerable expense, it is now possible to live longer and be sick less frequently or at least less dangerously. In the past, most people paid their own doctors' bills, although health care for the indigent has always been provided by public action or private philanthropy. Since the war, the proliferation of health insurance has given some form of collective but private insurance to three-quarters of our 182 million people. This has greatly reduced pressure for a national health service along British lines. For the aging, whose health-care needs stand in inverse proportion to their capacity to pay or insure, public insurance has finally been initiated and needs to be expanded. The total annual expenditure on health is estimated at over $25 billion, a little more than on education. Of this, about $6 billion is public.

So much for the allegation that the "new needs" are all public needs. Now for some further statistics on the public store, which is said to have been neglected. Some of them could make an investor in private growth stocks envious. Research expenditures (mainly for defense and atomic energy) have gone from about $1 billion to over $8 billion in the last ten years. Federal grants to the states have advanced from $2.2 billion to $7 billion during the same period. Social-security benefits rose from $1 billion to over $10 billion. All in all, public cash outlays (federal and state) advanced from $61 billion to $134 billion over ten years, 57 percent faster than the GNP.

For those who feel about public spending the way Mark Twain felt about whiskey, these figures may still look slim. (Mark Twain thought that while too much of anything was bad, too much whiskey was barely enough.) To others, the data may suggest that the advocates of more public spending have already had their way. Could their present discontent be the result of not keeping their statistics up-to-date? In one of his recent pamphlets, Arthur M. Schlesinger, Jr., claims that the sum of the many neglects he observes (including defense) could be mended by raising public expenditures by $10 to $12 billion. That is well below the increase in public cash outlays that actually did take place in one single fiscal year, from $118.2 billion in 1958 to $132.7 billion in 1959. In the three fiscal years 1957–59, these outlays went up more than $31 billion, though the advance slowed down in 1960. More facts and less indignation might help to attain better perspective.

Some parts of federal, state, and local budgets have expanded less rapidly than those cited—in many cases fortunately. The massive buildup in defense expenditures from the late 'forties to the 'fifties has squeezed other programs. Unfortunately, on the other hand, some programs that both political parties have favored—including aid to education, to depressed areas, for urban renewal—have been delayed unduly by the vicissitudes of politics. But the figures as a whole lend little support to the thesis that politicians don't spend enough, and that the government store is not expanding fast enough.

THE CITIZEN IN THE STORES

The two stores—private and public—work very hard these days to capture the business of the citizen-taxpayer. Here is what he hears as he walks into the private store:

"The principal advantage of this store," the private businessman says, "is that you can shop around and buy exactly what you want. If I don't have

215

it I'll order it. You, the consumer, are the boss here. To be sure, I'm not in business for charity but for profit. But my profit comes from giving you what you want. And with competition as fierce as it is, you can be sure the profit won't be excessive."

If the proprietor has been to Harvard Business School, he will perhaps remember to add something about the invisible hand which in a free economy causes the self-seeking of competitors to work for the common good. He will also, even without benefit of business school, remember to drop a word about the danger of letting the public store across the street get too big. It might endanger freedom.

As the citizen turns this sales talk over in his mind, several points occur to him. Without denying the broad validity of the argument, he will note that quite often he has been induced to buy things he did not really need, and possibly to neglect other, more serious needs. Snob appeal and built-in obsolescence promoted by expensive advertising don't seem to him to fit in with the notion that the consumer is king. Looking at the brand names and patents and trademarks, he wonders whether most products are produced and priced competitively instead of under monopoly conditions. The invisible hand at times seems to be invisible mainly because it is so deep in his pocket.

Bothered by these doubts, the citizen walks across the street and enters the public store.

"Let me explain to you," says the politician who runs it—with the aid of a horde of hard-working bureaucrats doing the chores. "The principles on which this store is run are known as the political process, and if you happen to be familiar with private merchandising they may seem unusual, but I assure you they work. First of all, almost everything in this store is free. We simply assess our customers a lump sum in the form of taxes. These, however, are based largely on each customer's ability to pay, rather than on what he gets from the store. We have a show of hands from the customers once a year, and the majority decides what merchandise the store is to have in stock. The majority, incidentally, also decides how much everybody, including particularly the minority, is to be assessed for taxes.

"You will observe," the politician continues, "that this store is not run for profit. It is like a co-operative, run for the welfare of the members. I myself, to be sure, am not in politics for charity, but for re-election. But that means that I must be interested in your needs, or you would not vote for me. Moreover, there are some useful things that only I can do, with the help of the political process, and in which you and every citizen have an interest. For instance, everybody ought to go to school. I can make them go. Everybody ought to have old-age insurance. I can make that compulsory too. And because I don't charge the full cost of the service, I can help even up a little the inequalities of life.

"By the way," the politician concludes, "if there is any special little thing you want, I may be able to get it for you, and of course it won't cost you a nickel."

216

The citizen has some fault to find with the political process too. He notes that there is not even a theoretical claim to the benefits of an invisible hand. Majority rule may produce benefits for the majority, but how about the other 49 percent? Nor is there the discipline of competition, or the need for profits, to test economy of operation. There is no way, in the public store, of adjusting individual costs and benefits. And the promise to get him some small favor, while tempting, worries him, because he wonders what the politician may have promised to others. The political process, he is led to suspect, may be a little haphazard.

He asks himself how political decisions get to be made. Sometimes, obviously, it is not the majority that really makes a decision, but a small pressure group that is getting away with something. He will remember that—after payments for major national security and public debt interest— the largest single expenditure in the federal budget is for agriculture, and the next for veterans. He may also recall that one of the first budgetary actions of the new Administration was to increase funds for agriculture by $3 billion.

THE EXPANDING BELT

Next, the citizen might consider the paralyzing "balance-of-forces" effect that often blocks a desirable reshuffling of expenditures. The allocation of public funds reflects the bargaining power of their sponsors, inside or outside the government. A classical example was the division of funds that prevailed in the Defense Department during the late 'forties. Army, Navy, and Air Force were to share in total resources in a way that would maximize military potential. By some strange coincidence, maximum potential was always achieved by giving each service the same amount of money. It took the Korean War to break this stalemate.

What is the consequence of the balance-of-forces effect? If the proponents of one kind of expenditure want to get more money for their projects, they must concede an increase also to the advocates of others. More education means more highways, instead of less; more air power means more ground forces. To increase a budget in one direction only is as difficult as letting out one's belt only on one side. The expansion tends to go all around. What this comes down to is that politicians are not very good at setting priorities. Increases in good expenditures are burdened with a political surcharge of less good ones.

The last-ditch survival power of federal programs is a specially illuminating instance of the balance of forces. If a monument were built in Washington in memory of each major federal program that has been discontinued, the appearance of the city would not be greatly altered. In contrast, when the Edsel doesn't sell, production stops. But the government is still reclaiming land to raise more farm surpluses and training fishermen to enter an occupation that needs subsidies to keep alive. Old federal programs never die, they don't even fade away—they just go on.

217

The citizen will remember also the ancient and honorable practice of logrolling. The unhappy fate of the Area Development bill illustrates it admirably. As originally proposed, the bill sought to aid a limited number of industrial areas where new jobs were badly needed. It got nowhere in the Congress. Only when it was extended to a large number of areas with less urgent or quite different problems, were enough legislators brought aboard to pass it. Because of the heavy political surcharge with which it had become loaded, President Eisenhower vetoed the bill. A bill was finally enacted early this year, long after aid should have been brought to the areas that needed it.

Finally, the citizen might discover in some dark corner of his mind a nagging thought: Any particular government program may be a blessing, but could their cumulative effect be a threat to freedom? He has heard businessmen say this so often that he has almost ceased to pay attention to it. He rather resents businessmen acting the dog in the manger, trying to stop useful things from being done unless they can do them. He is irritated when he hears a man talk about freedom who obviously is thinking about profit. And yet—is there any conclusive rebuttal?

THE CITIZEN'S FAILURES

The citizen would be quite wrong, however, if he blamed the politician for the defects of the political process. The fault lies with the process, or better with the way in which the process, the politician, and the citizen interact. The citizen therefore would do well to examine some of his own reactions and attitudes.

First, when he thinks about taxes, he tends to think of them as a burden instead of as a price he pays for a service. As a body, the nation's taxpayers are like a group of neighbors who decide to establish a fire department. Because none is quite sure how much good it will do him, and because each hopes to benefit from the contribution of the rest, all are prudent in their contributions. In the end they are likely to wind up with a bucket brigade.

But when it comes to accepting benefits, the citizen-taxpayers act like a group of men who sit down at a restaurant table knowing that they will split the check evenly. In this situation everybody orders generously; it adds little to one's own share of the bill, and for the extravagance of his friends he will have to pay anyhow. What happens at the restaurant table explains—though it does not excuse—what happens at the public trough.

Finally, in his reaction to public or free services, the citizen takes a great deal for granted, and seldom thinks of the cost. Public beaches mistreated, unmetered parking space permanently occupied, veterans' adjustment benefits continued without need—as well as abuses of unemployment compensation and public assistance—are some examples. This applies also, of course, to privately offered benefits, under health insurance, for instance. The kindly nurse in the hospital—"Why don't you stay another day, dearie, it

218

won't cost you anything, it's all paid for by Blue Cross"—makes the point.

By removing the link between costs and benefits, the political process also reduces the citizen's interest in earning money. The citizen works to live. If some of his living comes to him without working, he would be less than rational if he did not respond with a demand for shorter hours. If these public benefits increase his tax burden so that his overall standard of living remains unchanged, the higher taxes will reduce his work incentive. Why work hard, if much of it is for the government?

THE POLITICAL DOLLAR AT A DISCOUNT

These various defects of the political process add up to an obvious conclusion: the dollar spent by even the most honest and scrupulous of politicians is not always a full-bodied dollar. It often is subject to a discount. It buys less than it should because of the attrition it suffers as it goes through the process, and so may be worth only 90 cents or 80 cents and sometimes perhaps less. The private dollar, in too many cases, may also be worth less than 100 percent. But here each man can form his own judgment, can pick and choose or refuse altogether. In the political process, all he can do is say Yes or No once a year in November.

The discount on the public dollar may be compensated by the other advantages of government—its ability to compel, to subsidize, to do things on a big scale and at a low interest cost. Whether that is the case needs to be studied in each instance. Where these advantages do not apply, the private market will give better service than the political process. For many services, there is at least some leeway for choice between the private and public store—health and retirement, housing, research, higher education, natural-resource development. Defense, on the other hand, as well as public administration, public works of all kinds, and the great bulk of education—while perhaps made rather expensive by the political process—leave no realistic alternative to public action.

The argument I have offered is no plea to spend more or less on any particular function. It is a plea for doing whatever we do in the most effective way.

SOME QUANTITATIVE HISTORY

Francis M. Bator

Simply to add up all the money paid out each year by public agencies as recorded in their accounts is not a very revealing exercise. Not all spending is alike; to derive insight from expenditure figures one must distinguish, at the least, between two kinds: "exhaustive" expenditure (G) and "nonexhaustive" expenditure (N).

"Exhaustive" expenditure, so-called, is spending that "absorbs" goods and services. It consists of *purchases* by government of goods and services from business and households (e.g., of typewriters and B-52's, and of the services of construction companies and of civil servants). Its total is a measure of the net claim of government on current production and hence of the volume of output not available for personal consumption or private investment. It also measures the volume of production not subject to a "market test," i.e., to a purchase by a private buyer.

"Nonexhaustive" expenditure is spending that absorbs no output but redistributes income or assets. Made up of interest on the public debt, of such transfer payments as unemployment compensation, unrestricted cash grants to veterans, old-age and retirement benefits, and of federal grants-in-aid to state and local governments, nonexhaustive expenditure is best thought of as the obverse of taxes. Like taxes, it redistributes "dollar votes"; and unlike purchases of goods and services, it does not constitute a claim on labor or other scarce resources. It does not, as do, e.g., the wages of civil servants, represent payment for current services rendered. (The cost of administering programs of nonexhaustive expenditure is, of course, a part of purchases of goods and services.)[1]

Article is from Francis M. Bator, *The Question of Government Spending*, New York: Harper and Bros., 1960, pp. 9–28. Copyright © by Francis M. Bator, reprinted by permission of Harper & Row, Publishers.

[1]The distinction between exhaustive and nonexhaustive expenditure is not in all cases clear, even in concept. Moreover, the available statistical information does not always fit the categories even where there is no intrinsic ambiguity. How, for instance, is one to treat government enterprises which produce for sale to private buyers? While it is the burden of "net" in "net resource-absorbing expenditure" that one must not count in their expensable purchases on current account (e.g., the expenses of a profitable municipal power plant), one cannot completely ignore such enterprises—they are not all profitable. Any publicly subsidized excess of expenses over sales revenue in running, say, post-offices or post-exchanges, or, for that matter, some private facility, implies government resource absorption. The amount of the subsidy, however, is a very poor measure of such "absorption" and hence I shall follow the Commerce Department practice of excluding "subsidies less current surplus of government enterprises" from exhaustive expenditure. Where such exclusion makes a significant quantitative difference, footnotes contain alternative calculations combining "subsidies less surplus" and purchases of goods and services.

Except for a brief look at the magnitude and composition of non-exhaustive expenditure (N), primary attention in what follows is on the first category, government purchases of goods and services (G). But it is well to emphasize that neither G nor indeed *total* public spending (E, i.e., G + N) should be thought of as that will-o'-the-wisp: a measure of the volume of resources the allocation of which is in some sense "determined" by government. Both exhaustive and nonexhaustive expenditure affect allocation: the first by directly bidding for resources, and both by altering the disposable incomes and asset-positions of individuals, business firms, and units of government. But so do a host of other governmental measures which entail no public spending or lending, such as the licensing of broadcast bands, tariffs, policing of airplane safety, and the like. Anything that affects the profitability of some activity or the composition of private spending, whether directly, as do taxes, or more indirectly by altering the pattern of prices or availabilities (of, say, mortgage money or sugar), will have more or less pervasive effects on supply and demand throughout the economy.[2]

On the other hand, it is G and not the *total* of public spending (E) which measures the volume of resources "absorbed" by government; to use the ratio of total government spending to gross national product, E/GNP, as an indicator of the public claim on output, as is frequently done, is most misleading. The nonexhaustive components of spending do not constitute such a claim; it would be possible for the ratio to exceed 100 percent, though the government was absorbing only a fraction of GNP, with private consumption and investment taking the rest.

NONEXHAUSTIVE EXPENDITURE (N)[3]

What has been the history since 1929 of all-government, federal, and state-local nonexhaustive spending? What are the interesting trends? The most striking thing about the series on all-government nonexhaustive spending is the tremendous increase between 1929 and 1957. N grew fifteenfold (from under $1.7 billion per annum to $25.5 billion in 1957) as compared with a tenfold increase in purchases of goods and services (G), a somewhat more than fourfold increase in gross national product, and a 40

---

[2] To think sensibly about the question of how many dollars' worth of output are "influenced" by government purchases, one should think about it in the way one would think about an urn filled with marbles. How many of ninety black marbles in an urn containing a hundred marbles have their positions influenced by the ten white marbles? The relationships are likely to exhibit mutual interdependence. The resource-composition of personal consumption is as much a cause as a consequence of the resource-composition of the government's share in output.

[3] To economize on space I make liberal use in all that follows of the symbols G (for all-government exhaustive expenditure) and N (for all-government nonexhaustive expenditure). Some use is made also of FG and FN, to represent federal exhaustive and nonexhaustive spending; and of SG and SN for the corresponding state-local magnitudes. GNP stands for gross national product and E (used only a few times) for total government spending, i.e., for G + N.

percent increase in population. Even if corrected for inflation-caused shrinkage in the dollar yardstick by say 85 percent (using the price index for GNP), the rise in the annual volume of purchasing power subject to interpersonal transfer via government has been dramatic. In 1957, 23 percent of public expenditure consisted of nonexhaustive spending, as compared with 17 percent of a much smaller total in 1929.

What explains the fifteenfold rise in government nonexhaustive expenditure since 1929? It is evident from the composition of N that social security and World War II must take much of the blame—with an assist by the Korean War. Between 88-100 percent of annual nonexhaustive spending since 1929 has consisted of transfer payments and of interest on the public debt, with transfers in 1957 taking 72 percent (about par for the postwar decade) and interest 23 percent. Of the interest, over four-fifths is attributable to the financing of World War II—i.e., about $5 billion of a 1957 total of $6 billion. And of the $18.4 billion of transfers that year, a fourth was accounted for by cash grants to veterans, and the other three-fourths by direct relief and by benefit payments from the various social insurance trust funds (e.g., old-age and survivors, unemployment, railroad retirement, federal civilian pensions). In 1957, then, a little more than half of all nonexhaustive spending reflected the cost of social security, and another third (plus) was a heritage of the war and of Korea.[4]

In view of the role of war finance and of the social security programs of New Deal vintage, it is not surprising that the lion's share of postwar nonexhaustive expenditure has been federal. In 1929 interest paid by state-local governments made up $0.5 billion of a total government interest bill of $0.9 billion; by 1957 the federal government paid $5.5 billion of the $6 billion total. (State-local interest payments, net of interest receipts, have shown no trend rise at all since 1929.) And of transfer spending since 1947, the federal government has been responsible for about three-fourths. In 1957, for instance, the federal component came to 80 percent of the $18.4 billion total—about the same percentage as in 1929, when the federal share in transfers was 78 percent (of a $0.9 billion total). (During most years of the mid- and late 1930's, in contrast, the federal share fluctuated between a third and a half.)[5]

---

[4]The all-government interest bill (net) came to $0.9 (+) billion in 1929, $1.3 billion in 1941, $4.5 billion in 1946, remained under $5 billion until 1952, and then rose to $6 billion in 1957. The attribution of four-fifths of the 1957 amount to war finance is based on the rise in the net federal debt between 1940 and 1945 relative to the increase in net all-government debt between 1929 and 1957. For the data, see *Economic Report of the President*, January, 1959, p. 194.

[5]Federal net interest payments totaled $0.4 billion in 1929, $0.8 billion in 1941, $4.2 billion in 1947 (fiscal), and $5.5 billion in 1957.

Federal benefit payments from the various social insurance funds rose from $44 million in 1929 to a pre-1945 peak of $835 million in 1940, to $1.3 billion in 1945, approximately $2.2 billion in 1947 and 1948, up to $6.1 billion in calendar 1950 (due to the 1949 recession); went down to $4.4 billion in calendar 1951, up again to $5.6 billion in calendar 1953 and to $11.2 billion in the recession-ridden calendar year of 1957. The big

Moreover, the above comparisons do not tell the whole story. An appreciable fraction of state-local transfers is financed by *federal* grants-in-aid to state and local governments. Rising from a 1929 level of $0.1 billion to $1.5 billion in 1947 and $3.6 billion in 1957, such grants constitute an intra-governmental transaction; hence they do not show up in the net total of all-government nonexhaustive spending. But in the postwar period they have accounted for 10-15 percent of the nonexhaustive expenditures of the federal government (with no trend)—percentages well below the 1933-1943 figures, but above the 1929 ratio of 9 percent. (In calendar 1957, $1.3 billion of the $4.1 billion of federal grants to state and local govermnents went for highway and other transport; $1.8 billion for social security and welfare services—this helped finance state-local outlays of $2.9 billion; a little less than $0.3 billion was used for education, and the rest to help finance miscellaneous other state and local activities.)[6]

A few additional facts about postwar trends in nonexhaustive expenditure might be noted:

While interest on the public debt continued to grow during the postwar decade (from $4.5 billion in 1946 to $6.0 billion in 1957), national income—the sum total of wages, salaries, professional and proprietors' income, profits and interest—grew even faster. In 1946, 2.47 percent of the national income was subject to redistribution from taxpayers to holders of government bonds. By 1957 the ratio was down to 1.67 percent, above the 1929 figure of 1.12 percent, but not appreciably higher than in 1939 (1.66 percent) and of course much lower than during the worst of the depression. The ratio of the *federal* component of interest to national income, in turn, while it tripled between 1929 and 1957, has fallen sharply since 1946, from 2.31 percent to, e.g., 1.53 percent in 1957.

---

increase in various veterans' disability and compensation payments—the second major category of federal transfers—followed World War II ($0.5 billion in 1939, $6.9 billion in 1946, $4.3 billion in calendar 1951, and $4.7 billion in calendar 1957).

State and local transfers—these consist of two kinds of social insurance payments: government pensions and cash sickness compensation, and of direct relief—rose from $218 million in 1929 to $1.0 billion in 1937, $1.6 billion in 1946, and 4.0 billion in calendar 1957. In the postwar period relief payments have made up about two-thirds of the total.

[6]There is still another category of nonexhaustive expenditure—"subsidies less current surplus of government enterprises." (Subsidies consist of government payments to farmers, payments for the exportation and diversion of surplus agricultural commodities, shipping and housing subsidies, the wartime subsidy programs administered by the C.C.C. and the R.F.C., and subsidy payments to air carriers.) "Subsidies less surplus" would be particularly troublesome—subsidies do reflect some absorption of resources by government, i.e., a partial short circuit of private markets—were it not that in the postwar, until 1957 at least, the total did not amount to a significant proportion of N. Excluding 1957, the postwar average was negative; and 1956 and 1957 were the only postwar years during which the total came to more than $0.3 billion (or more than 1.8 percent of N). On the other hand, the total does hide more than it reveals. Surpluses realized by government enterprises generally offset the often sizable subsidies involved in the agricultural program. (In calendar 1957, agricultural subsidies alone ran to $2.5 billion.) Moreover, federal subsidies-less-surpluses have generally been larger than the all-government total—the state-local figures have all been negative.

What about transfer payments? For all governments taken together, transfers involved 6 percent of national income in 1946 and 5.1 percent in 1957. (The 1929 ratio was 1.04 percent; that in 1939, 3.45 percent.) In 1957 federal transfers alone came to 4.06 percent of national income, as compared with 5.09 percent in 1946. (In 1929, the ratio was 0.79 percent.)

In Summary

Nonexhaustive expenditure, i.e., spending which does not constitute a claim on resources and does not short-circuit private market allocation of resources, has accounted for between one-sixth and one-third of total government spending since the war, with the ratio generally higher than in 1929 and much higher than during the war. N has been especially significant in the federal budget. The ratio of federal nonexhaustive expenditure to total federal spending has ranged between a quarter and a half during the last ten or so years, with social security, veterans' benefits, and interest on the government debt taking the lion's share. Again, none of these programs should be thought of as diverting substantial resources from private consumption or private capital formation. As will be argued below, the "economic" case for or against nonexhaustive expenditure must, in the first instance, hinge on ethical issues of income distribution.

EXHAUSTIVE EXPENDITURE

The second category of public spending—government purchase of goods and services (G)—is quite another matter. It does divert resources from production for private account; indeed, it is the best measure of the volume of resources "absorbed" by government, of current production not submitted to the test of a sale to a private buyer. What has been its history since 1929?[1]

All-Government Totals

The rise in public purchases, G, though not of the same order as in nonexhaustive expenditure, is again imposing. In 1957, G was ten times what it had been in 1929—less than during the height of the war in 1943-1944, but three times its 1947 level. Some of the increase reflects inflation-caused shrinkage in the unit of measure; in "real" terms, G* (all "deflated" series will be marked by an asterisk) has also grown, but by a factor of four rather than ten. It increased by two-thirds during the 1930's, by a multiple of five

---

[1]In a conveniently tidy world, the total of government purchases would correspond more or less exactly to the volume of resources that would be available to increase the production of private consumer goods and services, and of capital goods on private account, *if* exhaustive public expenditure were kept to zero. In the disorderly world in which the national income statistician must do his work, this is not quite the case: some of the services of the government, e.g., road maintenance to truckers, are not "final" goods but intermediate to private production; they are, in effect, inputs required by producers to maintain the current level of their output for private use. Since we have no good measure of the value of such governmentally produced intermediate services, all G will be treated as though it were "final." On this count, G overstates the sacrifice in forgone personal consumption and private investment.

between 1939 and 1944, then declined by 1947 to about one-and-a-quarter times its 1939 level only to double again between 1947 and 1957. (Figure 1 contains the "deflated" figures, which measure exhaustive spending in terms of the 1957 price level.)

FIGURE 1

GROSS NATIONAL PRODUCT AND GOVERNMENT PURCHASES OF GOODS
AND SERVICES, 1929, 1939–1946, 1947 f–1957 f
(Billions of 1957 f Dollars)

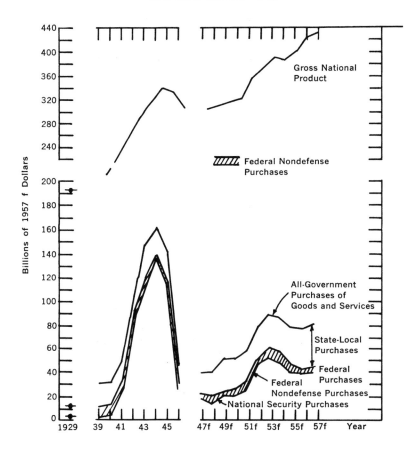

Of course G* is not the only thing that has increased since 1929. Population too has grown, as has total "real" output, GNP*. For perspective, it is well to look at G* per head of population, and at the ratio of public purchases to GNP. (See Figure 2.)

In terms of 1957 prices, government purchases of goods and services per head of population rose from $169 in 1929 to $498 in 1957, i.e., by a factor of three. Per capita "real" gross national product, in turn, increased about one-and-a-half times, from $1,587 to $2,545. The *share* of government purchases in total output during the same three decades rose from 8.1 percent to 19.6 percent. This last, the ratio of G to GNP in 1957, was substantially greater than the corresponding ratio in 1939 (14.6 percent) and greater also than the 1947-1951 ratios (12.7-15.9 percent). On the other hand, it is well below the 23 percent share of government in GNP during the height of the Korean War effort in 1953, and cannot compare with the 1943 ratio, when government exhaustive spending took 46 percent of the national output.[2]

FIGURE 2

PER CAPITA GROSS NATIONAL PRODUCT AND GOVERNMENT EXHAUSTIVE
EXPENDITURE 1929, 1939-1946, 1947 f-1957 f
(1957 f Dollars)

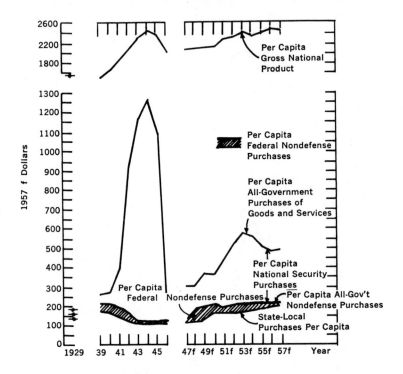

The time pattern of the statistics on per capita G^* is also what one might expect, given the weight of defense during the war and since 1949 (Figure 2). During the 1930's, G^* per head rose, albeit in zigzag fashion, from $169 in 1929 to $256 in 1939. Then came the wartime years of rapid expansion; by 1944 annual government purchases of goods and services in

---

[2]The above ratios are of G to GNP rather than of G^* to GNP^*. For technical reasons the ratio of two undeflated figures which belong to the same year is a better indicator of what is wanted than are the "deflated" ratios. (It happens that the G^*/GNP^* ratio increased less between 1929 and 1957 than the G/GNP ratio—from 10.6 percent [rather than 8.1 percent] to 19.6 percent. The prices of G-type goods rose more than the average of all final-product prices.)

real terms hit a peak of $1,223 for every head of population. With demobilization, G* per capita fell to $300 in 1947 (17 percent higher than in 1939), only to rise again to a postwar high of $587 during the Korean War (1953). And, although the Eisenhower administration managed by means of federal economies following the armistice to make G* per capita fall—to $498 in 1957, the 1957 level still exceeded that in 1947 by two-thirds. "Real" all-government exhaustive expenditure per head rose faster in the defense-ridden postwar decade than during the depression.

Nondefense Totals

The series on total government purchases is not a bad guide to the history of spending for defense and war, but it leaves hidden the rather more intriguing story of public expenditure for other than security.[3] Instead of the fourfold increase shown by total G* between 1929 and 1957, *nondefense* public spending in real terms only a little more than doubled, rising from $18.9 billion in 1929 to $39.8 billion in 1957. Moreover, when matched against the rise in nondefense gross national product, i.e., against the rise in the total nondefense output of the economy, the *share* of government increased only from 7.5 percent in 1929 to 10.3 percent in 1957. Indeed, the ratio of nondefense G to nondefense GNP during the postwar years remained well below the 1939 and 1940 figures of 13.4 percent and 12 percent. It appears, in other words, that of the resources left over for private and public "civilian" consumption and capital formation—left over, that is, after military provision for survival—we have been committing in the postwar period only a slightly larger fraction to such communal uses as schools, roads, sanitation, urban renewal, etc., than we did in 1929, and a smaller share than in 1939 and 1940. (In calendar 1953, the one postwar year for which I have comparable estimates, the share of government in nondefense output—the ratio of nondefense G to nondefense GNP—was lower in the United States than, e.g., in capitalist West Germany (15.1 percent), welfare conscious England (14.5 percent), socialist Sweden (14.3 percent), and capitalist Belgium (11.7 percent). As among the six countries for which I made the calculation, only the Canadian ratio (10.6 percent) was lower than our 11.2 percent (with only national-defense-proper subtracted). Our 1957 ratio of 10.8 percent was just barely higher than Canada's.[4]

---

[3]Figures 1 and 2 contain the relevant figures: "total national security" expenditure (TNS) in current and in deflated (1957) prices (TNS*); nondefense public expenditure, i.e., G* minus TNS*; nondefense G* per capita; nondefense GNP*, total, per capita, and per household; and the share of nondefense G in nondefense GNP. TNS is equivalent to what the Department of Commerce labels "national security" (adjusted to a net-of-sales basis). It includes in addition to the Budget Bureau's "national defense" and "international affairs and finance plus defense support" some expenditures on the merchant marine. GNP* minus TNS* measures the volume of total output available for nondefense use.

[4]During World War II public G-type spending for other than defense fell both in absolute amount (in real terms) and as a proportion of nondefense GNP; we cut back *communal* civilian consumption and investment more than personal consumption. During the Korean War, however, nondefense G* and the proportion of nondefense G to nondefense GNP fell only between 1950 and 1951 and then only slightly.

The *per capita* figures of real nondefense spending are also of interest. (*See* Figure 2.) During the 1930's, nondefense G* per head of population rose from $155 in 1929 to $233 in 1939. After a wartime decline to $118 (in 1945) it began to rise once again, passing its 1929 level in 1947 but remaining well below the 1939 figure of $233 until 1954, when it hit $236. But 1954 marks the record. In 1955 and also in 1957, nondefense G* per head fell off again, if only a little. In 1957, at $234 we devoted about the same volume of resources per head of population to civilian-type public use as in 1939 despite the fact that total (real) civilian output per capita had risen from $1,514 in 1939 to $2,281 in 1957. (Nondefense GNP* per *household* was $7,826 in 1957; of this we devoted $803 to *public* consumption and investment. The corresponding 1940 figures were $6,117 and $840.)[5]

Federal vs. State-Local Civilian Purchases[6]

What in all this has been the role of the federal government? Spending for national security is, of course, virtually all federal. But what about exhaustive spending on other than defense—e.g., on conservation, public health, and public works? Do the figures indicate a trend of federal budgetary encroachment on state-local civilian functions?

Whatever the trend, the federal share in nondefense exhaustive spending is strikingly small; of all civilian-type G, the federal government was the source of only 8.1 percent in 1929 and 12.2 percent in 1957. True, in most peacetime years in between, the proportion was considerably higher: 33 percent or so in 1939 and 1940; 20-28 percent in the late 1940's; 23 percent in 1953 and 1954. But since 1954 Washington's percentage has been falling fast; in 1957 it was only a little over a third of what it had been in 1939-1940 and lower than in any year for which the figures are available (1929, 1939-1957) save 1929 and 1945. Even if one takes into account that some state and local exhaustive expenditure is financed by federal grants-in-aid—and that in 1957 the state-local share in nondefense G was less (by a twentieth!) than in 1929—these figures hardly suggest an imminent federal "takeover." (As a

---

[5]The 1939–1957 per capita comparison is not affected even if one adds to real nondefense purchases of goods and services the somewhat ambiguous category of spending which the Commerce Department labels "subsidies less surplus of government enterprises" (adjusted for price level change). In 1939 the *sum* of real public purchases and subsidies came to $242 per capita; the corresponding 1957 figure was $241. On the other hand, in 1954 all-government "subsidies less surplus" was negative; the sum of the two categories amounted to only $232, *less* than in 1957. However, to compare the $241 in 1957 with $232 in 1954 is to overstate the difference. Much of the increase in "subsidies less surplus" between 1954 and 1957 was due to the agricultural price-support operations of the Commodity Credit Corporation, some of which involved the finance of foreign aid through the disposal, at a loss, of surplus crops via the so-called Public Law 480 program. If one adds to purchases only nondefense subsidies, the 1957 total comes to about $239. (To deflate "subsidies less surplus" I used the Commerce Department's implicit deflator for "foreign marketings and C.C.C. loans" and the deflator for GNP, in appropriate mixture.)

[6]*See* Figures 1 and 2 for the figures on nondefense FG* (total and per capita) and for the ratios of nondefense FG to nondefense G and nondefense GNP.

matter of fact, even if one takes *total* G, defense and all, Washington's fractional share has fallen in every year since 1953; in 1957, at 58.7 percent, it was no higher than in 1947-1950.)[7]

What about the *absolute* level of federal civilian purchases? In 1929 Washington absorbed $13 of a per capita nondefense GNP* of $1,573. By 1957, civilian output had grown to $2,281 per head; the federal government's share, at $29, had increased somewhat faster. But $29 was hardly a record. In 1939 and 1940 the total of real nondefense purchases had been $71 per capita, and in all nonwar years since then, save two, it ranged between $35 and $56. Moreover, the 1954-1957 trend was sharply negative. (The percentage share of the federal government in civilian GNP in 1957, at 1.3 percent, was a third of what it had been in 1939 and 1940 and at its lowest level, save 1951, since 1946. Per *household*, federal nondefense spending in 1957 took $98 of a total civilian output of $7,826; in 1940 the corresponding figures were $270 and $6,117.)[8]

---

[7]The federal share in the combined total of public nondefense purchases *plus* "subsidies less surplus of government enterprises" has been rather greater: 9.1 percent in 1929; 38-40 percent in 1939-1940; 26-31 percent in the late 1940's; 26 percent, 20 percent, 21 percent, and 19 percent in 1954-1957. Even in the combined total, however, and despite the big rise in federal agricultural subsidies in 1957, the federal government's share in 1957 was half of what it had been in 1939-1940, and fell by a fourth between 1954 and 1957. It was also lower than in any of the years 1929, 1939-1957, except, of course, 1929. (Note that these are not truly nondefense statistics: except for 1954-1957 I have no way of knowing how much of "subsidies less surplus" was defense-connected.)

Federal vs. state-local comparisons are, of course, complicated by federal grants-in-aid to state and local governments. The Department of Commerce treats all such grants as federal *nonexhaustive* expenditure; grant financed state-local exhaustive spending is booked as SG. Yet to the extent that federal grants-in-aid are ear-marked for specific kinds of exhaustive spending (e.g., highways), the question of which level of government really absorbs the resources is meaningless: decision and control are shared. Since the actual administering and purchasing are apt to be by state-local governments, and also because I do not have data on what proportion of federal grants-in-aid is tied to specific kinds of purchases by the recipient, I here follow Commerce Department practice.

[8]The size of the decline in real federal civilian purchases between 1954 and 1957—from $55 to $29 per capita—is misleading. About four-fifths or so of the decline reflects a sharp fall in G-type expenditure on agriculture, a fall which was in part offset by a rise in federal agricultural subsidies. However, even if one adds federal "subsidies less surplus" (appropriately deflated) to federal nondefense purchases of goods and services, the resulting series shows a sharp downward trend between 1954 and 1957 (from $60 per capita to $46) and a very sharp decline from the 1939 total of $87. (With agricultural foreign-aid subsidy taken out, the 1957 figure is $44; there was no such subsidy in 1954. The section on "functional shares" below contains an explanation of how agricultural price-support operations are treated in the national income accounts.)

It should be noted that the broad pattern of the history of nondefense FG* is not at all sensitive to small variations in the statistics, i.e., to variations of, say, $1—$4 on a per capita basis. This is important, because the FG* minus TNS* (total national security) series is of slightly dubious ancestry. TNS was deflated not by an index of its own (I know of none), but by the index for FG. Since most of FG is made up of TNS, the *relative* distortion in TNS* is almost certainly negligible. But a given absolute error that is small in relation to a large number could be substantial relative to a small number; hence results based on fine differences in FG* minus TNS* would have to be taken with a grain of salt. On the other hand, the nondefense ratios of FG to G and to GNP are based on current-price series, hence are not on this account distorted. The all-government series, too, are relatively immune—civilian FG constitutes only a small fraction of nondefense G.

Functional Shares: 1957

To people conditioned to think of public spending as a euphemism for waste the fact that there has been since 1939—in fact, since 1929—no substantial rise in the fractional share of government in civilian output is of small comfort; any increase in the absolute magnitude of G is bad. But the open-minded might be inclined to explore further. On what kinds of things has the government spent our money?

Figure 3 shows the breakdown as among broad categories. Of the all-government total of $87.1 billion, some $44.6 billion went for *national defense* proper and $2.1 billion for *international affairs and finance* (i.e., for

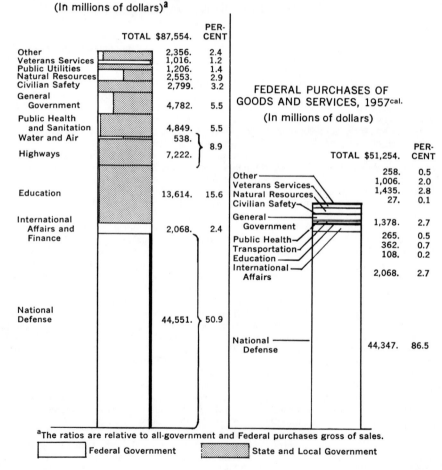

ALL-GOVERNMENT PURCHASES OF
GOODS AND SERVICES, 1957cal.
(In millions of dollars)a

	TOTAL $87,554.	PER-CENT
Other	2,356.	2.4
Veterans Services	1,016.	1.2
Public Utilities	1,206.	1.4
Natural Resources	2,553.	2.9
Civilian Safety	2,799.	3.2
General Government	4,782.	5.5
Public Health and Sanitation	4,849.	5.5
Water and Air	538.	8.9
Highways	7,222.	
Education	13,614.	15.6
International Affairs and Finance	2,068.	2.4
National Defense	44,551.	50.9

FEDERAL PURCHASES OF
GOODS AND SERVICES, 1957cal.
(In millions of dollars)

	TOTAL $51,254.	PER-CENT
Other	258.	0.5
Veterans Services	1,006.	2.0
Natural Resources	1,435.	2.8
Civilian Safety	27.	0.1
General Government	1,378.	2.7
Public Health	265.	0.5
Transportation	362.	0.7
Education	108.	0.2
International Affairs	2,068.	2.7
National Defense	44,347.	86.5

aThe ratios are relative to all-government and Federal purchases gross of sales.

☐ Federal Government   ▨ State and Local Government

conduct of foreign affairs, "informational activities," and foreign economic assistance plus defense support [$1.8 billion]). In all, 53 percent of government purchases of goods and services in 1957 was accounted for by these two "national security" categories, with the federal government responsible for virtually all.[9]

By far the largest "civilian" item was *education*. It absorbed $13.6 billion—33 percent of nondefense public purchases. All but $0.1 billion of that was state and local G, but the federal contribution was augmented by some $0.27 billion in grants-in-aid. (Of the $13.6 billion, which came to around $280 per household, $8.8 billion went for wages and salaries, $2.8 billion for construction, and $2 billion for "other purchases.") Eleven and four tenths billion dollars represented the cost of primary and secondary education.

The second largest civilian item, *transportation*, cost $7.76 billion, with the highway program taking 18 percent of all civilian G ($7.2 billion), and water and air transport another 1.3 percent ($0.54 billion).[10] Of the total for transportation, only $0.36 billion consisted of federal purchases, strictly defined; but $1.28 billion of the state and local commitment for highways was financed by federal grant. At any rate, for all governments taken together, education and the highway program used up 52 percent of all nondefense exhaustive expenditure.

The next two largest items were (1) *public health and sanitation* ($4.85 billion, i.e., 12 percent of nondefense G, with the federal government responsible for only a small fraction); and (2) *general government*, i.e., the administrative cost of running the government ($4.78 billion, or 12 percent of civilian G). Of the last, $1.38 billion measures the cost of the federal government and $3.4 billion that of all state and local governments. Adding *civilian safety:* police, fire protection, prisons, etc., which took another 7 percent ($2.8 billion, virtually all state and local), the above categories — education, transport, general government (overhead, if you wish), sanitation and public health, and police and fire protection —used up 82 percent of all nondefense G.

The bulk of the remainder was split three ways. *Natural resources* took $2.6 billion (6.2 percent of nondefense G), with three-quarters going to "conservation and development" and the rest to "recreational use of resources" and "other." *Public utilities*, i.e., transit, electricity and, most important, water and gas, took another $1.21 billion (3 percent). Last,

---

[9]The sum of the two categories is somewhat less than "total national security" (when TNS is gross of sales). (It should be noted, incidentally, that the percentages given in the text are relative to G gross of sales, i.e., $87.554 billion. The reason is that the functional components are available only on a "gross of sales" basis. The sum of the components will not exactly equal the given totals because of rounding.)

[10]In addition to expenditure on the merchant marine, the "water transport" category includes spending on harbor construction, inland waterways, etc. Air transport, in turn, covers C.A.A. activities, construction and operation of civilian airfields, etc.

veterans' services cost $1.02 billion (2.5 percent), with federal veterans' hospitals and medical care taking four-fifths.[11]

---

[11]Exhaustive expenditure on agriculture in calendar 1957 was only $0.26 billion. The rest of the $3 billion of spending on agriculture consisted of subsidies. For discussion of the treatment of C.C.C. price-support operations, *see* the section on Agriculture.

Since this book was first written (in the summer and autumn of 1958) the Commerce Department has completed and published a series on the functional composition of government purchases which covers, in addition to 1957, the years 1952–1956 (U.S. Income and Output, 1958). The major changes in the composition of G between calendar 1952 and 1957 were as follows: The share of defense plus international affairs fell from 63 percent to 53 percent; the share of education in nondefense G rose from 27.6 percent to 33.3 percent; that of highways from 15.8 percent to 17.6 percent; veterans' services fell from 4.2 percent to 2.5 percent; and G-type expenditure on agriculture from 3.6 percent to 0.6 percent (after reaching 12 percent in 1953). Besides national defense, absolute declines occurred in the dollar amounts devoted to: international affairs and finance; veterans' services; exhaustive expenditure on agriculture; "water transport"; and "housing and community redevelopment." (Spending on the last fell from $581 million in 1952 to $185 million in 1957.) All such absolute declines are especially significant since they occurred in the face of rising prices and hence indicate much larger "real" reductions.

INCOME REDISTRIBUTION UNDER THE SOCIAL SECURITY SYSTEM

Elizabeth Deran

The social security tax, which at first glance may appear a straight-forward, simple levy treating all taxpayers alike, on closer examination turns out to be characterized by a number of striking inequalities. The effective rate of tax, combined with the matrix of benefit provisions, leads to redistribution of income among several overlapping groups. Whether the inequalities enhance or worsen the equity of the tax must be decided on a primarily subjective basis, but before useful judgments can be made, the exact nature of the differences need to be spelled out. This article will identify some of the major inequalities built into the social security system.

EFFECTIVE RATE OF TAX BY INCOME CLASS

Since its inception in 1939, the social security tax in this country has always taken the form of a flat rate applied up to some specified maximum base, after which the rate drops to zero. Unlike other taxes related to income, the OASDHI[1] tax does not allow adjustments for the personal situation of the taxpayer, and instead of taxing income (more narrowly, earnings) *after* appropriate exemptions and deductions have been taken, taxes instead the bottom slice.

Statutory Effective Rates

As a consequence of this unusual base, the statutory effective rate on earnings takes the general form given by the expression:

$$y = r,\ x \le M;\ \frac{rM}{x},\ x > M$$

where r represents the statutory flat rate; x, total earnings; M, the maximum base. That is to say, the rate of tax is proportional up to the specified maximum of taxable earnings, after which it becomes a decreasing monotonic function and therefore regressive.

Several such curves, with values of r and M in force at selected points in the history of the social security tax, are shown in Figure 1. Since, as the

---

The author is senior research analyst, Tax Foundation, Inc. The views expressed are her own and do not necessarily reflect those of Tax Foundation.

Article is from *National Tax Journal*, Vol. 19 (September, 1966), pp. 276–85. Used with permission of publisher and author.

[1]OASI (Old Age and Survivors Insurance) until 1956; OASDI ("Disability" added) from 1956 through 1965; OASDHI ("Hospital" added) from 1965 on.

figure shows, the rate has increased more rapidly than the base, over the years the gap between the effective rate on lower levels of earnings and on higher levels has widened. That is to say, if αr is the rate in the later year and βM the maximum base in the later year, such that $\alpha > \beta > 1$, then

$$r - \frac{rM}{x} < \alpha r - \frac{\alpha r \beta M}{x}$$

when $x \geq M + \beta M$. For example, under the 1937 provisions, the gap between the effective statutory rate on earnings of \$3,000 and of \$20,000 was 0.85 percentage points; under the 1955 provisions, 1.58 percentage points; under the 1966 provisions, 2.81 percentage points.

FIGURE 1

EFFECTIVE RATE OF OASDHI[a] TAX BY EARNINGS LEVEL,
SELECTED YEARS, 1937–1987

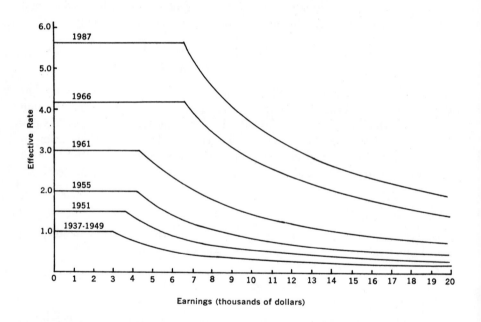

Earnings (thousands of dollars)

[a]OASI only prior to 1956; OASDI only prior to 1966.

Effective Rate on Family AGI

Figure 1, however, gives a misleading impression of the true effective rate of the social security tax. For one thing, it merely shows the tax as a fraction of taxable *earnings*, excluding from the base a number of items which commonly are considered income.[2] Also, in some ways it is more meaningful to consider the effective rate on *family* income, since single persons represent but a small proportion of all taxpayers.

[2]Among the more important income items not subject to the OASDHI tax are capital gains, dividends, interest, and rent.

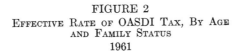

FIGURE 2
EFFECTIVE RATE OF OASDI TAX, BY AGE
AND FAMILY STATUS
1961

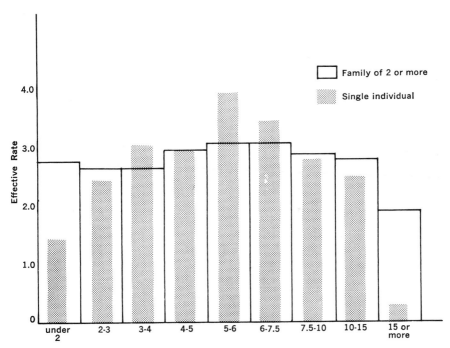

Adjusted Gross Income Class (thousands of dollars)

Figure 2, which derives from computations based on unpublished material collected by the Bureau of Labor Statistics in its 1961 consumer expenditure survey, shows how the statutory effective rate on earnings is modified by consideration of all types of income and the family unit. The rate for single persons illustrates the effect of relating tax payments to reportable income under federal income tax provisions, rather than earnings taxable under OASDHI alone. The effective rate on families shows in addition the consequence of multiple earners in a family.

The effective rate of the tax when taken with respect to adjusted gross income is markedly different from the effective rate of the tax with respect to earnings. Figure 1 showed a top rate in 1961 of 3 percent for all earnings categories up to $4,800, with gradually declining rates for earnings above that amount. In contrast, Figure 2 shows for that same year an effective rate (for single persons) of 1.5 percent on the lowest AGI category, a top rate of 4.0 percent for the category of AGI between $5,000 and $6,000, a gradual decline to 2.5 percent for the category of $10,000 to $15,000 and then a sharp drop to 0.3 percent for AGI of more than $15,000. That is to say, compared with Figure 1, Figure 2 shows generally lower effective rates in the smaller income categories, higher rates in the middle and moderately high income categories and a much lower rate for the highest income category.[3]

The effective rate on family AGI is higher than the effective rate on the AGI of single persons in income categories up to $3,000 and income categories in excess of $7,500. This relationship suggests (but of course does not prove) that in these categories more than one member of the family earned taxable wages. Because the social security maximum base applies to the earnings of an individual, a family with earnings in excess of the maximum taxable base will be taxed more heavily if both the husband and the wife have earnings than if only one member of the family is employed. For example, under the 1966 rate of 4.2 percent and maximum base of $6,600, a man earning $10,000 would be taxed a total of $277, for an effective rate of approximately 2.8 percent. A second family in which the husband and wife each earns $5,000 would pay a total tax of $420, for an effective rate equal to the statutory rate of 4.2 percent and 1.4 percentage points higher than the first family's rate.

In 1961 the effective rate on family AGI was highest for that income category just above the maximum base, but whether this relationship persists under the new base cannot be determined at this time.

In general, then, it would appear that the effective rate of the social security tax rarely corresponds to the statutory rate. The effective rate is lower when computed on income rather than on taxable earnings alone, and higher on families with more than one wage-earner.

TAX PAYMENTS IN RELATION TO BENEFIT LEVELS

When taxes are linked as directly to benefits as is the case under the social security system, the temptation to analyze the tax in relationship to benefits becomes irresistible. While one cannot trace an *economic* relationship which causes a particular kind of expenditure to result from this or any other form of tax, still in the case of the social security tax there exists a legal and institutional link. Admittedly, the relationship between the payroll tax and the social security benefits which it presently finances could be nullified by Congress at any time. With only slight changes in the ground rules, social security benefits could be paid out of general revenues while payroll tax collections could be earmarked for the school lunch program, the Peace Corps, or any other program which suited Congress' fancy. No economic forces would operate automatically to annul such congressional action. Nonetheless, the institutional bond between tax payments and benefits in the United States today has become so strongly cemented that joint analysis seems justifiable.

---

[3]The most obvious and important explanation for the difference between the two figures stems from the fact that even for single individuals the income base used in Figure 2 is larger than the earnings base used for Figure 1. But another difference stems from the complication that tax payments in Figure 2 include the self employment tax, at 1.5 times the rate of employee tax alone. Since collections from the self employment tax in 1961 represented only about 7 percent of total collections, however, any distortion resulting from its inclusion should not be excessively large, unless a disproportionate number of the self-employed are single.

Under the present provisions governing benefit levels, taxpayers are treated differently on the basis of several criteria. The amount of benefits which any given taxpayer will receive depends on the average level of his earnings and his family condition. On the other hand, the amount of tax which he pays depends on his level of earnings and his occupation (which usually reflects the number of years he has spent in covered employment). A merging of these two sets of conditions leads to a wide range of percentages expressing, for individual taxpayers, total tax payments as a proportion of total benefits.

Tax Payments and Benefits by Earnings Level

The social security system has had a redistributive effect related to earnings built into it ever since its inception, with benefit levels relative to average earnings generally weighted in favor of low earnings levels.

In a recent article in the *National Tax Journal*, Ernest C. Harvey dealt with one aspect of this redistributive effect. Unfortunately, he somewhat obscured the significance of his investigation by a confusing choice of nomenclature, calling what is essentially a tax payment-benefit relationship the effective rate of taxation.[4] It also seems to me that Mr. Harvey developed a needlessly sophisticated method. Figure 3 illustrates a more straightforward approach which yields almost identical results with only a few simple percentage computations. This figure, which graphs the simple percentages resulting from a division of present OASI primary benefit levels by the associated average taxable wage, shows a curve which is almost a mirror image of the curve Mr. Harvey so laboriously obtained.[5] Both curves illustrate the point that the beneficiary with a history of low earnings gets relatively more pension for his

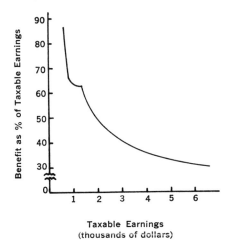

FIGURE 3
OASI PRIMARY BENEFIT AS PERCENT
OF AVERAGE TAXABLE EARNINGS

Benefit as % of Taxable Earnings

Taxable Earnings
(thousands of dollars)

---

[4]Mr. Harvey defines the effective rate of the social security tax as the rate "adjusted for differences in the relationship between contributions and benefits attributable to those contributions." ("Social Security Taxes—Regressive or Progressive?" *National Tax Journal* (December, 1965), pp. 408–414.) I believe that most economists would consider the effective rate of a tax as the total tax divided by some measure of total income in the case of a tax related to income or earnings, or by some measure of value in the case of a tax levied on commodities. This is the sense in which effective tax was treated above.

[5]Rate, base, and pension levels Mr. Harvey used in his computations have been superseded by the Social Security Amendments of 1965. The slight difference in contour between the two curves results from an increase in the overall redistributive effect which Congress authorized in the 1965 amendments.

237

tax dollar than does the high earner; i.e., the system redistributes income in favor of the low wage earner. For instance, a taxpayer earning a yearly average of $6,600 receives an annual benefit equivalent to about 30 percent of his taxable wages, while someone earning only $2,400 receives benefits amounting to 45 percent. This advantage is even more marked for very low wages; the pension amounts to about 66 percent of average taxable wages of $800; 75 percent of $700 and 88 percent of $600.

Benefit Levels Related to Family Status

But to conclude, solely on the basis of either Figure 3 or Mr. Harvey's computations, that the social security system is progressive, would be to overlook a number of aspects which are equally relevant to the question. The relationship between earnings levels and benefits tells only a small part of the story. The ratios shown in Figure 3 only apply to either a single beneficiary or a married couple when both worked in covered employment. While no direct data are available, it is possible to impute the proportion of such beneficiaries at about 45 percent of all beneficiaries.[6] All the others presumably were receiving benefits enlarged by their family situation.

It is instructive to examine some hypothetical cases in which pension levels are related to the beneficiary's family status. In Table 1, actual historical rates and bases were used to compute total tax payments for imaginary beneficiaries retiring in 1966. It was assumed that beneficiaries always earned at least as much as the maximum base, to prevent redistributive effects related to average earnings from obscuring redistributive effects related to family circumstances.

The first eight cases show the added benefits granted on the basis of a beneficiary's status as a spouse or parent. For instance, if an unmarried beneficiary who has been covered by OASDI since its outset lives for 10 years after he retires (an arbitrary period chosen for comparison purposes only), his total tax payments at 3 percent compound interest will represent 21.3 percent of his total benefits discounted at 3 percent. The same percentage holds for a married couple, both of whom worked until age 65. In contrast, the tax payments of a married man whose wife never worked for pay amount to only 14.2 percent of 10 years of benefits. That is to say, the married man who was able to keep his wife out of the labor force receives a bonus of half-again the amount received by the single individual or the working couple. Moreover, if there are dependent children in the household—perhaps rare, but not unheard of—the percentage decreases yet more, with the total depending on the age of the children, as shown by cases 3-5.

---

[6]For instance, in 1964, the latest year for which appropriate figures are available 10.7 million or 58.8 percent out of a total of 18.2 million beneficiaries receiving OASDHI payments could have been in the category depicted by Figure 3. The balance of the beneficiaries were dependents of one type or another. Since 2.6 million of these dependents were spouses (not counting widows or widowers), then no more than 8.1 million or less than 44.5 percent received primary benefits alone.

TABLE 1

EMPLOYEE TAX PAYMENTS AS PERCENT OF BENEFITS UNDER OASI,
SELECTED CATEGORIES OF BENEFICIARIES

Category of Beneficiary	Total Employee Tax Payments Plus 3 Percent Interest 1937–1965[a]	Total Benefits, Discounted at 3 Percent 1966–1975	Total Tax Payments as Percent of 10 Years of Benefits[a]
1. Single individual, 65	$2,877	$13,479	21.3
2. Married man, wife never employed, both 65	2,877	20,224	14.2
3. Married couple, both employed, both 65	5,754	26,958	21.3
4. Married man (65), wife (62, never employed), child (15)	2,877	22,461	12.8
5. Married man (65), wife (62, never employed), 2 children (15 and 16)	2,877	23,100	12.5
6. Married man (65), wife (35, never employed), 2 children (3 and 5)	2,877	30,868	9.3
7. Married man, wife receives less than half-support, has noncovered earnings (both 65)	2,877	20,224	14.2
8. Married woman, husband receives less than half-support, has noncovered earnings (both 65)	2,877	13,479	21.3
9. Farm worker,[b] wife never employed (both 65)	2,030	20,224	10.0
10. Military serviceman,[c] wife never employed (both 65)	1,566	20,224	7.7
11. Self-employed individual (nonfarm)[b]	3,045 (d)	13,479	22.6 (d)
12. Self-employed farmer,[e] wife never employed (both 65)	2,525 (d)	20,224	12.5 (d)
13. Dentist,[c] wife never employed (both 65)	2,349 (d)	20,224	11.6 (d)

[a]To take account of employer portion of tax, multiply by two.
[b]Not covered until 1951.
[c]Not covered until 1956.
[d]No separate employer tax. Figure given includes entire payment on behalf of individual.
[e]Not covered until 1955.
Source: Computations based on data from Social Security Administration.

Examples 7 and 8 illustrate the interesting quirk in the benefit provisions that in some instances payment levels can depend on the beneficiary's sex. A man whose wife receives noncovered earnings (i.e., dividends, rental income, etc.) which provide more than half her support may nonetheless claim her as a dependent spouse. A woman whose husband is in precisely the same situation is treated as a single individual and therefore receives no additional payments whatever for her spouse.

Benefit Levels Related to Occupation

Uneven as the treatment on the basis of marital and family conditions may be, the differences still are not nearly so marked as those which result from the beneficiary's occupation. The reason for occupational differences can easily be deduced from Table 2, which gives the dates on which major extensions of coverage took effect. For instance, it will be seen that workers

239

in commerce and industry paid OASI taxes for some 14 years before other segments of the economy began to be gathered into the system. Nearly 20 years elapsed between the beginning of the system and the coverage of lawyers and most medical professionals. And yet the hypothetical dentist in Table 1 was fully insured by 1966 and qualified for retirement benefits on the same footing as his cousin who worked in commerce and industry—and hence paid social security taxes—since 1937.

TABLE 2

MAJOR CHANGES IN COVERAGE UNDER OASDI, 1935–1966

Effective Date	Compulsory Coverage Added	Elective Coverage Added
1937.........	All workers in commerce and industry, except railroads, in continental U.S., Alaska, and Hawaii	None
1951.........	Self-employed (except farm and professional), regularly employed farm and domestic workers, Federal civilian workers not under retirement program, Americans employed outside U.S. by American employers, residents of Puerto Rico and Virgin Islands	State and local government employees not under retirement system: employees of nonprofit institutions
1955.........	Farm self-employed, professional self-employed (except lawyers and medical professionals), most farm and domestic workers	State and local government employees under retirement system, ministers
1956.........	Lawyers, dentists, optometrists, chiropractors, osteopaths, veterinarians, and other medical professionals (except doctors of medicine) materially participating farm landlords, Armed forces	....
1959.........	Most crude gum workers	....
1961.........	Peace Corps volunteers, residents of Guam and Samoa	....
1965.........	Doctors of medicine	....
1966.........	Hospital interns	....

Source: Social Security Administration.

Examples 9-13 in Table 1 illustrate the effect of occupation on the total tax payments as a percent of benefits. Examples 9 and 10 are comparable to 2 except for occupation. Yet a farm worker's percentage is 50 percent smaller than that of a worker in commerce and industry; the military serviceman's is only one-third as much.

The differences between the self-employed and other beneficiaries are more difficult to identify, primarily because of the special rate which applies to the former. If, for comparability, the employer's share of the tax is also considered, then the percentage for a widowed self-employed grocer is about half that for his counterpart in commerce and industry. Similarly, a self-employed married farmer, not covered until 1955, enjoys a percentage just slightly more than half that of, say, a lathe operator and his wife; a married dentist, covered since 1956, only 40 percent as large as that of the married lathe operator.

240

Clearly, these examples could be expanded almost endlessly, using various combinations of marital status, number and age of children, and occupation. For the most extreme result possible, one could contrast a single individual in commerce and industry vis-à-vis a Samoan with enough very young children to qualify for maximum benefits for a long period. But the intent here has not been so much to point to "horrible examples" as to call attention to the everyday, ordinary results which ensue because the variables governing tax liability differ from the variables governing benefit levels.

Intergeneration Transfers

Table 1 hints at another interesting facet of the social security system. The occupational contrasts depend primarily on the date of initial coverage relative to date of retirement. For the individual entering the labor force today, occupation by and large will make little difference in his payment-benefit ratio. That is to say, beneficiaries who were relatively old when their occupation fell under social security coverage receive a windfall. The windfall, however, is not confined to those coming under coverage in the 1950's or later; it is merely larger for such beneficiaries. For the fact is that no one retiring in 1966 could have been covered—i.e., could have paid OASI taxes—his full working life, unless by some anomaly he did not enter the working force until the age of 38.

Even the most "unfavorable" percentage in Table 1 is a good bargain, particularly considering that no deduction has been made for the value of the disability and survivors insurance which has been in force since 1956. Under the most extreme assumption possible, that all of the employer's share of the tax is shifted to the beneficiary, even the single individual in commerce and industry, if he lives 10 years after he retires, will get back more than double the amount he and his employer paid in. Moreover, Medicare, for which no allowance was made in the computation of total benefits, more than likely improves the beneficiary's chance of living even longer and thus increases the probable benefit total yet more.

One man's windfall can often be another man's loss. In the case of the social security system, the windfalls enjoyed by today's beneficiaries are subsidized by younger participants. That is to say, the present system results in an intergeneration transfer, an income redistribution from young to old. *Ceterus paribus*, the younger the taxpayer, the higher the tax payments as a percent of benefits, and vice-versa.

It is difficult to isolate the intergeneration redistribution in any systematic way, simply because there exists a more or less continuous spectrum of tax payment-benefit percentages related to age and occupation. Table 3, however, illustrates the general principle.[7] Percentages similar to

---

[7]The figures in Table 3 do not take into account the full intergeneration transfer effect, since they apply to beneficiaries who have been in covered employment either their full working lives or since the outset of the social security system. This condition will not be met by most self-employed until 1995; farm self-employed, 1999; lawyers and most medical professionals, 2000; doctors of medicine, 2009, to cite only a few examples.

those in Table 1 are computed for beneficiaries retiring in 1963, 1965, and various years in the future, with the benefit totals based on actual life expectancies.

TABLE 3

VALUE OF TOTAL EMPLOYEE TAX PAYMENTS AND BENEFITS, AND TAX PAYMENTS
AS PERCENT OF BENEFITS[a]
SELECTED RETIREMENT YEARS, 1962–2010

Year of Retire- ment	Value of Tax Pay- ments at 3 Percent Interest[b]	Value of Benefits Discounted at 3 Percent[c]			Value of Tax Payments as Percent of Value of Benefits		
		Single Male	Married Male	Single Female	Single Male	Married Male	Single Female
1962.....	$ 1,885	$15,548	26,234	18,144	12.1%	7.2	10.4
1965.....	2,580	16,054	27,092	18,966	16.1	9.5	13.6
1970.....	4,312	17,416	29,401	19,395	24.8	14.7	22.2
1980.....	9,406	18,621	31,445	21,055	50.5	29.9	44.7
1990.....	15,341	19,103	32,262	21,746	80.3	47.6	70.5
2000.....	22,502	19,947	33,693	22,853	112.8	66.8	98.5
2010.....	28,531	20,429	34,510	23,406	139.7	82.7	121.9

[a]Based on Social Security Law as amended, in 1965. Excludes employer tax.

[b]Assumes worker is employed (as an employee) at maximum covered earnings in all years after 1937, or after attaining age 20, if later. Excludes portion of tax earmarked for health insurance. Tax payments are the same for single male, married male, and single female.

[c]Assumes worker is alive at age 65 and retires at that time (attaining age 65 at the beginning of the year). Married worker and his wife are the same age.

Source: Unpublished computations prepared by Ray M. Peterson, vice president and associate actuary, The Equitable Life Assurance Society of the United States.

A single male retiring in 1962 would pay taxes worth 12.1 percent of the benefits he will receive if he lives out his normal span of years. The percentage rises to 16.1 percent for a single male retiring in 1965; by 1970, the percentage rises to 24.8 percent. By 1980, his taxes would amount to slightly more than half of his benefits. By the year 2000, taxes more than cover benefits. By 2010, taxes exceed benefits by $8,000, not counting the employer portion of the tax. In that year, the value of the combined tax would exceed the value of benefits by about $36,000, clearly identifying the source of the windfalls shown in Table 1.

CONCLUSION

Popular belief assumes that the OASDHI tax is regressive; Mr. Harvey claimed, on the contrary, that the tax is progressive. But several of the points emerging from the preceding discussion cast doubt on both viewpoints.

In brief, the major redistributive factors built into the social security system are the following:

1. The effective tax rate, which—
   (a) Decreases as the taxpayer's income level increases, particularly if nontaxable income items loom large or earnings exceed the maximum base.
   (b) Increases when there is more than one family member with taxable earnings.

2. Total tax payments over the taxpayer's entire working life, which—
   (a) Vary directly with the level of taxable earnings, but not necessarily with the level of income.
   (b) Are lower if the taxpayer's occupation has not been covered ever since he entered the working force.
   (c) Are lower if he is delayed in entering the working force—as, for example, by earning a college degree.
   (d) Are higher the later he is due to retire.
3. Total benefits, which—
   (a) Are higher in absolute terms, but lower as a percent of earnings, if the beneficiary's earnings have been relatively high, and vice-versa.
   (b) Are higher if the beneficiary is married and/or has dependent children.
   (c) Vary directly with longevity.

By plucking out suitable portions of the evidence, one can "prove" either the popular idea or Mr. Harvey's contention. Point 1a nicely illustrates the former; point 2a reinforces the latter. But reflection on the remaining points suggests, as so often happens, that real life is not amenable to simple theoretical classifications.

Most economists probably would expect that 1b, 2a, and 3a redistribute income in favor of low-income taxpayers, but that 1a, 2b, 2c, 3b, and 3c operate in the opposite direction and that 2d is indeterminate. However, there probably is no rigorous method (or suitable information) one might use to measure even approximately the extent to which any one of the above effects offsets another. The problem of estimating the relative importance of each factor with a view to determining the net effect of redistribution likely must remain insoluble.

While uncertainty is vexing, honest recognition of its existence is preferable to deceptive attempts to find a pattern where none exists. Condemnation or praise of the social security system on the basis of its income redistribution—a common practice—begins to look like a meaningless exercise. Nor do any workable "cures," except possibly the passage of time, recommend themselves. For the time being, apparently the wise course is to put aside personal equity considerations, and concentrate on other aspects, in making judgments about this tax.[8]

---

[8]For an examination of the effects of the OASDHI tax on resource allocation, growth, economic stability, etc., see: *Economic Aspects of the Social Security Tax*, New York, Tax Foundation, 1966.

CHAPTER IV

SOME STRATEGIC CONTEXTS OF

PUBLIC FINANCE AND BUDGETING:

ANALYTIC MODELS AND

ACTUAL PATTERNS OF DECISION-MAKING

Economists once made life simple for themselves. They let assumptions take the place of descriptions. Thus classical economists assumed widespread consumer knowledge, more or less perfect competition between producers, and rational decision-making by both producer and consumer. Under such conditions, even in the relatively short run, people reflected what they valued by the prices they were willing to pay for any array of goods. There was little need for strategy in all this, little need for long-range planning. Economic Man got what he could while he could, basically. This is an elemental strategy.

Similarly, public finance and budgeting would be simple indeed if some cousinly assumptions were made. Classical Budgeting Man could spring from a small handful of assumptions. The assumptions include:

1. Relatively complete and comparable knowledge by both voters and policy makers about what individuals and groups want and how to get it;

2. Meaningful comparisons between alternative programs or agencies so that scarce budget dollars can be assigned in terms of such criteria as the relative efficiency of attaining social ends of various orders of preference; and

3. Rational decision-making by both voters and policy makers.

We have long since learned that simplicism in economics does not help in either understanding what is or prescribing what should be. Thus a consumer's knowledge about what he does want is far from perfect, and he is perhaps best off in this area. Comparatively, at best, his knowledge about the degrees to which alternative products meet his specific needs is imperfect.

A few massive enterprises also have a great advantage in shaping particularly the short-run tastes of the great multitudes, as by advertising that exploits our deepest needs to be loved or admired. The assumptions of the classical economist, in short, must be modified or rejected.

244

This section hopefully helps encourage a sophistication about public finance and budgeting similar to that achieved in economics. Basically, the focus here is dual: on analytical models of decision-making; and on actual patterns of decision-making.

The broad approach here is usefully framed in terms of two models of decision-making that are relevant to all of administration. Table I sketches the properties of the two models. Basically, the Rational Comprehensive model of decision-making is consistent with the ideal assumptions detailed above for Economic Man and Budgeting Man. Classical Economic Man, for example, has the knowledge of values and reality demanded by the Rational Comprehensive model. In addition, because all consumers and producers are assumed to have small and relatively equal shares of influence in the model's marketplace, everyone's knowledge and desires are afforded full and equal but minor play. There is no especial need for alternative strategies under these conditions.

The Successive Limited Approximations (SLA) model of decision-making stands in sharp opposition. Economic Man and Budgeting Man would not find the SLA model congenial. Indeed, they would be immobilized by conditions like those assumed by the SLA model. Thus the SLA model implies incomplete knowledge of what is desired and how it may be obtained. Here alternative strategies take on considerable signifiance, and chance and insight play major roles.

The selections below in various ways reflect and elaborate these two basic models of decision-making. Some cautions are appropriate. Of course, the connections between the selections and the models usually are in terms of "more or less." That is, the selections tend to reflect more of one model than the other; they reflect differences in degree more than in kind. As a related caution, neither model is more appropriate than the other in all cases. Thus the SLA model is clearly inappropriate where the assumptions of the Rational Comprehensive model can be met in reality, as in the solution of a linear programming problem which yields the lowest transportation costs of moving specified quantities of specific goods between known points having different freight charges. Here also the issue is one of greater or lesser usefulness rather than all or none. The relevant art is determining those circumstances under which one model or the other is more appropriate, not trumpeting the one and excoriating the other. The two models have their specific uses while they vary significantly in their general applicability.

Specifics may help establish the value of the two models of decision-making as analytical end-points that various commentators approach but variously modify. Two pieces by Arthur Smithies, for example, reflect one variety of ideal-cum-modification. Thus the pieces accept the general ideal of the Rational Comprehensive model while they also develop some of the complexities of approaching the ideal in practice. Thus his brief "Conceptual Framework for the Program Budget" presents a brief list of the components of his systemic notion of planning, programming, and budgeting; and his "Budgeting and the Decision-Making Process" adds detailed counterpoint about practical difficulties in attaining his ideal system without essentially changing that ideal.

TABLE 1

Two Models of Decision-Making

Rational Comprehensive Model	Successive Limited Approximations Model
1a. Values or objectives are determined and clarified separately, and usually before considering alternative policies.	1a. Objectives and action alternatives are considered to be inter-twined.
1b. Policy-formation is approached through ends-means analysis, with agreed-upon ends generating a search for appropriate ways of attaining them.	1b. Means-end analysis is often inappropriate because means and ends are not distinct.
1c. A "good" policy is therefore one providing the most appropriate means to some desired end.	1c. A "good" policy is one about which various analysts agree, without their agreeing that it is the most appropriate means for some objective.
1d. Every important relevant factor is taken into account.	1d. Analysis is limited in that important possible outcomes and important values are neglected.
1e. Theory often is heavily relied upon.	1e. Successive comparisons greatly reduce the need for theory.

Based on Charles E. Lindblom, "The Science of Muddling Through," *Public Administration Review*, Vol. 19 (Spring, 1959), pp. 79-88.

The issue facing Smithies is an aged one. At which point, if ever, does the ideal so conflict with the existing or the possible that it is appropriate to adopt another ideal? Clearly, Smithies does not feel the reservations he notes are great enough. The fact remains, however, that he provides substantial evidence of the problems confronting Rational Comprehensive approaches to finance and budgeting. Some of these problems are unique and circumstantial, but some exist almost everywhere and apparently most of the time. For example, Smithies' notions of both "horizontal division" of an organization by function and "vertical division" of an organization by levels reflect a ubiquitous practical roadblock to approaching the Rational Comprehensive model. In essence, organizations tend to fragment in two basic ways: "up and down" between different hierarchical levels; and "across" between units at the same level performing different organization activities. Both varieties of fragmentation reduce the degree to which planning, programming, and budgeting can be delicately articulated and integrated into a comprehensive system. Note only that the different needs and problems of the various fragmented subgroups may not be expressed and compared, even if those needs and problems are comparable, compatible, and can be met. Suborganizations will develop within any agency, that is, and their members will tend to "play close to their chests" with financial and budgeting data. The point holds "for horizontal" relations with peers as well as for "vertical" relations with superiors and headquarters units dealing with finance and budgeting.

What some observers see as deviations, others see as normal and perhaps as desirable. Barber and Wildavsky illustrate the point in terms of their approaches to "incrementalism," which has a strong flavor of the Successive Limited Approximations Model of Table 1. Thus Smithies requires a statement of the nation's goals before he begins budgeting. An incrementalist, in a rough but approximate sense, looks first at what the budget was last year and in the few preceding years. The incrementalist's basic budgeting rule thus becomes: "base level, plus or minus." This basic rule is crude, but it may also be realistic and the most that can be expected in many cases.

The selections below provide two perspectives on incrementalism. Thus Barber looks long and hard at the criteria policy makers actually used in making "budget decisions" in response to a problem situation imposed by the experimentor. Barber's "Complexity, Synopticism, Incrementalism, and the Real Questions" reports some of the results of an ingenious laboratory experiment with real governmental decision-making groups. Since the decision-making groups were local boards of finance, Barber in effect gives us a look at incrementalism from the "top, down." Wildavsky's "Ubiquitous and Contingent Strategies" provides a "bottom, up" complement. Essentially Wildavsky details the ways in which government agencies seem well advised to act so as to maximize the chances of getting favorable consideration from those who have formal control over appropriations, particularly legislators.

Viewing budgeting as comprehensive or as incremental is no mere play on an emphasis. For many purposes, the theoretical and practical differences are substantial. First, the two views differ because their proponents are looking at

247

somewhat different things in somewhat different ways. Thus incrementalists tend to stress how things actually are. However, comprehensive budgeters are given to emphasizing how they ought to be. Budgeters of the two persuasions, consequently, are liable to find themselves at odds on a wide range of issues. The "is" and the "ought," in short, commonly do not coincide, Indeed, the predisposition to emphasize one or the other may reflect basic unyielding personality differences.

Second, "strategy" is all-important to the incrementalist view while it is distinctly secondary in any comprehensive approach to budgeting. The comprehensive approach tends strongly to seek support for a program in terms of its consistency with national objectives. Its bias thus is toward articulating those objectives, and perhaps complaining if movement toward them is sluggish. Although this view admits of some exaggeration, the incrementalist seeks strategies that are acceptable even if agreement about objectives has not been achieved or is in fact unlikely or impossible. Illustratively, one can seldom easily speak of "national objectives" but life must go on regardless. Of course, agreement about objectives probably always is desirable. Failing that, the question is: Is there some program we can agree is a good one, lack of agreement about objectives notwithstanding?

In sum, proponents of the two views about budgeting and financial decisions will find themselves leaning in opposite directions. The contrast is not absolute. For strategies are relevant in the comprehensive approach; and objectives cannot be neglected by the incrementalist. Usually, however, the emphases are so opposed that the contrast is all but absolute.

Third, deep philosophical differences may underlie the two approaches to budgeting and financial decisions. Thus the incrementalist position is more at home with a "pluralist" concept of what the basic form of government is and/or ought to be. The comprehensive approach inclines more toward some form of "elitism" as a descriptive and/or prescriptive guide for governance. Again the point must not be pushed to extremes, for "pluralism" and "elitism" may have developmental ties. For example, "too much" pluralism may in practice lead to social and political chaos. In such a case, pluralism may then lead to elitism.

The theoretical differences between the two approaches to budgeting decisions, in any case, may reflect or be strongly reinforced by the philosophies or world views of the individuals espousing them. The differences in approach in such a case may rightly be called ultimate.

A final selection points up other significant theoretical and practical differences between the incremental and comprehensive approaches to budgeting. That selection is Charles E. Lindblom's "Decision-Making in Taxation and Expenditures." Lindblom essentially compares a number of characteristics of the federal budgeting processes with certain norms supported by orthodox budgeting principles. He provides detail on the major slippages between practice and principle, moreover.

Lindblom does not despair that reality and the norms of orthodox budgeting practice are at significant odds. The closing part of his argument, in fact, sketches several senses in which decision-making about budgets is better off

248

for the differences between what actually happens and what is often accepted as desirable. Lindblom develops his position via an analysis of coordination through "partisan mutual adjustment" in which he often finds a rationality and effectiveness that others have argued can be found only in a comprehensive approach to budgeting. Lindblom also suggests that a commitment to the comprehensive approach can be dangerous as well as misguided in the many cases in which the required means-ends analysis is awkward or impossible. In sum, he sees means-ends analysis as most applicable to "low-level problems." Much that is of budgetary and financial significance in governance does not qualify as "low-level problems," however. And therein lies the rub of a general commitment to the comprehensive approach as Lindblom sees it.

CONCEPTUAL FRAMEWORK FOR THE PROGRAM BUDGET

Arthur Smithies

The need for program budgeting arises from the indissoluble connection between budgeting and the formulation and conduct of national policy, or the policy of a state, a city, or a town, as the case may be. Governments, like private individuals or organizations, are constrained by the scarcity of economic resources at their disposal. Not only the extent to which they pursue particular objectives, but the character of the objectives themselves, will be influenced by the resources available. On the other hand, the extent to which the government desires to pursue its objectives will influence the resources it makes available to itself by taxation or other means. Planning, programming, and budgeting constitute the process by which objectives and resources, and the interrelations among them, are taken into account to achieve a coherent and comprehensive program of action for the government as a whole. Program budgeting involves the use of budgetary techniques that facilitate explicit consideration of the pursuit of policy objectives in terms of their economic costs, both at the present time and in the future.

To be more specific, a modern government is concerned with the broad objectives of defense; law and order; health, education, and welfare; and with economic development, together with the conduct of current business operations, notably the Post Office. No government, whatever its resources, can avoid the need for compromises among these objectives. No country can defend itself fully against all possible external threats. It takes certain risks with respect to defense for the sake of increasing the domestic welfare of its citizens. It must also compromise between the present and the future. The more actively it promotes defense and welfare at the present time, the more it may (under certain conditions) retard the long-run economic development of the country, by curtailing both private and public investment in the future. The country will be frustrated in the pursuit of all its objectives if it neglects the effective maintenance of law and order. Yet, compromises are made in this area also. No country supports a police force that will detect every crime, and no country enforces every law up to the limit.

Moreover, the character of each major program will depend on the total resources the government can appropriate to its purposes. A small country (at the present time) cannot afford nuclear weapons. Few countries can, or at any rate do, attempt to educate as wide a segment of their population as does the United States. However, countries may vary in their willingness to pursue their national objectives. With much smaller natural resources, the Soviet Union is prepared to make efforts comparable to those of the United States in both the fields of defense and education.

The task of making the necessary compromises among various objectives is the function of planning, programming, and budgeting. To make those compromises it is necessary that the various government activities be expressed in terms of a common denominator, and the only common denominator available is money. It is difficult to compare the relative merits of an additional military division and an additional university. It is often more feasible to compare the relative merits of spending an additional billion dollars in one direction or the other. But to make that comparison it is necessary to know how much an additional billion dollars will add to military strength and how much to university education. While defense and education cannot be measured in simple quantitative terms, quantitative information can throw light on the consequences of spending money in various directions.

There are, however, a multitude of ways in which money can be spent on defense or education. To make intelligent comparisons, each of these major functions must be broken down into meaningful subfunctions. Modern defense at least requires considerations in terms of strategic forces and limited war forces. Education must be broken down at least into primary, secondary, and tertiary education. Major programs should thus be considered in terms of subprograms, and at the end of the scale one reaches the manpower, material, and supplies used by the government in support of these activities. Such considerations and calculations should lead to the concept of resources (money) used in "optimal" or preferred ways to achieve policy objectives.

Some government decisions relate only to the immediate future in the sense that if they turn out to be wrong, they can be readily reversed. Others, however, relate to a distant future that can be only dimly foreseen. Pure research, particularly, is in this category, since its consequences are, in the nature of the case, unknown. But governments nevertheless must make critical decisions with respect to the resources they devote to particular kinds of research as well as to research in the aggregate. At a lower order of difficulty, critical decisions with respect to transportation, resource development, and the development of weapon systems relate to the next decade rather than the next year. All budgeting is essentially a matter or preparing for the future, but modern budgeting involves long-range projections into a highly uncertain future.

The basic point of view of this book is that a government can determine its policies most effectively if it chooses rationally among alternative courses of action, with as full knowledge as possible of the implications of those alternatives. The requirement of choice is imposed on it by the fact that any government is limited by the scarcity of resources. It is fundamental to our culture that rational choice is better than irrational choice. The government must choose not only among various courses of government

251

action, but also between the government's total program and the private sector of the economy. The task of choice is not rendered easier by the fact that a substantial part of the government's program is designed to affect the future performance of the private economy. The primary purpose of program budgeting is to facilitate the making of these difficult choices.

Planning, programming, and budgeting is the focus of the process of comparison and coordination. In line with the foregoing paragraphs it involves:

1. Appraisals and comparisons of various government activities in terms of their contributions to national objectives.
2. Determination of how given objectives can be attained with minimum expenditure of resources.
3. Projection of government activities over an adequate time horizon.
4. Comparison of the relative contribution of private and public activities of national objectives.
5. Revisions of objectives, programs, and budgets in the light of experience and changing circumstances.

These operations are inherent in any planning, programming, and budgetary process. Program budgeting involves more explicit recognition of the need to perform them than has been traditional. It also involves the application of new analytical techniques as an aid to the exercise of the human judgment on which choices must ultimately rest.

It should be clear from this statement of the budgetary problem that the traditional distinction between policymaking and budgeting, or between setting of goals and deciding on how to attain them, is inadequate and misleading. While the government can have a general desire and intention to defend the country, it cannot have a defense objective that is operationally meaningful until it is aware of the specific military implications of devoting resources to defense; and as part of that awareness, it should know the consequences of using defense resources in alternative ways. The question of allocative efficiency is thus intimately bound up with the question of the determination of goals. An adequate programming system must serve both purposes.

BUDGETING AND THE
DECISION-MAKING PROCESS

ARTHUR SMITHIES

This chapter is designed to provide the analytic framework of this study—to bring out the relation of budgeting to the whole process of decision-making. Almost every governmental decision has budgetary implications since the process of decision-making almost invariably involves the allocation of scarce resources among alternative uses. Resources can be used privately or diverted by taxation or other methods to government use, and, if so diverted, they are allocated among a variety of government uses. A major thesis of this study is that the entire process of decision-making is improved to the extent that these choices are made explicitly and deliberately. Or if the Government desires to exempt a particular program from exposure to competition for funds, the decision to do so should be expressly made. The first purpose of this chapter is to elaborate this central argument.

The second purpose is to discuss the decision-making process, and the budgetary process in particular, from the viewpoint of the structure and procedures of a complicated organization. Although my concern is with the Federal Government, it is convenient at this stage to discuss the problem in more general terms and to work out principles of organization that can later be applied to the specific problem of the Federal budget. This chapter is thus designed merely to provide a basis for analysis. In no sense is it intended to provide a full description of the government decision-making process.[1]

STAGES IN THE
DECISION-MAKING PROCESS

The process of decision-making by an organization can be represented as a continuing process consisting of six stages: determination of policy objectives, planning, programming, budget formulation, budget (or program) execution, budget (or program) review. These categories are reflected in varying degrees in an organization's structure and procedures. For instance, in the national defense organization each stage can be readily identified. At the opposite extreme, the proprietor of a business may carry out all the stages himself. In other instances the stages shade into each other. In any

---

Article is from Arthur Smithies, *The Budgetary Process in the United States*, New York: McGraw-Hill Book Co., 1955, pp. 20–34. Copyright © 1955 by Committee for Economic Development. Reprinted with permission of author and publisher.

[1]This chapter has been greatly influenced by Herbert Simon's *Administrative Behavior*, New York: The Macmillan Company, 1947, and Paul H. Appleby's *Big Democracy*, New York: Alfred A. Knopf, Inc., 1945. But neither of these authors can be held responsible for the conclusions reached.

event, it is useful for analytical purposes to consider the decision-making process in these terms. These are first discussed on the assumption that each of them is carried out by the organization as a whole. Later the distribution of functions within the organization is considered.

The determination of policy objectives is a subject that is largely outside the scope of this study. The political and social processes of a country result in the adoption of national objectives with respect to national defense, resource development, social security, and payment of benefits to veterans. These objectives may be formally expressed in legislation, such as the G.I. Bill of Rights, or they may be expressed equally forcefully in the general political consciousness of the country—as is the case with major foreign-policy objectives. Policy objectives may be deeply rooted in a country's history and tradition; they may emerge as compromises among conflicting political forces; or they may result from general consideration of the national interest.

It is important to recognize, however, that governments as well as other organizations must frequently make decisions in an aura of great uncertainty, with respect both to the situations that have to be met and the results that different courses of action may produce. In the area of foreign policy, for instance, the Government may be unable to define its objectives precisely since the intentions and objectives of other countries are imperfectly known. Only after some course of action has been taken and has proved to be a move in the right or the wrong direction may it be possible to reduce uncertainty with respect to the future. Determination of policy objectives may therefore consist largely in extensions or reversals of what has been done in the past, based on the experience of the past. Consequently an effective review of past performance is an important factor in the determination of policy objectives.

Furthermore, objectives in the future may be changed as a result of actions taken in response to present attitudes. Social security, for instance, was adopted as a program in the 'thirties in response to the attitudes that then existed. But its operation for almost two decades has substantially altered national attitudes toward the program. If the consequent new decisions are to be well founded, this process of change in national attitudes should be based on as clear an understanding of past operation of the programs concerned as is feasible.

The adoption of a particular objective of policy inevitably implies a decision on the urgency or importance of that objective. When the Government decides that a change in defense policy is desirable, it must also form some notion of how desirable. And in that connection it forms some notion of how far it is prepared to sacrifice other objectives in order to attain its new objective. But such notions are vague and imprecise at the policy-formation stage. It is the purpose of the subsequent stage of the decision-making process to make them precise and thereby to formulate a unified program that will achieve the most satisfactory compromise among the various objectives of policy.

Planning, as the term is used here, means the preparation of alternative plans that will further particular policy objectives in varying measure and that are within the reasonable bounds of feasibility. Proposals to fortify the moon or to provide family allowances of $10,000 a year may be consistent with established policy objectives, insofar as those objectives have been made precise, but they may be generally considered to be so far outside the bounds of feasibility that they should be contemplated by visionaries rather than by planners.[2] As examples, military planners design an array of stategic plans to further foreign-policy objectives. City planners devise alternative methods of coping with a traffic problem. Or regional planners may produce a variety of approaches to the economic development of a region. Planning in this sense may be related to particular policy objectives or to a variety of objectives.

Programming denotes a further step in the direction of finality and feasibility, and may involve selection among alternative plans or a combination of elements from a number of plans. When a program is adopted to achieve a particular policy objective or if, for instance, the President announces a comprehensive program, it is implied that the program is considered feasible and can be carried out. The aspect of feasibility that is of most concern to us here is, of course, the willingness of the organization to bear the cost of the program. Both particular and comprehensive programs, however, are frequently promulgated before they have been exposed to the rigorous tests of budgeting. One reason for this situation lies in the operations of a complex organization, which will be examined later.[3] Another arises from the fact that it is frequently desirable to program for a period into the future, longer than the period for which it is feasible to prepare budgets. Budgets to be useful must relate to a future that is reasonably foreseeable. It may nevertheless be desirable to program for a future that can only be foreseen dimly —provided that the program is subject to revision as the future unfolds.

Basic decisions that greatly influence the size of the budget may be taken at the programming stage. As dramatic examples, the distribution of the defense program among the three Services and of the Air Force program among the various commands are budgetary questions, since the national objective is to obtain the most efficient use of resources devoted to defense. While these questions are largely settled before a budget is prepared, the programming decisions should be based on the relative costs of the various defense alternatives.

The formulation of a budget is an extension of the programming stage. Programs become expenditure programs and thus are expressed in terms of a common denominator, money. They can then be compared with each other

---

[2]Needless to say, the word "planning" as I use it here has no connotation of central control of economic activity. I am using it rather in the sense in which it is used in military circles.

[3]*See* "Organizational Structure and Procedures and the Decision-Making Process" section of this article.

and with their cost in terms of taxation or of borrowing with greater precision than is feasible in the earlier stages of the process. Furthermore, the question of economy—the attainment of given program results at minimum costs—can be effectively considered only when all the elements of the program are expressed in terms of money.[4]

The comparisons and calculations that comprise the formulation of the budget are likely to call for revision of programs, since more light is thrown on implications of those programs than was previously available. On the other hand, if the budget in a particular year fails to provide for the year what is called for by a longer-term program, the program may nevertheless be adhered to and may exert an upward pull on the budget in the following year. The budgeting stage is the first point at which rational economic calculation—consideration of how scarce resources can best be allocated among various alternative uses—comes fully into play. Although these comparisons enter in the earlier stages to some extent, they cannot be fully carried out until all programs are considered together and are expressed in a common denominator. The major thesis, stated above, that expenditure commitments for any particular program should not in general be made until this stage is reached rests on the view that this process of rational calculation and comparison can further the total objectives of an organization.

Budget or program execution should be regarded as a separate stage in the decision-making process since, even in a budget for as short a period as a year, it is impossible to prescribe what is to be done with complete specificity or to provide for all contingencies. The objectives of the budget can be more nearly achieved if there is some discretion exercised in the execution of the budget than if it is followed slavishly. During the budget period, external factors may require minor revisions in policy objectives, and possibilities of economy may become apparent that could not be foreseen at the time the budget was prepared. Successful execution of the budget therefore requires scrupulous adherence to its intent but departure from its detail where necessary to give effect to its intent. In the course of the execution of the budget new methods for achieving economy and efficiency in the conduct of operations should be tested and explored. This should be the continuing purpose of administrative management based on actual experience. The talents and techniques required for this task are essentially different from those required to secure an efficient allocation of the budget among the various programs.

Budget or program review has three main purposes. In the first place, expenditures should be reviewed from the point of view of their legality and propriety. Such a review is the traditional purpose of an audit of the

---

[4]Money is used as the common denominator for budgeting because in normal terms it represents in general the cost of scarce resources. In times of extreme scarcity, such as total war, the money measure of scarcity becomes inadequate. Budgeting in terms of critical scarce factors such as manpower or strategic materials then tends to replace monetary budgeting; it is usually called "programming" rather than "budgeting."

organization's accounts. In the second place, a review of actual performance provides a link between the past and the future in the determination of policy objectives and the formulation of a budget. In the third place, a review of actual performance is essential for the purposes of administrative management. And the kind of review required for this purpose may be different from that needed for programming purposes. For instance, a classification of expenditures by purposes or functions is needed for the formulation of a budget. But the traditional classification by organization units or objects may be more suitable for administrative management.

The behavior of the organization depends on the way in which it performs each of these operations and the ways in which it relates them to each other. One organization may make virtually all its decisions at the policy-making stage. Its determination of objectives may also involve determination of its program. In other words, it leaves the allocation of resources among alternatives to look after itself. Another may be so preoccupied with costs and economy that it loses sight of its purposes and objectives. Organizations may vary also in the degree to which they permit review of the past to influence their future plans. Some may look only to the future and forget the past. The behavior of others may depend far more on the forces of inheritance and tradition than on the shifting contemporary scene.

Organizations can also differ widely in the way in which they define their policy objectives. In some the objectives may be defined with precision, and the subsequent stages of the process may consist mainly of refinements and elaborations of the initial determination. The "firm" of the economics textbooks, for instance, has a single objective—to maximize profits. When the supply and cost conditions faced by the firm are assumed to be known, its program can be worked out by mere computation. At the opposite extreme, it is difficult if not impossible to define with any precision the policy objectives of a university. Its policies grow out of the activities of members of the faculty who are motivated by a general belief in the university's traditions and purposes. Yet their ideas of policy may vary widely. In fact, the success of the university may be held to depend on the existence of such a variety of viewpoints. Nevertheless the university's resources are limited, and, despite the diversity of its objectives, the university must adopt a definite budget program. Clearly the formulation of the budget has more serious policy implications for the university than for the hypothetical firm. In government, the role of budget formulation usually falls somewhere between these extremes.

How an organization combines the several stages of the decision-making process depends largely on its basic purposes and on temperaments and attitudes of the individuals who comprise it. Such factors may be decisive in the simpler forms of organization, such as the small New England town meeting, where all members of the town deliberate together. The analysis of their behavior then falls within the province of the social psychologist. The economist, however, can still point to the degree to which rationality enters the decision-making process. He can say to the town, "If you want to act more rationally, you will stress the formulation of a definite budget more heavily than you now do." He may also be prepared to say, "In my judgment you will be better off if you make more conscious selections among alternatives than you now do, and I can suggest to you some habits of thought that will assist you to do so."

The behavior of the more complicated organizations—of which the Federal Government may well be the most complicated—depends not only on the attitudes and habits of thought of their members but also on their formal procedures and structures. The rules under which an organization operates and the relationships established among its parts have an important bearing on the ways in which the various parts of the decision-making process affect its total behavior. Proposals for improvement in the process must therefore consist largely of suggestions for procedural and structural changes.

ORGANIZATIONAL STRUCTURE AND PROCEDURES AND THE DECISION-MAKING PROCESS

Discussion of the government decision-making process and of budgeting in particular has frequently tended to take an unduly simplified view of the structure of an organization and the distribution of functions within it. For instance, the relations of the legislature with the executive have often been embodied in these familiar statements: the legislative determines policy; the executive formulates a budget to carry out that policy; the legislature considers and enacts the budget; the executive executes the budget; the legislature reviews the accounts of the executive.

That formulation conveys the impression of a simple sequence of technical operations. Policy-making is disposed of in the first stage. Budgeting is merely a matter of determining the costs of the "policies determined by the Congress." Appropriation involves a technical review of the executive estimates and the formulation of detailed directives for the executive. Execution means carrying out both the letter and therefore the spirit of those directives. Review means an audit of the accounts of the executive from the point of view of their legality and propriety. This description is by no means a caricature of traditional views. It is faithfully reflected in the procedures of the appropriations committees and in the procedural association of budgeting with accounting to the exclusion of its association with policy formation. Whether or not this approach ever furnished an adequate guide to organization, it is thoroughly inadequate for a government performing its modern functions. The legislature does not distill policy once and for all out of the air. Policy objectives are being continually revised in the light of experience and the changing needs of the situation. The legislature is largely influenced in this respect by the recommendations of the executive.

The formulation of a budget is far more than a translation of predetermined objectives into financial terms. Policy objectives—particularly in the defense area—may, of necessity, be capable of definition only in imprecise terms. Consequently, when the legislature undertakes to review the executive budget, it has more to do than merely check details. It must decide whether it approves or wishes to alter the program content of the executive budget. Or, as occurs in the parliamentary system of government, the legislature surrenders the right to amend the budget but retains the right to dismiss the executive and in that way to get a new budget. Furthermore, the need to relate expenditures to revenues makes it impossible to regard budgeting as a mere translation of policy into financial terms. Only the peculiar conditions of the nineteenth century made it possible to overlook this essential point in connection with the Federal Government.

The budget enacted by the legislature cannot be formulated in complete detail. The executive must be permitted discretion to adapt the program to the needs of a changing situation as it unfolds, subject to the overriding policy objectives established by the legislature. It follows that review should be much more than a matter of accounting or auditing as commonly understood. For the legislature to perform its functions properly, it needs to appraise the total performance of the executive within the areas of executive discretion. Finally, the executive cannot be treated as a whole. The operation of the decision-making process depends heavily on the relations of the chief executive and his subordinate departments and on those of department heads with their subordinates. In the Federal Government the situation is even more complicated since the executive departments have responsibilities to the Congress in addition to their responsibilities to the President. Consequently a more elaborate view of organizational structure and procedures is needed—one that recognizes the continuing nature of the decision-making process, the thoroughgoing interdependence of the various stages, and, therefore, the fact that no single part of the organization is exclusively concerned with any one stage.

As groundwork for such an approach it is necessary to stress both the vertical and the horizontal aspects of the structure of an organization. The nature of its decisions will depend first on the hierarchical structure of the organization, that is, on the vertical division of functions. It will depend also on the horizontal arrangements made at each level in the hierarchy—on how legislatures or executives at any level divide and combine their activities with respect to policy objectives, budgeting execution, and review.

Vertical Division of Functions

An organization is normally divided vertically into a legislative or representative body, a chief executive, and executive departments and their subdivision. The need for a vertical division arises first from the fact that legislative bodies are normally too cumbersome to carry out completely some of the top-level functions in the decision-making process. While in some organizations the legislature is clearly superior to the chief executive, in others it shares top-level authority with him.[5] The latter situation is typified by the power of the President to veto laws passed by the Congress and by the power of the Congress to exert direct control over executive departments through formal or informal restrictions on the use of appropriations. Secondly, the vertical division arises from the need for specialization in the Executive Branch. Specialization necessarily means that discretion within defined limits is exercised by subordinate layers. If an upper layer gives complete instructions to a subordinate layer, no specialization will be achieved. Specialization also implies that a subordinate official sees less of the total picture than his superior. While he should be aware of the objectives of the whole organization, he is not competent to compete with his superiors in the performance of their functions.

The behavior of the organization will depend largely on the relationships and the lines of communication that are established among the successive layers in the vertical hierarchy. These fall within three main categories: (*a*) Directives, which flow down the organization. Directives, whether given to the executive by the legislature or by one executive level to another, have two main functions: first, they prescribe what shall be done; and second, they determine the degree of discretion that may be exercised at the subordinate level. (*b*) Recommendations, which flow up through the organization. The recommendation made by one level to the next above it depends first of all on the functions that are assigned to it; second, on its view of the policies that the organization should follow; and third, on the recommendations it receives from below. It should be emphasized that an executive is not likely to be performing his functions adequately if he merely transmits recommendations received from a subordinate. He presumably has a more complete knowledge of the policies of the organization as a whole than does his subordinate, and he should revise the recommendations he receives in the light of his greater knowledge. (*c*) Reviews and reports on past performance, which flow up through the organization—both to show how far directives have been carried out and to provide a guide to decisions for the future.

The nature of the vertical relationships differs widely among organizations. An army narrowly limits the areas in which subordinates may exercise direction and make recommendations. On the other hand, the policies and programs of a university are likely, in the main, to originate in the faculty. There is no rule for the optimum form of an organization for all purposes.

---

[5]I shall speak of the chief executive as a single individual for the sake of simplicity. It is important to realize, however, that this is merely a simplification. The chief executive may be a cabinet, as in the British Government. In some corporations the board of directors constitutes the chief executive. In others the president is the chief executive, while the board of directors acts rather as the representatives of the legislature (the shareholders). In still others chief executive authority may be vested in an executive committee. In the Federal Government the President is constitutionally the chief executive.

There is likely, however, to be an optimum structure of vertical relationships for an organization that is designed to serve some given purpose.

Horizontal Division of Functions

The need for a horizontal division of functions is most evident in a legislature. All the members of even the simplest legislative body cannot collectively perform the several decision-making operations. It therefore divides into committees, say, a policy and planning committee, a budget committee, and an execution and review committee. The nature of the legislature's decisions will depend both on the ways in which it divides the process and on the way in which it relates the decisions of the various parts to each other. For instance, one that divides its budgetary function between separate expenditure and revenue committees is likely to reach different decisions from one that has a single budget committee. And the way in which committees are coordinated may result in the policy and planning committee being stronger than the budget committee or vice versa.

The question of horizontal organization arises not only in legislatures but at every level of a vertical organization. An executive is concerned with policy objectives in areas where he can exercise discretion or can make recommendations to his superiors. He must submit a budget for his future activities. He must execute his budget when it is enacted. He must report on his operations. Within his own orbit the head of a division may be as much concerned with policy as the head of a government department. But the division head bases his policy recommendations and decisions on a narrower and more specialized set of criteria than does the head of the department. Horizontal arrangements thus give rise to the same kinds of questions in executive departments as in legislatures.

COMPLEXITY, SYNOPTICISM, INCREMENTALISM, AND THE REAL QUESTIONS

JAMES D. BARBER

Potentially at least, budgetary decisions are immensely complex. They can involve calculations covering the entire range of detailed governmental functions and operations, from the chemistry of water purification to the psychology of social work. Aaron Wildavsky's examples from the congressional budgetary process—e.g., should more money be spent on studies of homopoiesis or lymphomatosis[1]—could be matched at the local level. Potential complexities also exist in coping with relations among levels of abstraction, in assessing the implications of past actions for future ones, and in applying ethical standards to uncertain choices. In Chapter III, I shall try to show how various ambiguities in these matters provide opportunities for power strategies. Here the point is that the most determined budgeter can never hope to take into account all the complexities implicit in the decisions he must make.

Consider the "ideal" budget-maker. He begins by surveying the goals of the community, ranking them in order of importance and determining the temporal priority of each in relation to the others. He bases this initial step on a comprehensive knowledge of his town's economic, political, historical, and ecological character, projected into the future by means of appropriate techniques. Then he proceeds to determine the best means to these ends, making a detailed analysis of each department's resources, operations, and plans. Finally, he allocates funds among these activities in accordance with the priorities previously established and the probabilities of various unforeseen contingencies.

This "synoptic ideal"[2] is obviously impossible to obtain in its pure form, but it is often held out as a goal to be approximated as nearly as

---

Article is from James D. Barber, *Power in Committees*, Chicago: Rand McNally & Company, 1966, pp. 34–46. Reprinted with the permission of author and publisher.

[1]Aaron Wildavsky, p. 9, *The Politics of the Budgetary Process*.

[2]David Braybrooke and Charles E. Lindblom, *A Strategy of Decision: Policy Evaluation*, New York: Free Press of Glencoe, 1963, chap. 3. On synoptic versus incremental approaches, *see* also Charles E. Lindblom, "The Science of 'Muddling Through,'" *Public Administration Review*, Vol. 12 (1952), pp. 79–88; Yehezkel Dror, Charles E. Lindblom, Roger W. Jones, Mickey McCleery, and Wolf Heydebrand, "Governmental Decision-Making: A Symposium," *Public Administration Review*, Vol. 24 (1964), pp. 154–65; James W. Fesler, "Administration in the Federal Government," *Yale Papers in Political Science*, No. 6 (New Haven, Conn.: Yale University Press, 1963); and Rufus P. Browning, "Innovative and Non-Innovative Decision Processes in Government Budgeting," a paper delivered at the 1963 Annual Meeting of the American Political Science Association.

possible. Budget-makers are advised to move in this direction, to take into account as many facets of the problem as they can. At its worst, such advice is simply exhortation to try hard and do better. Analysts of actual budget-making processes as they are performed from day to day by human beings in official positions have come forth with a radically different picture of the budget-maker. In fact, they report, budgeters operate incrementally by restricting their attention to very small segments of the total problem, comparing a few alternative marginal departures from the existing situation, and considering only what can be done with readily available resources. While this view can be offered as a strictly empirical observation, it can also be used to elaborate a series of recommendations.

However, to concentrate on the stark contrasts between the synoptic ideal and the incremental reality is perhaps to miss some real questions of practical importance. The interesting questions regarding budget-making practices are:

1. Matters of Degree. The alternatives are not incrementalism versus synopticism, but more-or-less incrementalism versus more-or-less synopticism. To what extent can (should) the budgeter take into account a somewhat broader range of calculations than he does? To what extent can (should) he devote more of his time to marginal calculations at the expense of large and long-range considerations?

2. Matters of Method. There are any number of ways to simplify an excessively complex problem. What are the implications of choice among these various possibilities? What particular intellectual devices can (should) the budgeter adopt?

3. Matters of Rationality. Decision-makers may pursue strategies for simplification largely consciously, with an awareness based on rational choice, or largely unconsciously, in accordance with unexamined habits or predilections. Cognitive complexity is a psychological problem, a source of strain, which can be resolved by inadvertence or design, accidentally or purposefully.[3] The data to be presented next bear on these questions, and I shall come back later to some possible answers.

BUDGETARY CRITERIA

As will be recalled, each board of finance spent approximately thirty minutes in the small groups laboratory on a budget-reducing task, looking over its own most recent budget figures to determine where and by how much the total could be cut if this were necessary. These deliberations were tape recorded and, subsequently, complete, typed transcripts were prepared. To find out what criteria were actually employed as the members approved and rejected reductions, a content analysis of this material was performed. First,

---

[3] On conscious versus unconscious decision rules, *see* Karl W. Deutsch, *The Nerves of Government,* New York: Free Press of Glencoe, 1963, chap. vi.

TABLE 1

BUDGETARY CRITERIA:
PERCENTAGE OF COMMENTS EXPRESSING REASONS FOR
AND AGAINST PROPOSED REDUCTIONS

Reasons for Cuts

Magnitude and Change of Expenditures
Appropriation was increased in last budget..............16.8%
New item...11.8
Large item.. 9.1
Account shows surplus; current expenditure rate.......... 8.9

Subtotal..   46.6
Effects on Operations
Cuts will not hamper services........................13.6
Expenditure can be postponed........................ 8.9

Subtotal..   22.5
Uncertainty
Original appropriation based on rough estimate, was not
    considered carefully by BF.........................10.9
Funds may not be needed; can correct later.............. 6.3

Subtotal..   17.2
Other
Effect on tax rate................................... 4.7
Comparison with other departments.................... 2.3
Probable public reaction to cut...................... 1.6
Probable reaction of department to cut................ 1.3
Comparison with other towns.......................... 0.9
Competence or sincerity of requester.................. 1.3
Miscellaneous....................................... 1.6

Subtotal..   13.7

Total...   100 (N = 559)

Reasons against Cuts

Uncontrollable items
"Can't be touched"..................................27.4%
State requirements.................................. 8.1

Subtotal..   35.5
Appropriation Already Minimal
BF cut from last request............................10.5
BF considered last request carefully.................. 9.1
Appropriation has decreased.......................... 5.0
Request was minimal; tight........................... 4.3

Subtotal..   28.9
Effects on Operations
Cut will hamper services............................16.0
Effect uncertain, perhaps harmful..................... 7.4
Urgent; cannot be postponed.......................... 0.5

Subtotal..   23.9
Other
Probable public reaction to cut...................... 3.8
Effect on tax rate.................................. 2.4
Competence or sincerity of requester.................. 2.1
Probable reaction of departments..................... 0.2
Comparison with other departments.................... 0
Comparison with other towns......................... 0
Miscellaneous....................................... 3.3

Subtotal..   11.8

Total...   100.1 (N = 420) all comments which could be identified as favoring specific reductions were distinguished from those opposing specific reductions, giving totals of 559 and 420 respectively. Then these comments were assigned to categories meant to catch the main substantive content of each as this emerged inductively from the data. In Table 1, the frequencies of these comments are detailed. These figures and a freer perusal of the transcripts cast light on several board of finance techniques for simplifying an extremely complex set of problems.[4]

Criterion 1: Controllability

The distinction between controllable and uncontrollable costs is a preliminary criterion, applied when the members of the board attempt to decide where to focus attention rather than how much to cut. Certain expenditures have been committed by previous long-range decisions, or are tied in closely with basic legal requirements, or are mandatory accompaniments of other fundamental costs such as retirement funds or wage levels. Excluding these from consideration enables the board to devote its efforts to those matters on which it has discretion in the short run. This is the most frequent of the reasons advanced against cutting particular items. Obviously it can be a useful device when it is consciously applied from the beginning.

In a good many cases, however, the reasons for categorizing an item as uncontrollable are not clear. The borderlines between expenses which are irrevocably committed, those which could be affected by changes in other areas of the budget, and those which are thought to be difficult to change without disrupting essential services are not well defined. Often the members seem to be referring not to some fixed commitment but to a general *consensus* among themselves that changing an item would be undesirable. Typically, the item is mentioned, someone comments that it "can't be touched," all quickly agree, and they pass on to the next item. In these cases ambiguities in the meanings of controllability are not consciously explored, and it is possible for many specific appropriations to drift over into the uncontrollable category.

Criterion 2: Size and Increase

Most boards appear to recognize that cutting budget requests "across the board" by some fixed percentage or amount is, in the long run, destructive of budgetary rationality. The lesson is learned through a series of feedback processes. Over the years, such flat cutting teaches the requesting agencies to anticipate losing a fixed proportion of their requests, regardless of the merits of the case, and thus to adjust the requests accordingly. The budget reviewers eventually catch on to this ploy and automatically deduct the traditional "fat" or excess before beginning their real cutting. The requester may then be motivated to pad even more, and so on. Eventually both sides begin to lose confidence in one another, and to realize how ridiculous the game is becoming.

---

[4]Many of these themes are similar to those Wildavsky found at the federal level. *See* Wildavsky, *op. cit.*, chap. ii and iii.

The spiral may end with mutual confessions of sin, prayers for forgiveness, and oaths of reform. Judging from comments offered in the boards of finance discussions, across-the-board cutting is passé.

Generally, attention is fixed on the large items in the budget and those requests which have increased over the previous request and/or appropriation. Large requests indicate large and, thus, important programs and therefore, members conclude, large opportunities for savings. The focus is on agency *totals* as clues for the allocation of attention. This is the easiest way to distinguish among requests, and chopping down a large appropriation may pay off in money terms much more than many smaller-scale decisions.

There is, however, a hidden assumption in this line of reasoning which may be fallacious: that a large item contains roughly the same proportion of "fat" as the smaller items do—or perhaps more. This would be a valid conclusion if, for example, the requests were padded on a percentage basis, by adding, say, 10 percent. But otherwise the following proposition would probably hold for most departments: the larger the request, the more times it has been carefully reviewed during the request-making process. The board of education budget, almost always the largest single item, has filtered up to the board of finance through a long series of preliminary stages: teachers, principals, superintendent of schools, board of education budget committee, and full board of education. The tree warden, on the other hand, may bring his comparatively small but unreviewed request directly to the board of finance. Insofar as each successive review tends to reduce initial estimates, many large final totals may indicate budgetary muscle rather than fat.

The technique of concentrating on the large items, then, may be undertaken consciously, but it is often practiced without complete awareness of critical assumptions.

But, in fact, the board of finance may make few comparisons from department to department on the basis of size or any other principle. The main procedure in practice is to consider the budget *horizontally*—this year versus last year—rather than *vertically*—Department A versus Department B. Increased requests stand out; sometimes the difference between last year's and this year's request is calculated and entered on the budget forms in order to highlight this aspect. The operative assumption seems to be that stable expenditure levels are *prima facie* valid and need not be closely examined, while raises are suspicious and need detailed scrutiny. As a simplifying device, this technique reflects the much more general tendency for a person to notice objects in motion amidst a collection of fixed objects.

However, designating what is moving and what is still depends on a further specification: moving in relation to what? A *stable* or constant money figure may conceal marked instability in the level of services rendered, in real expenditure terms (considering prices), in changes in the revenue side of budgeting, and so forth. A *raise* in the salary schedule of 2 percent a year represents a *decline* in real incomes if the cost of living is going up 3 percent a year. If more state funds are made available for road work, a *stable* figure for the town highway department in fact represents an *increase*. In periods of increased welfare needs, as in a recession, a *stable* welfare expenditure conceals an actual *drop* in spending per case. Thus simplification by means of concentration on departures from previous spending levels risks distortion and substantive error in the budget. If most other conditions are stable, however, it offers one more way to cut down the burden of calculation.

Criterion 3: Concreteness

If asked to describe their procedures in budgeting, most members of the boards of finance would, I believe, refer to the above techniques in one form or another. The budgeter is usually aware that he uses such techniques—these are the reasons which he advances overtly. But frequently there is an aspect of each technique of which he remains unconscious: the bases for the reasons which he advances are seldom explored and, I think, seldom thought about. The remaining criteria to be discussed fall largely in the latter category of simplification techniques employed unconsciously, or at least according to no regular design.

When a person must make a decision in an ambiguous situation, he searches for some familiar element or set of elements with which he has had much experience, and concentrates on that. In a discussion of education, for example, the philosopher is apt to focus on the general goals, the psychologist on the learning process, and the economist on the marginal utility of various resource allocations. Board of finance members often bring to their official tasks considerable experience in practical affairs, gathered over years of business activity. This means that they are familiar with budgets and can quickly grasp the practical implications of budgetary details. But these very strengths may divert attention toward the concrete, down-to-earth details of a problem and away from certain less tangible but relevant matters.

Take the recreation budget, for example. Questions such as what variety of fencing is best for a playground, what it is reasonable to pay for grading a ball field, and the like are quite similar to those encountered in the course of business. But other matters of key import to the recreation program seem strange: Which of several alternative teenage sports programs would contribute most to the health and welfare of the youngsters? What balance should be struck between programs for the various age groups? These kinds of questions are in fact decided by the ways the board allocates funds. But they may be answered indirectly, without discussion or adequate information, because of the board's tendency to wrestle with physical details rather than policy alternatives. Many of the comments scored above as effects on operations are of this nuts-and-bolts variety.

Criterion 4: Immediacy

The pressure to keep the discussion in board meetings focused on the here and now is intense. Exaggerated in the laboratory situation, scarcity of time is a problem also in the normal budget deliberations, as the deadline for completing the budget approaches inexorably. The member who brings up the long-range picture, or who reaches too far back into the past for his illustrations, may be made to feel that he is interrupting an emergency meeting to introduce irrelevancies. This year's problems are bad enough without adding in those of a decade hence. Simplification is thus achieved by restricting attention to the present and near future.

Yet, of course, decisions made in the immediate context do shape long-run community developments. This is especially evident in large capital expenditures. When a bridge is built in a certain location, the town is, in effect, committed for years to come to a certain pattern of traffic flow in that area. Other land uses are excluded for a long time. Long-term effects on real estate values, business fortunes, and the like may be fixed. Attitudes expressed in the board of finance deliberations regarding community planning agencies often discount these implications but they cannot disprove them.

Viewing time in the other direction, if the board focuses only on what is immediate, it tends to eliminate much relevant evidence from the past. This is not to reintroduce all the complications which simplification techniques are meant to handle, but only to point out that there may be particular decisions upon which particular past experiences might bear, and that an unconscious decision to exclude from consideration everything that happened before last year may not be entirely reasonable. The key problem is one of information retrieval or feedback. Some relevant historical information will be stored in the minds of the members and they may be motivated to introduce it, but the imposition of group restraints on such expressions excludes this vital resource. Other information might be kept in systematic written form, readily available for reference when needed.

Here again, then, a device for simplifying complexity bears with it the possibility of introducing unnecessary additional complexities, as the same problems are encountered and muddled through again and again, without benefit of ordered hindsight.

We have negative evidence of another variety of immediacy or insularity as a criterion: the rather surprising lack of reference to experiences in other towns. The members of a board of finance focus on their own community almost exclusively. Fewer than 1 percent of the comments favoring cuts and none of those opposing cuts refer to comparisons with other towns. In part this is a result of lack of information, few boards being aware that comparative statistical data on town budgeting decisions are readily available. In part it reflects community pride—"Ours is a unique town"—and in part reasonable doubts about the transferability of findings from one setting to another. But among the 169 towns in Connecticut there are undoubtedly many which face similar problems in education, law enforcement, municipal financing, and so on. The small town of Bethlehem may gain little enlightenment from the teeming city of Bridgeport, but it might profit from a look toward Canaan or Bozrah or Hebron.

Criterion 5: Uncertainty

All of these criteria could be considered methods for reducing uncertainty. In a more complex way, however, the boards appear to use the certain-uncertain distinction itself as a simplifying device. We notice in Table 1 such items as "Original appropriation, based on rough estimate, was not considered carefully by BF," "Funds may not be needed; can correct later," "BF considered last request carefully," "Effect uncertain, perhaps harmful." The thrust of these comments seems to be that at any given time the board will (a) not reconsider decisions about which the members have been certain in the past, and (b) make new decisions, without feeling entirely certain about them, only if such decisions can be taken tentatively and any ill effects can be corrected later. The latter gambit is a prediction that in some cases (usually those involving small expenditures) risks can be progressively eliminated on the basis of future feedback. For example, most towns can expect to encounter sudden needs for additional snow removal funds from time to time, and to draw on various contingency funds to meet these needs as they arise. Money for hiring new school teachers, on the other hand, is needed once and for all near the first of the year in order to complete contractual arrangements. This invites gambling a bit with the snow but taking a cautious approach with the teachers.

The retrospective dimension of uncertainty as a criterion is somewhat simpler. The board looks back at its prior deliberations and recalls that in some cases decisions were made with considerable confidence and in others with considerable doubt. The more uncertain they were, the more willing they are to reconsider. On the surface this appears to be an obvious and reasonable way to proceed, but it is open to at least one kind of irrational inference. That is, estimates of past certainty may be based almost entirely on past effort—on the time and energy previously devoted to reviewing a request. Members seem to feel that if a problem was initially considered at great length the solution was very likely right, or at least that new deliberations on the problem are unlikely to improve the solution. In many cases this makes sense, but in others the fact that much effort went into the making of a decision may indicate that members had many doubts, that many contingencies had to be taken into account, and/or that opinions had to be substituted for missing information. In other words, effort expended is sometimes, but not always, an accurate index of results achieved.

Criterion 6: Dollars and Cents

Another way to simplify the complexity of a decision is to focus on its formal details—in this case, the figures on the pieces of paper at hand. The numbers provide the fundamental basis for calculation, the expression of wants and costs in comparable monetary units. And arithmetic furnishes the fundamental techniques for comparing this program with that one, this year with last year, and so on.

The danger inherent here is that of falling into a kind of symbolic reification in which the representation is cognitively detached from the thing represented, the link between symbol and reality forgotten. In budgeting it is possible to become so absorbed in dollars-and-cents calculations that one loses track of what the figures stand for. This problem arises especially when a great deal of time is spent on arithmetic in order to bring together a coherent set of requests. The numbers come to have a life of their own as they are summed and subtracted and divided. This can lead to mistakes in emphasis and interpretation; for example, a decision to cut a request from one department by a certain amount may be treated as a precedent of sorts for cutting another department by the same amount. The forest is lost sight of as the trees fall all around.

These six criteria for simplification in budgeting: (1) Controllability, (2) Size and increase, (3) Concreteness, (4) Immediacy, (5) Uncertainty, and (6) Dollars and cents appear to be the main ones employed by the boards of finance. Of course, any aspect of budgeting not attended to suggests a technique for reducing complexity—for instance, little attention is paid to revenue-raising problems or to public opinion in these deliberations—but these half-dozen criteria seem to shape budgeting most determinatively. They bring us back to the "real questions" raised earlier.

Close study of the discussion transcripts leads to the conclusion that if these boards err, it is not in the direction of the "synoptic ideal." We come away with the impression that far too little attention is devoted to the broader, longer-range implications of the decisions being made, and that evidence which could be highly useful is systematically ignored.[5] The temptation is strong to preach the gospel of the bigger picture, to urge more effort on all fronts. But this is unlikely to increase the effectiveness or rationality of the budgetary process. More to the point are considerations of how simplification can be accomplished without sacrificing so much of the larger dimensions of budgeting.

INCREMENTAL IMPROVEMENTS IN INCREMENTALISM

If the major problem for the budgeter is economizing his attention then strategic decisions—those which subsume or predetermine some aspect of many lesser decisions—are of prime importance.[6] Strategic decisions pay off in

---

[5]On the conservative tendencies of incrementalism, see John T. Lanzetta and Vera T. Kanareff, "Information Cost, Amount of Payoff, and Level of Aspiration as Determinants of Information Seeking in Decision-Making," Behavioral Science, Vol. 7 (1962), pp. 459–73; Randall B. Ripley, "Interagency Committees and Incrementalism: The Case of Aid to India," Midwest Journal of Political Science, Vol. 8 (1964), pp. 143–65; and Vernon Van Dyke, Pride and Power: The Rationale of the Space Program, Urbana: University of Illinois Press, 1964, chap. xvi.

[6]On strategic simplification, see Deutsch, op. cit., pp. 251–52; and Thomas C. Schelling, "Bargaining, Communication and Limited War," in The Strategy of Conflict,

savings in time and energy as the same types of problems come up repeatedly. For example, once a man decides to shave every morning, he need not concern himself further with the matter. The time taken to make this decision represents a saving, not a waste, of effort. The rule need not be applied rigidly; there will be occasions for breaking it. But by concentrating attention for a while on a recurrent problem and resolving it, one conserves mental energies for years to come.

For the boards of finance, and perhaps for other budget-making bodies, three kinds of strategic decisions appear to offer the best possibilities. None is new, but they are unevenly attended to.

1. Basic Policy and Timing Decisions

By consciously devoting time early in the budget process to determining the boundaries between all controllable and all uncontrollable costs, setting general cost-of-living salary adjustments, and the like, these matters are removed from the agenda of many meetings on specific budget items. Similarly, paying attention early to long-range community planning can dispose of conflicts which might otherwise crop up repeatedly. Timing decisions, particularly setting a schedule for the submission and consideration of requests, can save many an hour's *ad hoc* discussion about what to do next. The simple matter of setting a definite time for meetings—especially for *ending* meetings—removes another set of unnecessary uncertainties. Such cross-cutting decisions on specific, clearly defined topics offer much better possibilities for improvement than vague discussions of general goals or theories of administration.

2. Information-Processing Decisions

Part of the problem here is simply that of creating and collecting information: keeping accurate minutes, requiring reports from operating agencies, gathering statistics on various facets of town finance. The more serious problems involve organizing and communicating available information for maximum utility in making individual decisions. For example, one of the boards of finance regularly has before it, at budget time, a breakdown of the appropriations to each department over the last decade, including the percentage of the total town budget spent annually by each. Standardized budget forms facilitate quick access to relevant comparisons. By setting up a system for training new members and for distributing agendas and pertinent documents to all members for study before they come together at the meeting, the board can save much collegial learning time. Again, the significant pay-off results from *deciding*, consciously and definitely, how information is to be created, stored, and retrieved.

New York: Oxford University Press, 1963, pp. 53–80. On similar simplification techniques in Congress, *see* Ralph K. Huitt, "Congressional Organization and Operations in the Field of Money and Credit," in William Fellner *et al.* (eds.), *Fiscal and Debt Management Policies*, Englewood Cliffs, N.J.: Prentice-Hall, 1963, particularly pp. 436–40.

3. Delegation Decisions

The possibilities of delegation are largely unexploited by most boards of finance. Yet it is evident that much relevant research could be farmed out to finance officers, department heads, and clerks. If a program budget, in which each requesting agency spells out in simple narrative form the main services rendered in the past year and the program for the next year, is submitted, the members of the board will not have to dig this information out of the requesters at joint meetings. Research and recommendations on long-term community trends can also be delegated. And perhaps the biggest saving in time could be accomplished by assigning simple calculation tasks to a clerk with a desk calculator. The man-hours consumed by problems in simple arithmetic add up impressively in many boards.

These are, of course, matters of detail on which there can be valid disagreement. The point which needs to be stressed is that analysis of such methods offers better possibilities for the incremental improvement of incrementalism than does a focus on grand alternative models of decision-making. If the goal is rational efficiency in exercising the power of the purse, such mundane moves have much to recommend them. If the purpose is to attain a position of power in the framework of town government, other devices ... may be called for.

UBIQUITOUS AND CONTINGENT STRATEGIES

AARON WILDAVSKY

What really counts in helping an agency get the appropriations it desires? Long service in Washington has convinced high agency officials that some things count a great deal and others only a little. Although they are well aware of the desirability of having technical data to support their requests, budget officials commonly derogate the importance of the formal aspects of their work as a means of securing appropriations. Budget estimates that are well prepared may be useful for internal purposes—deciding among competing programs, maintaining control of the agency's operations, giving the participants the feeling they know what they are doing, finding the cost of complex items. The estimates also provide a respectable backstop for the agency's demands. But, as several informants put it in almost identical words, "It's not what's in your estimates but how good a politician you are that matters."

Being a good politician, these officials say, requires essentially three things: cultivation of an active clientele, the development of confidence among other governmental officials, and skill in following strategies that exploit one's opportunities to the maximum. Doing good work is viewed as part of being a good politician.

Strategies designed to gain confidence and clientele are ubiquitous; they are found everywhere and at all times in the budgetary system. The need for obtaining support is so firmly fixed a star in the budgetary firmament that it is perceived by everyone and uniformly taken into account in making the calculations upon which strategies depend.

"Contingent" strategies are particular; they depend upon conditions of time and place and circumstance; they are especially dependent upon an agency's attitude toward the opportunities the budgetary system provides for. Arising out of these attitudes, we may distinguish three basic orientations toward budgeting in increasing order of ambition. First, defending the agency's base by guarding against cuts in old programs. Second, increasing the size of the base by moving ahead with old programs. Third, expanding the base by adding new programs. These types of strategies differ considerably from one another. An agency might cut popular programs to promote a restoration of funds; it would be unlikely to follow this strategy in adding new programs. We shall take up ubiquitous and contingent strategies in turn.

Article is from Aaron Wildavsky, *The Politics of the Budgetary Process*, Boston: Little, Brown and Company, 1964, pp. 64–84. Reprinted with permission of author and publisher.

CLIENTELE

Find a Clientele. For most agencies locating a clientele is no problem at all; the groups interested in their activities are all too present. But for some agencies the problem is a difficult one and they have to take extraordinary measures to solve it. Men and women incarcerated in federal prisons, for instance, are hardly an ideal clientele. And the rest of society cares only to the extent of keeping these people locked up. So the Bureau of Prisons tries to create special interest in its activities on the part of Congressmen who are invited to see what is going on. "I wish, Mr. Bow, you would come and visit us at one of these prison places when you have the time. ... I am sure you would enjoy it." The United States Information Agency faces a similar problem—partly explaining its mendicant status—because it serves people abroad rather than directly benefiting them at home. Things got so bad that the USIA sought to organize the country's ambassadors to foreign nations to vouch for the good job it said it was doing.

Serve Your Clientele. For an agency that has a large and strategically placed clientele, the most effective strategy is service to those who are in a position to help them. "If we deliver this kind of service," an administrator declared, "other things are secondary and automatic." His agency made a point of organizing clientele groups in various localities, priming them to engage in approved projects, serving them well, and encouraging them to inform their Congressmen of their reaction. Informing one's clientele of the full extent of the benefits they receive may increase the intensity with which they support the agency's request.

Expand Your Clientele. In order to secure substantial funds from Congress for domestic purposes, it is ordinarily necessary to develop fairly wide interest in the program. This is what Representative Whitten did when he became a member of the Appropriations Committee and discovered that soil conservation in various watersheds had been authorized but little money had been forthcoming: "Living in the watersheds ... I began to check ... and I found that all these watersheds were in a particular region, which meant there was no general interest in the Congress in this type of program. ... It led me to go before the Democratic platform committee in 1952 and urge them to write into the platform a plank on watershed protection. And they did." As a result, Whitten was able to call on more general support from Democrats and increase appropriations for the Soil Conservation Service watersheds.

Concentrate on Individual Constituencies. After the Census Bureau had made an unsuccessful bid to establish a national housing survey, Representative Yates gave it a useful hint. The proposed survey "is so general," Yates said, "as to be almost useless to the people of a particular community. ... This would help someone like Armstrong Cork, who can sell its product anywhere in the country ... but will it help the construction industry in a particular area to know whether or not it faces a shortage of customers?" Later, the Bureau submitted a new program that called for a detailed enumeration of metropolitan districts with a sample survey of other areas to get a national total. Endorsed by mortgage holding associations, the construction material industry, and Federal and state housing agencies, the new National Housing Inventory received enthusiastic support in Congress where Representative Preston exclaimed, "This certainly represents a lot of imaginative thinking on your part. ..." In another case the National Science Foundation made headway with a program of summer mathematics institutes not only because the idea was excellent but also because the institutes were spread around the country, where they became part of a constituency interest Congressmen are supposed to protect.

Secure Feedback. Almost everyone claims that his projects are immensely popular and benefit lots of people. But how do elected officials know? They can only be made aware by hearing from constituents. The agency can do a lot to ensure that its clientele responds by informing them that contacting Congressmen is necessary and by telling them how to go about it if they do not already know. In fact, the agency may organize the clientele in the first place. The agency may then offer to fulfill the demand it has helped to create. Indeed, Congressmen often urge administrators to make a show of their clientele.

> SENATOR WHERRY: Do you have letters or evidence from small operators ... that need your service that you can introduce into the record. ... Is that not the test on how much demand there is for your services?
>
> RALSTON (Bureau of Mines): Yes. ... If it is important, as a rule they come to talk.

When feedback is absent or limited, Congressmen tend to assume no one cares and they need not bother with the appropriation. "... A dozen or more complaints do not impress me very much. ... We cut this out last spring and we did not hear any wild howls of distress. ..." When feedback is present it can work wonders, as happened with the Soil Conservation Service's Small Watershed program. Representative Andersen waxed enthusiastic:

> ... Will you point again to Chippewa-Shakopee? I know that project well because it is in my district. I wish the members of this subcommittee could see that Shakopee Creek watershed as it is today. The farmers in that neighborhood were very doubtful when we started that project. Now many of them tell us, Mr. Williams, that the additional crops they have obtained ... have more than repaid their entire assessment. ...

Guarding the treasury may be all right but it becomes uncomfortable when cuts return to haunt a Congressman. This is made clear in Representative Clevenger's tale of woe.

> CLEVENGER: I do not want to economize on the Weather Bureau. I never did. I do want an economical administration. ... I have been blamed for hurricane Hazel. My neighbor, who lived across the road

275

from me for 30 years, printed in his paper that I was to blame for $500 millions in damage and 200 lives. . . . His kids grew up on my porch and yet he prints that on the first page and it is not "maybe." I just "am." He goes back to stories that related to cuts that I made when I was chairman of the Committee.

Most agencies maintain publicity offices (under a variety of titles) whose job is to inform interested parties and the general public of the good things the agency is doing, creating a favorable climate of opinion. There may be objections to this practice on the part of Congressmen who do not like an agency and/or its programs, but those who favor the agency consider it desirable. House subcommittee Chairman Kirwan urged this course on the Bureau of Indian Affairs in connection with its Alaskan Native Service, a worthy but not overly popular program. "Why don't you make some arrangement to tell the Americans every year," Kirwan suggested, "instead of telling this committee what is going on? If you write a letter when you go back to Alaska . . . I will guarantee you the press will get it." The Weather Bureau was urged to put out some publicity of its own by Representative Flood, who observed that

> . . . forecasts . . . were obviously, literally and figuratively all wet. Somebody pointed out in this [*New York Times*] editorial where this . . . forecast has been "a little cold, a little wet, a little snow, but not bad." . . . But something took place which . . . dumped the whole wagonload of snow on Broadway and made them very unhappy. This happened repeatedly over a period of 30 days, which did not make you look very good, if I can understate it. . . . All right. Why do you not prepare a statement for the many newspaper readers in the area and point out to them that you know the problem is there, and that this is what you want to do about it. . . .

A final example comes from a student who wrote away for a summer job and received in reply a letter from an administrator refusing him on account of budgetary limitations. "Because of our inadequate funds at this critical time," the official wrote, "many students, like yourself, who would otherwise receive the professional training that this work provides, will be deprived of that opportunity. . . . Only prompt action by Congress in increasing these funds can make the success of our mission possible."

Divided We Stand. The structure of administrative units may be so arranged as to obtain greater support from clientele. It may be advantageous for a department to create more bureaus or subunits so that there are more claimants for funds who can attract support. "We have had the rather disillusioning experience that too often when we create a new agency of Government or divide up an existing agency," a Representative concluded, "that we wind up with more people on the payroll than we ever had before. . . ." There can be little doubt the division of the NIH into separate institutes for heart research, cancer research, and so on has helped mobilize more support than lumping them together under a general title with which it would be more difficult for individuals to identify.

United We Fall. The Weather Bureau is an example of an agency that did rather poorly until it took the many suggestions offered by its supporters in Congress and established a separate appropriation for research and development. The new category was the glamorous one and it was easier to attract support alone; being lumped in with the others hurt its appeal. Indeed, putting projects under the same category may be a way of holding down the expenditures for some so that others will not suffer. One of the imposing difficulties faced in building up the Polaris missile program was the fear that it would deprive traditional Navy activities of resources.

Advisory Committees Always Ask for More. Get a group of people together who are professionally interested in a subject, no matter how conservative or frugal they might otherwise be, and they are certain to find additional ways in which money could be spent. This apparently invariable law was stated by Representative Thomas when he observed that "All architects [doctors, lawyers, scientists, Indian chiefs] are for more and bigger projects, regardless of type. I have not seen one yet that did not come into that classification."

Advisors may be used to gather support for a program or agency in various ways. They may directly lobby with Congress or the President. "I happened to have lunch with Dr. Farber (a member of the quasi-governmental advisory committee of the NIH) the other day," Congressman Fogarty reveals, "and I learned there is considerable sentiment for these (clinical research) centers." Congressman Cederberg did not know of "anyone who would in any way want to hamper these programs, because I had lunch with Dr. Farber. ..." Advisors may provide a focus of respectability and apparent disinterest to take the onus of self-seeking from the proponents of greater spending. They may work with interest groups and, indeed, may actually represent them. They may direct their attempts to the public media of information as anyone can see by reading the many columns written by Howard Rusk, M.D., a writer on medical subjects for the *New York Times*, requesting greater funds for the NIH.

Do Not Admit Giving in to "Pressure."

CIVIL AERONAUTICS BOARD OFFICIAL: ... One of the reasons there has been such substantial expansion in local airline service, believe it or not, is largely due to the members of Congress.

REPRESENTATIVE FLOOD: I hope you are talking about Hazleton, Pa.

CAB OFFICIAL: I am talking about Pennsylvania as well as every other state. I do not want to leave the impression here that there has been undue pressure or that we have been unduly influenced by members of Congress, but we have tried to cooperate with them.

REPRESENTATIVE FLOOD: I do not care what the distinction is.

But if They Press Make Them Pay.

CAB OFFICIAL: ... Senator ... if there are any members of Congress apprehensive about the increasing level of subsidy, this has not been evident to the Board. ... I cannot think of any local service case in

277

which we have not had at least 15, 20, or 25 members of Congress each one urging an extension of the local service to the communities in his constituency as being needed in the public interest. ... We felt that they, if anyone, knew what the public interest required ... as to local service ... with full knowledge that this would require additional subsidy.

Avoid Being Captured. The danger always exists that the tail will wag the dog and the agency must exercise care to avoid being captured. Rival interests and Congressmen may be played against each other. New clientele may be recruited to replace the old. The President and influential Congressmen may be persuaded to help out. Or the agency may just decide to say "no" and take the consequences. Dependence upon the support of clientele, however, implies some degree of obligation and the agency may have to make some compromises. The interests involved may also have to compromise because they are dependent upon the administrators for access to decisions, and they may have many irons in the fire with the agency so that it is not worth jeopardizing all of them by an uncompromising stand on one.

Spending and Cutting Moods. Unfortunately, no studies have been made about how cutting and spending moods are generated. Yet changes in the climate of opinion do have an impact on appropriations. Possibly a great many groups and individuals, working without much direct coordination but with common purpose, seize upon events like reaction to World War II controls and spending to create a climate adverse to additional appropriations, or upon a recession to create an environment favorable for greater expenditures.

Budget Balancing and End-Runs. It is clear that the slogan of the balanced budget has become a weapon in the political wars as well as an article of belief. This is not the place to inquire whether the idea has merit; this is the place to observe that as a belief or slogan budget balancing is one determinant of strategies.

When the idea of a balanced budget becomes imbued with political significance, the Administration may seek appropriations policies that minimize the short-run impact on the budget although total expense may be greater over a period of years. In the Dixon-Yates case a proposed TVA power plant was rejected partly because it involved large immediate capital outlays. The private power plant that was accepted involved much larger expenditures over a 25 year period, but they would have had comparatively little impact during the Eisenhower Administration's term of office.[1]

When clientele are absent or weak there are some techniques for making expenditures that either do not appear in the budget or appear much later on. The International Monetary Fund may be given a Treasury note that it can use at some future date when it needs money. Public

---

[1]*See* the author's *Dixon-Yates: A Study in Power Politics*, New Haven, Conn.: University Press, 1962.

buildings may be constructed by private organizations so that the rent paid is much lower in the short run than an initial capital expenditure. The Federal Government may guarantee local bond flotations. An agency and its supporters who fear hostile committee action may also seek out ways to avoid direct encounter with the normal budgetary process. This action is bitterly opposed, especially in the House Appropriations Committee, as back-door spending.

I do not mean to suggest that getting constituency support is all that counts. On the contrary, many agencies lay down tough criteria that projects must meet before they are accepted. The point is that there are ordinarily so many programs that can be truly judged worthwhile by the agency's standards that its major task appears to be that of gaining political support. Priorities may then be assigned on the basis of the ability of the program and its sponsors to garner the necessary support.

CONFIDENCE

The sheer complexity of budgetary matters means that some people need to trust others because they can check up on them only a fraction of the time. "It is impossible for any person to understand in detail the purposes for which $70 billion are requested," Senator Thomas declared in regard to the defense budget. "The committee must take some things on faith." If we add to this the idea of budgeting by increments, where large areas of the budget are not subject to serious questions each year, committee members will treat an agency much better if they feel that its officials will not deceive them. Thus the ways in which the participants in budgeting try to solve their staggering burden of calculation constrains and guides them in their choice of means to secure budgetary ends.

Administrative officials are unanimously agreed that they must, as a bare minimum, enjoy the confidence of the appropriations committee members and their staff. "If you have the confidence of your subcommittee your life is much easier and you can do your department good; if you don't have confidence you can't accomplish much and you are always in trouble over this or that." How do agency personnel seek to establish this confidence?

Be What They Think They Are. Confidence is achieved by gearing one's behavior to fit in with the expectations of committee people. Essentially, the desired qualities appear to be projections of the committee members' images of themselves. Bureaucrats are expected to be masters of detail, hard-working, concise, frank, self-effacing fellows who are devoted to their work, tight with the taxpayer's money, recognize a political necessity when they see one, and keep the Congressmen informed. Where Representative Clevenger speaks dourly of how "fewer trips to the coffee shop ... help make money in most of the departments ...," Rooney demonstrates the other side of the coin by speaking favorably of calling the

Census Bureau late at night and finding its employees "on the job far later than usual closing hours." An administrator is highly praised because "he always knows his detail and his work. He is short, concise, and to the point. He does not waste any words. I hope when it comes to the economy in your laundry soap it is as great as his economy in words."

To be considered aboveboard, a fair and square shooter, a frank man is highly desirable. After an official admitted that an item had been so far down on the priority list that it had not been discussed with him, Senator Cordon remarked, "All right, I can understand that. Your frankness is refreshing." An administrator like Val Peterson, head of the Federal Civil Defense Agency, will take pains to stress that "There is nothing introduced here that is in the field of legerdemain at all ... I want ... to throw the cards on the table. ..."

The budget official needs to show that he is also a guardian of the treasury: sound, responsible, not a wastrel; he needs to be able to defend his presentations with convincing evidence and to at least appear to be concerned with protecting the taxpayer. Like the lady who gets a "bargain" and tells her husband how much she has saved, so the administrator is expected to speak of economies. Not only is there no fat in his budget, there is almost no lean. Witness Dewey Short, a former Congressman, speaking on behalf of the Army: "We think we are almost down to the bone. It is a modest request ... a meager request. ..." Agency people soon catch on to the economy motif: "I have already been under attack ... for being too tight with this money. ..." Petersen said. "I went through it [a field hospital] very carefully myself to be sure there were no plush items in it, nothing goldplated or fancy."

If and when a subcommittee drops the most prevalent role and becomes converted into an outright advocate of a program, as with the Polaris missile system, the budget official is expected to shoot for the moon and he will be criticized if he emphasizes petty economies instead of pushing his projects. Democratic Subcommittee Chairman Kirwan and ranking Republican Jensen complained that the Bureau of Land Management did not ask for enough money for soil conservation. "It is only a drop in the bucket," Kirwan said, "they are afraid to come in." "This committee has pounded for the seven years I know of," Jensen responded, "trying to get them to come in with greater amounts for soil conservation and they pay no attention to it." The norm against waste may even be invoked for spending, as when Kirwan proclaimed that "It is a big waste and loss of money for the U.S. Government when only 6 million is requested for the management of fish and wildlife." In 1948 the head of the Cancer Institute was told in no uncertain terms, "The sky is the limit ... and you come in with a little amount of $5,500,00. ..." It is not so much what administrators do but how they meet the particular subcommittee's or chairman's expectations that counts.

Play It Straight! Everyone agrees that the most important requirement of confidence, at least in a negative sense, is to be aboveboard. As Rooney once said, "There's only two things that get me mad. One is hare-brained schemes; the other is when they don't play it straight." A lie, an attempt to blatantly cover up some misdeed, a tricky move of any kind, can lead to an irreparable loss of confidence. A typical comment by an administrator states, "It doesn't pay to try to put something over on them [committee members] because if you get caught, you might as well pack your bags and leave Washington." And the chances of getting caught (as the examples that follow illustrate) are considerable because interested committeemen and their staffs have much experience and many sources of information.

Administrators invariably mention first things that should not be done. They believe that there are more people who can harm them than can help and that punishments for failure to establish confidence are greater than the rewards for achieving it. But at times they slip up and then the roof falls in. When Congress limited the amount of funds that could be spent on personnel, a bureau apparently evaded this limitation in 1952 by subcontracting out a plan to private investors. The House Subcommittee was furious:

> REPRESENTATIVE JENSEN: It certainly is going to take a house-cleaning ... of ... all people who are responsible for this kind of business.
> OFFICIAL: We are going to do it, Mr. Chairman.
> REPRESENTATIVE JENSEN: I do not mean "maybe." That is the most disgraceful showing that I have seen of any department.
> OFFICIAL: I am awfully sorry.

If a committee feels that it has been misled, there is no end to the punitory actions it can take. Senator Hayden spoke of the time when a bureau was given a lump-sum appropriation as an experiment. "Next year ... the committee felt outraged that certain actions had been taken, not indicated in the hearings before them. Then we proceeded to earmark the bill from one end to the other. We just tied it up in knots to show that it was the Congress, after all, that dictated policy."

Four months after a House subcommittee had recommended funds for a new prison, a supplemental appropriation request appeared for the purchase of an institution on the west coast that the Army was willing to sell. Rooney went up in smoke. "Never mentioned it at all, did you?" "Well," the Director replied, "negotiations were very nebulous at that time, Mr. Rooney." "Was that," Rooney asked, "because of the fact that this is a first-rate penal institution ... and would accommodate almost 1,500 prisoners?" It developed that Rooney, catching sight of the proposed supplemental, had sent a man out to investigate the institution. The supplemental did not go through.

281

Integrity. The positive side of the confidence relationship is to develop the opinion that the agency official is a man of high integrity who can be trusted. He must not only give but must also appear to give reliable information. He must keep confidences and not get a Congressman into trouble by what he says or does. He must be willing to take blame but never credit. Like a brand name, a budget official's reputation comes to be worth a good deal in negotiation. (This is called "ivory soap value," that is, 99 and 44/100% pure.) The crucial test may come when an official chooses to act contrary to his presumed immediate interests by accepting a cutback or taking the blame in order to maintain his integrity with his appropriations subcommittee. It must not be forgotten that the budget official often has a long-term perspective and may be correct in trying to maximize his appropriations over the years rather than on every single item.

If you are believed to have integrity, then you can get by more easily.

> ROONEY: Mr. Andretta [Justice Department], this is strictly a crystal ball operation; is it?
> ANDRETTA: That is right.
> ROONEY: Matter of an expert guess?
> ANDRETTA: An expert guess. . . .
> ROONEY: We have come to depend upon your guesswork and it is better than some other guesswork I have seen.

A good index of confidence is ability to secure emergency funds on short notice with skimpy hearings. No doubt Andretta's achievement was related to his frequent informal contact with Rooney.

> ROONEY: I am one who believes we should keep in close contact with one another so we understand one another's problems.
> ANDRETTA: I agree.
> ROONEY: You very often get in touch with us during the course of the year when you do not have a budget pending, to keep us acquainted with what is going on.
> ANDRETTA: Exactly. . . .

Make Friends: The Visit. Parallel in importance to the need for maintaining integrity is developing close personal relationships with members of the agency's appropriations subcommittee, particularly the Chairman. The most obvious way is to seek them out and get to know them. One official reports that he visited every member of his subcommittee asking merely that they call on him if they wanted assistance. Later, as relationships developed, he was able to bring up budgetary matters. Appropriations hearings reveal numerous instances of personal visitation. A few examples should suggest how these matters work: Representative Jensen: "Mr. Clawson [head of the Bureau of Land Management] came in my office the other day to visit with me. I don't know whether he came in purposely or whether he was just going by and dropped in, and he told me that he was asking for considerably more money for . . . administrative

282

expenses and we had quite a visit. . . ." A subordinate employee of that bureau showed that he had caught the proper spirit when he told Representative Stockman, "If you would like some up-to-date information from the firing line, I shall be glad to call at your office and discuss the matter; will you like for me to do that?"

When columnist Peter Edson editorially asked why the Peace Corps did so well in appropriations compared to the difficult times had by the State Department and the Agency for International Development, he concluded that Sargeant Shriver, head of the Corps, "has tried to establish congressional confidence in him and his agency. Of the 537 members of Congress, he has called on at least 450 in their offices."

The Pay-Off. Wherever possible, the administrators seek to accommodate the Congressman and impress him with their interest and friendliness. This attitude comes through in an exchange between a man in the Fish and Wildlife Service and Senator Mundt.

> OFFICIAL: Last year at the hearings . . . you were quite interested in the aquarium there [the Senator's state], particularly in view of the centennial coming up in 1961.
>
> MUNDT: That is right.
>
> OFFICIAL: Rest assured we will try our best to have everything in order for the opening of that centennial.

The administrator recognizes and tries to avoid certain disagreeable consequences of establishing relationships with Congressmen. The Congressman who talks too much and quotes you is to be avoided. The administrator who receives a favor may get caught unable to return one the following year and may find that he is dealing with an enemy, not just a neutral.

I'd Love to Help You but . . . Where the administrator's notion of what is proper conflicts with that of a Congressman with whom it is desirable to maintain friendly relations, there is no perfect way out of the difficulty. Most officials try to turn the Congressman down by suggesting that their hands are tied, that something may be done in the future, or by stressing some other project on which they are agreed. After Representative Natcher spoke for the second time of his desire for a project in his district, Don Williams of the Soil Conservation Service complimented him for his interest in watershed activity in Kentucky but was "sorry that some of the projects that were proposed would not qualify under the . . . law . . . but . . . they are highly desirable."

The "it can't be done" line was also taken by the Weather Bureau in an altercation with Representative Yates.

> WEATHER BUREAU OFFICIAL: We cannot serve the public by telephone . . . because we cannot put enough telephone lines or the operators to do the job. . . . We expect them [the public] to get it through the medium of newspapers, radio, television. If you have six telephones you have to have six people to deal with them. You have no idea. . . .

YATES: Yes; I do have an idea, because I have been getting calls from them. What I want to do is have such calls transferred to you. ... But as long as you have only one phone, I shall get the calls and you will not. ...

WEATHER BUREAU OFFICIAL: We find we must do it on the basis of mass distribution.

Sometimes, action may be delayed to see if the committee member will protest. The Weather Bureau tried for a while to cut off weather reports from Savannah to the northern communities that constitute its major source of tourists despite the fact that the Bureau's House subcommittee chairman represented that city.

REPRESENTATIVE PRESTON: I wrote you gentlemen ... a polite letter about it thinking that maybe you would (restore it) ... and no action was taken on it. Now, Savannah may be unimportant to the Weather Bureau but it is important to me. ...

WEATHER BUREAU OFFICIAL: I can almost commit ourselves to seeing to it that the Savannah weather report gets distribution in the northeastern United States.

Give and Take. At other times some compromise may be sought. Secretary of Commerce Averell Harriman was faced with the unpalatable task of deciding which field offices to eliminate. He first used internal Department criteria to find the lower one-third of offices in point of usefulness. Then he decided which to drop or curtail by checking with the affected Congressmen, trying to determine the intensity of their reactions, making his own estimate of whom he could and could not afford to hurt. Harriman's solution was a nice mixture of internal and political criteria designed to meet as many goals as possible or at least to hold the Department's losses down.[2]

Truth and Consequences. In the end, the administrator may just have to face the consequences of opposing Congressmen whose support he needs. Even if he were disposed to accommodate himself to their desires at times, he may find that other influential members are in disagreement. He may play them off against one another or he may find that nothing he can do will help. The best he may be able to do is to ride out the storm without compounding his difficulties by adding suspicions of his integrity to disagreements over his policies. He hopes, particularly if he is a career man, that the Congressmen will rest content to damn the deed without damning the man.

Emphasis. The administrator's perception of Congressional knowledge and motivation helps determine the kind of relationships he seeks to establish. The administrator who feels that the members of his appropriations subcommittees are not too well informed on specifics and that they

---

[2]Kathryn Smul Arnow, *The Department of Commerce Field Offices,* The Inter-University Case Program, ICP Case Series, No. 21, February, 1954.

evaluate the agency's program on the basis of feedback from constituents, stresses the role of supporting interests in maintaining good relations with Congressmen. He may not feel the need to be too careful with his estimates. The administrator who believes that the Congressmen are well informed and fairly autonomous is likely to stress personal relationships and demonstrations of good work as well as clientele support. Certain objective conditions may be important here. Some subcommittees deal with much smaller areas than others and their members are likely to be better informed than they otherwise would be. Practices of appointment to subcommittees differ between House and Senate and with passing time. Where Congressmen are appointed who have direct and important constituency interest at stake, the information they get from back home becomes more important. If the composition of the committee changes and there are many members without substantial background in the agency's work, and if the staff does not take up the slack, the agency need not be so meticulous about the information it presents. This situation is reflected in the hearings in which much time is spent on presenting general background information and relatively little on specifics.

Subcommittee and Other Staff. Relationships of confidence between agency personnel and subcommittee staff are also vital and are eagerly sought after. Contacts between subcommittee staff and budget officers are often frequent, intensive, and close. Frequency of contacts runs to several times a day when hearings are in progress, once a day when the bill is before the committee, and several times a month during other seasons. This is the principal contact the committee staff has with the Executive Branch. Even when the staff seeks information directly from another official in the agency, the budget officer is generally apprised of the contact and it is channeled through him. Relationships between ordinary committee staff members and Budget Bureau personnel are infrequent, although the people involved know one another. The top-ranking staff members and the Budget Bureau liaison man, however, do get together frequently to discuss problems of coordination (such as scheduling of deficiency appropriations) and format of budget presentation. At times, the BOB uses this opportunity to sound out the senior staff on how the committee might react to changes in presentation and policy. The staff members respond without speaking for the committee in any way. There also may be extensive contact between committee staff and the staff attached to individual Congressmen, but there is not a stable pattern of consultations. House and Senate Appropriations Committee staff may check with one another; also, the staff attached to the substantive committees sometimes may go into the financial implications of new bills with appropriations staff.

When an agency has good relations with subcommittee staff it has an easier time in Congress than it might otherwise. The agency finds that more reliance is placed on its figures, more credence is given to its claims, and more opportunities are provided to secure its demands. Thus one budget officer received information that a million-dollar item had been casually dropped from a bill and was able to arrange with his source of information on the staff to have the item put back for reconsideration. On the other hand, a staff man can do great harm to an agency by expressing distrust of its competence or integrity. Asked if they would consider refusing to talk to committee staff, agency officials uniformly declared that this refusal would be tantamount to cutting their own throats.

DECISION-MAKING IN TAXATION AND EXPENDITURES

CHARLES E. LINDBLOM

INTRODUCTION

The planners of this conference believed that it might be possible eventually to formulate more workable standards for government tax and expenditure decisions by interweaving a search for clarification of actual decision processes with a search for workable norms. In undertaking such a project as they proposed, I am accordingly pursuing a refinement of normative economics in a roundabout way. Most of what I have to say will be positive, not normative and, for that matter, will be more derived from political science than from traditional economics. The facts to be alluded to are on the whole familiar. The norms sought are of two kinds: for taxers and spenders and for designers of decision-making machinery. Given the purposes of such Universities-National Bureau conferences as this one, I take it that in the interpretation of facts, hypotheses will often be welcome. If at critical points in the argument I fall back on the plea for additional research, I assume I am within my scholarly rights.

1. CONTEMPORARY PRACTICES AND NORMS

Beginning then with facts, let us take note of some characteristics of government expenditure and taxation decisions in the United States, especially in the federal government, that are significant to economists.[1]

1. Legislative decisions that authorize expenditures are typically made without benefit of any formal machinery that brings budgetary considerations to bear on them. The authorization committees of the Congress on one hand, and the appropriations committees, on the other, are relatively independent of each other and not locked in close cooperation.

2. The costs and benefits of authorized programs are not typically weighted against each other, systematically and explicitly, when legislative decisions are made.

3. Policy-making is not systematically and explicitly viewed as a problem in the choice among alternative means for the achievement of desired ends. Even in decisions in which the necessity of allocating scarce

---

Article is from National Bureau of Economic Research, *Public Finances: Needs, Sources, and Utilization*, Princeton, N.J.: Princeton University Press, © 1961, pp. 295–323. Reprinted with permission of Princeton University Press.

[1]Most of the characteristics of decision making to be listed are familiar. All can be documented in Arthur Smithies, *The Budgetary Process in the United States*, McGraw-Hill Book Co., 1955.

funds might appear to make the means-ends problem especially acute, decision-making is not typically marked by explicit comparison and deliberate choice among means. The military's penchant for the "best" of everything—the best planes, the best mess kits, the best gloves—is coming to be the classic example of reluctance to evaluate means in the light of ends. Points 2 and 3 are, of course, merely two aspects of the common failure of government decision-makers to employ an adequate concept of cost.

4. Some major expenditure or taxation policies are set or altered as an accident or by-product of other decisions. That is to say, a policy is not always a decision; it is often simply upon us without deliberate and explicit choice. A "decision" to run a surplus or deficit is, for example, often not a decision at all but simply an outcome.

5. More generally, many of the financial and other implications of a decision are ignored when a decision is made. The decision-maker, whether administrator or legislator, permits pressure of work and limits on his own concerns to confine his attention to less than all of the important relevant variables.

In the budgetary process, most of us see a partly realized, partly potential, technique for making expenditure and taxation decisions more rational. This brief list of characteristics of financial decisions can be extended to note certain aspects of budgeting.

6. Many major explicitly financial decisions are outside the budgetary process. Tax decisions are, of course, wholly outside; so also deficiency appropriations. And in wartime, as might be expected, appropriations to the military are so generous that availability of physical supplies, not budgetary considerations, set expenditure rates.

7. As many economists have noted, there is in the federal budgetary machinery no explicit provision for coordinating revenues and expenditures.

8. Formal congressional review of the budget is concentrated in appropriations subcommittees whose interests are focused on segments of the budget considered largely in isolation from other segments.

9. Neither the appropriations committee as a whole nor the Congress as a whole gives extended formal consideration to the budget as a whole, nor does the appropriations committee as a whole play a strong coordinating role for the subcommittees.

10. Moreover, even in considering segments of the budget, the subcommittee members are repeatedly drawn into scrutiny of details rather than of the major expenditure alternatives, although this phenomenon varies from one subcommittee to another.

11. Being torn between two possibilities—using budgetary scrutiny for detailed administrative control or using it for planning broad public policy—legislators are drawn toward the first to a degree that reduces significantly their explicit attention to the latter.

12. Congress does not enact the budget as a whole at the termination of budget review but instead enacts a series of appropriations bills.

13. Budgeting is marked by conflict between President and Congress, between the two houses of Congress, and among subcommittees.

Familiar as these provisions are, they are essential to what follows.

The accepted contemporary norms for the budgetary process reflect widespread dissatisfaction with the characteristics of the budgetary process just summarized. I would expect widespread agreement on such a list of norms as the following, taken from Smithies (page references are to Smithies) though altered somewhat in emphasis and presentation. Some are norms for taxers and spenders; some are norms for designers of decision-making machinery. Some are general norms, and some are norms pertaining to coordination, which is a special aspect of decision making.

1. Governmental objectives should be as clearly and explicitly defined as possible (25ff.).

2. Alternative policies should be explicitly regarded as alternative means toward the achievement of objectives (28).

3. Specifically, expenditure decisions should be made explicitly and deliverately in the light of all the objectives they are intended to achieve (16).

4. In the interests of a rational comparison of alternatives, final expenditure decisions should not be made until all claims on the budget can be considered (16).

5. Revenue and expenditure decisions should be deliberately coordinated (192).

6. For each expenditure, some systematic and deliberate appraisal of benefits and costs should be made (12ff.).

7. Policy-making, including budgetary policy-making, should achieve a unified policy (23).

8. A comprehensive overview of policy-making on expenditures and revenues should be attempted (16, 25).

9. All taxation and expenditure decisions should be somehow embraced in the budgetary process (175ff.).

10. Specifically, the legislature should undertake a comprehensive, unified, rather than segmented, review of the budget (164, 169, 193).

11. Decisions should be made on the basis of a cooperative division of function between the legislature and the executive (45).

For present purposes, it does not matter that some of these norms overlap others and that some are more specific statements of others. It is important, however, to observe that a few central principles run through this and similar lists to be found elsewhere in the literature. In such lists economists reveal themselves as esteeming, not surprisingly, such conventional principles as:

1. A comprehensive overview of factors relevant to a decision.

2. Clarity of definition of social objectives.

3. A means-end approach to policy.

4. Deliberate and explicit choice among policies.

5. A calculation and minimization of cost.

6. Reason and cooperation rather than arbitrariness, coercion and conflict.

7. A unified decision-making process for decisions that are highly interdependent.

Most, perhaps all, of the listed norms are applications in varying degrees of specificity of these more fundamental principles.

2. DISCREPANCY BETWEEN PRACTICES AND NORMS

For all the immediate appeal of both norms and underlying principles, an objection to them is that they do not emerge from a skeptical analysis of the actual decision-making process, good and bad, in government but appear instead to be derived from a paradigm of a rational decision process. They stem from criticisms of government decision-making that take the form of observations that the process is not what one would suppose a rational process to be.

Reconsider now in this light the characterizations of decision-making with which this paper opened. They are invariably read as shortcomings of decision-making, although I did not present them as such. They are thought to be shortcomings, I suggest, not on a demonstration of their effects but by implicit or explicit appeal to obvious standards of rationality. Or look again in this light at the seven underlying principles on which the norms rest. Why are they as persuasive as they are? Because, again, they represent almost universally accepted ideas on how to be rational in any kind of problem-solving.

It is possible that we are all betrayed by these obvious standards for rational problem-solving. Perhaps they are more limited in their applicability than we have thought. Although one's ideas of what is rational suffice to predict that using a milk bottle to drive spikes into 4 X 4's will ordinarily be inferior to using a hammer, one cannot be confident for such a complex process as governmental decision-making that such principles of rationality as comprehensiveness of overview, explicitness of choice, means-ends calculations, and clarity of definition of objectives are appropriate. These are standards drawn largely from our own intimate experiences with small scale, relatively more simple, problem-solving.

That conventional norms do indeed follow paradigms of rational processes rather than reflect independent diagnosis of decision-making and that they may lead us astray can be illustrated. It is a commonplace norm that revenue and expenditure decisions should be coordinated through some formal congressional machinery now lacking. Why? Because fiscal policy is a powerful device for economic stabilization, from which it seems "logically" to follow that Congress should have formal machinery for taking account of the fiscal consequences of a prospective surplus or deficit. But is it in fact true that Congress is without methods for coordinating revenue and expenditure decisions? No, it is only without *formally prescribed* procedures, and we should know by now that informal operating procedures are often superior to formal. And is Congress typically unaware of a deficit when it occurs? No, except to the degree that fact-collecting cannot keep up to date in any organization. Do such deficits and surpluses as do occur (other than those justified by stability considerations) appear at random? No, they are probably the result of a combination of congressional attitudes toward fiscal policy and pressures upon Congress. Do then "economically unwise" surpluses and deficits demonstrate a need for formal coordination? No, not unless formal coordination can be shown to be an intermediate step to the achievement of changed congressional attitudes and to the restructuring of pressures on congressmen.

What is it about government decision-making that might make "obvious" principles of rational choice inappropriate? A first answer is that complex decision-making is molded by limitations on human problem-solving capacities not taken account of in the conventional picture of rational choice.

Consider man's limited capacity to undertake usefully a comprehensive overview of the variables relevant to a complex decision. If sufficiently ambitious, all attempts at a comprehensive overview run into two major limits: first, man's limited intellectual ability, that is, his limited ability to grasp, calculate, and remember; and, second, limited information. Some problems lie so far beyond these two limits that it would be irrational for man to attempt an informed and reasoned solution to them; better he flip a coin, adopt a rule of thumb, or decide by any of several "arbitrary" means.

Commonplace though not trivial decisions as to whether to marry, what occupation to choose, or how many children to produce are not so much comprehensively calculated as resolved through a limited evaluation; or they are drifted into, unthinkingly decided, taken as by-products of other decisions, or settled by rule of thumb. While the role of what might be called "reason" in such decisions might well be increased for some people in some circumstances, I see no evidence that these decisions would always be more rational (unless "rational" is defined as "reasoned") if approached through an inevitably only partly successful comprehensive overview of the relevant variables. I would not be so foolish as to make the attempt myself and did in fact satisfy myself with a very limited view of the variables.

If these relatively simple personal decisions call for intellectual capacities and knowledge beyond our reach, all the more so do complex governmental decisions. The federal budget document runs to 2,000 pages, and prints of committee hearings on it cover many thousands more. It is not at all obvious, and indeed doubtful, that any man or committee can achieve a sufficiently intimate understanding of the budget as to make the thousands of comparisons and evaluations required in a genuinely comprehensive overview, even if these printed materials were all one were required to master. In fact, of course, one cannot understand the variables relevant to budgetary decisions without knowing, grasping, remembering, and relating to the decisions a prodigious amount of information about government, the economy, and the wishes of the citizenry.

These difficulties do not mean that men think and express conspicuously irrational thoughts when faced with the budget, or that they flee in panic, or that the budgetary process comes to a grinding stop. They do mean, however, that most budgetary decisions are in fact made in ways economists are accustomed to call arbitrary, that thousands of important comparisons are never in fact made, that many major issues never come to the attention of decision-makers, and that such agreement as various decision-makers reach is less owed to the exhaustiveness of their scrutiny of the budget than to common ideology, prejudice, or even common ignorance when they all miss the same relevant issues that might have divided them.

If this is true, as can easily be documented and as I should like to see documented by research, then it does not at all follow that even more ambitious attempts at comprehensiveness of overview, as is conventionally recommended, will increase the elements of rationality in government taxation and expenditure decisions. It is quite possible that overtaxing man's limited capacities still further will make the situation worse.

An objection to this line of argument springs to mind. It is that limits of man's capacities have been pushed back by dividing up the decision-making process, that is, by factoring out subdivisions of the decision tasks. It is true, everyone agrees, that limits on man's problem-solving capacity can indeed be pushed back by factoring out parts of problems and enlisting the cooperation of a number of individuals or groups, each of whom attacks its own assigned part of the problem. If it were not for this possibility, even the small federal budgets of earlier decades would have been beyond our grasp. But pushing back the limits is not the same as eliminating them. Hence, even with subdivision of the decision-process in the administration and in Congress, a $70 billion budget presents a staggering decision-making problem. Is it not obvious that, even with subdivision, thousands of important comparisons are not made and many major issues are not brought to the attention of decision-makers?

We can see why subdivision only pushes back but does not remove limits by looking at subdivided decision-making processes. Observers report such familiar difficulties as the following:[2] (1) Coordination of subdivisions is a continuing task of top decision-makers; (2) Substantial interdependent elements that cannot be factored out remain the responsibility of top decision-makers; (3) Appropriate lines of division are unstable, as changing conditions create new patterns of interdependency; (4) Difficulties of communication, many of which are intended by subordinates, misrepresent to top decision-makers the facts required for their decisions; (5) Motivational difficulties, illustrated by divergence between organizational goals as seen by top decision-makers and as seen by subdivisions, inevitably distort decisions. If this last point is not clear, it predicts, for example, that appropriations subcommittees take a segmental view of the budget not only because they lack a strong central coordinating committee, but also in large part because a subdivision or subcommittee inevitably takes on goals and attitudes of its own.

---

[2]*See* for example, Ely Devons, *Planning in Practice*, Cambridge: Cambridge University Press, 1950.

Now, again, these difficulties in subdividing the task of comprehensive overview do not mean that decision making becomes chaotic when subdivided. They simply represent specifications of *limits* on man's capacities to carry off successfully a comprehensive overview of a complex problem. And to return to our main point, they buttress the allegation that government decision-making is molded by limits on man's capacities that are not taken account of in contemporary conventional norms and principles.

Another illustration of the failure of conventional norms and principles to take sufficient account of the facts is that government officials often cannot cast a policy problem into a means-ends framework, as the norms require.

An immediate and obvious difficulty on this score is that decision-makers, to say nothing of the electorate, do not in fact wholly agree on objectives or values.[3] To be sure, on many they agree roughly; but the scope of government decision-making is not limited to their areas of agreement. Nor do men generally aspire to universal agreement on objectives of social policy, prizing instead diversity and change. Still, it may be questioned, do we not agree that governments shall take as their working objectives those preferred by the majority? Do we not consequently enjoy a working agreement on objectives of governmental policy?

This is a question of fact, and for several reasons the answer is no. In the first place, it has been shown that majority rule is a process through which it is not usually possible for citizens to indicate preferences on specific policies.[4] If a winning candidate differed from his defeated opponent on, say, an issue in foreign policy (among other issues that divided them), it does not follow that those who voted for him favored his stand on the foreign policy issue. Hence, neither the winning candidate nor anyone else can say what policy objective is to be taken, by majority rule, as the government's objective.

Second, most policy choices open to government, including almost all budgetary choices, are never even raised during election campaigns as campaign issues. Again, therefore, a public official is without a clearly defined governmental objective. Third, even in abstract principle we do not in fact agree on majority rule as a basis of working agreement. For in a large number of decision-making situations, citizens differ as to how far the equality principle implicit in majority rule ought to be compromised to take account of differences in intensity of preference among citizens and differences in their circumstances. We have even gone so far in the United States as to subject some policy decisions to a vote in which only farmers in particular categories participate. And, of course, the United States Constitution makes numerous systematic provisions for inequality, as in its basis for representation of

---

[3] For present purposes, I shall use interchangeably such terms as "values," "objectives" (including "constraints"), "goals," and "ends."

[4] R. A. Dahl, *A Preface to Democratic Theory*, Chicago: University of Chicago Press, 1956, pp. 124 ff.

senators and the bicameral legislature. On all these counts, it is clear that government decision-makers are often without clear instructions from the electorate on policy objectives.

At one extreme, the impossibility of a means-end approach to policy is clear when one decision-maker's mean is another's end. To one decision-maker or citizen, for example, tax reduction comes to play such a role in his thinking that we can only call it an end or objective for him. To another, tax reduction is considered simply as one of several means to an objective like full employment. A government such as ours survives because it takes advantage of agreement among two such individuals where it finds it; to require them to agree with each other on which is end and which is means and then ask for their agreement on both ends and means is not only to pose insuperable problems of calculation to them but also to endanger political stability. The political scientists tell us democracies cannot be fussy about the terms on which their citizens reach agreement.

I should like these specific failures of the conventional principles to take account of the character of government decision-making to be taken as illustrative of two more general failures that will become clearer as we move through succeeding stages of the analysis. The failure to account for man's limited capacities and for the frequent impossibility of casting a problem into a means-end framework is sufficient to reveal the possibility that conventional norms and principles have not taken sufficient account of either (1) the sheer complexity of government decision-making or of (2) the special problems of handling values or objectives. Almost any other specific aspect of decision-making we might have looked into will reveal the same two underlying problems: complexity and special difficulties in evaluation.

It was suggested above that our ideas of what is rational in problem-solving are derived in large part from introspective observation of our own problem-solving processes from which many of the complexities of collectivities, including certain value problems, are absent. In addition, recent new insights into decision-making carry a powerful bias. With few exceptions, the formal theory of decision-making has not faced up to the possibility that complexity can outstrip limited intellectual capacity.[5] And the success of conventional principles in such sophisticated applications as operations research have perhaps tempted us to forget the limited competence of these applications and the possibility that extremely complex rational decisions have to be approached quite differently. Aware of this, Charles Hitch writes:

> I would make the empirical generalization from my experience at RAND and elsewhere that operations research is the art of suboptimizing, i.e., of solving some lower-level problems, and that difficulties increase and our special competence diminishes by an order of magnitude with every level of decision-making we attempt to ascend. The sort of simple

---

[5] *See* the survey: Ward Edwards, "The Theory of Decision-Making," *Psychological Bulletin* (July, 1954), pp. 380–417. The older theory has, of course, been extended, through statistical and mathematical theory, to deal more adequately with limitations on information.

explicit model which operations researchers are so proficient in using can certainly reflect most of the significant factors influencing traffic control on the George Washington Bridge, but the proportion of relevant reality which we can represent by any such model or models in studying, say, a major foreign-policy decision, appears to be almost trivial.[6]

3. INCREMENTAL DECISION-MAKING

We need now to pause to make clear and rather exact the significance of the fact that conventional principles do not face up to either the complexity of decision-making or its special value problems. A common but too quickly despairing inference is that we have no alternative but to press on as far as possible toward comprehensive overviews of our collective problems, toward clarification of objectives, toward structuring each decision as a means-end problem, toward deliberateness and explicitness of choice, and the like. Those who make this inference will grant that man's capacity to employ these methods successfully is indeed limited, that government expenditure and taxation policies, therefore, will at best be none too good; but they may somewhat paradoxically take heart from the discrepancy between practice and norm by believing that the only continuously serviceable norms are those impossible to reach.

But *if* for rational decision-making there is any alternative to comprehensiveness, the means-end approach, deliberateness and explicitness, and the like, the more sensible inference would be to employ these methods only when their limits permit and to employ an alternative when available. A big "if," it will be replied. Let us see. A fundamental characteristic of the literature on expenditure and taxation decisions is that it has not explored the possibility of alternatives, as I now propose to do.

There are a number of ways in which a decision-maker, within government or out, can approach a rational decision that departs considerably from the practice of the conventional principles outlined above.[7] Herbert Simon, for example, has constructed a model of "satisficing" rather than maximizing. It takes account of limits on man's cognitive capacities, by simplifying both the welfare or payoff function and the process of search for a satisfactory solution.[8] Its implications for government decision-making procedures remain to be explored but are not, I should think, trivial.

Problems of resource allocation in wartime led E. A. G. Robinson to the hypothesis: "The golden rule of all planning is that it must be done in terms of the scarcest of the resources."[9] This, the "bottleneck principle," is

---

[6]Charles Hitch, "Operations Research and National Planning—A Dissent," *Operations Research* (October, 1957), p. 718.

[7]It is apparent by now that I am not going to define rationality. The reader is invited to supply his own definition, for I think what I have to say about rationality is as true for one concept of it as for another among the common definitions.

[8]Herbert Simon, "A Behavioral Model of Rational Choice," *Quarterly Journal of Economics* (February, 1955), pp. 99–118.

[9]D. N. Chester (ed.), *Lessons of the British War Economy*, Cambridge: Cambridge University Press, 1951, p. 57.

hardly more than a hint at still another model of rational decision-making; but it may be the germ of a principle for drastically simplifying a complex problem so that it can be as rationally decided, for all the makeshift appearance of the decision, as through an inevitably futile attempt to comprehend all the complexities of the problem.

Still other ways of simplifying decision-making tasks to avoid irrationalities might be mentioned. Among them is one I have elsewhere described in some detail under the label of the incremental method.[10] I suggest that it is actually the most common method through which public policy decisions, including decisions on taxes and expenditures, are approached. That it is a method commonly practiced has led us to take it for granted rather than formalize it in terms like those that formalize incremental consumer choice, to which it is obviously related.

The incremental method is characterized by its practitioner's preoccupation with: (1) only that limited set of policy alternatives that are politically relevant, these typically being policies only incrementally different from existing policies; (2) analysis of only those aspects of policies with respect to which the alternatives differ; (3) a view of the policy choice as one in a succession of choices; (4) the *marginal* values of various social objectives and constraints; (5) an intermixture of evaluation and empirical analysis rather than an empirical analysis of the consequences of policies for objectives independently determined; and (6) only a small number out of all the important relevant values.

Of these six characteristics, the first three are recognizable characteristics of political decision-making, as practiced by both officials and most policy-minded academic analysts. I shall not linger over them except to point out that anyone whose approach meets the first three conditions has enormously simplified his policy problems compared to what they would be if he literally and strictly followed the conventional prescription to attempt a comprehensive overview. The fourth and fifth strike at the value problem in policy-making; and the sixth strikes at the general complexity of policy analysis, although in what appears to be a shocking way.

Let us first consider problems of handling values. In the incremental method, political decision-makers handle values through marginal comparisons in the same way that consumers do. Although economists describe rational consumer behavior by reference to utility surfaces, indifference curves, demand schedules, and the like, a rational consumer need know nothing about them. He need not first determine his indifference curve for oranges and apples and subsequently decide his purchase policies accordingly. Nor need he first try to comprehend all possible product mixes (or even a few alternative product mixes), then decide which one he prefers, and only then make those purchases necessary to attain the preferred mix. The rational

---

[10]Charles E. Lindblom, "Policy Analysis," *American Economic Review* (June, 1958), pp. 298–312.

consumer proceeds directly to marginal comparison of alternative specific purchases. The way in which we economists can, for our own professional purposes, conceptualize consumer choice obscures the great difference between what the consumer can be conceived of as having done but does not actually do—ascertain a function, then choose so as to maximize it—and what he actually does—simply compare policies at the margin and choose directly the preferred policy.

Like the consumer, the incremental decision-maker in governmental affairs does not make use of a utility function, in his case a social welfare function. He does not think in terms of "all the variables that might be considered as affecting welfare: the amounts of each and every kind of good consumed by and service performed by each and every household, the amount of each and every kind of capital investment undertaken, and so on."[11] He can hardly be said to know even a point or two on such a function because he does not think in terms of alternative social states; and, if he can be said to value one social state higher than another, this fact is more to be inferred from his choices than said to control them. He makes specific choices, as does the consumer, at the margin.

Similarly, incremental decision-makers closely intermix empirical and value elements in choice as do consumers. We may describe a consumer who buys a car as having decided upon such a purchase policy in order to attain such objectives or values as speed of movement, ready accessibility of transportation, improved status, and conformity, as well as the pleasures of novelty, display, color and form, and acquisition itself. To decide whether to buy a car and, if so, which car, requires then that he both choose among combinations of such values as these and empirically investigate the consequences of alternative purchase policies for the attainment of each of these values. Thus he must make two kinds of choices: (1) the preferred value-mix and (b) the purchase best suited to the attainment of the preferred value-mix. In actual fact, however, he makes these two choices simultaneously when he decides upon his purchase; he does not in one choice determine the preferred value-mix and then make his purchase in its light.

Moreover, he would find it difficult to describe, even to himself, his preferences among the objectives except by pointing to the purchase made and those rejected. Furthermore, he would confess that many of the objectives or values served by his purchase appeared to him as relevant only after alternative purchase policies began to compete in his mind. He did not, for example, first consider buying a car in order to satisfy his esthetic senses, but esthetic values quickly became relevant once he contemplated buying a car.

Although it is customary to analyze values as a first step in policy-making, it is a characteristic of the incremental method that such an analysis

---

[11]Abram Bergson, "Socialist Economics," in H. S. Ellis (ed.), *A Survey of Contemporary Economics*, New York: The Blakiston Company, Inc., 1947, p. 417.

is cursory, short-lived, and only a prefatory clarification of a few of the many goal-values that will be affected by policies to be considered. Sometimes such an analysis is omitted entirely. Either at once or very quickly in incremental decision-making, the analysis turns directly to alternative policies. *Predicting* consequences of alternative policies and *evaluating* the consequences then become intertwined to the degree that, as in consumer choice, only in the final choice among policies is the final choice among objectives or values itself made.

For example, many policy analysts find it extremely difficult to decide how much inflation they are willing to tolerate in order to achieve some specified reduction in unemployment except in contemplation of some particular set of policy alternatives offering marginally different prospective amounts of inflation and unemployment. Or, again, none of us do very well in describing to others—or even to ourselves—the relative value of economic security and rapid economic growth. But we make the choice when confronted with alternative policies offering different increments of the two values. Again, we do not determine our welfare function, then choose, but instead choose directly and, in so doing, simultaneously both indirectly define a part of a welfare function and maximize it.

It is also a characteristic of the incremental method that the decision-maker is much more tentative about his objectives or values than he is considered to be in conventional models. He counts on policy choices to lead him to fresh perceptions about values, he expects to learn about his values from his experiences with pursuing and enjoying them, and he is inclined to think that in the long run policy choices have as great an influence on objectives as objectives have on policy choices.[12]

If incrementalism is a method through which a single decision-maker can rationally evaluate alternative policies, it also offers a solution to the problem of disagreement among decision-makers on values. Incrementalism sidesteps problems posed by disagreement on values because decision-makers deal directly with policies, as has just been explained; no virtue attaches, as it does in the conventional method, to prior discussion of and agreement on objectives or values.

This characteristic of incrementalism makes agreement possible in at least three distinguishable ways. First, ideological and other differences in values that loom large when considered abstractly do not necessarily stand in the way of agreed marginal values. Second, the practice of evaluating only in

---

[12]How then distinguish, it might be asked, a rational and irrational decision? The conventional model defines a rationally chosen policy by its relation to a set of objectives. A rational policy, for example, is one that attains its objectives, or maximizes the probability of doing so, or is, by warranted beliefs, best suited to attainment of its objectives. But since for complex public policy decisions, the decision-makers' objectives are defined by the policy choice he makes, the principal characteristic of the rational decision—perhaps the defining characteristic—turns on the accuracy of the decision-maker's predictions about the outcome of his policies. We shall, however, say more about this below.

actual choice situations often leads decision-makers to reconsider values in the light of practical constraints, and reconsideration often moves them toward agreement. Third—and much more important—individuals can often agree on policies even if they hold conflicting values. A group of decision-makers can agree, for example, on the desirability of a sales tax without agreeing on objectives; they may have quite different values and reasons in mind. It will be shown in a later section that incrementalism makes still another attack on the problem of disagreement: sometimes incremental policy-makers are coordinated by methods that do not require them to agree with one another on either values or policies.

As for the general problem of complexity in policy-making, the most drastic simplification of complex problems achieved in incremental decision-making is, as already indicated, through outright neglect of important consequences of policies. Neglect of important variables is so widely preached against that it may be worthwhile to make the point that all policy analysts practice such neglect and intend to go on doing so. In academic policy analysis, we economists routinely leave a mound of unfinished business for the political scientist, sociologist, or psychologist to attend to; and we only sometimes remember to qualify our results accordingly. We leave to the psychologist, for example, the appraisal of malingering when we analyze the desirability of liberalizing benefits under unemployment compensation. Less obvious but no less common is every policy analyst's neglect of imponderables, even when they are considered to be important. Beyond these omissions are many others, some of which appear at least superficially to be arbitrary or random, others of which are traceable to our ignorance. Examples are extremely long-run consequences for family solidarity of increasing urbanization achieved as a result of agricultural expenditures (or restrictions of expenditures) that induce farmers to leave the land; short-term consequences for corporate concentration of military procurement decisions; and consequences for the development of socialized medicine of liberal expenditures on veterans' medical care.

If important consequences are neglected, can the method still be described as one suitable for rational decision-making? Or is omission of important consequences a proof of irrationality? Whatever one's concept of rationality, I suggest that the answer in principle is clear. If the consequences are not neglected in the processes by which policies are determined, then that they are neglected by any given decision-maker is not evidence of irrationality in decision-making. Less cryptically, if values neglected by some decision-makers are the concern of other decision-makers, public policies taken together can be rational. We often permit the fallacy of composition to obscure this insight. Or, to put it another way, we often miss this point because we have applied to politics a confusion of partial and general equilibrium analysis.

Consider a hypothetical example. The President and some of his advisers agree on a greatly expanded program of highway expenditures. Their objectives are national defense, reduction of highway congestion for civilians, and economic development. Consequences of the program for the parity of the 50 states as recipients of federal funds are ignored, as are possible consequences for auto fatalities, design of automobiles, profits of existing toll roads, destruction of homes and recreational areas, sales of automobiles, sales of home furnishings, character of home life, participation in organized religion, and so on.

When the program is presented to Congress, if not before, some of the neglected values will be spoken for by, representatives of the states or of toll-road authorities. These interests may come to terms immediately with the original proponents of the program, not necessarily by each representative's taking into account each other's values but by agreement directly on modifications of the program. Other interests will wait until congressional consideration of the program is underway, and still other interests will be brought to bear on the administrative officials eventually responsible for implementing the program. And years later, when it becomes apparent to churchmen that too many people are out driving on Sunday rather than attending religious services, they will stir themselves to find ways of combating the tendency. When they do so, they will not necessarily associate the tendency with the earlier highway program, and it is not at all necessary that they do so in order to deal with their problem.

I intend the example to do no more than show the possibility that decisions can be rational even if each decision-maker ignores important values, if only the values neglected at one point are attended to at another. It is not necessary to show that all values are given equal consideration; they are not in the conventional method. Nor is it necessary to show that their inequalities are systematic or are understandable in terms of some formula; they are not in the conventional method. Nor is it necessary to show that all important values are brought somehow to bear on each decision, even if not on each decision-maker. For sometimes a neglected value will move no one to action until a decade later when it becomes clear that it is being endangered.

The example I chose was not after all very hypothetical; the processes illustrated are familiar. Let us, therefore, explore further the possibility that interconnections among decision-makers in actual fact accomplish rational decision-making despite the apparent irrationalities of each decision taken by itself. We turn thus to an aspect of decision-making that can be posed explicitly as the problem of coordination.

4. COORDINATION THROUGH PARTISAN MUTUAL ADJUSTMENT

Coordination is worth exploring for several reasons. First, we have been lead into it by an exploration of ways in which decision-makers simplify their problems and hence achieve a rationality that would be denied them if they tried to comprehend their problems fully. The possibilities that decision-makers are achieving some notable degree of rationality through the practice of what we have called the incremental method depend in large part on how the decisions are related to each other. Second, quite aside from incrementalism, coordination is an aspect of decision-making with its own special difficulties usually not sufficiently distinguished from decision-making in general. Third, in the study of expenditure decisions, budgeting usually emerges as the dominant coordinating process, and we shall want later to reconsider budgeting in the light of alternative coordinating mechanisms actually in use or potentially useful.

One group of possible coordinating devices includes, of course, the very same procedures that have already been described for decision-making generally; the conventional method with its attempt at comprehensiveness of overview; and the alternative methods for simplifying decision-making, i.e., bottleneck planning, satisficing, and incrementalism. These are all similar in that, if they are used for coordinating decisions, the principal coordinating mechanism is a centrally located mind or centrally located, closely cooperating group of minds. Consideration of their prospects for achieving rational coordinating decisions raises the same questions as we have already raised about them, and I shall consequently pass them by with only two comments.

With respect to the conventional method, because limitations on rationality are posed both by value conflicts and by the complexity of problems, these limitations would appear to be even more serious in the case of coordinating decisions than for decisions generally. With respect to the incremental approach to decisions, it is indeed a possible coordinating method; but, because one of our claims for it is that individual decision-making irrationalities are compensated for by characteristics of a coordinating mechanism appropriate to it (and yet to be explored), to defend incrementalism itself as an approach to coordinating decisions is, though not impossible, difficult.

To what extent the coordination of, say, total federal revenues and expenditures—they are coordinated, even if not ideally—is accomplished through this first group of coordinating methods is not clear. As we have seen, the absence of formal machinery for a centrally comprehended coordinating decision does not prove the absence of central coordination. Assuming some degree of central coordination, achieved perhaps through informal consultation, we do not know what mixture of such approaches as the conventional and the incremental is employed. In any case, inspection of such a problem in coordination as this one would quickly lead us to believe that a second type of coordination, not marked by central comprehension, is also exploited.

The second type, so far as I know, has been best elaborated, though with some troublesome ambiguities in presentation, by Michael Polanyi in a little known essay in which he attempts to generalize from market coordination processes.[13] This is a method in which each of a number of decision-making centers desiring a solution to a commonly recognized problem that cannot be centrally solved independently makes an adjustment to the positions taken at each other decision-making center. A long succession of such independent adjustments eventually achieves a solution to the problem when no center needs make a further adjustment. Polanyi draws an explicit analogy with certain forms of mathematic problem-solving.

His assumption, on which he perhaps wavers, that participants in such a process recognize a common problem and deliberately cooperate is an assumption explicitly to be denied in describing still a third kind of coordination: the mutual adjustment of partisan decision-makers. In this kind of coordination, adjustments to each other are made by decision-makers who do not share common criteria, differ in the values they think important, do not necessarily cooperate with each other or recognize any common problem. It is an especially significant kind of coordination for incremental decision-makers because, to the extent that they simplify their problems by concentrating on some values to the exclusion of others, they become the very kind of partisan we have just described. It is in this third kind of coordination that we shall find the mechanisms through which incremental decisions are often made parts of a larger rational policy-making process.

Partisan mutual adjustment is commonplace for coordination of any two or more of such individuals and groups as the President, Director of the Budget Bureau, individual legislators, congressional committees and subcommittees, administrators at various levels, and countless private groups. At least three major types of partisan mutual adjustment can be distinguished although any one individual or group is often simultaneously engaged in all three.[14]

Atomistic. This first type is suggested by atomistic mutual adjustment in the hypothetical purely competitive market. Each decision-making group simply ignores the repercussions of its decisions on other groups in deciding upon its own policies. The decision-maker may or may not know that his decisions have repercussions for other groups; in either case he ignores them. It follows that he does not attempt to manipulate other groups. In the example above, protagonists of a highway program can simply ignore the consequences of their policies for church groups, for taxpayer associations, or for wildlife conservationists. Typically, a group acts atomistically with respect to some but not all other groups. The atomistic method is, I think,

---

[13]Michael Polanyi, "Manageability of Social Tasks," *The Logic of Liberty*, Chicago: University of Chicago Press, 1951.

[14]It will be apparent to many that in exploring these processes I am following the tradition of the pluralists in political theory. But my professional interests in the application of the results of these inquiries to problems of collective expenditure and other economic decisions turns my interest toward the calculation aspects of these processes rather than the control aspects. More concretely, where a political scientist asks whether these processes safeguard us against an overconcentration of power, I ask whether they can aid us in rational choice.

the equivalent of Polanyi's method except for what I believe to be his assumptions of a common recognition of a problem and of deliberate cooperation.

In the atomistic method, each partisan group will find itself constantly adjusting its policies as it finds that other groups have created the need for an alteration in its course of action. A continuing process of mutual adjustment could conceivably work through successive approximations to an equilibrium in which no further moves are necessary; but, equilibrium tendencies or not, it interlocks the various groups whose policies are consequential for each other.

Deferential. In this adjustment process, each decision-maker avoids any policy that would constrain or adversely affect another group. In our own private affairs, each of us is accustomed to leaving unchallenged to each of our associates certain areas of personal choice. Similarly, there develops in the political arena a set of mutual concessions of jurisdiction or authority among decision-makers, individual or group. In addition, private citizen and public policy-maker alike defer in order to avoid adverse counter moves. In such a process as this, decision-makers seek a way to attain their objectives in the areas of free movement left open by the activities of other decision-makers. Some congressmen will not pursue their policy objectives if they turn out to challenge the President's program; and similarly in some areas of choice formally open to the President, he will defer, say, to a congressional coalition. Again, decisions are closely interlocked by this process of mutual adjustment.

Strategic. In this method, decision-makers manipulate each other in a variety of ways. They may do so by partisan discussion, in which they try to win other decision-makers over to their preferred decisions by whatever purely verbal appeals they think might be effective. This kind of discussion differs from discussion that proceeds in the light of agreed objectives or end values, and its possibilities for achieving coordination throw, I suggest, a new light on the loose but stimulating older concept of democracy as government by discussion. It is the kind of discussion in which an advocate of tax reduction in the Senate might appeal to his high-expenditure colleague not through values shared but by calling the colleague's attention to facts favorable to tax reduction or by reference to his colleague's values or objectives.

Second, decision-makers may manipulate each other by the exchange of effective threats and promises. The Pick-Sloan plan for the Missouri River is an example of the product of an exchange of promises, in this case between the Army Engineers and the Reclamation Bureau. An exchange of threats and promises is a common outgrowth of partisan discussion, but I mean to define partisan discussion to exclude it, so that it can be seen as distinct. Such an exchange I shall refer to as bargaining, following, in so doing, one common usage. Partisan discussion and bargaining, as I have defined the latter, are typically intermixed.

Third, they may manipulate each other by a variety of pressures on each other beyond partisan discussion and bargaining, that is, by injuring, forestalling, or crippling each other directly. For this no intercommunication is required, as in partisan discussion and bargaining; and the frustrated group or decision-maker may not even know the source of the frustration. Here, as also in bargaining, one of the principal strategies is to form an alliance or coalition. Among several advantages gained through alliance, one is that, where one group is without a direct method of influence on a third, it may use a second as an instrument, as when the President is induced by one group to dismiss the head of an agency that stands in the way of the first group. The National Wildlife Association and the American Forestry Association are examples of a pair of conflicting decision-making groups both powerless to make legislation and administrative decisions alone, hence both engaged in building alliances with legislators, other interest groups, and individual voters.

How often these methods for partisan mutual adjustment achieve a rational coordination of decisions is not realized. That they interlock decisions made at various points in the body politic is clear enough; that they are methods for interlocking a multiplicity of incrementally approached decisions is also clear. In addition, whatever its defects, partisan mutual adjustment achieves whatever coordination it does achieve without making coordination a staggering intellectual task. To the extent achieved, coordination is a by-product of decision-making, as in market processes. Nor does coordination, so achieved, make staggering demands for information, because the facts needed to achieve an intellectual coordination are required by no one. Finally, coordination so achieved does not depend upon agreed objectives or values. In short, partisan mutual adjustment strikes at both the complexity problem and the values problem.

But what if the interlocking of decisions is without any perceivable desirable pattern? It has to be shown that coordination so achieved is rational in some sense going beyond what we have already said. I suggest the following hypotheses:

1. *Partisan mutual adjustment is a process through which any value held to be important by any group of people can be made influential on policy-making.* The common objection that not all important interests are participant in each decision is, for reasons discussed above, not valid; it is sufficient for the truth of this hypothesis that each interest be somewhere influential.

2. *It often achieves a satisfactory weighting of conflicting values or interests in policy-making.* Because, as argued above, there is no agreed formula for weighting of conflicting values in our society, any one of a large range of possible systems of weights is no less satisfactory by any agreed standard than another. And since any system of weight used in conventional methods of coordination is to a degree arbitrary, it need only be shown that the system of weights used in mutual adjustment is sometimes better.

While accidents of strategic position and other factors will produce a wide variety of weight from one policy area to another, a supporting hypothesis is that policy will respond relatively more to widely shared and/or intensely held values than to less widely shared and/or less intensely held values and that, consequently, values will in effect often be weighted in a satisfactory way. This supporting hypothesis is all the more probable because of the practice of groups to form alliances around common or adjacent interests. It does not imply that all individuals express their values and the intensity of their values by the degree to which they participate in the mutual adjustment of groups in the political arena. On the contrary, a satisfactory system of weights could evolve from the mutual adjustment of groups representing a small minority of citizens if the distribution of values and intensities among the participating minority corresponded roughly to its distribution in a larger population consisting of citizens not indifferent to policies even if not participating. Again, the system of weights does not have to meet any very restrictive conditions in order for it to be satisfactory in the light of alternative methods of coordination.

3. *In particular, the weighting of interests in mutual adjustment meets the requirements of consent.* Put down roughly, for brevity's sake, the hypothesis takes account of the alleged precondition of democratic government: that citizens must agree on certain fundamental values and procedures, despite their disagreements on others. Societies can be thought of as purchasing this agreement, or consent to continuation of democratic government, by conceding to each interest group whatever it requires as a price for its consent. (If too many groups demand too high a price, their demands cannot be met, and democratic government is impossible.) Mutual adjustment is a process in which, when the intensity of frustration of group interests threatens democratic consent, the fact is plain; and the option is open to other groups to pay the necessary price. This is an aspect of mutual adjustment much to be prized, I suggest, even if it is sometimes converted into blackmail, as perhaps it has been in the fight against desegregation.

These three hypotheses deal directly with the suspicion almost all of us entertain that mutual adjustment is an arbitrary coordinating mechanism. I suggest that they are sufficient both to call into question the widespread view that central coordination is generally superior and to argue the desirability of comparative study of the two methods, with the hope of discovering just when the one is superior to the other.

Three additional hypotheses throw further, though indirect, light on the value of mutual adjustment as a coordinating process.

4. *Partisan mutual adjustment clarifies citizens' perception of their own preferences and leadership's knowledge of citizens' preferences.* I can only allude briefly to competition among potential group leaders for followers as having the effect of stimulating each leader to outdo his rivals in articulating for the group its preferences and its best avenues toward their gratification.

5. *It also often dissipates conflict stemming from narrow or hastily considered views of group interests by group members.* The search for allies in multilateral bargaining, for example, puts enormous pressure on group leaders to find a way of defining a group's interest so that it can be

harmonized with the interests of potential allies. Mutual adjustment will often achieve not merely a compromise of interests but what Mary Parker Follett has called an integration of interests.[15]

6. *Whether mutual adjustment is or is not more coercive than centrally achieved coordination depends upon the rules of the game by which the mutually adjusting groups play.* In view of some tendencies to stress the coercive aspects of mutual adjustment, it is relevant to emphasize its contribution to winning consent, to point up the inevitability of coercion in central coordination, and finally to point out that, while mutual adjustment could and does under some rules lead to violence, as between nations, in other circumstances it can be and is played by rules that respect traditional constraints on the use of coercion.

5. IMPLICATIONS FOR NORMS AND PRINCIPLES

We now turn to the implications of all the foregoing for norms and principles for decision-makers and designers of decision-making machinery in the field of taxation and expenditure decisions. To the extent that incrementalism together with partisan mutual adjustment is a set of processes for rational decision-making, its first implications for norms and principles in decision-making are already obvious from the foregoing discussion. Although these first implications are destructive more than constructive, to go very far beyond them requires research and reflection that has hardly yet been attempted and which has in fact been inhibited by the common preoccupation with conventionally conceived decision-making.

The first and obvious implication is that, to the extent that incrementalism and mutual adjustment are defensible, every single one of the conventional norms explicitly listed in the early pages of this paper is invalidated. Some of them are reduced to norms appropriate to particular circumstances in which central comprehension is possible; others are entirely inappropriate.

It would be tedious to discuss each in turn; inspection of them in the light of the foregoing argument should be sufficient. But it may be helpful to recapitulate some principal points of the foregoing argument as explicit comment on each of the seven listed principles on which the more numerous prescriptions rest. Each of the seven is in some substantial way invalidated.

A. Comprehensive Overview. It follows from all the foregoing that deliberate omission of important relevant values from the analysis of a decision is desirable for sufficiently complex decisions, or for decisions in which decision-makers cannot agree on values; and the circumstances in which each omission is satisfactory increase with the adequacy of partisan mutual adjustment for the coordination of the decisions so made.

B. Defined Social Objectives. For collective decisions, they cannot be defined if they cannot be agreed upon, as is typically the case for large-scale

---

[15]H. C. Metcalf and L. Urwick (eds.), *Dynamic Administration: The Collected Papers of Mary Parker Follett,* New York: Harper & Row, Publishers, 1942, pp. 31 ff.

social choice. Often social objectives can be defined only through actual marginal policy choices by individuals or by groups within which values are agreed upon. It is then sufficient that such individuals and groups agree on policy, even if they do not agree on objectives; and atomistic and deferential mutual adjustment achieve policy-making even without agreement on policy. Hence the principle is often inappropriate in that it defines a quite unnecessary requirement for rational collective choice.

C. Means-End Approach. Where values cannot be agreed upon, it is not desirable that participant decision-makers look upon their problem as a collective means-end problem; it is sufficient that they simply find a basis for agreement without regard to which variables are means and which are ends. Or it is sufficient in some types of mutual adjustment, such as atomistic and deferential, that they see the policy problem only as a problem of adaptation of means to their own private partisan ends. Moreover, since ends and means are simultaneously finally chosen in incremental policy-making, it is not desirable that policies be chosen as means to previously clarified ends. Finally, it is desirable that ends be considered as quite tentative and that they be reformulated with each policy choice in such close interconnection that it can be said that ends follow choice of means as much as means follow choice of ends.

D. Deliberate and Explicit Choice. It is desirable that some policies be set as a by-product of partisan mutual adjustment rather than deliberately and explicitly. Just as we do not have in a price system a deliberate and explicit choice among resource allocations but permit allocation to be determined as a by-product of a multiplicity of market decisions, so policy on, say, income distribution in the United States may be an example of a policy best achieved as a by-product of more particular decisions on factors affecting income distribution. Or, for another example, it may be desirable to let the aggregate size of the military budget emerge as a by-product of decisions on specific expenditure programs and not raise the aggregate as an explicit problem at any time. On values and objectives, it follows from comments on the means-end approach that values or objectives should quite commonly not be made the object of explicit and deliberate choice but should be chosen implicitly at the margin through an actual policy choice and should not be articulated as an unnecessary obstruction to agreement on policy.

E. Unified Decision Process. This normative principle, specifying the general appropriateness of hierarchical forms of organization to knit decision-makers together, simply leaves no room for coordination through partisan mutual adjustment.

F. Reason and Cooperation. The whole point of the argument of this paper might be reduced to the proposition that reason runs out, cannot bear the burdens imposed on it, therefore has to be employed in the light of its limitations. A general prescription to employ reason in decision-making, however persuasive, is less wise than a prescription to use reason in establishing such decision-making machinery as reduces the demands made

307

on reason and achieves a coordination of only partly reasoned decisions through processes of adjustment other than those that go on in the human mind.

Because partisanship is an asset (because it simplifies), conflict becomes not a problem but a method of coordination. Conflict is as useful, therefore, as cooperation. Conflict between the President and Congress, for example, or between two administrative agencies is, within limits still to be explored, to be prized as an essential element in partisan mutual adjustment.

G. *Calculation and Minimization of Cost.* This principle requires more extended comment than given to the others, although the principal grounds for qualifying the principle are inferrable from the above comments on the means-end approach.

Let us take the example of expenditures for inspection of income tax returns, an allegedly clear case in which a larger expenditure than at present would easily recoup its cost in increased tax receipts. Assume that those making the decision are divided among those who want the increased receipts and are willing to expand the necessary funds to accomplish their objective, those who welcome an opportunity to weaken income taxation, and those who, while favorably disposed to income taxation, are not happy about the extent to which its enforcement requires detailed investigation of personal affairs by revenue officials. Each can calculate costs as he sees them, both monetary and intangible. Typically, at some stage a policy will in fact emerge; but, given the assumption that their values differ, they will not have aggregated their values into a pay-off or welfare function (assuming, of course, they do not have an overriding agreed value in the form of such a function). Hence the policy finally arrived at by agreement or by other mutual adjustment is just that—a policy, not their response to an agreed compromise or aggregation of their conflicting values.

Given this solution to their problem, it cannot be asked and answered whether the costs of achieving a social objective were minimized or not, except by the arbitrary injection of the personal values of the observer who asks the question. In this case, a prescription that costs be calculated and minimized could be appropriate only for the partisan problem-solving of the participant decision-makers, which is not the way in which such a prescription is ordinarily intended. As a prescription intended for some collectivity like the House of Representatives, it is not operational, for the House as a whole cannot agree on what is value received and what is cost.

To go further, it would not even always be desirable, even if possible, for the House to agree on an aggregating rule for conflicting values so that, in the light of such an aggregation, choices could be made that did maximize values received or minimize costs. For presumably such a rule would itself be a product of partisan mutual adjustment. To minimize costs under such circumstances would therefore be simply to make policies consistent with prior partisan adjustment of conflicting values. It is not at all clear that this is to be preferred to the direct partisan mutual adjustmnet of policy conflicts

308

without prior resolution of value differences. The arbitrary element is only more apparent in the one method than in the other.

The same line of argument holds for choice among expenditures on, say, heavy bombers, medium bombers, and missiles of various kinds. It is easy to advocate the policy of providing the biggest bang for a buck; but, in the absence of agreement among bargainers for various branches of the military or among congressmen on just what weapon has the biggest bang, the prescription reduces to the advice to the partisan interests to minimize costs or maximize objectives as they narrowly see them, or else the prescription is again nonoperational.

One appropriate alternative prescription in cases such as these is that expenditures should be undertaken that participant decision-makers can voluntarily agree on, assuming only that each participant has, in his own limited view, acted economically. Another appropriate prescription is simply that each decision-maker act economically and that their independently decided courses of action be coordinated (policy achieved as a by-product) through atomistic, deferential, or some type of strategic adjustment not even requiring their agreement, assuming only that the process of adjustment meets certain conditions.

Still further, let us assume no disagreement whatever on values but a problem so complex as to go beyond the successful comprehension of any individual or committee. Under these circumstances, breaking the problem down into its aspects and throwing decisions into the hands of partisan groups linked through mutual adjustment may still be desirable. If so, the appropriate prescription is, again, not that costs be calculated but that the policy be that on which the participants can agree or be that policy achieved as a by-product of mutual adjustment without agreement. Here the impossibility of achieving a value aggregation in the light of which costs can be minimized stems not from conflict but from complexity. . . .

. . . .

CHAPTER V

SOME ADMINISTRATIVE CONTEXTS OF

PUBLIC BUDGETING AND FINANCE:

PERSPECTIVES ON INTERNAL AND EXTERNAL

CONTROL OF AGENCY SPENDING

Expenditure processes wend their way—often torturously—from agency request through final audit of the agency's spending. This section focuses on a paramount part of those processes. That focus is on the diverse ways and means of exercising control over public spending. Scrutiny usually is multiple, for complex "internal controls" manned by its own employees exist to monitor the spending of each public agency. And should or lest those internal controls fail, "external controls" also have been developed. Figure 1 lists major control elements of both kinds. The particular emphasis here is on the nonlegislative controls. The distinction of internal vs. external controls is not watertight, and complex feedback loops exist. The two types of controls serve, however, as a first approximation of that which exists.

Roy E. Moor's "The Expenditure Process" describes the overall system to which internal and external controls are applied. He begins with the formal legislative decision to spend public monies and ends with the audit of the ways in which the monies actually were spent. There are many possible hang-ups within that long interval. For example, the Bureau of the Budget is a vigilant defender of the interests of the presidency (and of the Bureau's own interests as well), but that vigilance extends in complex ways beyond the legend in Figure 1: "External Controls: Budgetary Processes." As a matter of policy, for example, budgetary apportionments are set up. That is, usually on a quarterly basis, Bureau officials help determine schedules to expend specific portions of an agency's budget. The apportionment has direct purposes: to facilitate fiscal planning, as by the

310

FIGURE 1

Some Prominent Features of the Flow-Chart of the Control over Agency Spending

External Controls: Budgetary Processes	Internal Controls: Regulating Processes	External Controls: Auditing Processes
External executive control:	Budget Controls	Contract renegotiation: as by the Renegotiation Board
Bureau of the Budget	Agency Budget Office	
Overall budget preparation	Requests	External audit: Government Accounting Office
Oversight of legislative activities	Allotments	
Monitoring formal executive-legislative contacts	Program Controls	External regulation: substantive and appropriations committees and sub-committees of Congress
Negotiating allotments for spending by executive agencies	Planning	
	Evaluation	
External legislative control:	Cost Controls	
Substantive and appropriations committees and sub-committees of Congress	Agency Accounting Office	
	Cost accounting	
Statutory legislation	Production Controls	
Authorizations to spend	Scheduling and production control	
	Work standards	
	Quality control	
	Evaluation of Controls	
	Agency Auditing Office	
	Internal audit	

Treasury in its concern about when payments will be required; and to prevent an agency from launching an unwise "buying spree" toward the end of a fiscal year to spend all available monies.

Moor's summary introduction "The Expenditure Process" reflects a complex scene. It is a picture of attempted integration within the presidency at the onset of the spending cycle. And yet Moor's piece also presents a picture of complex fragmentation or parceling out of various phases of the spending processes, as to legislative sub-committees. Thus a General Accounting Office sits at the terminal end of the spending cycle, and the GAO is accountable in law and largely in practice to the Congress. The whole reflects a peculiarly American stamp. The relevant summary is not who controls the spending process but that many people and offices share in its control in complex ways under incredibly complicated conditions.

The overall picture of the spending process is given kaleidoscopic detail by a number of sources. Carl W. Tiller's "Agency Budget Problems" begins the task of providing such detail. His zone of interest includes the external controls exercised by the Bureau of the Budget over agency spending. Moreover, Tiller's focus also touches on the complex relations that exist within an agency as it seeks to apply internal controls to the spending of its component units. The total picture is one of great potential for Bureau/agency friction, as well as one of potential for friction between (for example) budgeting and accounting staffs within the same agency. For example, Tiller reports that budgeting and accounting personnel even in the same agency do not share close formal and informal relations. The "good guys" and the "bad guys," in sum, cannot be defined solely in terms of who sits inside and who is outside an agency.

Note that Tiller writes both as an observer describing what exists and as a professional budgeting official prescribing what ought to exist. Thus he speaks of "the regrettable diffusion of budget responsibility in a number of agencies." Empirically, as an observer, he refers in this excerpt to "the splitting up of the former functions of budget offices." Evaluatively, as a budgeting professional, Tiller regrets that there "are many aspects of the job of helping executives reach decisions which used to be lodged in the budget staff but are now found elsewhere." Empirically, the cause may lie in the behavioral and organizational dynamics emphasized in the following two chapters. For example, budget staffs in agencies just might identify with their fellow professionals at department headquarters or in the Bureau of the Budget. To the degree that agency budget staffs are powerful, then, they might seem as interested in pleasing headquarters or Bureau contacts as much as in serving the line officials in their own agency. Operating officials within the agency might not always have the same interests, however.

Perhaps more centrally, one major cause of Tiller's regret about the falling from power of some budget agencies is the increasing relevance of "internal auditing." What is this activity? And why has it attracted so much attention recently? First, Army Regulations illustratively define "internal audit" as "the independent appraisal activity within the Army for the review of financial accounting and related operations as a basis for constructive service to command and management at all levels." In general, second, the sharply-greater concern with "managerial controls" inside the executive agencies of the federal government since World War II underlies the growing importance of the internal audit. Earlier perhaps the dominant emphasis was on external control by the presidency through budgetary tools. Still earlier, the emphasis was on legislative control of administration.

This general approach to the growing concern about internal audit can be given more specific roots. The head of each executive agency of the federal government, for example, has responsibility for establishing and maintaining an adequate system of internal control. The lesser contemporary problem is the tight budgeting of monies for spending on intra-agency activities. The contemporary task is more to see that very large amounts are spent effectively and legally, often by complex tiers of contractors and sub-contractors working for (but not in) a public agency. Roughly, per dollar spent, less money now goes into the kind of internal activities, many of them mundane, that budgeting offices coped with historically. "Cost consciousness" is the major cry, moreover, and most budgeting agencies are not well-staffed for cost-cutting services. Relatedly, government agencies now increasingly face the task of presenting "one face" to contractors. Here again internal audit is more crucial than budgeting. Crudely, the end of the spending pipeline is a strategic spot to police the overall system of internal control of large volumes of "outside spending." Internal audit is at the end of the pipeline, and budgeting is at the front.

Proponents of the crucial role of the internal audit have labored hard to reinforce history. History helped mightily, no doubt of it. One observer isolated three powerful historical trends supporting an enlarged role for internal audit:[1]

1. The General Accounting Office has been active in unearthing deficiencies of management, especially in relation to contracts with outside organizations. Agency managements thus were motivated to discover and remedy the deficiencies before GAO review. Hence the growing importance of internal audit.

2. Congress gives close attention to reports of the GAO, and reports of alleged irregularities also get wide publicity. For obvious reasons, then, executive agencies have been anxious to isolate irregularities by internal audit.

3. Consequently, internal audit commonly has enjoyed access to top management, who are anxious lest irregularities be suppressed within the hierarchy of their own organizations.

Other historical forces were at work. The recent large-scale introduction of automatic data-processing equipment, for example, probably aided internal audit. Such powerful machines encouraged a systemic and overall view of managerial control. The location of internal audit in the agency spending process, again, permitted unusual opportunities for systemic oversight. At any rate, perhaps most basically, supporters of internal audit have emphasized the broad aspects of

---

[1] Daniel Borth, "Accounting in the Federal Government," The Federal Accountant, Vol. 13 (June, 1964), pp. 32–33.

managerial control which are such a challenge in today's public organizations. And these advocates also have attempted to tie internal audit closely to top management. Overall, proponents of internal review did not default on their opportunities.

To be sure, there are strong ebbs as well as flows in the overall tide toward an increasing emphasis on internal audit. Three particular resisting factors will be stressed here. First, the early history of auditing in the federal government is overall one of punitiveness and restriction. Consider the early and strong tendency of the General Accounting Office to attempt to control expenditures as well as to audit them. During the period up until World War II, roughly, Schulsinger reports that rather than emphasing reports to Congress the GAO tended to intervene in executive processes as government officials. These officials could attempt to undo the transaction, or they could personally reimburse the government. This GAO approach was well designed to alienate administrative officials. As Schulsinger concluded:

> By the use of the disallowance power, GAO personnel were able to substitute their conclusions of law and fact for those of agency administrators having responsibility for the conduct of government activities. Their authority to do this was frequently questioned, but their power was only in rare instances effectively limited.[2]

Such early history of auditing has not been completely lived down. Memories (and myths) die slowly in government.

Auditing still carries a certain stigma to many operating officials, although times have changed. Beginning in 1949, for example, the GAO began a "comprehensive audit" program. The number of GAO employees shrank by some 60 percent between 1946 and 1953, largely due to a sharply-diminished concern for checking individual transactions at a central office to find evidences of failures to follow procedures or the law, or to find evidences of failures to supply "adequate" evidence that public monies were expended properly. In contrast, as Schulsinger notes, the "comprehensive auditor" worked at the site of operations rather than at a remote Washington GAO desk. His sights also were raised. As Schulsinger explains, "the comprehensive auditor" cut down substantially the amount of voucher examination, or other scrutiny of individual transactions, and concentrated instead on surveying management procedures and controls generally, with a view to helping management develop its own controls.[3]

Second, and relatedly, auditing's history reflects a concern with errors untempered by a recognition that some are unavoidable either in actual fact or because of cost. Spending a dollar to prevent a 10 cent error illustrates the point at issue, and the early history of federal auditing (or perhaps its mythology) is full of examples. Understandably, operating officials were concerned about such

---

[2]Gerald G. Schulsinger, *The General Accounting Office: Two Glimpses*, Inter-University Case Program Series No. 35. University, Ala.: University of Alabama Press, July 1956, p. 4.

[3]*Ibid.*, p. 5.

an auditing approach. Illustratively, one business executive complained about the repeated citation in audits of errors of omission and commission. He explained that he did not advocate error for error's sake. Rather, he criticized the "usual implication" that these things should never occur. "Perhaps they should not," he explained, "and it may be that with superhuman effort on our part they would not, but to prevent their occurrence may well cost five or ten times as much as it would if we were to take the risk of their occurrence on a self-insurance basis." The executive drove his point home. "On the whole," he concluded, "we may sometimes find it more economical not to try to prevent every mistake but to operate on the philosophy that, when we do err, we will uncover the error and guard against its repetition in the future.[4] *This "management orientation" stands in sharp historical opposition to the "auditing orientation," although some of the sharper edges of the difference have worn away over time.*

Third, the philosophy underlying the early history of auditing was one of centralization. In contrast, decentralization is an increasingly common answer to providing managerial control. And never the twain do meet. To be sure, things are far removed from those days when the GAO demanded to examine all relevant papers relating to all expenditures at GAO headquarters. But the practice of auditing still reflects some bias toward a centralized system. This may once have endeared auditing to top executives. However, centralized systems often have their significant liabilities as organizations grow larger. This fact powerfully encourages top management to go slowly in augmenting the role of internal auditing.

Haver E. Alspach provides detailed counterpoint to the general trends sketched above. Alspach is the General Auditor of the Ford Motor Company, and brings formidable qualifications to his theme of "Internal Auditing Today and Tomorrow." Alspach reflects the lofty aspirations of the internal auditor, while he stresses the quid pro quo that will permit achieving those aspirations. That is, Alspach argues that internal auditing will pay its way not so much in the traditional sense of a post-audit of expenditures, of a kind of discovering of open organizational barn doors through which the monetary horses have already fled. Rather, attaining Alspach's aspirations for the internal auditor will require the development of methods and systems for control that will alert management with an immediacy beyond that possible in most of today's organizations. To extend the earlier metaphor, the internal auditor must determine where the financial barn doors may be, when they are likely to be left open, and which doors are more expensive to close than are the runaway horses that may escape. Additionally, all this intelligence must be available well before the actual fact.

Whether or not Alspach is correct in assessing the developing role of the internal auditor, there seems no question that he need not search for challenges. The challenges to financial reporting abound and, if anything, become evermore important.

---

[4]Dudley E. Browne, "Uses and Misuses of Accounting in Reducing Costs," *The Federal Accountant*, Vol. 13 (December, 1963), p. 60.

Some specific sense of the newer problems facing today's internal auditor is reflected in the sharply-increased tendency of government agencies to contract-out for goods and services. Victor K. Heyman well outlines the related problems in his "Government by Contract: Boon or Boner?" Contracting-out has some real advantages in many cases, but it always implies problems of controlling costs and encouraging efficiency. With cost-plus-fixed fee contracts, for example, a government agency motivates little or no contractor concern for efficiency. Sensitive government accounting and auditing controls patently are necessary. If incentive contracts are used, on the other hand, great care must be taken in setting targets lest the contracting party make great profits or lose its organizational shirt. Again, sensitive financial controls are vital.

If an agency's internal controls are not adequate to the job, as Figure 1 shows, further protection is available. The focus here is on the external post-audit provided by the General Accounting Office. Other external controls exist, of course, and they may be powerful. Thus congressional investigating committees can have a massive impact, for good or ill.

Any realistic approach to the General Accounting Office must reflect forces-in-opposition, for that agency has been and perhaps must be Saturday's child. While monitoring executive agencies, the GAO is an arm of Congress that strives to assure that public monies have been adequately spent. Beyond that simple statement, little can be written that is simple or incontestable. Thus the GAO does more than provide reports about irregularities, which characterizes the "independent audit" of business organizations. Although not in the executive branch, moreover, the GAO has power over executive agencies. The GAO has not been above using that power, in addition, as in voiding payment of vouchers for services provided or goods delivered. Hence the GAO has been a major storm center, and feelings about it can become intense in both proponent and opponent.

Two selections below fittingly provide opposed vantage points on the GAO. Both contributions reflect the richness of that agency's past and its promise. Frank H. Weitzel's "Comptrollership Trends in the Federal Government" is oriented toward the challenges facing comptrollership and toward its promise in meeting those challenges. The wealth of detail Weitzel provides cannot be adequately summarized. Basically, he reflects the complex backgrounds out of which the GAO evolved its mission-and-role. All in all, the GAO is an institution developed under inhospitable conditions to handle a job that desperately required doing. Weitzel emphasizes GAO's significant advances under those conditions, and foresees its greater future promise.

The GAO gets much the worse of it in Joseph Harris' "The General Accounting Office: Functions and Issues." Clearly an advocate of presidential leadership, Harris comes down hard on the GAO and its past, while noting the marked recent improvements in its relationships with executive agencies. That the external audit is provided by the GAO, that the GAO's role involves more than some control over executive agencies, and that the GAO is basically Congress's creature, are hard facts for Harris. He never becomes reconciled to them.

The selections by Weitzel and Harris are usefully framed in the context of the special report from The Federal Accountant on "Fifteen Years of Progress." That report suggests some of the diverse senses in which both authors have firm handholds on reality. That is, the special report considers the Joint Financial Management Improvement Program, a cooperative effort involving the Bureau of the Budget, the Department of the Treasury, and the GAO. The report clearly reflects the significant problems of financial control in the federal government. In addition, the report clearly reflects 15 years of progress in coping with financial problems by agencies of government that do not always have the same interests and have on occasion been on opposed sides of issues. The special report reflects some of the fruits of creative collaboration in public management, while it also implies the difficulties inhibiting effective problem-solving when several large organization units are involved.

THE EXPENDITURE PROCESS
Roy E. Moor
AUTHORIZATION

The first step toward determining the nature and amount of Federal expenditures is to make decisions on the functions which the Government should perform. In a few instances, the decisions are so basic that they are accepted without specific legislation. However, in the great majority of cases, the Congress explicitly enacts statutes authorizing a particular activity to be carried out. These authorizations may not include any financial details, but they are nevertheless an indication of congressional intent and thus can have significant economic effects.

Some authorizations are permanent. For example, in 1935 the Congress enacted a permanent authorization whereby 30 percent of all customs receipts are allocated to the Agricultural Marketing Service for the purpose of expanding domestic and foreign market outlets for farm commodities. Other authorizations are for specified periods and must be renewed if necessary. For example, the national defense education program, as enacted in 1961, is for two years only.

In general, authorizing legislation is enacted before funds are granted, and the financial aspects of a Government activity are considered separately by the Congress. Therefore, an agency which has been given responsibility for a function must typically request further legislation to obtain operating funds. However, in some instances, authorizing statutes also provide financial authority. For example, the Federal-Aid Highway Act not only initiated the Federal highway program but also allowed the Bureau of Public Roads to commit the Government to make specific grants for highway construction. All Government corporations are allowed by statutory authorization to make expenditures from the receipts of their own operations.

APPROPRIATIONS

The Constitution of the United States states that—

> No money shall be drawn from the Treasury but in consequence of appropriations made by law; and a regular statement and account of the receipts and expenditures of all public money shall be published from time to time.

This constitutional requirement represents the cornerstone of the Federal budgetary process.

The Government—like most individuals and businesses—typically commits itself to expenditures before the expenditures are actually made. For

---

Article is from *The Federal Budget As An Economic Document*, Washington, D.C.: U.S. Government Printing Office, 1962, pp. 7–24. Printed for the Joint Economic Committee, Congress of the United States.

example, when an agency hires an employee, a commitment exists to pay a salary before the salary is paid. Similarly, when an agency lets a contract, a commitment exists to make payment at a later time when the contract is fulfilled. Before any Government agency can make an expenditure, permission must be obtained from the Congress to commit or obligate the Government for the expenditure. The legislation which grants this authority to commit the Government is referred to as "obligational authority."

In March or April each year, the Bureau of the Budget begins to develop preliminary estimates of anticipated future expenditures. Sometimes these estimates are requested from the individual agencies; sometimes the Bureau of the Budget itself initiates the preparation of the estimates. The estimates include all of the types of outlays which will be associated with future activities of each agency, regardless of the persons receiving the expenditures or the purposes for which the expenditures are made. For example, the judiciary branch might estimate the amounts of expenditures which it will make for printed materials even though a substantial portion of the actual printing will be done by the Government Printing Office or other Government agencies. The estimates are made both for programs already authorized and for new programs which will be proposed. The estimates are reviewed by the Bureau of the Budget and, in consultation with the agencies, consolidated estimates for the entire Government are based upon the requests for "new obligational authority." Each January, the President submits to the Congress figures which, in his judgment, indicate the needs for the entire Government for new obligational authority in order to enter into commitments during the 12-month period beginning on the following July 1. The combined statement of all these requests represents "The Budget of the U.S. Government."

Several features of this budget should be noted. First, the new obligational authority does not reflect estimates of cash outflows during the forthcoming fiscal year. Rather, the amounts represent requests by the agencies for permission from the Congress to obligate the Government to future expenditures. The actual cash outflows may occur several years after the period for which the permission to obligate was granted. Second, the budget consists of estimates which are subject to several types of changes. The most obvious type of change is that the Congress will not grant exactly the amounts of new obligational authority requested. Also, the estimates of the agencies—made initially in March or April of one year for the period beginning in July of the following year—may not accurately indicate the actual needs for obligational authority for the activities of the Government. To the extent that actual circumstances vary from those predicted and additional obligational authority seems necessary, the President may make requests for supplemental obligational authority.

Despite these characteristics, the budget does represent a statement of Presidential proposals. As such, it serves as one advance indication of the potential economic impact of the Government on the private sector. The

319

budget can be used as a planning instrument not only by the Congress and the other agencies of Government but also by all those businesses and individuals which will be affected by Government decisions.

The budget is disintegrated as soon as it is received by the Congress. The document is referred to the House Appropriations Committee, separated into parts, and further referred to various subcommittees of the Appropriations Committee. These parts become the basis for the various appropriations bills that pass through Congress. The budget as a single document is not considered by the Congress in one piece of legislation. Each subcommittee of the Appropriations Committee holds hearings, draws up an appropriation bill, reports it to the full committee, and the bill proceeds through the normal legislative channels. Most appropriation bills are finally enacted around the end of June and early July.

Following the completion of each congressional session, a set of revised budget estimates, based on the appropriation bills enacted, is published by the Bureau of the Budget. This publication is generally referred to as "Midyear Budget Review." This document provides further indication of the Government's future expenditure intentions.

The new obligational authority provided by the Congress in the various appropriation bills are of several types. The most common form is the ordinary appropriation. An appropriation allows a Government agency (1) to commit the Government by orders, contracts, and so forth for specific types and amounts of future expenditures and (2) to make the future expenditures as the commitments are fulfilled.

Appropriations are granted in various forms. "One-year appropriations," which are the most common form, allow an agency to incur obligations within only one fiscal year, the grant expiring at the end of the year. However, if the obligations are incurred in the year, obligated balances of such appropriations remain available indefinitely for the making of expenditures in payment of the obligations. A typical example would be salaries and expenses of the FBI.

"Multiple-year appropriations" are available for the incurring of obligations for a specified period of time in excess of one year, with the obligated balances remaining available indefinitely for the making of expenditures in payment of the obligations. These appropriations are used primarily for programs of an unusual seasonal nature, for example, the Sugar Act program of the Commodity Stabilization Service.

"No-year appropriations" are available for both obligation and expenditure until the purpose is accomplished. This type of appropriation is used primarily for certain types of benefit payments and for construction of projects where a time limit would not add appreciably to the system of expenditure control. An example is the general construction by the Corps of Engineers in the Department of Defense.

"Current indefinite appropriations" are appropriations in which both the obligations and subsequent expenditures are indefinite in amount. These

320

appropriations may be available on a one-year, multiple-year, or no-year basis. The amounts involved in these appropriations are determined in various ways. Sometimes, the amounts are tied to particular receipts, and are frequently set in the enabling authorizations. For example, all advance deposits to cover payments of fees are appropriated each year for certification, inspection, and other services of the Food and Drug Administration. In other cases, the amount of the appropriation is determined by other factors. For instance, the appropriation to the Post Office Department is based on the difference between estimated postal receipts and authorized obligations.

"Permanent appropriations" are those in which additional amounts become available from year to year under existing law, without new action by Congress. Their availability may be limited to one-year or multiple-years, or be of a no-year type. Some of these permanent appropriations are enacted through ordinary legislation; others are in appropriation acts. Some permanent appropriations involve definite amounts for obligation and expenditure. For example, an endowment of $50,000 is given each year to each State and Puerto Rico for agricultural and mechanical arts instruction in colleges. Others are permanent indefinite appropriations where the amount becoming available for obligation and expenditure is not specified in the law, but is determined by other factors, e.g., the amount of receipts from a specified source. An example is the allocation of 30 percent of customs receipts to the Agricultural Marketing Service mentioned earlier. Alternatively, the determination may be simply on the basis of financial need, e.g., interest on the public debt.

Another type of obligational authority is the contract authorization. These authorizations have the first feature of an appropriation, i.e., they allow an agency to incur specific obligations, but they provide no power to make the expenditures associated with the obligations. Hence, an agency with contract authorization must make a subsequent request to the Congress for an appropriation to liquidate the obligations.

Contract authorizations are used generally where more than a year is expected to lapse between the time an obligation is placed and the time expenditures become necessary. A contract authorization may be enacted currently by Congress; those which appear in substantive law are current for the first year and permanent thereafter. Typically, they are definite in amount, e.g., the amount of air-navigation facilities that can be contracted for in a particular year. However, sometimes they are indefinite in amount, e.g., the contracts for the building in connection with extension of the Capitol. Alternatively, the contract authorizations may be permanent, and these are usually in substantive law. Some of these provide for specific amounts to be obligated for a limited number of years, e.g., grants for slum clearance and urban renewal. Others provide for renewal each year with no time limit, e.g., education and welfare services for Indians in Alaska.

Due to the existence of contract authorizations, another type of appropriations are those to permit the payment of obligations incurred under

321

previously granted contract authorizations, i.e., "appropriations to liquidate contract authorizations." These are authorizations to make expenditures only, and are not authority to incur additional obligations. Hence, these authorizations are not included in new obligational authority.

Some obligational authority is in the form of authorizations to expend from debt receipts. Some of these authorizations are in appropriations bills. However, many of the authorizations are not in appropriations bills and these are frequently referred to as "backdoor financing." They are generally provided in one of three ways. First, the Treasury may be authorized to provide public debt receipts to an agency, often in exchange for notes of the agency. Since the dollar balances in the bank accounts of the Treasury are not distinguishable by sources, whether obtained from taxes or from borrowing, this type of authorization represents, in essence, an appropriation to commit and to spend Government funds just like any other appropriation. Second, the Treasury and an agency may receive authorization to cancel notes issued by the agency to the Treasury. The effect of this authorization is to restore the authority previously used by the agency to "borrow" from the Treasury, i.e., to obligate and to spend additional Federal funds. Third, an agency may obtain an authorization to borrow directly from the public. Since this type of authorization is granted by the Congress, it means, in essence, that the agency can obtain funds by increasing the outstanding debt of the Federal Government. All three of these forms of authorizations may be considered and recommended to the Congress by committees other than the Appropriations Committees.

Some obligational authority is "no-year" in the sense that the agency may use the grant of authority to obligate at any time in the future. Most appropriations, however, are limited in time—usually to one or two fiscal years. In these cases, an agency which does not obligate itself to the full extent of its appropriations within the limited period must request an extension or reappropriation for a further period if the intention still exists to make the commitment. There are also reauthorizations of contract authority and reauthorizations to expend from debt receipts.

Table 1 indicates the amounts of total new obligational authority proposed by President Eisenhower for the fiscal year 1962 and the general categories of these amounts.

TABLE 1
TYPES OF NEW OBLIGATIONAL AUTHORITY, FISCAL 1962
(in millions)

Type	Current Authorizations	Permanent Authorizations	Total
Appropriations	$70,315	$9,188	$79,503
Authorizations to expend from debt receipts	793	211	1,004
Contract authorizations	...	340	340
Reappropriations	(^{1})	20	20
Total	71,108	9,759	80,867

[1]Less than $500,000.
Source: The 1962 Budget, pp. 14–15.

It is essential to recognize that Table 1 shows only request for new obligational authority. There is, at any point in time, an outstanding amount of existing obligational authority which has not yet been fully consumed by expenditures. Most of these existing obligational authorities will already have been used to create commitments but the final expenditures under the commitments will not have been made. Table 1 indicates the increment of obligational authority that President Eisenhower considered should be added to the amount which was estimated would be in existence on July 1, 1961.

Figure 1 shows these relationships. It was estimated in January 1961 that unspent obligational authorizations on July 1, 1961, would be approximately $74 billion. President Eisenhower requested $80.9 billion of new obligational authority be made available for the fiscal year 1962. If this total were granted by the Congress, agencies would then have $154.9 billion of

FIGURE 1
1962 EXPENDITURES RELATED TO AUTHORIZATIONS BY CONGRESS
(in billion dollars)

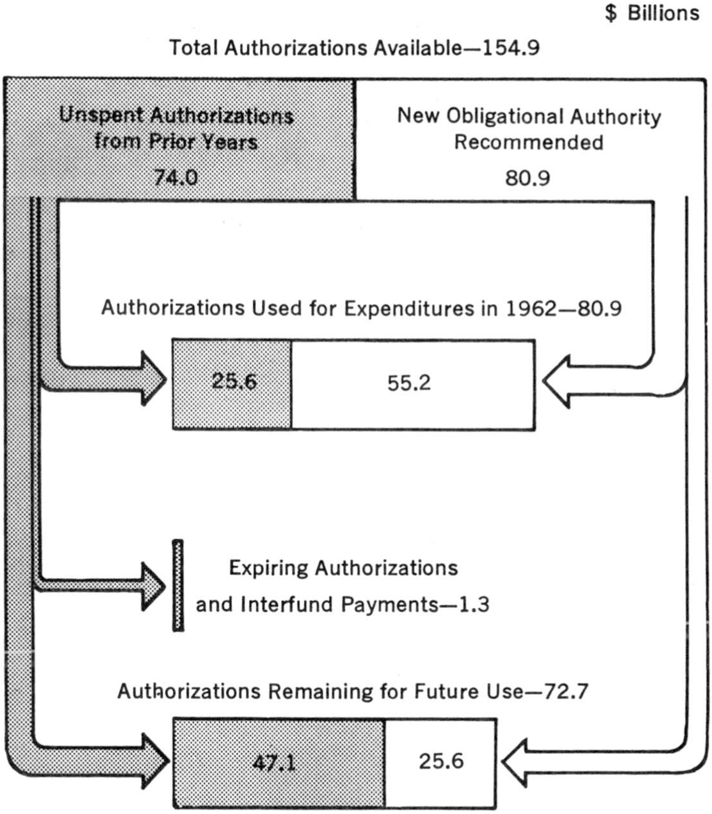

$ Billions

Total Authorizations Available—154.9

Unspent Authorizations from Prior Years
74.0

New Obligational Authority Recommended
80.9

Authorizations Used for Expenditures in 1962—80.9

25.6   55.2

Expiring Authorizations and Interfund Payments—1.3

Authorizations Remaining for Future Use—72.7

47.1   25.6

Source: "1962 Federal Budget in Brief," p. 58.

obligational authority from which to make expenditures. It was further estimated that, of the total amount, $80.9 billion would result in expenditures, during fiscal 1962. The total expenditures in fiscal 1962 would include $25.6 billion in liquidation of obligational authority already granted by the Congress and $55.2 billion in liquidation of the new obligational authority requested by President Eisenhower. Expiring obligational authorizations would have consumed another $1.3 billion of the previously appropriated authorizations. Hence, out of the $154.9 billion granted and requested, $72.7 billion was expected to be used for expenditures in fiscal years after fiscal 1962.

APPORTIONMENT

The enactment of an obligational authority by the Congress does not require the immediate establishment of a Treasury bank account to the credit of a Government agency. There are several steps between enactment of an obligational authority and cash outlay by the Treasury, and it would be poor business practice to hold cash idle while each of these steps is being consummated. As Figure 1 suggests, the interval between the grant of an obligational authority and the expenditure may be quite long, up to several years. If the Treasury were to hold amounts in bank balances for all of these future expenditures, the cost to the Government would equal the interest on the national debt that could be retired by these balances. Hence, the Treasury uses its funds almost immediately as it receives them to meet daily expenditure needs, regardless of outstanding obligational authority. If current receipts exceed claims against the Treasury arising from expenditures, as customarily happens during major taxpaying periods, debt obligations can be reduced. If the flow of cash claims begins to drain the relatively small Treasury bank balances at a faster rate than the incoming flow of cash receipts, the Treasury must go to the money markets and borrow funds.

The first step in the budgetary process after obligational authority has been enacted typically involves apportionment of the authority. This apportionment is done by the Bureau of the Budget, usually on a quarterly basis. The agencies determine in the first instance the rate at which they wish to obligate the Government to future expenditures, but the Budget Bureau reviews these plans before apportioning the authority to be sure the rate is consistent with the amount of obligational authority for the entire year. The Bureau may modify apportionments requested by the agencies if the requests do not seem appropriate. Hence, the Bureau has the ability to hold the use of obligational authority to lower levels than those enacted by the Congress. Since the congressional grants of obligational authority are rather general, considerable potential power rests with the Budget Bureau to control the direction and timing of Government expenditures. This power has been exercised to achieve economic objectives only in rare cases, but it represents a significant latent force for controlling the economic impact of the Government on the economy.

A second level of apportionment occurs within agencies once the obligational authority is distributed by the Bureau of the Budget. Agency heads determine the rate of allotments by months or quarters to the various administrative units within the agencies. As a result, additional restrictions may be placed on the use of obligational authority granted by the Congress.

OBLIGATION

An agency usually commits the Government only after apportionment of obligational authorizations have been made. However, there are several exceptions. Continuing employment represents a commitment which presumably exists before the apportionment. In some instances, agencies issue letters of intent in advance of apportionment, and a number of specific situations are described in the law under which orders with private firms can be placed even before appropriations.

Government statistics indicate amounts of "obligations incurred," i.e., commitments made by the Government during certain periods. The figures include not only commitments for purchases of goods and services from the private economy but also intragovernmental transfers, grants to State and local governments, and purely financial transactions. For example, the agencies may show obligations incurred to the Government Printing Office or interest owed to the Treasury as a result of borrowings from the Treasury.

The incurring of obligations is a significant step in two senses. It is typically the first point at which specific arrangements are made with those private firms and individuals that will be affected by the ultimate expenditures. Hence, to the extent that the private sector has not already begun to adjust during the previous stages of budget decision making, it must begin to react when obligations are incurred, since the commitments become binding on both the private sector and the Government. For the same reason, the incurring of obligations is also the last step in the budgetary process at which the Government has complete discretionary control over its expenditures. From this point forward, the amount and flow of expenditures is influenced by both parties to the transactions, not merely the Government.

Letters of intent are, in effect, interim devices by which a seller is instructed to begin production even though a detailed contract has not yet been signed. The purpose of these letters is to expedite production. They were extensively used during World War II and had significant economic effects in advance of the incurring of obligations. However, the use and importance of such letters has been substantially reduced in recent years.

Procurement procedures of Government agencies are generally governed by two laws: The Armed Services Procurement Act of 1947 and the Federal Property and Administrative Services Act of 1949, as amended.

325

The first of these acts provides that:

Purchases of and contracts for property or services covered by this Act shall be made by formal advertising. However, the head of an agency may negotiate such a purchase or contract, if—

(1) it is determined that such action is necessary in the public interest during a national emergency declared by Congress or the President;

(2) the public exigency will not permit the delay incident to advertising;

(3) the aggregate amount involved is not more than $2,500;

(4) the purchase or contract is for personal or professional services;

(5) the purchase or contract is for any service by a university, college, or other educational institution;

(6) the purchase or contract is for property or services to be procured and used outside the United States and the Territories, Commonwealths, and possessions;

(7) the purchase or contract is for medicine or medical supplies;

(8) the purchase or contract is for property for authorized resale;

(9) the purchase or contract is for perishable or nonperishable subsistence supplies;

(10) the purchase or contract is for property or services for which it is impracticable to obtain competition;

(11) the purchase or contract is for property or services that he determines to be for experimental, developmental, or research work, or for making or furnishing property for experiment, test, development, or research;

(12) the purchase or contract is for property or services whose procurement he determines should not be publicly disclosed because of their character, ingredients, or components;

(13) the purchase or contract is for equipment that he determines to be technical equipment whose standardization and the interchangeability of whose parts are necessary in the public interest and whose procurement by negotiation is necessary to assure that standardization and interchangeability;

(14) the purchase or contract is for technical or special property that he determines to require a substantial initial investment or an extended period of preparation for manufacture, and for which he determines that formal advertising and competitive bidding might require duplication of investment or preparation already made or would unduly delay the procurement of that property; or

(15) the purchase or contract is for property or services for which he determines that the bid prices received after formal advertising are unreasonable as to all or part of the requirements, or were not independently reached in open competition, and for which (A) he has notified each responsible bidder of intention to negotiate and given him reasonable opportunity to negotiate; (B) the negotiated price is lower than the lowest rejected bid of any responsible bidder, as determined by the head of the agency; and (C) the negotiated price is the lowest negotiated price offered by any responsible supplier;

(16) he determines that (A) it is in the interest of national defense to have a plant, mine, or other facility, or a producer, manufacturer, or other supplier, available for furnishing property or services in case of a national emergency; or (B) the interest of industrial mobilization in

case of such an emergency, or the interest of national defense in maintaining active engineering, research, and development, would otherwise be subserved; or

(17) negotiation of the purchase or contract is otherwise authorized by law.

The Federal Property and Administrative Services Act of 1949 establishes almost identical requirements.

EXPENDITURES

Cash outflows begin to occur in some cases almost simultaneously with the incurring of obligations. In other instances, the interval between the initial commitment and the final expenditure related to the commitment can be several years. These differences in lag times can be explained by the differences in types of expenditures which the Government makes.

The Government makes some expenditures which involve virtually no use of productive resources. These expenditures include purchases of existing assets, interest payments on the national debt, and security benefits, unemployment compensation, certain farm subsidies, and various other outlays. In these instances, expenditures typically are concurrent with—or immediately follow—commitments since no process of production is required prior to payment.

The Government also makes expenditures for goods and services produced by the Government itself. In these cases, the Government pays the productive factors as their services are being used—not as the final goods and services are received. Hence, there are two potential lags in these types of expenditures: the interval between commitment and expenditure and between expenditure and completion of the goods or services. However, because of the nature of the goods and services produced directly by Government, these two lags are typically short or nonexistent. For example, the Agriculture Department incurs an obligation to Forest Service employees that it will pay wages and salaries during the course of a fiscal year. The wages and salaries are paid monthly or biweekly after the services have been provided by the employees. Therefore, the Government may receive the benefits of, for example, an improved mountain trail after the commitment to spend but before the expenditure. On the other hand, results of forest research may not become available until a number of years after the expenditures associated with the research.

Government expenditures involving minimum use of productive resources and expenditures involving direct Government employment of such resources must be distinguished from purely intragovernmental transfers. The latter, which involve merely changes in the internal bookkeeping of the Government, are only examined in this study to the extent they reflect possible future economic consequences. The Government expenditures must be examined because they have a direct impact. For example, when an

327

amount is debited to the Treasury's account and credited to a Social Security Administration account, the economy is unaffected. But when the Social Security Administration makes payments to individuals, the payments clearly do affect the economy. Similarly, an apportionment by the Bureau of the Budget to the Forest Service allowing it to incur obligations is, in a sense, an intragovernmental transfer which is only important as an indication of future Government action. A basic assumption throughout this study is that the productive resources employed by the Government are drawn from the private sector. Hence, payments by a Federal agency to its employees—as well as to private owners of resources—are treated as expenditures to the private economy, not as intragovernmental transfers. This approach is similar to that used in the Federal budget.

In addition to expenditures which involve little use of resources and those where the resources are employed directly by the Federal Government, there is a third category of expenditures in which the resources are employed on behalf of the Government by the private sector. This production in the private sector of goods and services for sale to the Government is not usually reflected in Federal budget data as the production proceeds, despite the fact that the Government is clearly affecting the economy.

The Federal Government, just as a private business firm, does not usually pay for goods until the items have been delivered, inspected, and approved. Hence, the expenditures in these cases occur after the use of productive resources.

However, some Government agencies which contract for work to be done in the private sector are allowed to make payments to the private contractors prior to final delivery. Such payments are usually restricted to large orders for heavy equipment where the production requires substantial addition to the working capital of the private producer. The payments in these cases are of two types. "Progress payments" can usually be made up to 75 percent of the value of the contract or 90 percent of labor and material alone, and no interest is charged the contractor on such payments. It has been estimated that almost one-third of total military expenditures for procurement and production in fiscal 1954 were in the form of progress payments.

"Advance payments" are made before work begins on a contract but are typically provided only when no other contractor is available to do the work without advance payments. In general, a 6 percent per annum interest is charged on advance payments. The payments are deposited in special bank accounts and withdrawals by a contractor are supervised. Advance payments were quite important during World War II, but are relatively insignificant at present. To the extent these two types of payments are made, however, data on Government expenditures presumably reflect more precisely the use of resources by the private economy.

In general, there are two reasons for the lags between initial authorizing of expenditures and final payments to the private sector. The first lag is usually administrative. A period of time is necessary for the agencies to prepare and obtain approval of apportionment requests, to draw up specifications for orders, and to award contracts. It was estimated that during the World War II defense buildup this administrative lag varied from a week to five months. This lag depends in part on the newness of the program. The average period was reduced from approximately a year in the first Public Works Administration to 100 days in the second PWA program. Such changes in the length of the lag period during the course of an expenditure program are typical and must be considered in measuring the economic effects of Government contracts and expenditures.

A second, and more significant, lag is due to technological factors. It takes time for a contractor to obtain the necessary resources, to draw plans, to negotiate subcontracts, and to solve technical difficulties. It has been estimated that for military items, the interval between contract settlement and the time the first units are completed at the scheduled rate of production varies from six months in the case of uniforms to over two years for bombers and fighters. A further delay occurs after delivery for inspection, paperwork, and disbursements.

The lags for soft goods services are, of course, much shorter than for hard goods. The period between obligations and expenditures for such items as salaries, travel, and printing usually is only a few months at most.

The rate of expenditures can be changed in several ways. Federal contracts may be canceled, although the Government may lose its existing investment in a project or may have to pay damages to a contractor for unrecoverable cost in these cases. Most contracts allow for subsequent changes by the Government which may serve to expedite or slow the rate of expenditures.

RENEGOTIATION

Renegotiation is a process of determining what part, if any, of the profits realized from contracts and subcontracts is excessive. To the extent that such profits are determined to be excessive, they are returned to the Government in the form of refunds. Statutory renegotiation of defense contracts and related contracts dates back to 1942. Presently, renegotiation is conducted by the Renegotiation Board.

It is important to note that renegotiation of contracts is quite limited in scope. First, renegotiation applies only to contracts with certain agencies of the Government and to the related subcontracts. These agencies presently are the Department of Defense, Maritime Administration, Federal Maritime Board, General Services Administration, National Aeronautics and Space Administration, and the Atomic Energy Commission. Second, a number of limitations are set forth in the Renegotiation Act so that certain contracts with the specified agencies are excluded. These exemptions include contracts and subcontracts for many agricultural commodities, for products of mines, oil and gas wells, contracts with common carriers, public utilities and tax-exempt organizations.

Renegotiation is conducted not with respect to individual contracts but with respect to the receipts or accruals of a contractor under all renegotiable contracts and subcontracts in an entire fiscal year.

No fixed formula or preestablished rates are used in determining excessive profits. Each contractor is treated as an individual case. In general, six factors are considered in measuring excessive profits: the efficiency of the contractor, reasonableness of cost and profits, amount and source of public and private capital employed, the extent of risk assumed, the nature and extent of the contribution to the defense effort, and the character of the business.

Under the law some contractors are required to file information with the Renegotiation Board. In fiscal 1960, approximately 17,400 contractors filed such information. Of these 17,400, about 13,400 were not examined in detail. About 3,000 more were withheld at central headquarters for further screening. This left approximately 1,000 cases to be assigned to the regional boards which actually do the examining for excessive profits.

The firms which were determined to have the $52.7 million of excessive profits had total renegotiable sales of $4,583.1 million and renegotiable profits of $401.6 million.

In addition to the determinations of excessive profits, contractors subject to renegotiation made voluntary refunds and price reductions of $77.8 million. However, both the figures for determinations of excessive profits and for voluntary refunds are made before adjustments in Federal income taxes.

AUDIT

The auditing of expenditures is done in the first instance at the agency level. Each agency has an auditing officer as well as a budget officer and the auditing process is continuous. Many agencies have both a preaudit of expenditures prior to payment and a postaudit after payment. However, the major auditing of Government accounts is done by the General Accounting Office, an agency of the Congress. Very broad powers have been vested in the GAO and in the Comptroller General of the United States who directs its activities. These powers include the authority to decide most questions involving a payment to be made by any agency of the Government; to audit and settle all public accounts; to settle, adjudicate, and adjust all claims for and against the Government; to prescribe systems and procedures for administrative appropriation and fund accounting; and to investigate all matters relating to receipts and disbursements of public funds, including the right to examine any pertinent books, documents, papers, and records of any Government contractors or subcontractors. All decisions of the Comptroller General are final and conclusive upon the executive branch in the settlement of public accounts. The responsibility is upon agency heads to maintain adequate systems of accounting and internal control, but these must conform to principles and standards prescribed by the Comptroller General.

Within these broad powers, GAO performs several types of functions. All wholly owned and mixed-ownership Government corporations are subject to an annual audit by GAO. In addition, the GAO conducts audits on a selective basis of all other Government activities, either by functional or agency categories. The Comptroller General also makes many specific analyses of administration and expenditures by particular Government agencies for the benefit of the Congress.

AGENCY BUDGET PROBLEMS

Carl W. Tiller

Budgeting in the Federal Government serves as a means, both at the national level and at the individual agency level, of weighing choices and determining priorities. Since governmental programs cannot be carried on without money, the necessity for making decisions about money forces decisions about program and efficiency. Implicit in nearly every decision on obligating or spending money is a decision on what will be done with the money. And what will be done with the money involves decisions as to program and the degree of managerial efficiency which is contemplated.

The inevitability of the budget cycle is another aspect of budgeting which contributes to decision making within Government. Whether an executive is ready to make decisions or not, budget time comes around at least annually and forces administrators into decisions they might otherwise prefer to postpone.

BASIC BUDGET CONSIDERATIONS

The Government's approach to budgeting reflects its keen awareness of the importance of careful planning and of the vital role budgeting plays in national decision making. National decision making involves plans, not merely forecasts. The budget is not primarily a forecast, although there are forecasting elements within it—for example, what the tax yield will be at present rates. Essentially that which the President budgets, that which an agency head budgets, and that which subordinates budget, are a series of plans and proposals, not merely a set of forecasts of what is likely to happen.

Each spring programs under way and those proposed for adoption are evaluated in terms of feasibility, need, progress and cost. A five-year forward projection is made during this spring preview period and shortly thereafter each agency head is given a planning target or series of targets to be used as a guide in the development of detailed agency financial and program plans. These combined agency financial and program plans are thoroughly reviewed during the fall months of the year in a process which culminates the following January with the President's submission of the Budget of the United States to the Congress.

Congress of course also uses the budget process, as a way not only to make decisions about the budget itself but also to make decisions about the scope and nature of an agency's program. For many agencies, the budget process provides the one regularly recurring opportunity for congressional

Article is from *The Federal Accountant*, Vol. 13 (September, 1963), pp. 58–67. Used with permission of publisher and author.

appraisal of what has been taking place and is proposed to take place in the agency.

In order that budgets may represent good plans, it is necessary that the budget process lead to well-considered decisions on program needs. A budget should be so prepared and presented that it focuses consideration on the missions to be performed and on the steps which are necessary to perform those missions. For example: What is needed in order to have an appropriate defense posture? What are the needs for successful operation of a system of mail delivery? What should be the national program of reforestation? What are the Government's needs with respect to immigration and customs matters? The budget process must bring to attention and obtain decisions annually on over 5,000 programs of the Government.

These decisions are influenced, and necessarily so, by consideration of available resources. There is never as much money in sight as would be needed to carry out all of the programs which the various program administrators think desirable. Sometimes there are not enough persons available with skills of the type needed for specialized programs, particularly in such areas as research and engineering. Budgeting therefore must assist executives in setting priorities and determining the best allocation of available resources. Decisions on the budget as a whole are also influenced by the nation's economy and considerations of the role that the budget should play in the nation's economy. Budget presentations of the agencies might well give attention to the relationship between program proposals and the state of the nation's economy.

One of the hardest phases of budgeting occurs when two or more objectives seem to come into conflict. Such a clash takes place many times in the preparation of the President's budget. For example, the objective of a bigger program to meet national goals with respect to education may conflict with the objective of reducing the budget deficit. Again, the objective of reducing the gold outflow may conflict with the objective of economizing. Which objective should yield and which should triumph—to hold down payments abroad or to hold down total payments? The answers do not come easily, for there is no exactly right answer; decisions must be reached in the light of weighing the circumstances and alternatives in each individual case.

AGENCY BUDGET OFFICERS

Agency budget-making necessarily involves the participation of all senior officials in the agency but the agency's budget officer is its general focal point for budgetary endeavors. By the very nature of the budgetary process, the budget officer in most agencies has the major responsibility for reviewing and integrating the agency's budget and thus exerts a rather considerable influence on agency decisions. Among the various facets of a budget officer's responsibilities, these five may be distinguished as having special importance:

1. To aid the process of executive decision making, including decisions on programs, administrative requirements and finances.

2. To present the proposed program and financial plan of the agency, or of his segment of the agency, to subsequent reviewing authorities.

3. To communicate decisions made and guidance adopted at higher levels, with reference to program and finances, to and through his organization.

4. To influence decisions through his own store of information, analysis and advice.

5. To provide a focal point within his organization for efforts to obtain efficiency, eliminate waste and to see that the Government gets the highest possible return on every dollar spent.

In his budget-making responsibilities, the agency budget officer typically functions in a staff capacity and his contribution to decision making constitutes what probably is his most important role. Decision making requires facts, alternatives, evaluation of possible consequences and recommendations from subordinates. A competent budget officer accordingly draws on accountants, statisticians, line operators and many others within his agency for the factual data needed for budget presentations. Effective budget presentation involves a statement of and consideration of alternatives, both with respect to ways to accomplish the agency mission and with respect to the probable consequences of spending more or less than proposed for the purpose within the fiscal year.

Agency budget officers could make greater contributions to decision making if they gave more attention to the possible consequences of alternatives and submitted data thereon along with their recommendations. A consideration of alternatives is a basic part of the budget evaluation that occurs in the Bureau of the Budget, as policy issues are readied for the President's consideration. Above all, budget officers should remember that no budget is really made by the budget staff; it is made by the principal executive in charge of the Government agency concerned and should be made in the light of relative needs, alternatives and possible consequences.

SOME AGENCY PROBLEMS IN BUDGETING

Budgeting, involving as it does estimates of an uncertain future, is inherently a difficult process but not all of the problems encountered by agency budget staffs as they seek to carry out their responsibilities can be attributed to the uncertainty of the future. Many of the problems can be characterized as organizational in nature and some of the most troublesome problems are of an individual agency's own making. For discussion purposes, however, agency problems in budgeting will be considered under three general headings: Problems of Environment; Problems Inherent in the Budget Process; and Problems Relating to Budget Presentation.

An overall comment pertinent to all three of these headings concerns the regrettable diffusion of budget responsibility in a number of agencies. Too often in the last ten years or so, budget staffs have been stripped of significant portions of their responsibility. There are many aspects of the job of helping executives reach decisions which used to be lodged in the budget staff but are now found elsewhere. While "empire building" should be avoided, the splitting up of the former functions of budget offices may result in less coordinated staff work and perhaps less adequate budget plans. It is most important that there be the greatest possible coordination between the budget staff and other agency staffs concerned with planning, management, accounting, statistics, reporting and related activities.

Problems of Environment

A basic group of agency budget problems can be associated with the environment in which budgeting occurs. Probably the most common problem in this category relates to horizons and time span. Modern society has become so complex the Government simply cannot do a good job of budgeting by considering only one year at a time. It is difficult, however, to get some agency executives to look very far into the future. In the national interest, there must be more appraisal of long-range objectives and more long-range programming (even though firm decisions and commitments of money may not come for long periods of time) as a basis for sound annual budgets.

Some of the multi-year plans that have been presented to the Bureau of the Budget the past three budget seasons have been very good, but on the whole the quality of these plans has been disappointing. There has not been adequate multi-year planning on the part of the doers, the line officials in the agency who are going to carry out the plans and who really should initiate much of the planning. An over-concern with day-to-day operations—and lack of concern with long-run objectives—is a significant roadblock in the path towards better budgeting.

Probably a majority of the Government's agency budget officers consider as one of their problems the fact that they are always working in a "tight budget" environment. This criticism is the reverse of what the public generally thinks about the budget as a whole. Actually, the budget is always tight, but consideration is always given to worthwhile programs and financial needs. No agency is kept from voicing its aspirations in its budget submission for the President's consideration, although there may be disagreement as to how worthwhile are particular proposals.

Perhaps no catalog of agency budget problems would be complete without noting that an almost universal problem is lack of success in getting all the program authority and financial resources that an agency wants. Because any one agency's needs must be weighed against other needs and against overall factors relating to the fiscal policy and the nation's economy, it is not possible to budget as much for some programs as might seem warranted. But, after taking account of such elements of decision making, an agency officer may still improve his performance by establishing with

335

successive reviewing levels the highest degree of confidence in his integrity. There is no substitute for confidence in the integrity of the budget presentation and in the integrity of the budget officer personally—confidence that his facts and figures are accurate, honest, reliable and completely frank. Of course, integrity alone is not enough; an agency must also have worthwhile programs, and worthwhile and genuine financial needs, in order to get its budget proposals accepted at successive levels of review.

Problems Inherent in the Budget Process

A very common complaint is that the budget process is too long—that it is too spread out, beginning too soon and ending too late. For no apparent reason, some agencies begin their annual budget process as early as February—17 months before the fiscal year starts. In every agency the overall process is undoubtedly too long and too spread out, and too many man-hours are devoted to it. There is a widespread need for critical self-evaluation of the budget process at various levels within Government.

A related problem is the difficulty of obtaining firm decisions at the time they are needed. Even when the process starts early, it becomes difficult to get decisions nailed down at the various levels of review. This is probably more characteristic of legislative program items in the budget than of continuing programs, but it applies to both. Are decisions being sought at an earlier stage than is absolutely necessary? How can decisions be obtained promptly when they are really needed? The answers to these questions may seem elusive, and they probably are, but part of the difficulty undoubtedly lies in too little attention to these areas within the agencies themselves.

Another problem, and a very serious one for many reasons, is the delay in congressional action on legislation and appropriations, which slows down preparation of the next budget. Even though most budget officials agree that budgeting should be done from a zero base, it is desirable to know what the congressional attitude has been toward the last budget before the next one is prepared, or at least before decisions on it become final. Congressional delays on the budget in recent years have been aggravated by the practice of requiring annual authorizations—the double budget system—for more and more programs. Almost 35 percent of the dollars in the latest budget are for programs on which Congress requires annual authorizations before the appropriations may formally be acted upon under the rules of Congress. That is, the agency must first present a request for legislation to extend the expiration date of a law or to authorize a larger amount to be appropriated, and obtain needed legislation, before the appropriation process can move very far. Late appropriations have become a common and unfortunate handicap for agency operations as well as for both budget execution and preparation of the following budget.

One final problem with respect to the budget process is that budget personnel are tied up the year around in too many routines. Not only is the annual budget preparation process itself long, but there are so many supplementals and budget amendments, special forecasts, special analyses, reports and other duties, that budget personnel have too little opportunity to think, to plan and to evaluate carefully. There is a need for more fortitude to keep the budget process in the normal cycle, and to eliminate consideration of supplemental estimates and budget amendments which should have been planned earlier or might wait until the next fiscal year. Perhaps, too, some of the routines of reports and some of the special analyses might be shifted from budget staffs to other portions of an agency organization.

Problems Relating to Budget Presentation

By far the most frequent criticism made of budget presentations is that too much detail is required. Part III of the Budget Appendix (details of personal services) might well be an early candidate for omission. But, as in the case of many other details, the law requires it, and members of Congress may well need such detail even if others find little need for it as a part of the printed budget documents. Often detail presently required stems from a real interest in Congress—for example, in budgets for automobiles—that in part has arisen because of past abuses of discretion by particular agencies or officials.

Some agencies express concern that budget submissions must include classifications of data that are of no particular interest to them. But they may overlook the fact that some classifications of data which are not of direct managerial interest in the agency may be of importance in managing the Government as a whole. Decision making with regard to the relation of Federal finances to the economy involves the analysis of information on the economic impact of Government transactions, even though an individual agency may not find such information vital in its own day-to-day operations.

Incidentally, agency personnel might be surprised if they knew how often the Bureau of the Budget resists requests and suggestions that additional details, classifications and other data be obtained from the agencies. The budget submissions are handy vehicles for carrying annual reports and statements of plans on a variety of subjects that are important but may make the total budget submission burdensome instead of helpful.

Another budget problem is the fact that the data obtained by budget offices are not always in the best form. A few budget submissions still need "activity" classifications that reflect the programs carried out, and they need data on the cost of carrying out those programs and on the changes in the resources available for future program needs. Many agencies still need to develop or improve their measures of program accomplishment. This is true also at various levels within many agencies.

Lack of appropriate accounting and budget liaison is still a problem in some agencies. Accounting offices sometimes give their budget offices data in a form that has to be reworked for presentation to a higher level, and budget assistants who rework the material may know what the required form is but often do not really know how to put the data into that form. The result is

337

the compilation of queer and inaccurate budget schedules and statements, which must be revised subsequently. With respect to "actual year" data, there can be little reason for an accounting office not to provide the data in the form required for review and submission to other levels, and those in the budget office ought to use their time to better advantage than reworking data that comes from the accounting offices.

Inadequate budget justifications are a more general problem, applying to estimate material which department and bureau budget officers receive as well as to some they create. Many words saying that this is needed and that is needed do not demonstrate need, but this problem goes beyond the financial management community. Line officials may have legitimate program needs and legitimate financial needs, but some of them have not learned how to communicate their needs in a way that enables someone else to appraise and evaluate those needs wisely. More should be done to help officials outside the financial management community to learn how to explain and justify their needs.

COMMON OBJECTIVES

Throughout the budgetary process, agency budget officers and the staff of the Bureau of the Budget have a great common interest. Budgeteers at various "levels" are working in staff capacities for "line" officials who have the ultimate responsibility. All participants in the budget process thus have a common interest in seeing that the data and the considerations for decision making are presented in such a way that wise conclusions can be reached by those in decision-making roles.

By working together, agency budget officers and staff examiners in the Bureau of the Budget can do much to improve budget procedures. Their interests are mutual in making the budget process more effective as a means toward reaching decisions and providing for their execution. Many improvements have been made in the past 15 years and a few changes may have been made which have not represented progress. Additional improvements can be made if everybody concerned will undertake to cooperate in solving basic problems, working together towards the objective of making the budget process a better servant of those with responsibility for making Government decisions—both in the Executive Branch and in Congress.

INTERNAL AUDITING TODAY AND TOMORROW

Haver E. Alspach

The "Statement of Responsibilities" promulgated by the Institute of Internal Auditors contains a generally accepted definition of internal auditing which reads as follows:

> Internal auditing is an independent appraisal activity within an organization for the review of accounting, financial and other operations as a basis for service to management. It is a managerial control, which functions by measuring and evaluating the effectiveness of other controls.

This definition highlights the modern concept that internal auditing is an appraisal activity and a managerial control. It is appropriate, therefore, to examine in this context the problems and opportunities that the auditor faces today and tomorrow in providing the greatly expanded service which management requires under modern operating conditions. Meanwhile any erroneous conception of the auditor as a spy, a gumshoe or a nit picker should be for all time dispelled.

Significantly, but not surprisingly, auditing in Government has much in common with auditing in business. Both have many of the same objectives, principles and techniques. Certainly the purposes of the Federal Government Accountants Association, in particular, are compatible with the managerial control concept of internal auditing. Its general research objective, "The conduct of research which will lead to the development of improved financial management techniques," and its bylaw provision which states as an objective:

> To aid in the improvement of accounting and auditing in the Federal Government through promoting appropriate utilization of accounting methods and techniques for purposes of management control and accountability to the public

confirm this. In the statements which follow, therefore, the frequent references to "business" and "the business world" should be considered as interchangeable with "Government" insofar as internal auditing is concerned.

BROAD CHALLENGE OF AN EVOLVING ENVIRONMENT

It is important to identify certain of the developments that characterize the era in which we live and the era into which we are entering as a basis for suggesting how the internal auditor can meet the challenge of these

Article is from *The Federal Accountant*, Vol. 13 (September, 1963), pp. 114–27. Used with permission of publisher and author.

developments. This moreover must be done repeatedly if we are to keep abreast of our asserted purpose of assisting management in attaining its own managerial objectives. In regard to the future, however, little more can be done than present some of the problems and raise some of the questions that we and our successors may have to face in a future environment of more complicated technology, extended communications, an increased tendency toward larger enterprises, expanded international commerce, and a higher level of expectation for performance in the business world.

Let us examine a few of the factors that require present and future consideration. One factor that has been exerting a great influence for some time and that we will all have to consider in making our plans for the future is the accelerated rate of change on all fronts, including the business world. Until the recent past, change in business came at a rather moderate pace. But that time of gradual change—of slow evolution—is behind us. Tremendous acceleration in the progress of science and technology in just a decade has made the rate of change so rapid that our only hope of keeping up with new developments is to foresee them well in advance. The internal auditor must certainly keep his thinking adjusted to look forward—not backward—if he is even to maintain his usefulness to management, let alone increase it.

Of course all of the problems of business will not be new. Many of them will be called by the same old names, but we shall have to avoid the error of trying to solve them in the same old way. Spiraling costs are perhaps a good case in point. It might be argued that costs have already been cut to the bone and that nothing further can be done in this area. Before we adopt a negative attitude, however, should we not consider the possible parallel situation that has developed in the scientific and engineering fields? Our scientific people have time after time improved on what was previously thought perfect, have accomplished the impossible, and have developed the unbelievable. This they have done by availing themselves of all the new applicable scientific knowledge they can find. Can we not take a page from the book of the researcher and engineer and apply the resources at our disposal for cutting costs and solving other business problems? I think there is only one answer to that question—we must do so.

Any consideration of the problems ahead for internal auditors is necessarily closely related to the problems ahead for management. As I have mentioned, one of the most compelling of these is the rapidly increasing rate of change. Professor R. W. Revans expressed it in a recent article in *The Internal Auditor* as follows: "A major problem among managers today is to develop improved methods of control so that the effectiveness of their policies and the hindrances to their fulfillment can be known as clearly and as quickly as possible." How are we to apply this principle both as regards the running of our own internal auditing organization and the fulfillment of our objective of rendering adequate service to our managements under changing conditions?

340

A broad answer to this question is supplied by Professor Revans when he suggests that whatever part we play will be largely determined, not by what management expects of us, but by what we can exhibit to the managers. In auditing—as in everything else—supply is a major force in creating demand. If management is to be pushed to the limit of its resources to keep abreast of its own problems, it has little time to sit down and work out what kind of salvation it prefers. What management needs is ready-made help. Such help, if in competent supply, will also be in immediate demand. This, then, is our broad challenge; we must sharpen our capabilities so that we may be able to provide the help which management requires, and we must further take the initiative in offering our services rather than expecting the invitation to come from management.

ECONOMY IN AUDIT ENDEAVOR

To cope with this challenge we must indulge in some critical self-examination. We must recognize that we do not have unlimited resources of manpower, time or capabilities. We must apply some of the same type of thinking that goes into solution of scientific and research problems to which I have previously alluded.

It seems reasonable to believe that internal auditors will continue properly to have responsibility for certain financial and protective functions. Should we not, however, make every effort to discharge these functions as economically as possible so that the time saved can be directed to other and perhaps more productive matters? Three possibilities for effecting such economies will be discussed to illustrate how productive an economy-oriented approach can be.

First, have we assumed more responsibility in the protective area than is desirable? Is it not possible that management has abdicated some of its responsibilities for self-appraisal by shifting an undue portion of protective functions to the internal auditor? To the degree that this condition exists, we should recognize it and should be sufficiently objective to call upon operating management to again assume active responsibility for some of these functions which may have passed to auditors by default. The restoration of protective functions in the operating structure would provide some of the time we are looking for to devote to other important matters.

Second, let us not be too reluctant to give up old and cherished ideas as to the depth of auditing effort that is required to adequately test a given area. For example, we must examine fully the possibilities of statistical sampling—a procedure which should not be followed blindly but utilized after close scrutiny of the fields where it is most applicable. Sampling principles in turn may often be applied at a greatly accelerated pace if integrated with the operations of electronic data processing systems. In our auditing at Ford we have made use of sampling in several ways, including application at a centralized computer activity handling payroll transactions

341

for 146,000 employees and in connection with the selection of balances for confirmation at a location maintaining 190,000 receivable accounts. In addition, our Finance Staff Operations Research Department has studied the feasibility of determining total inventory value by projecting the results of counting a statistically selected sample of items. This study indicated that satisfactory accuracy should be achieved by statistical sampling techniques, and one of our divisions has since requested authorization to use these techniques as the basis for adjusting its replacement parts inventory in lieu of annually counting all parts.

Third, to achieve economies of time, we should apply tough thinking to traditional concepts as to frequency of audit. Is there any magic about auditing once every six months, once a year or at any other specified interval? Here again we must pursue an enlightened and scientific approach and not merely fall into the easy path of past concepts. In making decisions regarding both frequency and depth of audit, it is important not to overlook the work being done by other staff activities or by public accountants. We can often serve management more effectively and economically by coordinating our effort with other groups than we can by blindly insisting that we—as internal auditors—directly cover all the bases.

These three suggestions do little more than scratch the surface in a very limited area. Many, many more ideas can be generated.

CHANGING EMPHASIS IN AUDIT ENDEAVOR

As our environment changes, it is becoming increasingly important that we re-examine the scope of some of our basic auditing practices. Management needs to determine not only that items reflected on the books are still there but that they are profitably used; not only that salaries are paid to persons who in fact exist, but that these persons are giving value for what they are paid. Determinations are needed not only as to whether inventories are properly valued but also whether the organization can operate more profitably at reduced levels of inventory; not only whether bills are paid upon proper authority but whether the supplies or services were worth what we paid for them and whether they were necessary for effective operation. These points are elementary and probably are representative of the previously-mentioned responsibilities which management should build into the operating and financial control system rather than leave to internal auditors. In fact our responsibility may well lie not so much in the area of post audit, but more in the area of devising methods whereby management can be reliably informed with an immediacy not now possible.

This concept can readily be related to the application of operations research which, although perhaps not too clearly defined to date, has emerged as a new and accepted technique useful in solving management problems. It is a broad approach requiring precise facts, varied knowledge and mathematical skill. It resolves a mass of information concerning a problem into an orderly pattern and makes it possible to apply scientific and mathematical techniques in the solution. Alternative courses of action can be evaluated and compared. As auditors, we may not be able to play a direct part on the research team, but we should be able to visualize the use of this approach to management problems.

With reference to the earlier comment that we may often better serve management's needs by coordinating our efforts with those of other groups, what are some of these groups that engage in management counseling activities of a type similar to those performed by internal auditors? As one example, there seems to have been a trend recently on the part of systems and procedures organizations to claim management auditing as an important part of their work. Also, management consultant organizations have been in operation for many years and public accounting firms have become increasingly interested in management services. Furthermore, in most organizations—at least in the larger ones—there are staff specialists in such areas as purchasing, production control and finance who conduct operational reviews in their assigned fields.

All of these groups—including internal auditors—have interests in, and abilities to perform, management counseling activities, and it borders on the absurd to take a position that such activities are the prerogative of any one group. Even if we felt this to be so, there is no assurance that our managements would concur. However, we as internal auditors are in a position to influence management's selection of who is to perform these activities under varying circumstances. This provides us with an opportunity for exhibiting a top management attitude, which means considering the genuine needs of our organization and not solely our own immediate interests. While we should not back off from tasks that we can most appropriately perform, we must be statesmenlike enough to recognize that there may be areas where other groups can operate more economically and perhaps more effectively. In such instances, the truly management-oriented auditor has a responsibility to recommend that the matter be handled by representatives of some other group.

Regardless of the auditing philosophies adopted in our respective organizations, each of us must indulge in periodic self-appraisal as to whether internal auditing is serving a necessary and useful purpose. In making this appraisal we cannot afford to get overly preoccupied with techniques, procedures and administrative details—important as these factors are. It is essential that we never lose sight of the broad objective of internal auditing which, simply stated, is improvement of the business. This improvement may take many forms including better controls or a higher level of efficiency. The evaluation of our job places on us the responsibility of being constantly alert to the changing needs of management and of modifying our internal auditing effort to meet those needs. This is not an easy task and requires strong personal perseverance and frequent reappraisal, taking advantage of all the resources at our disposal.

In the Institute of Internal Auditors' "Statement of Responsibilities" we already have a concept that is perhaps larger than our performance. If we equip ourselves to produce effectively under the changing conditions that lie ahead, the question of access to new operating areas will become academic. Our present measure of objectivity will be completely outmoded if we can grasp the larger concept of scientific rationale where the empirical approach is discarded and where nothing is without challenge until proven in all respects. We have come a long way with "cut and try" methods but we have a long way to go before we can honestly say that we are employing the scientific method.

APPLYING SCIENTIFIC METHODS TO AUDITING

How does one go about applying the scientific method to internal auditing? First, it is necessary to adopt an open and skeptical frame of mind. From that point the individual must apply himself to defining the problem areas, using judgment in separating the major areas from the minor areas. He must then be willing to put in a lot of plain hard work in increasing his knowledge of the principles and facilities available for solving the problems. Not the least important factor at this point is the very real necessity for honest self-examination to determine whether he has the capabilities to do each particular job. I think you will all agree that it is extremely dangerous for the internal auditor—and for the organization which employs him—to pose as an expert in fields beyond his capabilities. On the other hand he should never cease his efforts to expand these capabilities and to exploit them fully.

This brings us to the basic premise that the need for continuing individual education is never-ending and that the opportunity for personal development is unlimited. It can be said that continuing education for the professional is most effective where professional experience is shared. Many of the avenues for sharing experience have been, and I am sure will continue to be, provided through the Federal Government Accountants Association, the Institute of Internal Auditors and other professional associations functioning in broad financial management fields.

AUDIT RESPONSIBILITY AT
FORD MOTOR COMPANY

Regardless of the degree of technical skill developed by the auditor, he cannot do a fully satisfactory job unless he operates within an effective administrative framework. In discussing matters of organization and administration, I shall deal in specific terms—namely how we approach the job at Ford Motor Company. While we are certainly not so brash as to claim that our organization and methods are ideal, we do feel that our internal auditing is well suited to a large industrial enterprise and provides a significant service to management.

The General Auditor's Office of the Ford Motor Company is a component of the central corporate staff, and the General Auditor reports directly to the Vice President-Finance. Our central corporate staff is vested with the responsibility of developing overall policies, supplying functional direction to the operating divisions, and coordinating Company-wide activities. Domestic production and warehousing operations are conducted at approximately 100 divisional and plant locations distributed throughout the United States, and credit operations are handled by approximately 120 offices. In addition, Ford conducts activities of various kinds through domestic and foreign subsidiaries having about 40 locations. Inasmuch as each of these locations is subject to audit, the responsibilities of the General Auditor's Office include coverage of some 260 clients.

In order to provide the greatest possible service to management and to our 260 clients, consistent with maintaining the audit staff at a reasonable numerical level, we are called upon to conduct various types of audits. However, under the Company's decentralized form of organization, the greater portion of audit coverage is accomplished by what may be termed "responsibility" audits. Audits of this type consist of a general review of most financial functions and selected operating activities for which local executives have management responsibility.

Although our responsibility audits are by no means confined to the limitations of what are commonly termed "balance sheet" audits, the financial statements do form the working basis. Our program for responsibility audits includes selected analyses of transactions recorded in all accounts, a review of local practices for compliance with prescribed policies and procedures, and an appraisal of the system of internal control. In addition, we place considerable emphasis on evaluating the effectiveness of budgetary reporting and the accuracy of product costing. We also make a survey of plant protection, the handling of scrap, and the receiving, storing and shipping of materials. Other activities examined are purchasing, traffic, employee suggestion plans, records retention and forms control. We continuously encourage our staff to give particular attention to the constructive phase of auditing, which includes among other things the development of recommendations for improved procedures, cost savings through more efficient clerical and operating methods, and paperwork simplification.

In regard to the frequency of responsibility audits we have attempted to maintain a pattern which takes cognizance of the relative importance of the locations being examined. Under this principle, intervals between audits normally range from 15 to 18 months, in the case of larger locations, to as much as 24 to 36 months in the case of smaller locations where there are only limited accounting functions. Of course this pattern may be varied to recognize unusual conditions.

Another important effort is the conducting of feature audits. This type of audit is usually employed in connection with staff activities or in those quasi-operating areas which are not identified as separate accounting

345

locations but which carry on activities of a financial or operating nature. For example, such an audit is performed in the pension section of the insurance department of the Treasurer's Office. Other audits in this category would include the observation of annual physical inventories and reviews of the compilation and costing of such inventories, reviews of activities such as purchasing, traffic, stockholder records and employee feeding operations, sales office examinations, audits of the control aspects of major construction projects, and the like.

Responsibility and feature examinations comprise the major portion of our audit work. However, the General Auditor's Office also conducts special audits or investigations on its own initiative or at the request of management. Essentially the same program and approach are followed in audits of foreign activities.

AUDITING APPROACH AT FORD MOTOR COMPANY

In conducting our activities in the field, there is no surer way to promote *bad* relationships with operating personnel than for an auditor to keep all developments to himself during a six or eight weeks' examination and then, at the last minute, confront the plant accounting executive with a long list of deficiencies. In order to maintain *good* public relations during the course of our audits, we make every effort to keep personnel at the locations apprised of our findings as the field work progresses. We feel that this is *extremely* important in order to resolve any disagreements as to facts and, more particularly, to obtain the cooperation and confidence of the people being audited. It is our practice to have the in-charge senior write up any audit findings on a progressive basis as each portion of the audit program is completed. One copy of these write-ups is given to the plant controller in line with our policy of keeping him currently advised. Another copy is furnished the audit manager for use in his interim review of the progress of the audit work.

At the conclusion of the audit field work, a closing conference is held, attended by the manager and controller of the audited activity and by the audit staff personnel and audit manager engaged on the assignment. At this conference the draft of the report is read to local management and each audit finding is discussed for the purpose of resolving any differences of opinion regarding the facts to be presented in the formal report. Also, by means of this conference local management is informed in advance regarding the findings to be included in the report and therefore is in a position to commence action for correcting the deficiencies reported.

It is of course generally agreed that audit reports must be factual, concise, well organized, clearly written and attractively presented. Our approach to reporting at Ford is to use the exception method; we tell management *only* about those things which are *not* satisfactory. Because of this, the audit staff has sometimes been accused by operating personnel of having a one-track mind. However, we feel that this method of reporting directs attention to those areas requiring correction and that, in the absence of adverse comments, the report reader may assume that other areas are satisfactory.

Our reports are written in essay or narrative form. Financial statements and schedules are not included except in unusual circumstances where the use of such information is essential in reporting the results of the examination. It is also our practice not to include *minor* deficiencies arising from clerical errors or inadvertent procedural deviations. These items are, however, called to the attention of local management and an informal written list of these deficiencies is submitted for their use in effecting corrective action.

In regard to the issuance of reports, we feel that time is of the essence and strongly subscribe to the adage that there is nothing so stale as yesterday's newspaper. Consequently, our standards require that a report be issued not later than six working days after completion of the audit field work, and we generally equal or improve upon that standard.

Our reports are directed to the Vice President-Finance. Copies are also distributed directly to divisional management, interested central staff personnel, and to the Company's outside public accountants. The Central Staff Controller's Office transmits copies of the reports to the appropriate divisional controller with a letter requesting a formal reply regarding the corrective action taken. The responsibility for following up and ultimately closing the reports also rests with the Central Staff Controller's Office. However, the General Auditor receives copies of all correspondence concerning the reports and has the opportunity to express an opinion regarding the acceptability of the corrective action.

COROLLARY FUNCTIONS

An important aspect of our activity is the coordination of internal auditing coverage with that of the Company's outside public accountants. While the internal auditing work is in no way subordinate to, or directed by, the public accountants, they do place considerable reliance on our coverage in their determinations as to whether procedures are followed, whether internal control is effective and similar matters. It is for this reason that copies of our reports are distributed to the public accountants and the timing of our audits is coordinated with theirs.

As might be expected also, many cooperative relationships exist internally with other central staff activities. The General Auditor's Office has no *direct* responsibility for developing or issuing financial or operating procedures, although naturally we generate recommendations relative to these matters in the course of our audit work. However, the auditing staff is *often* asked to review proposals before procedures are issued or changed. In addition, on our own initiative or upon request, we frequently consult with

347

the Controller's Office, Treasurer's Office, Industrial Relations, Purchasing, Legal, Production Control and other staff activities for the purpose of clarifying or amending existing policies and procedures. In our opinion, this function of consultation is an important part of the internal auditing activity and is another example of management's acceptance of our services.

PRODUCTIVE RESULTS ESSENTIAL

It must be emphasized that management—whether at Ford or elsewhere—does not blindly place confidence in the value of internal auditing. Each management must be sold by a continuing demonstration of high-class performance and productive results. By this I do not wish to imply that internal auditing should be oversold or overrated. However, I do feel that the internal auditor can contribute greatly to the successful operation of an enterprise and can be looked to as a source of constructive assistance rather than cold criticism.

This standing is not easily *attained* or automatically *maintained*. Internal auditing does not flourish for its own self or because of pretty reports. It exists only because of worthwhile service to management, and acceptance depends upon the skill with which the job is performed. The internal auditor, no less than the sales manager or the manufacturing manager, is a part of the team and he must produce first-class results to stay on the team—and this will be true whether we are speaking of internal auditing today *or* tomorrow.

AUDITORS IN GOVERNMENT

While there has been significant improvement in administrative management during the past few years that has resulted in sizeable savings in administrative operations, the Committee would like to see a greater use of contract-review auditors, internal auditors, and other management specialists to eliminate unnecessary work, obtain more favorable prices for the Government in the maintenance contracting area, and develop more realistic work measurement factors to evaluate the work production of various offices engaged in routine administrative work.

With increased attention to these areas, it could be expected that some of the flagrant examples of waste discovered annually by the General Accounting Office could be avoided.

Source: House Appropriations Committee in reporting out the Department of Defense Appropriation Bill for 1964.

GOVERNMENT BY CONTRACT: BOON OR BONER

Victor K. Heyman

The time appears to be rapidly approaching when the employees of the federal government, like the classic iceberg, are nine-tenths "invisible." Even today, a rough estimate of federal employment would be in the neighborhood of eleven million workers, only five million of whom are direct military and civilian federal employees.[1] The remaining workers are obtained by means of contracts, grants, and similar instruments.

Much is known about the problems of administering the regular government agencies, but very little is known about administering the large numbers of people and activities brought into the federal service by contract. In this paper we are concerned with the benefits and problems of the latter; that is, the problems of control, economy, and policy and the benefits obtained by contracting with "private" institutions for services of an administrative, managerial, or scientific nature. We will take for granted that the federal government needs the services under study.

EXTENT OF CONTRACTING OUT

Before the problems and benefits to the government of contracting for services can be intelligently grasped, it is necessary to provide some information as to the extent of such contracting. The major portion of it is for research and development, weapons systems management, and technical supervision of weapons programs, although considerable amounts of contracting are for the management and operating of government-owned facilities, management analysis and similar consultant services, educational activities, foreign technical assistance, and miscellaneous other services.

Research and Development

The trend throughout the government is toward increased contracting for research and development. In general, there are three major types of

Note: This article is based on work performed by the author for The Brookings Institution and a paper delivered by him at the 1960 Annual Meeting of the American Political Science Association.

Article is from *Public Administration Review*, Vol. 21 (Spring, 1961), pp. 59–64. Used with permission of publisher and author.

[1]This figure is obtained by means of the following equation: gross federal expenditures are to gross national product as gross federal employment is to total U.S. employment. Thus $80 billion/$480 billion equals 11.17 million federal employees/67 million workers. Admittedly this is only a very rough estimate.

research and development programs.[2] First, the government finances research which is of the contractor's choice—generally of a basic or fundamental nature and generally with universities.

In the second category of research contracts are those in which the government goes to the contractors for research designed to solve particular problems arising in the agency's performance of its mission.

Finally, there are the research and development contracts calling for the contractor to manage and operate government-owned facilities. These will be discussed later.

In all, more than thirty agencies and departments of the federal government contract for research and development. The federal government in fiscal year 1960 spent by way of this kind of contract 77 percent of its $7.7 billion research and development funds, in 1959 it was 76 percent and in 1958 it had been only 74 percent.[3] Considering that the total amount of money allotted for research and development has been climbing rapidly, the money spent on research and development contracts has grown significantly both in total size and in percentage.

Weapons Systems Management and Technical Supervision

The military departments have had an extremely difficult time deciding on the most appropriate way to integrate military requirements and control with industrial planning and organization. At one extreme was the Army's use of its own facilities and know-how to take the Redstone and Jupiter missiles from basic requirement through the production of prototype missiles. At the other extreme was the "weapons systems management" concept which, as conceived in 1952 by the Air Force Research and Development Command (ARDC), put onto a single contractor the full responsibility for designing and producing a complete weapons system ready to perform its specified function.

Between these two extremes many other ways of integrating industry and the military have been attempted. The Navy has four major patterns of industrial relations ranging from the Air Force weapons systems management concept to almost the Army's arsenal concept. In any case, it is clear that the military has contracted for a wide range of functions which give the contractors tremendous power.

The list of nonindustrial type facilities owned by the government and managed and operated by private contractors is large and growing. The military departments and the Atomic Energy Commission have made the most use of such contracts, but other agencies also use them. This type of

---

[2]This tri-partite categorization of research and development contracts is taken from National Science Foundation, *Government-University Relationships* in Federally Sponsored Research and Development, National Science Foundation, Vol. 58, No. 10, 1958, p. 9.

[3]National Science Foundation, *Federal Funds for Science, VIII.* The Federal Research and Development Budget, Fiscal Years 1958, 1959, 1960, National Science Foundation, Vol. 59, No. 40, 1959, pp. 46, 48, 50.

arrangement overlaps to a considerable extent the contracting for research and development, since under the latter practice, the government may also provide rent-free facilities for the use of the contractor.

Management Analysis and Consultant Services

The government obtains the services of all kinds of experts by means of contracts. The Defense Department has used extensively such contracts.[4] Departments and agencies have contracted with private firms to come in, review the operations or prospective operations of the agency, and to tell it how it should be organized, what its accounting or cost analysis system should be, what electronic equipment it ought to have. Contracts have also been given for the teaching of courses in management analysis, the establishment of procedures for prediction of supply and demand for agency services and/or materials, and the analysis of industrial facility availability and private management competence for undertaking government work. These contracts are comparatively small, ranging normally in five and six figures and let on a negotiated fixed price basis with redetermination permitted.[5]

The so-called "think groups" are usually classified as consultant-type services. The Air Force established the first of these groups, the RAND Corporation. RAND started with five people; it now has more than 800. Its first contract in fiscal year 1948 was for $2,750,000, and its fiscal year 1960 contract was approximately $13,500,000. Groups similar to RAND include the Operations Research Office, Johns Hopkins University (Army); MITRE Corporation (Air Force); Institute for Defense Analysis (Department of Defense); Human Relations Research Office, George Washington University (Army); and the Naval Warfare Analysis Group and Operations Evaluation Group, Massachusetts Institute of Technology (Navy).

Educational Services

Educational services are more and more required by the federal government. Frequently these are obtained by direct hire procedures, but there appears to be a trend toward hiring educational institutions on a cost-reimbursement basis, with or without profit. Although there are no exact figures available, educational services obtained by contract probably cost more than $5 million a year.

Technical Cooperation

Another important area of contracting is that for technical cooperation services. ICA let contracts totaling more than $63 million of its $303

[4] U.S. House, 86 Cong. 2 sess., Committee on Appropriations, Hearings before the Subcommittee ... on *Department of Defense Appropriations for 1961*, pt. 7, pp. 175–85.

[5] U.S. House, 85 Cong. 2 sess., Committee on Post Office and Civil Service, Hearings before the Subcommittee on Manpower Utilization ... on *Manpower Utilization in the Federal Government*, p. 283. Especially useful here is U.S. House, 86 Cong. 2 sess., Committee on Appropriations, Hearings before the Subcommittee ... on *General Government Matters Appropriations for 1961*, pp. 144–67.

million project assistance budget for fiscal year 1960 for educational and technical services. More than 44 percent of the technicians working abroad on this program are contractors' employees. As of March 31, 1959, fifty-two universities were providing Point Four educational assistance abroad. Numerous other private profit and nonprofit institutions have provided services of various types for ICA.[6]

PROBLEMS AND BENEFITS

Benefits

There can be no question that the government has obtained the use of facilities and individuals through contracting that otherwise might not be available to it. Experience and knowledge of types not prevalent in government are constantly on tap. All functions performed in the "private" sector of the economy are available as and when needed. Faced with demands for services as never before, accompanied by the clamor to prevent "big government," legislators and administrators have developed a device that at the outset could be all things to all people, and may very well be the only possible manner of pleasing both those who want a small government and those who want big new governmental programs. The government, following Vannevar Bush's policy in the World War II Office of Scientific Research and Development, has used talent where it could be found with a minimum of disruption. The use of contracts allows short-term projects to be carried on without a regular staff with which the "government would be saddled." It allows full flexibility of personnel policies and salaries, fringe benefits, and working "atmosphere," which can be changed as the work changes. People with fresh ideas are free to be hired and released without a single civil service regulation being applied. Whole institutions and their prestige can be hired when needed, in effect temporarily "nationalizing" them. The glamor of the independent "unbiased" source can be acquired to sell ideas to an agency's staff, Congress, or the public (as in management analysis work). Special equipment for special projects need not be bought, only to lie unused at the end of the program. People who would not work for the government because of salary, red tape, pension and personal commitments, etc., are obtainable.[7]

---

[6]U.S. House, 86 Cong. 1 sess., Committee on Appropriations, Hearings before the Subcommittee ... on *Mutual Security Appropriations for 1960*, p. 1208. Figures on use of contract employees from ICA Statistics and Reports Branch, July 26, 1960.

[7]The following sources were useful in determining the advantages of the contracting system: Bureau of the Budget Circular A-49, *Use of Management and Operating Contracts* (Feb. 25, 1959); Lee A. DuBridge, "Science and Government," *Chemical and Engineering News*, Vol. 31 (Apr. 6, 1953), pp. 1384–90; U.S. House, 85 Cong. 2 sess., Committee on Post Office and Civil Service, Hearings before the Subcommittee on Manpower Utilization ... on *Manpower Utilization in the Federal Government*, pp. 108, 136; U.S. House, 86 Cong. 1 sess., Committee on Appropriations, Hearings before the Subcommittee ... on *National Aeronautics and Space Administration Appropriations for 1960*, pp. 171–72; *Senate Report 139*, 85 Cong. 1 sess., pp. 31–33.

Contracting out is thus a system that allows the government to farm out a complete range of administrative and executive responsibilities accompanied by money, authority, and responsibility. These advantages are real and immense and, given the demands for services and for the continuation of a "free enterprise" system, probably essential.

Problems of Cost and Control

Nevertheless, the government, and therefore those who demand the services, must pay a price for these advantages. The first problem is that the government will never be able to attain the knowledge and experience to perform its assigned functions with civil service and military personnel if it contracts for them every time they are needed. If an agency makes contracts in order to obtain any of the many advantages mentioned, it thereby prevents its own people from acquiring the knowledge useful or necessary for performing the same or similar work at another time. It is providing an opportunity (particularly in research and development work) for patentable inventions to be created, the ownership of which is a serious source of conflict and unpleasantness.

Secondly, the incentives to efficiency in most of these contracting operations are quite small, and in some cases negative. Since most research and development is done on a cost-plus-fixed-fee (CPFF) basis, a contractor who accepts such a contract "to get in on the ground floor" has little inducement to keep his costs at a minimum. The more he experiments, the more he learns, and with little or no out-of-pocket expenses. He, in essence, receives an education at government expense, and the government may well pay for more research on a particular project than it needs or wants. When it is also considered that the research and development contract is quite often the forerunner of the production contract, much of which is on a fixed-price incentive basis (i.e., the government and the company share in any "saving" below the "target price"), the research contractor has a positive incentive to boost his research and development costs as high as possible so that the production target price will similarly be set high. This presents a very difficult control problem.[8]

The price of economy may come as high as the proverbial price of freedom—eternal vigilance. The Atomic Energy Commission in its early years attempted to instill a nebulous patriotic and nonremunerative concept of satisfaction in its contractors to increase efficiency under CPFF contracts. This apparently failed badly, and the AEC was forced to assume greater supervisory responsibilities over its contractors. The Air Force, which has

---

[8]*House Report 1959*, 86 Cong. 2 sess., pp. 33–35. This observation was made by the House Armed Forces Committee, Special Subcommittee on Procurement Practices of the Department of Defense. The fact that the Air Force has consistently underestimated the cost of CPFF research and development contracts by an average of 18 percent and the Navy has underestimated such costs "significantly" suggests that the problems of cost control have not been solved. *Ibid.*, p. 35.

attempted to contract for the performance of functions in as bold and imaginative a fashion as did the AEC, may learn the same lesson.

The third problem is that the simple dependence of the government, particularly the military, on contractors may be most undesirable. The Department of Defense and the three military services already find themselves heavily dependent on their "think group" contractors, like RAND, and would be severely handicapped without them. The NASA has said that it would need five years to replace the facilities and manpower now possessed by its CPFF contractor, Jet Propulsion Laboratory of the California Institute of Technology, and the experience and know-how of this group could not be so easily replaced.[9] With such dependence, what happens if the contractor and the government disagree as to fee, patent rights, or any of the many other features of the contract? At least one congressional committee finds it "difficult to conclude otherwise" than that all impasses are resolved in favor of the contractor.

The dependence of the government on civilian contractors in time of war may prove embarrassing at best. Today civilian contractors are even operating at military bases overseas. Contractor personnel are needed to set up missile bases, to help train military personnel, and to analyze technical problems beyond the capabilities of the military. As time passes, perhaps, the military will gain experience and need less contract support on any particular missile system. Nevertheless, in view of the rapid rate of obsolescence of new systems, it has yet to be demonstrated on a sustained basis that the military can perform its required functions without large amounts of contract support. In time of war, what is to guarantee that such support will be available when needed?

A fourth problem connected with contracting for services is that of salaries. As function after function is contracted, the bidding price of good personnel goes up and the government finds itself unable to hire and keep good men at civil service salaries. Contract research and development centers have taken from the federal government approximately 12,000 employees per year in recent years, seriously reducing the government's "in-house" capabilities. The NACA-NASA has suffered acute losses of top personnel since January, 1955. More than 250 GS 11-16 personnel were lost to industry, seventy-three to just three companies. They had a median service of eleven years with government. Such losses are certainly felt in the ability of the government to provide services for itself.[10]

It is frequently suggested that the practice of contracting for services is in large part forced on the government because of the need to pay higher

---

[9]U.S. House, 86 Cong. 1 sess., Committee on Appropriations, Hearings before the Subcommittee ... on *National Aeronautics and Space Administration Appropriations for 1960*, p. 99.

[10]U.S. House, 86 Cong. 2 sess., Committee on Post Office and Civil Service, Hearings before the Subcommittee on Manpower Utilization ... on *Manpower Utilization in the Federal Government*, pp. 13–14, 24ff.

salaries than Congress will permit. The Institute for Defense Analysis, the Defense Department's "think group," was largely created for just this reason. The salary problem is most severe for personnel with many years of experience, particularly if they have executive and managerial ability. The median salary increases for the top NASA officials who went to private industry was one to three thousand dollars. The exceptional younger man is also a difficult person for the government to get and hold. Direct government employment becomes increasingly unattractive as contractors' salaries become distinctively better than government salaries.

One of the ironic features of the present situation is that the government is indirectly paying these people what it will not pay them directly. At the same time, it is creating centers of competition which raise the price for good people higher than would be the case with direct hire. It cannot be overlooked that the government, directly and indirectly, is the primary market for most of them. A more orderly procedure might, perhaps, allow sufficient savings to train enough new personnel to supply the entire market. The pirating taking place by contractors against the government, and among themselves, may well be an important disrupting factor in the very functions which the government desires to see performed quickly and effectively. It certainly would seem to be an inflationary factor. Individual government agencies seem to feel that the advantages of uncoordinated and extensive contracting are worth this price, but from an overall viewpoint, are the advantages such as to be worth the risk of destruction of the civil service system?

Problems of Policy

From a policy point of view, the effects of contracting for services may be equally disagreeable. The Attorney General has pointed out that:

> This Government must be deeply concerned with the future of competitive enterprise, and it is important that its share of this activity [research and development] be administered to promote competition within the limits possible under the urgency and complexity of the defense program. ... (W)hat indications are available warn that the Government expenditures may not run counter to the industry trend toward concentration, but in some degree may reinforce it.[11]

Since the advanced stages of the research and development phase blend into the early stages of the production phase, most private firms have viewed research and development contracts as the admission price for the subsequent "follow-on" production contracts. These companies frequently complain that the profits from research and development contracts are too

---

[11]Cf. *Report of the Attorney General* (Nov. 9, 1956), pt. 1, "Government Sponsored Industry Research." This part of the report is reprinted in full in U.S. House, 86 Cong. 1 sess., Committee on Science and Astronautics, Hearings before the Subcommittee on Patents and Scientific Inventions ... on *Property Rights in Inventions Made Under Federal Space Research Contracts*, p. 896.

small, since many customary business expenses are nonreimbursable.[12] To the extent that this is so, the government can only contract with those companies that can afford to delay their profit-making and engage in weapons production, and this usually means larger businesses.[13]

When the government gives contracts to a corporation in amounts exceeding $1.9 billion a year, it is creating a great center of power over which it has only limited control. Subcontracting takes place under practically all of the large contracts, and in most cases the "prime" contractor has considerable latitude as to where and with whom he will subcontract. The laws requiring special consideration for small business and depressed areas in government contracting do not apply to subcontracting by prime contractors unless the agencies make them apply. In many cases small business has felt that the agencies have taken a dim view of any such requirement.

Along the same lines, the prime contractor has considerable latitude as to whether he will make or buy subsystems and, if left alone, will frequently "make" whatever he can—whether or not he has the capability at the start of the contract—so long as the contracting agency does not object and he can meet his deadlines. How desirable is it to place the well-being of small-business sheep in the paws of the big-business lion?

Still another policy problem is the changing relations between government and industry. Many small businesses today are totally dependent on government contracts. RAND, ORO, STL, etc., are for all intents and purposes government organizations, except that they are not government owned, their personnel are not civil service and are not subject to the Hatch Acts, and they are not protected against a sudden decision by the government to end the contract. One author, in attempting to characterize the changing government-industry relationship, called it a "new federalism,"[14] another called it a "partnership," while a Congressman who would not have much use for high-sounding phrases simply said it is not free enterprise. Perhaps it is a "missing link" between socialism and private capitalism. From a policy standpoint, is it desirable?

A further point of concern from the viewpoint of public policy is the effect government contracting is having on the nation's educational institutions. Colleges and universities and their associated research centers are receiving approximately $760 million per year for the conduct of government research and development work alone.[15] They are operating and managing a number of government facilities and are constantly loaning personnel for high-policy consultations. The military services each have contracts with well over one hundred institutions of higher learning for basic research alone.

---

[12]*Aviation Week* (Mar. 9, 1959), p. 217.

[13]*Report of the Attorney General* (Nov. 9, 1956), *op. cit.*, pp. 888–904.

[14]Don K. Price, *Government and Science*, New York: New York University Press, 1954, p. 46.

[15]National Science Foundation, *Federal Funds for Science*, Vol. 8, *op. cit.*, p. 50.

Such a widespread use of educational institutions as contractors cannot help but bring about fundamental changes in the American educational system, and these must be examined from a policy standpoint.

CONCLUSION

The critical tone of many of the preceding comments should not be taken as disparagement or condemnation of the system of contracting for services. In an age of international and intranational interdependence, many of the problems mentioned are unavoidable. Professor Marver Bernstein has noted in another connection that the government-nongovernment dichotomy has "ceased to exist," and also that "many government employees are so closely connected in their official duties with the work of private firms that they are in part industry personnel."[16] As we have noted, the same thing has happened in reverse to employees of private firms. The risks of conflicts of interest are immense, but no very desirable alternative presents itself.

No simple formula can be given as to when the government should contract for services, or whether it should at all. Perhaps contracting is the answer to the modern counterpart of the problems for which the government corporation was created in an earlier day. However, the effectiveness and efficiency of this system which, like Topsy, "just grow'd," need to be questioned and examined until we learn at least as much about it as we know about the problems of administering the regular government agencies.

---

[16]Marver H. Bernstein, "Conflicts of Interest in Federal Employment," a paper prepared for delivery at the Annual Meeting of the American Political Science Association, 1959, p. 13.

COMPTROLLERSHIP TRENDS IN THE FEDERAL GOVERNMENT

Frank H. Weitzel

The progressive infusion of modern comptrollership concepts into executive agencies of the Federal Government ranks as one of the more notable developments of recent decades. Since World War II perceptive leadership in many Government agencies and in the Congress has successfully transformed a veritable hodgepodge of archaic fiscal procedures into a dynamic management force of vital significance in the conduct of governmental affairs. The tangible achievements of these years, as well as some of the remaining shortcomings, are marshalled in the Joint Financial Management Improvement Program's recent fifteenth anniversary report,[1] which is appropriately entitled *Fifteen Years of Progress*. Unlike many official reports, this outstanding fifteenth anniversary report is highly readable and warrants the thoughtful attention of every citizen interested in the financial activities of his government.

There is now widespread, although not universal, recognition of the fact that modern accounting and statistical data provide the only effective means by which responsible executives can direct and control operations beyond the range of their own personal observation and supervision. Since accumulation of essential data is a basic part of the comptrollership process, many of the Government's financial management improvements in the past fifteen years are inherently accounting improvements. As accounting improved, however, attention was focused more on the use of data than on its accumulation and the accounting horizon thus was extended to the vital field of management applications. Today the predominant accounting emphasis in Government is on the application of financial data to ongoing activities, in keeping with the forward-looking approach characteristic of modern comptrollership.

COMPTROLLERSHIP AND CONTROLLERSHIP SYNONYMOUS IN GOVERNMENT

Although in the Federal Government "comptrollership" is more commonly used than "controllership" to designate financial management

---

Article is from *The Federal Accountant*, Vol. 13 (June, 1964), pp. 4–23. Used with permission of publisher and author.

[1]This comprehensive 102-page report is currently available for 35 cents from the Superintendent of Documents, Washington, D.C.: U.S. Government Printing Office, 20402. Highlights were summarized in *The Federal Accountant* (March, 1964), pp. 127–38.

functions, the two forms are equally appropriate from a substantive standpoint and both are in official use. Occasionally an attempt is made to attribute some special significance to one or the other form of spelling but nothing in the ancient and somewhat cloudy derivation of the two forms would seem to justify any distinction. No doubt, the general governmental preference for the "comptrollership" form stems from its use by the First Congress in early legislation establishing accounting positions in the Government.

When the position or function involved is created by law, the specific provisions of the statute and not the form of spelling determine the nature of the duties to be performed. Thus a specific denotation should not be inferred from the use of one or the other form of designation for positions established by law unless clearly justified by the applicable language of the statute or its legislative antecedents.

EARLY DEVELOPMENT OF COMPTROLLERSHIP IN GOVERNMENT

The concept of comptrollership in the Federal Government is a very old one, actually predating the Constitution itself by a number of years. In 1781, during the Revolutionary War, congressional ordinances placed the business of the Treasury under a superintendent of finance and provided for a comptroller, a treasurer, a register and auditors. The offices of comptroller and auditor were abolished in 1787 but equivalent positions were soon revived under the Constitution when an early act of the First Congress established the Treasury Department with a secretary as head and a comptroller, an auditor, a treasurer and a register.[2] The comptroller and the auditor served as accounting officers in roles designed to implement the constitutional safeguard of legislative control of the purse, as set out in the clause in Article I, Section 9, which reads: "No Money shall be drawn from the Treasury, but in Consequence of Appropriations made by Law." It was their responsibility to apply whatever limitations and requirements Congress might prescribe with respect to the use of public funds.

In the next century the number of accounting officers grew to two comptrollers and six auditors, with their respective staffs. Most of the additional officers were added in 1817 by an act which provided for settlement of all Government claims and accounts in the Treasury Department.[3] The Dockery Act of 1894 consolidated the accounting system under the Comptroller of the Treasury and gave him appellate powers over the six auditors who settle the public accounts, as well as authority to render decisions in advance of payment when requested by department heads or disbursing

[2] 1 Stat. 65.
[3] 3 Stat. 366.

officers.[4] The 1894 act also empowered the Comptroller to prescribe the forms for keeping and rendering all public accounts other than postal.

A far-reaching change occurred in 1921 when the Budget and Accounting Act[5] created central budget and accounting offices, the first in the Executive Branch and the second in the Legislative Branch. This act, still in effect in amended form, was the first comprehensive legislation ever to pass in the comptrollership field and constituted a major forward step toward sound financial management in the Federal Government. Prior to this act no provision existed for a coordinated budget system in the Federal Government and no procedures had been developed for the formulation of a meaningful annual summary of the Government's prospective revenues and estimated expenditure needs.

When the Treasury Department was established in 1789, the authorizing statute made it the duty of the Secretary of the Treasury "to prepare and report estimates of the public revenue, and the public expenditures." However, early attempts by the Secretary of the Treasury to exercise financial leadership met with formidable resistance and his activities in this area became little more than those of a mere transmittal agent who relayed to Congress the individual appropriation requests formulated in the various executive departments and agencies. This situation continued unchanged, for all practical purposes, until enactment of the Budget and Accounting Act of 1921 created within the Treasury Department a central budget organization designated the Bureau of the Budget and made the President the business manager of the Executive Branch of the Government.[6]

By other provisions of this memorable act the General Accounting Office was created in the Legislative Branch to provide an agency "independent of the executive departments" for the purpose of checking the Government's financial transactions. Its principal functions today stem from the basic responsibilities assigned to the Comptroller General in this act and consist of prescribing accounting principles, standards and related requirements; cooperating in the development of accounting systems; reviewing agency accounting systems and approving those that conform to prescribed standards; making audits and investigations; rendering legal decisions; settling claims and accounts; and furnishing reports and assistance to Congress.

MODERN BUSINESS CONCEPT OF COMPTROLLERSHIP

During the past century a number of factors combined to enhance the status of financial executives in American business, including:

(1) Growing size and complexity of industrial organizations;

---

[4] 28 Stat. 205.

[5] 42 Stat. 20.

[6] The Bureau of the Budget and all its functions were transferred to the Executive Office of the President by Reorganization Plan No. 1, 1939, 5 U.S.C. 133t, note.

(2) Increasing taxation of and expanding regulatory jurisdiction over business activities; and

(3) Widening separation between management and ownership interests.

At the same time an insistent demand for better management practices brought with it an inescapable need for more adequate accounting and more effective management control information. Particularly since the turn of the twentieth century financial ability has become an increasingly important consideration in the conduct of business.

As these forces exerted increasing influence on the business environment, the comptrollership function expanded accordingly and became in time the focal point for planning and control in business enterprise. One of the most comprehensive current definitions of this function, and undoubtedly the most authoritative to be found in business practice, is that developed by the Committee on Ethics and Eligibility Standards of the Financial Executives Institute and approved by its National Board of Directors in September, 1949. The Institute's six-point definition distinguishes six major areas of comptrollership activity:

1. To establish, coordinate and maintain, through authorized management, an integrated plan for the control of operations.

2. To measure performance against approved operating plans and standards, and to report and interpret the results of operations to all levels of management.

3. To measure and report on the validity of the objectives of the business and on the effectiveness of its policies, organization structure and procedures in attaining those objectives.

4. To report to government agencies as required, and to supervise all matters relating to taxes.

5. To interpret and report on the effect of external influences in the attainment of the objectives of the business.

6. To provide protection for the assets of the business ... in part through ... establishing and maintaining adequate internal control and auditing.

This six-point definition, being appropriately broad in concept, affords an excellent measure of how closely the modern comptrollership function in Government parallels that in business. All six of these areas have a comptrollership counterpart in Government because, through the years, the major forces at work in the governmental environment were similar to those in business. While Federal agencies of course do not report to "government agencies" in quite the same sense that business firms must, every Federal agency nevertheless is required to report to a number of other Government organizations external to itself and usually considers the prescribed reporting requirements every bit as onerous as business firms regard theirs. As to external influences generally, mention need only be made of the increasing attention being focused on the relationship between the Federal budget and the national economy.

BASIC INFLUENCES ON COMPTROLLERSHIP IN GOVERNMENT

Comptrollership in the Federal Government inevitably has been affected by the wide diversification of governmental activities and by the extensive scope and unparalleled volume characterizing a great many of them. During the depression years of the 1930s numerous programs of action were initiated in varied economic fields, involving the Government in large-scale banking, lending, utility, insurance and housing endeavors. Even before the United States became embroiled in World War II, large increases in Federal spending were highlighting inadequacies in the Government's systems of financial management, and the astronomical levels Federal spending reached during the war further emphasized the need for more adequate financial management procedures.

Over the years, governmental accounting in the United States had been directed almost exclusively toward ensuring that obligations and expenditures were legally authorized and within the appropriations provided by Congress. While this objective was and still is essential, the manyfold increase in the variety and magnitude of Federal activities focused attention as never before on the absolute necessity of adequate property and cost accounting in the Federal Government. At the same time there was a growing awareness of the need for better management generally throughout Government. This growing awareness crystallized in the appointment of the first Hoover Commission whose studies created wide popular interest in performance budgeting to deal with the cost of programs or functions on an accrual basis rather than mainly with estimates and liquidations of obligations.

These forces were being manifested increasingly throughout this period in a changing approach to audit responsibility, particularly on the part of the General Accounting Office. Of far-reaching impact was the Comptroller General's decision in the late 1940s to depart from the traditional detailed centralized audit and embark on a program of comprehensive audits conducted at the site of operations, aimed at determining how the audited entity was carrying out its financial responsibilities.

GOVERNMENT CORPORATION CONTROL ACT

Early in this course of events Congress enacted the Government Corporation Control Act of 1945 "to bring Government corporations and their transactions and operations under annual scrutiny by the Congress and provide current financial control thereof."[7] This landmark legislation required both "business-type" budgets and annual audits "in accordance with the principles and procedures applicable to commercial corporate transactions."

---

[7]59 Stat. 597.

Under its provisions corporate budgets were to be supported by accounts that provided full cost information and were to include actual and projected balance sheets, income statements and statements of sources and applications of funds, as well as "such other supplementary statements and information as are necessary or desirable to make known the financial condition and operations of the corporation." Similar guidance was prescribed for the annual corporate audits to be made on behalf of Congress by the General Accounting Office.

In response to the audit mandate conferred by this act, the Comptroller General established a Corporation Audits Division in the General Accounting Office and staffed it with professional accountants experienced in public practice. The audits of this new division soon demonstrated the practical advantages of following auditing procedures perfected over the years by the national public accounting firms. The division's initial reports, based on these procedures, were most favorably received by Congress and it was the patent success of this new program that largely influenced the Comptroller General several years later to extend the comprehensive audit approach to executive agencies generally.

Many of these early corporate audit reports emphasized the importance, both to the corporation itself and to the Government generally, of an effective comptroller organization. A 1946 report on the Reconstruction Finance Corporation,[8] for example, included the following recommendation:

> We believe that the creation of the position of controller in the RFC is an absolute necessity. We believe also that the assignment of responsibilities and authorities to this position should be sufficiently broad to assure that the RFC and the Government of the United States will derive at least as great a value from the accounting function as is now derived by the most progressive of private American business corporations.
>
> The functions of the controller should be conceived as being fundamentally separate from those of the treasurer, and both the chief auditor of the Company and the budget officer should be made subordinate to the controller. The accountability of the treasurer would be established by such a concept, and the tedious task of coordination of the accounting, budgeting and auditing functions would be avoided at the top management level.

Two months after this recommendation was made the Reconstruction Finance Corporation established an "office of controller" as a major division within the corporation and shortly afterwards appointed an individual of outstanding qualifications to head the new office. The newly-appointed controller was made responsible for budget preparation and administration; accounting policies, procedures and operations, including financial reporting; internal auditing; economic analyses and statistical studies; insurance functions; and planning the organizational structure of the corporation.

---

[8]House Document No. 674, 79 Cong., 2 sess.

JOINT FINANCIAL MANAGEMENT
IMPROVEMENT PROGRAM

One of the greatest single factors in the development of comptroller-ship in the Federal Government has been the Joint Financial Management Improvement Program[9] undertaken with congressional support in 1947 to improve Federal financial management in all of its aspects. This continuing program involves every Federal agency and has produced numerous improvements of lasting benefit under the leadership of the Comptroller General of the United States, the Secretary of the Treasury, and the Director of the Bureau of the Budget. The leaders of this program insisted from the beginning that accounting systems should be geared to the needs of management and they encouraged a systematic agency approach to financial management, especially in the internal audit and budget processes and the provision of adequate accounting information to support budget justifications.

The progressive concepts fostered by this program are reflected broadly through the Federal Government in agency accounting systems that give appropriate attention to the cost of doing business and utilize accrual and cost data in combination with other available management tools to achieve the most efficient agency operation. Although many agency systems have not yet attained the degree of perfection necessary for the Comptroller General's certification of conformance with required standards, the substantial progress that has been achieved confirms the inherent soundness of the continuing emphasis on the establishment in every agency of a comptroller organization manned by qualified and able personnel capable of and responsible for dealing with financial management from the standpoint of operating factors.

The emphasis under the program on the importance of linking these organizations to top management to bring them close to management considerations as they evolve has encouraged numerous agencies to establish comptroller positions in the top management echelon where a comptroller can function most effectively.

The fifteen annual progress reports issued to date under the Joint Financial Management Improvement Program frequently highlight the concerted effort made over the years to provide a better basis for comptrollership activity. This effort has ranged from assistance to the Civil Service Commission in establishing new financial executive position standards and advice on financial training to technical projects aimed at improving accounting support of budgets and fully synchronizing programming, budgeting, accounting and reporting.

---

[9]This program was identified originally as the Joint Program for Accounting Improvement and was renamed in 1959 in recognition of the fact that the work being done under the program was broader than the original name implied.

FIRST HOOVER COMMISSION RECOMMENDATIONS

Another notable development in 1947 was the launching of a concerted effort to devise an efficient and economical plan for carrying out authorized governmental activities. By unanimous vote in July of that year Congress established a bipartisan Commission on Organization of the Executive Branch of the Government, later popularly known as the Hoover Commission when former President Hoover accepted the position of commission chairman. The authorizing statute directed the Commission to submit to Congress plans for:

> Limiting expenditures to the lowest amount consistent with efficient performance of essential services, activities and functions.
> Eliminating duplication and overlapping of services, activities and functions.
> Consolidating services, activities and functions of a similar nature.
> Abolishing services, activities and functions not necessary to the efficient conduct of government.
> Defining and limiting executive functions, services and activities.

With much of its attention directed towards the current financial activities of the Government, in consonance with this strong emphasis on management improvement, the Commission, after thorough analysis, adjudged the governmental budgeting and accounting systems of the day more a handicap than a help to good management. At the root of the problem, the Commission reported, was an antiquated budget system little modified since the days of Alexander Hamilton. Because the budget was composed essentially of lists of items to be paid for, rather than of objectives to be accomplished, it failed to disclose how much an activity cost and how that cost compared with those of similar activities. The accounting system was found to be equally deficient, in part the result of undue centralization of routine bookkeeping operations.

The Commission's chief proposal for improving financial management involved refashioning the budget to a "performance basis" which would set forth clearly in terms of functions, projects or activities how the requested amount was to be spent. Other major proposals recommended that the primary responsibility for accounting systems be clearly placed in the Executive Branch of the Government and that site audit be substituted for centralized voucher examination. These important recommendations appeared not only in the Commission's Budgeting and Accounting Report, but also in many of the reports dealing with other matters. In the report on the National Security Organization, for example, the Commission's first recommendation proposed:

> a. That full power over preparation of the budget and over expenditures as authorized by the Congress be vested in the Secretary of Defense, under the authority of the President.
> b. That the Secretary of Defense direct and supervise a major overhaul of the entire budget system; that the budget be of a perfor-

mance type with emphasis on the objectives and purposes to be accomplished rather than upon personnel, supplies, and similar classifications; that uniform terminology, classifications, budgetary, and accounting practices be established throughout all the services along administrative lines of responsibility, so that fiscal and management responsibility go together.

NATIONAL SECURITY ACT AMENDMENTS

Less than three weeks after the first Hoover Commission submitted these recommendations on the National Security Organization, President Truman requested Congress to increase the authority of the Secretary of Defense. The National Security Act of 1947 had provided a basis for some unification of the military services and for coordinating military policy with foreign economic policy but further improvements were needed to overcome the following rather startling state of affairs pointed out in a Hoover Commission task force report:

> The committee feels that it is justified in saying that our military budget system has broken down. The budgetary and appropriation structures of the Army and Navy are antiquated. They represent an accumulation of categories arrived at on an empirical and historical basis. They do not permit ready comparisons, they impede administration, and interfere with the efficiency of the Military Establishment. Congress allocates billions without accurate knowledge as to why they are necessary and what they are being used for.

At the request of the Senate Committee on Armed Services, the chairman of the Commission task force making this report drafted a proposed new title to the National Security Act which would establish in the Department of Defense and the three component military departments comptroller organizations to carry out comprehensive financial management functions. The proposed title promised greater economy and efficiency in the military establishment and prescribed that budgets be presented and administered on a performance basis. These proposals were accepted without significant change and were enacted into legislation as part of the National Security Act Amendments of 1949.[10]

Under this new legislation, the financial provisions of which became Title IV of the National Security Act, the Army, Navy and Air Force were required to organize and conduct their budgeting, accounting, progress and statistical reporting, and internal audit, consistently with the Defense Comptroller's operations, as specifically outlined in the law. The responsibilities of the Defense Comptroller, by statute an Assistant Secretary of Defense, have been substantially enlarged by the Secretary of Defense. In addition to the responsibilities specifically designated by law, the comptroller was made responsible for two important management analysis functions:

---

[10]63 Stat. 578.

(1) Evaluating the administration and management of approved policies and programs; and (2) Recommending appropriate steps which will provide in the Department of Defense for more effective, efficient and economical administration and operation, will eliminate unnecessary duplication or will contribute to improved military preparedness.

Several years ago these functions were further expanded to include assisting the Secretary of Defense, components of the Department of Defense and other agencies of the Federal Government in evaluating defense programs by:

> *First*, developing measures of resource utilization and methods of characterizing resource limitations and availabilities, in such a way as to make it possible to answer quickly and accurately questions about the costs and feasibility of a variety of alternative programs of force structures, weapons systems, and other military capabilities projected over a period of several years;
>
> *Second*, assembling and consolidating data as to pertinent nonfinancial programs of the Department of Defense and translating them into financial programs which can be presented in various forms so as to show the total financial implications of currently approved, new or alternative programs; and
>
> *Third*, presenting the information so obtained so as to point up the fiscal implications of alternative programs and the problems of choice involved.

This assignment to the comptroller of a broad role for active participation in major management functions is a very significant development. This concept, if given proper encouragement and implementation, could lead to a general strengthening of comptrollership concepts throughout Government.

BUDGET AND ACCOUNTING PROCEDURES ACT

One year after Title IV was added to the National Security Act, the Budget and Accounting Procedures Act of 1950[11] gave further impetus to the comptrollership concept. This general legislation recognized the need for accounting systems which would provide a reliable base for managerial decisions and for the first time in Federal law made the head of each executive agency primarily responsible for all budgeting and accounting functions within his agency. With respect to accounting and auditing, this act specifically required each agency head to establish and maintain systems of accounting and internal control designed to provide full disclosure of agency financial results, adequate financial information for agency management, effective control over and accountability for all agency funds and assets, reliable accounting results for budgetary purposes, and suitable integration of agency and Treasury accounting. Under its provisions also the Comptroller General is required to cooperate with executive agencies in the development

---

[11]64 Stat. 832.

of their agency systems and with the Treasury Department in the development of a system of central accounting and reporting, and to approve these systems when they meet his prescribed basic requirements.

In determining his auditing procedures and the extent of his detailed examination of documents, the Comptroller General is enjoined by this act to give due regard to generally accepted principles of auditing, including consideration of the effectiveness of accounting organizations and systems, internal audit and control, and related administrative practices. Specific authority was provided for the retention of documents at agency offices where they are normally kept so that audits might be conducted at the site of operations. Under these auditing provisions, the amount of detailed work can be regulated in the light of the effectiveness of agency accounting systems and of administrative application of statutes and other legal requirements in carrying out financial transactions.

The Comptroller General used the authority provided in this 1950 act to discontinue voluminous duplicating accounts previously maintained in the General Accounting Office. The particular responsibilities formerly carried out through the discontinued procedures are more effectively served by auditing the accounts maintained by the Treasury Department and other agencies and by establishing appropriate requirements for the maintenance of agency systems. Thus the legislation itself and the actions taken under it have exerted a two-fold influence on the development of comptrollership in the Federal Government:

> *First,* they have fixed on the head of each executive agency responsibility for functions which can best be carried out at agency level by an effective budget and accounting organization.
>
> *Second,* they have progressively freed executive agencies from many external requirements which previously had hampered the full growth of effective budget and accounting organizations.

POST OFFICE DEPARTMENT FINANCIAL CONTROL ACT

The Post Office Department Financial Control Act of 1950[12] did for the Post Office Department what the Budget and Accounting Procedures Act did for the Government as a whole. It transferred the administrative accounting and reporting functions previously performed by the General Accounting Office for the Department to the Postmaster General and imposed upon him the responsibility to establish and maintain adequate systems of accounting and internal control. The General Accounting Office was given the responsibility of prescribing accounting principles, cooperating in systems development and performing a comprehensive independent audit.

---

[12] 64 Stat. 460.

SECOND HOOVER COMMISSION RECOMMENDATIONS

Three years following these basic legislative reforms, in July of 1953, another bipartisan commission was established to appraise the organization and activities of the Executive Branch of the Government. While the public law establishing this new special commission was similar in most respects to the one which six years earlier established the first Hoover Commission, it specified two additional areas that this second commission, also headed by former President Hoover, should consider in recommending legislative or administrative action to promote greater economy and efficiency in Government: (1) Eliminating nonessential services, functions and activities which are competitive with private enterprise; and (2) Relocating agencies responsible directly to the President into departments or other agencies.

In carrying out its broad mandate, the second Hoover Commission—formally, as before, the Commission on Organization of the Executive Branch of the Government—carefully surveyed progress made in adopting improved financial management practices since the report of the first Hoover Commission. The Commission's studies documented the substantial progress that had been achieved during the intervening years but indicated that further progress was needed. The resulting report, rendered after two years of critical appraisal, included a series of 25 recommendations for the further development of financial management in Government.

Major proposals in the Commission's report centered around broadening the use of costs in the financial affairs of Government and strengthening the comptrollership organizations servicing the President and the heads of executive agencies generally. The Commission strongly endorsed the objectives and activities of the Joint Financial Management Improvement Program but noted the comparatively limited participation of the Bureau of the Budget in the joint effort. It accordingly recommended that the Bureau's participation in the Joint Improvement Program be strengthened through the establishment of a new staff office under an Assistant Budget Director to provide appropriate leadership in comptrollership matters to executive agencies of the Government. The powers and duties suggested for this new office were enumerated in the Commission Report as follows:

> To develop and promulgate an overall plan for accounting and reporting, consistent with broad policies and standards prescribed by the Comptroller General. These broad policies and standards should continue to be developed in cooperation with the Executive Branch.
>
> To expedite, guide and assist in the introduction of modern accounting methods in the executive agencies consistent with the overall plan.
>
> To set reasonable but definite time schedules for performance and to watch progress.
>
> To stimulate the building of competent accounting and auditing organizations in the executive agencies and to assist actively in the

selection, training and retention of capable personnel.

To report at least annually to the Budget Director with respect to the status of accounting in each of the executive agencies.

This proposal followed the basic view held by the first Hoover Commission that comptrollership functions are inherently part of management and therefore must evolve within the environment in which management operates. Both Commissions fully accepted the modern concept that accounting and budgeting are interrelated aspects of financial management and sought through their respective recommendations to establish a common system of accounting and budgeting throughout Government. The General Accounting Office also supported this concept in commenting on the Commission's recommendation that a new staff office be established in the Bureau of the Budget. After referring to the Joint Financial Management Improvement Program and to the specific responsibilities of the Comptroller General and agency heads under the Budget and Accounting Procedures Act of 1950, the Comptroller General stated:

> It is our view that primary reliance must, of necessity, continue to be placed upon the head of each executive agency because of the fact that accounting is an integral part of total management responsibility and any effort to obtain improvements must have the full support of agency management to be successful. However, the added emphasis on getting the job done Governmentwide, contemplated by the above recommendation, could be very helpful in expediting progress if appropriately carried out.

A related Commission proposal stressed the importance of establishing agency comptroller organizations throughout the Federal Government. The Commission recommended that, to provide more effective financial management, there be established in all principal agencies and major subdivisions thereof the position of comptroller which would embrace the following duties and functions:

> To direct the setting up and maintenance throughout his agency of adequate accounting and auditing systems and procedures in conformity with the provisions of the Budget and Accounting Procedures Act of 1950.
> To direct the recruitment, training and development of qualified accounting personnel.
> To develop and be responsibile for reliable and informative financial reports for (1) internal management purposes and (2) distribution to Congress and to other executive departments and agencies.
> To direct the preparation and review execution of budgets prepared at operating levels for the information of top management which is responsible for budget policies.

After preparing a comprehensive analysis of the second Hoover Commission's budget and accounting recommendations, the Bureau of the Budget in 1956 presented to the President specific plans for carrying out the Commission's recommendations. In so doing the Director of the Bureau of the Budget conceded that he should exercise stronger leadership in comptrollership matters, and with the President's approval and added appropriation support from Congress for this purpose, he instituted an expanded program to encourage accounting reform throughout Government.

The recommended new staff office in the Bureau of the Budget was established in April of 1956 but no directive action was taken centrally to implement the companion recommendation relating to agency comptrollership organizations. This latter recommendation, most authorities felt, was properly directed to the responsible agency heads for their consideration. Any imposition of a fixed pattern of organization, whether by legislative or administrative action, would conflict with the guiding principle that agency heads must have the authority to control the internal organization of their agencies. In the years since this recommendation was made, many agencies have acted individually to establish comptroller offices and otherwise strengthen financial management functions in consonance with the objectives sought by both Hoover Commissions.

COMPTROLLERSHIP'S CURRENT STATUS

To date a significant number of Federal agencies have combined all or most of their financial management functions under the direction of an official at the top level of management who usually, but not always, bears the title of comptroller. This realignment of financial functions has not stopped at the top, but in agencies such as the Defense Department, the Post Office Department and the General Services Administration has extended into the field organizations.

As matters now stand, the comptroller's span of operations and status in an agency vary from agency to agency. The greatest difference seems to be in the placement of the budgeting and internal audit functions. In the case of budgeting, the separate status it not infrequently has may be attributable in part to the fact that development of the budget function generally preceded the development of the accounting function, as a result of a provision in the Budget and Accounting Act of 1921 requiring each agency to appoint a budget officer.[13] Internal auditing, on the other hand, came along much later and had to be fitted into an existing and often well-entrenched financial management pattern. By far the most important consideration, however, is that the budget officer and internal auditor be positioned where they can function in an independent and unbiased manner regardless of whether they report directly to the top manager.

Lest the reader gain the impression that no further progress needs to be made in the development of comptrollership responsibilities and functions in the Government, let him ponder this extract from the Joint Financial

---

[13]Repealed as a specific requirement by Section 102(f) of the Budget and Accounting Procedures Act of 1950, 64 Stat. 832.

Management Improvement Program's report previously referred to, *Fifteen Years of Progress:*

> There are two major areas in which progress has not been adequate nor as rapid as it should be. These involve establishing accrual accounting systems that are tailored to the needs of the agency and are in keeping with prescribed principles and standards, and making effective use of cost information for the purposes of internal agency management.
>
> With respect to accounting systems in civilian agencies, for example, the Comptroller General to date has approved 46 complete systems out of 133 subject to approval. In the last 5 years, however, only six have been added to that group. Furthermore, none of the major departments have all their accounting systems approved. In the budgeting area, while most agencies now are presenting cost based appropriation requests, many still use obligation instead of cost data as the basis for day-to-day management of operations. Much work remains to be done, therefore, to reach the goals established in legislation and sought by the joint program.

In recognition of this situation, the Comptroller General, in a letter of May 19, 1964, to the heads of Federal departments and major agencies, said:

> Many changes and improvements in Federal agency accounting practices have been made since 1950. In the nearly 14 years that have gone by, however, the number of executive agency accounting systems that have been modernized, improved, and brought into conformity with the requirements of law and the broad principles and standards prescribed by our Office is disappointingly small.[14]

The Comptroller General urged each agency head to arrange for an appropriate review of the status of financial management improvement work within his organization with a view to accomplishing needed further progress. The House Committee on Government Operations expressed its interest in this letter and in the extent to which the executive agencies had carried out their responsibilities under the Budget and Accounting Procedures Act of 1950 and related legislation. The Committee's Subcommittee on Executive and Legislative Reorganization held hearings on July 2 and July 28, 1964, at which the Comptroller General and representatives of the Treasury Department and the Bureau of the Budget appeared and testified as to their appraisal of the progress already made and the further steps which need to be taken.

Undoubtedly much more can and should be done to provide improved financial management and meet the objectives envisioned by Congress and the Executive Branch in this area. Nevertheless, comptrollership has come of age in the Federal Government where comptrollers frequently occupy positions of responsibility quite comparable to those held by their counter-

---

[14]B-115398; coverage of this letter is included "Inside Government Department," in *The Federal Accountant,* Vol. 13 (June, 1964).

parts in industry. In the perspective of these developments the accelerating trend toward more effective comptrollership organizations can be expected to continue in future years. There is every reason to believe that Federal agencies will find it advantageous to strengthen comptrollership functions as required to improve agency management. Their action in this respect undoubtedly will be influenced by the extent to which top management makes use of the services an effective comptroller can render and by the extent to which the comptrollers themselves respond to management needs.

THE GENERAL ACCOUNTING OFFICE: FUNCTIONS AND ISSUES

Joseph P. Harris

The present-day General Accounting Office describes itself as:... a nonpolitical, nonpartisan agency in the legislative branch of the Government created by the Congress to act in its behalf in examining the manner in which Government agencies discharge their financial responsibilities with regard to public funds appropriated or otherwise made available to them by the Congress and to make recommendations looking to greater economy and efficiency in public expenditures.[1]

The GAO is an establishment of about 4,700 people, the majority of whom are accountants, auditors, lawyers, and investigators. Employees are recruited on a merit basis, following examinations given by the Civil Service Commission. GAO headquarters in Washington, where the bulk of these employees are assigned, is a large, modern building near—but not on—Capitol Hill. About 1,800 GAO employees are assigned to regional and field offices in some 20 principal U.S. cities, and a small group of about 80 scrutinize expenditures abroad from offices in Paris and Tokyo. Appropriations for the support of the GAO have currently run about $43 million annually. Most years, the GAO reports that it has collected for the government, from improper or disputed payments, sums exceeding its appropriation, not to mention even greater savings made in departmental budgets by GAO's recommendations.[2]

CONTROL OF THE ACCOUNTING SYSTEM

In a business firm, establishment of the accounting system is ordinarily a management function, and the role of the external auditor is to

---

Article is from Joseph P. Harris, *Congressional Control Of Administration*, Washington, D.C.: The Brookings Institution, 1964, pp. 135–52. Used with permission of author and publisher.

[1]U.S. General Accounting Office, *Functions of the U.S. General Accounting Office*, Report for the Senate Committee on Government Operations, 87 Cong., 2 sess. (1962), p. 1.

[2]For fiscal 1962, the GAO reported collections of over $48 million. The total reported for fiscal years 1950–62 was $708 million. In 1962, the GAO also took credit for savings of $114 million in agency operations. *See* Comptroller General, *Annual Report . . . 1962*, pp. 243–255.

Without entering the question deeply, it might be observed at this point that the value of an auditor generally is not measured by sums collected or recovered. Since auditors in the business world do not have authority to disallow expenditures, collections are not attributed to them, although their work may lead indirectly to recovery of funds in serious cases of fraud or malfeasance.

374

report to the directors and stockholders on the accuracy of the accounts and the adequacy of the system. In the federal government, by contrast, the auditor—the Comptroller General—has authority in his own right to prescribe the principles and control the standards of accounting in the executive agencies.

The Budget and Accounting Act of 1921 transferred to the Comptroller General some of the central bookkeeping functions previously performed by the Treasury (Sec. 304), and further instructed him to "prescribe the forms, systems, and procedure for administrative appropriation and fund accounting in the several departments and establishments, and for the administrative examination of fiscal officers' accounts and claims against the United States" (Sec. 309).[3] For many years the General Accounting Office used this as authority for imposing on the departments quite rigid requirements as to the kinds of accounts to be kept, reports to be made, and procedures to be followed leading to GAO approval and issuance of the "warrants" by which certain central bookkeeping transactions were accomplished. Departments and agencies increasingly complained that the GAO's system was archaic and cumbersome; that the GAO, the Treasury, the Budget Bureau, and their own internal administrative needs imposed conflicting and overlapping accounting requirements; and that the system did not accommodate the kind of internal financial control and reporting procedures that modern accounting can provide as aids to management.

Establishment of the Joint Program in 1948 reflected agreement among the interested parties, including the Comptroller General, that reform of the accounting system was needed. Although the Hoover Commission's proposal for legislation to switch primary responsibility for the accounting system to the Executive branch was rejected, the Act of 1950 was a compromise that preserved the ultimate authority of the Comptroller General but encouraged modernization and provided for greater recognition of the role and responsibility of executive agencies in shaping their accounting systems.

A carefully worded section (111) declared it to be the policy of Congress that:

(a) The accounting of the Government provides full disclosure of the results of financial operations, adequate financial information needed in the management of operations and the formulation and execution of the Budget, and effective control over income, expenditures, funds, property, and other assets.

(b) Full consideration be given to the needs and responsibilities of both the legislative and executive branches in the establishment of accounting and reporting systems and requirements.

(c) The maintenance of accounting systems and the producing of financial reports with respect to the operations of executive agencies, including central facilities for bringing together and disclosing informa-

---

[3] 42 Stat. 23–24.

tion on the results of the financial operations of the Government as a whole, be the responsibility of the executive branch.

(d) Emphasis be placed on effecting orderly improvements resulting in simplified and more effective accounting, financial reporting, budgeting, and auditing requirements and procedures and on the elimination of those which involve duplication or which do not serve a purpose commensurate with the costs involved.

(e) The Comptroller General of the United States, the Secretary of the Treasury, and the Director of the Bureau of the Budget conduct a continuous program for the improvement of accounting and financial reporting in the Government.[4]

Pursuant to this declaration, the Comptroller General was instructed to consult the Secretary of the Treasury and the Director of the Budget and to prescribe the "principles, standards, and related requirements" for accounting in the agencies. The agency heads, however, were given responsibility for actually establishing and maintaining systems and procedures to provide appropriate control of funds and data for reporting, budgeting, and internal management needs. The systems so established must conform to the principles and standards set by the Comptroller General, who was instructed to review and report on them from time to time. The Comptroller General, however, was instructed to perform his functions in a manner conforming with the declaration of policy and permitting the executive agencies to fulfill their responsibilities under the act.

Since 1950, proceeding through the Joint Program, the GAO and the agencies have cooperated in gradual elimination of obsolescent methods and requirements and installation of accounting and reporting procedures that provide a more effective form for management control as well as external audit and evaluation. The GAO's current position is that basic responsibility for the particulars of any agency system rests with the agency. Its own concern is with broad principles and standards. For several years the GAO maintained a special Accounting Systems Division to work with the agencies; this activity is now assigned to a combined Accounting and Auditing Policy staff. The GAO's ultimate authority over the accounting system is exercised in several ways. Statements of "principles and standards" are issued to the agencies in manual form.[5] There is also a long-range program of review of agency and bureau accounting systems, leading to the Comptroller General's official "approval" of systems fully meeting the GAO's standards. As of June 1962, 41 of the 128 identifiable separate accounting systems in the Executive branch had been so certified, and approval had been given to major parts of 15 other systems.[6] Both "approved" and "unapproved"

---

[4]64 Stat. 834.

[5]U.S. General Accounting Office, *General Accounting Office Policy and Procedures Manual for Guidance of Federal Agencies* (5 vol., looseleaf, originally issued 1957, with occasional supplements), Title 2.

[6]Comptroller General, *Annual Report ... 1962*, p. 50.

systems are subject to GAO review and comment in the course of ordinary audits or special investigations.

For the long run, there remains some question whether even this degree of auditor control of the accounting system is consistent with or gives encouragement to proper exercise of what should be primarily an executive management responsibility. However, the ambiguity of the Act of 1950 has permitted a balance between executive and GAO interests that for the time being seems tolerable to both parties.

AUDIT, SETTLEMENT, AND LEGAL INTERPRETATIONS

The heart of the power of the Comptroller General lies in his statutory authority to audit and settle the accounts of executive officers, including the making of legal interpretations incidental thereto, with his determinations final and conclusive upon the Executive branch. About the propriety of his auditing the accounts there can be no question, for this is the essence of the function of a legislative auditor, although there is room for debate about the scope, manner, and criteria of the audit. But the combination of auditing with binding power of legal interpretation and settlement is the crux of historic controversy about the Comptroller General, and the source of much of the day to day friction between the General Accounting Office and the executive agencies.

Audit

With some limited exceptions specified by statute, the auditing authority of the GAO extends to all activities, financial transactions, and accounts of the federal government. It includes the records of contractors having contracts negotiated without advertising, their subcontractors' records, and the records of certain recipients of federal assistance in the form of loans, advances, grants, or contributions. All officers of the government are required by law to make their records available and to cooperate with the GAO. The law requires an annual audit of certain specified agencies, and the accounts submitted by accountable officers must be examined within three years if individuals are to be held liable for improper expenditures (except in case of fraud or criminality). Within these broad limits, the Comptroller General has wide discretion to determine the frequency, detail, and procedures for auditing.[7]

Congress's general policy with respect to accounting and auditing, as expressed in Sec. III (d) of the Act of 1950, is that:

> The auditing for the Government, conducted by the Comptroller General of the United States as an agent of the Congress, be directed at determining the extent to which accounting and related financial

---

[7]See: *Functions of the U.S. General Accounting Office, op. cit.,* pp. 9–10.

reporting fulfill the purposes specified, financial transactions have been consummated in accordance with laws, regulations, and other legal requirements, and adequate internal financial control over operations is exercised, and afford an effective basis for the settlement of accounts of accountable officers.

Sec. 117 (a) of the act, with specific respect to auditing, makes a broad grant of authority to the Comptroller General but gives him certain guidance:

> In the determination of auditing procedures to be followed and the extent of examination of vouchers and other documents, the Comptroller General shall give due regard to generally accepted principles of auditing, including consideration of the effectiveness of accounting organizations and systems, internal audit and control, and related administrative practices of the respective agencies.

With the authorization and encouragement of this act, auditing procedures have been greatly modernized in recent years. For the first two decades of the GAO, practically all of the auditing was done at its own offices, to which agencies were required to ship all the necessary papers and documents. Beginning with some exceptions made for government corporations and emergency programs in the 1930's, and continuing increasingly since World War II, there has been a trend toward conducting the audits in the operating agency offices where the books are kept—what GAO calls "site audits" as distinguished from "centralized audits."[8]

GAO now has auditing groups on a continuing basis in the headquarters of many agencies, and has its own field staffs examining agency operations all over the country and abroad as well. Although most of the auditing now is done on the site, some classes of expenditures, such as transportation, are still audited centrally, and a few agencies are still required to send all of their vouchers and related documents to GAO for centralized audit.

Along with the shift in location of audits has gone a broadening of the scope and purposes of auditing. The traditional GAO audit—sometimes called a "desk audit" or "voucher audit"—consisted basically of a careful scrutiny of the papers on each transaction to assure that all expenditures had been legally made and documented. This was a laborious operation, requiring a large clerical staff and inevitably leading to a great deal of bickering over detail with the operating agencies. Furthermore, it had only a limited usefulness. A congressional committee staff report noted that although it "resulted in the recovery of substantial amounts of funds improperly expended, it was only incidentally conducive to an analysis of the effectiveness and economy of the management of the agencies." Since 1950, the GAO has moved toward a policy of "comprehensive audits" in which

---

[8] As noted, the first Hoover Commission condemned the "deluge of paper work" at the GAO, and the Act of 1950 contained some permissive language encouraging GAO to make more use of the site audit.

emphasis is not on the individual transactions but on the soundness of the agency's accounting and financial management system and the efficiency of its operations generally. This has made possible the gradual elimination of several thousand clerical employees at the GAO. Some agencies and classes of expenditure, however, still receive a detailed and less than comprehensive audit, and even in the comprehensive audit some individual vouchers are checked, although increasingly on a sampling basis.

These developments have significantly improved the quality and usefulness of the auditing and reduced some of the old frictions between the GAO and the departments. Difficulties still arise, however, because of the confusion of control and audit functions assigned the GAO by statute and the persistent tendency of both Congress and the GAO to extend the auditing to the point where it conflicts with executive functions. A sense of the wide sweep of the auditing operation may be gained by examining what the GAO announces as the elements of a comprehensive audit.

1. A study of the pertinent laws and legislative history to ascertain congressional intent as to the purpose of the activities engaged in by the agency, their intended scope, the manner in which they are to be conducted, and the extent of the agency's authority and responsibility.

2. A review of the policies established by the agency (and to the extent applicable by the central control agencies) to determine whether they (a) conform to the intent of Congress, and (b) are designed to carry out the authorized activities in an effective and efficient manner.

3. A review of the procedures, practices, form of organization (particularly as to the segregation of duties and responsibilities), and system of reporting, review, and inspection as well as other elements of internal control to determine whether they (a) provide reasonable assurance of control over expenditures, receipts and revenues, and assets, (b) assure the accuracy, reliability, and usefulness of financial data, including the budget statements and supporting data presented to the Bureau of the Budget and the Congress, (c) promote operational efficiency, (d) result in adherence to prescribed policies, and (e) assure compliance with the requirements of applicable laws, regulations, and decisions.

4. A review and analysis, by activities, of receipts and revenues, expenditures, and the utilization of assets together with all related control processes as a basis for evaluating the effectiveness with which public funds are applied and properly utilized. This will include comparison of performance with budget estimates and with results of prior periods and evaluation of costs of performance in relation to accomplishments.

5. The examination of individual transactions, the confirmation of balances with debtors, creditors, and depositaries, and the physical inspection of property to the extent necessary to determine whether (a) transactions have been consummated in accordance with applicable laws, regulations, and decisions, and have been correctly classified, (b) resources and financial transactions have been properly accounted for, and (c) control processes of the agency are functioning effectively.

6. The exploration and full development of all important deficiencies encountered and the presentation of appropriate recommendations for corrective action by the Congress, where needed, agency heads, or the

control agencies such as the Bureau of the Budget, the Civil Service Commission, and the General Services Administration. This will include the reporting of any programs undertaken or transactions completed without authority of law which were disclosed during the audit as well as the stating of exceptions against accountable officers and the making of collections resulting from illegal or otherwise improper expenditures.[9]

As the GAO notes in a subsequent section, "While the goal is an evaluation of the discharge of the agency's financial responsibilities, the scope of the comprehensive audit extends to all of an agency's operations and activities *and to all of their aspects.*"[10] Particularly to be noticed is the declared right to compare agency policies and activities with legislative intent, to assess agency organization, and to evaluate efficiency by various means including comparing performance with budget estimates. Although it clearly is the function of legislative auditors to point out any executive actions contrary to law, it is doubtful whether this should include attempts to delve into legislative history and intent beyond a plain reading of the statutes. Executive officials in charge of programs are ordinarily in close touch with the committees that originate relevant legislation and are just as well situated as outside auditors to judge legislative intent; if they disregard legislative wishes they are also in position to be brought to account without the assistance of auditors.

It is equally doubtful whether auditors should venture into the realm of general departmental policies that do not directly involve the financial and accounting matters in which auditors are professionally competent. Similarly, it can be questioned whether independent auditors should undertake to determine whether the form of organization is suitable, or to make general evaluations of performance, efficiency, and effectiveness of administrative operations. Auditors should report wasteful practices that come to their attention, but their training does not thereby qualify them to express judgments on the overall efficiency of operations.

An efficiency audit requires a specially qualified staff and is best conducted as an internal audit responsible to management. The Comptroller General has encouraged and assisted the departments in instituting internal audits for this and other purposes, which is commendable, but there is an important distinction between the internal audit, a tool of management, and the external audit, which is to serve the legislature. The present broad sweep of the auditing function puts a substantial burden on executive agencies to cooperate and comply with the Comptroller General's regulations. This may be in accord with the preferences of Congress, but there is room for doubt whether this approach serves Congress well or leaves an administrator with the discretion he needs if he is to be held responsible for the effectiveness of operations.

---

[9]U.S. General Accounting Office, *General Accounting Office Policy and Procedures Manual for Guidance of Federal Agencies*, Title 3, Sec. 2020.20.

[10]*Ibid.*, Sec. 2020.30. (Italics added.)

Settlement

The extended scope of the auditing function would not be so controversial if the Comptroller General were only empowered to report his findings and express his doubts about administrative policies and operations to the appropriate executive officials and Congress, and leave it to them to make the necessary adjustments. The rub, however, is that he also is empowered to settle the accounts—and in the course thereof to state exceptions and disallow expenditures—of executive officers. This gives him a strong sanction for enforcing his interpretations of the law and views about sound administrative procedure on the departments. To be sure, the power of disallowance is exercised in connection with specific items of expenditure which the Comptroller General considers improper under the law; he cannot disallow all the expenditures of a billion-dollar program merely because he considers it inefficiently managed. Nevertheless, the fact that the departments must eventually settle with the GAO requires them to give great weight to its views on all questions of policy and procedure, even when they involve matters on which the department's competence and judgment ought to be superior.

As mentioned above, a proposal to transfer the power of settlement to the Executive branch was central to FDR's 1937 attack on the GAO, and has been revived at various times since. Congress and the GAO, however, have always angrily resisted and successfully repulsed such efforts. In their view, the meaning of legislative control is to have the agent of Congress in position to prevent or recover specific expenditures he believes improper; authority merely to report such events after the fact would be no control at all. The fact that this interference with particular transactions weakens executive responsibility and denies Congress a truly independent post-audit is not impressive to many legislators.

Legal Interpretations

Making decisions as to whether or not particular transactions are in accord with the law and regulations is, of course, the essence of the settlement function. There is great room for differences, however, in the manner of exercise of that function. Whether the auditor construes the law broadly or narrowly, whether he is subject to any check or guidance in his constructions, whether the burden of proof in case of disagreement is on the auditor or the spending officer, and whether there is any appeal or ultimate recourse from the determinations of the auditor—these are all questions of moment and controversy.

In the course of settling accounts and passing on expenditures and claims, the Comptroller General issues legal decisions on the propriety, under all relevant laws, of past transactions. He also is authorized by law to give advance opinions on the legality of proposed transactions when asked to do so by department heads or disbursing officers. In order to avoid the danger of a disallowance, the departments usually secure advance clearance on any new type of activity, expenditure, or procedure about which there can be any doubt. In recent years, the Comptroller General has issued over 6,000 legal decisions and reports annually, the most important of which are published in *The Decisions of the Comptroller General*, a weighty series of annual volumes.

These decisions constitute an administrative code of great scope and complexity. They involve interpretations and applications of federal statutes, treaties, state and foreign laws, and administrative regulations—not to mention the judgment of the GAO concerning sound administrative and financial practice. Many decisions relate to provisions of law designed to control administrative matters of personnel, financial management, travel, use of government property, and other details. Others, however, are concerned with Congress's intent concerning major governmental programs.[11] This formidable body of interpretations tells executive officers what they can and cannot do, limits their discretion, and circumscribes the methods, procedures, and activities which they utilize in the discharge of their functions.

Executive officials have always complained that the interpretations and decisions of the Comptroller General were unduly restrictive, a drag on effective administration. They claim that the habitual tendency of the General Accounting Office is to resolve all doubts against the administrators; that statutes granting authority to administrators are construed narrowly, while statutes stating restrictions are construed broadly; and that when the statutes are silent the GAO is reluctant to give the departments latitude to choose the most effective means of implementing the purposes of the law. The GAO's restrictions, it is claimed, manifest a negative attitude toward administration and government activity in general. These complaints are less common nowadays than in the McCarl era, but continue to be made.

While it is probably inevitable that administrators will be restive under any kind of external controls, many observers—including this author—feel that on the whole many of the executive complaints are justified. In its approach to administrative matters, the GAO does have a tendency to rule against actions or procedures unless they are expressly authorized by law or are clearly essential to the conduct of authorized programs. The GAO's restrictions often seem to go beyond the reasonable requirements of protecting the public purse, and amount to a substitution of the Comptroller General's judgment for that of the responsible administrators, even on matters about which the administrators are best situated to

---

[11] It might be emphasized that these interpretations are by no means confined to the appropriation statutes that were the initial historic concern of the legislative auditor. In a recent year, these provided a basis for only 12 percent of the Comptroller General's decisions. Other sources were: contracts, 30 percent; civilian personnel, 12 percent; military pay and allowances, 18 percent; transportation, 17 percent; and other matters 10 percent. *See* Comptroller General, *Annual Report, . . . 1959*, p. 277.

judge. The result is a serious limitation on administrative discretion, approaching a transgression on the constitutional authority of the Executive branch.

The GAO's usual reply is that such criticisms are nonsense, since it is merely enforcing the letter of the law and the intent of Congress; the proof is that Congress seems happy with the GAO's performance; and anyone dissatisfied with the GAO's interpretations can urge Congress to clarify or change the law.

The tendency of Congress—or at least of those portions of Congress attentive to such matters—to approve of the GAO's restrictive interpretations must be conceded. The difficulty is that this puts an almost overwhelming burden on the departments to challenge or have modified any rulings they feel to be unfair. If the Comptroller General has ruled adversely in an advance opinion, the department risks a disallowance if it proceeds. Ordinarily, a disallowance is conclusive. In rare instances a disallowance can be upset by somehow getting the case into court, but this is a risky course for the accountable officer, and even if he is vindicated the results may be applicable only to this one case and will not secure a change in the general rule.

A safer course is for the department to attempt to persuade Congress to modify the statutes to provide clear authority for what it wishes to do. But this takes time and effort. Legislative committees have crowded agendas, such problems often involve technicalities that are difficult to explain, and Congress is generally reluctant to upset the Comptroller General's rulings, particularly if the Comptroller General takes the position—as he frequently does—that the law should not be changed. In many instances the departments have secured legislation of this sort, after some delay, but they are able to make this effort only occasionally and on the most important matters. The more usual course is to acquiesce in the Comptroller General's rulings and try to find alternative, even though less effective, ways of achieving the same purposes.[12]

Completely aside from its effect on administration, the result of this situation is that Congress does not get an adequate review of what has happened in the close cases. Departments that are displeased or placed in difficult situations by the Comptroller General's rulings find it hard to get Congress to review the matter. If the Comptroller General does agree with what the department wishes to do, he becomes a party to the transaction. Where then is Congress's independent post-audit?

---

[12]An example of this sort of sequence occurred after the Comptroller General ruled in 1939 that departments could not provide off-the-job training for government employees unless specifically authorized by law to do so, a ruling which seriously hampered training programs of the departments during World War II. This and subsequent rulings restricting the authority of departments to conduct training programs led eventually to passage of a general government employees training act—but not until 1958.

Statutory Exceptions

Although Congress has not been willing to take away the control functions of the Comptroller General for governmental activities in general, it has over the years exempted certain agencies and programs from his control when his decisions encountered strong criticism, or the Executive branch made an unusually strong case for greater flexibility. This has ordinarily been accomplished by providing that the determinations of the executive officers shall be conclusive, subject to review only by the courts. For example, Congress has exempted certain payments to veterans, soil conservation payments, commodity credit benefits, and certain activities of the State and Defense Departments. Interpretations of the revenue laws involved in determining customs and internal revenue assessments are not open to the Comptroller General's review, although he audits revenue accounts to check on payments into the Treasury.

An interesting exception was made in the Contract Settlement Act of 1944, which Congress passed over the Comptroller General's objections. This act was adopted in part on the recommendation of Bernard M. Baruch and John M. Hancock, two highly respected figures in the world of finance, who contended in a report to the Office of War Mobilization that conversion of industry from war to peace would be seriously impeded if all the anticipated war contract settlements were to be subject to audit and adjustment by the Comptroller General.[13] A compromise was reached which permitted such settlements to be negotiated conclusively by executive agencies, without adjustment by the Comptroller General. The Comptroller General, however, was permitted to examine the settlements after they were made and report his findings to Congress—and to the Department of Justice if fraud was suspected.

A somewhat similar principle was used to settle a long controversy over the auditing of agencies organized in the form of government corporations, such as the TVA, the Reconstruction Finance Corporation, and the numerous corporate agencies used in government credit operations. For many years the Comptroller General had sought to apply to these agencies his full powers of audit and settlement of accounts, while the corporations resisted in the name of the administrative flexibility which had been sought in using the corporate form of organization in the first place. Finally Congress reached a settled policy in the Government Corporation Control Act of 1945, which made these agencies subject to a commercial-type audit to be conducted by the Comptroller General at the corporate offices.[14] Under this act, the Comptroller General reports to Congress on the adequacy of the accounts and any expenditures he believes to have been unauthorized by

---

[13]John D. Millett, *Government and Public Administration*, New York: McGraw-Hill Book Co., 1959, p. 183.

[14]59 Stat. 597.

law, but he does not have the power to settle accounts and enforce his interpretations of law directly on the corporations, except as that power is elsewhere given him by separate legislation.

REPORTS AND SERVICES TO CONGRESS

The legislative history of the Act of 1921 indicates that the primary objective Congress sought in establishing the General Accounting Office was to provide itself with a trusted source of information about the way in which public funds were being used in the executive departments.[15] To this end, the act authorizes the Comptroller General to investiage "all matters relating to the receipt, disbursement, and application of public funds" and requires him to make an annual report to Congress on the work of the GAO, including recommendations on any financial legislation he considers necessary and any other "recommendations looking to greater economy or efficiency in public expenditures." He also is required to report from time to time on the adequacy of financial control in the departments, and "every expenditure or contract made by any department or establishment in any year in violation of law." Other special investigations and reports may be made on the request of Congress or its committees.

The President and the Bureau of the Budget may also request reports and information from the Comptroller General, and the GAO on its own initiative makes many reports and recommendations on matters of lesser importance directly to particular departments.

This adds up to a formidable body of reporting. In fiscal year 1962, for example, the GAO submitted 271 reports on audits and investigations to Congress, or congressional committees, or individual members. In the same year 548 reports went directly to agency officials.[16] These reports are of different types. Audit reports on government corporations relate to the accounts of a particular fiscal year, and resemble the reports customary on commercial corporate firms. Reports on ordinary executive departments and agencies, however, do not relate to a specific period, but are the result of the GAO's intermittent audits, investigations, or special studies of departmental operations.

The Comptroller General provides a number of important services to Congress in addition to audit reports on executive agencies. Special reports on executive transactions or programs are made at the request of legislative

---

[15]Rep. James W. Good, chairman of the House committee sponsoring the legislation, said: "The officers and employees of this department (*sic*) will at all times be going into the separate departments in the examination of their accounts. They will discover the very facts that Congress ought to be in possession of and can fearlessly and without fear of removal present these facts to Congress and its committees." (Quoted in *Financial Management in the Federal Government, op. cit.*, p. 300.)

[16]Comptroller General, *Annual Report ... 1962*, pp. 265–285.

committees, or individual members.[17] Members of the GAO staff are frequently detailed to committee staffs—most frequently those of the Government Operations and Appropriations committees—to assist with investigations or analysis of legislation on financial matters. During fiscal year 1962, 158 lawyers, accountants, auditors, or investigators were so assigned for varying periods, at a total cost of over $400,000. The GAO keeps constant watch on bills introduced in Congress. Its 1962 *Annual Report* notes 445 reports with comments on proposed legislation to legislative committees, and 23 hearings in which staff members testified.[18] These services are prized highly by most legislators, as the record of any hearing involving the GAO will demonstrate.

There are a number of unsatisfactory aspects of the GAO's auditing and reporting system, and its relations with Congress generally. For one thing, because audit reports in most cases do not relate to the accounts for a particular time period, Congress is not provided with the information it needs to hold executive officials accountable for their use of funds. This difficulty is accentuated by the fact that audit reports are often made after a considerable time has elapsed, and the departments claim that they already are aware of the deficiencies reported, or that appropriate corrective measures are under way. It is often difficult to tell just who has detected the weakness and what the current status of the matter is.

Another problem is that the scope of the reports—which grows out of the scope of the audits themselves, as discussed above—often is so wide that they involve matters of policy and administration that go beyond the professional competence and normal functions of auditors. Many examples can be cited.

In 1955, and for several years following, the audit reports on the Tennessee Valley Authority included statements of opposition to legislation then being proposed which would authorize TVA to sell revenue bonds to finance construction of steam plants and other power facilities. The Comptroller General recommended that "agencies of the Government, other than the Treasury Department, should not be authorized to borrow from the public for purposes of the nature involved in the proposed legislation and that financing of such activities should be by appropriation."[19] Thus the Comptroller General stepped into a policy matter that did not involve probity in the use of funds, or even administrative efficiency, but did involve him in a highly political public-private power controversy. However, he takes the position that any diminution of regular annual congressional control of funds is his business to oppose, regardless of the broader policy objectives involved.

---

[17]"This type of work is given a very high priority and the performance of such work, particularly for congressional committees, has become a very important part of the work of the Office." *See* U.S. General Accounting Office, *Functions of the General Accounting Office, op. cit.*, p. 23.

[18]Comptroller General, *Annual Report . . . 1962*, pp. 17–26.

[19]Comptroller General, *Annual Report . . . 1956*, p. 145.

GAO reports have often been highly critical of both policy and administration of the politically controversial foreign aid programs. Some of its indictments of loose administrative procedures do, indeed, seem well founded. Other reports, however, involve matters of judgment and policy. An audit report of 1959 on the Development Loan Fund, for example, commented adversely on the criteria on which development loans were being made to several countries. Another recent report questioned the procedures by which the Department of Defense and the Joint Chiefs of Staff determined the level of military forces in certain friendly countries that we were aiding. Inasmuch as such decisions involve both military considerations and political maneuvers in the East-West struggle, this hardly seems a sphere for the auditors.

Reports on the Department of Agriculture in recent years provide several examples of GAO's tendency to get into policy matters. In 1959 the Secretary of Agriculture was criticized for setting the export price for cotton at too high a level to bring about a large sale abroad. For foreign policy reasons, the department was refraining from dumping large quantities of cotton on the world market, but the GAO thought such a pricing policy contrary to the intent of Congress. In 1957 the GAO ventured into the perennially controversial topic of the amount of grazing to be permitted on the public lands, and adequacy of the fees charged for such grazing.

In 1962 the Comptroller General told a congressional committee that the GAO had called to the attention of the Secretary of Health, Education, and Welfare the fact that procedures for testing and control of new drug products were different in the biologics program of the National Institutes of Health from those of the drug control programs administered by the Food and Drug Administration.[20] Inasmuch as these programs involve quite different kinds of products, with different technical problems and different historical patterns of government-industry relationships, there is some doubt about the significance of such a discovery by the auditors.

Difficulties arising from the broad scope of the Comptroller General's audit reports are accentuated by the way in which they are handled and used by Congress. There is no single committee of Congress, or in either house, with the sole function of receiving, conducting inquiries, and recommending action on the basis of these reports. The Legislative Reorganization Act of 1946 made the Committees on Government Operations of the two houses the principal recipients of these reports, but matters concerning appropriations are reserved to—and jealously guarded by—the two Appropriations Committees; many other Committees also request and receive GAO reports from time to time.

Thus there is no single point of responsibility, no systematic and comprehensive review of the GAO's work as a whole. Sometimes the

---

[20]*Independent Offices Appropriations for 1963*, Hearings Before the House Committee on Appropriations, 87 Cong., 2 sess. (1962), Part 2, pp. 7–8.

Comptroller General's reports are picked up and provide a basis for important inquiries by the committees. At other times when he reports there seems to be no one listening. Committee chairmen or individual members tend to request or seize on the reports which suit their own purposes—usually those that provide the most anti-executive pay dirt. Thus the tendency of the GAO to stray into policy matters adds fuel to the constitutional conflict between President and Congress or the fratricidal conflict between legislative and executive wings of the majority party.

FIFTEEN YEARS OF PROGRESS: JOINT FINANCIAL MANAGEMENT IMPROVEMENT PROGRAM

THE FEDERAL ACCOUNTANT

Some fifteen years ago a cooperative improvement effort—then known as the Joint Program for Improving Accounting in the Federal Government—was started. It began by reason of agreements reached among the top financial officials in the United States Government: the Comptroller General, the Secretary of the Treasury and the Director of the Bureau of the Budget. Officially established in October, 1948, this program had the avowed purpose of establishing more efficient and effective financial systems in the Federal Government.

In working toward that goal, effort centered first on improving accounting operations. In the 1950s, however, the work being done under the program obviously was broader than the name implied. The use of accounting information for program decisions, for budgeting, and for reporting and control, focused attention on problems in those areas and stimulated corrective action. Accordingly, the name was changed to the Joint Financial Management Improvement Program.

Today this program is a continuing force for working out financial management and control problems in the areas of programming, budgeting, accounting and reporting. It is concerned with conforming agency practices to established requirements, and dealing with the challenges of new programs, an ever-changing Government structure and advancing technology. The work continues as a cooperative effort of all executive agencies, operating under the combined leadership of the Bureau of the Budget, the Treasury Department and the General Accounting Office.

From the beginning, Congress has had an active interest in the program. The Budget and Accounting Procedures Act of 1950, for example, updated the Budget and Accounting Act of 1921 and related legislation, and gave statutory recognition to the joint program. Other important legislation was enacted in 1949 and 1950, and more recent laws clarified policies and requirements in the financial management field.

Besides the interest of individual congressmen, the Appropriations and Government Operations Committees in particular have worked closely with the joint program—both in getting it underway and in bringing about desired reforms. Many budget and accounting proposals of the first Hoover Commission—created by Congress—were reflected in the initial improve-

Article is from *The Federal Accountant*, Vol. 15 (March, 1964), pp. 127–138. Used with permission of publisher.

ment activities of the joint program. A similar group, the second Hoover Commission, also issued a report of findings and recommendations in the financial management area in 1955. This report cited important gains made by the joint program but recommended that it be strengthened to obtain faster progress. In addition, the report led to amendments of basic legislation that laid a groundwork for modernization of Federal financial management systems.

Since it began, the joint program has been regarded as a continuing effort of great importance to more efficient management. Changing programs, concepts and techniques continuously pose new problems. A major aim has been to remain flexible and maintain a capability that will keep abreast of the times—so that the financial management practices of Government do not become outmoded by changing conditions.

The goals and objectives of the program have remained fairly constant over the years. Though restated from time to time, the continuing overall goal has been to improve financial management practices in a way that will best meet the needs of the Legislative and Executive Branches. That goal, in turn, can be broadly summarized in these major objectives:

> 1. Strengthen organizational facilities and staff capabilities to provide for effective and economical financial management throughout the Government.
> 2. Establish accounting systems on the accrual basis to provide full disclosure of assets, liabilities, income and expense, and to develop financial data needed for effective management of operations at all levels of Government.
> 3. Establish financial planning and budgeting techniques that are integrated with programming, accounting and reporting practices into a single management system—one that supports budget estimates, stimulates economical program management, permits evaluation of the cost of performance, provides for efficient use of resources, and results in effective control of appropriations, funds, obligations, expenditures and costs.
> 4. Establish internal control methods appropriate to agency management needs, including timely and meaningful reports on financial results and progress performance, and suitable facilities for internal audit.
> 5. Integrate agency financial management systems with the requirements of the Federal budget and Treasury's central accounting processes to permit efficient development of accurate and useful Governmentwide reports showing the status of funds, financial results, economic impact and the costs of performing Government functions.

After fifteen years of the joint program, to what extent have these objectives been reached? How effective has this cooperative effort been? What results—in terms of ultimate benefits—have been obtained?

While this report is concerned primarily with highlighting significant improvements in Federal financial management practices during the past fifteen years, a balanced presentation requires that the progress made be viewed in relation to the total objectives of the joint program. There are two major areas in which progress has not been adequate nor as rapid as it should be. These involve establishing accrual accounting systems that are tailored to the needs of the agency and are in keeping with prescribed principles and standards, and making effective use of cost information for the purposes of internal agency management.

With respect to accounting systems in civilian agencies, for example, the Comptroller General to date has approved 46 complete systems out of 133 subject to approval. In the last five years, however, only six have been added to that group. Furthermore, none of the major departments have all their accounting systems approved. In the budgeting area, while most agencies now are presenting cost-based appropriation requests, many still use obligation instead of cost data as the basis for day-to-day management of operations. Much work remains to be done, therefore, to reach the goals established in legislation and sought by the joint program.

Despite these kinds of problems, this program has proved to be an effective force in Federal financial management. Today, in contrast with 1948, financial management is more clearly a working partner of general management; budgeting is program oriented and incorporates improved planning techniques; responsibility accounting is better accepted; financial reporting is more clearly tied to programs and increasingly reflects performance in relation to plans; cost consciousness in management gradually is becoming more evident; and auditing generally is centered on management effectiveness rather than legalistic document review. In 1961, the Senate Committee on Government Operations gave recognition to the advances brought about by this program. In its report on Financial Management in the Federal Government (Senate Document No. 11,[1] issued in February, 1961), the committee stated:

> Many improvements in budgeting, accounting, and reporting have resulted from the work done under the joint program and the committee is vitally interested in its continued progress.

Not all of the gains, of course, are attributable to staff directly engaged in the joint program. Improvements were brought about by a number of people with different interests—operating managers, program experts, technicians, economists, budget staff, accountants, auditors, etc. Many advances were made through the initiative of such people in individual agencies. Some were made possible by the basis for cooperation provided in the structure of the joint program. Others came about as a direct result of joint studies and recommendations. All, however, combine to reflect the significant changes that have taken place in the past fifteen years.

The benefits obtained from these changes are difficult to measure. Savings sometimes can be identified with individual improvements on a

---

[1]This outstanding 369-page report, distributed through the Superintendent of Documents, U.S. Government Printing Office, is now out of print.

one-time basis or over a period of time. In many cases, however, the most valuable contribution is the better management that is brought about by the change. This kind of return cannot be measured in dollars—yet it can be most significant in terms of its impact on program operations.

Overall, one of the best measures of results was provided by the House Post Office and Civil Service Committee. Its Subcommittee on Manpower Utilization compared the number of personnel in financial management at the end of fiscal years 1950 and 1957. A report on that study—House Report No. 2512—was released in August, 1958. While this report noted that comparable data were not available from the Defense Department, it pointed out that civilian agencies had reduced the number of financial management personnel by more than 15 percent in the seven years under review. This meant a decrease of over 6,000 personnel, from 39,644 to 33,552. By applying a minimum average salary for financial personnel, this reflects an estimated saving in annual salary costs alone of more than $30 million. The report also stated:

> It is significant that, in a number of instances, reductions were made in financial management personnel through more effective systems and procedures despite level or increased program activities of the departments and agencies. This information clearly indicates that: (1) increased program activities and appropriations do not automatically mean an increase in financial management personnel is required; and (2) real economies in the use of manpower are possible where effective effort is made to modernize and streamline agency financial management functions.

To this philosophy the Joint Financial Management Improvement Program wholeheartedly subscribes. There is much to be done in working toward established goals. Simplification and modernization are the keynotes of this continuing effort.

FIFTEEN YEARS OF PROGRESS

In the late 1940s, financial operations in the Federal Government were unduly complex and generated a mass of red tape. There were inadequate communications among the central agencies and conflicting requirements in numerous instructions to the operating agencies. Budgeting and accounting generally were uncoordinated. The budget placed restrictions on buying specific things and controls were dedicated almost completely to complying with legal limitations on the use of funds. Agencies were required to use restrictive accounting and reporting procedures that gave little or no attention to the financial data needs of operating managers. Auditing largely dealt with a legalistic examination of a multitude of vouchers. The net effect was to hinder rather than to help management.

Faced with these conditions, the joint program initially took action to clear out the red tape at the top levels of Government—in effect, to first "put the house in order." One of the first steps was to update legislative requirements.

PROGRESS IN MODERNIZING LEGISLATION

When the joint program began, the Budget and Accounting Act of 1921 was the principal basic law in this field. In addition, certain central accounting operations were based on the Dockery Act of 1894 and legislation that established the Treasury Department in 1789. These were supplemented by many other laws, such as the Antideficiency Act—Section 3679 of the Revised Statutes—and the Government Corporation Control Act of 1945. Thus Federal financial management in 1948 was based on a "patchwork" of legislation, much of which had little applicability to twentieth century problems.

In this setting, the central agencies joined with congressional staff to modernize legal requirements. This produced the Budget and Accounting Procedures Act of 1950. President Truman called this bill:

... the most important legislation enacted by the Congress in the budget and accounting field since the Budget and Accounting Act, 1921, was passed almost 30 years ago.

The new legislation repealed 106 outdated laws. Beyond that, it strengthened Bureau of the Budget management responsibilities and authorized the budget to include data on the functions and activities of Government (the "performance budget" concept of the first Hoover Commission); clarified the responsibilities of the General Accounting Office, the Treasury Department, and each executive agency in accounting and reporting; and restated the auditing responsibilities of the General Accounting Office—authorizing audits to be performed at the site of agency operations.

Other significant Governmentwide legislation in this field included:

The amendments of the Antideficiency Act in Section 1211 of the General Appropriation Act for fiscal year 1951. This spelled out more precisely Bureau of the Budget and executive agency responsibilities for control of appropriated funds. It required each agency to establish a system of administrative control subject to approval by the Budget Director, and to report to the President and Congress any case in which money was used in excess of authorized limits.

To further strengthen fund controls, Section 1311 of the Supplemental Appropriation Act for fiscal year 1955 was enacted to improve the quality of obligation data, that is, firm commitments against appropriated funds. In this legislation, congressional committee staff, with the cooperation of the General Accounting Office and the Bureau of the Budget, developed statutory criteria by which the validity of an obligation is determined.

Public Law 84–798 was enacted in July 1956, to simplify agency accounting requirements and procedures for settlement of claims. This legislation was worked out by congressional committee staff and joint program representatives, based in part on a proposal of the second Hoover Commission.

The recommendations of that commission also led to passage of Public Law 84–863 in August, 1956. The combined efforts of congressional and joint program staff produced this legislation, which established in law the principle of using costs in preparing and executing a budget, and the requirement for developing agency accounting systems on the accrual basis to produce data on assets, liabilities and the results of operations.

With respect to individual agencies, joint program staff worked with Congress to develop several important laws passed during this same period. These included:

The Federal Property and Administrative Services Act of June, 1949, which created the General Services Administration. From the financial management standpoint, this law required monetary accounting for property and provided for General Accounting Office-General Services Administration-executive agency cooperation in establishing suitable systems for that purpose.

In August, 1949, the National Security Act Amendments of 1949 were passed. Title IV of that law outlined specific provisions for financial management in the Department of Defense. It called for comptroller organizations throughout the department, authorized use of working capital and management funds, directed adoption of performance budgeting, and provided for use of uniform classifications and systems.

One year later the Post Office Department Financial Control Act of 1950 was enacted. This law made the Post Office responsible for its own administrative accounting and reporting functions, and provided a solid foundation for establishing modern financial management systems in that department.

Meanwhile, the three central agencies took coordinated steps to lay out clearer ground rules and to make the financial systems in Government a more responsive tool of management. This was done either jointly or by each one in terms of its own responsibilities—as appropriate for each particular situation. The accomplishments of the past fifteen years are too numerous to recount. Examples can be given, however, of some of the more significant events that took place.

PROGRESS IN FEDERAL BUDGETING

Budgeting in the Federal Government has gone through tremendous changes in the past fifteen years—in both the kind of budgeting used and the way the annual budget is presented. Essentially, budgeting is a decision-making process in which responsible officials make determinations on what is to be done in relation to available money and other resources. This involves preparing plans, obtaining financing and carrying out approved plans in accordance with decisions made.

Broadly speaking, the Federal budget is a presentation to Congress and the general public of the President's judgment on a work program for the coming fiscal year and the financing needed to carry out his proposals. This plan is set forth in relation to the national economy, against a background of results of operations in the past fiscal year and a revised outlook for the year in progress. The Bureau of the Budget has the primary role in this process and is responsible for improving related management practices.

Probably the most far-reaching change in budgeting was the shift to the performance approach. This affected the entire process, including formulation, presentation and execution. It began in 1949, following a recommendation of the first Hoover Commission that the Federal budget present the programs to be carried out and identify the costs of those programs.

For many years, though some agencies gave supplemental information on activities or projects, budget requests centered on objects or things to be purchased, such as salaries, travel costs, payments for rents and utilities, etc. This gave no idea of what the items were to be used for, nor what the results would be. The idea of performance budgeting was to identify the nature and character of work performed, and to use that as the primary basis for decision making. Accordingly, the Bureau of the Budget refashioned the Federal budget for fiscal year 1951 to show programs and activities under each appropriation request and to introduce workload and other performance information in narrative form.

Agency budget presentations over the years concentrated on obligation information, showing when orders were placed. In carrying out an approved budget, agency financial systems were set up for detailed control of obligations, to keep from spending more than the limits set in congressional appropriations. This generally satisfied legal requirements. The systems did not, however, fully serve as a budget and management tool because they failed to develop financial information that would provide better disclosure and be more useful to managers in making operating decisions. Performance budgeting called for information on program costs and the value of available resources (money and materials on hand), as well as obligation and disbursement data. This would give responsible officials a better basis for management and provide an improved picture of program performance and the resources on hand in agencies.

As part of the conversion to performance budgeting, action also was taken to simplify the appropriation structure—under which Congress gives agencies authority to spend. With the approval of Congress, more than 200 appropriations were eliminated by changes and consolidations in the 1951 budget, followed by another reduction of over 50 items the following year. While retaining essential controls in Congress, these adjustments simplified the agencies' accounting job and permitted managers to use available resources more effectively in program operations. The Bureau of the Budget since has continued to work toward simplified agency appropriation patterns, attempting to maintain an appropriate balance between congressional control and agency flexibility in use of appropriated funds.

In addition, the programs established for the performance budget were set up within broad functional categories already in use. This permitted summarizing agency programs in major categories of services performed by the Federal Government. To improve the communication of such data to the general public, the Bureau of the Budget since January, 1950, has been issuing a "Budget in Brief"—a pamphlet that presents in popular form the most significant program and financial information in the annual budget.[2] Through these techniques the taxpayer is given a capsule picture of what he might expect in the way of performance during a fiscal year.

PROGRESS IN ACCOUNTING AND AUDITING

Accounting in the Federal Government also has changed significantly over the last fifteen years. One of the early and most important developments in the joint program was a change in the basic approach to accounting and financial control.

Today, managerial accounting is the major goal. This means fashioning accounting systems to develop accrual, cost and fund information that meets the operating needs of responsible officials at the various levels of management. At the same time, it seeks full disclosure and essential safeguards over all available resources. This contrasts markedly with pre-1948 emphasis on across-the-board uniformity and preoccupation with detailed fund controls, which generated unnecessary paperwork and duplicate recordkeeping. Of equal importance is the recognition that financial control must necessarily rest at the point of operations and be supplemented by a modern audit approach that serves higher level information and control needs.

The General Accounting Office has basic responsibilities in these areas. It has played a prominent role in developing and applying these concepts. ... One of the basic changes that emerged from early joint program activities was a shift in the General Accounting Office approach to its job of laying out accounting requirements for operating agencies. Authority for this was provided in the Budgeting and Accounting Procedures Act of 1950. It permitted the Comptroller General to prescribe accounting principles and standards to guide individual agencies in developing their own accounting systems, rather than to prescribe uniform procedures for use by all agencies.

The initial development work was done by the General Accounting Office, with assistance from the Treasury Department, the Bureau of the Budget and the operating agencies. Statements of principles and standards were progressively issued by the Comptroller General in the early 1950s.

---

[2] These reports are made available annually for a nominal sum (currently 35 cents) through the Superintendent of Documents, Washington, D.C.: U.S. Government Printing Office, 20402.

They were designed to provide a framework flexible enough to permit accounting to be fitted to the needs to be served, to stimulate the highest standards of accounting and financial reporting, and to encourage continued orderly improvement of all phases of Federal financial management.

The establishment of accounting principles and standards is not, however, a one-time action. The original statements ultimately were incorporated in Title 2 of the General Accounting Office Manual.[3] Revisions and additions have been made from time to time to reflect experience and later developments. Such changes will continue to be made.

The Budget and Accounting Procedures Act of 1950 provides that accounting systems developed by executive agencies shall be approved by the Comptroller General when he deems them to be adequate and in conformity with his prescribed principles, standards and related requirements. Procedures for obtaining such approvals are furnished in the General Accounting Office Manual.

At the end of fiscal year 1963, 133 organizations in civilian agencies had accounting systems that were subject to approval by the Comptroller General. At that date, complete systems in 46 of these had been approved; and parts of systems, covering such operations as payroll and property accounting, had been approved in 15 others. In the Department of Defense, only one complete accounting system has been approved—the one covering civil functions in the Army Corps of Engineers. Parts of systems have been approved in nine other instances, relating to such areas as pay and collection procedures.

Because of subsequent legislation and refinements in prescribed requirements, most systems approved the last fifteen years need reexamination and updating in the light of current requirements. For example, some of the approved systems do not incorporate accrual accounting to the extent contemplated by Public Law 84-863, approved in August, 1956. Therefore, while 46 complete systems have been approved by the Comptroller General as adequate in the light of legislation and conditions as they existed at the time of approval, this does not necessarily reflect the number that would be deemed adequate when measured against current requirements. In recognition of this situation, the General Accounting Office is considering a program of reexamining approved systems and, for those cases that do not meet current requirements, withdrawing approval until the necessary changes are made.

In fiscal year 1963, 15 complete systems submitted to the General Accounting Office for review or approval had to be returned to the agencies

---

[3]This manual, officially designated the *General Accounting Office Policy and Procedures Manual for Guidance of Federal Agencies,* is available on a subscription basis (which includes automatic distribution of changes as issued) for $15.00 from the Superintendent of Documents, Washington, D.C.: U.S. Government Printing Office, 20402; Title 2, "Accounting Principles and Standards of Internal Auditing Guidelines," may be subscribed to separately but currently is out of print pending revision.

because they did not meet current requirements. The principal deficiencies commonly found were:

> 1. A failure to design and operate the accounting systems in a manner appropriate for use of cost-based budgeting practices—particularly for internal management purposes.
> 2. A failure to convert to an integrated cost-based system and, in lieu thereof, adding supplemental procedures to produce accrual information at annual intervals.

PROGRESS IN CENTRAL FINANCIAL OPERATIONS

Many advances have been made since 1948 in the central financial operations of the Federal Government. With the Budget and Accounting Procedures Act of 1950 as the mainspring, the objectives have been to simplify the ways in which funds are made available for use; to establish a more efficient system of accounting for the Government as a whole; and to develop Governmentwide reports that provide full financial disclosure—in a way that best serves the users of the data.

Accounting operations in the Federal Government today bear little resemblance to those of 1948. Gone is the central papermill— and related red tape—that stemmed from outmoded legislation (some of which dated back to the eighteenth and nineteenth centuries). The former rigid requirements on operating agencies, which existed primarily to satisfy burdensome central fiscal needs, have been removed. They have given way to a simplified structure of broad summary central accounts, supported by agency financial systems that are set up basically to meet management needs at the agency level. This avoids duplication, places accountability for funds at the responsible level, and more efficiently provides better data for agency management and for central financial reports.

The Treasury Department is primarily responsible for the central accounting, reporting and related financial operations. ... The present central accounting system, installed progressively in the early 1950s, is based on reports of cash transactions by disbursing, collecting and administrative offices. Generally, it furnishes an accounting for all cash assets and liabilities, reflects expenditures in terms of either checks issued or cash payments and shows receipts on the basis of collections by collecting officers. This contrasts with previous practices, which provided for recording expenditures when checks were issued or paid and receipts on the basis of warrants and advices of deposit from banks.

One effect of this improvement was to afford a positive basis for reconciliation with transactions recorded in agency accounting systems. Another was to provide consistent data for use in various Governmentwide reports. To illustrate the latter, the annual budget used to include large unexplained adjustments to make budget totals agree with data shown in the Treasury central reports. Beginning with the 1954 budget, such adjustments were eliminated by reason of this change and coordinated action under the joint program.

In recent years, a number of changes have been made in ... [the annual combined statement of receipts, expenditures and balances] ... to produce a more informative presentation. These include, for example, an analysis of unspent appropriations to identify how much had been used to place orders and how much was still available for that purpose; information showing the use of foreign currencies, as reflected in a foreign currency accounting, control and reporting system put into effect by the Treasury Department in 1953; and a balance sheet as of the close of each fiscal year, showing the cash assets and liabilities of the Government as related to cash receipts and expenditures.

Basic current reporting of the nation's finances is accomplished through daily and monthly Treasury statements. Until February, 1954, only a daily statement was used to report on receipts, expenditures and the Government's surplus or deficit. Under that practice, considerable difficulty was experienced in trying to tie the data back to other Treasury and agency reports. A joint study of the problem led to adopting a policy of using a monthly as well as a daily report for this purpose. Under this policy, the daily statement shows only the Government's cash assets and liabilities in the account of the Treasurer of the United States, and related cash deposits and withdrawals; and the monthly statement reflects classified receipt and expenditure data plus the budget surplus or deficit. This change had the advantage of tying directly to the central and operating agency accounts, and permits accurate comparisons with other Treasury reports and budget estimates.

In 1961 a joint team of central agency representatives completed a study of Governmentwide financial reports. That team inventoried existing reports, identified the users and their needs and developed recommendations for a coordinated system that would adequately serve the users' interests. The most recent result of that study is *Treasury Circular No. 1073*, released in May, 1963. That circular established a new monthly report of gross obligations in the agencies, classified by object of expenditure. Such Governmentwide data were determined to be necessary for more effective analysis of the economic impact of Government operations on the private economy.

Another area substantially improved in recent years is the development of balance sheets in Federal agencies. This provides a good illustration of the interrelationships of various improvement actions of the joint program. Under the Governmentwide modernization program conducted by the Bureau of the Budget, the agencies are required to develop financial property information and other data used to prepare a balance sheet. The General Accounting Office principles and standards provide criteria for this work. *Treasury Department Circular No. 966* requires all agencies to submit balance sheets for their operations at the end of each fiscal year. This circular previously applied only to Government corporations and revolving funds, but was extended in June, 1956, to all operating agencies. The data furnished by the agencies in response to the circular are used in the Treasury Department's annual combined statement of receipts and expenditures, on a basis consistent with information reflected in the annual budget; and provide source data for information submitted by Treasury to the House Committee on Government Operations for use in its annual report on real and personal property owned by the Government.

PROGRESS IN STRENGTHENING STAFF RESOURCES

As the joint program moved ahead, it was recognized that the most modern financial management systems would be of little value unless qualified people were available to use the systems properly and keep them up to date. In other words, the system itself would not do the job; success depended on the people that operated the system. The revised financial management practices introduced since 1948 called for high calibre finance personnel who were "management minded," that is, staff who recognize that their responsibilities included seeking out the needs of program managers and fashioning efficient systems to meet program requirements as well as provide necessary fund controls.

The Civil Service Commission has primary responsibilities in the Federal personnel field, including classification standards and training. In view of the problems posed by adopting modern financial management concepts, the joint program joined with the Commission to bring about better job standards in this field and to improve the quality of financial personnel by introducing more extensive education and training activities.

PROGRESS IN AGENCY DEVELOPMENT OF SYSTEMS

The Budget and Accounting Procedures Act of 1950 placed greater financial management responsibilities in operating agencies and provided more flexibility for developing systems consistent with the objectives of that act. The joint program provided leadership and assistance in the transition from former rigidly prescribed practices and procedures.

While effective fund controls continued as a necessary requirement, the joint program emphasizes the need for developing improved management data and reorienting managers to control programs in terms of costs. In so doing, it stressed the idea of matching information produced by accounting systems with the data requirements of planning, budgeting and operating personnel. Overall, the end objective has been use of a single management system that conforms to requirements and is suited to the needs of agency management—one that instills a cost consciousness in agency staff and produces more efficient program results.

Progress toward this goal has been made since 1948, but much remains to be done. There is tremendous diversity in the size and nature of Government operations—as much as can be found in all private industry. This means many different kinds of systems are needed.

In the budget area, all agencies adopted program classifications as a necessary step to convert to performance budgeting. Since then, continued emphasis has been given to refining classification, adopting cost budgeting techniques and strengthening management along program and performance lines. This includes, for example, simplifying financing to give management more flexibility; installing planning practices to better allocate and control resources; and using meaningful financial and program data to more effectively present requirements and control planned operations.

Accounting improvement work in the agencies the past fifteen years centered on developing accounting as a more effective tool of management. Objectives include establishing systems that show results in terms of operating responsibilities and produce accurate and meaningful data suited to internal and external management needs. This involves adopting modern accrual accounting practices, establishing monetary property records, providing effective fund control information and developing cost data useful for better program management. Consideration also is given to efficiency of the system, with particular attention to the economies possible in data processing applications.

CHAPTER VI

SOME BEHAVIORAL CONTEXTS OF

PUBLIC FINANCE AND BUDGETING:

DIFFERENCES AND SIMILARITIES BETWEEN

PEOPLE AS DOMINANT THEMES

The study of human behavior must wrestle with two apparently contradictory strains. For genetic reasons, as well as philosophical ones in the Western civilizations, the uniqueness of the individual must be stressed. However, it is also clear that if people do differ in many significant ways, they are also similar in equally significant senses. Perhaps more precisely, many people in fact behave similarly under enough conditions that one would be foolish to insist in principle on the unmodified uniqueness of the individual. Such behavioral similarities in no way deny that people are also unique in significant senses.

There is no settling the tension between uniqueness and similarity. Behavioral science must continually seek generalizations that respect individual uniqueness. At the same time, however, behavioral scientists must frame their concept of human uniqueness in ways that do not require neglect of what is similar enough in nature that it cannot be ignored.

Public finance and budgeting similarly are in the differences/similarities business. The pieces reprinted in this chapter establish the point in diverse ways. By way of introductory support of the point, note only that budgets set goals. Immediately, then, the budget-maker is involved in balancing the differences and similarities of those people subject to the budget. Will any thousand individuals best respond to a "tight" budget and work frantically even though the budget is realistically unattainable? Or does Sam work best when he experiences the success of "bringing a project in under budget," and the more so the better as far as he is concerned? Setting a "loose" budget is appropriate in such a case, even

402

though it is unrealistically high. The practical difficulty of course, is that the budget-maker can seldom have it both ways. He must be acutely conscious of that point where enough people will respond similarly and positively to the standards he offers.

Chris Argyris' "What Budgeting Means to People" goes right to the heart of an important set of differences that characterize relations with budgeting and finance personnel in organizations. In short, those specially charged with responsibility for budgeting or finance are likely to see their activity in different ways than those performing other activities of which budgeting and financial considerations constitute only a part. What one sees, goes the shorthand version of the point, is determined by where one sits.

The differences between the perceptions of those in budgeting and line foremen often are sharp, as Argyris develops them. For example, he compares the perceptions of the two types of organization members concerning this theme: What are the uses of budgets? As might be expected, budgeting personnel see their activity as crucial and strategic. Budgeting is "the watchdog" of the firm. Consequently, it closely identifies with top management via supplying the data required for overhead control. Foremen have a sharply different view. Budgets tend to complicate the foreman's job of dealing freely with individual cases, and budgeting personnel are seen as uninformed and pretentious, and sometimes as malicious.

These differences in perceptions suggest the delicacy of relations of budgeting and finance personnel with other organization members, especially because perceptual differences are reinforced by a wider family of issues that could reduce effectiveness. Thus Argyris develops a list of major bones of contention between budgeting and line supervisors. Some of these complaints are pretty clearly what may be called "objective dilemmas." That is, they exist as an inherent part of budgeting and finance activities. The problems of handling objective dilemmas, whether more or less acute, will exist. Other difficulties may derive from "standard practices," that is, from established ways of doing things. Standard practices may be changed, of course. Thus this second class of difficulties may be sharply reduced if organization members are willing.

The variety of difficulties deriving from "objectives dilemmas" and from "standard practices" may be illustrated briefly. Patently, for example, budgeting and finance personnel monitor money. Since money is the lifeblood of all organizations, both business and government, budgeting and finance often will be where the heated action is. Examples cover a far broader range as well. Thus reports about meeting budgets must treat "ancient history." The interval during which the report is prepared may be shortened with "on-line" automatic data-processing equipment, but "ancient history" must be included. Other complaints are more or less clearly the results of "usual practices." That budget reports are full of "results" but few "reasons," for example, is often true but it also can be changed.

That there are no easy ways to solve the many issues faced by budgeting and finance personnel can be established briefly. Thus inherent issues will remain, of course. Their severity can be reduced, but only by getting mutual cooperation. Of course, the sharp differences in perceptions identified by Argyris suggest that getting cooperation will be difficult. "Usual practices" can be changed, but again only if free and open communication is possible. Sharp differences in perceptions close channels of communication, however, and perceptions are difficult to change. The magnitude of the challenge is plain.

Bold summary is possible. Given the sometimes-extreme differences in perceptions of budgeting people and those of foremen, the most reasonable prediction calls for considerable stress and inefficiency in coping with complaints, whether they derive from "objective dilemmas" or from "usual practices." The summary might have to be softened as the organization, the level, and the job are varied. What Argyris saw in four factories does not necessarily apply to Universal Organizations. Even with such qualifications however, striking commonalities exist between Argyris' results and many actual organizations.

Notice we are firmly back in the differences/similarities business, based upon the preceding summary paragraph. The point may be made explicit in two sentences. Students and practitioners can neglect only at their own peril the differences in perceptions that Argyris isolates. Nor can students or practitioners neglect the marked similarities between other organizations and those described by Argyris in his article.

Andrew C. Stedry provides useful elaboration on the differences/similarities theme. Excerpts drawn from his Budgetary Control and Cost Behavior variously approach the crucial role of "levels of aspiration" in budgeting. Stedry surveys the applicable literature and finds it wanting for his purposes. Consequently, he designed a laboratory experiment to test the validity of a variety of hypotheses about levels of aspiration, performance, and kinds of budgets.

The issues confronted by Stedry may be put in skeletal form. Basically, all people tend to develop "levels of aspiration," internalized standards of performance toward which they are committed to strive. "Estimates of performance" must be distinguished from levels of aspiration, in addition. For example, consider a major leaguer who could realistically be a .400 hitter in baseball. He might be motivated to extend himself only when he is below .350, however, his aspiration level in this case would be below his own realistic estimate of performance. Of course, estimates of performance may coincide with levels of aspiration.

There is no tentative raising of the issue of levels of aspiration. Immediately, a host of important questions begs for attention. What happens to his performance if an individual settles on a level that is easy to achieve? Or simply impossible? And do some people habitually overestimate or underestimate their actual performance? With what consequences in each case? Such questions imply great challenges to the behavioral sciences, and far outstrip the available answers in theory or practice, but such are the questions which daily confront budgeters and financial officers.

Fortunately, some useful behavioral benchmarks exist. For example, an individual will tend to decrease his level of aspiration in response to failure. The practical implications seem direct. Budgets ought not be so demanding that they preclude success. If budgets are impossibly high, individuals will tend to reject them. Levels of aspiration may be lowered, as a consequence, by an approach that seeks to raise them.

Despite our existing knowledge, much remains to be learned about the interaction of internal estimates of performance, internal levels of aspiration, and externally-imposed budgets. Consider only that in budgeting an external demand is more or less imposed on the individual to accept a specific level of aspiration. The situation is complex, for the individual may estimate that the required performance is unattainable under any conditions. In addition, even if the subject (S) estimates he could attain the budget goal, S's own levels of aspiration may be such that he is unwilling to do all that might be necessary to attain the external goal. Of course, S could accept the external goal as his own internal level of aspiration. The likelihood of his doing so will be a direct function of the specific management practices used in formulating and administering the budget.

Matters could be further complicated, but it should be clear that it is a glorious can-of-worms that Stedry must sort out. The excerpts below suggest the real progress he made, and they also should suggest the value of a full reading of the original source.

If nothing else, one of Stedry's findings reported below has triggered a useful airing of differing points of view. Thus Stedry notes that the experimental subjects (Ss) who performed best in his experiment were individuals who first received their "high" performance budget imposed by the experimenter (E) and then set their own aspiration levels. The worst performers were those Ss who first set their own aspirations and then were given E's "high" performance budget. Stedry explains:

> An hypothesis which might satisfactorily explain this phenomenon is as follows: The high performing group formed its aspirations with the high budget levels in mind, while the low performing group rejected the high budget after forming aspirations with relation to their last performance. ... (Alternatively), the stress, at least for some subjects, was so high that they may have been "discouraged" and may have ceased to try to improve performance.

Other possibilities also exist, but Becker and Green in their "Budgeting and Employee Behavior" pick up the theme that "participation" in the making of budgets "can lead to better morale and increased initiative." Their analysis usefully covers much ground, starting with the basic belief that "participation" is no panacea but that it can produce beneficial results under specified circumstances. Roughly, participation is one way of increasing the chances that an employee's level of aspiration will be more or less consistent with the demands and standards in an organization's budget. Without participation, a wide divergence of individual aspirations and formal goals is more likely.

Care must govern any conclusions about the efficacy of "participation," because the associated phenomena are complex. Becker and Green argue that sufficient employees respond similarly enough to "participation" that under specified conditions the student of organization for many practical purposes gives less attention to the differences that patently do exist between individuals. Directly, the management use of "participation" often can increase the likelihood that Ss will accept a budget as their own internal level of aspiration. The generalization does not hold (for example) for all individuals or all cultures, but it apparently applies quite broadly. Of course, participative techniques also could generate resistance to management's budget, as by permitting group forces to mobilize when employees come to feel that management is employing pseudo-participation whose results are only accepted when they coincide with management's desires. Participative techniques generally have more sanguine effects, however.

If Becker and Green stress the similarities between people in organizations this is no sign that our dual theme of differences-similarities can be scrapped. Thus Stedry's "Reply" to Becker and Green clearly indicates that significant differences still exist between observers of budgeting and aspiration levels, despite the commonalities that the three researchers share. Not to be outdone, Becker and Green respond to Stedry with "A Rejoinder to A 'Reply',"[1] which is not reprinted in this volume. Quite sharply, they indicate their own version of the differences they perceive between their position and Stedry's.

Thus this section must end as it began, coping with the apposition of differences and similarities of the various behavioral contexts within which public finance and budgeting are performed. Hopefully, more has been accomplished than following this section's own tail. Epigrammatically, the level of aspiration of this chapter has been to introduce the reader to some of the behavioral complexities that probably will be essentially unravelled within our lifetimes. Today, however, these behavioral complexities remain as massive experiential Everests that defy the scientific mountain-climber. No student of administration, to justify the attention given here, can today remain unaware that the complexities are there and must be conquered.

---

[1]Selwyn W. Becker and David Green, Jr., "Budgeting and Employee Behavior: A Rejoinder to A 'Reply'," *Journal of Business*, Vol. 37 (April, 1964), pp. 203–205.

WHAT BUDGETING MEANS TO PEOPLE

CHRIS ARGYRIS

The purpose of the study is to examine problems and to raise questions concerning the possible human relations effects budgets have upon supervisors. Because of the nature of the problem this study cannot present final solutions to problems, nor answer questions in any definitive way. It can merely define a wider aspect of the budget problem and suggest possible solutions. Each controller must light up these approaches with his own experience. In short, this study, the first of its kind attempted by the Foundation, is primarily exploratory.

Because of the indefinable limits of the human problems in this area, the research team decided to focus its attention on how the supervisors feel about budgets and how the finance people feel about the same budgets. The group sought answers to questions such as these.

1. How do the finance people see their job?
2. What problems do the finance people see in relation to factory people? What problems don't they perceive?
3. Similarly, how do the factory supervisors see their job?
4. What problems do factory supervisors perceive in relation to the finance people and/or budgets? What problems don't they perceive?
5. What similarities and differences exist between factory people and finance people with regard to values, attitudes, and feelings toward budgets?

WHAT BUDGET PEOPLE THINK ARE:

The Use of Budgets

To the budget people, budgets have an extremely important function in the organization as the "eyes and the ears of the plant." They provide the answers to most questions and the budget people see themselves as the "answer men" of the organization. Consider the following examples:

First let me say that budgets are the watchdog of this company. What do I mean by that? Two things: First, if we have profit, there's no problem; Second, if we are losing money, what can we do about improvement—any kind of improvement?

We guard the fields. The budget department has to constantly strive to improve the goods and make the plant better. There is always room to make things better.

Article is from *The Impact of Budgets on People*, New York: Controllership Foundation, 1954, pp. 2–21. Reprinted with permission of author and publisher.

There is, therefore, an important emphasis made on budget people constantly finding things that are "sour," looking for weaknesses and, in general, looking for things that are wrong, not right.

Another emphasis is equally important. All the budget people interviewed insisted that the errors found and the weaknesses uncovered should immediately be sent to top management.

> If I see an inconsistency, I'll go to top management and report it. No, I never go to the supervisor in charge. It is our job to report any inconsistencies to the top management.

Once the information is in top management's hands, it is up to it to take action. In other words, budget results are primarily top management control instruments.

Coupled with the task of finding weaknesses and reporting them to top management is a third emphasis on doing the reporting soon. Budget results can be effective only when they are "hot off the griddle." Whatever pressure budgets may generate to "motivate" a factory man to better his record would be lost if action was not taken immediately.

> It's our philosophy that we've got to get these figures to top management when they're hot. They're no good when the job is cold. As it is now, with our records, top management can get the factory supervisors together and do something right away.

A fourth emphasis is on using the budget as a means for putting pressure on operating supervisors.

> As soon as we examine the budget results and see a fellow is slipping, we immediately call the factory manager and point out, "Look Joe, you're behind on the budget. What do you expect to do about it?"
> True, he may be batting his brains out already on the problem but our phone call adds a little more pressure—er—well, you know, we let them know we're interested.

Finally, budget people believe that budgets present a goal, a challenge to factory people. They think that without budgets factory people would have nothing "to shoot for"—would lack the help of a great motivating instrument. For example:

> Production budgets set the goals. The budgets, yes, the budgets, set a challenge for those fellows (factory). It's something for them to shoot for. They need something to shoot for. All of us need a goal.

In summary, budget personnel see budgets as performing at least the following important functions:

> 1. They are a means to make things better. There is always room for improvement. Inconsistencies, errors, weaknesses are constantly being discovered, examined, and reported to top management.

2. Properly used, they are a means of instituting improvements quickly. Budgets are of most value when their results are in the hands of top management as soon as possible.

3. They are a means of putting pressure on factory supervisors.

4. They provide a goal, a motivating force for the factory people.

The Differences Between Their Outlook and That of Factory Supervisors

If the budget people see any important differences between the outlook of operating people and themselves, such information should be of value in ascertaining how "basic" are the causes of misunderstanding between the budget and production parts of the organization.

The results indicate that budget people see some very basic differences. For example:

> I would say that factory people have a different outlook on life. They tend to be more liberal toward others.
>
> The financial people, on the other hand, look at life more coldly. To them, it's all figures. The only thing they look at is what amount of money is involved. It's the total figure that counts.
>
> The factory supervisors' outlook on things is different. They emphasize today. Yes, they're looking at only the short run. We have to look at things in the long run. We have to see the whole unit. They worry about their individual departments.
>
> I think you'd almost say there are personality differences between factory and finance. We (finance) tend to approach everything with figures. We have to. We've been trained that way. Factory people approach it without worrying about costs.
>
> Yes, there are differences. We (finance) have been trained to see things as they are—to study them logically and systematically. We've been trained to look at a problem and say, 'Well, this is it, one, two, three, bang, that's it.'

The differences described above may be clues for understanding the human problems that arise. For example, if the factory supervisors are, in fact, only interested in the short run and if the budget staff does not see the short run as being crucial, then trouble will arise. Similarly, if the budget staff has a basically different outlook on problems from the factory supervisors, this difference will tend to increase disagreements.

Their Problems With Factory Supervisors

The budget people were asked to describe what they felt was the most difficult problem they faced in their relationships with factory supervisors. The majority of the replies fell into a very consistent pattern. The most pressing problem was "selling" budgets to factory supervisors. The budget people believed that the task was almost insurmountable. It was interesting to see that the three most often stated reasons for this problem with factory supervisors were (a) lack of education on the part of factory supervisors, (b) lack of interest, and (c) misunderstanding and/or mistrust of budgets.

409

Some of the Solutions to These Problems

Most of the solutions suggested by budget people seem to revolve around educating, or training, factory people in the appreciation and use of budgets.

These are some of the suggestions:

1. Supervisors should be taught the use and need for budgets in the company and specifically in their departments.

2. If possible, budgets should be explained so the supervisor would know exactly how and why budgets are constructed the way they are. Most finance people were quick to caution against overwhelming the factory man with minute details of financial "buzz words." (They all pointed out that the explanations should be kept as simple as possible.)

3. Closely connected with the above is the budget staffs' desire that factory people have more acquaintance with, and therefore respect for, the everyday problems of the finance staff in administering budgets.

4. Interestingly enough, most of the top controllers believed that the problems of administering the budget would not be alleviated until finance people, as well as factory people, changed. They felt that the budget people should be given a thorough course in self-understanding and in understanding and getting along with others—in other words, a course in human relations.

These, then, are the human problems involved in the administration of budgets and what can be done about them, as seen by the budget people.

WHAT FACTORY SUPERVISORS THINK ARE:

The Use of Budgets

Just how important are budgets and budget departments to factory supervisors? Each factory supervisor was asked to name the department which affected him the most and then the second most important. Fifty-seven percent considered production control as number one and forty-five percent chose the budget department as number one. Of the fifty-seven percent who picked the production control department as number one, all but one supervisor chose the budget department as the second most important department.

It seems relatively safe, therefore, to say that budgets wield an important influence in the production supervisor's world. Here are some typical comments:

Well, if you want to study a department that has its clutches everywhere, go into the budget department. That's all over this plant.

In general, the supervisors close to the employees hardly ever used budgets. In fact, they suggested that the best way to cause trouble was to mention a budget directly or indirectly to the employees. The supervisors higher up in the line of authority did use them. Of course, their usage varied, but in general the budgets were used. We shall see subsequently that the amount of use by upper-level supervisors was closely related to the way they handled their subordinates.

Use by Top-Factory Supervisors

We have seen that front-line supervisors are not able to use budgets freely with their employees. Top-factory supervisors, on the other hand, seem to use budgets quite frequently and strongly on the supervisors below them.

Clearly, the closer one is to the employees, the less one can use budgets to increase production or arouse interest in production. If such is the case, one begins to wonder about the supervisor who is in the position of receiving all the pressure from above, but cannot pass on the pressure to the people below him. Does all this pressure stay with the supervisor?

Budget Problems

Although there may be some differences among levels of supervision in the use of budgets, all the supervisors, regardless of their rank, were pretty much agreed concerning the limitations of budgets. Some of the limitations mentioned were:

Budget Reports Only Include Results, not Reasons. Perhaps one of the greatest criticisms of budgets was the fact that they never included the reasons why they were not achieved by a certain supervisor. There was considerable feeling about this problem. Supervisors disliked intensely the fact that their departments would look "sick" on the budget while the reasons for the "sickness" were never published along with the results.

> Budgets never show the reasons why they have not been met. They never take into account all variables that affect production.

The budget might contain the finance man's explanation: e.g., "The reason 'why' this budget has not been met is excess labor costs, or too much waste of time getting the job ready to be produced, etc.," but such reasons were not the real explanations as seen by the supervisors. They wanted the budget to state why they had excess labor costs, or why it took too long to get the job ready.

In other words, the supervisor's why was never included. Only the why of the budget man was included.

The following supervisor sheds additional light on the subject. It is interesting to note that he realizes why the budgets are not broken down further. But it is perhaps more interesting to note that even though he understands why budgets give only the total picture, he still feels quite strongly about them. Such data cannot help but lead one to wonder if a knowledge about budgets will really alleviate the feelings about them.

> As I see it, budgets are for top management. Top management is only interested in the total picture. They just want to see the results. They're just interested in knowing if the goal has been met.

411

The deviations, the headaches are all ironed out for them at the end of the budget. But, you can bet your boots, they are not ironed out for me. They remain, to remind me of the many things that can go wrong in my department. It's like this: I'm in the forest. I see hundreds of different trees (problems) that go to make it up. Top management is up in the air looking down on the forest. They see a mass of green. Now the budget measures that mass of green, but they don't tell the top management anything about the different trees that make up the green. You might put it this way—my job is to worry about the feelings that go to make up these figures. Finance peoples' job is to worry about the figures without the emotions.

Emphasis on History. Another closely allied problem is that budgets emphasize past performance. Budgets are historical documents. As such, they are used primarily to project some predictions about the future based on the past.

Factory supervisors, on the other hand, place little emphasis on the past and hardly ever have time to think of the future. Their emphasis is on the present day-to-day situation.

Rigidity of Budgets. In addition to the emphasis on the past, supervisors felt there was an equally negative emphasis on rigidity of standards. Once established, budget people seemed to dislike changing standards. Most budget people, the factory supervisors stated, were inflexible.

This rigidity of the finance people, as seen by the factory supervisors, leads to some important feelings on the part of the latter. For example:

I'd say one of the biggest problems is that budgets are set up on past performance. Once they come up with a figure, they hate to leave it. Two years ago, my budget on errors was 100, now it's 150, but our production has increased a lot more.

Somehow the budget people freeze the figures in their minds and they just don't want to change.

Budgets Apply Pressure for an Ever-Changing Goal. One of the more important criticisms the factory people had was the feeling that the people who set the budgets were never satisfied. For example:

If I meet this budget, those guys up there will only raise it. Or, You can't let them know that you made the budget without too much trouble. If you do they'll up it as sure as hell.

These were typical remarks made by most of the factory supervisors. (In no case did the top-factory supervisor consider this to be a criticism.) It was quite obvious that the factory supervisors wondered when, if ever, the optimum level would be reached. For example:

They make a budget and then constantly increase it. There's too much of that constant raising and raising that thing. Pretty soon the boys catch on and figure out it's the same old stuff. So they don't respond.

The Implication that Budgets Motivate Supervisors to Do a Better Job. As we have seen earlier, the finance people perceive budgets as

412

goal-setters for factory supervisors. They feel that the supervisors are "kept on the ball" because of budgets. Some finance people suggest that factory supervisors would be "lost" without budgets. On the other hand, factory supervisors resent quite strongly being thought of as people who would lose their motivation if it were not for budgets.

Some of them agreed that budgets had a function of helping them accomplish their work, but few if any saw budgets as the creator of their motivation. To accept budgets as motivators is to imply that supervisors do not have adequate interest in their jobs. This is seen as an insult to a man's integrity and the factory supervisors resent it strongly. For example:

> I don't care much for budgets. I can use them, but I don't need them. My job is to get out the production, and I do the best I know how. What do I need budgets for? Now budgets can't help me in that.
> Budget! Well, I know this is the way the other fellows feel about it. They don't want to be bothered with them. We do our job, and we do the best job we can. That's it. No matter what comes out, we know we've done our best.

Budgets Are Not Realistic. Another important criticism made by factory supervisors was that some budgets were purposely kept high so that they were almost impossible to meet. The supervisors definitely and sincerely resent this practice. They resent it primarily for two reasons:

Such a practice places a supervisor in a situation where he can never succeed. One supervisor expressed this when he said:

> There's not much sense in setting a budget that's too high. What good is it? If a man doesn't meet it, he's going to say, 'to hell with it.' It's going to get him to think they're never satisfied. If you ever want to discourage a guy, just give him a budget you know he can't meet.

Such a practice implies that the company does not believe the supervisor's own desire to do a good job is sufficient to meet reasonable budgets. The unrealistic budget is used to spur supervisors on, but it does not work and is resented.

The Differences between Their Outlook and That of the Budget People

In the first part of this article some differences in outlook between financial people and factory people as seen by the financial people were described. What are the differences in outlook as seen by the factory supervisors?

The first four basic differences as seen by the factory supervisors have already been discussed. They were:

1. Finance people are primarily interested in the past and the future. They don't think of the present.
2. Finance people tend to be too rigid once they have set up their figures.

413

3. Finance people see only the total picture. They never see the many problems that go to make up the total picture. They worry only about end results.

4. Finance people tend to see life only as a set of figures. They take the emotions out of life and deal only with the cold figures.

Some other differences have not been previously mentioned:

5. Finance people cannot see the other person's point of view. They know almost nothing about the problems a supervisor is faced with daily.

6. Finance people have a language of their own. It is completely different from the language of the shop.

7. The final difference is more in the area of attitudes. It was best expressed by one supervisor who said:

A big problem with budget people, and all finance people for that matter, is that basically they are—well, let's see, yes—sarcastic.

I think that they think they're the whole show. If you're asking for our opinions, we think they have an overexalted opinion of their position.

Solutions to Some of These Problems

1. By far the most frequent and most stressed recommendation made by factory supervisors was that the finance people should learn to see the other person's point of view. The supervisors recommended that the finance people be given a "taste" of factory problems. Some typical comments were:

They are not fully acquainted with our everyday production problems. They don't realize our troubles and our difficulties. The best thing to do is to bring them down and see our problems.

I'd tell you what I'd teach them: to know my job. See the problems I have. Bring them down here and see what really goes on.

2. The financial people should undergo some training to learn that budgets are not final. They are merely opinions. One supervisor stated:

Yes, I could recommend a good thing. I wish they could have their thinking about budgets changed. They are too rigid. Budgets are statements of opinions not facts. That's their big trouble. They think budgets are facts.

3. The financial people should change their belief that the employee is lazy and wants to do as little work as possible. For example:

I'd like to see them change their attitude that employees are not out to get them (budget people) and do as little work as they can get away with.

4. Closely related to recommendation (3) above is one that recurred often: Finance people should change their belief that the best way to raise production is through pressure.

5. Financial people should be taught that they are not superior to factory supervisors. Some typical comments:

I'd deflate their ego—I'd give them something to take them down a peg.

BUDGETS AND FORMING LEVELS OF ASPIRATION

ANDREW C. STEDRY

Having established the need for a particular kind of budget whose aim is control, as opposed to planning or forecasting, it is now desirable to investigate the relationship between the control budget figure and actual performance.

... A "good" control budget is one which produces "good" results. If it is desired to minimize cost in a given department, and if a budget of $1000 produces a cost of $1001, and a budget of $300 produces a cost of $1000, the latter is a better budget. The magnitude of the budget figure is unimportant other than in terms of its impact on cost.

The budget is a goal imposed on an individual, who shall be called a "department head," by his supervisor or supervisors (management). To its attainment are occasionally attached positive rewards, but more frequently, negative rewards are attached to its nonattainment. If it could be assumed that the department head took the budget as his personal goal and worked toward this goal with maximum effort, the criterion of budget control for a single individual would be trivial—i.e., choose a cost goal at the technological minimum for the operation and let him work toward it. It is not difficult to visualize the effects of such a goal in practice. If there is negative reward attached to its nonattainment, some change must be made in the system or the department head will resign, be discouraged, or possible simply sabotage and oppose the system, perhaps soliciting the help of others to form a group for this purpose.[1] Regardless of the amount of positive reward attached to its attainment, the expected value of reward, statistically speaking, is zero; and the net expected value of rewards and penalties is negative.

In practice the budget may exist on paper at the technological minimum, and doubtless some budget or engineering departments may make just such forecasts for their own guidance. But in actual execution it is usual to secure assent of persons who are to be controlled so that some deviation or adjustment may be applied to this figure. This means that there is some "acceptable" level of cost which, in general, will be above the theoretical optimum. If cost descends below this level the performance is rated as meritorious, but if cost is above this level then there is an implied criticism

---

Article is from Andrew C. Stedry, *Budget Control and Cost Behavior*, ©1960. Reprinted by permission of Prentice-Hall, Inc., Englewood Cliffs, New Jersey.

[1]Cf. Chris Argyris, *The Impact of Budgets on People*, New York: Controllership Foundation, 1954.

which may receive explicit form when this fact is called to the department head's attention, and an investigation of causes supplemented by a report (perhaps by outsiders) may ensue. Reprimands, promotion passover, and dismissal are possibilities.

It is a postulate of this thesis that unwritten "acceptable levels" are the common bases of control budgets. Alternatively, there may be an acceptable rate of approach to the technological optimum, which in practice becomes the control element, and the cost level is then determined from the acceptable rate of improvement of the control budget.

Another hypothesis whose logic and empirical content will be investigated is that *a stationary budget[2] is not an effective control budget*. If the budget level is never attained, then some other criterion is in fact replacing it as a control element. If the level is consistently attained, the question of the possibility of consistently obtaining operation at a lower cost will never be answered, because there is no incentive to improve performance. If a level is obtained part of the time, either it must drift toward consistent attainment or nonattainment, or the percentage of the time it will be attained will become stable at some value which produces an acceptable balance of positive and negative reward for the department head. Another and related issue is whether anyone whose performance displays such characteristics would strive for the same reward balance at a lower budgeted cost level. It is part of the task of this thesis to provide a formal basis against which such questions may at least be asked (as they are not in the present literature) and thereby provide a start towards a formal theory of budgetary control. In particular, it is proposed to deal minimally with the question of budgetary level setting in order to focus on the dynamics which center about the question of when (and how) a budget should be changed.

THE BUDGET AS A DETERMINING FACTOR IN FORMATION OF ASPIRATION LEVELS[3]

When management presents the department head with a budget, it can only present its goal. It is a hypothesis of this thesis that management can increase the tendency of the department head to aim at or below this goal by increasing the positive reward associated with its attainment and/or increasing the negative reward associated with its nonattainment.

Management can enforce absolute compliance with the budget by dismissal for noncompliance. After this policy has been in effect for a short

---

[2] I.e., a budgeted cost for a given operation which does not change over time.

[3] My initial contact with aspiration levels was aided immensely by William H. Starbuck and his excellent survey of the field (W. H. Starbuck, "Level of Aspiration Theory and Market Behavior," Pittsburgh: Carnegie Institute of Technology, Graduate School of Industrial Administration, Behavioral Theory of Firm Project, Working Paper No. 7, November, 1957).

time, management would retain only the department heads who aimed at or below the budget and were successful at achieving their aims. It would seem, however, that for this procedure to be in operation without a decimation of supervisory personnel, the budget levels would need to be set for above expected cost in order to allow for random fluctuations. Such a procedure seems unlikely to cause the department head to drive his costs far below the budget, since safety will take priority over innovation. The fear of a lowering of the budget if he performs too well will undoubtedly dominate a desire to impress management with superior performance.[4] Barring this undesirable procedure, the budget may be considered at best a candidate for the department head's goal but more generally as one factor which operates in its determination. This level of cost toward which the department head strives will be termed his *aspiration level*.

EXISTING MODELS OF ASPIRATION LEVEL DETERMINATION

The definition of aspiration level which will be used here is consistent with the definition of J. D. Frank: "The level of future performance in a familiar task which an individual, knowing his level of past performance in that task, explicitly undertakes to reach ... "[5].

The assumptions of the model can best be comprehended in the following set of postulates for the behavior of a hypothesized department head.

1. If there is a *discrepancy* between the *expected actual level of expenditure* and the *aspired level of expenditure,* he will attempt to reduce this discrepancy by moving his aspiration level toward the actual level at a rate which depends on the size of the discrepancy.

2. In addition to the effect caused by the discrepancy, the *aspired level of expenditure* will be lowered in response to a lowering of the *budgeted level of expenditure.*

3a. The department head will be *encouraged* if the discrepancy (actual expected cost minus aspired cost) does not exceed some positive value known as the *discouragement point.*

3b. The department head will be *discouraged* if the discrepancy exceeds the *discouragement point* but does not exceed a larger value known as the *failure point.*

3c. If the value of the discrepancy exceeds the *failure point*, the system will cease to exist, or a new one will come into being; "the department head will resign."

4a. If the department head is *encouraged,* he will attempt to reduce a positive discrepancy by reducing the *expected actual level of expenditure;*

---

[4]Cf. C. I. Barnard, *The Functions of the Executive,* Cambridge: Harvard University Press, 1954.

[5]J. D. Frank, "Individual Differences in Certain Aspects of the Level of Aspiration," *American Journal of Psychology,* Vol. 47 (1935), p. 119.

he will react to a negative discrepancy by allowing expected cost to rise.[6]
The rate of reduction or increase depends upon the size of the
discrepancy.

4b. If the department head is *slightly discouraged*, he will reduce the
discrepancy by reducing expected cost at a lower rate relative to a given
discrepancy than he would if encouraged. If he is *moderately discouraged*,
he will allow expected cost to increase, but at a sufficiently small rate
that the discrepancy will not be increased. If he is *extremely discouraged*,
he will allow expected cost to increase at a rate which increases the
discrepancy.

Postulate 2 describes a situation in which the budget is a figure about
which there are several auxiliary points, each of which defines a particular
set of rewards. Using the Simon model of aspiration level determination, the
department head will find a point at which the rewards are "satisfactory."
He will then study the relationship of this point to the budget, find out
about how much it changes for a given change in the budget, and then
change his aspiration level accordingly, responding to changes in the budget.
Postulate 1 is essentially Lewinian in nature, in that the department head
may be interpreted as responding to a positive discrepancy as a reduction of
the perceived probability of success of the original aspiration, adjusting his
aspiration level in the direction of increased probability of success. The
discrepancy between the expected actual level of expenditure and the aspired
level of expenditure is appropriately termed a measure of *stress*, since clearly
the department head's "emotional tension, produced by frustration,"[7] varies
with the size of the discrepancy. A compromising of goals is a well-known
reaction to stress,[8] and hence postulate 1 may be interpreted directly as a
stress-reducing mechanism without considering the existence of subjective
probabilities.

Postulate 4a describes the department head as exhibiting another
"normal" form of reaction to stress—striving to improve performance. A
primary assumption of this model is that man is an improvable animal and
that, given sufficient motivation, cost reduction is a possibility. J. G. March
and H. A. Simon (Organizations, New York: John Wiley & Sons, Inc.) have
confined their discussion of improvement to an increase in search behavior.[9]
It is assumed here that improvement is possible through increased experience

---

[6]If a multiple commodity or multiple cost structure was hypothesized, it would be
assumed that negative stress in one area would direct attention to another. Cf. W.
Edwards, "Probability-Preference in Gambling," *American Journal of Psychology*, Vol. 66
(1954), pp. 349–364, and note chap. iii, p. 54, of this thesis.

[7]F. Ruch, *Psychology and Life*, Chicago: Scott, Foresman and Company, 4th ed.,
1953, p. 154.

[8]*Ibid.*, p. 162.

[9]But Cf. *Handbook of Experimental Psychology*, chap. xiii, Neal E. Miller,
"Learnable Drives and Rewards," where this same kind of search for improved situations
is ascribable to fear and anxiety ["Learnable Drives and Rewards," in *Handbook of
Experimental Psychology*, S. S. Stevens (ed.) New York: John Wiley & Sons, Inc., 1951, pp.
435–72].

with the task, diverting of effort from nonorganizational goals, development of increased "cost-consciousness" (diverting of effort from other organizational goals in which there is less stress), or mere harder work—all of which may be considered part of or in addition to search behavior. Postulate 3a notes a limitation on the amount of stress which the department head can tolerate and still devote his efforts to cost reduction at maximum effectiveness.

Postulate 4b describes the various stages of withdrawal within the range of stress denoted by postulate 3b. Caused by sublimation or ineffective effort due to stereotypy of response, the department head will be less successful in reducing costs. The neurotic response of extreme discouragement will eventually lead to ultimate withdrawal (postulate 3c), provided some change does not occur within the system. The assumption that exceeding the discouragement point will evoke one of only three types of behavior depending on the individual department head is made for the sake of simplicity rather than necessity.

To comprehend the more complex situations which are likely to be encountered in practice it would undoubtedly be necessary to complicate the model, and this would, in turn, vitiate the objective of simplicity and clarity which is a *sine qua non* of a theoretical formulation at this stage of scientific work in budget control and cost behavior. But simple as it is, the analysis here presented does present some highly plausible clarification. For instance, once the department head's goal-setting pattern has been established, a static budget will tend to produce stationary expected cost, subject only to random variation about an expected value, in a viable ongoing situation. It is evident, furthermore (and psychological considerations appear to be strong enough to warrant this conclusion), that management cannot choose a rate of budget reduction for a particular department independent of considerations of the motivation structure of the department's head. Although this would appear to be obvious, the emphasis in today's literature is on budgeted costs and their relation to technology and not on their relationship to the individual being budgeted.[10] Technological constraints are an additional factor which must be considered, but technology,[11] important though

[10]E.g., I. W. Keller, *Management Accounting for Profit Control*, New York: McGraw Hill Book Company, Inc., 1957, p. 98, states that, "The setting of standards is the responsibility of the technical staffs of a plant such as industrial engineers, design engineers, and chemists," although he later concedes that the foreman must agree that the standard is "fair." The problem of what to do if agreement is lacking, or what proportion of standards should be made to come into the area of questionable "fairness," is not related to the motivations of the individual concerned.

[11]In the literature of theoretical economics such technological factors (in the form of a production function) are accorded preponderant importance. But it must be remembered that the economic theory of the firm is based on a highly simplified model of the firm's "human" structure which, in turn, is justified by the fact that this model is designed primarily for analyzing "market" or general economic behavior and not the behavior of agents within a single firm.

it may be, does not obviate the necessity of also considering in any measure motives in a budgetary system which ultimately depend on some real consensus for their implementation. It is paradoxical that those who criticize mechanistic approaches to accounting (e.g., the research which treats human beings as servomechanisms[12]) fall into the trap of mechanistic approach themselves when applying (or explaining) rules of thumb to the problems of budgetary control.

The mathematics used in this chapter (and the logic with which it is associated) has been directed primarily to laying bare (and clarifying) certain issues which, though sometimes recognized in practice, are often concealed—or go completely unattended—in the existing literature on budgeting.[13] Certain by-products have also been achieved which will be explored in various ways in the chapters that follow. Thus certain issues involved in the strategy of setting budgets have been uncovered and related to each other in a way which related certain major factors to one another. Thus the budgeted amounts of the person to be controlled have been related to his actual cost performance with the aspiration levels acting as an intervening variable. Moreover, possible interactions between aspiration levels and cost performance have been examined. Finally, the objectives of those who seek to influence cost performance have been brought into the analysis, via the budgetary variables, in a way which raises most issues of strategy relative to the objectives of central management and thereby brings to the fore certain questions which are germane to adequate performance of the controller's office, as that office is now conceived.[14]

It is obvious, for example, that blanket budget reductions which are common in government bureaus and similar cost-saving "drives" in large corporations on a plant-wide scale are of dubious merit. Furthermore, the treatment of all subordinates "impartially" when it comes to budget demands, which essentially means treating them equally, regardless of their motivation structure, appears not only irrational from the cost standpoint but from the standpoint of welfare of the subordinates as well. For example, if a man at middle management level is directed to cut his budget, he may be able to "push" one man whose discouragement point is high to the limit

---

[12]*See*, for example, R. N. Anthony ["Cost Concepts for Control," *The Accounting Review*, Vol. 32, No. 2 (April, 1957)], who (rightfully) states that, "Human control systems cannot be so easily or so precisely designed as mechanical or electrical ones." Although he rejects the servomechanical analogy, he can only offer in substitution such comments as, "The method of constructing costs for control purposes is governed by management policy."

[13]Cf. e.g., J. B. Heckert, *Business Budgeting and Control*, New York: The Ronald Press Company, 1946. J. H. MacDonald, *Practical Budget Procedures*, Englewood Cliffs, N.J.: Prentice-Hall, Inc., 1939. This literature is almost completely occupied with the mechanics of budgeting to the point where it has assumed an almost standard form of presentation and development.

[14]Particular reference is made to the "control," as distinct from the "service," function in the sense in which these two terms are used in the controllership literature.

and by so doing avoid discouraging a few others whose discouragement points are lower, thus preserving morale and reducing costs further than he could by behaving "impartially." More specifically, if management desires to behave consistently over time, it must choose a more modest rate of budget reduction for the man who is easily discouraged than for the man who appears perpetually enthusiastic. Given two men with the same discouragement point, management must avoid discouraging the man who "when he is bad, is horrid," whereas the man who "when he is bad, is still slightly good" and doesn't give up easily can be kept on the verge of resignation for best cost results.

The models explored in this chapter indicate that an increase in stress, up to a point, is desirable in the reduction of costs. The assumption that standard costs must be "attainable," which pervades the current budget literature, is based on the assumption that the people who operate under them must be satisfied if they are to turn out a reasonable but unexceptional performance. But under even the very simple assumptions of the models in this chapter, it is evident that this need not be the case. Under certain circumstances the cost expected to be obtained by a department head must be above his aspirations in order to ensure that he will work diligently toward reducing costs. Insofar as budgets affect his aspirations this kind of behavior must be taken into account; references to "loose" and "tight" budgets, with blanket approvals of the latter and condemnation of the former, as is common in the literature,[15] are not an adequate basis for dealing with this problem. Pending an explicit quantitative characterization in particular circumstances, the equations used in the models of this chapter have at least established a provisional qualitative characterization which suggests, instead, that budgets should be set rather in a way which allows an effected department manager to achieve his aspirations part of the time. In conclusion we note that this opens a rather broad range of questions concerned with the value of accuracy and timeliness of accounting (as distinct from budgeting) reports in terms of both their immediate and ultimate consequences for cost behavior.

If, as is sometimes said, "Control exists in the minds of men rather than the books of account," then the theoretical model of this chapter helps to highlight and formalize the kinds of psychological concepts that need to be considered. Of course such formalisms, however logical or elegant, are not enough in and of themselves to justify a theory. An empirical foundation is greatly to be desired or, failing this, some kind of testing and validation is required. Apart from the study of Argyris[16], which does not really deal with the central problem of cost responses to budgetary control procedures, there

---

[15]Some authors entirely dodge this issue by favoring only "accurate" budgets, failing to make clear whether they are speaking of the budget as a planning instrument or a control instrument.

[16]Argyris, *op. cit.*

is (unfortunately) no systematic accumulation of evidence where the desired empirical foundation can be readily secured.

Failing access to a broadly based and systematic series of studies of managerial behavior under different budgeting arrangements, the following seem to be the best immediate alternative sources of empirical information: (1) studies that have been made of worker reactions to various incentive pay schemes, and (2) psychological (laboratory) studies (e.g., in aspiration level theory) which are more or less germane to the topic of interest. After these topics have been discussed in the sections immediately following, attention may be turned to one other source of information and possible validation. This information will be reported in the form of a laboratory experiment designed explicitly for the purpose of testing salient aspects of the theory which has now been advanced.

The studies presented in this chapter provide a crosssection of the evidence available about human behavior which might be applicable to an individual in a budget-controlled activity. More, of course, could be presented, but it is hoped that this brief survey will at least provide some background for the analyses and experiments which will be dealt with in the following chapters.

To summarize, there is evidence that individuals form either individual goals or estimates of their performance (or perhaps both). On the other hand, it is not precisely clear which of these is being formed at any given instant. These aspirations (or expectations) tend to be decreased following a failure in a previous trial in the same task, or increased by a success in that task. The aspirations are affected by external reference points other than performance, but this effect tends to decrease as experience with the task increases. (However, the effects of rewards have not been clearly determined.) The aspiration level is subject to change with success or failure on related tasks, but it is not clear whether the effects can be explained by stimulus generalization or by similarities of need.

Animal studies of motivation are a potential source of information, but the problems of inference relating them to human behavior are not solved even in general, so that use of information gleaned from these studies is of dubious value for the subject with which this thesis deals.

Experiments in utility maximization have used, as a basic premise the "rationality" of man. On the one hand, these studies are by and large oriented only to an individual's tastes and performance. On the other hand, there is no universal agreement on the basic postulates. Furthermore, these experiments have been conducted with amounts of money whose expected values are, as Dreze notes, in danger of being regarded as trivial by the subjects. This further attenuates the results secured (since they become even more difficult of extrapolation to an actual situation) and, hence, tends to reduce the reliability of conclusions that might otherwise be drawn.

Field studies have shown conflicting results, and only isolated examples of studies which indicate the possibility of introducing an adequate control scheme appear. A further weakness (from the standpoint of this study) is that almost all of the more substantial studies in this area have been directed primarily towards the behavior (motives, etc.) of production workers, as distinct from budgeting or budgeted management.

Business experience, though voluminous, tends to be so loosely phrased (or reported) and to contain such a mixture of complex and unresolved factors, that little can be gained, at this time, by a recitation or analysis of this experience. It therefore has seemed best to confine the presentation here to a single instance where the management has at least been more articulate than most. It is interesting—although, of course, not decisive—that this company (the Lincoln Electric Company) has issued its series of pronouncements in a form which is not wholly incompatible with the theory covered in the preceding chapter.

The brief survey of received evidence, analyses, and hypothesis (i.e., the survey just concluded) does not reveal any body of material which is sufficiently pointed either to validate or even to give satisfactory guidance for a theory of budgetary control of the kind which is of interest here. With this in view, an experiment was designed to see what could be uncovered by the laboratory techniques of experimental psychology when these are combined with the principles and tools of modern statistical inference, as exhibited by the theory of experimental design, and the tools provided by the analysis of variance, etc.

In the experiment which will now be reported, a major objective was to investigate relations that might exist between individual performance and aspiration levels and the relations that might also exist between these variables and the kind of "external"[17] goals which are represented by a budget of the kind commonly employed in management practice.

The results of the experiment have shown that performance in a situation where the attainment of a goal is rewarded and its nonattainment penalized is significantly affected by the type of budget chosen, the conditions of administration, and the way in which aspiration levels for the task are determined.

The experimental results indicate that an "implicit" budget (where the subject is not told what goal he must attain) produces the best performance, closely followed by a "medium" budget and a "high" budget. The "low" budget, which was the only one which satisfied the criterion of "attainable but not too loose," resulted in performance significantly lower than the other budget groups.

However, there is a strong interaction effect between budgets and the aspiration level determination grouping. The group of "high" budget subjects who received their budgets prior to setting their aspiration levels performed better than any other group, whereas the "high" budget group who set their

---

[17]*See* remarks in Existing Models of Aspiration Level Determination section regarding stress.

aspirations before receiving the budget were the lowest performers of any group.

An hypothesis which might satisfactorily explain this phenomenon is as follows: The high performing group formed its aspirations with the high budget levels in mind, while the low performing group rejected the high budget after forming aspirations with relation to their last performance. However, aspiration level data indicate that the low performing group had a much higher goal discrepancy so that, if anything, their goals were closer, on the average, to the budget than were the high performers.

The low performing group also had a very high achievement discrepancy score. If achievement discrepancy is interpreted as a measure of stress, this would give rise to an alternative hypothesis—viz. that the stress, at least for some subjects, was so high that they may have been "discouraged" and may have ceased to try to improve performance.

A major difficulty is involved in the use of achievement discrepancy scores. This results from the functional dependency of such scores upon performance. For example, a constant aspiration level would produce a negative correlation between achievement discrepancy and performance (ignoring the trivial case where performance equals aspiration level throughout). This conceptual deficiency of the current state of psychological theorizing makes it difficult to establish a causal relationship between this discrepancy and performance—as hypothesized in this model. It is, however, significant that the ordering of the stress (achievement discrepancy) corresponded fairly closely to the ordering of performance in spite of the opposing effect of the functional dependency.

It is also observed from the analysis that the size of the achievement discrepancy can be affected significantly by the size of the budget, a result which is consistent with the requirements for the validity of postulate 2 in the model of this chapter.

The investigation of the goal discrepancy also indicated a significant budget effect, and this again tends to corroborate postulate 2 since in the continuous model the two discrepancies are indistinguishable. A somewhat surprising (even though not statistically significant) effect is also present. This is the tendency of the groups who formed their aspiration levels without knowledge of the budget to come closer to their budget than is true for the group which had the advantage of the budget information supplied to them. A possible explanation is that a moderate departure from the budget can come about gradually in the groups that form aspirations first, while a departure in the other groups (since the budget is associated with reward) is likely to be a large shift downward.

The types of aspiration levels, under the procedures used, did play a part in performance differences. This was to be expected. But the fact that it did not play a part in the discrepancies which occurred requires some explanation. One possibility is that the greater variability of the aspirations noted in the aspirations of the β subjects (who did not have the budget when forming their aspirations), in spite of roughly the same average aspirations, may have produced a greater number of discouraged subjects (who had aspired to extremely high levels). In the group whose aspiration levels tended to remain close to the budget, there were relatively few extremely high or low discrepancies. Hence this group would tend to exhibit high but not intolerable levels which, according to postulates stated earlier, would lead to high performance as well.

Although not conclusive on the point, the study does shed some light on participative schemes of budgetary management insofar as these are connected to aspiration levels. The group which determines its aspiration level first, in the experimental situation, is closest to the solution proposed by MacGregor. He suggests that the department head should plan his budget and then take it to his supervisor who will give him his budget based on his estimate. The experimental data raise some questions as to the universal validity of this recommendation, for under the experimental situation if "management" decides on a "high" (performance) budget, its use of MacGregor's participation plan coincides with the worst possible result. On the other hand, it would probably help performance in a "low" budget situation.

This summary of the findings may now be concluded by a few observations on the causal connection between stress and performance. As already noted, the experiment did help to separate and distinguish between goal discrepancy and achievement discrepancy. The best that the data and subsequent analyses will bear on the subject of "stress" suggests only the possible use of achievement discrepancy as either a surrogate or a direct measure of stress. The value of the achievement discrepancy as a measure of stress is dubious and the effect of stress and/or achievement discrepancy on performance requires further documentation before such usage is fully warranted.

BUDGETING AND EMPLOYEE BEHAVIOR

SELWYN W. BECKER AND
DAVID GREEN, JR.

Writing in *Number, the Language of Science,* Tobias Dantzig observed: "The concrete has ever preceded the abstract. ... And the concrete has ever been the greatest stumbling block to the development of a science. The peculiar fascination which *numbers as individuals* have exerted on the mind of man from time immemorial was the main obstacle in the way of developing a *collective* theory of numbers, i.e., an arithmetic; just as the concrete interest in individual stars long delayed the creating of a scientific astronomy.[1]

And so it has been with budgeting, where for some there is still question on whether or not a theory has developed. Business budgeting is a twentieth-century innovation; its development has been characterized by a fragmentary literature and an emphasis on technique. A review of its history indicates that progress has largely been through learning from mistakes—a "cut-and-try" approach. In this paper we will review this history as a background toward an understanding of the relation of the budget to the motivations of those who effect and are affected by it. In a sense this will be an excursion—an attempt to determine "what the behavioral scientists can tell us or find out for us about ... the impact (of budgets) on people and on their aspirations."[2] In the process, we will point out that the attempt to make use of motivational factors in the budgeting construct raises many difficult and imperfectly understood problems. Further, we will attempt to explain why the style of managerial leadership is of critical importance in the choice of budget procedures—an issue largely overlooked. Also, we will consider the role played by the communication of performance results and the timing of budget revisions.

In the United States, budgeting by state and local government started with the municipal reform movements around the turn of the century. At the outset, the budget was viewed as an instrument of control—"control over the officers ... of administration by placing limitations on their authority to spend."[3] These early budgets were, and for the

---

Reprinted from "Budgeting and Employee Behavior" by Becker and Green by permission of The University of Chicago Press, Vol. 35, October 1962, pp. 392–402. © University of Chicago Press, 1962.

[1] 4th ed., New York: The Macmillan Company, 1956, chap. iii.

[2] David Solomons, "Standard Costing Needs Better Variances," *National Association of Accountants Bulletin,* Vol. 43, No. 4 (December, 1961), p. 30.

[3] Frederick A. Cleveland, *Chapters on Municipal Administration and Accounting,* New York: Longmans, Green & Co., 1909, p. 72.

most part still are, authorizations to spend—appropriations—for particular "objects of expenditure" such as personal services, commodities, travel, and the like. The appropriation was the "upper limit" much like a thermal control on a furnace—when the limit is reached the fuel, or, in the fiscal sense, the money is stopped. The upper limit was imposed through the approving of the budget by the governing body—the board, the council, the legislature, etc.

These governmental budgeting procedures provided for a second type of control—a restraint control. Each claim presented had to be approved for payment by the chief financial officer. The question of "what is a legal or bona fide obligation?" was resolved by considering (1) whether the budget document provided for such an expenditure, (2) whether sufficient funds were left in the appropriation to pay the claim, and (3) whether the necessary documents were on hand. To know if the remaining appropriation was sufficient, fairly elaborate records were maintained. To these were posted the dollar amounts of issued purchase orders as well as the specific expenditures.

Both types of transactions reduced the "available" balance. This was a practice of *clerical* control—a technique employed to insure the completeness of record and one that is still unique to governmental accounting (with the possible exception of retail "open-to-buy" records). To the extent that interim reports were prepared and distributed to department heads, rudimentary *communicative* control was practiced.

Governmental purposes were served well enough by these budget procedures. Revenue and expense forecasts were relatively simple. Because changes were not contemplated, the budgets were for fixed amounts for the designated time period. Where actual revenues fell short of the estimates, unilateral demands to cut expenditures by a designated percentage were issued—sometimes by resort to payless paydays.

Early business budgeting largely imitated governmental practice and technique. It began with "imposed" budgets[4] and the obvious controls—limit, restraint, clerical and communicative. During the early and middle 1930's, it became fashionable to speak of "budgetary control" and to view the budget as both (1) a financial plan and (2) "a control over future operations."[5] Also in the thirties, the inadequacies of the static budget became obvious when business activity took a sharp downturn and profits disappeared.[6]

---

[4]Imposed budgets have been characterized as ones "dictated by top management without the full participation of the operating personnel" (R. N. Anthony, "Distinguishing Good from Not-So-Good Accounting Research," in *Proceedings of the 22nd Annual Institute on Accounting,* Columbus: Ohio State University, 1960, p. 68).

[5]Eric Kohler, *A Dictionary for Accountants,* Englewood Cliffs, N.J.: Prentice-Hall, Inc., 1957, p. 75.

[6]F. V. Gardner, "How About That 1935 Operating Budget?" *Factory Management and Maintenance* (November, 1934); C. E. Knoeppel and E. G. Seybold, *Managing for Profit,* New York: McGraw-Hill Book Co., 1937, p. 206.

A budget form that provided for intraperiod changes in the level of sales or manufacturing was introduced and was called a flexible or variable budget. It attempted to provide "bench mark" numbers for a range of contemplated activity.

Primarily, budgetary control has been the attempt to keep performance at or within the acceptable limits of the predetermined flexible plan. In a sense the plan controls—but for how long? And how is the plan to be modified?

BUDGET PERIODICITY

The recurring cycle of early governmental and business budgets was simple. The budgets were imposed, there was performance, and the comparison of the performance against the budget influenced the next budget. The cycle could be depicted as follows:

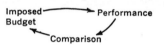

Ordinarily, the budget period was one year or two. The comparison of performance and budget often had curious results on the subsequent budget. Where expenditure was less than budget, there was a tendency to revise the subsequent budget downward. As a result, managers would engage in a spending spree the last few weeks of an appropriation year to avoid being cut down next year.

The budget period in business has also been calendar oriented—the quarter or twelve-week period extended twelve or fifteen months. Ordinarily, budget revisions are restricted to future periods. Later in the paper we will discuss reasons for cycling budget revisions on a basis other than the calendar.

BUDGET MODIFICATION

By 1930 it was recognized in business circles that imposed budgets "resulted in some dissatisfaction and advice was given to prepare them in the departments and have them revised or edited in the central offices."[7] Thus *participation* was introduced into the budgeting construct. It has been said that the "real values of participation at all management levels . . ., aside from better planning are the psychological values that accrue as the result of participation. A high degree of participation is conducive to better morale and greater initiative".[8]

---

[7]*Budgetary Control in Manufacturing Industries*, New York: National Industrial Conference Board, 1931, p. 52.

[8]B. H. Sord and G. A. Welsch, *Business Budgeting*, New York: Controllership Foundation, Inc., 1958, p. 97.

There is some evidence of the extent (and degree) to which participation is currently employed in business. Sord and Welsch interrogated managements of thirty-five companies to determine the level at which principal budget objectives were developed. No companies said they used totally imposed budgets. Six firms (17 percent) prepared objectives at higher levels and allowed subordinate managers to consider and comment on them before final adoption. Twenty-nine firms (83 percent) said they requested subordinate managers to prepare their own goals and objectives for review and approval at higher levels.[9]

Theirs obviously was a very small sample. Furthermore, it is questionable that the interrogatories used did, in fact, investigate participation. As Chris Argyris discovered, there is such a thing as "pseudo-participation." "That is, participation which looks like, but is not, real participation."[10]

Participation may have great value in improving budgets by drawing together the knowledge diffused among the participants, although we do not treat this objective here. Our interest is in participation as a useful technique for dealing with the psychological problems of employee satisfaction, morale, and motivation to produce; that is, the belief that increased participation can lead to better morale and increased initiative. The evidence supporting this belief will be evaluated, as well as other psychological effects associated with participation that may be of even greater importance. But first the question: What is participation? We will use the following definition: Participation is "defined as a process of joint decision-making by two or more parties in which the decisions have future effects on those making them."[11]

Participation
↓
Budget
↓
Performance
↓
Comparison

A collateral question: How does the introduction of participation affect the budget cycle? At first glance, it seems that the chart would appear as follows:

However, we believe this is too simple. Participation adds a separate "psychological path." Participation is *not* a single-value variable but rather is a concept encompassing several explicit variables. Instead of a simple cycle we have a sequence that might be depicted as follows:

---

[9] *Ibid.*, p. 95.

[10] *The Impact of Budgets on People,* New York: Controllership Foundation, Inc., 1952, p. 28.

[11] J. R. P. French, Jr., J. Israel, and D. As, "An Experiment on Participation in a Norwegian Factory," *Human Relations,* Vol. 13 (1960), p. 3.

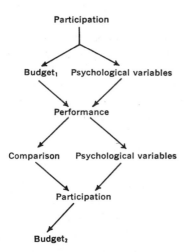

In paragraphs that follow we will attempt to identify these unspecified psychological variables by examining what we consider to be the relevant available research results. Before proceeding it is imperative to make one fundemental point: *Participation is not a panacea.*[12] Indeed, there is evidence to suggest that it is inappropriate in certain "environments." When participation is employed, the concept of control, as outlined above requires modification. Instead of the budget being the plan to which performance is conformed, compared, and evaluated irrespective of changes in environment (other than those provided for in the flexible budget), the plan is influenced, at least in part, by the environment. That is, control limits and informs those operating under the budget; in turn, they determine and limit the succeeding budget.

PARTICIPATION, MORALE, AND PRODUCTIVITY

In an industrial setting Coch and French investigated the effects of prior participation on production after work changes were introduced.[13] Difficulty of work and percentage of work changes were equated for a no-participation group (NP); for participation by representation (PR); and for a total participation (TP) group. With a prechange standard of sixty units per hour, after relearning, the NP group reached a level of fifty units per hour; the PR group sixty units per hour; and the TP group sixty-eight units per hour, or an improvement of about 14 percent over the standard rate. Another important finding was that 17 percent of the NP group quit their jobs in the first forty days after the change, and the remaining members of the group filed grievances about the piece rate, which "subsequently was found to be a little 'loose.'" There was one act of aggression against the supervisor from the PR group, none from the TP group, and no quits in either the PR or TP groups.

If employee turnover and stated grievances can be taken as a measure of morale, then it seems clear that the two groups that participated in the

---

[12]A useful discussion—"Participation in Perspective"—appears as chap. ix in *The Human Side of Enterprise* by Douglass McGregor, New York: McGraw-Hill Book Co., 1960.

[13]L. Coch and J. R. P. French, Jr., "Overcoming Resistance to Change," *Human Relations*, Vol. 1 (1948), pp. 512–32.

initiation of change were better disposed toward their job situations than was the no participation group.

Based only on this study one cannot decide if participation directly increased incentive to produce, as measured by subsequent productivity, or only improved morale, which in turn led to increased motivation. This is a point worth considering since morale is not perfectly correlated with productivity.

An inference about this relationship can be drawn after examination of a study by Schachter *et al.* on group cohesiveness and productivity.[14] (Group cohesiveness is usually defined as attraction to the group—desire to become or remain a member—and reluctance to leave the group. Another way of looking at cohesiveness might be the amount of "we" feeling generated in an individual as a result of his association with others.) Schachter and his associates experimentally created high and low cohesiveness in two groups. A task was chosen in which output could be easily measured. In half of each group subjects were individually given instructions designed to induce production at a high rate; the other half instructions designed to induce production at a low rate. It was found that group cohesion and acceptance of induction were significantly related. The high-cohesive groups more frequently accepted induction than did the low-cohesive groups. This was especially true of the negative induction, or "slow-down" situation.

The Coch and French study suggests that morale and/or productivity are enhanced as a result of employee participation in the initiation of change. The Schachter *et al.* study suggests that with participation held constant (all groups worked under constant conditions) change in productivity is related to group cohesiveness. Cohesiveness, it can be seen from the definition, is related to morale. Morale is most frequently defined as satisfaction with one's job, supervisors, and working associates. It has also been defined as the *degree* to which an employee identified himself as part of the organization. In either case morale and cohesiveness with a group imply some similar reactions and attitudes toward an organization or group.

Since participation affects morale (cohesiveness) and productivity, but cohesiveness without participation affects production, the most likely conclusion is that cohesiveness is dependent on participation but that changes in productivity are more directly related to cohesiveness.

ELEMENTS OF PARTICIPATION: PROCESS AND CONTENT

Let us consider participation as conceptually divisible into process and content. Process means the *act* of participating with the possible consequences stemming from the act; content is the *discussion topic* toward

---

[14]S. Schachter, N. Ellertson, D. McBride, and D. Gregory, "An Experimental Study of Cohesiveness and Productivity," *Human Relations*, Vol. 4 (1951), pp. 229–38.

which are generated the positive or negative attitudes. The *act* of participating enables the participants to know one another, communicate and interact with one another—conditions that easily can lead to increased cohesiveness. As we have seen, however, increased cohesiveness also can result in lower production if that is the sentiment of the cohesive group. Thus it becomes clear that the content of participation is an important determinant of final production levels. What should the content consist of and what should it accomplish? These questions can be answered on the basis of some data on group decision-making collected by Kurt Lewin and his students.[15] One experiment was designed to induce housewives to use previously unused foods (sweetbreads, etc.). Positive communications describing the foods were presented to two groups; one by the lecture method, the other by a group-discussion method. A subsequent check revealed that 3 percent of the women who heard the lectures served one of the meats never served before, whereas after group discussion, 32 percent served one of the meats. This experiment was repeated with a different leader, different groups, and a different food—milk—and yielded essentially similar results.

As compared to individual instruction and the lecture method, group discussion was superior in inducing change—a result attributed to the hesitancy of individuals to accept goals that depart from the group standard. Psychological nonacceptance of a goal by an individual virtually precludes its attainment by him.) The group-discussion method allows the group member to assess the standards of all other members so that, if the group apparently accepts a change, he too can accept it and retain his group membership.

It is clear that the content of participation should be directed toward setting a new goal with discussion of a sort sufficient to enable each participant to realize that the goal is accepted by the others in the group. The fulfillment of these conditions could serve as a definition of successful participation by (1) providing the opportunity for enough interaction so that a cohesive group can emerge and (2) directing the interaction so that each participant's analysis of the content will enable him to accept as his own those goals adopted by the group. Thus, we can see that the process and content of a participation program interact, and that such interaction can lead to one of several outcomes:

1. High cohesiveness with positive attitudes (goal acceptance), a condition of maximally efficient motivation;
2. Low cohesiveness with positive attitudes, an unlikely but possible condition that probably would result in efficient performance;
3. Low cohesiveness and negative attitudes, a condition resulting from unsuccessful participation that would tend to depress production within the limits of the integrity or conscience of each individual; and

---

[15] "Studies in Group Decision" in D. Cartwright and A. Zander (eds.), *Group Dynamics*, Evanston, Ill.: Row Peterson & Co., 1956, pp. 287–88.

4. High cohesiveness and negative attitudes, the occurrence most conducive to a production slow-down.

Level of Aspiration and Performance

Ideally, in the budgeting process, participation results in a plan of action including a proposed amount of accomplishment and an estimate of the costs to achieve it. If participation has been successful, then these proposed levels of cost and accomplishment are accepted as goals by the participants. In effect, these projected levels of achievement become the levels of aspiration of the managers of the organization. (In a smoothly running organization the managers induce acceptance of the same levels of aspiration in the members of their departments.)

Level of aspiration has been defined in the psychological literature as a goal that, when just barely achieved, has associated with it subjective feelings of success; when not achieved, subjective feelings of failure.[16] From an extensive review of the literature Child and Whiting summarize many findings into five conclusions:

1. Success generally leads to a raising of the level of aspiration, failure to a lowering.
2. The stronger the success the greater is the probability of a rise in level of aspiration; the stronger the failure the greater is the probability of a lowering.
3. Shifts in level of aspiration are in part a function of changes in the subject's confidence in his ability to attain goals.
4. Failure is more likely than success to lead to withdrawal in the form of avoiding setting a level of aspiration.
5. Effects of failure on level of aspiration are more varied than those of success.[17]

Recently Stedry has utilized this psychological variable in an attempt to establish some relations between level of aspiration, imposed budgets, and subsequent performance.[18] Stedry, not a psychologist, may have overlooked some of the relevant psychological literature. Seemingly he selected an inaccurate method of measuring aspiration level which weakens his several conclusions and recommendations. For his measure of level of aspiration, Stedry asked his subjects to express what they "hoped to achieve" on the next set of problems. Festinger found that the D score (the difference between performance and aspiration) was greater between performance and expressions of "like to get" than between performance and expressions of

---

[16]K. Levin, T. Dembo, L. Festinger, and Pauline Sears, "Level of Aspiration," in J. McV. Hunt (ed.), *Personality and the Behavior Disorders*, Vol. 1, New York: Ronald Press Co., 1944, pp. 333–78.

[17]J. L. Child, and J. W. M. Whiting, "Determinants of Level of Aspiration: Evidence from Everyday Life," in H. Brand (ed.), *The Study of Personality*, New York: John Wiley & Sons, 1954, pp. 145–58.

[18]Andrew C. Stedry, *Budget Control and Cost Behavior*, Englewood Cliffs, N.J.: Prentice-Hall, Inc., 1960.

"expect to get."[19] Diggory found the correlation between "hope" statements before and after failure significantly higher than statements of expectations before and after failure.[20] In other words, "hope" and "expect" represent different attitudes. Since level of aspiration is defined as the goal one explicitly undertakes to reach rather than the goal one hopes to achieve, it seems clear that Stedry's conclusions are based on an inaccurate measure of his major variable. Subsequently, Stedry has indicated his belief, based on questionnaire information, that his "subjects appeared . . . to have given the right answer to the wrong question."[21] In any event, his attempt is valuable heuristically because it highlights a possible relation between budgets, budgeting, and human motivational performance.

We have already hypothesized a relationship between participation and the formation of levels of aspiration. There remains a specification of the effects of level of aspiration on the remaining segments of the budget cycle.

After the budget has been adopted, the attempt to translate it into behavior constitutes the performance part of the cycle. The degree of effort expended by members of the firm as they attempt to achieve budgeted goals is partially dependent upon their levels of aspiration. Maximum effort will be exerted to just reach an aspired-to goal. In fact, according to level of aspiration theory if, for example, five units of effort are required to reach goal $x - 3$, ten units to reach goal $x - 2$, fifteen units to reach goal $x - 1$, and twenty-five units to reach goal x, the level of aspiration goal, an individual will expend the disproportionate amount of energy to achieve at level x to derive that subjective feeling of success. Thus we can see how a budget that is partially derived through a successful program of participation can result in greater expenditure of effort on the part of employees to reach goals specified in the budget.

Such expectations are not without foundation, of course. Bayton measured the levels of aspiration of three hundred subjects of roughly equivalent ability prior to their performance on seven arithmetic problems. He found that subjects with higher levels of aspiration followed with higher performance.[22] From a finding of this sort one cannot conclude that greater motivation to achieve is associated with the level of aspiration goal, but it is well known that increased motivation leads to increased effort, a condition usually followed by an increase in performance. We can thus find indirect support for our contention. Another bit of evidence may illustrate the point

---

[19]L. Festinger, "A Theoretical Interpretation of Shifts in Level of Aspiration," *Psychological Review*, Vol. 49 (1942), pp. 235–50.

[20]J. C. Diggory, "Responses to Experimentally Induced Failure," *American Journal of Psychology*, Vol. 62 (1949), pp. 48–61.

[21]Stedry, "Aspiration Levels, Attitudes, and Performance in a Goal-Oriented Situation," *Industrial Management Review*, Vol. 3, No. 2 (Spring, 1962), p. 62.

[22]J. A. Bayton, "Interrelations between Levels of Aspiration, Performance and Estimates of Past Performance," *Journal of Experimental Psychology*, Vol. 33 (1943), pp. 1–21.

further. Siegel and Fouraker set subjects to bargaining under bilateral monopoly conditions.[23] With no control of levels of aspirations, the subjects maximized their joint profits and split the profits nearly equally. However when high and low levels of aspiration were induced into the bargaining pairs (despite the fact that a better bargain meant more money for the subject), those with a low level of aspiration gained only about one-third of the joint profits. Thus, it seems clear that level of aspiration not only describes a goal for future attainment, but also it partially insures that an individual will expend a more-than-minimum amount of energy, if necessary, to perform at or above that level.

Depending, then, on the conditions under which a budget is drawn the budget can act as a motivating force and can induce better performance from the members of the organization. On the other hand, the budget can specify aims and goals so easy of attainment that the organization's members will be induced to produce at less than their usual capacity.

After the performance phase of the cycle a comparison is made between the costs and income previously predicted in the budget and the actually attained income and costs. We are not here concerned with how the comparison is made but rather with its utilization, since that may have considerable effect on employee behavior and morale.

Much has been written on the effect of communication within an organization. With reference to the comparison, or control, function of the budget, the use or misuse of communication can be critical especially when viewed in the context of participation and level of aspiration.

First and foremost, it is imperative for each participant to know whether he should feel subjective success or failure. If he is not informed of the results of the comparison he cannot know whether his striving for a particular level was worthwhile or not. Nor can he, in turn, pass on the word to his subordinates in whom he induced specific levels of aspiration. They, too, will not know whether to feel success or failure. We can see that communicating knowledge of results acts, in this case, as reward or punishment. It can serve either to reinforce or extinguish previous employee behaviors. Where subjects were given a learning task and provided knowledge of results, learning increased; but when knowledge of results was withheld performance fell, that is learning not only stopped but performance was decreased.[24] In discussing these results, Munn argued that "the rapid drop in performance which followed this point may be attributed to the loss of motivation which came with withdrawal of knowledge of results, not from forgetting what had been learned up to this point."[25]

---

[23]S. Siegel, L. Fouraker, *Bargaining and Group Decision Making*, New York: McGraw-Hill Book Co., 1960.

[24]J. L. Elwell and G. C. Grindley, "The Effect of Knowledge of Results on Learning and Performance," *British Journal of Psychology*, Vol. 29 (1938).

[25]N. L. Munn, *Psychology*, Boston: Houghton Mifflin Co., 1946.

Failure to communicate knowledge of results adversely affects not only performance but also morale. Leavitt and Mueller, in an investigation of effects of varying amounts of feedback, found that task accuracy increased as feedback increased. They also found that zero feedback is accompanied by low confidence and hostility while free feedback is accompanied by high confidence and amity.[26]

The question may now be asked: "So what if the employees don't know how they did? They already performed and the profit is recorded." The answer obviously concerns the effects this lack will produce on subsequent behavior and, more specifically, on the goals to be set in the succeeding budget.

The next budget will be affected because omitting feedback not only precludes certainty regarding a previous level of aspiration but also affects the subsequent level of aspiration. Most generally an individual will raise his level of aspiration after success and lower it after failure.

In the budgeting cycle, after the comparison phase, the new budget is started. The participating supervisors bring to the new participation situation all their new aspirations resulting from past feelings of success or failure. If they have been deprived of a rightfully achieved feeling of success, their subsequent aspirations are likely to be lowered. This could result either in a less efficient budget, that is, lower goals than could easily be achieved or, after disagreeable argument, an imposed budget from an adamant management. In the first case succeeding performance will be unnecessarily low; in the second, participation will be ineffectual with the possible result of poor performance and, almost certainly, lower morale. The *proper* budget cycle then is really a dual, interacting sequence of budgeting and psychological events. It can be depicted as follows:

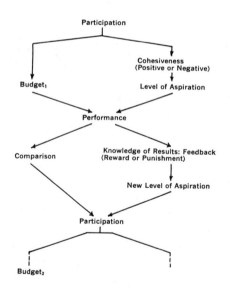

A successful participation budget does two things: (1) It induces proper motivation and acceptance of specific goals, and (2) It provides information to associate reward or punishment with performance. These lead

---

[26]H. J. Leavitt and R. A. H. Mueller, "Some Effects of Feedback on Communication," *Human Relations*, Vol. 4 (1951), pp. 401–10.

to new aspirations and motivations that set the stage for the next participation budget.

CONCLUSIONS

An understanding of the psychological variables stemming from participation is valuable, perhaps, for its own sake, but it is hardly likely to provide concrete assistance in a decision to institute such a program. We have seen that participation can lead to either increased or decreased output. It is not unlikely that the setting in which participation occurs is one determinant of the production outcome. Some organizations can be characterized as operating under relatively authoritarian leadership. By definition, participation is essential to democratic process and very probably is antithetical to an authoritarian organization. To illustrate the latter, assume that the various department heads participate in the decision-making process, prepare a budget, only to have it rejected by upper management without explanation other than that a more satisfactory budget is necessary. The best prediction here is that the participating group will be highly cohesive and hold negative attitudes toward management, a precondition to lowered output.

It is also likely that under authoritarian management status differences will be rigidly adhered to. If the participants in the budgeting process occupy different status levels influence on decisions will be directly related to status— the more status the more influence. Status differences would probably mitigate against high cohesiveness. Presumably status differences that did not affect the decision-making process would not preclude either a cohesive group or positive goal acceptance, especially if the occupants were secure in their positions or perceived the possibility of upward mobility.[27]

We do not wish to enter the controversy over the relative merits of various styles of leadership but merely wish to point to some possible limitations on the use of participation. In order to be successful, the participants must participate, that is, must have influence on the adopted decisions. If participation can be achieved under more or less authoritarian conditions, it is likely to be effective, just as it can be undermined (by disregard) with democratic leadership. Only management itself can determine whether it is worthwhile to initiate or continue the participation segment of the budgeted cycle.

At any rate, presuming an organization has determined that it can benefit from participation, are the psychological effects such that participation simply can be "grafted" onto existing procedures or are other changes

---

[27]Harold H. Kelley, "Communication in Experimentally Created Hierarchies," *Human Relations*, Vol. 4 (1951), pp. 39–56.

necessary? Or indeed, if no changes are necessary, are there any that can be made so that efficiency, motivation, and productivity will be enhanced?

Suggested changes in budgeting are not difficult to find. Stedry, recognizing the possible motivating forces produced by budgets, seems to suggest that "phony" budgets be prepared while the real budget is kept secret.[28] The "phony" ones would be designed to induce maximum motivation through a manipulation of level of aspiration. This plan would require different phony budgets for each department and, indeed, for each individual. If different budgets are viewed as discriminatory and unfair devices, company morale might suffer. Further, if already disgruntled employees learn that they were striving to attain phony goals the effectiveness of future budgets, real or phony, might be seriously impaired.

A knowledge of the effects of level of aspiration may lead to changes designed to increase employee motivation and output. The budget cycle characteristically is tied to an arbitrary time schedule. Even with no other information, this is defensible logically and perhaps economically as well. If, however, the budget is to be used as a control device (in the sense of prohibiting excessive expenditures) as well as a motivating device, then it clearly should be tied to the level of aspiration cycle rather than to a time schedule. We know that success leads to a rising level of aspiration and, generally, failure to a lowering. Failure can also result in "leaving the field," that is, psychological or physical withdrawal from the goal-oriented environment.

It is suggested here that much more frequent comparisons of performance and budget be made, including feedback to the employees of the results of the comparison. This recommendation is made for the following reasons: (a) If the performances meet or slightly exceed expectation, then level of aspirations will rise and budgets can and should be revised; otherwise employees will perform at the budget level when they could be performing at a higher budget level. Maximum efficiency can only be achieved by revising the budget upward. (b) If performances are just slightly below the budget expectations, budget changes are not necessary, but feedback is so that employees will continue to strive for the budget goals. (c) If performances are well below the budget, it may be well to revise the budget downward. If such revision is not made, employees' level of aspiration will fall, the budget will be viewed as unattainable, and output will fall. The danger here is that levels of aspiration and output may fall much more than is necessary. If the budget is revised downward just enough so that it is perceived as being attainable, then maximum output will be achieved again.

---

[28]*Budget Control and Cost Behavior*, pp. 5, 17, 41–42, and 71. Stedry does not use the term "phony."

BUDGETING AND EMPLOYEE
BEHAVIOR: A REPLY

Andrew C. Stedry

In their article "Budgeting and Employee Behavior" Selwyn W. Becker and David Green, Jr.,[1] present an amalgamation of psychological and accounting theory. The authors are concerned with the problem of employee response to budgetary modification and state that, for them, a major "interest is in participation as a useful technique for dealing with the psychological problems of employee satisfaction, morale, and motivation to produce; that is, the belief that increased participation can lead to better morale and increased initiative" (p. 394).

Implicitly in this quotation and explicitly in the following discussion they state that as fundamentals of their approach (a) "*participation is not a panacea*" [italics in original]. Indeed, there is evidence to suggest that it is inappropriate in certain 'environments,' and (b) that "participation is *not* a single-value variable but rather is a concept encompassing several explicit variables" (p. 395). It is not clear how, reasoning from these fundamentals, they arrive at a set of conclusions which, among other statements includes:

> A successful participation budget does two things: (1) it induces proper motivation and acceptance of specific goals, and (2) it provides information to associate reward or punishment with performance. These lead to new aspirations and motivations that set the stage for the next participation budget [p. 401].

The difficulty may lie in their assumptions about possible relationships between morale and motivation as they affect productivity and between participation and productivity within a framework of an organizational leadership style.

This commentary, while upholding the two fundamental points, questions the assumptions and the conclusions which rest upon them. For the moment, let us take "participation is not a panacea" and the following quotation:

> We do not wish to enter the controversy over the relative merits of various styles of leadership but merely wish to point to some possible limitations on the use of participation. In order to be successful, the participants must participate, that is, must have influence on the adopted decisions. If participation can be achieved under more or less authoritarian conditions, it is likely to be effective, just as it can be undermined (by

Reprinted from "Budgeting and Employee Behavior: A Reply," by Andrew C. Stedry by permission of The University of Chicago Press, Vol. 37, January 1964, pp. 195–202. © University of Chicago Press, 1964.

[1] *Journal of Business*, Vol. 35 (October, 1962), pp. 392–402. Page references to this article are given in parentheses in the text.

disregard) with democratic leadership. Only management itself can determine whether it is worthwhile to initiate or continue the participation segment of the budgeted cycle [p. 401].

In spite of some possible ambiguity in the above statement it seems almost impossible for them to advocate participation without entering the leadership-style controversy. Indeed, they had earlier stated, "By definition, participation is essential to democratic process and very probably is antithetical to an authoritarian organization" (p. 401). In view of the clear implications provided by Becker and Green that participation should be a part of budgeting practice (even though qualified occasionally to the effect that it should *really* be participation and that other changes—apparently in leadership style—may be necessary for success), it would seem to be of value to discuss some of the relevant literature.

LEADERSHIP STYLES AND PRODUCTIVITY IN BRIEF

While the evidence is generally mixed, several studies support the view that organizations with authoritarian structures are more effective in task performance than democratic ones. Experiments by Leavitt using the network apparatus developed by A. Bavelas indicated higher morale but lower productivity where communication patterns for problem solution offered more organizational freedom and individual autonomy—that is, democratic prototypes—than in more hierarchically structured patterns—that is, authoritarian prototypes.[2] Also using the Bavelas networks, Guetzkow and Dill found that part of learning to perform the experimental task was the development of a hierarchical (more authoritarian) structure with few communication channels and a rationalized leader from a less structured (more democratic) communication pattern with more avenues of communication.[3] Further experimentation of Leavitt (unpublished) indicates that those groups which began with a less structured organization, although they in effect chose their own leader, never "caught up" in performance with those groups which had initially been more hierarchically organized.

Such evidence is not, however, restricted to the laboratory. Morse and Reimer varied closeness of supervision of clerical workers.[4] One group's supervision was altered to a looser, more autonomic structure, while a second group's supervision was made closer and more detailed. While in the first group the workers had higher morale and exhibited more involvement and

---

[2]H. J. Leavitt, "Some Effects of Certain Communication Patterns on Group Performance," in Eleanore E. Maccoby, T. M. Newcomb, and E. L. Hartley (eds.), *Readings in Social Psychology*, New York: Henry Holt & Co., 1958, pp. 546–63.

[3]H. Guetzkow and W. R. Dill, "Factors in the Organizational Development of Task-oriented Groups," *Sociometry*, Vol. 20 (1957), pp. 175–204.

[4]Nancy Morse and E. Reimer, "The Experimental Change of a Major Organizational Variable," *Journal of Abnormal and Social Psychology*, Vol. 52 (1956), pp. 120–29.

commitment in their work than the second, marked improvement in productivity was observed in both groups with the more closely supervised group's improvement significantly *greater*. Several surveys have indicated that successful supervisors are more frequently observed among those who spend more time in supervisory activities, in particular in planning and skilled tasks, than in working with the men or other nonsupervisory duties.[5]

Further corroboration may be obtained from the work of Fiedler, who found in a variety of situations that leaders who remain distant and aloof from their subordinates are more successful than their counterparts who form close personal ties with (i.e., "relate to") their work groups.[6] While these results are again in the form of survey data, they are somewhat stronger than most inasmuch as the aloofness score utilized might be interpreted as a measure of a "conditioning variable" whose relative size remains fairly consistent across individuals in a variety of situations—that is, there are "high-aloofness people" and "low-aloofness people." In any event these studies cast serious doubt on theories of management which rely excessively upon improvement of the personal relationship of supervisor and subordinate. Such results, coupled with evidence cited above of the apparent efficacy of time spent in planning and supervising rather than working with men, clearly leads us to look beyond the man-manager relationship for a viable theory of effective supervision.

MORALE AND PRODUCTIVITY

Another assumption which appears vital to Becker and Green's discussion is the effect of various budgeting practices on morale.[7] The social-psychological evidence of a relationship between morale and productivity is drawn almost exclusively from survey data, thus making it impossible to determine whether (or in which situations) (1) high morale causes high productivity, (2) high productivity causes high morale, or (3) both high

---

[5]Cf. R. L. Kahn and D. Katz, "Leadership Practices in Relation to Productivity and Morale" in D. Cartwright and A. Zander (eds.) *Group Dynamics*, 2d ed., Evanston, Ill.: Row, Peterson & Co., 1960, pp. 554–71. It should be noted that the evidence presented is generally gleaned from survey data. E.g., although some consensus among the studies cited would tend to indicate that foremen who have "freedom" to plan ahead are higher producers, it is not clear whether this freedom reflects a recognition by their supervisors of their abilities or the converse. Also a statement (p. 563) that "high producing supervisors were predominantly employee-identified" would seem to conflict with the evidence (pp. 556–58), of the positive correlation of productivity with the amount of time spent supervising and planning—which would reflect, by contrast, a greater managerial orientation—than with time spent working with men. The difficulty here seems primarily methodological. The difficulties inherent in attempting to draw causal conclusions (albeit carefully) from first-order correlations of survey data are signal.

[6]F. E. Fiedler, *Leader Attitudes and Group Effectiveness*, Urbana: University of Illinois Press, 1958.

[7]Although they caution us that (p. 396) "morale is not *perfectly* correlated with productivity" [italics mine], they seem to imply (in direct references on pp. 394, 395, 396, 399, 400, and 402) its beneficial effects and improvement through feedback and/or participation.

morale and high productivity are caused by one or more other environmental contributors. The almost ubiquitous inference of the first causal determination is unjustified by the form of the evidence.[8] It is also of interest that the study of Morse and Reimer revealed an inverse relationship between morale and productivity where the experimentally manipulated variable, closeness of supervision, is the logical choice of an independent variable for causal implication if any is to be chosen. Two other interesting studies also show an inverse relationship. Goode and Fowler found negative correlations between morale and productivity of unskilled workers on an assembly line.[9] On the other hand, in one of the relatively few studies that deal with the morale and productivity of people other than workers or clerks, Weschler, Kahane, and Tannenbaum compared two divisions in an industrial research laboratory, one permissively and one restrictively led.[10] Although the permissively led group had much higher morale and made substantially higher estimates of their own productivity than did the restrictively led division, superiors rated the latter more highly than their own estimates and more highly than the former. The authors concluded that the director of the permissively led division "utilized the services of a high morale group and of satisfied people in the performance of tasks which his superiors did not consider of highest importance to the laboratory."[11]

It is not our intent here to resist the efforts of those who strive to make organizations better places to work. We wish merely to point out that the evidence relating to leadership style and the beneficial effects of morale is mixed.

PARTICIPATION—SOME EVIDENCE

To return more specifically to participation per se, the evidence does not bear out Becker and Green's implication that, as long as "participants participate" the effects will be beneficial.[12] Indeed, recent studies have shown that the effects of participation are heavily conditioned by personality and environmental factors.

---

[8]For a most thorough review of this evidence *see* R. Likert, *New Patterns of Management*, New York: McGraw-Hill Book Co. 1961. Before taking this evidence too seriously, however, the reader should be cautioned that it is not clear that all accounts are uniformly unbiased. For further discussion on this point *see* H. J. Leavitt's review of Likert's book in *Management Science*, Vol. 10, No. 1, pp. 162–64.

[9]W. J. Goode and I. Fowler, "Incentive Factors in a Low Morale Plant," *American Sociological Review* (1949), pp. 618–24.

[10]I. R. Weschler, M. Kahane, and R. Tannenbaum, "Job Satisfaction, Productivity and Morale," *Occupational Psychology*, Vol. 26 (1952), pp. 1–14.

[11]*Ibid*, p. 6.

[12]One can, of course, dismiss all evidence that does not support the participation hypothesis on the basis that in the case studied it was not *really* participation but "pseudo-participation." That this conclusion is generally arrived at ex post facto appears to be no deterrent (see Chris Argyris, *The Impact of Budgets on People*, New York: Controllership Foundation, 1958).

It is interesting to note that the study of French, Israel, and As,[13] which was intended to provide, in a different cultural setting, corroboration of the findings of Coch and French,[14] provided quite different results. Participation apparently improved *morale*, but *productivity* was unaffected. Although the authors indicate that the long-run effect of improved morale should be improved productivity, they present no evidence to this effect.[15] In short, the attempt to repeat the earlier study in a different organization in a different culture produced quite different results. Whether one cares to view the second study as indicative of mitigation of beneficial participation effects through national cultural translation, or merely through transfer to a different organizational culture,[16] the nonuniversality of the participation hypothesis of improved productivity should be clear.

In an attempt to isolate some of the variables conditioning the effects of participation, Vroom studied the relationship of participation to productivity of shipping supervisors.[17] While his results are drawn from survey data, the conditioning variables were obtained a priori from questionnaire information. He found that, where employees viewed participation as *legitimate*, productivity was higher under participative supervision, but, where it was viewed as not legitimate (e.g., evidence of "softness," inability to make decisions), observed productivity was lower. Vroom makes a convincing case for the persistence of such personality differences in the presence of quite dissimilar leadership styles. In light of this evidence we cannot conclude that participation will work for "all of the people all of the time" even if one were to alter situational variables so as to be more compatible with participation.

More recent evidence from a field experiment conducted by French, Kay, and Meyer is directly relevant to questions of participative budgeting, inasmuch as the amount of participation of goal-planning sessions was explicitly manipulated.[18] Results indicated that the differences in goal

---

[13]J. R. P. French, Jr., J. Israel, and D. As, "An Experiment on Participation in a Norwegian Factory," *Human Relations*, Vol. 13 (1960), pp. 1–13. Becker and Green borrow a definition from this article (n. 11, p. 394) but are unaware of, or do not care to present, the implications of their data.

[14]L. Coch and J. R. P. French, Jr., "Overcoming Resistance to Change," *Human Relations*, Vol. 1 (1948), pp. 512–32. Since Becker and Green devote a column to this study (pp. 395–96) we shall deal with it only in passing. The reader should be cautioned, however, as to the value judgments present even in their qualifying remarks, as epitomized by the paragraph on p. 396: "Based only on this study one cannot decide if participation directly increased incentive to produce, as measured by subsequent productivity, or only improved morale, which in turn led to increased motivation. This is a point worth considering since morale is not perfectly correlated with productivity."

[15]For discussion of a similar assertion, cf. H. J. Leavitt. review in *Management Science*. Unfortunately, the reader must be cautioned, in general, to examine the data rather than conclusions or summaries of results in this literature.

[16]It is not apparent that the original study was corroborated in any other domestic organization before "cross-cultural" corroboration was attempted.

[17]V. H. Vroom, *Some Personality Determinants of the Effects of Participation*, Englewood Cliffs, N.J.: Prentice-Hall, Inc., 1960.

[18]J. R. P. French, Jr., E. Kay, and H. H. Meyer, *A Study of Threat and Participation in a Performance Appraisal Situation*, New York: General Electric Co., 1962.

attainment between participatively set and nonparticipatively set goals were neither significant nor necessarily in the hypothesized direction (i.e., participation would improve goal attainment). Subsequent analysis of the same data by Kay revealed that those supervisors whom the manipulation had left unchanged from their previous perceived participation in goal setting (e.g., perceived low participation in normal working relationship and were in low participation experimental treatment) had significantly higher goal attainments than those who had previously perceived one level of participation and for whom the manipulation had changed (in either direction) the level of participation.[19] Thus in the only study to date which explicitly deals with the amount of participation as the independent variable in a budget-related situation, the only significant results relating to participation and performance are ex post and specifically oppose the hypothesis that a change *to* participative goal-setting will improve performance.

Thus it can be seen that, in their reliance on the "use" of participation, the attempt to enhance morale and hence productivity, and the consequent stress on "democratic" organization, Becker and Green are forced into a position antithetical to both their original fundamental points and much of the extant evidence.

ASPIRATION LEVELS AND PERFORMANCE

One might say that the character of existing psychological evidence is at the root of difficulty Becker and Green face in their attempt to extrapolate directly to problems in an industrial organization. This difficulty is particularly poignant in their discussion of aspiration levels and performance.

In general, psychological research dealing with goals has been directed toward the description and explanation of the goal-formation process. This research has dealt almost exclusively with the influence *on* aspiration levels of previous performance, success or failure in attainment of previous aspiration levels, other psychological variables, and cultural phenomena—for example, social norms. The emphasis has been placed on the process of goal formation and not on performance resulting from the formation of a particular goal. Explicit investigation of performance as a dependent variable has been rare; in psychological research the aspiration level has, with few exceptions, been treated as the dependent variable.[20] The study of performance as a function of an aspiration level that is in turn a function of a goal

---

[19]Communicated to the author in private correspondence.

[20]Becker and Green cite two of them: J. A. Bayton, "Interrelations between Levels of Aspiration, Performance and Estimates of Past Performance," *Journal of Experimental Psychology*, Vol. 33 (1943), p. 1; and S. Siegel and L. E. Fouraker, *Bargaining and Group Decision Making: Experiments in Bilateral Monopoly*, New York: McGraw-Hill Book Co., 1960.

(which is, at least in part, determined by an external source) has not, apparently, been of interest to psychologists.

Becker and Green seem quite concerned about an experiment I performed a few years ago in which I attempted to depart from the usual arrangement of dependent and independent variables in psychological research. For the reasons cited above it is quite reasonable that Becker and Green may have misinterpreted my experimental work.[21] After discussing the attributes of several different kinds of aspiration-level statements, they conclude: "Since level of aspiration is defined as the goal one explicitly undertakes to reach rather than the goal one hopes to achieve, it seems clear that Stedry's conclusions are based on an inaccurate measure of his major variable" (p. 398). Inasmuch as the study in question focused on budgeting-control problems, performance was chosen as the dependent variable. The experimental treatment (in a 4 × 3 factorial design) involved (1) the variation of the difficulty of goals presented by the experimenter and (2) variation of the presence or absence of the solicitation of a hope statement and the timing of the statement—before or after the presentation of the experimenter's goal. The observed experimental performance results showed significant differences between treatments in both variations and significant interactions were noted as well.[22] The inferences made for budgeting were drawn from these results. Recognizing that these results per se would not be of primary interest to psychologists, aggregated data on the results of the aspiration-level questionnaires were also presented. The reader may verify the tentativeness with which inferences from these auxiliary data were drawn.

I would like to pause a moment, however, to explain that the unanimity among psychologists on the wording of aspiration-level statements implied by Becker and Green simply does not exist. Even if we confine ourselves to those references which they cite, Festinger defines two measures of aspiration level based upon questions involving "like to get" and "expect to get."[23] Diggory uses both "hope" statements and "expect" statements as *measures of aspiration level.*[24] Neither author explicitly implies a preference for "expect." Intuitively, at least, "expect" implies prediction and either "try" or "hope" would seem closer to the "explicitly undertakes to reach" concept proposed by Frank.[25] Of particular relevance to a

---

[21]A. C. Stedry, *Budget Control and Cost Behavior*, Englewood Cliffs, N.J.: Prentice-Hall, Inc., 1960.

[22]For detailed results see *ibid.*

[23]L. Festinger, "A Theoretical Interpretation of Shifts in Level of Aspiration," *Psychological Review*, Vol. 44 (1942), pp. 235–50.

[24]J. C. Diggory, "Responses to Experimentally Introduced Failure," *American Journal of Psychology*, Vol. 62 (1949), pp. 48–61.

[25]J. D. Frank, "Individual Differences in Certain Aspects of the Level of Aspiration," *American Journal of Psychology*, Vol. 47 (1935), pp. 119–28.

discussion of an appropriate measure of aspiration level in dealing with performance are some misgivings about "expect" mentioned in a footnote by Bayton:

> Some investigators have questioned the key term used in the instructions given in those level of aspiration experiments which follow Frank's procedure. Irwin and Mintzer ... have indicated the inconsistency which exists among previous workers, since some asked their subjects to state what they expected to make, one asked what his subjects intended to make, another asked "What will you make?", and still another used "What will you try to make?" The present experiment employs the most consistently used term—"expect." Irwin in personal communication with the writer has raised the question of whether instructions asking the subjects to state what they expect to make have the same meaning as those requiring them to state what they are trying to make, and claims that if the incentive value of the level of aspiration is being studied the latter instructions should be used. Since Irwin and Mintzer demonstrate a difference in aspiration statement when their instructions asked for predictions as against hopes, support is given Irwin's criticism. However, the present experiment is designed to test the incentive value of the level of aspiration as it is generally conceived, and it therefore uses the term most consistently found in the instructions of other investigators.[26]

In dealing with budgeting research, it would seem a mistake to ignore the possibility of more than one kind of aspiration level being formed. While a prediction or expectation (probably closest to a forecast in budgeting parlance) might be formed, an intent to attain a budgeted performance which differs from an expected (median or mean value) performance might be held. Indeed, if the budget were equal to the expectation which would exist in the absence of the budget figure its purpose would be difficult to detect.[27] The question of a simultaneous existence of several levels of aspiration is not new. Gardner, for example, asks:

> Might not an individual in a task such as dart-throwing entertain at one and the same time a wild hope that he will make a perfect hit and a more prudent hope that he will at least hit the target, with perhaps an additional, selfconscious hope that he will not appear too awkward in the eyes of the experimenter? In other words, is there not considerable likelihood that an individual's aims on a given trial are manifold, fluctuant, ephemeral, and differing qualitatively as well as quantitatively, with those aims which involve a specific score often giving way to aims which cannot possibly be described in terms of score values?[28]

---

[26]Bayton, *op. cit.*, p. 3. It is unclear how, inasmuch as this article is cited by Becker and Green, a "term most consistently found" but obviously questioned as a measure could have been taken by them as irrevocably correct or accurate.

[27]An extended discussion of this point may be found in Stedry, *op. cit.*, chaps. i and ii.

[28]J. W. Gardner, "The Use of the Term 'Level of Aspiration,'" *Psychological Review*, Vol. 47 (1940), p. 65. This quotation appears in full in Bayton (*op. cit.*), cited by Becker and Green if selectively paraphrased by them (p. 399).

One can readily perceive the relevance of Gardner's remarks to a budgeting situation in which the simultaneous presence of a desire to do really well, a desire to "make the budget," and a desire not to fall below some minimally acceptable levels exists. The face validity of an expectation measure of a level of intended achievement (however often used by psychologists) is not apparent; the use of a single measure—prediction—in budgetary control research seems unnecessarily limiting if not unsound.

CONCLUSION

This discussion should not imply that the use of psychological constructs is undesirable in budgeting research. On the contrary, in the opinion of this writer not only psychological research but research emanating from all of the social sciences should be used where applicable—but should be used well.

Interdisciplinary work in its application of theory and findings to new contexts demands meticulous interpretation of previous studies lest potential for contribution be lost. A case in point is Becker and Green's treatment of the well-known study of Schachter and others, the conclusion of which reads in part: "In summary, the data indicate no necessary relationship between cohesiveness and high productivity.... Whether or not highly cohesive groups are more likely to develop standards of high production rather than low production is a separate question, but evidence from industrial studies . . . e.g., the slow down, indicates that this is not the case."[29]

Becker and Green, however, derive this summary: "Since participation affects morale (cohesiveness) and productivity, but cohesiveness without participation affects production, the most likely conclusion is that cohesiveness is dependent on participation but that changes in productivity are more directly related to cohesiveness" (p. 396).

The intermeshing of disciplines is valuable, regardless of the researcher's original training, if evidence is impartially selected and weighed in relation to both its original and new application. Further, the infusion of other disciplines is valuable only if the result creates new areas of potential exploration rather than fading indistinguishably into the current budgeting literature.

---

[29]S. Schachter, N. Ellertson, Dorothy McBride and Doris Gregory, "An Experimental Study of Cohesiveness and Productivity," *Human Relations*, Vol. 4 (1951), pp. 229–38.

CHAPTER VII

SOME ORGANIZATIONAL CONTEXTS OF

PUBLIC BUDGETING AND FINANCE:

PERSPECTIVES ON INDUCING AND

AVOIDING STRESS

Finance and budgeting are part of the vitals of any collective enterprise, and the influence is reciprocal. Patently, the style and efficiency with which finance and budgeting tasks are performed will leave their clear marks on the tone and effectiveness of the host organization. "The organization," however, is no passive receptor. The diverse properties of various organizations will influence, and sometimes determine, how budgeting and finance activities are performed. The latter point will be emphasized here, for its significance is seldom noted.

The posture of this section may be sketched broadly. Because of the jobs that budgeting and finance people must do, their contributions inherently are major stress-points in any organization. Because of the way the contributions of finance and budgeting typically are organized in collective enterprises, moreover, the worst is often made of relations that are inherently difficult. In part, the stress associated with budgeting and finance activities is unavoidable, for money and the ways it is to be spent are the obvious stakes, and feelings can be expected to run high even under the best of circumstances. This will always be so. In at least some major part, however, the stress commonly associated with budgeting and accounting is induced by the very organizational relations that men impose upon themselves. This need not always be so.

In its most elemental sense, then, the thrust of this section is toward more effective coping with the stress often generated in the performance of budgeting and finance activities. Specifically, that thrust has two component vectors. Thus descriptive materials will seek to better describe what stress often does exist. Hopefully, greater understanding of what exists may help reduce the sting of the inevitable. In addition, specific ways of moderating stress in budgeting and

448

finance activities also will be considered. In general, the restructuring of work will be the vehicle for moderating stress.

The comments above support a useful summary. As in the total volume, in short, the focus here is toward more effective action via increased understanding. Knowledge of what exists and of why it does, in sum, often permits changing what exists.

The excerpt from Keith Davis on "Staff Relationships" begins the task of illuminating how typical organizational arrangements imply a high potential for stress in budgeting and finance activities. Briefly, Davis distinguishes "Line" and "Staff" as primary and secondary to the accomplishment of an organization's objectives. This is the usual concept in both theory and practice. Budgeting and finance personnel generally are "specialist staff" in Davis' terminology, although they may also function as a high-level "general staff" as well. Like all staff activities, then, budgeting and finance begin the organizational race with the liability of being "secondary." Consequently, many staff officials strive mightily to disprove their organizational inferiority. The derivative potential for stress may be great. How can staff justify its existence? Well, staff could be very careful to discover irregularities at lower levels of organization and to report them upward to their superiors. The tactic is a two-edged sword, however. For focusing on Score-Card Questions places staff in a disciplining role with respect to those at lower levels of organization. In turn, this role may reduce staff's effectiveness in coping with Attention-Directing Questions and Problem-Solving Questions. The latter are more appropriate for demonstrating staff's usefulness to those at lower organizational levels. Circularly, then, staff may be further driven to seek top-level support via Score-Card activities. The circularity has patent self-heightening tendencies.

Other perspectives on the potential for conflict implicit in the staff role of budgeting and finance permit further insight. Consider that finance and budgeting do—and should—exercise considerable control over the activities of line and staff units as well. As Davis indicates, significant stress often derives from the actual exercise of control by those who are formally "secondary." Hence the typical and heated complaint by line officers that staff personnel should only help, but that in fact they also regulate and constrain line activities. Service and control being two sides of the same coin, the organizational separation of the two in the line-staff concept is awkward.

That budgeting and finance often do regulate and constrain line activities is abundantly clear in the excerpt from Gerald Schulsinger's "The General Accounting Office: Two Glimpses." The author provides introductory technical information about travel allowances, and a brief case study of how Ambassador Drew learned first-hand about the vigilance of public auditors in safeguarding the use to which public funds are put.

Two important considerations should influence the analysis of Schulsinger's contribution. First, the Government Accounting Office is formally accountable to Congress. It is not an executive agency, therefore. In business, an "outside" form of "certified public accountants" generally performs a post-audit.

The GAO review in this case was more in the nature of an executive audit, in that the GAO's action held up the disbursement of relevant monies. A post-audit would only indicate that questions about that disbursement seemed appropriate, after the expenditure has been made. The impact of the GAO in this case, consequently, is somewhat like that of an agency's "internal" budgeting and finance people as they go about their daily accounting or controllership activities. The basic difference is that the GAO provides its personnel with a protection—as Congress's watchdog rather than as employees of an executive agency—not available to an accountant challenging an expenditure within his own parent organization.

Second, the experience of Ambassador Drew should not be read as somehow typical. That is, the GAO has exercised similar but far more complex vigilance when the monies involved have totalled in the many millions of dollars. Rather, the case study illustrates the kinds of relations that may develop between budgeting and finance personnel and the organization units they service, even when the stakes are trifling. Trifles especially can be troublesome and can contaminate organizational relations. However common are experiences like those of Ambassador Drew, they can be aggravating and time-consuming. Such incidents can and do compound the stress that inherently exists in the delicate business of variously monitoring the spending of public monies. Travel expenses are a common focal item for conflict between financial offices and other organization units.

To summarize, the guiding principle of line-staff relations is in serious senses ill-suited to the realities of the regulation and constraint that are and should be exercised by financial and budgeting personnel. Nature abhors such imbalance, however. As usual, the incongruence of principle and practice is paid for in terms of a heightened potential for stress and perhaps for guilt.

People in organizations are eminently if often unconsciously realistic, and consequently they will tend to prepare for the worst in their interactions with budgeting and finance officials. Such preparations are often highly creative, but they are usually defensive in nature, and whether these preparations contribute to increased organizational effectiveness is problematic. Characteristically, also, these preparations generally focus upon somehow avoiding public evidence of ineffectiveness. Failing that, the focus is upon developing sources of support for the inevitable dark days when it will be necessary to fight to either establish that the figures are inaccurate, or to soft-peddle them. Commonly, either of these approaches requires firm and substantial political support.

Chris Argyris' "Budget Pressure: Some Causes and Consequences" suggests the richness of the ways in which security is sought. Argyris focuses on stress deriving from the use of budgeting to "keep the heat on" in an organization. His analysis clearly implies that such security often is paid for in terms of limitations on output and rigid organizational relations that defy change. Thus the creation of groups is a common way to seek security against the pressure of budgets, Argyris reports. Patently, however, such groups often provide security for members in organizationally-awkward ways such as keeping secret a labor-saving innovation. Similarly, the first-line supervisor must cope with the pressure supplied by budgeting personnel. He does so diversely: by channelling hostility into interdepartmental conflict; by punishing others, as via conflict in relations between line and staff; and by punishing himself, or "killing himself" at work. These patterns of coping, at best, imply mixed blessings and punishments for individuals and for their organizations.

"Budget Pressure" reflects the grim legacy of punitiveness in organizations. Basically, that is, Argyris documents the problems induced by the common definition of the success of budgeting and finance in terms of discovering, or attempting to prevent, the failure of others in the organization. The implied role for budgeting and finance is that of exerting pressure, and that role is likely to be an unattractive one for all immediately concerned. That is, few individuals like to pressure or to be pressured over even the short-run.

Whether or not individuals tend to shun pressure relations, in any case, no clear evidence supports their general usefulness. Much contrary evidence exists, indeed. Consider the common self-defeating circularity of punishment. Broadly, the search for security becomes more futile as it becomes more frantic. Line personnel try to protect themselves, as by forming groups. And budgeting personnel respond by seeking their security via more energetic efforts to isolate errors. But the latter tactic, in turn, merely heightens the defensiveness of the line. Of course, massive efforts by the hierarchy can break such circularities. Sometimes, indeed, just such massive efforts are necessary and justified in desperate cases. The most probable legacies of organizational hatchetings are a long-standing bitterness or an abject dependence on formal authorities. Each of these legacies has great costs.

A summary conclusion for budgeting and finance seems indisputable. Clearly, shaping organizations more to human needs will require minimizing the tension implicit in so structuring work that some can succeed only as others fail. Fortunately, the self-fulfilling tendencies sketched above do not seem to be a law of nature. Directly, a good part of the potential for stress in budgeting and finance activities derives from the orthodox structuring of work. Robert T. Golembiewski's "Accountancy As A Function of Organization Theory" attempts to illustrate the fullness of the proof of this important summary proposition. In addition, Golembiewski attempts to depict the broad outline of an alternative model for structuring work that permits the more human use of human beings. The alternative model eases the tension implicit in budgeting and finance activities in several important senses, as the article notes.

By way of introduction, two major considerations particularly recommend the unorthodox model. Basically, the alternative model increases the probability that budgeting and finance personnel can succeed as the line succeeds. Moreover, the alternative model is consistent with a wide range of research that permits substantial confidence in the usefulness of the alternative structure.

Detailed support for the major thrust of the selection by Golembiewski is provided by Simon and his collaborators in their "Centralization versus Decentralization In Organizing the Controller's Department." The excerpts below come

451

from the study of the controller's departments of several business firms with geographically-dispersed operations. The goal was to determine the effectiveness of different forms of departmental organization. A controller's department was considered effective as it: (1) Provides information services of high quality; (2) Provides these services at minimum cost; and (3) Facilitates the development of competent executives over the long-run, in both accounting and operating areas.

Wisely, Simon and his colleagues refrained from applying such criteria of efficiency as "adherence to orthodox principles of organization," for the article makes plain such a criterion would have been awkward. Consider here only, for example, that many of the controller's departments considered effective variously violated the traditional model for organizing work. That is, the effective departments tended to have variously-decentralized patterns of organization, such as those called for by the unorthodox model developed in the Golembiewski selection discussed directly above.

STAFF RELATIONSHIPS
KEITH DAVIS

A particular type of specialist is the staff expert. He is difficult to isolate and define because the term "staff" is used in many ways. For purposes of this book the staff is broadly defined as those activities which are supplementary to the primary functions of an organization. A manufacturing business exists primarily to produce and distribute goods—these are its line functions, and all others are staff. A retail store exists primarily to buy and sell merchandise—these are its line functions. Notice that in the first instance the purchasing activity is staff, but in the second case it is line. This is so because the primary functions of the two businesses are different. In government, a state employment office exists to place employees and process claims. These are its line functions.

GENERAL STAFF

There are two distinct types of staff, general and specialist. The general staff is an extension of the manager himself and may, therefore, be just as much a generalist as he is. General staff is represented by the assistant to a manager, such as the assistant to a division chief.[1] He aids his chief in any area of his chief's responsibility and serves as his agent in relating to other managers. His function carries no authority over others. Since he cannot delegate to others, no one owes responsibility to him; however, he may acquire considerable power in various ways. Perhaps he screens those who want to see his chief. Probably he spends more time with his chief than any of the managers the chief directs. He carries his chief's orders to others and may eventually feed in his own opinions rather than representing his chief's views. Since he reports directly to his chief, he especially carries implied power when dealing with managers two or three levels below; and since he gives no orders of his own, he can bypass to lower levels more easily than a line manager can. Unless his role and function are carefully defined, there may be confusion and friction; consequently, some organizations frown upon an "assistant-to" assignment (as distinguished from an "assistant manager" who serves his chief within the chain of command). Here is an example of the human difficulties involved.[2]

Article is from *Human Relations at Work* by Keith Davis. Copyright © 1962 by McGraw-Hill, Inc. Used by permission of McGraw-Hill Book Company.

[1]For an interesting discussion of the "assistant-to" relationship, *see* Thomas L. Whisler, "The 'Assistant-to' in Four Administrative Settings," *Administrative Science Quarterly* (September, 1960), pp. 181–216.

[2]Ernest Dale and Lyndall F. Urwick, *Staff in Organization*, New York: McGraw-Hill Book Company, Inc., 1960, pp. 173–174.

An Ivy League graduate without business experience became assistant to the president of an oil company. Viewing his position as one of high status, he ignored and snubbed the managers reporting to the president. He commanded them when he wanted information. He used stilted language and spoke in grand theories. Taking advantage of his rather ambiguous position, he avoided assignments and would not give clear-cut answers. Most important of all, he refused to learn from his past mistakes, a fact which assured his hasty departure.

SPECIALIST STAFF

General staff serves one manager, whereas specialist staff usually serves one specialized function (such as purchasing) as it applies to many managers and their departments. Specialist staffs contribute advanced expertness in a narrow area of activity. Other persons look to them for leadership because of their *expertise*. Specialist staffs, therefore, represent an *authority of ideas*, instead of line authority to issue orders. Their job is sometimes said to be to advise other units, but this is only one of three types of relationships they have, as follows:

1. Advisory—the staff guides others.
2. Service—the staff performs work for others.
3. Control—the staff regulates and constrains others.

As would be expected, each relationship sets a different pattern of human interaction, causing different types of human relations problems. One of the reasons that specialist staffs have so much difficulty in business is that they do not understand these different relationships and consequently do not vary their action to fit the situation. Though the concept of staff is quite old, it still is grossly misunderstood.

The three relationships are not mutually exclusive. As will be seen, a staff function as large as the personnel activity will usually have all three relationships. Neither are these relationships only with the line. A staff group, such as purchasing, buys for other staff units as well as line units.

Advisory Staff

The advisory staff is a specialized counsel to management. It acts at the request of management to help it prepare plans, study problems, and reach decisions. An example is a public relations department which helps an executive prepare a speech. The advisory staff is to the manager the least obnoxious of all because he is generally not compelled to consult it and he is not obligated to follow its advice. In the example just given, if the manager decides to change part of the speech after public relations has *advised* him about it, he is at liberty to do so because he is the *responsible* person. However, if public relations is a *control* staff, the manager may not change his speech without public relations approval.

A natural result of this relationship is that the staff is sensitive about its position. It feels insecure because it knows it can be "put out of business" unless it can convince people to use it. Since it cannot force others to seek its advice, it tries hard to "sell" its services, sometimes to such an extent that it becomes a nuisance. It feels, properly so, that it must justify its existence.

Advisory staff is established to help the manager who needs it; however, if he fails to consult it, its ideas are valueless because it goes unheard. Of course, that is just what many managers do. In order to assure that the staff is heard, the *doctrine of compulsory staff advice* is sometimes applied to important problems.[3] This doctrine requires that the line manager consult his staff before taking action. This in no way abridges his authority. He still decides what action shall be taken, but at least he cannot avoid the advice of the group established to give it. This doctrine permits the staff to reduce its selling function and spend more time on its specialty; however, it irks the manager because his decision is delayed pending advice. Though it is not used extensively, an example is the requirement that a supervisor consult the personnel department for policy guidance before he gives a worker a disciplinary suspension. The supervisor makes his own decision, but if he does not follow his staff's advice and if his action gets poor results, he is in the unfortunate position of having to answer to his chief for not following the advice he received. The result is that he tends to follow staff advice unless he has good reason to make an exception.

Service Staff

Service staff performs for a manager certain activities which have been separated from his job. In the true sense of the word, it performs a service. When a particular staff service is separated from a manager's job, he is then usually compelled to use the service staff, because to continue performing the work in his own department would be a duplication of function. Many staff activities have primarily a service relationship. Examples are the cafeteria and the purchasing function. An executive who wishes to make a purchase is required to use the purchasing staff. Though he has authority to specify the product, he does not buy it. Though he initiates the action, he does not perform the function.

It is apparent that service staff relationships are likely to cause more human relations problems than advisory relationships, because the service staff restricts the scope of a manager's actions. This point is illustrated by the relations between purchasing and production in a large factory. In this company the purchasing department buys all materials and services, except petty-cash items and small emergency items. The production organization, directed by a production manager, is the main consumer of these goods and services. It is assumed by top management that centralization of purchasing in one department permits better buying, use of materials, and over-all economies in purchasing. This is probably true, *but* these technical economies produce considerable human dislocation, as is the usual pattern.

---

[3]James D. Mooney, *The Principles of Organization*, New York: Harper and Brothers, 1947, pp. 119–121.

In the first place, the production manager and his superintendents have lost some of their authority. They are no longer the "big shots" that they used to be with vendors and their agents. Their feeling of importance is depreciated, and they probably receive fewer complimentary lunches and other favors from suppliers. On some occasions, they do not even have a supplier's catalogue and have to go to the purchasing department to borrow its catalogue. Production superintendents are still permitted to talk to salesmen, but they must be careful that they do not in any way obligate the company to purchase a particular item, because that is the purchasing department's function. Superintendents can go just so far with the salesman, and then the purchasing department takes over. No one is ever quite sure where the line is drawn between the superintendents' function and the purchasing department's. "Just so far" is a line difficult to define; consequently, bickering develops between the two. Purchasing people feel that superintendents sometimes "almost" obligate the firm without authority; so they discourage suppliers from dealing personally with superintendents and try to tag along when they do.

The production organization has authority to initiate purchase orders and, in most cases, to set product specifications. In an effort to hold more of their authority, production people often fix specifications to point toward a particular supplier. Purchasing men feel that their function has been usurped, because they want to have a choice of two or more suppliers; and the bickering starts all over again. Sometimes, of course, purchasing men make errors in transcribing specifications to a purchase order, which causes confusion, occasional shipment of an unacceptable product, and further complaints from the line. On other occasions, production people omit a necessary specification or state a wrong one. Production people, in self-defense, state that the error would have been caught if they dealt directly with the supplier. Purchasing men counter with, "You should know what you are doing in the first instance."

Frequently the production organization wants something in a hurry, and then it collides with the procedure. This is the system which purchasing has established for performing its service. Procedures are inherently slow, and production tends to chafe under these restrictions. Sometimes a production department inquires, "Why can't we get a priority?" Purchasing replies, "Your need is no greater than many other orders we have." Departments often feel, "You processed so-and-so's order before you took mine" or "You didn't place the order soon enough to allow for normal delays in making the deadline." These problems arise partly because of procedural restrictions but also because the purchasing organization serves many departments and therefore has a degree of choice whether to serve one department or another first. Considerable behind-the-scenes negotiating occurs to determine who will get the quickest and best service. The purchasing director has to "play his cards right" to keep from displeasing line managers.

The foregoing description of problems with the purchasing staff is multiplied all over the company by other service staffs. These problems do not imply that the service staff idea is unsuitable, because experience has already shown the necessity and usefulness of service staff in complex, functionalized organizations. What is needed is a better recognition and treatment of the human problems that result from the technical efficiencies of service staff groups.

Control Staff

At first glance, the term "control staff" appears to be ill chosen. Obviously, a staff manager has control of *his own subordinates* the same way that any other manager has control of his employees, but control of other people's subordinates is an entirely different type of activity. When a staff unit controls any activities of those outside its chain of command, this is called *staff control*. Note that staff control as it is described here differs from a *staff service*, such as purchasing. When staff performs a service function, it does the work with its own people; but when staff performs a control function, it exerts controls upon someone else's people as they perform the work. The control relationship is an environment in which many human relations difficulties develop. Many control situations give the staff a veto over line actions. It is natural for the line to resent this and speak of "the front-office clerks who have all the authority but none of the responsibility." Executives in one company are required to route certain expenditure requests through the controller's office (note that the name of this staff office is derived from the fact that it does control). The requests are vetoed (actually they are returned unapproved) by the controller if they exceed available funds or if he feels the funds were not allocated for the purpose stated in the request. Regardless of the propriety of this procedure, line personnel object to staff controls of this type, as illustrated by the cartoon, Figure 1. The four types of staff control will now be discussed.

Functional Control. This is accomplished by the staff's right to issue orders regarding some highly specialized part of someone else's job and to take appropriate action if he does not comply. It is an application of the functional foremanship idea developed by Frederick W. Taylor. When a staff unit is given functional control over any activity, it is *for that narrow activity*, serving as direct boss of the person who performs it. An example is a safety director in a hazardous industry who can order a worker to stop performing an unsafe operation, and this can be done without first getting approval of the worker's foreman.

The principal defect of staff control by functional authority is that unity of command is violated, so that two persons are responsible for a particular job and jurisdictional conflict tends to arise. Even if the jurisdiction of each is crystal clear, the person who has the principal responsibility often feels that his effectiveness is being hampered by the functional actions of the

457

second person. In any case, the employee who is controlled has two supervisors to please, and he may be confused regarding when the authority of each applies.

FIGURE 1

LINE PERSONNEL TEND TO RESENT STAFF CONTROLS*

"Hah! Accounting tried to walk all over me!"

*From *Manage* (June, 1955), p. 9. Used by permission.

Agency Control. In agency control the staff has no authority to issue orders in its name, but it may do so in the name of its line manager. In this case the staff is acting under general instructions from its manager, and he may not see the actual order until after it is issued. If an error is made, the staff is responsible to the manager; but the order stands as if it were issued by the manager, and those who follow it are protected until it is changed by the manager or his staff. An example is the daily bulletin of a military organization, which is issued by the adjutant, "For the Commanding Officer." Another illustration is the production control department which in one company prepares and issues in the name of the superintendent the production schedules and orders. The schedules tell each foreman what products his department will work on and what type of machine to use. Foremen follow this schedule as an order from the superintendent.

Policy Control. Policy control is heavily used in modern management. It works like this. A manager determines a policy and maintains normal follow-up through reports and personal contacts, but he recognizes that he cannot follow up to the extent necessary. Perhaps the subject is technical or nebulous, and he knows his associates will overlook certain variations because they lack technical competence or are too busy with their whole management job. Many routine interpretations may arise which require consistency in interpretation. The manager, therefore, instructs his staff to observe and check on this function and to enter into the situation when anything appears out of line. He usually also instructs his associates to refer to the staff when they observe variations or have questions of interpretation. This is something more than mere advice because the line person is supposed to follow the staff judgment unless he wishes to take the question to his manager. It is something less than agency, because the line person may appeal to his manager, in which case he is appealing the staff's judgment and not the manager's. Further, no question of an order is involved, as in the case of agency.

Policy control is evident in home office specialists who visit a field operation to observe and suggest. It is also the type of control usually exercised by auditors when checking past operations. The job of judging another person's performance is never a popular one, and it is made less so when it is done by staff. In this case the staff is actually an outsider who sits in judgment of the performers. It does not call the plays and it is not directly responsible for them, but it judges them. Those who are audited often feel that management is suspicious of them. Thus, when an auditor arrives, a manager asks, "Why should he check me? I'm honest." This viewpoint is more than simply a manager's vivid imagination, because staff persons sometimes do eye line management suspiciously and try to catch it in some indiscretion.

Procedural Control. In this instance the staff controls by sitting astride the chain of procedure—a procedure which has been established by management. In performing its function in that procedure, the staff may rebuff or veto something initiated by another manager. An illustration is the procedure for merit increases in a government office. A manager initiates a rate increase, but before it can be finally approved by his chief, it has to go to the personnel department for approval concerning compliance with the maximum rate limit for that job, time since last increase, and other applicable regulations. If the proposed increase does not comply, it is returned unapproved by the personnel department.

In a retail store all credit sales by salesmen are conditional and subject to approval by the credit department. Although this procedure is quite necessary to protect the company's accounts receivable, a salesman who makes a sale—only to lose it again because his customer cannot get the credit—is apt to feel that the credit department has stolen his commission.

And if he fails to make his quota for the month, the credit department gets the blame.

Factory inspection is an excellent example of procedural control. Though an inspector does not produce any goods, he determines their acceptability. If there is an incentive plan, his decisions usually affect earnings of employees, a fact which tends to increase the possibility of friction between him and the employees. The typical layman thinks that factory inspection is objectively done on the basis of mathematics and mechanics, but factory employees know that it has many chances for *subjective* judgment. An inspector can be "hard" or "easy" in dealing with employees. If he is tough and uncooperative, employees may become more intent on fooling him than maintaining quality. They will try to sneak defective work past him and otherwise beat him at his own game, which means that the original purpose of inspection—a quality product—is being negated. Thus procedural control can lead to its own defeat because of human difficulties arising therefrom.

Procedural and policy controls are perhaps used more than the other two types. It is evident that procedural control is especially powerful and, consequently, a potential hazard in line-staff relations. In a printing plant, for example, a scheduler cannot tell a foreman to stop the presses, but he can say that he will not accept the quality of product now being printed, hence effectively stopping the presses.

LINE-STAFF RELATIONS

The advisory, service, and control activities of staff require staff people to give part of their time to developing better human relations with others. The staff function is not only to provide specialized aid to management, but also *to provide that aid within an effective human relations climate.* Lacking suitable human relations, staff activities may disrupt more than they help. In performing their activities staff people need to understand three factors in their environment in order to respond effectively to those they serve. These factors are illustrated by reference to a production shop and its attendant staff groups.

The Staff's Position

The staff usually has a shorter chain of command to the top of the organization than a line group. It can reach the top easier when it wants to get the ear of top management. This is illustrated by one company in which the training supervisor has only two persons between him and the president, but the foremen with whom he deals have four persons intervening. Under conditions like this, staff specialists tend to enjoy more status and privileges than their line counterparts. Line supervisors are more cautious about conflict with a staff member because they feel sure he could win in a showdown because he is closer to top management.

460

Very often the staff is in a separate chain of command, which means that it is quite removed from the line and the line has scant recourse against it when a conflict arises, unless a line person is willing to appeal all the way to the top to a mutual supervisor of the two departments. The staff man in his separate chain of command can effectively short-circuit the line and carry reports to the top without going through the general foreman and the superintendent. The foremen become afraid they will be misrepresented or criticized to top management, so they tell the staff man as little as possible. This makes his job more difficult, and he becomes more critical of the foremen.

Most staff people enter the shop as specialists. In most cases they definitely know more *about their particular specialty* than a foreman. He has breadth of knowledge about many shop activities, and the staff has intensity of knowledge. Because of their specialized superiority, staff persons often get disgusted and impatient with a foreman who does not comprehend a staff plan. This conflict is aggravated by the fact that more staff people than line people have college training. In many cases the staff men were hired for their present job from outside the company and did not work their way up the way the foreman had to do. Because of its specialized superiority, the staff becomes the "I-know-how-to-do-it" group and the line becomes the "I-do-the-work" group. Line foremen resent intrusion by a group which always tells how to do the work but seldom does any of it.

The Staff's Way of Work

Other problems arise because of the staff's way of work. Generally it employs a different system of logic than the line. Its logics are coldly objective, with a few exceptions, whereas the foreman must work also with people. A particular staff is mostly concerned with a single logic such as mathematics, engineering, or economics, but the line is concerned with broad integration of both logical and human (non-logical) factors.

Staff groups in their intense specialized interest have a way of not telling the line what they are doing until they are ready to "spring" a new plan or procedure. Then they want it adopted in a hurry. They expect the foreman to understand in a few minutes what they have taken weeks or months to develop. If he is slow or resentful, they conclude that he is uncooperative.

The Staff's Effect on the Line

The staff has two significant effects on the line which cause human problems. It is an instrument of change and it eliminates workers. With regard to change, a common shop expression when certain staff groups appear is "Wonder what they are going to change this time?" Change is of such importance that it will be treated more fully in a later chapter.

The function of many staff groups is to reduce costs and increase efficiency, which sometimes results in improvements that make certain jobs

461

unnecessary. Regardless of all the staff's logic showing that its action in the long run will benefit workers in general, the particular worker who is displaced and his friends will not like the idea. Even when he is given work elsewhere in the company, he does not like being moved and perhaps having to learn a new skill. When labor–saving staffs enter the shop, each man sees a threat to his security. This is his *feeling*, even if logic will not support it.

The difficulties of line-staff cooperation are so great that some organizations have tried to abolish the line-staff concept altogether. Indeed, the complex conditions in advanced scientific firms make it difficult sometimes to distinguish line and staff. New organizational models are being developed to incorporate these new conditions, and it is likely that they will give more emphasis to *process relations* because the technological process itself is a basic determinant of how people must work together. Hybrids may develop with traditional line-staff structures superimposed to maintain focus on mission and control costs. But the line-staff concept will not give ground easily, because it offers genuine benefits especially in more traditional organizations. Improvements in human relations will make line-staff structures even more effective.

PROCESSING TRAVEL VOUCHERS: AN ILLUSTRATIVE CAMEO

GERALD G. SCHULSINGER

GLOSSARY OF TRAVEL TERMS

The *Travel Authorization* (T/A), or Travel Order, as it is sometimes called, is the document by which an agency authorizes a trip on the part of an employee or consultant traveling on behalf of the agency. It designates the points of departure and arrival, the mode of travel, and the appropriation to which costs should be charged. For certain employees, a T/A, valid for an entire fiscal year, may authorize as many trips "as may be necessary" without geographic limit, or within the continental U.S., or to and from stated points, but the typical T/A is for a trip only and circumscribes the period of time in which the trip must be taken as well as the route. Copies of each T/A are filed with the GAO.

The *Travel Request* (T/R), when duly filled out and signed, is a government form valid, upon presentation to a common carrier, for tickets to the destination designated on the T/R. Typically the traveler takes his T/A to the Transportation Office of his agency, which will then issue T/Rs conforming to it. The carriers periodically submit the used T/Rs to the GAO, which, after auditing them, authorizes payment directly to the carrier. The system saves the government traveler the necessity of tying up personal funds in tickets during the inevitable lags between trip and repayment from the government.

The *Travel Voucher* is the form on which the traveler, having completed his trip, records his expenses and requests a check for that part of his expenses which are compensable to him. Since the cost of tickets will generally have been covered by T/Rs, the major part of the compensation owed him will be *per diem* for expenses en route.

Per Diem is a flat sum which the government pays the traveler for food, lodgings, tips, and other costs incident to travel, in lieu of an itemized bill for each expense. *Per diem* rates vary according to the place of travel. In the summer of 1952, for example, *per diem* ranged from $6.00 per day in Iwo Jima, Korea, Nyasaland, Thailand, and various other places, to $30.00 per day in the Soviet Union. In the continental U.S. the maximum and normal *per diem* was then $9.00 per day. But an agency could allow less. Travellers making an extended stop-over or stay at one place were frequently limited to $7.00 for that portion of the trip. A common example is the consultant, whose home is

Article is from Gerald G. Schulsinger, *The General Accounting Office: Two Glimpses*, University: University of Alabama Press, 1956, pp. 13–19. Reprinted with permission of author and publisher.

designated as his duty station to put him in travel status, and who is called to Washington on a temporary appointment, not to exceed 90 days.

For employees of the United States Department of Agriculture and others travelling extensively in rural areas, the *per diem* was frequently less than the maximum.

A smaller *per diem* was frequently prescribed if the trip did not exceed 24 hours.

The Standardized Government Travel Regulations (SGTR) is a complex set of rules covering most civilian travel on behalf of the government. It is promulgated, in the main, by the Bureau of the Budget (the Comptroller General writes a small part of it), under authority of the Travel Expenses Act of 1949 and its statutory predecessors. But just as law is "made" as much by the judges who interpret it as by the legislators who write it, the government's travel regulations are "made" as much by the Comptroller General and his staff, who interpret them and control their application, as by the Bureau of the Budget, which is their primary author.

THE CASE OF MINISTER DREW

The Flight Home

Late in January of 1952, the Department of State appointed the Honorable Gerald A. Drew, then American Minister to the Hashemite Kingdom of the Jordan and a career diplomat of some 25 years experience, to the post of Director-General of the Foreign Service. His appointment took effect on April 1, 1952; and his resignation as Minister, one day earlier. In accord with Departmental custom, Drew was instructed to wind up his affairs at the legation to return to Washington at the beginning of March, and to spend 30 days in Washington on consultation status pending accession to his new position.

Drew spent February conducting legation business and attending the social functions by which diplomats mark the movements of their colleagues. He secured reservations for a flight leaving Beirut, Lebanon, Near Eastern terminus of Pan-American Airways, on Wednesday morning, February 27th. Since there is no commercial transportation between Amman, site of the legation, and Beirut, the Minister embarked in an official car on Monday morning, February 25th, for the ten-hour automobile trip to Beirut. He arrived there that evening and remained until Wednesday, a period of waiting later to be questioned by the GAO. On Wednesday afternoon, several hours late, the plane departed, arriving in New York a day later. Drew pushed on to Washington immediately. There he went on consultation status for 30 days, at the end of which his resignation as Minister and inauguration as Director-General were effected.

Following him, on the S.S. "Excambion" from Beirut, were Mrs. Drew and the accumulated luggage and household belongings of many years abroad. She arrived in Washington on April 4th.

464

Birth of the Voucher

Although the trip was over, much of the paper work was still ahead. On January 29, 1952, the Department of State had issued a Travel Authorization (T/A) valid from February 25 to April 5, 1952, authorizing Drew's trip from Amman and 30 days of consultation in Washington on a *per diem* basis. Copies of the T/A had gone to Amman, to several filing cabinets within the Department of State and to the GAO. At Amman, the legation had issued Travel Requests (T/Rs) to Mr. and Mrs. Drew. The original T/R's were presented to Pan American and the steamship line for tickets; the copies would later be submitted to the GAO.

In April, the new Director-General, probably with the aid of his secretary, filled out, in duplicate, the Travel Voucher. It was necessarily a lengthy document. It listed, both for himself and for Mrs. Drew, the precise time of arrival and departure along the trip, the claimed *per diem* as adjusted to the different rates applicable to each country through which they passed, and the amounts to be paid directly to the carriers. Drew's claim for himself and his wife, other than the cost of the tickets, came to approximately $471. The voucher, signed by Drew and approved by his former administrative superior, was sent with the carbon T/Rs attached to the Departmental Office of Finance, located in a low barracks-type building several blocks from the main offices of the Department. There a departmental auditor inspected it, approved it, and prepared a "Voucher and Schedule Form" listing the name of the payee and the amount payable. On the same forms were listed other payees on other vouchers and the amounts they were to receive. The certifying officer certified the Voucher and Schedule Form and sent it to Paul Banning, Chief Disbursement Officer of the Treasury. This action was, in effect, State's authorization to the Treasury to pay. In May the Treasury mailed a check for the proper amount to Drew. It also returned the original Voucher and Schedule Form to the State Department's Office of Finance where it rejoined Drew's original voucher for eventual submission to the GAO.

The GAO Group at State

GAO auditors assigned to Department of State accounts have moved from main GAO headquarters to a two-story wartime temporary building in which State's Office of Finance is also housed. Their presence there is in the nature of an experiment to test the savings made possible—and the problems raised—by eliminating the shipment of State's financial records to another part of the city and by putting the auditors on the site of operation, close to information in State's files, which could otherwise be obtained only by correspondence. Despite their presence on the scene, the auditors are not intended to operate a comprehensive audit; rather their main activity is voucher checking, and contact between the groups is largely limited to the exchange of information regarding particular vouchers.

When Drew's voucher arrived at the GAO office, it remained on the shelves while auditors worked on earlier vouchers and determined, on the basis of past performance, what kinds of vouchers to schedule for 100% audit. Travel vouchers, as always, were found to be rich sources of exceptions. The wanderings of State personnel, frequently crossing even within a single day, zones of varying *per diem* rates; the custom of scattering, and then collecting, household goods in various corners of the world; the large numbers of travelling temporary consultants who, in the opinion of the GAO auditors, were often not mindful of travel regulations; and the complexity of rules uniquely applicable to Foreign Service personnel—all tended to suggest that a scrutiny of travel vouchers would repay the auditors' efforts.

The Auditor Inspects

In January 1953, the bundle of vouchers of which Drew's was one reached the top of the pile. The service group took each voucher and attached it to the relevant T/A, previously filed with the GAO. The bundle was then given to the next auditor ready for a new supply—in this case Miss Marie Knight, an elderly auditor of many years service. Systematically she examined the vouchers, many of which recorded the journeys of diplomats to lands that were little more to her than names on a map. An experienced hand at the business, Miss Knight could ordinarily handle a hundred vouchers a day; few of them, obviously, involved as protracted a treatment as the one described in this case.

On reaching Drew's voucher, she checked for mechanical compliance, and then turned to its substance. Two items struck her attention:

1. The Minister had left the Amman legation on Monday morning for Beirut. The plane home from there was not scheduled to leave until Wednesday morning. Amman to Beirut is, by the Minister's own statement, a ten-hour trip. Thus he might have left Amman on Tuesday morning, and still have reached Beirut in time for the plane's departure. This would have saved the government $12, since *per diem* is calculated only from time of his departure from the embassy.

2. Mrs. Drew had arrived in Hoboken harbor on the S. S. "Excambion," with ten suitcases. She claimed compensation for $2.50 (25¢ per suitcase) spent in transferring them from the boat to the taxi at the pier, and another $2.50 spent in transferring them from the taxi to the Washington-bound train. The Standardized Government Travel Regulations (SGTR) permit compensation to the traveler for genuine baggage transfers, e.g., for trunks checked on a through ticket from one Chicago terminal to another. But porters' fees for hand luggage come within the range of expenses which the flat *per diem* rate is expected to cover. Miss Knight decided that Mrs. Drew's expenses came within the second category—porters' fees—and could not be separately compensated.

The Auditor Objects

Promptly she wrote out, in longhand, a draft of a notice of exception. It read as follows:

Per Diem claimed: 1/2 day at 9 dollars $4.50 (Feb. 25th)
                    1–3/4 days at 12 dollars $21.00 (Feb. 26th)
                                       $25.50

Allowable: 1/2 day at 9 dollars $4.50 (Feb. 26th)
            3/4 day at 12 dollars $9.00 (Feb. 27th)
                   $13.50

Employee could have left his official station at some time on February 26, 1952, in order to leave Beirut, Lebanon at 9 A.M. February 27, 1952, thus avoiding delay at Beirut . . .

The *per diem* in lieu of subsistence has been held to include all charges or fees to porters or baggagemen and reimbursement of above charges in addition to the *per diem* allowance is unauthorized. SGTR #44.

The total of disputed items came to $17, of which $12 represented the disputed *per diem* and $5 represented the claim for porters' fees.

Miss Knight's draft was initialed, after brief inspection by Mr. Sam Cosetta, her superior. Then neatly typed over the printed signature of the Comptroller-General on a standard form, the notice of exception, together with four carbons, went upstairs to the Review and Settlement Section, Office of Finance, Department of State—State's "exceptions" unit. There a clerk attached the notice to a form letter from Miss Rae Welch, chief of the section, asking the recipient to explain the questioned expenses. She sent the two documents to Drew. "I tell my people that unless the GAO is plainly wrong, send it on to whoever wrote the voucher and let him deal with it," says Miss Welch. "That person is the best source of information. I thought the Budget and Accounting Procedures Act would serve to eliminate some of these petty exceptions. The steps necessary to process these exceptions in order to clear the records cost more than is realized by refunds."

The Solution

When presented with the voucher and covering letter, the Director-General decided to suggest a compromise. On March 20th, he dictated the following reply:

Disallowance of the sum of $5 for transfer charges on baggage in N.Y. is accepted and check in that amount, payable to the Treasurer of the U.S., is attached.

With respect to the disallowance covering *per diem* at Beirut on 2/26/52 in the amount of $12, I should like to explain that it was essential to allow an extra day for this travel in view of the danger at that time that the mountains between Damascus and Beirut might unexpectedly be covered with snow. In this case it would be necessary to make a long detour north of Damascus through Syria in order to reach Beirut over a road not subject to being closed by snow. In addition it was necessary for me to spend the greater part of the day February 26 in consultation with Ambassador Locke concerning Point IV matters, and Minister Minor concerning political problems of mutual interest. (I was at that time American Minister to the Hashemite Kingdom of the Jordan.) It is assumed that this period is properly 'awaited sailing time' and that the GAO will remove the objection.

The reply was signed by Drew and sent by regular messenger from the main State building, where Drew works, to Miss Welch. She certified it, and sent it downstairs to Miss Knight. Miss Knight found both the check for the porters' fees and the explanation for the Beirut stopover satisfactory. Although the GAO maintains a file of information on each Foreign Service post, enabling her to verify the authenticity of the Director-General's claim that the road might have been closed by snow, she did not bother to refer to it.

"It isn't because he's a Director-General that we let it go," explained Mr. Cosetta. "We've taken exceptions to some very important people, and if the President of the United States was to make a mistake and overcharge, I have no doubt that we'd raise an exception, and I have no doubt that he would pay it. But we feel that most people are honest, and when they make a mistake it's because they don't know, or they're careless, or because they didn't fill the voucher out right. If he had just said so about the snow, or having to see this other ambassador, right on the voucher, we never would have questioned it."

Miss Knight's work was almost done. Her only remaining duty was to verify that the Director-General's check had been properly reported on State's cashier schedule. It was; Miss Knight then stamped the case CLOSED. Over a year after Drew and his wife had completed their trip, the covering papers were laid to rest.

BUDGET PRESSURE: SOME CAUSES AND CONSEQUENCES

CHRIS ARGYRIS

One of the most common of the factory supervisors' attitudes about budgets was that budgets were used as a pressure device to increase production efficiency. Many cases were cited to support this point. Finance people also admitted that budgets helped "keep people on the ball" by raising their goals and increasing their motivation. The problem of the effects of pressure applied through budgets seems to be the core of the budget problem.

THE CAUSES OF PRESSURE

Employees and front-line supervisors believe that the cause for pressure from the top is due to top management's belief that most employees are basically or inherently lazy. Employees and front-line supervisors also feel that top management believes that employees do not have enough motivation of their own to do the best possible job.

The interviews with top management officials revealed that the employees' beliefs were not totally unfounded, as a few quotations from some of the top management (both line and finance) make clear:

> I'll tell you my honest opinion. Five percent of the people work, ten percent of the people think they work. And the other eighty-five percent would rather die than work.
>
> I think there is a need for more pressure. People need to be needled a bit. I think man is inherently lazy and if we could only increase the pressure, I think the budget system would be more effective.

Such feelings, even if they are never overtly expressed toward employees, filter through to the employees in very subtle ways. Budgets represent one of the more subtle ways. Once the employees sense these feelings exist in top management, they may become very resentful.

THE EFFECTS OF PRESSURE

How do people react to pressure? In three of the plants studied factory supervisors felt they were working under pressure and that the budget was the principal instrument of pressure. Management exerts pressure on the workforce in many ways, of which budgets is but one.

Article is from Chris Argyris, *The Impact of Budgets on People*, New York: Controllership Foundation, 1954, pp. 14–22. Reprinted with permission of author and publisher.

Budgets, being concrete, seem to serve as a medium through which the total effects of management pressure are best expressed. As such they become an excellent point of focus for studying the effect of pressure on people in a working organization.

THE CREATION OF GROUPS

An increase in tension, resentment, suspicion, fear and mistrust may not be the only result of ever stronger management pressures transmitted to supervisors, and in turn, to employees. We know, from psychological research, that people can stand a certain amount of pressure. After this point is passed, it becomes intolerable to an individual. We also know that one method people have to reduce the effect of the pressure (assuming that the employees cannot reduce the pressure itself) is to join groups. These groups then help absorb much of the pressure and the individual is personally relieved.

The process of individuals joining groups to relieve themselves of pressure is not an easy one. It does not occur overnight. The development of a group on such a basis seems to have the following general stages of growth.

> *First,* the individuals "feel" the pressure. They are not certain, but they sense an increase in pressure.
> *Second,* they begin to see definite evidences of the pressure. They not only feel it, they can point to it.
> Since they feel this pressure is on them personally, they begin to experience tension and general uneasiness.
> *Next,* the people usually "feel out" their fellow workers to see if they sense the pressure.
> Finding out that others have noted the pressure, the people begin to feel more at ease. It helps to be able to say, "I'm not the only one."
> *Finally,* they realize that they can acquire emotional support from each other by becoming a group. Furthermore, they can "blow their top" about this pressure in front of their group. Gradually, therefore, the individuals become a group because in becoming a group they are able to satisfy these needs:
> 1. A need to reduce the pressure on each individual.
> 2. A need to get rid of tension.
> 3. A need to feel more secure by belonging to a group which can counteract the pressure.

In short, a new, cohesive group has developed to combat management pressure. In a sense, the people have learned that they can be happier if they combine against this management pressure.

Suppose now that top management, aware of the tensions which have been generated and the groups which have been formed, seeks to reduce the pressure. The emphasis on budgets is relaxed. Perhaps even the standards are "loosened." Does this then destroy the group? After all, it's primary reason for existence was to combat the pressure. Now, the pressure is gone. The group should eventually disintegrate.

The answer seems to be that the groups continue to exist!

The evidence for this is not as conclusive as it should be. Therefore, the following explanation should be considered primarily in the realm of inference and conjecture rather than scientific fact.

These factors seem to operate to keep the group in existence:

1. There is a "time lag" between the moment management announced the new policy and the time the workers put it into effect.

2. The individuals have made a new and satisfactory adjustment with each other. They have helped to satisfy each other's needs. They are, as the social scientist would say, "in equilibrium" with each other. Any attempt to destroy this balance will tend to be resisted even if the attempt represents an elimination of a "bad" or unhealthy set of conditions. People have created a stable pattern of life and they will resist a change in this pattern.

3. The individuals fear pressure will come again in the future. Because of this feeling, they will tend to create unreal conditions or to exaggerate existing conditions so that they can rationalize to themselves that pressure still exists and, therefore, the need for the group also exists.

PRESSURE ON FRONT-LINE SUPERVISORS

But what about the foreman? Strong pressures converge upon him. How does he protect himself from these pressures?

He cannot join a group against management, as his work force does. For one reason, he probably has at least partially identified himself with management. For another reason, he may be trying to advance in the hierarchy. Naturally, he would not help his chances for advancement if he joined a group against management.

The evidence of the previous chapters seems to indicate that the line supervisor cannot pass all the pressure he receives to his employees. Time and time again the factory supervisors stated that passing the pressure down would only create conflict and trouble which would lead to a decrease in production.

The question arises, where does the pressure go? How do the supervisors relieve themselves of at least some of the pressure? There is evidence to suggest at least three ways in which pressure is handled by the supervisors:

1. Interdepartmental strife. The foremen release some of the pressure by continuously trying to blame fellow foremen for the troubles that exist. "They are," as one foreman expressed it, "trying to throw the dead cat in each other's backyard."

In three plants observed, much time was spent by certain factory supervisors in trying to lay the blame for errors and problems on some other department.

2. Staff versus factory strife. The foremen released much of the pressure by blaming the budget people, production control people and salesmen for their problems. The data already presented concerning factory supervisors' attitudes towards budget people substantiate this point.

3. "Internalizing" pressure. Many supervisors who do not express their feelings about the pressure have in reality "internalized" it and, in a sense, made it a part of themselves. Such damming up of pressure seemed to be expressed in the following ways:

(a) Supervisor A is quiet, relatively nonemotional, seldom expresses his negative feelings to anyone, but at the same time he works excessively. Supervisor A can be found working at his desk long after the others have gone home. As one supervisor expressed it, "That guy works himself to death."

(b) Supervisor B is nervous, always running around "checking up" on all his employees. He usually talks fast, gives one the impression that he is "selling" himself and his job when interviewed. He is forever picking up the phone, barking commands and requesting prompt action.

Both of these types (or a combination of these types) are expressions of much tension and pent up emotions that have been internalized. People working under such conditions finally are forced to "take it easy," or they find themselves with ulcers or a nervous breakdown.

But that is not the end of the problem. Constant tension leads to frustration. A frustrated person no longer operates as effectively as he was accustomed. He finds that he tends to forget things he used to remember. Work that he used to do with pleasure, he now delegates to someone else. He is no longer able to make decisions as fast as he did months ago. Now he finds he has to take a walk or get a cup of coffee—anything to get "away from it all."

SUCCESS FOR BUDGET SUPERVISORS MEANS FAILURE FOR FACTORY SUPERVISORS

Students of human relations agree that most people want to feel successful. We observe people constantly defining social and psychological goals, struggling to meet them, and as they are met, feeling successful.

Finance and factory supervisors are no exception. The typical finance supervisor does his work as best he can. He hopes and expects just praise of this work from his superior. Most of his success comes, therefore, from his superior's evaluation. It is the "boss" who will eventually say "well done," or commend a promotion. In other words, a finance supervisor measures his success on his job, to a substantial degree, by the reactions of his superior.

The situation is the same for the factory supervisor. He also desires success. Like the finance supervisor, much of his success also derives from the comments and behavior the "boss" exhibits. In short, the factory supervisor is also oriented toward the top for an evaluation of how well he is doing his job.

What is the task of a good and successful finance supervisor? The reader will recall that the finance people perceive their task as being the watchdog of the company. They are always trying to improve the situation in the plant. As one finance supervisor said, "Always, there is room to make it better." And finally, the reader will recall the statement that, "The budget man has made an excellent contribution to this plant. He's found a lot of things that were sour. You might say a good budget man ... lets top management know if anything is wrong."

In other words, their success derives from finding errors, weaknesses, and faults that exist in the plant. But, when they discover these errors, weaknesses, and faults, they also single out a "guilty party" and implicitly, at least, accuse him of failure. This is true because in finding weaknesses, errors or faults in a certain department, one is at the same time telling the factory supervisors that "things aren't going along as well as they could be." This, naturally, gives many factory supervisors a feeling of failure.

To be sure, such an occurrence will not make every supervisor feel he has failed. Some supervisors do not worry much about their job. Therefore, we find that the supervisor who really feels the failure is the one who is highly interested in doing a good job.

REPORTING SHORTCOMINGS OF THE FOREMAN

The way in which these shortcomings are reported is also important:

Assume that finance man A discovers an error in foreman B's department. How is this error reported? Does the finance man go directly to the factory foreman? In the plants studied the answer, usually, is "no."

The finance man cannot take the "shortest" route between the foreman and himself. For one reason, it may be a violation of policy for a staff man to go directly to a line man. But, more important (from a human point of view), the staff man derives his success when his boss knows he is finding errors. Therefore, his boss would never know how good a job finance man A is doing unless it came to his attention. In short, perhaps because of organizational regulations but basically because much success in industry is derived from above, the finance person usually takes his findings to his own boss, who in turn gives it to his, and so on up the line and across and down into the factory line structure.

Taking the long way around has at least one more positive value for finance people. The middle and top management finance people also derive some success in being able to go to the plant manager and point to some newly discovered weaknesses in the factory. Therefore, not only one man obtains feelings of success, but all interested people up the entire finance structure obtain some feeling of satisfaction.

But, how about the factory people? The answer seems evident. They experience a certain sense of "being caught with their pants down."

Finally, to add insult to injury, the entire incident is made permanent and exhibited to the plant officials by being placed in some budget report which is to be, or has been, circulated through many top channels.

473

EFFECTS OF FAILURE ON PEOPLE

One might ask: What effects does this kind of failure have upon an individual? If they were insignificant, obviously we would not be concerned. Such is not the case. Feelings of failure can have devastating effects upon an individual, his work and his relationships with others.

Lippitt and Bradford, reporting on some ingenious scientific experiments conducted on the subject of success and failure, state that people who fail tend to:

Lose interest in their work.
Lower their standards of achievement.
Lose confidence in themselves.
Give up quickly.
Fear any new task and refuse to try new methods or accept new jobs.
Expect failure.
Escape from failure by daydreaming.
Increase their difficulty in working with others.
Develop a tendency to blame others, to be overcritical of others' work and to develop troubles with other employees.

On the other hand, people who succeed tend to:

Raise their goals.
Gain greater interest in the activity in which they are engaged.
Gain greater confidence in their ability in the activity.
Increase their persistence to future goals.
Increase their ability to cooperate and work.
Increase their ability to adapt readily to new situations.
Increase their emotional control.

In summary, we should point out that finance people aren't inherently "out to get them" as factory people in the plants described them. Rather, they are placed in a social organization where the only way in which they can receive success is to place someone else in failure.

ACCOUNTANCY AS A FUNCTION OF ORGANIZATION THEORY

ROBERT T. GOLEMBIEWSKI

Modern accountancy is ineluctably the product of a wide variety of environmental factors that shaped its tools and approach. This truism can prove very useful. For example, common opinion has it that significant changes in the scope and methods of accountancy must be made. The truism heading this paragraph, then, requires this important qualification: Any lasting changes in accountancy will depend in significant respects upon understanding these environmental factors and upon changing or eliminating them, where possible.

A recent article—"Organization Theory and the New Accountancy: One Avenue of Revolution"[1]—developed this point of view by considering one major environmental determinant that has left a deep impress upon accountancy. The present article attempts to satisfy numerous requests to present the argument in a journal in which both theorists and practitioners in accountancy will have a more convenient opportunity for study and comment. Mere repetition, of course, seldom has much to recommend it. Therefore, this article takes a different approach to demonstrating the importance of organization theory to accountancy, and to outlining how structural innovation can contribute fruitfully to the present reevaluation of the scope and methods of accountancy. The reader reasonably may move from this piece to the more detailed argument of the original article, and thence to the massive literature on behavior in organizations that underlays both analyses.[2]

PURPOSES, PROCEDURES, AND PROBLEMS OF ACCOUNTANCY: SOME HERITAGES OF THE TRADITIONAL THEORY OF ORGANIZATION

The purposes, procedures, and problems of contemporary accountancy can be approached in useful ways as a function of the traditional theory of organization. Figure 1 facilitates making this point in detail. This figure depicts the conventional organization of three "line" processes A, B,

---

Article is from *The Accounting Review*, Vol. 39 (April, 1964), pp. 333–41. Reprinted with permission of author and publisher.

[1]Robert T. Golembiewski "Organization Theory and the New Accountancy: One Avenue of Revolution," *Quarterly Review of Economics and Business*, Vol. 3 (Summer, 1963), pp. 29–40.

[2]Much of this literature is reviewed and synthesized in the author's *Organizing Men and Power: Patterns of Behavior and "Line-Staff" Models*, Chicago: Rand McNally & Co., 1967.

and *C*, and of one "staff" service *D*. Symbolically, the contributions of $A + B + C + D$ combine to yield product P_1. Note also that *M* designates the manager, and that each *S* refers to a first-line supervisor.

FIGURE 1

ORGANIZING A SIMPLE SET OF OPERATIONS IN TERMS OF THE
TRADITIONAL THEORY OF ORGANIZATION

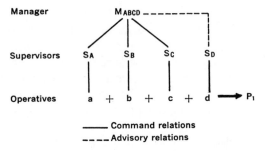

Figure 1 may be drawn with assurance and confidently taken to be a simplified analog of the kind of structure usually encountered in practice. For Figure 1 is based upon the well-known "principles" of the traditional theory of organization that guide most attempts at organizing. These "principles" include such propositions:

1. That work must be specialized in terms of functions at upper levels of organization and in terms of processes at lower levels.
2. That authority must be delegated by a single head to a sharply limited number of subordinates.
3. That supervision must be detailed and continuous.

The effects of these "principles" of organizing are clearly reflected in the purposes, procedures, and problems of accountancy. Some of the senses in which this is the case will be sketched below. For convenience, the emphasis will be upon internal reporting, as opposed to public accounting or the preparation of materials for annual reports and the like.

Purposes of Internal Reporting

Raising the question of the purposes of internal reporting easily could get out of hand. For the enumeration of such purposes is limited only by the ingenuity of the commentator. Let us keep tight rein on ingenuity here by restricting our attention to the several kinds of questions which a full-fledged system of internal reporting should be able to handle successfully. These questions, then, serve conveniently to outline the purposes of internal reporting. Following Simon and his collaborators,[3] three types of questions may be taken to outline the full range of challenges facing internal reporting:

1. Score-Card Questions: "Am I doing well or badly?"

---

[3]Herbert A. Simon, Harold Guetzkow, George Kozmetsky, and Gordon Tyndall, *Centralization vs. Decentralization in Organizing the Controller's Department,* New York: Controllership Foundation, 1954, pp. 3–4.

2. Attention-Directing Questions: "What problems should I look into?"

3. Problem-Solving Questions: "Of the several ways of doing the job, which is the best?"

The quoted illustrative questions, of course, are those that a "line" manager might ask himself and those that an internal accountant could help answer.

Procedures for Internal Reporting

These purposes of internal reporting, as it were, provide destinations rather than routes. There are numerous procedures that might be employed to achieve these purposes, that is. In general, however, the procedures actually employed have tended toward a stereotypic pattern. This fact does not reflect the rigid requirements of optimum efficiency in organizations. In fact, the stereotypic approach often significantly curbs efficiency, as will be demonstrated. The stereotypy of the procedures developed in pursuit of the major purposes of internal reporting, rather, reflects the domineering guidance of the "principles" of the traditional theory of organization and of the structure sketched in Figure 1.

The argument of this introductory paragraph is an important one, of course, and requires careful support. To this end, let the focus be upon one major procedural element that pervades so much of the practice of internal reporting in today's business and government agencies, the "line-staff" concept. I have elsewhere analyzed in some detail the classical "staff" model.[4] This classical model was dubbed the "neutral and inferior instrument" (NII) concept, for it prescribes that the "staff" man is outside the line of command, that he merely provides neutral advice or expertise, and so on. This terse characterization suffices for present purposes.

The NII concept of "staff" all but monopolizes the field in prescribing relations in contemporary organizations.[5] Evidence of the impact of this procedural device upon internal accounting is common, for example. Illustratively, and consistent with the NII model, the internal accountant commonly does not report "across" to a lower-level "line" official at his own level. In contrast, he reports *up* his own "staff" hierarchy of one or more superiors, the "staff" superior then reports *over* to the appropriate higher-level "line" official, and the latter in turn communicates *downward* to the "line" official directly concerned, the communication going through one or more levels of intermediate "line" supervision. More generally, much of the content of the role of the accountant engaged in internal reporting is defined in terms of the NII model.[6]

---

[4]Robert T. Golembiewski, "Toward the New Organization Theories: Some Notes on 'Staff'," *Midwest Journal of Political Science*, Vol. 5 (August, 1961), pp. 237–59.

[5]Dalton E. McFarland, *Cooperation and Conflict in Personnel Administration*, New York: American Foundation for Management Research, 1962, p. 18 and Table 19, p. 73.

[6]*See*, for example, David S. Brown, "The Staff Man Looks in the Mirror," *Public Administration Review*, Vol. 23 (June, 1963), pp. 67–73; and Chris Argyris, *The Impact of Budgets on People*, New York: Controllership Foundation, 1952.

The NII "staff" model did not just happen, of course. In all relevant particulars, it evidences the influence of the traditional theory of organization. Consider but a few factors that establish the point. At the very least, the NII model fits exactly such "principles" of the traditional theory of organization as specialization by function. In its crudest form, that model requires that the "line" specialize in "doing." "Thinking," or "planning," or some such, is reserved to the "staff."

Relatedly, only the NII model avoids a challenge to the unity of command underlying the traditional theory of organization. For the classical "staff" model claims both neutrality and inferiority, and both are necessary if the "principles" are to be respected.

This suggests the weakness of the NII model. Not that logical consistency with the "principles" was the only support of the NII model. That model was aided and abetted by the vigorous complaints of "line" officials around the turn of the century about sharing their authority with the new "staff" specialists. As Dale and Urwick described these complaints and their consequences:[7]

> So the fur flew, and harassed chief executives in business after business were driven into a hysteria of assurances that staff specialists were not meant to do what they had manifestly been hired to do. The line managers were solemnly told that the staff men were "purely advisory" and that no one need take their advice if they did not want to. . . .

Convenience, that is, proved a powerful reinforcement for logical consistency. Both together, however, hardly constitute scientifically desirable criteria for a "staff" model.

Problems of Internal Reporting

Internal reporting has suffered from this molding of procedures to the traditional theory of organization. In sum, the derived procedures proved inadequate to meet the three broad purposes of internal reporting as well as to surmount the mensural and motivational difficulties created by the traditional theory of organization. That is, the three purposes impose requirements different enough—*when the traditional theory of organization is respected*—that they tend to frustrate efforts designed to achieve all of them. Thus Simon and his co-workers noted the tendency of controller's departments to fulfill admirably one or another of the three purposes of internal reporting, while others receive less effective attention.[8]

The point here may be supported by outlining the demands of fulfilling each of the three purposes of internal reporting. Score-Card Questions, to begin, have attracted the lion's share of attention in organizations, and with

---

[7]Ernest Dale and Lyndall Urwick, *Staff in Organization*, New York: McGraw-Hill Book Co., 1960, p. 165.

[8]Simon, *et al., op. cit.*, pp. 3–4.

substantial reason. For the traditional theory of organization requires that an undue importance be placed on score-card data. Referral to Figure 1 helps explain this bias of the traditional theory. Simply, three "line" processes A, B, and C are involved in the production of item P_1. A "staff" service D—internal reporting, let us say—provides valuable service toward the same end. Therefore, crudely, $A + B + C + D = P_1$.

There are motivational and mensural problems aplenty in this simple formulation. Let us forsake comprehensiveness, and attempt to make the most of a single datum. That is, only M_{ABCD} oversees enough of the operations to make reasonable decisions on non-trivial matters related to production of P_1. Understandably, then M_{ABCD} will place great emphasis on score-card data. Many difficulties are implied and encouraged thereby. Three particular difficulties deserve spotlighting.

First, the traditional theory of organization encourages a separatism of the several units of organization while it requires that the efforts of each must be delicately integrated into a common flow of work. This works at cross-purposes, patently. Thus the units headed by S_A, S_B, S_C, and S_D have only tenuous responsibilities for P_1, the volume and the quantity of which is of obvious significance. The enduring interests of each of these units is more or less rooted in their own particular process or function. It could hardly be otherwise. For the traditional theory of organization stresses them, and individuals are paid to be interested in them. The difficulty, of course, is that total performance commonly comes off the loser in the effort to mesh such particularistic interests.

This phenomenon of separatism in organizations has been observed often, and it has been analyzed in telling detail.[9] We may, therefore, assume the incidence and significance of such organizational separatism and concentrate on its effects. When things go awry, as they often will, this situation obtains: M_{ABCD} will place increasingly great emphasis on score-card data; the individual supervisors will strive all the more mightily to have their own particular function or process appear in a good light, whatever this means for the total flow of work; and accountants will be forced to apply increasingly great pressure to unearth crucial data or to gain some measure of agreement about the allocation of costs. All this is natural enough, given the traditional theory of organization. But the dynamics tend to be self-defeating.

Second, these unfortunate dynamics do not reflect man's consistent and pervasive perversity. Rather, the traditional theory of organization tends to create an environment within which little better can be expected. Thus the traditional theory of organization forces the accountant to handle Score-Card Questions that are at least very difficult, if that theory does not create an

---

[9] James G. March and Herbert A. Simon, *Organizations*, New York: John Wiley & Sons, Inc., 1958, especially pp. 36–47; and Eliot D. Chapple and Leonard R. Sayles, *The Measure of Management* (New York: The Macmillan Company, 1961), especially pp. 18–45.

ersatz complexity that makes impossible any non-arbitrary assignments of costs to individual organization units. These Score-Card Questions, in the bargain, have great relevance for the lower "line," and great reliance often is placed in them by the upper "line." This outlines an unfortunate condition, and certainly one not likely to exhibit man at this cooperative best. The assignment of the cost of an error to A or B or C, for example, illustrates the kind of issues on which the mischief of the traditional theory is most patent.[10] Matters are delicate enough under the best of circumstances. Consider only one awkward feature of the traditional theory. Each "line" supervisor has a relatively large organization unit, all of whose members are bound by the tie of performing the same function or process. This datum implies the possibility of an organization unit waging substantial political warfare if it feels disadvantaged in the assignment of costs. Relevantly, a single unit in a structure like that in Figure 1 can disrupt the total flow of work. Ample evidence demonstrates that this leverage does not always go unutilized.[11]

The role of "staff" in such jostling for power must be conflicted. Let it not be said that the accountant always shrinks from the effort of developing the power necessary to play the game with some success.[12] An accounting unit hardly could meet the rigorous demands of the traditional theory of organization otherwise. Short of settling for a program of nagging obstructionism or of desperate devotion to minutiae, the effort to develop power—to be taken seriously by others in an organization—must be a constant one. The common reliance of the upper "line" upon internal reporting, in addition, simplifies matters for the accountant via "having the boss' ear." But note that this effort must remain a source of conflict for the "staff" man, even if it is successful. For the NII model does not legitimate such an active role, necessary though it may be. The "line," therefore, can seriously question the legitimacy of "staff's" exercise of power. And "staff" might feel guilty enough about its own efforts to resort to more or less elaborate subterfuges to assuage its discomfort. These conditions are not well designed to induce favorable working relations between "line" and "staff."

Third, score-card data often must be used in attempts to force the integration of operations complicated by the traditional theory of organization. Particularly because of the separatism by functions and processes prescribed by that theory, great demands are placed upon internal reporting as a means of goading cooperative effort or of assigning responsibility in its absence. This punitive motivational use of such data makes mensuration very difficult. For example, it can easily force organization units into a greater resort to devices of self-protection, thereby worsening the separatism already endemic to the traditional theory of organization and thereby

---

[10] For a case in point, *see* Argyris, *op. cit.*, pp. 17–19.

[11] Chapple and Sayles, *op. cit.*, pp. 89–97.

[12] Melville Dalton, *Men Who Manage*, New York: John Wiley & Sons, Inc., 1959, particularly chap. iii.

480

increasing the difficulties of meaningful internal reporting. As Worthy perceptively put the matter,[13] respecting the "principles" eliminates

"natural" standards of performance and management is forced to exercise considerable ingenuity in inventing controls which it can use for administrative purposes. Unfortunately, contrived controls such as these, so far from facilitating interdivisional cooperation (which is one of their purposes) often become themselves a source of conflict. The individual supervisor or executive is under strong compulsion to operate in such a manner as to make a good showing in terms of the particular set of controls to which he is subject, and often he does so only at the expense of effective collaboration across divisional lines.

This brief analysis is capable of terse summary. Score-Card Questions in an organization patterned after the classical theory have a punitive bias. Or to say almost the same thing, they tend to induce mechanisms of defense and self-protection. The point is crucial, for these products of generating score-card data outline just the conditions that make it very difficult to meet the other purposes of internal accounting. The point may be put in another way. Given the general acceptance of the traditional theory of organization, the collection of score-card data must preoccupy internal reporting. And to the degree that this is in fact true of any accounting unit the less likely is that unit to prove effective in handling Attention-Directing Questions or Problem-Solving Questions.

These are not merely logical surmises, be it noted. Relevant research leaves much to be desired. But this conclusion seems generally appropriate to the question of whether internal reporting should develop in the direction of more elaborate periodic score-card reports or toward strengthening special studies: ". . . further development of staff and facilities for special studies is a more promising direction of progress than elaboration of periodic accounting reports."[14] This conclusion reflects both a potential usefulness and a relatively unfilled need.

If this analysis is near the mark, then, merely calling for emphasis on Attention-Directing Questions and Problem-Solving Questions must prove abortive. For the traditional theory of organization remains undisturbed, with all that implies. Tersely, the procedures appropriate for Score-Card Questions under the traditional theory ill suit the requirements of the two former types of questions. The same is true of the tone of relations commonly induced in seeking score-card data, and perhaps of the personality characteristics appropriate for the effort under the traditional theory of organization. It might seem reasonable, as an alternative, to assign responsibility for each of the three purposes of internal reporting to separate

---

[13]James C. Worthy, "Some Aspects of Organization Structure in Relation to Pressure on Company Decision-Making," in L. Reed Tripp (ed.), *Proceedings of the Fifth Annual Meeting of the Industrial Relations Research Association*, IRRA Publication No. 10, 1953, p. 77.

[14]Simon, *et al., op. cit.,* p. 4.

units. This possibility is not considered here. Thus, among other consequences, it aggravates organizational separatism, raises jurisdictional questions, and invites overlap and duplication of effort. Moreover, for our purposes, this alternate approach is not very instructive although it might be the best accommodation possible under specific practical conditions.

This position may be supported parsimoniously. Consider Attention-Directing Questions. Thus Simon and his collaborators note that they require "direct and active channels of communication with the operating executives at those points in the organization where operations are being measured." The implied argument needs to be developed only briefly to suggest how the search for score-card data under the traditional theory of organization often fouls the delicate relations Simon sketches. The NII model of "staff," needless to say, greatly complicates just the kind of communication required, if the burdens of "up, over, and down" reporting do not in fact result in a hardening of the communicative arteries. Relatedly, the punitiveness and defensiveness that characterize so much of internal reporting do not provide much encouragement for the kind of interaction required by Attention-Directing Questions. Finally, the separatism fostered by the traditional theory of organization and the NII model does not predispose the component units of an organization to the continuing and sensitive co-operation required by the use of internal reporting to indicate the specific problems that "line" personnel might keep in mind.[15]

Much the same, if perhaps more pointedly, might be written of Problem-Solving Questions. They draw on a wide variety of information, including accounting data. They also require a high degree of mutual confidence, intimate knowledge of the needs of the affected units of an organization, and cooperative and continuing relations that permit timely studies. The traditional theory or organization, in general, would not be likely to do tender service to this catalog of prerequisites.

TOWARD A NEW ORGANIZATION THEORY

These few paragraphs sketch some dismal probabilities for cooperative effort, to be sure. Despair, however, is not necessarily in order. Indeed, it has proved possible for men of persistence and inventiveness to avoid the difficulties posed by the traditional theory of organization while meeting the full range of purposes of internal reporting. Guest, for example, provides an interesting record of just such a case of the fruitful cooperation of a new plant manager, his comptroller, and other "line" and "staff" officials in an organization that had suffered grievously from the full list of maladies sketched above.[16] Even in this case, however, some participants were pessi-

---

[15]On this point, see Argyris' analysis of interviews with budget officers in his *The Impact of Budgets on People, op. cit.*, chap. i.

[16]Robert H. Guest, *Organizational Change*, Homewood, Ill.: Richard D. Irwin, Inc., Irwin-Dorsey Series in Behavioral Science in Business, 1962.

FIGURE 2
ORGANIZING A SIMPLE SET OF OPERATIONS IN TERMS OF AN
UNORTHODOX THEORY OF ORGANIZATION

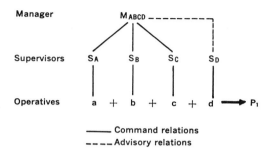

mistic. They felt a new era of good feeling would pass quickly with the transfer of the plant manager, who induced and sustained the changes by his skillful handling of men.

It would be foolish, of course, to place our hopes in managerial supermen. The good intentions of the vast majority of us are combined with lesser talents. Structural innovation can provide the continuing reinforcement of good intentions and average talents, however. Figure 2 sketches such a structure for the simplified set of processes considered in Figure 1. Notice that the focus in Figure 2 is upon what may be called "administrative entities," each of which contains all of the elements necessary for producing P_1. Figure 1, in contrast, stresses individual processes and functions. In this sense, a Figure 2 structure may be characterized as holistic, or integrational; a Figure 1 structure may be considered as particularistic, or fragmentary. To illustrate, each supervisor in Figure 2 controls all of the organizational elements necessary for P_1. The individual supervisors in Figure 1, however, each oversee only individuals performing a single activity required for P_1.

The unorthodox structure in Figure 2 is not merely an alternative to the traditional structure. It has been approached in numerous practical situations. Indeed, some aspects of the figure have been stressed by accountants as of great importance in the more effective use of accounting data for managerial control,[17] although such stress is not commonplace. Any organization with strong tendencies toward decentralization, moreover, will have important points of similarity with Figure 2. More or less typically, to illustrate, an accounting service (like D in Figure 2) will report directly to

---

[17]Consult, for example, Robert N. Anthony, *Management Accounting: Text and Cases*, Homewood, Ill.: Richard D. Irwin, Inc., 1960, 2d ed., especially pp. 320-33.

the "line" official at its level (S_1, for example) rather than upwards to unit D at headquarters. There are many variations in practice on the basic pattern, but their purpose is the same: to reduce time lags between observation and remedial action and to reduce the punitiveness both associated with the "up, over, and down" pattern of "line-staff" relations consistent with the traditional theory of organization.[18]

The several advantages of the structure in Figure 2 have been outlined in detail elsewhere. Here consider only one crucial sense in which internal reporting is facilitated. Thus the managerially significant measure of performance (e.g., variance from standard cost of the units headed by S_1, S_2, and S_3) is also a relatively simple accounting task. The more difficult task of determining the costs to be assigned A, B, C, or D within any unit of organization, moreover, is less significant. For a supervisor's status no longer will depend directly upon whether the charges go to A or B or C, as is the case in a Figure 1 structure. In addition, no supervisor will be threatened by the internal accountant's handling of this more difficult task. For the results of such inquiry can help the supervisor in more effectively managing the total administrative entity for which he is responsible. In a Figure 1 structure, in stark contrast, the results of such an inquiry inherently imply punishment of supervisors for imperfections in a total flow of work, of which any supervisor controls but a part, and for which he often has no clear and unambiguous responsibility. There is a world of difference between the two structures in this particular, needless to note.

There are other convenient features of the structure in Figure 2. Thus much of the pressure is taken off internal reporting—and off accountants!—because it is not used as a goad to superior (or more likely acceptable) performance. For now the units headed by the three supervisors can be compared in terms of simple and meaningful measures of performance.

Thus the relative value of the efforts of units headed by S_A, S_B, S_C, and S_D in Figure 1 can be approached only via arbitrary and often troublesome conventions that are all too vulnerable to sharp dealing. Moreover, these conventions often act as ceilings on performance, a happenstance that motivated one student to argue for the use of bogus budgets so as to avoid limiting effort.[19] In addition, developing or changing these conventions often will prove difficult and seem arbitrary, in that these conventions are not tied to the demands of work in any clear and direct way. The meaningful competition of the several comparable units in a Figure 2 structure, in pleasing oppositeness, should operate so as to induce an upward-orientation in what is considered an acceptable level of performance. The "pressure," in

[18]Harry D. Kolb, "The Headquarters Staff Man in the Role of a Consultant," in Mason Haire (ed.), *Organization Theory in Industrial Practice*, New York: John Wiley & Sons, Inc., 1962, pp. 143–46.

[19]Andrew C. Stedry, *Budget Control and Cost Behavior*, Englewood Cliffs, New Jersey: Prentice-Hall, Inc., 1960, especially pp. 17, 41–42, and 71.

a real sense, is sustained and yet seems natural in that it derives directly from work.

Consider also that a Figure 2 structure reduced the intensity of the forcefield within which internal reporting must take place. Any single unit in a Figure 1 structure, to approach the point, can exercise considerable power. Thus the unit headed by S_A, for example, could seriously disrupt the total flow of work. Indeed, output could fall to zero. In a Figure 2 structure, however, restrictions of output by one unit would disadvantage only members of that unit. Output would fall at most by $1/N$, where N is the total number of similar autonomous units. Realistically, units in a Figure 2 structure would hesitate to punish only themselves, a fact that reduces the probability of resistance by an obstreperous unit of organization.

Simple structure variations, that is to say, can have profoundly different consequences for behavior.

Such description might be extended, but it would come to the same point. The structure in Figure 2 is very congenial to filling the three purposes of internal reporting. Score-Card Questions, that is, are neither so crucial, nor so subject to arbitrary allocations, nor so likely to adversely color the relations of accountants and others, as Figure 1 structures. This of itself makes more probable a telling emphasis on Attention-Directing Questions and Problem-Solving Questions.

But the argument need not be made by default. More positively, the accountant d in the unit headed by S_1 patently has a continuing relationship with the several processes necessary to produce P_1; moreover, he has a direct stake in the successful performance of his unit. He is no longer an organizational "outsider" with interests quite different from those of the unit served, as in Figure 1 structures. He can communicate directly with the official at just the point at which operations are being measured. And it is definitely in the interest of accountant d to draw quick attention to opportunities to improve operations, to know and to anticipate needs, and to help study alternate ways of meeting them. For shoddy work will be subject to facile comparison with the performance of other units. The implied enlargement of the job of accountant d, in addition, also is attractive.[20]

This merely sketches the positive argument, of course. But it suffices to demonstrate that, following Figure 2, it is possible to challenge the full range of purposes of internal accounting with more optimism than one can muster when considering the traditional theory of organization.

SUMMARY

Internal reporting serves as a case in point of the intimate senses in which accountancy is a function of organization theory. The traditional

---

[20]For numerous examples of the efficacy of job enlargement, see Georges Friedmann, *The Anatomy of Work*, Glencoe, Ill.: Free Press, 1961, pp. 40–67.

theory of organization has the effect of directing attention to but one of the purposes of internal reporting, the asking of Score-Card Questions, and this at great cost to cooperative effort. An unorthodox theory of organization does not suffer from the same liabilities to the same degree. Of particular significance, this unorthodox theory of organization facilitates asking Attention-Directing Questions and Problem-Solving Questions that must receive a growing proportion of the attention of the accountant engaged in internal reporting, and this if only because electronic data processing will increasingly eliminate much of the accounting time heretofore devoted to Score-Card Questions.

Therefore, it seems appropriate that organization theory receive considerable attention by members of the accounting profession, which is presently in the throes of rethinking its scope and methods. For an inappropriate organization structure can frustrate the most worthy of intentions and, in any case, any fundamental changes in accountancy will require changes in the traditional theory of organization.

CENTRALIZATION VS. DECENTRALIZATION IN ORGANIZING THE CONTROLLER'S DEPARTMENT

HERBERT A. SIMON,
GEORGE KOZMETSKY,
HAROLD GUETZKOW, AND
GORDON TYNDALL

The study seeks to determine the *effectiveness* of different forms of departmental organization. Ideally, in a business concern the test of effectiveness is profit. But for testing the effectiveness of organizing the controller's department, the question cannot be approached in this direct fashion. Intra- and interdepartmental relations are too indirect and complex to be traced directly to profits. Hence, three indirect measures of effectiveness were used. A controller's department is effective to the extent that it—

> Provides informational services of high quality.
> Performs these services at a minimum cost.
> Facilitates the long-range development of competent accounting and operating executives.

INTRODUCTION · · ·

The words "centralization" and "decentralization" are used with a wide variety of meanings. One of these meanings, however, is fundamental to the others, and it becomes the strategically important one for this study:

> An administrative organization is centralized to the extent that decisions are made at relatively high levels in the organization; decentralized to the extent that discretion and authority to make important decisions are delegated by top management to lower levels of executive authority.

For example, a measure of the degree of centralization or decentralization in the whole production department would be obtained by observing the relative roles of the vice president for manufacturing, the factory manager, and the factory department head, respectively, in important production decisions. The greater the part of company top level executives in decision-making, the greater the centralization of organization; the greater the role of factory executives, or factory department executives, the greater

Article is from *Centralization vs. Decentralization In Organizing the Controller's Department*, New York: Controllership Foundation, Inc., August, 1954, pp. 1–2, 4–9, 13–17, and 18–19. Reproduced with permission.

the decentralization in organization to the factory or factory department levels.

Survey observations indicate that these controllers' departments enter the decision-making process primarily as suppliers and analyzers of information, and as consultants. Therefore, "centralization" and "decentralization" in the controllers' departments must be related to the levels in other departments to which such information, and analytical and consulting services are supplied.

The relative degree of centralization or decentralization of the controller's department depends on at least five factors:

1. *The structure of the accounts and reports.* A decentralized account structure is one that provides a maximum of information about individual subordinate organization units (for example, individual factory departments, or sales districts), by means of separate cost statements or profit and loss statements for individual units.[1]

2. *The geographical location of accounting functions.* Geographical decentralization means locating the personnel of the controller's department in the company's factories and district officers rather than largely at the home office.

3. *Formal authority relations.* Decentralization of formal authority means attaching accounting units directly to the operating units whose activities they are recording—for example, placing the factory controller under the authority of the factory manager.

4. *Loyalties.* Decentralization of loyalties means encouraging accounting personnel to regard themselves as members of the operating "team" to which they are providing service.

5. *Channels of communication.* Decentralization of communication means building up direct contact and communication between accounting personnel and the executives and supervisors of decentralized operating units—for example, direct communication between the factory accounting department and factory department heads or personnel.

This study showed rather conclusively that the same degree of centralization and decentralization is not desirable with respect to all five of these factors.

CENTRALIZATION AND DECENTRALIZATION OF THE ACCOUNT STRUCTURE

Two rather different kinds of decentralization are possible. One, which is sometimes called "responsibility accounting," consists in classifying actual and standard (or budgeted) costs according to the organizational unit primarily responsible for incurring the cost, and presenting periodic cost statements for each such unit. The other, sometimes described as "profit and loss accounting," consists essentially in treating interdepartmental and

---

[1]Decentralization, in this sense, is a function of the amount of detailed information supplied about individual organization units. The form in which this information is to be provided (e.g., the chart of accounts) will, of course, be determined primarily at top levels of the controller's department.

interdivisional transfers of manufactured and partially manufactured goods as "sales," thereby arriving at a profit and loss statement for individual organizational units like divisions, factories, sales districts, and sales branches.

Survey findings leave little doubt that *a decentralized account structure of one or the other of these two forms is desirable—at least down to the level of factory departments, sales districts, and individual sales branches.* A more difficult question is whether the decentralization should be in the direction of responsibility statements or profit and loss statements.

Where a company is divided into a number of relatively self-contained parts, each responsible for manufacturing and selling a group of products, profit and loss statements for these individual parts appear to be meaningful and effective. Decentralized profit and loss accounting runs into real difficulties when the parts of the company to which it is applied are not really self-contained—for example, when separate decentralized statements are prepared for manufacturing and for sales of the same products.

There are four main reasons for avoiding overelaboration of decentralized accounting reports: (*a*) Reporting items not controllable at the respective decentralized units is an unnecessary expense; (*b*) It decreases understanding of the reports and discourages operating men from using them; (*c*) It may lead to resentment; and (*d*) It often causes tardiness in issuance of the accounting reports.

No evidence was found that decentralized profit and loss statements are more effective than decentralized responsibility statements in promoting profit consciousness. It is suggested that profit consciousness is best promoted along two rather different lines:

> Informing executives and supervisors from time to time about the company profit picture, and the spread that is needed between costs and sales to maintain profits. But this does not require incorporating profit information in the periodic accounting reports, or arbitrarily allocating overhead items to individual statements.
>
> Developing further the problem-solving uses of accounting information which will help to educate executives and supervisors as to the profit consequences of specific decisions.

ORGANIZATION WITHIN THE CONTROLLER'S DEPARTMENT

> *There is generally much to be gained from separating, to a considerable degree within the controller's department, the personnel and units responsible for each of three major kinds of functions:*
>
> Bookkeeping, and preparation and distribution of periodic accounting reports.
> Assistance to the operating departments in current analyses of accounting information for score-card and attention-directing purposes.
> Participation in the use of accounting information for problem solving on a special-studies basis.

Perhaps the principal need for separating these functions is to maintain adequate administrative direction and control over the amount of time and effort that is devoted to the different kinds of tasks by accounting personnel. It was repeatedly observed that, when accountants had heavy supervisory responsibilities for report preparation in addition to analytical responsibilities, the pressures of supervision and deadlines led to a relative neglect of analytical work. As a result, when the functions are combined, the controller's department retains little control over the amount of effort that is given to each.

Combining the functions leads to a potential conflict between the accountant's function of providing service to operating departments, and his function of analyzing operations to provide valid and objective data for higher levels of management. Separating the record-keeping functions from analytical work is also an important supplement to an effective internal audit in reducing the dangers of collusion. It may also give the analytical personnel greater freedom to develop close working relationships with operating executives without a feeling of conflicting responsibilities.

Another reason for separating the functions is to allow greater flexibility for organizing each of them in the most economical and effective manner. If there is some organizational separation, each function can be located at the level or levels most appropriate for its particular task. Each can be centralized or decentralized to the extent that appears desirable, independently of the others.

CENTRALIZATION AND DECENTRALIZATION: CURRENT ANALYSIS

An essential condition for the attention-directing use of data is that the accounting reports be reviewed regularly and periodically in order to determine when performance is "off standard" and to initiate inquiries as to the reasons. A principal means for accomplishing this lies in the development of communication channels between the controller's department and the operating departments at the appropriate levels.

There are at least two directions in which the controller's department can take the initiative to strengthen the use of accounting services:

By doing an effective job of funneling reports upward from factories and sales units, and bringing them to the attention of top level executives, so that these executives, in turn, will use the reports in dealing with their subordinates.

By getting top management support for a regular, systematic interpretation of monthly cost variances to be prepared by operating men with the assistance of analysts from the accounting department. This will encourage a regular and growing contact between the controller's department and operating men at middle management levels.

490

Among the most essential direct communications channels between controller's and operating departments are those between the controller and the factory department head, the factory manager, the district and regional sales managers, and the top company executives responsible for production and sales.

Such channels can be developed by:

Giving accounting personnel duties that can only be discharged by working with operating men.

Giving these assignments high priority by separating them from record-keeping and supervisory functions.

Physically locating the accounting man close to his operating counterpart.

Using for these contacts accounting personnel who have adequate status and character to maintain the relationships on a basis of mutual respect, and who possess a thorough understanding of operations.

CENTRALIZATION AND DECENTRALIZATION: SPECIAL STUDIES

In the companies studied, a very great part of the "spade work" in investigating major operating problems is done by persons outside the controller's department; hence, to a large extent, these problems cut across departmental lines and have to be dealt with from a company-wide or factory-wide viewpoint. For this reason, the special studies work calls for more centralized communications than the current analysis work. An effective organizational arrangement appears to be to establish a unit for special studies in the company offices of the controller's department, and a smaller unit of the same sort in each of the larger factories or other major operating units.

Under most circumstances *the controller's department can most effectively bring its special skills to bear upon problems as a part of a team—formal or informal—that includes staff assistants to operating executives and members of other staff departments as well as accounting personnel.*

Formal procedures that required the preparation of "savings statements" as a basis for capital appropriations were very effective in bringing the controller's department into the decision-making process. Institution of a formal cost reduction program had this same general effect. This suggests that the use of accounting information for problem-solving purposes could be further extended by developing similar procedures in areas like production scheduling, market research, or quality control, which would give the controller's department a broader opportunity to participate formally in the investigatory process. It would also increase effective managerial use of the wealth of data available from the controller's department.

491

CENTRALIZATION AND DECENTRALIZATION: RECORD KEEPING

For the record-keeping units, the main questions of centralization and decentralization relate to the geographical location of the personnel. How far should the record-keeping and reporting functions be centrally located? How far should they be decentralized to factories and sales districts?

The most important consequences of centralization or decentralization of the records functions have to do with the accessibility of documents and the reliability of the source records. Both of these criteria point in the direction of relatively great geographical decentralization. To give access to detailed records, it is generally advantageous to decentralize record keeping to the locations where the major uses are made of the data. To get reliability, the accounting personnel who are responsible for recording and classifying data need to be as close as possible to the operating situations where the data originate.

There may be definite cost advantages in centralizing to the extent that is necessary for mechanization or clerical specialization. In the surveyed operations, most of these economies can be attained with units centralized to the factory or regional sales level. Further centralization apparently offers little additional gain from a cost standpoint. For this reason it should be possible to retain most of the advantages of decentralization mentioned in the previous paragraph without decentralizing so far as to incur serious clerical "diseconomies."

Questions of promptness, uniformity in classification of data, and auditing control are in most instances of small importance in determining the optimal degree of centralization and decentralization of record keeping.

Manufacturing Records

For manufacturing operations of any size, the volume of clerical work in a single factory is generally sufficient to permit the bulk of the accounting for manufacturing operations to be done at the factory. There remains the question of whether factory record-keeping activities should be further subdivided and decentralized into accounting units paralleling the several operating departments in the factory, or whether they should be assigned to centralized units corresponding to the major accounting activities. The conclusion reached from survey observations is that the net advantage lies on the side of the centralized structure within the factory, although the balance of advantages is less decisive in a very large factory with several separate products and production lines, than it is in a smaller factory.

When the purchasing function is centralized for the company as a whole, the question arises as to whether the accounts–payable work should be handled in the company offices or the individual factories. The project staff were unable to determine that there were important advantages, one way or another.

492

Sales Records

In sales accounting, the operations involving the greatest volume of clerical work are billing and the maintenance of accounts receivable. There are indications that, primarily for reasons of access to records, evident advantages exist in locating the accounts receivable in the same city or cities as the credit units. But to achieve clerical economy in posting to the accounts, the credit work should not be further decentralized than is absolutely necessary.

In none of these companies was the location of billing a particularly critical matter. When sales are made through company sales branches, locating the billing function with accounts receivable and collections seems generally satisfactory. In other cases, the advantages seem fairly balanced between billing at the factory or sending a copy of the shipping memorandum to a central billing unit located with accounts receivable.

FORMAL AUTHORITY OVER DECENTRALIZED ACCOUNTING OPERATIONS

There are two general types of arrangements of the lines of formal authority in the companies studied. In some, the factory controller or chief accounting executive[2] is completely under the formal authority of the company controller. In other companies he is "functionally" responsible to the company controller, "administratively" to the factory manager.

It was observed that when the accounting department lacks acceptance and active support from the top levels of the manufacturing department, it may be unsatisfactory to divide authority over the factory accountant between the company controller and the factory manager. But in organizations *where top executives of the operating departments regard the controller's services as important management tools, a system of divided authority appears to work as well as a plan in which the factory controller or district office manager reports solely to the company controller.*

Of greater importance than the lines of formal authority is the question of how much leeway should be given the accounting man, at a decentralized location, to run his own shop. Whether authority was centralized or decentralized, *it was found that the greatest service was provided to factory management when the factory accountant felt that he had authority to provide reports to the factory management as requested, within the minimum standards of accounting policy and procedure* laid down by the company controller's department.

---

[2]To avoid confusion of terms and to reduce necessity for lengthy, qualifying phrases, the term "factory accountant" is used in this report to designate the chief accounting and control executive in the factory. This is not intended to suggest that a division or factory controller's responsibilities are confined to accounting.

Whatever the formal arrangements, it seemed that appointments and removals of factory accountants are almost always a matter of negotiation and agreement between the controller's department and the factory manager. Admitting this joint responsibility, there is probably some advantage in placing the formal power of appointment in the controller's department.

Because of the nature of their duties, office managers in sales groups are more likely than factory accountants to regard themselves, and to be regarded, as members of the operating executive's staff. On the whole, the case for decentralized authority appears stronger in the sales than in the manufacturing area. But, where the normal lines of personnel movement lie within the accounting department, the office managers themselves tend to prefer having personnel and salary administration in the hands of the controller's department.

THE DEVELOPMENT OF ACCOUNTING PERSONNEL

In most organizations, promotion tends to be more or less "vertical." When a position is vacant, the tendency is to fill it by promotion from one of the positions immediately subordinate to it, or in a related part of the organization. If an organization is designed along the lines recommended above, a vertical promotion policy is likely to lead to difficulties. With the separation between analytical work and record-keeping functions, one group of accounting executives would, with vertical promotion, develop their analytical skills but acquire little experience in' supervision; another group would acquire supervisory skills with little chance to develop competence in analytical work.

Hence, *in an organization developed along the suggested lines, it is important that there be an intelligent and carefully administered plan for the horizontal transfer of potential supervisors and executives at several stages of their careers.* By horizontal transfer is meant promotion from analytic positions to supervisory positions in record-keeping units, and vice versa.

Personnel development for controllership functions is an organizational problem only to a limited degree. To a far greater extent it is a problem of providing men with training and experience, both prior to and during their employment, that will deepen and broaden their understanding of general business problems. One specific direction for progress is the broadening of pre-employment training for industrial accountants. A second direction is to develop further the opportunities for interdepartmental promotion of promising men. A third direction is to encourage the use of teams and "task forces" drawn from several departments to undertake major planning studies.

. . . .

THE MEANING OF CENTRALIZATION AND DECENTRALIZATION

"Centralization" is a word of many meanings. With reference to management problems, an administrative organization is *centralized* to the extent that decisions are made at relatively high levels in the organization, and persons at lower levels have relatively little discretion. Conversely, an administrative organization is *decentralized* to the extent that important delegations of discretionary and decision-making authority are made from higher to lower levels of the organization.

This study is particularly concerned with:

The degree of centralization or decentralization within the controller's department;
The relationship of this to the degree of centralization or decentralization within operating departments, particularly manufacturing and sales.

Centralization and Decentralization in Controllers' Departments

In some companies a factory accountant is given broad discretion to determine the accounting procedures to be used in the factory, or the kinds of reports to be prepared for the factory manager; in other companies, he is not. In the former case, therefore, there is relatively great decentralization *to the factory level* within the controller's department; in the latter situation there is relatively great centralization *to the company level* within the controller's department.

Centralization and Decentralization in Operating Departments

In some companies a factory manager is given broad discretion to determine manufacturing methods, to handle industrial relations, even, in some cases, to determine what the factory is to produce. The broader the scope of the functions over which the factory manager exercised discretion, the greater the decentralization *to the factory level* in the manufacturing department. In several of the companies studied (Westinghouse Electric is an example) there is an important intermediate stage of delegation between the company level and the factory level—the division. Certain matters are decentralized all the way to the factory, others only to the division. Similarly, on the sales side, in many companies the regional office constitutes an important level between the central company office on the one hand, and the district sales office, on the other.

Relationship Between Controller and Operating Department Decentralization

Effectiveness of centralization or decentralization of the controller's department is likely to depend on the relative centralization of operating departments of the company, particularly manufacturing and sales. For example, there would be little apparent point in supplying department

495

foremen with information that would help them schedule production if scheduling decisions are made at the factory or company level with little departmental participation.

What constitutes an effective relationship between the controller's department and operating departments? Is the most effective procedure to feed accounting, statistical and analytical information into the operating organization at the levels where the relevant operating decisions are being made? Or is it better to feed all accounting information in at the top levels of the operating organization, relying on the manufacturing and sales executives to transmit downward information needed for decisions at lower levels. How far should the analysis of data be an accounting responsibility; how far an operating responsibility? It is clear, then, that the study involves examination of centralization and decentralization of the broad accounting functions of controllership *in relation to* operating centralization and decentralization.

Degree and Elements of Centralization or Decentralization Are the Core of the Problem

Centralization may also vary within an administrative unit, some of its functions being centralized while others are decentralized. None of the seven companies studied had completely centralized organizations and functions. Particular activities within the seven companies were found to be centralized or decentralized *to a degree,* varying widely from unit to unit, and from function to function. Thus, posing the problem of centralization became a question of examining the *degree* of centralization and decentralization of the different decision-making functions. It also involved analyzing the *impact* of centralization on five important elements of accounting functions of the controller's department:

1. The *structure of the accounts and reports.* For example, whether the chart of accounts is broken down in such a way that a cost statement or a profit and loss statement can be drawn up for an individual factory or department within a factory.

2. The actual *geographical locations* where accounting functions are performed. For example, whether the records of factory costs are posted at the factory or in the company offices.

3. The *formal authority relations* between accounting personnel and operating personnel. For instance, whether the factory accountant reports to the company controller or to the factory manager.

4. The structure of *group loyalties.* Whether the factory accounting personnel regard themselves as part of the factory "team" or as part of the controller's department, for example.

5. The *channels used* by accounting and operating personnel *in communicating* with each other. For instance, whether the company controller and his home office subordinates communicate directly with the factory controller, or whether their communications with the factory are channeled through the factory manager.

The following paragraphs will attempt to clarify further what is meant by each of these five elements.

Decentralization of Accounts and Reports. The first element relates to the structure of the accounts and reports themselves. For example, in a company with a number of factories, the account structure is decentralized to the factory level if most costs for a factory are separately accumulated and a more or less complete income and expense statement prepared periodically for the factory. Similarly, if within each factory costs are accumulated for each department, the structure is decentralized down to the departmental level.

Decentralization of the accounting structure is aimed at the greatest possible decentralization of operating decisions but retaining the operating executive's responsibility for results—results that may be measured in terms of sales, profits, return on investment, or cost reduction.[3]

The idea that the account structure should be decentralized at least to the factory has gained wide acceptance in American industry. In selecting companies for study, the project staff was unable to discover one that did not go at least this far in decentralizing its accounts. Almost all accounting and operating executives of these companies were agreed that the factory manager's job is to make as large a profit as possible, within the limits of company policy, with the manufacturing facilities and investment available to him.

The device most generally used in these companies for securing accountability with a decentralized account structure is the budget, usually of the flexible type, and a monthly comparison of actual with budgeted expenditures. In most, but not all the companies, the determinants of the monthly production cost allowances are tied in directly to the system of standard production costs, adjusted for volume variance. Thus, when the actual manufacturing cost equals the standard, the actual expenditure equals the budget. In about half the companies, a profit and loss statement is prepared for each factory or group of factories in a division. Practice varies as to whether sales are entered in the factory profit and loss statement at actual sales price or at a standard price. One company calculates for each factory the ratio of profits to investment; another is planning to introduce a balance sheet prorating its total capital investment to its various manufacturing facilities, and treating each, on paper, as a separate "corporation."

Generally, decentralization of accounts is not carried as far in sales as in manufacturing. In one case, the manufacturing department "sells" its product to the sales department, and profit and loss statements are prepared for geographically decentralized sales units, but this is not general practice.

There is a wide range in the degree of completeness of the factory accounts. At one end of the range is a company in which purchasing of

---

[3]For a nontechnical discussion of the philosophy underlying decentralization of the account structure, *see* Perrin Stryker, "P & C for Profit," *Fortune* (April 1952), pp. 128 ff.

principal raw materials is centralized. The factory accounts show only the labor actually employed at the factory and operating supplies purchased locally. Material costs and allocations of the company sales and administrative expenses do not appear on the factory statements.

At the other end of the range is a company in which the factory statements include all manufacturing expenses, including materials priced at standard, together with a recirculated allocation of company sales and administrative expenses. The companies which have carried furthest the philosophy of fixing profit responsibility at the factory tend toward this structure of factory accounts.

Geographical Centralization and Decentralization. A second, and quite distinct element in decentralization is the *geographical dispersion* of bookkeeping and accounting functions to the actual locations where manufacturing and sales activities are carried on. It was this characteristic that a controller had in mind when he stated in an interview: "We have decentralized our factory cost figures. They keep their own records."

There is, of course, no necessary connection between the degree of decentralization of the account structure, as previously defined, and the geographical decentralization of accounting activities. It would be entirely possible to have the account structure decentralized to the departments, for example, and still have all of the original accounting documents forwarded to the central company offices for recording and preparation of reports. On the other hand, it would also be entirely possible to have virtually all the recording activities, including tabulating, carried on at the plants and district sales offices, but no separate cost reports prepared for these individual organizational units.

As a matter of fact, in the companies studied, those that have gone furthest in decentralization of their accounts and reports have generally gone furthest in geographical decentralization of accounting functions. This raises the question, to be discussed in later chapters, of whether there are compelling administrative reasons why these two aspects of decentralization should go hand in hand. Will the efficiency or effectiveness of accounting suffer if there is more or less geographical decentralization than decentralization of accounts? Or has this close connection come about simply through a lack of recognition that two separate sets of organizational decisions are involved here?

In the companies studied, a number of situations existed where these two kinds of decentralization have not been carried to the same organizational levels. The case of accounts receivable in Eastman Kodak has already been mentioned. Although the *accounts* are decentralized so that reports can be compiled for individual sales branches, the accounts receivable ledgers are maintained and posted in the company central offices. Comparison of National Works with Donora Works yields an example of varying practice in factory departments. The account structure is very similar in the two works, but at Donora many of the recording functions are handled by accounting units located out in the several works departments, while at National most of these functions are performed at the central works accounting offices.

Centralization and Decentralization of Authority. A third element in centralization and decentralization relates to the lines of formal authority in the organization. Viewing a multi-plant (or multi-division) company as a whole, it is decentralized if each factory operates as a more or less self-contained unit, with the factory manager responsible for all of the functions carried on within the factory, and having formal authority over all factory personnel.

If the industrial relations director in the factory or the head of the industrial engineering department reports to his counterpart in the company offices, instead of to the factory manager, the organization is centralized to that extent. Similarly, if the top accounting executive in the factory reports formally to the factory manager, accounting control is decentralized; if he reports to the company controller, it is centralized.

Again, this third element in centralization and decentralization may be quite independent of the two previously examined. Indeed, in the companies studied, decentralization of the account structure and geographical decentralization of accounting functions had always been carried further than the decentralization of authority.

In answering questions about formal authority, persons interviewed usually made a distinction between "administrative" authority and "functional" authority. By "administrative" authority they meant the day-to-day relation of a "boss" to his subordinates. This included work assignments, handling personnel and operating questions referred by subordinates, and settling questions involving relations among subordinates. By "functional" authority they meant the right to determine the technical aspects of the accounting function: the chart of accounts, report content and deadlines, bookkeeping procedures, and so on. Obviously, there is some possibility of overlap and of disagreement as to precisely which decisions fall in one category and which in the other. However, little confusion or disagreement was found in the operating departments as to the proper classification of matters which arose in daily operation.

. . . .

Group Loyalties. The formal authority relationships do not tell the whole story of whether the factory accountant operates as a member of a centralized accounting department or a member of a decentralized factory staff. His personal feelings of loyalty must be taken into account. On the organization chart, he might appear as a member of the accounting department, but in fact he might regard himself as a part of the factory management team; the reverse might be true.

It is not easy, in an interview with strangers, for a member of an organization to give a frank and objective appraisal of where his loyalties lie. Hence, the survey team attempted to assess a number of related pieces of

499

evidence to learn whether factory accountants regarded themselves primarily as members of the factory manager's "team" or the company controller's "team." For example, they were asked which of two reporting assignments with close deadlines would receive priority. The interviewer noted whether they spoke of the operating management of the factory as "we" or "they," and similarly, for the home-office accounting department. Whether or not informal lunch-time and other social groups tended to cut across the line between accounting and operations was observed and noted.

Appraisal of this evidence indicates that loyalty tends to be closely associated with the centralization or decentralization of formal authority. In general, the primary loyalty of the factory accountant is with the controller's department in those companies where formal authority in accounting is centralized. In those companies where formal authority is decentralized, the loyalties appear, on balance, to be with factory management. There were two factories, among those in companies with decentralized authority, where the factory accountants felt themselves more or less cut off from *both* the factory management and the controller's department. In these two situations, the factory accountants tended to regard themselves as subject to "cross pressure" from these two sources, rather than as having a strong allegiance to either.

The sample of seven companies and nine factories is far too small to permit a generalized assessment of the factors associated with centralized or decentralized loyalties and their relative importance. A few observations may be mentioned as explanatory factors.

Geographical separation from the home office appears to foster decentralized loyalties. In companies having distant branches, in California, for example, comments were frequently volunteered about the problems of maintaining home-office control over accounting operations in those branches.

Further, the feeling that "we are accountants, but they are operating people," appears to be a powerful force restraining the decentralization of accounting loyalties. Even in the situations with most decentralized loyalties, the accounting personnel felt strongly their responsibility for accurate reporting in accordance with *company* accounting procedures—including procedures they thought incorrect or inadequate.

A number of specific instances were observed where competing claims were made upon accounting personnel to adhere to the professional standards of accountancy on the one hand and, on the other, to get along with factory management by not reporting unpleasant facts. With one possible exception, all observed conflicts of this sort were resolved in favor of the standards of the profession.

Centralized loyalties were also fostered by the tendency of accounting personnel to look to the controller's department for chances of promotion. Except for Eastman Kodak, there was little transfer of accounting employees into manufacturing departments; there was more movement into sales department positions. Where interdepartmental promotions were relatively common, loyalties were more decentralized than elsewhere. Whether the opportunities for promotion are the cause, and the decentralized loyalties the effect, or vice versa, is hard to assess.

Centralization and Decentralization of Communication. Closely related to the question of centralization or decentralization of formal authority and of feelings of loyalty is the question of communications. Communications aspects of accounting organization will be considered decentralized to the factory if communications of the factory accounting personnel are more frequent with factory operating executives than with the headquarters controller's department. In the opposite case, the organization is considered centralized. Further, communication is not considered to be the routine flow of accounting documents and reports, but contacts by letter, telephone, or face-to-face for the purpose of assigning work, requesting information, settling problems of accounting procedure, and so forth. Both the amount and importance of such communication will be taken into account in assessing relative strength of communication channels.

As with other elements in decentralization, the pattern of communications within a plant or division may differ significantly from the organization of accounting communication for the company as a whole. At least one situation was found where communication for the *company as a whole* was relatively centralized—that is, communications between headquarters and factory control and accounting. However, *within the factory*, communication was relatively decentralized—in the sense that there was more communication between the factory accounting department and other factory departments than between the accounting department and the factory manager.

CHAPTER VIII

SOME TECHNICAL CONTEXTS OF

PUBLIC BUDGETING AND FINANCE:

TOWARD MORE EFFECTIVE CONTROL

Any system of public financial controls rests on an underlying technology of tools and approaches. It is to a diverse collection of these tools and approaches that this section turns. The collection includes the commonplace and the esoteric; it stresses definition of financial concepts as well as statistical tools; and it encompasses both individual techniques and their complicated combinations in sub-systems or systems of financial controls. While it is unrealistic to expect to be everything to all men, this section tries.

A first selection, "The Local Administrator as Budgeter," casts a wide net. It defines several types of budgets; it illustrates typical budget documents; and it establishes the intimate connection between estimating costs and developing a budget document. The emphasis in budgets may be on the various kinds of activities or services or equipment for which public funds are to be expended, as in the "line-item budget." The emphasis also may be upon the major objects or programs of public spending, as in "performance" or "program" budgets. Wherever the emphasis, "The Local Administrator As Budgeter" illustrates (if only in simple cases) the rudiments of budgeting.

As the objects of budgeting become more complicated, approaches and tools of analysis of corresponding power must be developed, for complexity requires that the total budget process be factored into manageable pieces. Factoring in turn, however, complicates the problems of somehow exerting overhead control, and of attempting to bring spending in individual areas into some coherent balance in terms of systemic criteria. The more individual factorings and sub-factorings, the greater the problems of control and coherence. For example, at Factoring I the executive may be convinced that he prefers more spending on A than B. But if a_1, a_2, and a_3 all contribute to A, the budgeter in Factoring II again must develop criteria to assign dollar priorities. So it may go

502

for many additional factorings. In the process, the criteria for choice are likely to become more explicit, and judgments about desirable priorities may shift in complex ways. Consequently, a goal may be considered desirable in Factoring I, but subprograms necessary to achieve that goal may not gain corresponding support in later factorings because alternative uses of monies are somehow more justifiable at that level.

If the mental picture projected is one of a duality, of a kind of tug-of-war between irreconciliables, the sentences above have communicated what they intended. Roland N. McKean handles some of the complexities of the factoring problem in his "Criteria of Efficiency In Government Expenditures." He develops the notion of "suboptimization," of the factoring of spending decisions into sub-parts because no one or no system can meaningfully compare all relevant alternatives. He concludes that, in the absence of some general criteria, difficulties will plague our attempts at factoring.

Factoring will always pose problems but, to some degree at least, we can determine which problems we must face. For example, all budgetary decisions require factoring of some sort, so factoring problems there must be. However, different approaches to budgeting raise different factoring problems.

The different factoring problems of various approaches to budgeting may be outlined briefly. Traditionally, for example, the chief executive issues a call for estimates, which are generated from below. Thus a strict line-item budget might list "10 stenographers at $4500 each." This line-item is the product of many factorings beginning at low levels of organization whose requests were aggregated and perhaps trimmed as they rose through a hierarchy. An overhead authority seeking control probably would attempt to control the number of stenographers. Even if the executive controlled this factoring, his victory would be a slim one indeed, for that executive must be more concerned with what the stenographers do than with how many there are. What the stenographers would do under a strict line-item budget, however, was decided in earlier factorings. Checking the validity and specifics of decisions made in these early factorings poses a difficult problem for the executive. Moreover in these early factorings, agencies develop internal consensus about, and commitment to, specific programs. This consensus and commitment often are difficult for any executive to change.

Roughly, each additional factoring further restricts the top executive's meaningful control. And traditional budgeting procedures restrict the executive to later factorings. As Schick observes:[1]

> In budgeting, which is committed to the established base, the flow of budgetary decisions is upward and aggregative. Traditionally, the first step in budgeting, in anticipation of the call for estimates, is for each department to issue its own call to prepare and to submit a set of estimates. This call reaches to the lowest level capable of assembling its own estimates. Lowest level estimates form the building blocks for the next level where they are aggregated and reviewed and transmitted

[1]Allen Schick, "The Road to PPB: The Stages of Budget Reform," *Public Administration Review*, Vol. 26 (December, 1966), pp. 257–58.

upward until the highest level is reached and the totality constitutes a department-wide budget. Since budgeting is tied to a base, the building-up-from-below approach is sensible; each building block estimates the cost of what it is already doing plus the cost of the increments it wants. (The building blocks, then, are decisional elements, not simply informational elements as is often assumed.)

In sum, the line-item budget makes it difficult for the top executive to influence those factorings which he must particularly control. This is an awkward combination.

Under a "program budget," in contrast, the executive can and must influence early factorings. This may enhance his control, for this kind of budget in the first factoring deals with decisions made by the executive about the priorities of various programs, with what will be done. Hence the common designation "PPB" (Planning-Programming-Budgeting). Later factoring must refine how program objectives will be achieved and which specific mix of resources will be used, of course. These later factorings are difficult for the top executive to control, but he also has less interest in them. As Schick observes:[2]

PPB reverses the informational and decisional flow. Before the call for estimates is issued, top policy has to be made, and this policy constrains the estimates prepared below. For each lower level, the relevant policy instructions are issued by the superior level prior to the preparation of estimates. Accordingly, the critical decisional process—that of deciding on purposes and plans—has a downward and disaggregative flow.

The comparison above of the two approaches to budgeting is greatly simplified, but Allen Schick's contribution remedies this simplicism. Schick provides a detailed look at Planning-Programming-Budgeting, which most broadly is an attempt to take advantage of the top executive's control over early factorings in the expenditure process. Schick's "The Road to PPB: The Stages of Budget Reform" carefully illustrates the arguments supporting program budgeting, speculates on its probable advantages, and makes some educated guesses about what changes in the processes of public spending are implied by PPB. Overall, the implied changes are significant. Thus they require that policy be made before budget estimates are solicited. Consequently, the premium is on doing in rough form—from the top, down—the planning and programming on which budgets will be based. A line-item budget, in crude but useful opposition, lessens the top executive's control over planning and programming.

In addition to being able to decide what kinds of factoring problems we will cope with, considerable progress has been made in how well we can cope with whatever factoring problems we face. For example, Gene H. Fisher's "The Role of Cost-Utility Analysis In Program Budgeting" introduces the kind of tools required to make policy prior to the detailed preparation of budget estimates. Just such pre-preparation (to use Schick's term) is required by PPB, of course. Fisher discusses and illustrates one application of "cost-utility analysis" that

---

[2]*Ibid.*, p. 258.

facilitated making a policy decision before detailed budget estimates were requested from executive agencies. Revealingly, only six weeks were available to compare the cost benefits of several alternative military policies. Without question, some large multiple of six weeks would have been required if the agencies in question had been asked to submit detailed budget estimates. Moreover, agency personnel might have developed a commitment to a specific alternative which the President or high-level defense officials might in turn have to violate later because of broader considerations.

Cost-utility analysis is merely one of a numerous arsenal of powerful analytic tools which have become available largely since World War II. John W. Pocock's "Operations Research: A Challenge to Management" provides a summary introduction to several prominent new mathematical techniques in this growing analytic arsenal. Among their many other uses, such techniques provide some of the more sensitive analysis and control required by today's complex budgeting and financial decisions.

Various systemic uses of new management techniques also have been developed. Perhaps most prominent among these is PERT, whose prime applications have been in scheduling and controlling complex interdependent events such as the development of the Polaris missile. Ivars Avots describes this system for scheduling and control in "The Management Side of PERT." PERT applications make particular use of the computer. For example, PERT networks commonly include many hundreds of individual events, each with its own estimated completion time and complex interdependencies with other events. Should the completion of a particular event be delayed, computer runs can reveal the impact of that delay on the total set of events, help re-schedule by permitting choice between alternative adaptions to unanticipated delays, and the like.

Benjamin J. Mandel shows that public budgeting and finance can be aided in more humble ways. Techniques need not be as esoteric as queuing theory; computations need not challenge a sophisticated computer; and problems need not be of such overwhelming dimensions as the Polaris program. Mandel's "How to Apply Sampling In Voucher Examinations" relates statistical techniques to voucher-checking that has been so much a source of irritation over the years. Congress' authorization to use sampling methods rather than 100 percent inspection is another reflection of a new attitude toward public budgeting and finance. As Mandel gently indicates, however, this attitudinal change must be complemented by increased knowledge and skills of relevant specialists whose training was narrower. In this case, most auditors apparently lacked the statistical skills necessary to take advantage of the Congress' authorization. Mandel thus illustrates the commonplace need to reinforce changed attitudes with appropriate skills, even as new skills challenge old attitudes.

THE LOCAL ADMINISTRATOR AS BUDGETER
Frank P. Sherwood and
Wallace H. Best

To fully understand the budget process in your city it is necessary to have an understanding of the various types of budgets. In your career as supervisor you will hear reference made to such terms as current or operating budgets, capital budgets, long-range capital improvement programs, line-item budgets, performance budgets, and program budgets.

CURRENT AND CAPITAL BUDGETS

In most cases the current budget (or operating budget as it is often called) covers municipal operations for a year period. It may be contrasted to the long-term or capital budget, which is concerned with the acquisition of land and rights-of-way and the construction of major public works such as public buildings, streets and bridges, sewer systems, off-street parking, and public utilities. The current or operating budget pays for such things as salaries; materials and services, such as street repair materials, mimeographing services, stationery; and other items essential to the continuing maintenance of the city plant.

The capital budget is distinguished from the current budget in various ways:

1. It represents a long-range plan of capital investment only.
2. It does not have the annuality of the current budget. Projects may be programmed for six years ahead and the effects of the capital program are much longer than that.
3. It is not adopted and executed in the same way as the current budget. The general goals are approved for a six-year period but are subject to yearly revision. The capital projects program for the coming year is made a part of, and executed through the current operations budget.

All-too-often a city provides for capital improvements only when the need in a particular case has become sufficiently acute to dramatize the extraordinary expenditure which is usually required. Thus, the city's financial resources may be exhausted by provision for a few capital items, while other needs are neglected.

In contrast to this haphazard method a comprehensive plan (usually drawn up by the planning department or planning commission after con-

---

Article is from *Supervisory Methods In Municipal Administration*, Chicago, Ill.: The International City Managers' Association, 1958, pp. 255–64. Used with permission of publisher and authors.

sultation with the various departments of the city government and submitted to the citizens of the community for their suggestions and advice) will indicate what things are needed; the relative importance of the various items; and the location, character, and scale of what is to be done to satisfy these needs. The long-range capital improvement program will schedule these items over a period of years so that they can be provided as needed, within the limits of the financial resources of the community.

FIGURE 1
EXAMPLE OF LINE-ITEM BUDGET

PUBLIC SAFETY FUND
EXPENDITURES

Account Number	Account Title	1956 Actual	1957 Actual	1958 App'ns
2-1	Police Department			
A	Salaries	$387361	$417407	$451460
B-11	Heat and Light	11741	11215	11800
B-21	Telephone and Telegraph	4387	4523	4500
B-23	Postage	18	38	40
B-24	Travel and Training	339	462	950
B-26	Freight	40	75	100
B-29	Ambulance Service	9600	11370	14880
B-37	Doctor and Hospital	2221	819	2500
B-41	Legal Notices	33	30	100
B-45	Printing	498	471	500
B-62	Investigations	4	...	100
B-65	Court Costs and Fees	...	42	100
B-71	Office Equipment Repairs	593	347	600
B-72	Bldg. and Bldg. Equipment Repairs	1619	1405	2000
B-92	Towels and Laundry	149	67	150
B-93	Dues	15	21	25
B-95	Disinfectants	332	300	350
C-11	Office Supplies	2187	2094	2550
C-21	Gasoline and Oil	10117	10072	10500
C-22	Motor Vehicle Supplies and Repair	6497	5738	6500
C-41	Jail Food	2972	2797	3000
C-42	Janitor Supplies	108	190	250
C-8	Medical Supplies	4	6	25
C-112	Wearing Apparel	4560	4602	6400
C-113	Photo Supplies	845	688	1100
C-114	Radio Repair and Supplies	...	...	1500
C-12	Other Supplies	1315	1680	1300
D-11	Motor Vehicle Insurance	1568	1732	1780
C-12	Building and Content Insurance	149	149	200
Z-1	Office Equipment	528	155	1100
Z-2	Motor Vehicle Equipment	2853	16818	12400
Z-12	Other Equipment	1300	2944	1800
	Total	$453953	$498257	$540560

LINE-ITEM BUDGET

In most cities the budget is regarded primarily as a financial and accounting device with expenditure estimates for various departments being submitted and reviewed as money estimates. Requests are supported mostly by the detailing of objects to be purchased such as materials, supplies, equipment, and salaries to be paid. The validity of the request is judged largely on the basis of comparison with previous expenditure experience. This is the line-item type of budget, based on appropriations to each "object" classification (materials, supplies, equipment, and salaries, for example). Figure 1 illustrates one example of a line-item type of budget.

PERFORMANCE BUDGET

In recent years the term "performance budget" has been widely adopted to identify a concept of the budget as a device for planning city programs of service. This terminology was first used by the Hoover Commission in recommending the adoption of improved budgetary techniques by the Federal Government:

> We recommend that the whole budgetary concept of the Federal Government should be refashioned by the adoption of a budget based upon functions, activities, and projects; this we designate a 'performance budget.'
> Such an approach would focus attention upon the general character and relative importance of the work to be done, or upon the service to be rendered, rather than upon things to be acquired such as personal services, supplies, equipment, and so on. These latter objects are, after all, only the means to an end. The all-important thing in budgeting is the work or the service to be accomplished, and what that work or service will cost.[1]

Thus the goal of the performance budget is to reach beyond the dollars alone and the mere objects of purchase, to the end result of governmental operation—the services to be performed.

Performance Budgets and Program Budgets

In essence there is little distinction between performance budgeting and program budgeting. As a matter of fact, the budgeting identified as performance budgeting in the Hoover Commission report was first known as program budgeting (see Figure 2).

Building Expenditure Estimates. Not so long ago the department head in a city with a large annexation program was bemoaning the fact that he could not operate his department on the funds "they gave him." The council's reaction was "we gave you everything you asked for." When the department head pointed out that the council had not provided for the services required for the annexed areas the council's reply was "tell us how much it will cost to service that area and we'll see that you get the money." This placed the department head in a dilemma: all he knew was that he was short on manpower and equipment. He wanted more dollars but when he had to say how many dollars he threw up his hands in confusion.

---

[1]United States Commission on Organization of the Executive Branch of the Government, *Report Number 7: Budgeting and Accounting*, Washington, D.C.: U.S. Government Printing Office, 1949, p. 8.

The line-item approach shows how many clerks are to be hired, how much travel money will be spent, how much will go for printing, mimeographing, paper, typewriters, and stationery. This is a clear and explicit type of budget, but with no precedent for his guidance the department head is not helped out of his dilemma by the line-item practice. A new and different approach is needed.

FIGURE 2
EXAMPLE OF PROGRAM-TYPE BUDGET

PERSONNEL DATA	Actual 1955–56	Esti-mated 1956–57	Budget 1957–58
REGULAR POSITIONS			
Clerk Typist 2........	1	1	1
Clerk Stenographer 2...	1	1	1
Semi-Skilled Laborer....	1	1	1
Sidewalk Const. & Rep. Frmn...............	1	1	1
Cement Finisher.......	1	1	1
Street Inspector........	6	6	6
Street Inspector-Supervisor..............	1	1	1
TOTAL REGULAR POSITIONS......	12	12	12
MAN YEARS PAID.	11.8	11.8	11.9
OVERTIME HOURS PAID...............	564	528	528

EXPENDITURE RECAP	Actual 1955–56	Esti-mated 1956–57	Budget 1957–58
PERSONAL SERVICES			
Regular Payroll........	44,988	47,475	48,098
Overtime Payments....	1,078	1,075	1,075
TOTAL PERSONAL SERVICES......	46,066	48,550	49,173
NON-PERSONAL EXPENSE			
Inspectors Bus Tickets..	750	750	750
Materials Used by Repair Crew..........	287	845	800
Maintenance City Property...............	35,623	43,425	46,350
Sidewalk Assessment Work...............	14,030	23,000	20,000
TOTAL NON-PERSONAL EXPENSE........	50,690	68,020	67,900
OUTLAY			
Major Installation.	5,958	....	5,700
TOTAL DIVISION..	102,714	116,570	122,773

— CITY OF HARTFORD —
ANNUAL BUDGET
PUBLIC WORKS
CURBS AND WALKS   31–11

All activity of the Sidewalk Division has been combined in code 31–11 including the office staff previously reflected in 31–01, the repair crew formerly in 31–12, and sidewalk assessment work once charged to 31–17. However, curb and walkwork included in paving projects is absorbed in the street maintenance account.

This division inspects the condition of all sidewalks, curbs, driveways, ramps, house numbers, street signs, parking meters, and water and gas gates along 215 miles of city streets. Orders are sent to property owners to repair walks and drives. In the event of non-compliance, the city may order the work done and the bill charged against the owner. Revenue code 7316 reflects the amount of reimbursement.

Installation of sidewalk and drive on the north side of Allen Place along the cemetery, $2,700, and replacement of walk at South Green, $3,000, are included in outlay. The maintenance program is outlined below:

CITY RESPONSIBILITY	Actual 1955–56	Esti-mated 1956–57	Budget 1957–58
WORK MEASUREMENT			
Curbs–lin. ft........	13,351	21,363	22,000
City-owned walk–sq. ft............	4,394	5,500	5,500
City-accepted walks–sq. ft...........	3,995	5,000	5,000
COST			
Curbs..............	$30,913	$37,395	$39,600
City-owned walks ...	2,460	3,445	3,500
City-accepted walks.	2,250	2,585	3,250
TOTAL..........	$35,623	$43,425	$46,350

PRIVATE RESPONSIBILITY			
Walks and drives–sq. ft..............	20,844	33,424	30,770
Cost..............	$14,030	$23,000	$20,000

THE PERFORMANCE APPROACH

The performance approach calls for a budget in which the appropriation figures bear a clear relation to service standards, volumes of work to be performed, methods of performing such work, and the cost element required by such standards and volume.

Performance data has sometimes been called "what we're going to do" data. The supervisor who has been crucified by the newspapers because he didn't remove snow during last winter's snow storm or because the streets flooded due to inadequate cleaning of sewer mains or catch basins will have a happier life if he develops a budget with the "what we're going to do" approach.

The supervisor needs both accounting data and performance data. The accounting division can furnish the dollar amounts required in developing expenditure estimates. Performance data consists of organization charts, work programs, and units for measuring these programs. Accounting information may help the supervisor correlate and interpret the performance data but most of the performance information must be developed by the individual supervisors.

The supervisor first must identify his current program size. He may know, for example, that the city has a policy of removing snow only after a four-inch fall or cleaning catch basins every five years, but perhaps the policies were laid out when there were not as many parking meters and cars or before so much road construction was underway as to create an added burden of dirt on the streets. When the program size has been clearly identified the next step is to compute the costs for the current program and programs of alternate sizes. In this way he can provide an expenditure estimate based on adequate study. The final appropriation can then be proposed by his department head and the chief administrator and determined by the council on the basis of helpful and understandable information.

Measuring Activities

At the heart of any program or performance budget is an adequate system of measurement. In preparing a performance-type budget request the supervisor, if he wishes to clean all residential streets once every two weeks, must have information available which will enable him to compute "how much" gasoline, oil, materials, and supplies will be needed for that schedule; "how many" man-hours will be needed to achieve the program; and "how much" new equipment must be purchased if the program is to be accomplished. The "how much" and "how many" call for measurements. Figure 3 shows the units of measurement commonly used in public works and public utility departments. These units provide the public works supervisor with information needed to make a start on measuring the activities of his work group.

All supervisors have rules or standards of operation which they consciously or subconsciously apply to their operations. These standards usually have been developed through years of experience. However, there is a tendency to judge entirely on the basis of past experience and neglect the important factor of changing conditions. In refuse collection, changes in the packaging of foods, method of heating homes, family size, and disposal methods have a bearing on standards.

A recent example of extenuating circumstances affecting the standard is shown in a case concerning water meter readings. The supervisor checked the daily progress of the meter readers by applying his rule-of-thumb: an average of 150 meters to be read each day. The average readings dropped off from this figure until the supervisor began transferring his readers. He discovered that the problem still persisted. Finally in desperation the meter readers asked the supervisor to come with them on their rounds. The supervisor found that the readers were having difficulty getting into the homes. More and more housewives were working, and the callbacks had nearly doubled since the 150-per-day standard was set. The supervisor adjusted his schedule so the readers would read at times when people were at home.

Production standards supply supervisors with a definite means of determining when the work load fluctuates upward to a point where more manpower should be added, or downward to a point where surplus manpower should be removed. Two earlier chapters have described the techniques developed for the improvement of methods of doing work. These techniques are available to the supervisor in developing production standards. In using them, if he discovers the job is not being done in the most efficient manner, or that the most efficient method is not being used, then the faulty operations must be corrected before production standards can be determined.

There are three approaches to standard setting: the man-hour approach (Figure 4 below shows this approach); the cost accounting approach (see Figure 5, especially the line headed "Washing Luminaires,"— the total unit cost shown at the end of the line provides a relatively scientific foundation for projecting future costs); and the ratio of personnel approach (under this system the number of personnel required is related to a definite organization index,—thus, in the federal government recent standards call for one personnel employee to every 110 civilian workers, and one person performing payroll, leave, and retirement activities for each 235 civilian employees). Whichever of these three approaches is decided upon, it becomes the basis for building the expenditure estimates.

Nonmeasurable Activities

While it is true that the supervisor has many tools to measure his activities, there are inevitably some activities which defy measurement. Only a portion of governmental activity is amenable to production measurement. An administrator, for example, cannot be expected to produce a prescribed number of "decisions" per day. However, the supervisor should make every effort to "measure" in order to increase the efficiency and effectiveness of his operation.

CONTROLLING THE BUDGET

If the supervisor spends too much his excess will reduce the city's surplus; that is, unless his excess costs are offset by some other supervisor's better cost control. A good supervisor never relies on this because he doesn't want to gain the reputation of always having to be bailed out.

FIGURE 3
Units of Measurement

PUBLIC WORKS AND UTILITIES DEPARTMENT UNITS OF MEASUREMENT APPLICABLE TO COST ACCOUNTING

Title: Function Activity Operation	Unit of Measurement	Title: Function Activity Operation	Unit of Measurement
Inspection Services		Placing Road Materials	
Building Inspection	each	(Solids)	sq. yd. or ton
Smoke Abatement Inspection	each	Low-type Bituminous Streets	
		Scarifying, Grading, Shaping	sq. yd.
Sewer Operation and Maintenance		Rolling	sq. yd.
Sewer Operation		Placing Road Materials	
Sewer Operation		(Solids)	sq. yd. or ton
Pumping	000 gal.	Placing Road Materials	
Purification and Treatment	000 gal.	(Liquids)	gal.
Sludge Disposal	tons	Patching	each
Laboratory		Paved Streets	
Laboratory Testing and		Removing Old Pavement	sq. yd.
Inspection	each	Rolling	sq. yd.
Sewer Maintenance		Placing Road Materials	
Storm Sewer Lines		(Solids)	sq. yd. or ton
Excavating	cu. yd.	Placing Road Materials	
Filling	cu. yd.	(Liquids)	gal.
Removing Pipe	l. ft.	Placing, Finishing Concrete	
Laying Pipe	l. ft.	(Pave.)	sq. yd.
Sheeting and Bracing	sq. ft.	Placing, Removing Forms	
Cleaning	l. ft.	(Pave.)	l. ft.
Sanitary Sewer Lines		Patching	each
Excavating	cu. yd.	Curbs and Gutters	
Filling	cu. yd.	Patching	each
Removing Pipe	l. ft.	Resetting and Removing	l. ft.
Laying Pipe	l. ft.	Roadsides	
Sheeting and Bracing	sq. ft.	Cutting Grass, Weeds, and	
Cleaning	l. ft.	Brush	sq. yd.
Combined Sewer Lines		Culverts	
Excavating	cu. yd.	Major Fixture Replacement	each
Filling	cu. yd.	General Repair and	
Removing Pipe	l. ft.	Maintenance	each
Laying Pipe	l. ft.	Sidewalks	
Sheeting and Bracing	sq. ft.	Placing, Finishing Concrete	
Cleaning	l. ft.	(Pave.)	sq. yd.
Catch Basins		Placing, Removing Forms	
Laying Brick	000 brk.	(Pave.)	l. ft.
Laying Stone	00 blk.	Patching	each
Sewer Manholes		Laying Brick	000 brk.
Laying Brick	000 brk.	Laying Stone	00 blk.
Laying Stone	00 blk.	Resetting and Removing	l. ft.
Open Drains and Brooks		Street Cleaning	
Laying Brick	000 brk.	Machine Sweeping	mi.
Laying Stone	00 blk.	Hand Sweeping	mi.
House Connections Mainte-		Flushing and Dust Laying	mi.
nance		Sweepings Disposal	ton
General Repairs	each	Winter Maintenance	
Thawing	each	Sanding	mi.
Cleaning and Inspecting	each	**Sanitation**	
House Connection, Con-		Garbage Collection and Disposal	
struction		Collection	ton
Excavating	cu. yd.	Set Out and Set Back	each
Filling	cu. yd.	Incinerator Operation	ton
Laying Pipe	l. ft.	Incinerator Bldg. Operation,	
Tapping	each	Maintenance	
Gates and Valves		Dry Refuse Collection and	
Major Fixture Replacement	each	Disposal	
General Repairs	each	Collection	ton
		Set out and Set Back	each
Maintenance of Thoroughfares,		**Parks, Parkways and Cemeteries**	
Appurtenances		Parkways, Maintenance	
Alleys		Parkway Tree Maintenance	
Removing Old Pavement	sq. yd.	Planting	each
Scarifying, Grading, Shaping	sq. yd.	Trimming and Removal	each
Rolling	sq. yd.	Inspection and Spraying	each
Placing Road Materials		Other Maintenance	
(Solids)	sq. yd. or ton	Cutting Grass, Weeds, and	
Placing Road Materials		Brush	sq. yd.
(Liquids)	gal.	Planting Grass	sq. yd.
Placing, Finishing Concrete		Spreading Fertilizer	sq. yd. or ton
(Pave.)	sq. yd.	Parks and Playgrounds,	
Placing, Removing Forms		Maintenance	
(Pave.)	l. ft.	Paths and Drives	
Patching	each	Scarifying, Grading, Shaping	sq. yd.
Unpaved Streets		Rolling	sq. yd.
Excavating	cu. yd.	Placing Road Materials	
Filling	cu. yd.	(Solids)	sq. yd. or ton
Scarifying, Grading, Shaping	sq. yd.	Placing Road Materials	
Rolling	sq. yd.	(Liquids)	gal.
		Patching	each

FIGURE 4

MAN-HOUR APPROACH TO STANDARD SETTING

Forms and Instructions Used by Los Angeles
for Performance Analysis by Man-Hours

Form CAO-9

PERSONNEL REQUIREMENTS - CITY OF LOS ANGELES

Function: Protection to Persons & Property Code No. 20

Subfunctions: Structural Regulations 21

Department: Building and Safety Code No. 21.1

Activity: Bldg. Permits & Inspections 21.11

			Last Completed Year				Current Year (Est.)				Next Year (Est.)					
(1)	(2)	(3)	(4)	(5)	(6)	(7)	(8)	(9)	(10)	(11)	(12)	(13)	(14)	(15)	(16)	(17)
Code No.	Description	Work Unit	Work Units	Personnel	Total Man-Hours	Man-Hours Per Unit	Work Units	Personnel	Total Man-Hours	Man-Hours Per Unit	Work Units	Man-Hours Per Unit	Total Man-Hours	Overtime Man-Hours	Regular Man-Hours	Personnel
.110	Administration....	B	......	3.9	8083	......	......	4.0	8352	......	......	......	8352	......	......	4.0
.111	Plan Checking.....	Bld. Pl. Ck'd	16809	41.8	87334	5.20	15456	39.9	83358	5.40	15500	5.50	85250	1200	82750	40.2
.112	Public Counter.....	" " Issued	60297	18.0	39463	0.65	47790	19.0	39672	0.83	50000	0.89	42750	......	......	20.5
.113	Zoning Enforcement....	" "	60297	10.0	20984	0.35	47790	11.0	22968	0.48	48000	0.50	24000	......	......	11.5
.114	Board Reports.....	Reports	10665	3.8	7934	0.74	10810	4.0	8382	0.77	11000	0.75	8250	......	......	4.0
.115	Inspections........															
.1150	Administration......	B	......	3.5	7308	......	......	3.8	8004	......	......	......	10440	......	......	5.0
.1151	Inspections.......	Inspections	370691	60.4	126020	0.34	348416	59.7	124584	0.36	350000	0.36	126000	......	......	60.3
.1152	Masonry Inspections.....	Inspection	17076	6.3	13050	0.76	19284	7.0	14616	0.76	20000	0.75	15000	......	......	7.2
.1153	Relocation.......	Applications	1462	5.0	10440	7.14	1444	5.0	10440	7.23	1500	7.25	10875	......	......	5.2
.1154	Maintenance and Occupancy....	Surveys	44659	27.6	57612	1.29	44716	31.7	66160	1.48	51000	1.40	71400	......	......	34.2
.1155	Parapet Walls.....	Surveys	1096	3.0	6264	5.71	850	3.0	6264	7.40	900	7.22	6500	......	......	3.0
.1156	Slum Clearance & Rehabilitation....	H	......	......	......	......	......	......	......	......	......	......	10440	......	......	5.0
.116	Clerical........	Documents	107831	41.6	86798	0.80	94936	39.4	82290	0.87	100000	0.88	88000	......	......	42.1
.117	Investigation & Prosecutions....	Cases	317	4.0	8352	26.35	334	4.0	8352	25.00	8750	1.00	8750	......	......	4.2
	TOTALS	......	......	228.9	479642	......	......	231.5	483442	......	......	......	516007	1200		246.4

Subactivities

513

FIGURE 5

COST ACCOUNTING AS APPLIED TO STREET LIGHT MAINTENANCE
COSTS IN SAN DIEGO

FUNCTION: STREETS
DEPARTMENT: PUBLIC WORKS
ACTIVITY: STREET LIGHT MAINTENANCE
MAINTENANCE STANDARDS:

WASHING LUMINAIRES—2 TIMES PER YEAR
LAMPING   —2 TIMES PER YEAR
PAINTING STANDARDS —BIENNIALLY

UNIT COSTS

OPERATION	UNIT Man-hours	RATE PER Man-hour	UNIT LAB. COST	UNIT MAT'L	UNIT EQUIP.	TOTAL UNIT COST
Washing Luminaires.	0.23	$1.29	$0.30	$0.01	$0.02	$0.33
Lamping..........	0.39	2.11	0.82	0.96	0.12	1.90
Painting Standards..	0.77	2.23	1.71	1.04	0.08	2.83

NUMBER OF STREET LIGHTS IN SERVICE..........................5010

Washing luminaires	5010	× 2	×	$0.33	=	$ 3,307.00
Lamping	5010	× 2	×	1.90	=	19,038.00
Painting standards	5010	÷ 2	×	2.83	=	7,089.00

ROUTINE MAINTENANCE BUDGET.........................$29,434.00

For the supervisor to carry his share of the load he needs to know two things: what expenses are in his budget, and where he stands in money spent at each mile post along the way. Proper charging helps in the effort to control expenses. When right account numbers are applied the supervisor knows what has gone into each set of figures reported back to him. Thus, he can read the score better when he is sure he knows what is in each account.

Oftentimes the supervisor would like to have every kind of expense shown separately but this usually costs too much for the accounting division to supply, and would also be too burdensome. That is why some small amounts are grouped. It adds some difficulty to the supervisor's task of keeping fully informed about the necessary details because there is trouble in remembering what is in each total. For this reason, the supervisor should ask the accounting division to tell him exactly what kinds of expenses are to be charged into each group total.

Many expenses the supervisor controls directly, some only indirectly. There may be expenses he can do nothing about: rent and depreciation are among those. Light, heat, and power are others he cannot do much about unless he has meters in his department. Yet the great majority of expenses he can do something about.

Many supervisors develop expense charts on which they plot the trend in expenses in order to carefully observe their year-to-date costs. Some are constantly analyzing their operating methods in order to determine the weak spots.

Each departmental budget in addition to being a plan for provision of services, is a part of the whole cost-control plan of the city. Budgets are created to hold expenses within limits and to avoid a deficit. In order to hold the line the best procedure is to plan out expenditures before the money is spent. Costs must be foreseen and controlled. Each supervisor will regulate the flow of expenditures by standards of his own that control his rates of spending. "Beating" the budget, or meeting service standards with less money than is available in the budget, is an excellent way to show your ability as a supervisor.

CRITERIA OF EFFICIENCY IN GOVERNMENT EXPENDITURES

Roland N. McKean

A good deal of progress has been made in certain analytical techniques, for example, those of estimation and computation, that can help us choose efficient courses of action. But one aspect of seeking efficiency, that of devising appropriate criteria or tests of preferredness, is almost as troublesome as ever. Moreover, it is a crucial aspect of choosing efficient policies; for with or without painstaking measurements and sophisticated computational techniques, poor criteria can lead to some very peculiar choices. As a simple illustration, consider the criterion and one of the choices of the efficiency expert in the play *The Pajama Game:*

> While I am still in bed I shave
> And the lather drips and the bed gets wet,
> And, oh, what a lousy shave I get
> But think of the time I save.[1]

But let us turn to more serious problems of choice and criterion difficulties. In this paper, I shall discuss a major complication in the devising of criteria, a few generalizations about appropriate tests of preferredness, and their application to specific governmental problems of choice. These remarks apply particularly to the use of quantitative analysis—whether called economic analysis, operations research, or systems analysis—in seeking efficient government programs and activities.

In comparing alternative government operations or courses of action, we cannot apply what might be called ultimate criteria. Thus we cannot apply such tests as "maximum well-being from available resources." Without more precise definitions, this is merely saying that we want the best. And when we spell out tests of preferredness more precisely, we find that we are using proximate criteria—that is, practicable tests which are not necessarily or obviously consistent with ultimate goals. The fact that we have to use such criteria makes it easy to adopt erroneous ones.

Article is from *Federal Expenditure Policies for Economic Growth and Stability,* Washington, D.C.: U.S. Government Printing Office, 1957, pp. 252–57. Printed for the Joint Economic Committee, Congress of the United States. Footnote numbers have been changed and some footnotes are omitted.

[1]*The Pajama Game,* book by George Abbott and Richard Bissell, music and lyrics by Richard Adler and Jerry Ross, New York: Random House, 1954, p. 125.

SUBOPTIMIZATION AND CRITERIA[2]

There is a major complication in the process of choosing that multiplies the possibilities of going astray. This complication is the fact that we inevitably have to break our problems of choice into manageable pieces or subproblems. As some have put it, the process of choosing efficient courses of action is a process of suboptimization. In a government or department, one man or one committee cannot possibly examine all problems of choice simultaneously and select each course of action in the light of all the other decisions. The task is divided among various persons along hierarchical lines, some of the broader policy choices being made by high-level officials or groups, and others being delegated to lower levels. Similarly analysis-making must be broken into manageable pieces, since it is impossible for a single analysis to examine all of the alternatives. Thus comparisons of possible courses of action always pertain to parts of the government's problem. Other parts of the overall problem are put aside for the moment, decisions about some matters being neglected, specific decisions about others being taken for granted. The resulting analyses are intended to help in finding optimal, or at least good, solutions to subproblems: in the language of systems analysis and operations research, they are suboptimizations.

Figure 1 may help to show precisely what is meant by suboptimization and what kind of difficulties are involved. In the allocation of money for forest development among its component activities (labeled "Sub-problem 2"), what should be done depends in part upon decisions at other levels. That is, the best allocation of these funds depends partly upon the way the whole Federal budget is allocated and partly upon the way forest management, fire suppression, and pest control are carried out. Nevertheless, decisions at all these levels cannot be made simultaneously. To be sure, each decision will not be made in complete ignorance of the others. But the allocation of funds for forest development may be made more or less independently of decisions about new operating procedures, work layout, and equipment. In the selection of specific fire suppression equipment (sub-problem 3), the allocation of the forest budget, a higher-level choice, and the selection of detailed operating procedures, a lower-level choice, will probably not be accomplished at the same time. Similarly, analysis intended to assist in such decisions inevitably looks at pieces of the Department's problem, with many other facets of the overall problem temporarily fixed or ignored, because of the sheer size and complexity of the Department's operations.

Piecemeal analysis and decision-making have their advantages. For one thing, as problems are broken down into smaller parts, more detail can be taken into account. A high degree of decentralization is often desirable so that the "man on the spot" can decide about many matters. In analysis, somewhat

---

[2]For many of the points mentioned here, see Charles Hitch, "Suboptimization in Operations Problems," *Journal of the Operations Research Society of America* (May, 1953), pp. 87–99.

FIGURE 1
SUBOPTIMIZATION AT DIFFERENT LEVELS

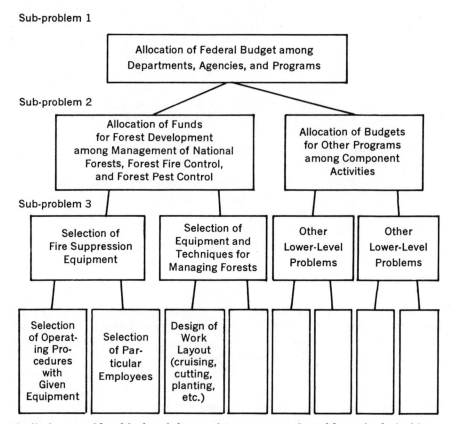

Sub-problem 1

Sub-problem 2

Sub-problem 3

similarly, considerable breakdown of governmental problems is desirable so that the models used in estimating results can be "on the spot," that is, less aggregative and more nearly correct in their predictions than departmentwide models would be. On the other side of the fence, there is a danger inherent in piecemeal analysis, one whose importance can hardly be overemphasized. This danger is that the criteria adopted in lower-level problems will not be closely related to higher-level criteria. As mentioned before, proximate criteria would have to be used in any event; but since problems must be examined a piece at a time, a whole hierarchy of possible criteria comes into play, and potential inconsistencies are abundant.

For example, consider sub-problem 3—the selection of fire suppression equipment for the national forests. This problem of choice is somewhat removed from top-level policy formation. In the case of fire trucks, maximum capacity (e.g., rate of flow that pumps can maintain) per dollar cost may seem like a plausible criterion. Yet there is no assurance that this test is consistent with overall aims. Suppose one engine costing $10,000 can maintain a flow of 10,000 units of water per minute—a capacity of 1 unit per dollar cost. Another engine costing \$50,000 can maintain a flow of 25,000 units of water per minute—a capacity of one-half unit of water per dollar cost. Is there good reason for choosing the former engine? Is this test closely correlated with higher-level criteria? No, not necessarily. The smaller engine may simply be an inexpensive way to let fires get out of control.

The higher-level criterion—that is, our overall goal in forest development and forest-fire control—is something like maximum profits to the Nation or, more specifically, maximum net value of output. Physical output, such as the volume of water that can be pumped per minute, need not be highly correlated with value of output. Moreover, even when output is in value terms, the ratio of output to cost, i.e., output per dollar cost, has no particular relationship to maximum net value of output. Since ratios permit the scale of output or cost to wonder willy-nilly, nothing insures their consistency with higher-level tests. It is always hazardous, therefore, to use them as criteria.

SOME REMARKS ON PROPER CRITERIA

So much for "suboptimization" and the fact that one must be extremely wary in devising criteria. What of a constructive nature can be said? If output and costs can be measured in the same unit—that is, dollars—a suitable criterion form is maximum output minus costs. For instance, in selecting fire suppression equipment and methods, the test can be maximum value of output; that is, timber and property saved, minus costs. In order to estimate value of output, of course, one cannot examine fire trucks (or tools for constructing fire breaks, or fire-finder devices) in isolation. In those circumstances, only a measure of physical output could be devised. It is necessary instead to fit the fire trucks (or other equipment being considered) into the system in a realistic context and estimate the value of assets saved annually with the alternative kinds of equipment. The kind that yields maximum value minus costs or, if the budget is fixed, maximum value for the given budget, is the most efficient.

To be sure there are supplementary considerations that cannot be embraced in a practicable test of economic efficiency. One major consideration of this sort is uncertainty. Which equipment is to be preferred if type A is more efficient on the average but type B gives a higher probability of avoiding catastrophic fires? Other supplementary considerations, for example, so-called intangibles, are always present. Nonetheless, the preceding test of economic efficiency is certainly a major consideration—one that is highly relevant to the final choice. This is more than can be said for many plausible criteria.

If output and costs cannot be measured in the same units, it is impossible to maximize value of output minus costs. This is the typical situation in defense activities, various loan programs, social security programs, and many other activities that provide special services to the public. Prices that are widely acceptable cannot be given to these outputs. Voters and officials have to attach values to various programs, at least implicitly, but one man's evaluation need not always be valid for other persons. In the case of such activities, analyses have to express output in physical terms, and the use of output minus costs (e.g., 20,000 patent applications processed minus $10 million) as a criterion becomes impossible.

The next best procedure appears to be to fix either the costs or the output at a reasonable scale. The test can then be minimum cost of achieving the specified physical output (e.g., patent applications processed, capability in particular military missions) or maximum physical output for the given cost. These two criterion forms are equivalent if the size of either gain or cost is the same in the two tests. If the test of maximum gain for a $50 budget points to the policy that yields a gain of 100, then the test of minimum cost to achieve a fixed gain of 100 will point to the same policy—the one that achieves the gain of 100 at a cost of $50. The choice between these two criterion forms depends mainly upon whether it is gain or cost that can be fixed with the greater degree of correctness.

This leads us to a most important question: How does one determine the right achievement or budget? If the achievement or budget is set uncritically, the test is not necessarily consistent with higher level criteria. In many problems of choice, the size of the budget or the scale of the mission is fixed by higher authority. In these circumstances, whichever is fixed can indeed be taken as given. If neither is fixed, one must try to select the mission or budget that seems reasonable in the light of higher level objectives. This calls for careful inquiry into those higher level objectives and their relationship to the mission or budget under consideration. Another possible procedure is to try several budget sizes or mission levels. If the same equipment is preferred for all task levels or budgets, that system is dominant. If the same course of action is not dominant, the use of several tasks or budgets is nonetheless an essential step, because it provides the policymaker with vital information.

APPLICATION TO SPECIFIC PROBLEMS

What implications do these observations have concerning the comparison of specific alternatives? Let's look briefly at two problems that confront government officials periodically: (1) Choosing among alternative sizes of the budget for forest management, and (2) choosing among alternative personnel policies in government. In determining the efficient size of the forest-management budget, we can devise sensible monetary measures of both output and cost. In this problem, then, a proper test would be similar to the criterion that private firms presumably use—maximum expected profits or, in other words, maximum gains minus costs (given whatever constraints exist). That is, choose the scale of timber planting, cutting, and selling that would yield the greatest excess of gains (discounted to their present value over costs (similarly discounted). The Forest Service sometimes prepares analyses employing this sort of test; yet in this problem, and in many other investment choices, less meaningful criteria are often employed. Note that it is misleading to use a benefit-cost ratio as a test in this case (as in most others). Unless applied with special constraints and solely to small increments in the budget, maximizing such a ratio would favor restricting operations to a small but golden opportunity—say, cutting a small amount of high-quality and easily accessible timber. Common sense would rule out this extreme, but the point is that the ratio would have little significance.

The second problem, determining personnel policies (e.g., in the military) is one in which output under alternative arrangements cannot satisfactorily be measured in dollars. If we slice off one particular part of the problem, i.e., setting the pay structure, a proper criterion is minimum cost of obtaining a designated set of services (i.e., physical output). The designated set of services should be consistent with the functions and tasks that are to be performed. The cost, of course, should not be confined to the coming year's expenses, but should be the present value of the costs for at least several years ahead. This example too is one in which appropriate criteria have been adopted, at least in some instances. With respect to military personnel, the Cordiner report has made use of a criterion similar to the one above in comparing its proposed pay structure with the existing one.

Suppose we examine other alternatives in determining personnel policies. The designated set of services, for civilian as well as military activities, should be called into question, too. We should like to eliminate overstaffing, to find more economical combinations of men and equipment, to design equipment and methods of operation that make more efficient use of personnel. For such purposes, the minimum cost of obtaining specified services will not serve as a criterion. Nor will such tests as physical output per worker, gain-cost ratios, or the minimum cost of doing some casually specified job. The test would have to be, in very general terms, the minimum cost of performing a function or mission that is specified carefully in the light of higher level criteria. To state that such a criterion form should be used is to leave the hard work still ahead, namely, putting down those appropriate specifications of the function to be carried out. But the hard work is there because the problem is hard. To avoid it by adopting nonsense criteria will not lead to sound choices.

The problems just mentioned—determining personnel policy and the forest-management budget—are but two of myriad choices that must be made in deciding upon government expenditures. In each of these choices, criterion selection is a crucial aspect of either analyzing the problem quantitatively or of just thinking about the alternatives. And in this matter of criterion selection, it is imperative that we draw on economic principles, together with caution and commonsense, instead of adopting the first plausible test that occurs to us.

THE ROAD TO PPB: THE STAGES OF BUDGET REFORM

ALLEN SCHICK

Among the new men in the nascent PPB [Program Planning Budgeting—Ed.] staffs and the fellow travellers who have joined the bandwagon, the mood is of "a revolutionary development in the history of government management." There is excited talk about the differences between what has been and what will be; of the benefits that will accrue from an explicit and "hard" appraisal of objectives and alternatives; of the merits of multiyear budget forecasts and plans; of the great divergence between the skills and role of the analyst and the job of the examiner; of the realignments in government structure that might result from changes in the budget process.

This is not the only version, however. The closer one gets to the nerve centers of budget life—the Divisions in the Bureau of the Budget and the budget offices in the departments and agencies—the more one is likely to hear that "there's nothing very new in PPB; it's hardly different from what we've been doing until now." Some old-timers interpret PPB as a revival of the performance budgeting venture of the early 1950's. Others belittle the claim that—before PPB—decisions on how much to spend for personnel or supplies were made without real consideration of the purposes for which these inputs were to be invested. They point to previous changes that have been in line with PPB, albeit without PPB's distinctive package of techniques and nomenclature. Such things as the waning role of the "green sheets" in the central budget process, the redesign of the appropriation structure and the development of activity classifications, refinements in work measurement, productivity analysis, and other types of output measurement, and the utilization of the Spring Preview for a broad look at programs and major issues.

Between the uncertain protests of the traditional budgeteer and the uncertain expectations of the *avant garde*, there is a third version. The PPB system that is being developed portends a radical change in the central function of budgeting, but it is anchored to half a century of tradition and evolution. The budget system of the future will be a product of past and emerging developments; that is, it will embrace both the budgetary functions introduced during earlier stages of reform as well as the planning function which is highlighted by PPB. PPB is the first budget system *designed* to accommodate the multiple functions of budgeting.

The author is indebted to Henry S. Rowen and Paul Feldman of the Bureau of the Budget and to the many Federal officials who guided him during a summer's sojourn along the road to PPB.

Article is from *Public Administration Review*, Vol. 26 (December, 1966), pp. 243–58. Used with permission of publisher.

THE FUNCTIONS OF BUDGETING

Budgeting always has been conceived as a process for systematically relating the expenditure of funds to the accomplishment of planned objectives. In this important sense, there is a bit of PPB in every budget system. Even in the initial stirrings of budget reform more than 50 years ago, there were cogent statements on the need for a budget system to plan the objectives and activities of government and to furnish reliable data on what was to be accomplished with public funds. In 1907, for example, the New York Bureau of Municipal Research published a sample "program memorandum" that contained some 125 pages of functional accounts and data for the New York City Health Department.[1]

However, this orientation was not *explicitly* reflected in the budget systems—national, state, or local—that were introduced during the first decades of this century, nor is it *explicitly* reflected in the budget systems that exist today. The plain fact is that planning is not the only function that must be served by a budget system. The *management* of ongoing activities and the *control* of spending are functions which, in the past, have been given priority over the planning function. Robert Anthony identifies three distinct administrative processes, strategic planning, management control, and operational control.

> *Strategic planning* is the process of deciding on objectives of the organization, on changes in these objectives, on the resources used to attain these objectives, and on the policies that are to govern the acquisition, use, and disposition of these resources.
> *Management control* is the process by which managers assure that resources are obtained and used effectively and efficiently in the accomplishment of the organization's objectives.
> *Operational control* is the process of assuring that specific tasks are carried out effectively and efficiently.[2]

Every budget system, even rudimentary ones, comprises planning, management, and control processes. Operationally, these processes often are indivisible, but for analytic purposes they are distinguished here. In the context of budgeting, *planning* involves the determination of objectives, the evaluation of alternative courses of action, and the authorization of select programs. Planning is linked most closely to budget preparation, but it would be a mistake to disregard the management and control elements in budget preparation or the possibilities for planning during other phases of the budget year. Clearly, one of the major aims of PPB is to convert the annual routine of preparing a budget into a conscious appraisal and formulation of future goals and policies. Management involves the pro-

---

[1] New York Bureau of Municipal Research, *Making a Municipal Budget*, New York: The Bureau, 1907, pp. 9–10.

[2] Robert N. Anthony, *Planning and Control Systems: A Framework for Analysis*, Boston: Allyn and Bacon, Inc., 1965, pp. 16–18.

gramming of approved goals into specific projects and activities, the design of organizational units to carry out approved programs, and the staffing of these units and the procurement of necessary resources. The management process is spread over the entire budget cycle; ideally, it is the link between goals made and activities undertaken. *Control* refers to the process of binding operating officials to the policies and plans set by their superiors. Control is predominant during the execution and audit stages, although the form of budget estimates and appropriations often is determined by control considerations. The assorted controls and reporting procedures that are associated with budget execution—position controls, restrictions on transfers, requisition procedures, and travel regulations, to mention the more prominent ones—have the purpose of securing compliance with policies made by central authorities.

Very rarely are planning, management, and control given equal attention in the operation of budget systems. As a practical matter, planning, management, and control have tended to be competing processes in budgeting with no neat division of functions among the various participants. Because time is scarce, central authorities must be selective in the things they do. Although this scarcity counsels the devolution of control responsibilities to operating levels, the lack of reliable and relied-on internal control systems has loaded central authorities with control functions at the expense of the planning function. Moreover, these processes often require different skills and generate different ways of handling the budget mission, so that one type of perspective tends to predominate over the others. Thus, in the staffing of the budget offices, there has been a shift from accountants to administrators as budgeting has moved from a control to a management posture. The initial experience with PPB suggests that the next transition might be from administrators to economists as budgeting takes on more of the planning function.

Most important, perhaps, are the differential informational requirements of planning, control, and management processes. Informational needs differ in terms of time spans, levels of aggregation, linkages with organizational and operating units, and input-output foci. The apparent solution is to design a system that serves the multiple needs of budgeting. Historically, however, there has been a strong tendency to homogenize informational structures and to rely on a single classification scheme to serve all budgetary purposes. For the most part, the informational system has been structured to meet the purposes of control. As a result, the type of multiple-purpose budget system envisioned by PPB has been avoided.

An examination of budget systems should reveal whether greater emphasis is placed *at the central levels* on planning, management, or control. A *planning orientation* focuses on the broadest range of issues: What are the long-range goals and policies of the government and how are these related to particular expenditure choices? What criteria should be used in appraising the requests of the agencies? Which programs should be initiated or terminated, and which expanded or curtailed? A *management orientation* deals with less fundamental issues: What is the best way to organize for the accomplishment of a prescribed task? Which of several staffing alternatives achieves the most effective relationship between the central and field offices? Of the various grants and projects proposed, which should be approved? A *control orientation* deals with a relatively narrow range of concerns: How can agencies be held to the expenditure ceilings established by the legislature and chief executive? What reporting procedures should be used to enforce propriety in expenditures? What limits should be placed on agency spending for personnel and equipment?

It should be clear that every budget system contains planning, management, and control features. A control orientation means the subordination, not the absence, of planning and management functions. In the matter of orientations, we are dealing with relative emphases, not with pure dichotomies. The germane issue is the balance among these vital functions at the central level. Viewed centrally, what weight does each have in the design and operation of the budget system?

THE STAGES OF BUDGET REFORM

The framework outlined above suggests a useful approach to the study of budget reform. Every reform alters the planning-management-control balance, sometimes inadvertently, usually deliberately. Accordingly, it is possible to identify three successive stages of reform. In the first stage, dating roughly from 1920 to 1935, the dominant emphasis was on developing an adequate system of expenditure control. Although planning and management considerations were not altogether absent (and indeed occupied a prominent role in the debates leading to the Budget and Accounting Act of 1921), they were pushed to the side by what was regarded as the first priority, a reliable system of expenditure accounts. The second stage came into the open during the New Deal and reached its zenith more than a decade later in the movement for performance budgeting. The management orientation, paramount during this period, made its mark in the reform of the appropriation structure, development of management improvement and work measurement programs, and the focusing of budget preparation on the work and activities of the agencies. The third stage, the full emergence of which must await the institutionalization of PPB, can be traced to earlier efforts to link planning and budgeting as well as to the analytic criteria of welfare economics, but its recent development is a product of modern informational and decisional technologies such as those pioneered in the Department of Defense.

PPB is predicated on the primacy of the planning function; yet it strives for a multi-purpose budget system that gives adequate and necessary attention to the control and management areas. Even in embryonic stage, PPB envisions the development of crosswalk grids for the conversion of data

525

from a planning to a management and control framework, and back again. PPB treats the three basic functions as compatible and complementary elements of a budget system, though not as coequal aspects of central budgeting. In ideal form, PPB would centralize the planning function and delegate *primary* managerial and control responsibilities to the supervisory and operating levels respectively.

In the modern genesis of budgeting, efforts to improve planning, management, and control made common cause under the popular banner of the executive-budget concept. In the goals and lexicon of the first reformers, budgeting meant executive budgeting. The two were inseparable. There was virtually no dissent from Cleveland's dictum that "to be a budget it must be prepared and submitted by a responsible executive . . ."[3] Whether from the standpoint of planning, management or control, the executive was deemed in the best position to prepare and execute the budget. As Cleveland argued in 1915, only the executive "could think in terms of the institution as a whole," and, therefore, he "is the only one who can be made responsible for leadership."[4]

The executive budget idea also took root in the administrative integration movement, and here was allied with such reforms as functional consolidation of agencies, elimination of independent boards and commissions, the short ballot, and strengthening the chief executive's appointive and removal powers. The chief executive often was likened to the general manager of a corporation, the Budget Bureau serving as his general staff.

Finally, the executive budget was intended to strengthen honesty and efficiency by restricting the discretion of administrators in this role. It was associated with such innovations as centralized purchasing and competitive bidding, civil service reform, uniform accounting procedures, and expenditure audits.

THE CONTROL ORIENTATION

In the drive for executive budgeting, the various goals converged. There was a radical parting of the ways, however, in the conversion of the budget idea into an operational reality. Hard choices had to be made in the design of expenditure accounts and in the orientation of the budget office. On both counts, the control orientation was predominant.

In varying degrees of itemization, the expenditure classifications established during the first wave of reform were based on objects-of-expenditure, with detailed tabulations of the myriad items required to operate an administrative unit—personnel, fuel, rent, office supplies, and other inputs. On these "line-itemizations" were built technical routines for

---

[3]Frederick A. Cleveland, "Evolution of the Budget Idea in the United States," *Annals of the American Academy of Political and Social Science*, Vol. 62 (1915), p. 16.
[4]*Ibid.*, p. 17.

the compilation and review of estimates and the disbursement of funds. The leaders in the movement for executive budgeting, however, envisioned a system of functional classifications focusing on the work to be accomplished. They regarded objects-of-expenditure as subsidiary data to be included for informational purposes. Their preference for functional accounts derived from their conception of the budget as a planning instrument, their disdain for objects from the contemporary division between politics and administration.[5] The Taft Commission vigorously opposed object-of-expenditure appropriations and recommended that expenditures be classified by class of work, organizational unit, character of expense, and method of financing. In its model budget, the Commission included several functional classifications.[6]

In the establishment of a budget system for New York City by the Bureau of Municipal Research, there was an historic confrontation between diverse conceptions of budgeting.

In evolving suitable techniques, the Bureau soon faced a conflict between functional and object budgeting. Unlike almost all other budget systems which began on a control footing with object classifications, the Bureau turned to control (and the itemization of objects) only after trial-and-error experimentation with program methods.

When confronted with an urgent need for effective control over administration, the Bureau was compelled to conclude that this need was more critical than the need for a planning-functional emphasis. "Budget reform," Charles Beard once wrote, "bears the imprint of the age in which it originated."[7] In an age when personnel and purchasing controls were unreliable, the first consideration was how to prevent administrative improprieties.

> In the opinion of those who were in charge of the development of a budget procedure, the most important service to be rendered was the establishing of central controls so that responsibility could be located and enforced through elected executives. ... The view was, therefore, accepted, that questions of administration and niceties of adjustment must be left in abeyance until central control has been effectively established and the basis has been laid for careful scrutiny of departmental contracts and purchases as well as departmental work.[8]

Functional accounts had been designed to facilitate rational program decisions, not to deter officials from misfeasance. "The classification by 'functions' affords no protection; it only operates as a restriction on the use

---

[5]*See* Frank J. Goodnow, "The Limit of Budgetary Control," *Proceedings of the American Political Science Association*, Baltimore: The Association, 1913, p. 72; also William F. Willoughby, "Allotment of Funds by Executive Officials, An Essential Feature of Any Correct Budgetary System," *ibid.*, pp. 78–87.

[6]U.S. President's Commission on Economy and Efficiency, *The Need for a National Budget*, Washington, D.C.: U.S. Government Printing Office, 1912, pp. 210–213.

[7]Charles A. Beard, "Prefatory Note," *ibid.*, p. vii.

[8]New York Bureau of Municipal Research, "Some Results and Limitations of Central Financial Control in New York City," *Municipal Research*, Vol. 81 (1917), p. 10.

which may be made of the services."[9] The detailed itemization of objects was regarded as desirable not only "because it provides for the utilization of all the machinery of control which has been provided, but it also admits to a much higher degree of perfection than it has at present attained."[10]

With the introduction of object accounts, New York City had a three-fold classification of expenditures: (1) by organizational units; (2) by functions; and (3) by objects. In a sense, the Bureau of Municipal Research was striving to develop a budget system that would serve the multiple purposes of budgeting simultaneously. To the Bureau, the inclusion of more varied and detailed data in the budget was a salutary trend; all purposes would be served and the public would have a more complete picture of government spending. Thus the Bureau "urged from the beginning a classification of costs in as many different ways as there are stories to be told."[11] But the Bureau did not anticipate the practical difficulties which would ensue from the multiple classification scheme. In the 1913 appropriations act:

> there were 3992 distinct items of appropriation. ... Each constituted a distinct appropriation, besides which there was a further itemization of positions and salaries of personnel that multiplied this number several times, each of which operated as limitations on administrative discretion.[12]

This predicament confronted the Bureau with a direct choice between the itemization of objects and a functional classification. As a solution, the Bureau recommended retention of object accounts and the total "defunctionalization" of the budget; in other words, it gave priority to the objects and the control orientation they manifested. Once installed, object controls rapidly gained stature as an indispensable deterrent to administrative misbehavior. Amelioration of the adverse effects of multiple classifications was to be accomplished in a different manner, one which would strengthen the planning and management processes. The Bureau postulated a fundamental distinction between the purposes of budgets and appropriations, and between the types of classification suitable for each.

> ... an act of appropriation has a single purpose—that of putting a limitation on the amount of obligations which may be incurred and the amount of vouchers which may be drawn to pay for personal services, supplies, etc. The only significant classification of appropriation items, therefore, is according to persons to whom drawing accounts are given and the classes of things to be bought.[13]

---

[9]"Next Steps ...," op. cit., p. 39.

[10]"Next Steps ...", op. cit., p. 67.

[11]"Some Results and Limitations ...", op. cit., p. 9.

[12]"Next Steps ...", op. cit., p. 35.

[13]Ibid, p. 7.

Appropriations, in sum, were to be used as statutory controls on spending. In its "Next Steps" proposals, the Bureau recommended that appropriations retain "exactly the same itemization so far as specifications of positions and compensations are concerned and, therefore, the same protection."[14]

Budgets, on the other hand, were regarded as instruments of planning and publicity. They should include "all the details of the work plans and specifications of cost of work."[15] In addition to the regular object and organization classifications, the budget would report the "total cost incurred, classified by *functions*—for determining questions of policy having to do with service rendered as well as to be rendered, and laying a foundation for appraisal of results."[16] The Bureau also recommended a new instrument, a *work program*, which would furnish "a detailed schedule or analysis of each function, activity, or process within each organization unit. This analysis would give the total cost and the unit cost wherever standards were established."[17]

Truly a far-sighted conception of budgeting! There would be three documents for the three basic functions of budgeting. Although the Bureau did not use the analytic framework suggested above, it seems that the appropriations were intended for control purposes, the budget for planning purposes, and the work program for management purposes. Each of the three documents would have its specialized information scheme, but jointly they would comprise a multipurpose budget system not very different from PPB, even though the language of crosswalking or systems analysis was not used.

Yet the plan failed, for in the end the Bureau was left with object accounts pegged to a control orientation. The Bureau's distinction between budgets and appropriations was not well understood, and the work-program idea was rejected by New York City on the ground that adequate accounting backup was lacking. The Bureau had failed to recognize that the conceptual distinction between budgets and appropriations tends to break down under the stress of informational demands. If the legislature appropriates by objects, the budget very likely will be classified by objects. Conversely, if there are no functional accounts, the prospects for including such data in the budget are diminished substantially. As has almost always been the case, the budget came to mirror the appropriations act; in each, objects were paramount. It remains to be seen whether PPB will be able to break this interlocking informational pattern.

By the early 1920's the basic functions of planning and management were overlooked by those who carried the gospel of budget reform across the nation. First generation budget workers concentrated on perfecting and

[14]*Ibid*, p. 39.
[15]"Some Results and Limitations . . .", *op. cit.*, p. 7.
[16]*Ibid.*, p. 9.
[17]"Next Steps . . .", *op. cit.*, p. 30.

spreading the widely approved object-of-expenditure approach, and budget writers settled into a nearly complete preoccupation with forms and with factual descriptions of actual and recommended procedures. Although ideas about the use of the budget for planning and management purposes were retained in Buck's catalogs of "approved" practices,[18] they did not have sufficient priority to challenge tradition.

From the start, Federal budgeting was placed on a control, object-of-expenditure footing, the full flavor of which can be perceived in reading Charles G. Dawes' documentary on *The First Year of the Budget of The United States.* According to Dawes,

> the Bureau of the Budget is concerned only with the humbler and routine business of Government. Unlike cabinet officers, it is concerned with no question of policy, save that of economy and efficiency.[19]

This distinction fitted neatly with object classifications that provided a firm accounting base for the routine conduct of government business, but no information on policy implications of public expenditures. Furthermore, in its first decade, the Bureau's tiny staff (40 or fewer) had to coordinate a multitude of well-advertised economy drives which shaped the job of the examiner as being that of reviewing itemized estimates to pare them down. Although Section 209 of the Budget and Accounting Act had authorized the Bureau to study and recommend improvements in the organization and administrative practices of Federal agencies, the Bureau was overwhelmingly preoccupied with the business of control.

THE MANAGEMENT ORIENTATION

Although no single action represents the shift from a control to a management orientation, the turning point in this evolution probably came with the New Deal's broadening perspective of government responsibilities.

During the 1920's and 1930's, occasional voices urged a return to the conceptions of budgeting advocated by the early reformers. In a notable 1924 article, Lent D. Upson argued vigorously that "budget precedure had stopped halfway in its development," and he proposed six modifications in the form of the budget, the net effect being a shift in emphasis from accounting control to functional accounting.[20] A similar position was taken a decade later by Wylie Kilpatrick who insisted that "the one fundamental basis of expenditure is functional, an accounting of payments for the services performed by government."[21]

[18]*See* A. E. Buck, *Public Budgeting,* New York: The Macmillan Company, 1929, pp. 181–88.

[19]Charles G. Dawes, *The First Year of the Budget of the United States,* New York: Harper & Row, Publishers, 1923, preface, p. ii.

[20]Lent D. Upson, "Half-time Budget Methods," *The Annals of the American Academy of Political and Social Science,* Vol. 113 (1924), p. 72.

[21]Wylie Kilpatrick, "Classification and Measurement of Public Expenditure," *The Annals of the American Academy of Political and Social Science,* Vol. 133 (1936), p. 20.

Meanwhile, gradual changes were preparing the way for a reorientation of budgeting to a management mission. Many of the administrative abuses that had given rise to object controls were curbed by statutes and regulations and by a general upgrading of the public service. Reliable accounting systems were installed and personnel and purchasing reforms introduced, thereby freeing budgeting from some of its watchdog chores. The rapid growth of government activities and expenditures made it more difficult and costly for central officials to keep track of the myriad objects in the budget. With expansion, the bits and pieces into which the objects were itemized became less and less significant. while the aggregate of activities performed became more significant, With expansion, there was heightened need for central management of the incohesive sprawl of administrative agencies.

The climb in activities and expenditures also signaled radical changes in the role of the budget system. As long as government was considered a "necessary evil," and there was little recognition of the social value of public expenditures, the main function of budgeting was to keep spending in check. Because the outputs were deemed to be of limited and fixed value, it made sense to use the budget for central control over inputs. However, as the work and accomplishments of public agencies came to be regarded as benefits, the task of budgeting was redefined as the effective marshalling of fiscal and organizational resources for the attainment of benefits. This new posture focused attention on the problems of managing large programs and organizations, and on the opportunities for using the budget to extend executive hegemony over the dispersed administrative structure.

All these factors converged in the New Deal years. Federal expenditures rose rapidly from $4.2 billion in 1932 to $10 billion in 1940. Keynesian economics (the full budgetary implications of which are emerging only now in PPB) stressed the relationship between public spending and the condition of the economy. The President's Committee on Administrative Management (1937) castigated the routinized, control-minded approach to the Bureau of the Budget and urged that budgeting be used to coordinate Federal activities under presidential leadership. With its transfer in 1939 from the Treasury to the newly-created Executive Office of the President, the Bureau was on its way to becoming the leading management arm of the Federal Government. The Bureau's own staff was increased tenfold; it developed the administrative management and statistical coordination functions that it still possesses; and it installed apportionment procedures for budget execution. More and more, the Bureau was staffed from the ranks of public administration rather than from accounting, and it was during the Directorship of Harold D. Smith (1939–46) that the Bureau substantially embraced the management orientation.[22] Executive Order 8248 placed the President's imprimatur on the management philosophy. It directed the Bureau:

---

[22]See Harold D. Smith, *The Management of Your Government*, New York: McGraw-Hill Book Co., 1945.

to keep the President informed of the progress of activities by agencies of the Government with respect to work proposed, work actually initiated, and work completed, together with the relative timing of work between the several agencies of the Government; all to the end that the work programs of the several agencies of the executive branch of the Government may be coordinated and that the monies appropriated by the Congress may be expended in the most economical manner possible to prevent overlapping and duplication of effort.

Accompanying the growing management use of the budget process for the appraisal and improvement of administrative performance and the scientific management movement with its historical linkage to public administration were far more relevant applications of managerial cost accounting to governmental operations. Government agencies sought to devise performance standards and the rudimentary techniques of work measurement were introduced in several agencies including the Forest Service, the Census Bureau, and the Bureau of Reclamation.[23] Various professional associations developed grading systems to assess administrative performance as well as the need for public services. These crude and unscientific methods were the forerunners of more sophisticated and objective techniques. At the apogee of these efforts, Clarence Ridley and Herbert Simon published *Measuring Municipal Activities: A Survey of Suggested Criteria for Appraising Administration*, in which they identified five kinds of measurement—(1) needs, (2) results, (3) costs, (4) effort, and (5) performance—and surveyed the obstacles to the measurement of needs and results. The latter three categories they combined into a measure of administrative efficiency. This study provides an excellent inventory of the state of the technology prior to the breakthrough made by cost-benefit and systems analysis.

At the close of World War II, the management orientation was entrenched in all but one aspect of Federal budgeting—the classification of expenditures. Except for isolated cases (such as TVA's activity accounts and the project structure in the Department of Agriculture), the traditional object accounts were retained though the control function had receded in importance. In 1949 the Hoover Commission called for alterations in budget classifications consonant with the management orientation. It recommended "that the whole budgetary concept of the Federal Government should be refashioned by the adoption of a budget based upon functions, activities, and projects."[24] To create a sense of novelty, the Commission gave a new label—performance budgeting—to what had long been known as functional or activity budgeting. Because its task force had used still another term—program budgeting—there were two new terms to denote the budget

---

[23]Public Administration Service, *The Work Unit in Federal Administration* (Chicago: The Administration, 1937).

[24]U.S. Commission on Organization of the Executive Branch of the Government, *Budgeting and Accounting*, Washington, D.C.: U.S. Government Printing Office, 1949, p. 8

innovations of that period. Among writers there was no uniformity in usage, some preferring the "program budgeting" label, others "performance budgeting," to describe the same things. The level of confusion has been increased recently by the association of the term "program budgeting" (also the title of the RAND publication edited by David Novick) with the PPB movement.

Although a variety of factors and expectations influenced the Hoover Commission, and the Commission's proposals have been interpreted in many ways, including some that closely approximate the PPB concept, for purposes of clarity, and in accord with the control-management-planning framework, performance budgeting *as it was generally-understood and applied* must be distinguished from the emergent PPB idea. The term "performance budgeting" is hereafter used in reference to reforms set in motion by the Hoover Commission and the term "program budgeting" is used in conjunction with PPB.

Performance budgeting is management-oriented; its principal thrust is to help administrators to assess the work-efficiency of operating units by (1) casting budget categories in functional terms, and (2) providing work-cost measurements to facilitate the efficient performance of prescribed activities. Generally, its method is particularistic, the reduction of work-cost data into discrete, measurable units. Program budgeting (PPB) is planning-oriented; its main goal is to rationalize policy making by providing (1) data on the costs and benefits of alternative ways of attaining proposed public objectives, and (2) output measurements to facilitate the effective attainment of chosen objectives. As a policy device, program budgeting departs from simple engineering models of efficiency in which the objective is fixed and the quantity of inputs and outputs is adjusted an optimal relationship. In PPB, the objective itself is variable; analysis may lead to a new statement of objectives. In order to enable budget makers to evaluate the costs and benefits of alternative expenditure options, program budgeting focuses on expenditure aggregates; the details come into play only as they contribute to an analysis of the total (the system) or of marginal trade-offs among competing proposals. Thus, in this macroanalytic approach, the accent is on comprehensiveness and on grouping data into categories that allow comparisons among alternative expenditure mixes.

Performance budgeting derived its ethos and much of its technique from cost accounting and scientific management; program budgeting has drawn its core ideas from economics and systems analysis. In the performance budgeting literature, budgeting is described as a "tool of management" and the budget as a "work program." In PPB, budgeting is an allocative process among competing claims, and the budget is a statement of policy. Chronologically, there was a gap of several years between the bloom of performance budgeting and the first articulated conceptions of program budgeting. In the aftermath of the first Hoover report, and especially during the early 1950's, there was a plethora of writings on the administrative advantages of the performance budget. Substantial interest in program budgeting did not emerge until the mid-1950's when a number of economists (including Smithies, Novick, and McKean) began to urge reform of the Federal budget system. What the economists had in mind was not the same thing as the Hoover Commission.

In line with its management perspective, the Commission averred that "the all-important thing in budgeting is the work or service to be accomplished, and what that work or service will cost."[25] Mosher followed this view closely in writing that "the central idea of the performance budget . . . is that the budget process be focused upon programs and functions—that is, accomplishments to be achieved, work to be done."[26] But from the planning perspective, the all-important thing surely is not the work or service to be accomplished but the objectives or purposes to be fulfilled by the investment of public funds. Whereas in performance budgeting, work and activities are treated virtually as ends in themselves, in program budgeting work and services are regarded as intermediate aspects, the process of converting resources into outputs. Thus, in a 1954 RAND paper, Novick defined a program as "the sum of the steps or interdependent activities which enter into the attainment of a specified objective. The program, therefore, is the end objective and is developed or budgeted in terms of all the elements necessary to its execution."[27] Novick goes on to add, "this is not the sense in which the government budget now uses the term."

Because the evaluation of performance and the evaluation of program are distinct budget functions, they call for different methods of classification which serves as an intermediate layer between objects and organizations. The activities relate to the functions and work of a distinct operating unit; hence their classification ordinarily conforms to organizational lines. This is the type of classification most useful for an administrator who has to schedule the procurement and utilization of resources for the production of goods and services. Activity classifications gather under a single rubric all the expenditure data needed by a manager to run his unit. The evaluation of programs, however, requires an end-product classification that is oriented to the mission and purposes of government. This type of classification may not be very useful for the manager, but it is of great value to the budget maker who has to decide how to allocate scarce funds among competing claims. Some of the difference between end-product and activity classifications can be gleaned by comparing the Coast Guard's existing activity schedule with the proposed program structure on the last page of Bulletin 66-3. The activity structure which was developed under the aegis of performance budgeting is geared to the operating responsibilities of the Coast Guard: Vessel Operations, Aviation

---

[25]*Ibid.*

[26]Frederick C. Mosher, *Program Budgeting: Theory and Practice*, Chicago: Public Administration Service, 1954, p. 79.

[27]David Novick, *Which Program Do We Mean in "Program Budgeting?"* Santa Monica: The RAND Corporation 1954, p. 17.

Operations, Repair and Supply Facilities, and others. The proposed program structure is hinged to the large purposes sought through Coast Guard operations: Search and Rescue, Aids to Navigation, Law Enforcement, and so on.

It would be a mistake to assume that performance techniques presuppose program budgeting or that it is not possible to collect performance data without program classifications. Nevertheless, the view has gained hold that a program budget is "a transitional type of budget between the orthodox (traditional) character and object budget on the one hand and performance budget on the other."[28] Kammerer and Shadoan stress a similar connection. The former writes that "a *performance* budget carriers the program budget one step further: into *unit costs.*"[29] Shadoan "envisions 'performance budgeting' as an extension of . . . the program budget concept to which the element of unit work measurement has been added."[30] These writers ignore the divergent functions served by performance and program budgets. It is possible to devise and apply performance techniques without relating them to, or having the use of, larger program aggregates. A cost accountant or work measurement specialist can measure the cost or effort required to perform a repetitive task without probing into the purpose of the work or its relationship to the mission of the organization. Work measurement—"a method of establishing an equitable relationship between the volume of work performed and manpower utilized"—[31] is only distantly and indirectly related to the process of determining governmental policy at the higher levels. Program classifications are vitally linked to the making and implementation of policy through the allocation of public resources. As a general rule, performance budgeting is concerned with the *process of work* (what methods should be used) while program budgeting is concerned with the *purpose of work* (what activities should be authorized).

Perhaps the most reliable way to describe this difference is to show what was tried and accomplished under performance budgeting. First of all, performance budgeting led to the introduction of activity classifications, the management-orientation of which has already been discussed. Second, narrative descriptions of program and performance were added to the budget document. These statements give the budget-reader a general picture of the work that will be done by the organizational unit requesting funds. But unlike the analytic documents currently being developed under PPB, the narratives have a descriptive and justificatory function; they do not provide

---

[28]Lennex L. Meak and Kathryn W. Killian, *A Manual of Techniques for the Preparation, Consideration, Adoption, and Administration of Operating Budgets*, Chicago: Public Administration Service, 1963, p. 11.

[29]Gladys M. Kammerer, *Program Budgeting: An Aid to Understanding*, Gainesville: University of Florida Press, 1959, p. 6.

[30]Arlene Theuer Shadoan, *Preparation, Review, and Execution of the State Operating Budget*, Lexington: University of Kentucky Press, 1963, p. 13.

[31]U.S. Bureau of the Budget, *A Work Measurement System*, Washington, D.C.: U.S. Government Printing Office, 1950, p. 2.

an objective basis for evaluating the cost-utility of an expenditure. Indeed, there hardly is any evidence that the narratives have been used for decision making; rather they seem best suited for giving the uninformed outsider some glimpses of what is going on inside.

Third, performance budgeting spawned a multitude of work-cost measurement explorations. Most used, but least useful, were the detailed workload statistics assembled by administrators to justify their requests for additional funds. On a higher level of sophistication were attempts to apply the techniques of scientific management and cost accounting to the development of work and productivity standards. In these efforts, the Bureau of the Budget had a long involvement, beginning with the issuance of the trilogy of work measurement handbooks in 1950 and reaching its highest development in the productivity-measurement studies that were published in 1964. All these applications were at a level of detail useful for managers with operating or supervisory responsibilities but of scant usefulness for top-level officials who have to determine organizational objectives and goals. Does it really help top officials if they know that it cost $0.07 to wash a pound of laundry or that the average postal employee processes 289 items of mail per hour? These are the main fruits of performance measurements, and they have an important place in the management of an organization. They are of great value to the operating official who has the limited function of getting a job done, but they would put a crushing burden on the policy maker whose function is to map the future course of action.

Finally, the management viewpoint led to significant departures from PPB's principle that the expenditure accounts should show total systems cost. The 1949 National Security Act (possibly the first concrete result of the Hoover report) directed the segregation of capital and operating costs in the defense budget. New York State's performance—budgeting experiment for TB hospitals separated expenditures into cost centers (a concept derived from managerial cost accounting) and within each center into fixed and variable costs. In most manpower and work measurements, labor has been isolated from other inputs. Most important, in many states and localities (and implicitly in Federal budgeting) the cost of continuing existing programs has been separated from the cost of new or expanded programs. This separation is useful for managers who build up a budget in terms of increments and decrements from the base, but it is a violation of program budgeting's working assumption that all claims must be pitted against one another in the competition for funds. Likewise, the forms of separation previously mentioned make sense from the standpoint of the manager, but impair the planner's capability to compare expenditure alternatives.

THE PLANNING ORIENTATION

The foregoing has revealed some of the factors leading to the emergence of the planning orientation. Three important developments influenced the evolution from a management to a planning orientation.

536

1. Economic analysis—macro and micro—has had an increasing part in the shaping of fiscal and budgetary policy.
2. The development of new informational and decisional technologies has enlarged the applicability of objective analysis to policy making. And,
3. There has been a gradual convergence of planning and budgetary processes.

Keynesian economics with its macroanalytic focus on the impact of governmental action on the private sector had its genesis in the under-employment economy of the Great Depression. In calling attention to the opportunities for attaining full employment by means of fiscal policy, the Keynesians set into motion a major restatement of the central budget function. From the utilization of fiscal policy to achieve economic objectives, it was but a few steps to the utilization of the budget process to achieve fiscal objectives. Nevertheless, between the emergence and the victory of the new economics, there was a lapse of a full generation, a delay due primarily to the entrenched balanced-budget ideology. But the full realization of the budget's economic potential was stymied on the revenue side by static tax policies and on the expenditure side by status spending policies.

If the recent tax policy of the Federal Government is evidence that the new economics has come of age, it also offers evidence of the long-standing failure of public officials to use the taxing power as a variable constraint on the economy. Previously, during normal times, the tax structure was accepted as given, and the task of fiscal analysis was to forecast future tax yields so as to ascertain how much would be available for expenditure. The new approach treats taxes as variable, to be altered periodically in accord with national policy and economic conditions. Changes in tax rates are not to be determined (as they still are in virtually all States and localities) by how much is needed to cover expenditures but by the projected impact of alternative tax structures on the economy.

It is more than coincidental that the advent of PPB has followed on the heels of the explicit utilization of tax policy to guide the economy. In macroeconomics, taxes and expenditures are mirror images of one another; a tax cut and an expenditure increase have comparable impacts. Hence, the hinging of tax policy to economic considerations inevitably led to the similar treatment of expenditures. But there were (and remain) a number of obstacles to the utilization of the budget as a fiscal tool. For one thing, the conversion of the budget process to an economic orientation probably was slowed by the Full Employment Act of 1946 which established the Council of Economic Advisers and transferred the Budget Bureau's fiscal analysis function to the Council. The institutional separation between the CEA and the BOB and between fiscal policy and budget making was not compensated by cooperative work relationships. Economic analysis had only a slight impact on expenditure policy. It offered a few guidelines (for example, that spending should be increased during recessions) and a few ideas (such as a shelf of public works projects), but it did not feed into the regular channels of budgeting. The business of preparing the budget was foremost a matter of responding to agency spending pressures, not of responding to economic conditions.

Moreover, expenditures (like taxes) have been treated virtually as givens, to be determined by the unconstrained claims of the spending units. In the absence of central policy instructions, the agencies have been allowed to vent their demands without prior restraints by central authorities and without an operational set of planning guidelines. By the time the Bureau gets into the act, it is faced with the overriding task of bringing estimates into line with projected resources. In other words, the Bureau has had a budget-cutting function, to reduce claims to an acceptable level. The President's role has been similarly restricted. He is the *gatekeeper* of Federal budgeting. He directs the pace of spending increases by deciding which of the various expansions proposed by the agencies shall be included in the budget. But, as the gatekeeper, the President rarely has been able to look back at the items that have previously passed through the gate; his attention is riveted to those programs that are departures from the established base. In their limited roles, neither the Bureau nor the President has been able to inject fiscal and policy objectives into the forefront of budget preparation.

It will not be easy to wean budgeting from its utilization as an administrative procedure for financing ongoing programs to a decisional process for determining the range and direction of public objectives and the government's involvement in the economy. In the transition to a planning emphasis, an important step was the 1963 hearings of the Joint Economic Committee on *The Federal Budget as an Economic Document.* These hearings and the pursuant report of the JEC explored the latent policy opportunities in budget making. Another development was the expanded time horizons manifested by the multiyear expenditure projections introduced in the early 1960's. Something of a breakthrough was achieved via the revelation that the existing tax structure would yield cumulatively larger increments of uncommitted funds—estimated as much as $50 billion by 1970—which could be applied to a number of alternative uses. How much of the funds should be "returned" to the private sector through tax reductions and how much through expenditure increases? How much should go to the States and localities under a broadened system of Federal grants? How much should be allocated to the rebuilding of cities, to the improvement of education, or to the eradication of racial injustices. The traditional budget system lacked the analytic tools to cope with these questions, though decisions ultimately would be made one way or another. The expansion of the time horizon from the single year to a multiyear frame enhances the opportunity for planning and analysis to have an impact on future expenditure decisions. With a one-year perspective, almost all options have been foreclosed by previous commitments; analysis is effective only for the increments provided by self-generating revenue increases or to the extent that it is feasible to convert funds from one use to another. With a longer time span, however, many more options are open, and economic analysis can have a prominent part in determining which course of action to pursue.

So much for the macroeconomic trends in budget reform. On the microeconomic side, PPB traces its lineage to the attempts of welfare economists to construct a science of finance predicted on the principle of marginal utility. Such a science, it was hoped, would furnish objective criteria for determining the optimal allocation of public funds among competing uses. By appraising the marginal costs and benefits of alternatives (poor relief versus battleships in Pigou's classic example), it would be possible to determine which combination of expenditures afforded maximum utility. The quest for a welfare function provided the conceptual under-pinning for a 1940 article on "The Lack of a Budgetary Theory" in which V. O. Key noted the absence of a theory which would determine whether "to allocate x dollars to activity A instead of activity B."[32] In terms of its direct contribution to budgetary practice, welfare economics has been a failure. It has not been possible to distill the conflicts and complexities of political life into a welfare criterion or homogeneous distribution formula. But stripped of its normative and formal overtones, its principles have been applied to budgeting by economists such as Arthur Smithies. Smithies has formulated a budget rule that "expenditure proposals should be considered in the light of the objectives they are intended to further, and in general final expenditure decisions should not be made until all claims on the budget can be considered."[33] PPB is the application of this rule to budget practice. By structuring expenditures so as to juxtapose substitutive elements within program categories, and by analyzing the costs and benefits of the various substitutes, PPB has opened the door to the use of marginal analysis in budgeting.

Actually, the door was opened somewhat by the development of new decisional and informational technologies, the second item on the list of influences in the evolution of the planning orientation. Without the avail-ability of the decisional-informational capability provided by cost-benefit and systems analysis, it is doubtful that PPB would be part of the budgetary apparatus today. The new technologies make it possible to cope with the enormous informational and analytic burdens imposed by PPB. As aids to calculation, they furnish a methodology for the analysis of alterna-tives, thereby expanding the range of decision-making in budgeting.

Operations research, the oldest of these technologies, grew out of complex World War II conditions that required the optimal coordination of manpower, material, and equipment to achieve defense objectives. Opera-

[32]V. O. Key, "The Lack of a Budgetary Theory," *The American Political Science Review*, Vol. 34 (1940), p. 1138.

[33]Arthur Smithies, *The Budgetary Process in the United States*, New York: McGraw-Hill Book Co., 1955, p. 16.

tions research is most applicable to those repetitive operations where the opportunity for qualification is highest. Another technology, cost-benefit analysis, was intensively adapted during the 1950's to large-scale water resource investments, and subsequently to many other governmental functions. Systems analysis is the most global of these technologies. It involves the skillful analysis of the major factors that go into the attainment of an interconnected set of objectives. Systems analysis has been applied in DOD to the choice of weapons systems, the location of military bases, and the determination of sealift-airlift requirements. Although the extension of these technologies across-the-board to government was urged repeatedly by members of the RAND Corporation during the 1950's, it was DOD's experience that set the stage for the current ferment. It cannot be doubted that the coming of PPB has been pushed ahead several years or more by the "success story" in DOD.

The third stream of influence in the transformation of the budget function has been a closing of the gap between planning and budgeting. Institutionally and operationally, planning and budgeting have run along separate tracks. The national government has been reluctant to embrace central planning of any sort because of identification with socialist management of the economy. The closest thing we have had to a central planning agency was the National Resources Planning Board in the 1939-1943 period. Currently, the National Security Council and the Council of Economic Advisors have planning responsibilities in the defense and fiscal areas. As far as the Bureau of the Budget is concerned, it has eschewed the planning function in favor of control and management. In many States and localities, planning and budgeting are handled by separate organizational units: in the States, because limitations on debt financing have encouraged the separation of the capital and operating budgets; in the cities, because the professional autonomy and land-use preoccupations of the planners have set them apart from the budgeteers.

In all governments, the appropriations cycle, rather than the anticipation of future objectives, tends to dictate the pace and posture of budgeting. Into the repetitive, one-year span of the budget is wedged all financial decisions, including those that have multiyear implications. As a result, planning, if it is done at all, "occurs independently of budgeting and with little relation to it."[34] Budgeting and planning, moreover, invite disparate perspectives: the one is conservative and negativistic; the other, innovative and expansionist. As Mosher has noted, "budgeting and planning are apposite, if not opposite. In extreme form, the one means saving; the other, spending."[35]

Nevertheless, there has been some *rapprochement* of planning and budgeting. One factor is the long lead-time in the development and procure-

[34]Mosher, *op. cit.*, pp. 47–48.
[35]*Ibid.*, p. 48.

ment of hardware and capital investments. The multiyear projections inaugurated several years ago were a partial response to this problem. Another factor has been the diversity of government agencies involved in related functions. This has given rise to various *ad hoc* coordinating devices, but it also has pointed to the need for permanent machinery to integrate dispersed activities. Still another factor has been the sheer growth of Federal activities and expenditures and the need for a rational system of allocation. The operational code of planners contains three tenets relevant to these budgetary needs: (1) planning is future-oriented; it connects present decisions to the attainment of a desired future state of affairs; (2) planning, ideally, encompasses all resources involved in the attainment of future objectives. It strives for comprehensiveness. The *master plan* is the one that brings within its scope all relevant factors; (3) planning is means-ends oriented. The allocation of resources is strictly dictated by the ends that are to be accomplished. All this is to say that planning is an economizing process, though planners are more oriented to the future than economists. It is not surprising that planners have found the traditional budget system deficient,[36] nor is it surprising that the major reforms entailed by PPB emphasize the planning function.

Having outlined the several trends in the emerging transition to a planning orientation, it remains to mention several qualifications. First, the planning emphasis is not predominant in Federal budgeting at this time. Although PPB asserts the paramountcy of planning, PPB itself is not yet a truly operational part of the budget machinery. We are now at the dawn of a new era in budgeting; high noon is still a long way off. Second, this transition has not been preceded by a reorientation of the Bureau of the Budget. Unlike the earlier changeover from control to management in which the alteration of budgetary techniques *followed* the revision of the Bureau's role, the conversion from management to planning is taking a different course—first, the installation of new techniques; afterwards, a reformulation of the Bureau's mission. Whether this sequence will hinder reform efforts is a matter that cannot be predicted, but it should be noted that in the present instance the Bureau cannot convert to a new mission by bringing in a wholly new staff, as was the case in the late 1930's and early 1940's.

WHAT DIFFERENCE DOES IT MAKE?

The starting point for the author was distinguishing the old from the new in budgeting. The interpretation has been framed in analytic terms, and budgeting has been viewed historically in three stages corresponding to the three basic functions of budgeting. In this analysis, an attempt has been made to identify the difference between the existing and the emerging as a difference between management and planning orientations.

---

[36]*See* Edward C. Banfield, "Congress and the Budget: A Planner's Criticism," *The American Political Science Review*, Vol. 43 (1949), pp. 1217–1227.

In an operational sense, however, what difference does it make whether the central budget process is oriented toward planning rather than management? Does the change merely mean a new way of making decisions, or does it mean different decisions as well? These are not easy questions to answer, particularly since the budget system of the future will be a compound of all three functions. The case for PPB rests on the assumption that the form in which information is classified and used governs the actions of budget makers, and, conversely, that alterations in form will produce desired changes in behavior. Take away the assumption that behavior follows form, and the movement for PPB is reduced to a trivial manipulation of techniques—form for form's sake without any significant bearing on the conduct of budgetary affairs.

Yet this assumed connection between roles and information is a relatively uncharted facet of the PPB literature. The behavioral side of the equation has been neglected. PPB implies that each participant will behave as a sort of Budgetary Man, a counterpart of the classical Economic Man and Simon's Administrative Man.[37] Budgetary Man, whatever his station or role in the budget process, is assumed to be guided by an unwavering commitment to the rule of efficiency; in every instance he chooses that alternative that optimizes the allocation of public resources.

PPB probably takes an overly mechanistic view of the impact of form on behavior and underestimates the strategic and volitional aspects of budget making. In the political arena, data are used to influence the "who gets what" in budgets and appropriations. If information influences behavior, the reverse also is true. Indeed, data are more tractable than roles; participants are more likely to seek and use data which suit their preferences than to alter their behavior automatically in response to formal changes.

All this constrains, rather than negates, the impact of budget form. The advocates of PPB, probably in awareness of the above limitations, have imported into budgeting men with professional commitments to the types of analysis and norms required by the new techniques, men with a background in economics and systems analysis, rather than with general administrative training.

PPB aspires to create a different environment for choice. Traditionally, budgeting has defined its mission in terms of identifying the existing base and proposed departures from it—"This is where we are; where do we go from here?" PPB defines its mission in terms of budgetary objectives and purposes—"Where do we want to go? What do we do to get there?" The environment of choice under traditional circumstances is *incremental;* in PPB it is *teletic.* Presumably, these different processes will lead to different budgetary outcomes.

A budgeting process which accepts the base and examines only the increments will produce decisions to transfer the present into the future with

---

[37]Herbert A. Simon, *Administrative Behavior*, New York: The Macmillan Company, 1957.

a few small variations. The curve of government activities will be continuous, with few zigzags or breaks. A budget-making process which begins with objectives will require the base to compete on an equal footing with new proposals. The decisions will be more radical than those made under incremental conditions. This does not mean that each year's budget will lack continuity with the past. There are sunk costs that have to be reckoned, and the benefits of radical changes will have to outweigh the costs of terminating prior commitments. Furthermore, the extended time span of PPB will mean that big investment decisions will be made for a number of years, with each year being a partial installment of the plan. Most important, the political manifestations of sunk costs—vested interests—will bias decisions away from radical departures. The conservatism of the political system, therefore, will tend to minimize the decisional differences between traditional and PPB approaches. However, the very availability of analytic data will cause a shift in the balance of economic and political forces that go into the making of a budget.

Teletic and incremental conditions of choice lead to still another distinction. In budgeting, which is committed to the established base, the flow of budgetary decisions is upward and aggregative. Traditionally, the first step in budgeting, in anticipation of the call for estimates, is for each department to issue its own call to prepare and to submit a set of estimates. This call reaches to the lowest level capable of assembling its own estimates. Lowest level estimates form the building blocks for the next level where they are aggregated and reviewed and transmitted upward until the highest level is reached and the totality constitutes a department-wide budget. Since budgeting is tied to a base, the building-up-from-below approach is sensible; each building block estimates the cost of what it is already doing plus the cost of the increments it wants. (The building blocks, then, are decisional elements, not simply informational elements as is often assumed.)

SOME BASIC DIFFERENCES BETWEEN BUDGET ORIENTATIONS

Characteristic	Control	Management	Planning
Personnel skill	Accounting	Administration	Economics
Information focus	Objects	Activities	Purposes
Key budget stage (central)	Execution	Preparation	Pre-preparation
Breadth of measurement	Discrete	Discrete/activities	Comprehensive
Role of budget agency	Fiduciary	Efficiency	Policy
Decisional-flow	Upward-aggregative	Upward-aggregative	Downward-disaggregative
Type of choice	Incremental	Incremental	Teletic
Control responsibility	Central	Operating	Operating
Management responsibility	Dispersed	Central	Supervisory
Planning responsibility	Dispersed	Dispersed	Central
Budget-appropriations classifications	Same	Same	Different
Appropriations-organizational link	Direct	Direct	Crosswalk

543

PPB reverses the informational and decisional flow. Before the call for estimates is issued, top policy has to be made, and this policy constrains the estimates prepared below. For each lower level, the relevant policy instructions are issued by the superior level prior to the preparation of estimates. Accordingly, the critical decisional process—that of deciding on purposes and plans—has a downward and disaggregative flow.

If the making of policy is to be antecedent to the costing of estimates, there will have to be a shift in the distribution of budget responsibilities. The main energies of the Bureau of the Budget are now devoted to budget preparation; under PPB these energies will be centered on what we may term *prepreparation*—the stage of budget making that deals with policy and is prior to the preparation of the budget. One of the steps marking the advent of the planning orientation was the inauguration of the Spring Preview several years ago for the purpose of affording an advance look at departmental programs.

If budget-making is to be oriented to the planning function, there probably will be a centralization of policy-making, both within and among departments. The DOD experience offers some precedent for predicting that greater budgetary authority will be vested in department heads than heretofore, but there is no firm basis for predicting the degree of centralization that may derive from the relatedness of objectives pursued by many departments. It is possible that the mantle of central budgetary policy will be assumed by the Bureau; indeed, this is the expectation in many agencies. On the other hand, the Bureau gives little indication at this time that it is willing or prepared to take this comprehensive role.

CONCLUSION

The various differences between the budgetary orientations are charted in the table presented here. All the differences may be summed up in the statement that the ethos of budgeting will shift from justification to analysis. To far greater extent than heretofore, budget decisions will be influenced by explicit statements of objectives and by a formal weighing of the costs and benefits of alternatives.

THE ROLE OF COST UTILITY ANALYSIS IN PROGRAM BUDGETING

Gene H. Fisher

Program budgeting as envisioned in this book involves several essential considerations. The primary ones may be summarized under three main headings: structural (or format) aspects, analytical process considerations, and data or information system considerations to support the first two items.

The *structural* aspects of program budgeting are concerned with establishing a set of categories oriented primarily toward "end-product" or "end-objective" activities that are meaningful from a long-range-planning point of view.[1] In such a context emphasis is placed on provision for an extended time horizon—some five, even ten or more, years into the future. These characteristics are in marked contrast with conventional governmental budgeting, which stresses functional and/or object class categories and a very short time horizon.

Analytical process considerations pertain to various study activities conducted as an integral part of the program-budgeting process. The primary objective of this type of analytical effort is to systematically examine alternative courses of action in terms of utility and cost, with a view to clarifying the relevant choices (and their implications) open to the decision makers in a certain problem area.

Information system considerations are aimed at support of the first two items. There are several senses in which this is important, the primary ones being (1) progress reporting and control and (2) providing data and information to serve as a basis for the analytical process—especially to facilitate the development of estimating relationships that will permit making estimates of benefits and costs of alternative future courses of action.

The present chapter is concerned primarily with the second of the items listed above: analytical process considerations. That an analytical effort is an important part of program budgeting (at least as practiced in the Department of Defense) is made clear in a recent statement by Secretary of Defense McNamara:

As I have pointed out in previous appearances before this Committee, in adding to a Defense program as large as the one we now have, we soon

---

Reprinted by permission of the publishers from David Novick, editor, *Program Budgeting*, Cambridge, Mass.: Harvard University Press, Copyright 1964, 1965, by The RAND Corporation.

[1] In many instances, end products may in fact be *intermediate* products, especially from the point of view of the next higher level in the decision hierarchy.

encounter the law of diminishing returns, where each additional increment of resources used produces a proportionately smaller increment of overall defense capability. While the benefits to be gained from each additional increment cannot be measured with precision, careful cost/effectiveness analyses can greatly assist in eliminating those program proposals which clearly contribute little to our military strength in terms of the costs involved.

This principle is just as applicable to qualitative improvements in weapons systems as it is to quantitative increases in our forces. The relevant question is not only "Do we want the very best for our military force?", but also, "Is the additional capability truly required and, if so, is this the least costly way of attaining it?"

Let me give you one hypothetical example to illustrate the point. Suppose we have two tactical fighter aircraft which are identical in every important measure of performance, except one—Aircraft A can fly ten miles per hour faster than Aircraft B. However, Aircraft A costs $10,000 more per unit than Aircraft B. Thus, if we need about 1,000 aircraft, the total additional cost would be $10 million.

If we approach this problem from the viewpoint of a given amount of resources, the additional combat effectiveness represented by the greater speed of Aircraft A would have to be weighed against the additional combat effectiveness which the same $10 million could produce if applied to other defense purposes—more Aircraft B, more or better aircraft munitions, or more ships, or even more military family housing. And if we approach the problem from the point of view of a given amount of combat capability, we would have to determine whether that given amount could be achieved at less cost by buying, for example, more of Aircraft B or more aircraft munitions or better munitions, or perhaps surface-to-surface missiles. Thus, the fact that Aircraft A flies ten miles per hour faster than Aircraft B is not conclusive. We still have to determine whether the greater speed is worth the greater cost. *This kind of determination is the heart of the planning-programming-budgeting or resources allocation problem within the Defense Department* [italics supplied].[2]

Numerous analytical approaches may be used to support the total program-budgeting process. Here we shall focus on one of them: cost-utility analysis. Before turning to this subject, however, a few of the other types of analysis should be noted briefly.

In terms of the types of problems encountered in the total program-budgeting process, perhaps one might think of a wide spectrum going all the way from the most major allocative decisions on the one hand, to progress reporting and control on the other. Major allocative decisions involve such questions as, Should more resources be employed in national security in the future, or in national health programs, or in preservation and development

---

[2]From the introduction of the Statement of Secretary of Defense Robert S. McNamara before the Committee on Armed Services on the Fiscal Year 1965–1969 Defense Program and 1965 Defense Budget, January 27, 1964, *Hearings on Military Posture and H. R. 9637*, House of Representatives, 88 Cong. 2 sess., Washington, D.C.: U.S. Government Printing Office, 1964.

of natural resources, etc.?[3] Ideally, the decision makers would like to plan to allocate resources in the future so that for a given budget, for example, the estimated marginal return (or utility) in each major area of application would be equal. But this is more easily said than done; and at the current state of analytical art, no one really knows with any precision how the "grand optimum" might be attained. In the main, the analytical tools now available—particularly the quantitative ones—are just not very helpful in dealing directly with such problems. Intuition and judgment are paramount.

At the other end of the spectrum—progress reporting and control—the main problem is to keep track of programs where the major decisions have *already been made*, to try to detect impending difficulties as programs are being implemented, and to initiate remedial actions through a feedback mechanism when programs are deemed likely to get out of control in the future. Numerous techniques are available for dealing with these types of program-management problems. Examples are the following: financial and management accounting techniques;[4] network-type systems for planning, scheduling, progress reporting, and control;[5] critical-path methods (within the framework of a network-type system);[6] Gantt chart techniques for program planning and control;[7] and various program-management reporting and control schemes developed in recent years in the Department of Defense to help program managers in the management of complex weapon system development and production programs.[8]

The area between the ends of the spectrum is a broad and varied one, offering the opportunity for applying a variety of analytical techniques. These techniques are focused primarily toward problem areas short of dealing with determination of the "grand optimum," although they can be of real assistance in sharpening the intuition and judgment of decision makers in grappling with the very broad allocative questions. Technically, this is called

---

[3]For example, *see* Arthur Smithies, *Government Decision-making and the Theory of Choice*, P-2960, Santa Monica, Calif.: The RAND Corporation, October, 1964.

[4]*See* Robert N. Anthony, *Management Accounting*, Homewood, Ill.: Richard D. Irwin, Inc., 1960, chaps. xiii to xv.

[5]One example is the so-called PERT system. For a description, *see: USAF PERT, Volume I, PERT Time System Description Manual*, September, 1963; and *USAF PERT, Volume III, PERT Cost System Description Manual*, December, 1963, Washington, D.C.: Headquarters, Air Force Systems Command, Andrews Air Force Base, 1963.

[6]*See* James E. Kelly and Morgan R. Walker, "Critical-Path Planning and Scheduling," *Proceedings of the Eastern Joint Computer Conference*, Ft. Washington, Pa.: Manchly Associates, Inc., 1959, pp. 160–173; and F. K. Levy, G. L. Thompson, and J. D. Wiest, *Mathematical Basis of the Critical Path Method*, Office of Naval Research, Research Memorandum No. 86, Pittsburgh, Pa.: Carnegie Institute of Technology, May 30, 1962.

[7]L. P. Alford and John R. Bangs, *Production Handbook*, New York: Ronald Press, 1947, pp. 216–229.

[8]For a good example, *see: Systems Data Presentation and Reporting Procedures (Rainbow Report)*, November 1, 1961 (with revisions as of March 9, 1962), Program Management Instruction 1–5, Washington, D.C.: Headquarters, Air Force Systems Command, Andrews Air Force base, 1962.

"suboptimization," and it is here that the analytical efforts are likely to have the highest payoff.[9]

In cases where a wide range of alternative future courses of action needs to be examined in a broad suboptimization context, the main subject of this chapter, cost-utility analysis,[10] may well be the most useful analytical tool. However, in other cases where the suboptimization context is much narrower and a wide range of alternatives is not available, the problem may be one of examining relatively minor variations *within* an essentially prescribed future course of action. The suboptimization context may be relatively narrow for numerous reasons—severe political constraints, lack of new technology to provide the basis for a wide range of alternatives, etc. Here, something akin to capital budgeting[11] techniques may be most appropriate.

In many instances, the above-mentioned techniques may have to be supplemented by other methods. For example, in numerous major decision problems it is not sufficient to deal only with the *direct* economic consequences of proposed alternative future courses of action, ignoring their possible indirect or spillover effects. In such instances, it may well be vitally important to consider indirect economic effects either on the economy as a whole or on specified regions or sectors of the total economic system. Certain transportation problems involve considerations of this type.[12] Also, in the case of certain national security and space decisions, especially in the higher echelons of the decision hierarchy, it is often necessary to consider possible regional or industry sector economic impacts associated with alternative weapon system development and procurement choices.[13] One way to deal with such problems is through the use of macroeconomic models that attempt to take into account key interactions among important components of the economic system: for example, interindustry (input-output) models for the economy as a whole,[14]

---

[9]For a discussion of suboptimization, *see* Charles Hitch, "Suboptimization in Operations Problems," *Journal of the Operations Research Society of America*, Vol. 1, No. 3 (May, 1953), pp. 87–99; and Charles J. Hitch and Roland N. McKean, *The Economics of Defense in the Nuclear Age*, Cambridge, Mass.: Harvard University Press, 1960, pp. 396–402.

[10]Sometimes called "systems analysis"; e.g., *see* Roland N. McKean, *Efficiency in Government Through Systems Analysis*, New York: John Wiley & Sons, Inc., 1958.

[11]For example, *see* Joel Dean, *Capital Budgeting*, New York: Columbia University Press, 1951; Harold Bierman, Jr., and Seymour Smidt, *The Capital Budgeting Decision*, New York: The Macmillan Company, 1960; and Elwood S. Buffa, *Models for Production and Operations Management*, New York: John Wiley & Sons, Inc., 1963, chaps. xiii and xiv.

[12]For example, *see* Brian V. Martin and Charles B. Warden, "Transportation Planning in Developing Countries," *Traffic Quarterly* (January 1965), pp. 59–75.

[13]See *Convertibility of Space and Defense Resources to Civilian Needs: A Search for New Employment Potentials*, compiled for the Subcommittee on Employment and Manpower of the Committee on Labor and Public Welfare, Senate, 88 Cong., 2 sess., Washington, D.C.: U.S. Government Printing Office, 1964. Note especially Part III, "National Adjustments to Shifts in Defense Planning," and Part IV, "Studies in Regional Adjustment to Shifts in Defense Spending."

[14]W. W. Leontief *et al.*, *Studies in the Structure of the American Economy*, New York: Oxford University Press, 1953.

and various types of regional models dealing with parts of the total national economy.[15]

Thus it is clear that numerous analytical methods and techniques exist that may be used to support various facets of the total program budgeting process. We have dealt with this point at some length to emphasize that the subject of this chapter, cost-utility analysis, is not the only analytical tool that might be used in program budgeting.

Let us now turn to our central theme. In the following paragraphs, cost-utility analysis is discussed in somewhat general and abstract terms. Illustrative examples are presented later in this book in several of the "case study" chapters—e.g., in the chapters on defense, natural resources, and education.

WHAT IS COST-UTILITY ANALYSIS

Attempting to define cost-utility analysis poses somewhat of a semantics problem. Numerous terms in current use convey the same general meaning but have important different meanings to different people: "cost-benefit analysis," "cost-effectiveness analysis," "systems analysis," "operations research," "operations analysis," etc. Because of such terminological confusion, in this chapter all of these terms are rejected and "cost-utility analysis" is employed instead.

Cost-utility analysis, as envisoned here, may be distinguished by the following major characteristics:

1. A most fundamental characteristic is the systematic examination and comparison of alternative courses of action that might be taken to achieve specified objectives for some future time period. Not only is it important to systematically examine all of the relevant alternatives that can be identified initially, but also to *design additional ones* if those examined are found wanting.[16] Finally, the analysis, particularly if thoroughly and imaginatively done, may at times result in modifications of the initially specified objectives.

2. Critical examination of alternatives typically involves numerous considerations; but the two main ones are assessment of the cost (in the sense of economic resource cost) and the utility (the benefits or gains) pertaining to each of the alternatives being compared to attain the stipulated objectives.

3. The time context is the future (often the distant future—five, ten, or more years).

---

[15]For example, *see* Walter Isard *et. al.*, *Methods of Regional Analysis: An Introduction to Regional Science*, Boston and New York: Technology Press of Massachusetts Institute of Technology and John Wiley & Sons, Inc., 1960.

[16]E. S. Quade, *Military Systems Analysis*, RM—3452—PR, Santa Monica, Calif.: The RAND Corporation, January 1963, p. 1.

4. Because of the extended time horizon, the environment is one of uncertainty (very often great uncertainty). Since uncertainty is an important facet of the problem, it should be faced up to and treated explicitly in the analysis. This means, among other things, that wherever possible the analyst should avoid the use of simple expected value models.

5. Usually the context in which the analysis takes place is broad (often very broad) and the environment very complex, with numerous interactions among the key variables in the problem. This means that simple, straightforward solutions are the exception rather than the rule.

6. While quantitative methods of analysis should be used as much as possible, because of items 4 and 5 above,[17] purely quantitative work must often be heavily supplemented by qualitative analysis. In fact, we stress the importance of *good* qualitative work and of using an appropriate combination of quantitative and qualitative methods.

7. Usually the focus is on research and development and/or investment-type decision problems, although operational decisions are sometimes encountered. This does not mean, of course, that operational considerations are ignored in dealing with R&D and investment-type problems.

8. Timeliness is important. A careful, thorough analysis that comes six months after the critical time of decision may be worth essentially zero, while a less thorough—but thoughtfully done—analysis completed on time may be worth a great deal.

ILLUSTRATIVE EXAMPLE OF COST-UTILITY CONSIDERATIONS IN A MILITARY CONTEXT

... there are people who believe that any analytical effort of value to a decision maker dealing with major problems may prove exceptionally difficult, perhaps impossible. Two reasons in support of this belief are (1) an extremely complex environment, along with a host of nonquantifiable variables; and (2) a short deadline to complete a study.

No doubt there are such instances. However, we have taken the position that even in rather severe cases, *something* can be done; and that this something may often be very useful in spite of the lack of extensive calculations of utility and cost. In this appendix, an example having the above characteristics is selected deliberately to illustrate the kind of analysis that might be done.[1] The example is a military one, extracted from an actual study conducted at The RAND Corporation some time ago. To avoid a security classified discussion, much of the substantive material has had to be suppressed. However, it is hoped that enough of the essential content of the problem is preserved so that a few of the more important points can be illustrated.

---

[1]Some years ago such an example might have been regarded as atypical. In today's environment, however, it is probably a most typical example.

[17]And also because of inadequate data and information sources.

General Statement of the Problem

Basically, the problem may be stated as follows:

1. Investigate the possible role of long-endurance aircraft (LEA)[2] for use in new weapon (or support) systems to perform a variety of Air Force missions in the 1970–1975 time period.

2. In each mission area compare LEA-type systems with alternative possibilities, including missile as well as aircraft systems.

3. Investigate the possibilities for *multipurpose* use of the LEA; i.e., of developing a basic aircraft and adapting it to several mission areas. What are the cost savings? What degradations, if any, in utility (system effectiveness) might be incurred in a given mission area by using a multipurpose vehicle rather than one "optimized" to that particular mission?

4. Assess the implications for possible new development programs to be initiated in the near future, with a view to initial operational capability in the early 1970's.

5. Consider the time to do the study: about *six weeks*.[3]

Further Consideration of the Problem

The statement of the problem as outlined above appears fairly straightforward, although the short time period for doing the study imposes a significant constraint. However, even preliminary thinking about the problem soon leads to a set of considerations, which in turn rapidly lead to the conclusion that the problem is a difficult one. Some of the more important considerations are outlined in the following paragraphs.

A wide range of possible mission area applications might be considered; for example: strategic bombardment, limited war, defense against submarine-launched ballistic-missile attack, air defense of North America (against the air-breathing threat), command and control, satellite launching platform, antisatellite-missile launching platform, air transport, and intelligence and/or reconnaissance patrol applications.

The future environment (1970–1975) in practically all the mission areas is very uncertain. In limited war, for instance, what kinds of limited-war scenarios[4] should we consider? Obviously, we cannot single out one that is

---

[2] A long endurance aircraft is one designed specifically to remain airborne in unrefueled flight for a prolonged period of time—in some cases several days. Usually the emphasis on long endurance involves compromises in certain of the other performance characteristics, especially speed and cruise altitude.

[3] In all fairness it should be pointed out that The RAND Corporation had in previous years done a considerable amount of work on the technical and design aspects of LEA. However, work on *system* applications of LEA was somewhat more limited. In any event, six weeks was a short time to do a study of this type, at least by RAND standards. But time to do a study is relative. In a military staff environment in the Pentagon, six weeks would no doubt be considered a relatively long time.

[4] Here "scenario" essentially means the context or setting within which the particular type of war is assumed to take place; for example, the geographic area, the political environment at the beginning of the conflict, the political objectives to be attained, the constraints on weapons (nuclear weapons or not?), the sanctuaries, if any, etc.

551

"most probable." A range of scenarios must be considered. This range should not necessarily be chosen on the basis of likelihood, but rather to illustrate possible roles for the LEA.

Within most of the mission areas, there is a wide range of alternative systems to be considered—even including the Navy's proposals for an advanced Fleet Ballistic Missile (Polaris) system in the strategic area. (Some of the more relevant alternatives are discussed later.)

After only slight initial examination, it becomes obvious that the most critical considerations do not concern the LEA vehicle itself, but rather the *payload subsystems* that have to be developed and procured to give an LEA system its capability in a given mission area. There are exceptions: probably command and control, for example. But, in general, the payload subsystems have the more interesting and difficult technical problems; and preliminary cost analysis indicated that the development cost for a subsystem in a given area (such as strategic bombardment) would be considerably greater than for the total development program for the LEA itself. In short, what initially is specified as mainly an aircraft problem rapidly turns primarily into a subsystem type of problem.

The main characteristics of an LEA are extended airborne capability (endurance), large payload, and long range.[5] These are so-called positive characteristics. The main negative ones are low speed and possibly constraints on altitude capability. Therefore the analyst should think immediately about mission applications where the positive characteristics are desired and where low speed is not a handicap or perhaps is even desirable (e.g., in certain types of intelligence/reconnaissance operations). One example is a mission area where airborne patrol operations are important. Another is a situation where vulnerability on the ground to an initial enemy attack is a problem, and an alternative basing scheme is required. The LEA used as an airborne platform provides such a scheme. But there are still other possible alternative basing schemes: ground mobility, water-based platforms (surface), water-based platforms (submersible), etc. These alternatives would have to be taken into account in the analysis.

From this partial list of considerations, it is clear that the problem at hand is indeed a complex one. The real question is what can be done with it in the short period of time available for analytical effort. For illustrative purposes, let us take one mission area—strategic bombardment—and consider some of the more relevant factors.

Some Considerations in the Strategic Bombardment Area

In considering whether currently planned strategic systems for the early 1970's should be supplemented, two major intelligence-type uncertainties are paramount:

1. Whether the enemy is likely to achieve technological advances such

---

[5]There are trade-offs among these, of course.

that his offensive capabilities will render U.S. fixed base (hardened) missile systems vulnerable on the ground to a first strike.

2. Whether the enemy is likely to achieve a reasonably effective defense against intercontinental ballistic missiles (an AICBM capability) during the early 1970 time period.

Although the analyst cannot *resolve* these uncertainties, he can and should trace out their implications, enumerate the relevant alternatives that might be used to meet them, and possibly suggest ways to hedge against them.

With respect to the first uncertainty (item 1), it is clear that the LEA would be of interest if the problem is one of seeking alternative basing schemes to avoid or reduce vulnerability on the ground. The LEA could be used as a standoff missile launching platform in a system having a substantial part of the force on continuous airborne alert. With respect to the second uncertainty (item 2), the LEA offers no *unique* features; but it could be used as an airborne platform from which low-altitude penetrating missiles (to avoid AICBM defenses) could be launched. When items 1 and 2 are combined, however, it could be that an LEA system (with low-altitude penetrating missiles) might be attractive. But such a system would have to be compared with the alternatives.

What are some of the relevant alternatives? The following is an illustrative list.

For the case in which the prime objective is to reduce initial vulnerability to a surprise attack, the alternatives are:

1. LEA used as a standoff platform for launching airborne ballistic missiles (ALBM's) in a system having a substantial part of the force on continuous airborne alert.
2. Land mobile (truck and/or rail) ballistic-missile systems.
3. Water mobile (barge) ballistic-missile systems.
4. Incremental fleet ballistic-missile (Polaris) force. (Incremental to the currently planned Polaris force.)
5. *More* Minuteman missiles to try to compensate for their ground vulnerability by having a bigger force. (Incremental to the currently planned Minuteman force.)

For the case in which the main purpose is to have a system that can penetrate enemy ICBM defenses, the alternatives are:

1. Low-altitude penetrating missiles launched from an airborne platform—an LEA or some other aircraft.
2. Land-based (fixed) ballistic-missile systems with low-altitude penetrating re-entry devices.
3. Land-based (fixed) ballistic-missile systems with multiple warhead (possibly including decoys) re-entry devices to confuse the enemy ICBM defense.
4. Sea-based ballistic-missile systems with low-altitude penetrating re-entry bodies or with multiple warhead capability.

For a combination of the above two cases, that is, where the main concern is about the initial vulnerability of U.S. strategic systems and about the enemy having an AICBM capability, the alternatives are:

1. LEA used as a standoff platform for launching low-altitude penetrating missiles in a system having a substantial fraction of the force on continuous airborne alert.

2. Land mobile (truck or rail) ballistic-missile systems with low-altitude penetrating re-entry devices or with multiple warhead re-entry bodies.

3. Water mobile (surface) ballistic-missile systems with low-altitude penetrating re-entry devices or with multiple warhead re-entry bodies.

4. Same as item 3 except *below* the surface platform—for example, submarines or submersible barges.

The main problem is to conduct an analysis to compare the above alternative on a cost-utility basis, with a view to determining preferred alternatives under certain assumed scenarios. Ideally, this would proceed somewhat as described below. (We assume a fixed utility conceptual framework; a fixed budget context could be used instead.)

An enemy target system(s) is specified to be destroyed with some probability of success (say, 90 percent). Campaign analyses are conducted to determine the size force that would be required for each alternative to do the specified task. This involves determination of the number of U.S. weapons surviving the initial enemy attack, determining the force that is successfully launched to make the responding strike on the specified enemy target system, assessment of losses to the enemy defenses, calculation of target destruction, and the like.[6] Given the resulting force size calculations, we then proceed with a resource analysis to determine the *total system cost* (research and development, investment and operating cost) for each of the alternatives required to do the job specified initially. These system costs can then be compared, to try to determine which alternative is likely to accomplish the given task at the lowest cost. Finally, the analyst might repeat the analysis for varying levels of initial enemy attack and varying types of U.S. responses, and then conduct a qualitative analysis to supplement the quantitative work.

The preceding discussion is in the realm of a "hard-core" cost-utility analysis, one that is not easy to do and is certainly very time consuming. Because only six weeks were available in this particular problem for the entire study, the analysis was far from complete. The real question is what *can* be done, if anything, within these limitations. We maintain that a great deal can be done far short of a type of analysis involving a relatively complete set of calculations of utility and cost.[7] For one thing, a mere *enumeration* of all the relevant alternatives may be very helpful. And better yet, if we can next furnish data and information bearing on utility and cost of these alternatives.

---

[6] It should be emphasized that these campaign analyses are very *difficult and time consuming.*

[7] Recall that our objective in analytical work is *not* to "make the decision," but rather to try to *sharpen* the decision maker's intuition and judgment.

Summary Analyses of Cost and Utility.   One thing that can be done is to develop summary analyses of cost and utility and present them along with a qualitative statement of some of the key implications. Examples are contained in Figure 1 and Table 1.

FIGURE 1
TOTAL SYSTEM COST VERSUS FORCE SIZE FOR ALTERNATIVE SYSTEMS
A, B, C, D, AND E

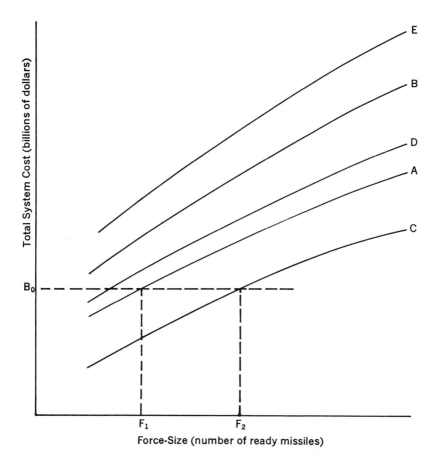

Figure 1 shows total system cost (research and development, investment and operating cost[8]) versus force size for several alternative systems. In this example force size means number of missiles in position ready to go. In the case of a system like Minuteman, it means number of missiles in silos ready to fire. In the case of an LEA system carrying airborne air-to-surface missiles, it means number of missiles continuously airborne on station ready to go. Used in conjunction with data pertaining to utility (as in Table 1), system cost versus force size curves can be useful.

[8]Operating cost is usually computed for a fixed period of years, say, five or seven.

555

TABLE 1
SELECTED DATA BEARING ON UTILITY CONSIDERATIONS FOR ALTERNATIVE SYSTEMS
A, B, C, D, AND E

	ALTERNATIVE SYSTEM				
DESCRIPTION	A	B	C	D	E
Quantitative information:					
Effective range (n mi)...........................					
Cruise speed (kn)...............................					
Penetration speed (kn)..........................					
Warhead yield (MT).............................					
Circular error probability (CEP).................					
Single shot kill probability:					
Against soft targets...........................					
Against hard targets...........................					
Extended strike option time (days)...............					
"					
"					
etc.					
Qualitative information:[1]					
"Show of force" capability.......................					
Multidirectional attack capability................					
Ground vulnerability............................					
In-flight vulnerability...........................					
Controlled response capability...................					
"					
"					
etc.					

[1]Some of these items have quantitative aspects, but they are very difficult to assess in a study with a short time deadline.

For example, suppose that alternatives A and C are in the same "ball park" with respect to certain key utility variables—say, penetration capability and single shot kill probability—but that C is clearly more vulnerable to an initial enemy strike than is A. The difference in the system cost curves for A and C in Figure 1, then, essentially represents what we pay for getting reduced vulnerability. But there are other ways to play this game. Suppose the decision maker has a given budget (B_0 in Figure 1) to spend for supplementation of the already planned strategic forces. For B_0 he can get a force size of F_1 for alternative A, or a much larger force (F_2) of system C. He may judge that the larger force of C may more than compensate for its higher vulnerability. Or he may decide that F_2 of C is roughly equivalent to F_1 of A and decide to go for C for other (qualitative) reasons: for example, C may have more of a show of force capability than A, or be preferable from a controlled response point of view.

In any event, *the decision maker is clearly in a better position to sharpen his intuition and judgment with the benefit of* Figure 1 and Table 1.[1] This is an illustrative example of what was meant earlier in this appendix when we indicated that there are numerous things that can be done between the extremes of no analysis whatever and "hard-core" cost-utility analysis. The

[9]It is assumed, of course, that a textual discussion goes along with the figure and the table, so that the decision maker can profit from any interpretive comments that the analyst may make.

above example is certainly far short of the detailed analysis, but it nevertheless may be useful.

A Purely Qualitative Analysis. Quite often a purely qualitative comparison—especially when used as a supplement to the kind of analysis presented above—can be very useful. An illustrative example is contained in Table 2.

TABLE 2
SYSTEM COMPARISON
(Illustrative example)

| Alternative system | INVULNERABLE TO | | | USEFUL FOR | | | | |
	Improved Enemy ICBM's	AICBM Defense	Air Defense	Hitting Known Hard Targets	Penetrating for Recce-Strike	"Show of Force"	Time on Station (days)	Alert Capability[1]
A......	No	No	Yes	No[2]	No	No	Unlimited	No
B......	No	Somewhat	Yes	Possibly	No	No	Unlimited	No
C......	Yes	Yes	Somewhat	Yes	No	Yes	2–3[3]	Yes
D.....	Yes	No	Yes	No	No	Yes	2–3[3]	Yes
E......	Yes	Yes	Yes[4]	Yes	No	Yes	2–3[3]	Yes
F......	Yes	Yes	Somewhat	Yes	Yes	Yes	2–3[3]	Yes
G......	Yes	No	Yes	No	No	No	90	Yes
H.....	Yes	Yes	Yes[4]	Yes	No	No	90	Yes
I......	No	Yes	Yes	Yes	No	No	Unlimited	No

[1]Number of missiles on station can be increased in times of tension.
[2]Poor CEP and low yield.
[3]Assuming no refueling on station
[4]With existing Soviet Union defenses.

The various alternatives are listed in the stub of Table 2, and in the body various qualitative comments are made regarding certain key capability characteristics for each of the alternative systems. In cases where a large number of alternatives are under consideration, such information can be useful in "weeding out" those cases that are likely to be of little interest and in selecting those items for further and more detailed deliberation.

A Subsystem Illustrative Example. Subsystem considerations are often of paramount importance in a given decision problem, particularly when uncertainties are present. In our present illustrative example, assume that one of the alternatives under consideration is a long-endurance aircraft (LEA) system utilizing a chemically fueled low-altitude penetrating missile (LAPM) launched from the LEA airborne platform located in a standoff position outside enemy territory. Assume further that we are somewhat uncertain about the gross weight versus low-altitude range relationship for this new LAPM, which is not yet developed and which, if developed, would not be operational until some six years from now. Upon examination, suppose that the analyst finds that LAPM gross weight is very sensitive to low-altitude range, and that this relationship can be graphed for two cases: an "optimistic" curve and a "conservative" relation between weight and range. See Figure 2. (We note that a rather severe weight penalty is incurred in moving from a range permitting coverage of 70 percent of the enemy target system (R_0) to one permitting a 95 percent coverage (R_1).)

FIGURE 2
LAPM Gross Weight versus Low Altitude Range

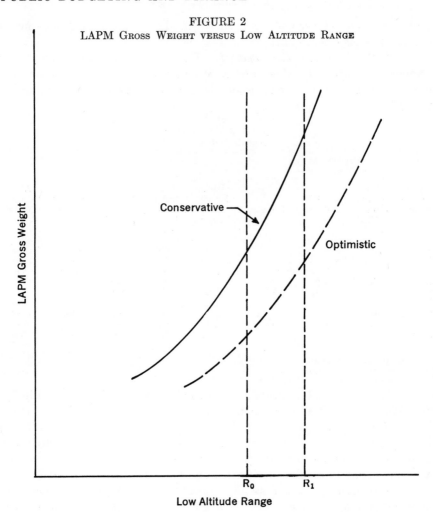

R_0 = LAPM range permitting coverage of 70% of the enemy target system

R_1 = LAPM range permitting coverage of 95% of the enemy target system

It may be instructive to explore the consequences of the relationships portrayed in Figure 2. As an illustrative example, let us consider a sensitivity analysis of total system cost as a function of the key variables in Figure 2 and two additional variables: force size (defined as total number of missiles in the system that are continuously airborne on station), and the average fly-out distance from base to station.[10] The results may look something like Figure 3.

---

[10]The importance of average fly-out distance from base to station (U.S. bases are assumed) depends on the strategic scenario being considered. If a quick response to an initial enemy first strike is desired, a long fly-out distance would be required. If not, a short fly-out distance might suffice.

FIGURE 3
Total System Cost versus Force Size for Various Cases

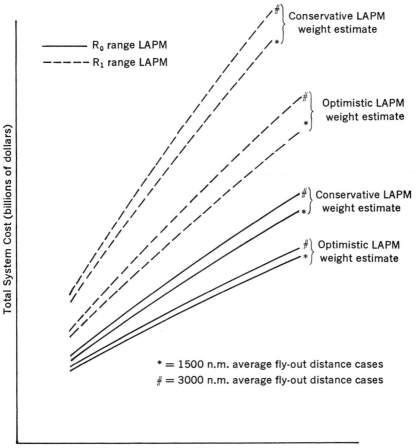

Number of Missiles Airborne on Station

From Figure 3 it is clear that we have examples of both sensitivity and relative *in*sensitivity. Total system cost is *very* sensitive to LAPM range (and hence gross weight), and it is fairly sensitive to whether the optimistic or conservative estimate of the weight versus range curve is used. Also, these sensitivities seem to increase as total force size increases. On the other hand, total system cost is relatively insensitive to average fly-out distance from base to station.[11]

The marked sensitivity to low-altitude range (and hence missile gross weight) is not surprising. As missile weight increases, the number of missiles

---

[11]This is not always the case. Here we are assuming a relatively efficient LEA platform from the standpoint of endurance. For less efficient LEA's total system cost can be relatively more sensitive to average fly-out distance from base to station.

that can be carried per LEA decreases. This means that to obtain a given total force of missiles continuously airborne on station, a larger number of LEA's must be procured. The total system cost spirals upward not only because of increased aircraft and missile procurement, but also because of increased number of personnel, facilities, supplies, etc.

Here we have an example of how a relatively simple analysis of subsystem characteristics can contribute toward sharpening intuition and judgment about the impact on the total system. In this case it might suggest certain component research and development programs that would result in a more favorable relationship between LAPM gross weight and low-altitude range—for example, research in propulsion components for LAPM-type missiles.

Research and development in component areas may be significant. In cases where major uncertainties (or other reasons) make it difficult to make a compelling argument for immediate initiation of development for the *total* system, the analysis may suggest relatively inexpensive *component* development programs that will in effect provide somewhat of a hedge against some of the major uncertainties in the problem.

OPERATIONS RESEARCH: A CHALLENGE TO MANAGEMENT

John W. Pocock

Operations research as an approach to the solution of business and industrial problems is in the headlines today. The power of its unique approach is repeatedly emphasized, yet few can agree on exactly what this approach is. The great variety of its analysis techniques is emphasized, yet few are familiar with more than two or three. The tangible worth of such analysis to the profit-seeking manager is touted, yet specific case material is still relatively scarce.

A synopsized and panoramic picture of operations research may provide some immediate appreciation of the total effort in business applications today and serve as background for the specific discussions that follow.

SEARCH FOR BASIC LAWS

. . . .

Every one of us, looking around at some apparently confused activity in the world about us, has probably felt that "there ought to be a law"—some underlying relationship which explains that particular activity and allows us to bring chaos under control. Such a thought may occur to us while we are involved in a traffic jam on the way to a football game or while we are standing in line at a cafeteria. We have the feeling that there must be some basic principle that could help solve the knotty problems we are wrestling with.

This feeling is an essential and basic motivation of all thinking people and has been in the mind of man from time immemorial. The ancient Persians felt it when they looked up at the stars and attempted to determine some rule for describing their erratic courses. The astronomer Brahe was similarly motivated when he brought together all the massive data concerning the movement of the stars and planets. So was Keppler as he carried on and worked these data into his studies. But Newton came along with his development of the laws of gravity and the laws of motion before the underlying "law of the heavens" was understood—and he had to invent differential and integral calculus to do it.

. . . .

Article is condensed from American Management Association, *Operations Research: A Basic Approach*, Special Report No. 13, New York: 1956, pp. 7–10 and 12–19. Used with permission.

TRANSFER OF EXPERIENCE

This illustrates a fundamental point in operations research that should be brought out early: The experience of a scientist in one field is quite often directly translatable to the totally alien work of a scientist in another field. This transfer, which has quite often led to the use of mixed terms, suggests that the fruits of scientific labor are also translatable into the problems of business operations.

One problem of long standing in scientific research has been this matter of communication between fields of knowledge and the derivation of fundamental laws across all fields. For example, the original work of Darwin has been found to contain data that would have permitted the discovery of the Mendelian principles. However, it remained for the historians to discover this fact, since the scope and experience of Darwin himself did not include the mathematical-statistical insights that Mendel was able to bring to the problem.

Similarly, much of the work that engineers and scientists have done in extensive research activities over the past decade has provided us with new tools and new methodologies that, given proper translation, can be applicable to analysis of business problems.

BODY OF ANALYSIS TECHNIQUES

It has been truly stated that "no war, no strike, no depression can so completely destroy an established business or its profits as new and better methods, equipment, and materials in the hands of an enlightened competitor." Operations research is essentially such a new and better method in the analysis of business operations. However, this new and powerful body of analysis techniques which has been developed over the past 15 years is often cloaked in the formidable language of mathematics; thus the basic approach is often obscured.

As an organized endeavor, operations research originated in England about 1939 as a basis for involving the location of English interception radar. By 1942, the techniques had achieved wide acceptance by top British military planners. The United States soon found, after its entry into the war in 1941, that a similar scientific approach was necessary in the planning of Army, Air Force, and Navy operations. Such projects as improving patterns of search activities for submarines, evaluating equipment performance, and establishing bombing patterns for most effective and efficient attack were undertaken.

In the late 1940's, industry became interested in operations research, and experimentation was undertaken in some of our larger companies. Its extension has been on the increase during the past several years.

AN OVERALL DEFINITION

Definitions of new areas of activity are generally not fruitful avenues of discussion. This is particularly true of operations research, where scientists are prone to argue at great length concerning a precise meaning. The problem is further compounded by the relative immaturity and newness of operations research, which makes any particular definition exact for only an instant of time. At this point in the history of its development, operations research is an attitude, an approach, a concept. It takes new shape each day.

For our purposes, an overall, rather than a specific, definition will be most appropriate. Thus:

Operations research is a scientific methodology—analytical, experimental, quantitative—which, by assessing the overall implications of various alternative courses of action in a management system, provides an improved basis for management decisions.

This definition is given more meaning if we consider basic characteristics of the operations research approach. These characteristics may be listed as follows:

1. Operations research is concerned with the problems of business operations as a system.
2. Operations research utilizes the scientific method in that it is analytical, experimental, and quantitative.
3. Operations research borrows successful methodologies from all the various branches of science.
4. The operations research approach almost invariably involves model building, which is fundamental to the scientific approach. There are many types of models—simulation, mathematical, physical.
5. An operations research study almost invariably involves predicting the effects of alternate courses of action.

Operations research utilizes successful techniques wherever they are found. The professional approaches employed in engineering, mathematics, statistics, physics, economics, and biology have all been found useful in operations research projects. In fact, the use of these various professional disciplines is so widespread that there is a strong inclination for a person to see in operations research those elements with which he is familiar. This often leads him to define operations research in the terms of his own profession. "We have been doing these things for years" is a characteristic remark.

IMPACT OF OPERATIONS RESEARCH

There are four major areas that have been penetrated to some extent by operations research: military, industrial, academic, and consulting.

Operations research has to date found its greatest use and development in the *military services*. It is well-developed activity in each of the service branches and is being expanded continuously into various operating units. Military operations research applications with business situation parallels have been concerned with such typical problems as:

What kinds of weapons and how many of each should the military have in order to accomplish its objective at lowest cost?

How can the Army best allocate each budgetary dollar allowance among its various activities?

How can the Army best deploy troops and weapons in a given situation to place it in the position of greatest line gain?

.   .   .   .

METHODOLOGY: PRINCIPAL TECHNIQUES

Operations research seeks to discover regularities in apparently unrelated or random activities. In this research, existing techniques of analysis in many fields of science are drawn upon; and new techniques, peculiar to operations research, are being developed and refined by basic researchers.

The pattern of regularity is generally represented as a "model," which is often mathematical in nature. Certain typical situations, repeatedly met, have inspired development of typical models, or techniques, for solution. Some of the more well-known techniques may be listed as follows:

1. Linear programming.
2. Queueing theory.
3. Game theory.
4. Search theory.

5. Symbolic logic.
6. Information theory.
7. Value theory.

Perhaps a simple example (which can scarcely be viewed as highlevel opsearch) will illustrate the main points of the operations research approach.

An abrasive manufacturing company owned seven warehouses, of varying capacities, at widely spread locations. In May, 1953, its single plant was totally destroyed by fire. The problem arose as to whether to rebuild at the present location or seek a location that would make the most effective use of the existing warehouses. The solution of this problem was aided by borrowing the center-of-gravity technique from physics.

In Figure 1, we have a physical representative of our problem. In the center is the old plant, which has burned to the ground. The seven warehouses are labeled with the letters A through G, inclusive; these will remain as located. In the lower left-hand corner, we have noted the plant output required, on a monthly basis, for each warehouse. Our problem is to balance out the distribution pattern so that our new plant will be located in such a way as to provide minimum distribution costs.

The objective, therefore, is to minimize the freight charges. It has been found that, under certain conditions, a satisfactory approximation in determining our ideal plant location is given by the following equations, in

564

which we assume that the *rates are equal in all directions* and that *all routes have approximately the same divergence from the straight line:*

$$x = \frac{x_aA + x_bB + x_cC + x_dD + x_eE + x_fF + x_gG}{A + B + C + D + E + F + G}$$

$$y = \frac{y_aA + y_bB + y_cC + y_dD + y_eE + y_fF + y_gG}{A + B + C + D + E + F + G}$$

These equations may be referred to as a model of our problem. The solution, using the values from Figure 1, puts our new plant at $x - 5$, $y = 7$.

This example, of course, is greatly simplified by reduction to a single variable—distance. If we desire to bring in other variables, such as freight rates, time of service rates, and so on, it obviously becomes more complicated and the solution may be affected accordingly.

Linear Programming

The center-of-gravity technique, which we have just discussed, is only a method of illustrating the approach that is made to problem solution. Generally, more refined methods will be required to handle the more complex problems found in real life. Linear programming is such a method, and may be best defined as a technique for determining the optimum allocation, or use, of limited resources to achieve some desired objective. The resources may be defined as the money a company has available for use, the plant or individual machine capacity, the advertising budget, and so forth; the desired objective may be the lowest cost or highest profit possible resulting from the way in which the resources are used.

The characteristics of the linear programming techniques must be considered as to their limitations on the problem solution. First, they assume, for the most part, that a linear or straight-line relationship exists among the variables. Second, the limits of variation must be fairly well established. Third, the volume of calculations that must be performed is often so extensive that an electronic computer is essential.

Linear programming has been applied to:

1. Lower distribution costs from factories to warehouses.
2. Provide better utilization of production facilities.
3. Provide a better method for sales planning.
4. Provide improved price-volume relationships.
5. Determine a better product mix.

Perhaps a simple example will illustrate the nature of a linear programming problem, though not the nature of the detailed solution.

A sugar-refining company had three factories and four warehouses, all geographically separated. A problem existed as to the proper utilization of production and storage facilities in order to achieve minimum freight costs in shipping the finished product from the three factories to the four warehouses. The opsearch unit of the consultants employed to solve this problem used linear programming to obtain an answer.

FIGURE 1
EXAMPLE OF CENTER OF GRAVITY ANALYSIS

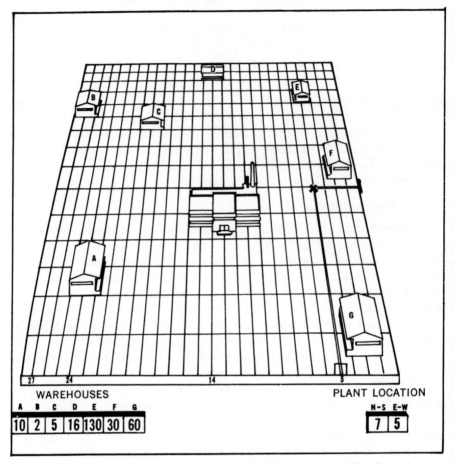

Figure 2 is a graphic representation of the problem. The factories are shown in Roman numerals I to III, and the warehouses are lettered *A* through *D*. If we assume that we can "allocate" the production of any of the factories to any of the warehouses, we may draw the arrowed lines shown. The block in the lower left-hand corner indicates the rates or cost of shipping one unit of output from a given factory to a given warehouse. The bottom row, with the numbers 5, 60, 40, and 105, represents the capacity in terms of production units for each of the three plants. This totals 105. The fourth row with the numbers 35, 10, 35, 25, and 105, represents the requirements for shipments of each of the warehouses on the same unit-of-time basis. Our problem is to allocate the plant capacities (that is, the production) to the warehouses so that we satisfy their requirements and minimize shipping costs.

The block in the lower right-hand corner of Figure 2 represents the solution to this problem. The numbers shown indicate the optimum allocation of production to the warehouses. If this plan were followed, the minimum cost of shipping would be realized.

Linear programming is one of the most powerful and broadly used techniques in the opsearch kit, but some difficulties arise in its use. It is important always to recognize the limitations of the model. The work involved in establishing the necessary equations is usually a task for a well-trained opsearcher, and the technique and solutions sometimes require inspired improvisation. A further limitation of the method occurs when the variables cannot be considered linear. There is, however, considerable work under way to expand the basic technique to more generalized problems and to simplify the mechanics. Linear programming promises to be a standard tool for a long time to come.

FIGURE 2

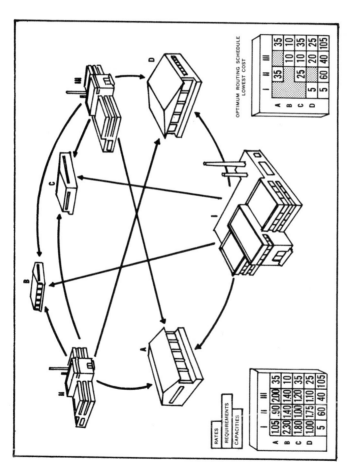

Queueing Theory

Queueing theory develops the relationships that are involved in waiting in line. Customers awaiting service, planes waiting to land, machines

567

awaiting the repair crew, items of a production line awaiting inspection—all are typical of the problems that may be approached by the methods of queueing theory.

For an example—an electric company decided to build a factory for the manufacture of television sets. Management could and did define the required plant capacity. However, a problem existed as to the best balance, in terms of cost, between the assembly lines and the servicing operation where the sets were tested and aligned. In other words, it was necessary to minimize the formation of costly stack-ups of unserviced sets or the improper utilization of service capacities. The consulting firm called on to assist in the solution of this problem used the queueing-theory approach to come up with the estimate of cost balance involved (Figure 3).

The television sets—all requiring alignment checks and, often, more lengthy service—are shown progressing down the final assembly line. They are moved to the service area for checking. When there are several unusually troublesome sets in a row, the servicing capacity is temporarily exceeded, and a pile-up of sets awaiting service occurs. The problem is that of figuring out the cost of total waiting—that is, the cost of tolerating the "queue" or the stack of goods shown in Figure 3 and balancing this cost against the cost of building enough service capacity to lessen the likelihood of the "queue."

Applications of queueing theory have shown great power in explaining the rational behavior of many important "waiting" situations. However, applications have been technically restricted by the relatively limited development of basic theory. The ability to handle more complex and generalized situations promises to be of ever-increasing importance but is growing very slowly. For the moment, the use of queueing theory is best left to the professional analyst.

Game Theory

The study of competition between two main factions establishes a mathematical model that can be manipulated for the purpose of determining one player's best strategy and most likely gain. So far, this technique and its application have been developed chiefly by the military, although some work has been done in applying game theory to the timing of advertising.

Search Theory

The study of minimizing the effort required to locate an object—or search theory—arose chiefly from the military problem of locating enemy submarines with limited detection resources. To date, it has had a very limited application to specialized marketing situations.

Symbolic Logic

The algebra of logic substitutes symbols for words, propositions, classes of things, or functional systems. There have been only faltering attempts to apply this technique to business problems; however, it has had

FIGURE 3

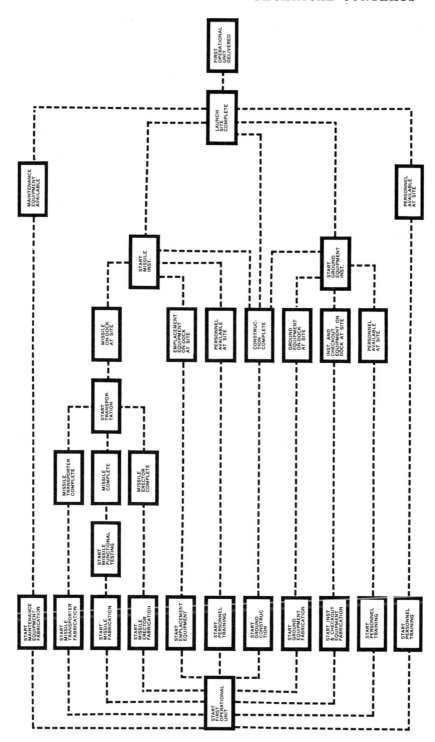

extensive implications in the logical design of computing machinery.

Information Theory

An analytical process transferred from the electrical communications field to operations research presumes to evaluate the effectiveness of information flow within a given system. Despite its application mainly to communications networks, it has had an indirect influence in stimulating the examination of business organizational structures with a view to improving information or communication flow.

Value Theory

Value theory is a process of assigning numerical significance to the worth of alternative choices. To date, this has been only a theoretical concept, and is in the status of elementary model formulation and experimentation. When and if developed, this technique should be most helpful in assessing the worth of the various conclusions in the decision-making process.

THE MANAGEMENT SIDE OF PERT

Ivars Avots

No management technique has ever caused so much enthusiasm, controversy, and disappointment as PERT. Within the past two years PERT or, to use its full name, Program Evaluation and Review Technique, developed originally for the United States Navy as part of the Polaris program as a mathematical method for defining the minimum time for completion of a complex project, has moved from the realm of production theory to the solid status of becoming a contract requirement in the nation's major defense programs.

It has also entered the business world where it is referred to not only as PERT but sometimes as "network analysis" and "critical path planning," depending upon the industry in which it is employed. Specific aspects of PERT theory have become items of controversy and concern in management circles. In addition, hundreds of thousands of dollars have been spent only to find in some cases that a given approach to PERT was not feasible within the context in which its use was planned.

What are the reasons which have caused PERT to make an impact unlike that of any other management technique? What has management learned about the application and limitations of this technique? What can be expected of PERT in the future? These are some of the questions managers need answered if they are to avoid the cost of experimentation. This article attempts to provide these answers with particular attention to problems of implementation on large programs.

PERT burst upon the management horizon in 1958 when it became part of the Polaris program. It was developed by the firm of management consultants, Booz, Allen & Hamilton for the Navy in order to coordinate the thousands of activities and individual processes required to bring to completion the complex project of creating a missile which could be fired under water.

The Air Force also adopted this technique. Its initial name for this program was PEP (Program Evaluation Procedure). Now it uses the same terminology as the Navy for its program evaluation technique. In the construction industry this method of networking time and procedures is called the Critical Path Method.

Despite the dissimilarity in nomenclature, all perform essentially the same logistical function of getting each of the components of a complex procedure completed at the precise time and delivered to the exact proper

Reprinted from the *California Management Review*, Vol. IV, No. 2, Winter 1962. Copyright 1962 by the Regents of the University of California.

place to be smoothly integrated into the final fabrication and launching of the product. The obvious advantages of such a technique, its streamlining of production, its essential tidiness and economy, its promise of optimum use at all times of men and material have made it a "natural" for business use wherever and whenever practicable. It is these very factors which have contributed to management's enthusiasm for PERT and also provided background for some of its controversies.

Foremost among them is the change in basic management philosophy which characterizes PERT against other management techniques. While it is true that considerable attention has been given in their day to bar charts, improvement curves, and other techniques, all of these were deterministic in nature. Planning resulted in a static system against which status was measured.

Introduction of PERT suddenly brought a change in traditional management thinking. The new technique did not look forward to meeting a schedule, but accepted uncertainty as part of the system. The effects of this change can be identified both in the enthusiasm for the technique as well as in resistance to it. Both conditions are often observed side by side even within the same organization.

THE SELLING POINTS OF PERT

Writers in technical publications have cited a complete line of selling points for the PERT technique. High on the list is the system's ability to predict the impact of schedule status. While other systems record status at a given time and require separate analysis to determine its effect on program objectives, PERT readily provides this information.

Moreover, PERT is primarily an analytical planning rather than a control method, and therefore does not suffer from the stigma associated with some management control techniques. In fact, as much as 60 percent of the benefits of PERT have been ascribed to its planning function rather than to its use as a control media.

This is because PERT forces integration of planning and thereby shows significant benefits even before it is used as a control tool. In the control area, PERT format cuts across organizational lines, eliminating the effect of defensive interpretation of reports along the lines of responsibility. At the same time, however, activities selected for the network usually recognize changes in responsibility and form the basis for positive control.

PREDICTIVE QUALITY

As a background for our discussion of PERT limitations, let us take a closer look at each of these selling points. Four features of the PERT technique give it the unique predictive quality which is not shared by other management control techniques. They are:

Critical path analysis
Program status evaluation
Slack determination
Simulation

A typical PERT network is shown in Figure 1. The critical path is the longest series of activities which must be performed from the beginning to the end of the network. Obviously, there can be more than one critical path for a program, and, depending on the completion status of individual activities, the critical path may change.

THE CRITICAL PATH

The advantage of the critical path is not only the fact that it permits determination of the effects of any schedule delays on program completion, but it also brings into use the exception principle focusing management attention to those areas where schedule maintenance is critical. When problems arise, critical path analysis highlights the areas where action must be taken to maintain overall program schedule.

As work progresses and status information is obtained, the PERT technique shows the time required to reach any event in the network. Together with the critical path analysis, this feature permits rapid evaluation of program status. Considering the fact that the status information can be integrated from a large number of sources and cover various levels of program effort, benefits to management can be quite significant.

TIME TRADE-OFF

Time estimates are assigned to the activities in a PERT network on the basis of normal manpower assignment and resource allocation. When compared to the concurrent critical path, some activities require less time and therefore possess a certain amount of slack. Listing of activities having slack identifies the area of effort where trade-off in time, resources, or technical performance may improve the schedule along the critical path.

At any time during the program, the effect of proposed schedule changes can be easily simulated by the computer. This feature permits management to examine detail activities, especially those critical to the program, for possible adjustments resulting in schedule or cost improvement.

ANALYTICAL PLANNING METHOD

Observers have rightfully noted that for maximum benefits PERT application must start during or before the planning phase of a new program. The major reason for this is the fact that networking forces integration of planning and helps to discover innumerable conditions which, in a complex program, may easily be overlooked.

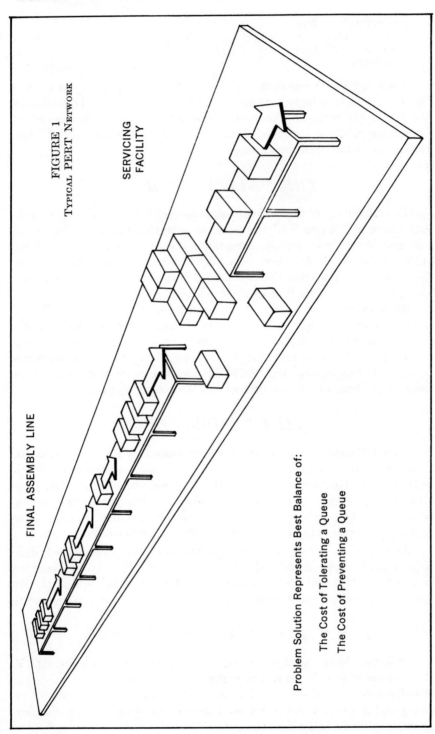

FIGURE 1
TYPICAL PERT NETWORK

FINAL ASSEMBLY LINE

SERVICING
FACILITY

Problem Solution Represents Best Balance of:

The Cost of Tolerating a Queue

The Cost of Preventing a Queue

The PERT network consists of a series of interrelated symbols representing principal events and activities in a program. An event is shown by a box and an activity is indicated by a line or arrow connecting events. When time estimates are assigned to activities, it is possible to compute the critical path of the program, as well as identify activities which have slack time. These may be extended without affecting program schedules.

Traditional program planners are usually skeptical about any benefits the PERT technique may give them, and quite often there is open antagonism on their part to use of the technique. They maintain that phasing charts and master schedules have been refined to a point where they can sufficiently cover the programming of complex efforts.

However, in some cases where PERT has been applied to a going program, the planning incompatibilities which have been detected have staggered even the proponents of the technique. As a result of networking, one defense manufacturer found that the existing plan called for placing of two missiles on the same launcher on the same day.

PERT has pointed out beyond any doubt the serious weaknesses of traditional scheduling methods when applied to a program such as major missile development, manufacture, and test. In a PERT network, where each event must be preceded and followed by another event, complex relationships and interdependencies can be identified. It is the discipline of planning logic required to develop a network which forces a planner to take a new look at his task, and in the process, opens to him significant new horizons.

POSITIVE CONTROL

In its entirety, a PERT network normally covers a program from its inception to at least the completion of the first article. Unlike schedules which tend to be related to organizational responsibilities, the network cuts across organizational lines. One week, the design group may be in the line of critical path, another week the line may have shifted, and the test group may be pacing the schedule. Whatever the case, management can readily identify the problem areas and initiate corrective action.

Although the network approach puts emphasis on the total program rather than particular elements, it should be remembered that if the network is sufficiently detailed, each of these elements, described by events and activities, can often be related to a functional organization or even a budget number.

NETWORKING

To permit this, events selected for a network must include those events which represent a change in responsibility for activities within the network. In other words, each activity needs to be identified with a particular organization. By comparison of actuals with activity estimates, the performance of each group can be evaluated, and causes for schedule difficulties can be pinpointed to responsible organizations.

Another contribution and selling point which cannot be overlooked results from the fact that networking requires adoption of positive and unambiguous definitions of all events and activities. Getting everybody in a large organization to talk the same language can be a difficult task, and if this can be accomplished as a side effect of PERT networking, it certainly deserves consideration.

Early in the development of PERT, statisticians recognized that although the technique was superior to existing flow and bar charting techniques for program planning and control, it had basic mathematical weaknesses. They also recognized that because of these weaknesses, careful decisions would have to be made as to the scope and method of application of the technique.

This recognition is well illustrated by the present PERT applications in the Boeing Company. Dictated by specific program characteristics and customer requirements, the applications on Minuteman, Dyna-Soar, and Bomarc programs are basically different in their approach and coverage, highlight different problems of application, and also show different degrees of success.

LIMITATIONS OF PERT TECHNIQUE

Some of the limitations of PERT application are very rudimentary. For example, because of its "time to completion" variable, PERT cannot be used when it is not possible to estimate the occurrence of events. This is true of any project in which there is a reasonable expectancy that a break-through in the state-of-the-art may change the sequence of events at any given stage of development. Alternate routes or paths are therefore required, both of which need to be followed to a point of no return.

Similarly, PERT cannot be used on activities which are under a recurring cycle, such as in manufacturing. PERT networks usually stop with the completion of the first production article at which point the traditional scheduling techniques or the line-of-balance method takes effect. This range of applicability is very real, and should be kept in mind throughout development of a PERT program.

MILITARY PROJECT EXPERIENCE

From the standpoint of limitations, it is of particular interest that PERT has never been implemented on a total weapon system. For example, on the Polaris program, certain portions were networked and reported on, but the Navy concedes that at no time did a total Fleet Ballistic Missile System network exist. The reasons for this are several:

1. *Accuracy of the Model.* The network model does not yield itself to the incorporation of computer checks, and there is no known method for verification of the logic of a network. For this reason, accuracy of the network depends on the process of preparing it. In practice, network development involves cycling through computer runs, progressive evaluation, and detection of possible inaccuracies, followed by revisions.

2. *Data Handling.* When network size exceeds approximately 5,000 events, it becomes difficult to maintain the purity of computer input and quick system response. A large number of events means that a large

number of people are involved in the processing of network data. Consequently, the exposure to error becomes greater. Time required for the PERT cycle also increases.

3. *Computing Large Networks.* Experience shows that it is almost impossible to manually calculate networks larger than 700 events. Therefore, larger networks, such as those for a major weapon system, require a computer. The number of events which can be economically handled by the computer depends on the amount of data which the computer can process in high-speed memory without extensive use of magnetic tapes. For example, the IBM 7090 computer has a storage capacity of 32,000 words. This capacity provides for approximately 10,000 activities or events. When networks exceed this size, it is necessary to utilize magnetic tape storage. Use of magnetic tape considerably increases the required number of computer passes and the associated cost.

4. *Summarization and Integration.* Large networks are awkward to handle. There is no known method for summarization or reducing the size of a network to a smaller equivalent net. Also, it is difficult to automatically assemble separate networks into a master network and compute it. This can be accomplished only through a special computer program and extensive cross-referencing.

5. *Reporting.* As the size of networks increases, the technique of translating computer outputs into management information becomes more difficult. Theoretically, network outputs identify problem areas as well as indicate where trade-offs in resources may be desired. While this information can be visualized when networks are small, reporting techniques have not been developed to the extent that similar use can be made of large networks. This factor limits PERT as a management tool on major programs.

PERT AS A MANAGEMENT PROBLEM

The nature and the far-reaching effects of the limitations of the PERT technique are such that the total problem cannot be left to the program planner or to an operations research man. Any large scale implementation of the technique has to follow careful analysis and soul searching and demands careful attention from top management.

Even when a company is required to adopt PERT by the military customer, it is necessary to keep an objective view point. For example, a degree of enthusiasm would help to accelerate the application of network analysis to routine projects, such as installation of a piece of machinery, design of a generator, or construction of a building. However, it would be foolish to use the same approach to a major weapon system. When exercised apart from experience and existing knowledge of limitations, enthusiasm may cause unsound PERT applications which result in unnecessary cost, adverse psychological effect, and possible delay in the implementation of a workable PERT system.

MUST RIDE HERD ON IT

The limitations also make it obvious that active adaptation of PERT in any company will cause a considerable amount of developmental research in the technique and may result in the support of particular approaches by various parts of the organization. For this reason, especially if the company is large, PERT is not a technique which, like most management techniques, can be turned over to the departments for implementation. It requires continuous top management attention and guidance during the implementation period.

If this is not done, time and effort are lost when several departments attempt to solve similar problems, and the situation is even more serious when, upon implementation, it is discovered that the system will not work in total or includes portions which are incongruous with the overall system. Top management attention is also important if the use of PERT techniques is required by a military customer or a major military prime contractor. In this case, definitive policy is required regarding the level of detail which will be effectively reported under the system.

Top management involvement in PERT is not restricted to overall guidance and policy formulation. Whenever more than one PERT application takes place in a company, certain technical problems immediately become apparent which need overall coordination. For example, the events in a PERT network can be numbered serially, sequentially, or at random. Computer programs are in existence to handle a network of each type. However, once a particular computer program is adapted by a company, it becomes impractical to introduce variations for each internal application. It should be easy to issue a company policy prescribing the use of a particular numbering system; however, such action would not solve the technical problem.

Major PERT networks may be tied into similar networks at other companies and selected data submitted in card form to military services which have their own PERT staffs. Unless the numbering systems are compatible, application of the technique will result in large workload and undue increase in cost. Unless top management is ready to assist subordinates and outside organizations to come to mutually acceptable terms, there will be disagreement, wasted effort, and an unfavorable impression on involved parties outside the company. Typical of the PERT technical problems, on which management attention will continue to be centered, are matters of system networking, scheduling, and reporting to management. Here are some of the facts concerning each of these problems.

SYSTEM NETWORKING

The usual approach to PERT on a major program starts with an overall master network. However, some people feel that this network may never be computed, and would serve primarily as a map for the selection of critical functional or subsystem areas in which detail networks would be developed. The critical path would be computed from the detail networks after practically all elements of the program have been covered. The master network would be adjusted as more definitive information becomes available in the detail networking process.

Another approach, sponsored mainly by the Boeing Company, takes the viewpoint that critical program areas cannot always be determined from a broad master network without actually computing a critical path. If functional areas are selected and networked in detail, interfaces between such functional networks are not readily apparent and integration of such networks may be extremely difficult. Even if integration is accomplished, such networks may not yield correct results and yet, because of the inability to check the network's logic, the computations have to be taken at face value.

An alternative approach recommended by the proponents of this viewpoint is to expand the master network in subsystem areas only and to use the master network for all computations. While such network would not have detail coverage in specific critical areas, it is believed to give a more dependable picture of the overall program.

Although PERT was developed basically as a planning and control tool, attempts have also been made to use it as a scheduling technique. Theoretically, PERT networks are a convenient base for preparation of bar charts and detail schedules. Networking should precede any bar charting of the program from the top down and may, in fact, eliminate the need for more bar charts and master schedules. When networks are established at proper detail, they can be used for end-to-end scheduling.

PERT AS SCHEDULING TECHNIQUE

While this theoretical approach is feasible on relatively simple programs, it breaks down when the complexity of the program is large, as in the case of major missile efforts. To utilize PERT as a scheduling tool on a complex program would require networking of hundreds of thousands of activities. Even at our advanced stage in computer technology, it is not practical to handle such vast networks. As the pressures arise to include more and more detail into the networking effort, management must recognize the limitations of the technique and draw a line.

A definition as to what PERT application should accomplish must be made and the level of detail to which the technique should be extended must be outlined. The Boeing Company, which unsuccessfully tried the scheduling approach on its Dyna-Soar program, has come to the conclusion that in the present state of development, PERT techniques cannot be used for detailed scheduling of large programs, and their application to such programs should be limited to planning and control purposes.

REPORTING TO MANAGEMENT

The principal objective of PERT reports is to call management attention to situations requiring decisions and action. In small, manually computed networks, status information can be reflected on a bar chart or some other easily visualized form. When larger programs are covered, the reporting output necessarily is in machine printout form which does not have the visibility required for analysis.

The situation is almost paradoxical since large programs which demand quick action by top managers, necessarily generate a greater amount of reporting paper. Since there is no method to summarize networks automatically, the process of extracting data, analyzing and then displaying these data requires progressive evaluation and permits some defensive interpretation along the way.

THE BIG PICTURE

In approaching any of these problems, management must avoid focusing on a small number of exceptions and give all its attention to the workability of the total program. It should always be kept in mind that one of those features which makes PERT excel over other techniques is the fact that it cuts across organization lines and looks at the total program. Detail logic and accuracy may have to be overlooked in order to arrive at a workable PERT program. The network should not be expected to be perfect in every detail to make it complete. As a mathematical model, the network should be sufficiently true to reality to yield practical solutions through exercise of its predictive quality.

COST OF PERT

Extensive application of PERT techniques obviously is expensive. Skilled technical personnel are required to plan networks, and engineering and operating men must take time to explain activities to planners and to make time estimates. Data processing and computer costs are impressive, to say the least.

The Special Projects Office of the Navy estimated it cost them $200,000 a year in computer time to conduct bi-weekly analyses of the Polaris program. While one contractor has priced its contractual PERT requirements at $300,000, other firms feel that PERT can replace a portion of the traditional planning tasks and that very little additional cost is involved.

This, of course, depends on the complexity of the program and the level of detail which may be handled within the limitations discussed earlier. The Air Force has estimated that PERT costs average 0.5 percent of total cost on research and development programs and 0.1 percent of total major programs generally.

Less Costly Than Coffee Breaks

In one instance, the Air Force found that engineering time consumed in contractor's PERT activity was less than a fourth of the time authorized for coffee breaks. This does not sound like much, however, just ten minutes per engineer per day amounts to over $300,000 a year when applied to one of the major missile programs.

To date, insufficient consideration has been given to the costs of large scale PERT applications. There is no doubt that only small applications can claim to offset these costs with savings in planning and scheduling. It is also true that on some programs, especially in construction, critical path planning can yield immediate tangible savings. For example, the Catalytic Construction Company credits network planning with a 25 percent reduction in cost on an $800,000 project. In most applications of PERT, however, the dollar savings are not quite so tangible. Costs, nevertheless, are real and should be considered in determining an optimum level of application for PERT.

OUTLOOK FOR PERT

During the first two years of PERT, discussions on the subject were limited to the technical journals and companies where the technique was being applied. Early in 1961, the technique suddenly emerged as a major selling point of several management consultants. Courses on the subject were announced. American Management Association organized a briefing seminar, and the Aerospace Industries Association formed a PERT task group.

The Department of Defense initiated efforts to achieve some standardization in PERT requirements of the military services. All these activities affected the growth of the technique, shaking out some of the marginal features, such as three time estimates and computation of variance, and advancing the extension of PERT to resource factors.

Resource Incorporation

Incorporation of resource factors, especially cost and manpower is currently the immediate problem in PERT development. From a theoretical standpoint, resource incorporation is not a serious problem. However, the issue becomes clouded when the methods of data collection and assignment to activities come under consideration.

To begin with, introduction of resource factors will further limit computer capacity and the number of events which can be economically processed. Resource application, therefore, will be more easily accomplished on some programs than on others. For example, programs differ in the desired level of detail in cost estimating and collection. If the networks were to be maintained at a gross level, the major problem in cost incorporation may well be that of identifying existing accounts with activities in the network, rather than assigning new account numbers to activities.

Until the problems of planning and control nature are successfully solved in PERT applications to large programs, the incorporation of costs, manpower, reliability, etc., cannot take place. These factors should be incorporated only on smaller networks where PERT technology has been sufficiently developed.

General Systems Theory Needed

From a long-range standpoint, the potential of PERT extends even beyond resource incorporation. In the past few years, both industry and government have recognized a growing need for a general systems theory which would consolidate the existing scientific management methods and thereby extend the field of management sciences. Russell D. Archibald of Hughes Aircraft Co. has pointed out that PERT may be an important step toward the development of such a theory, at least in the area of project-type programs. When all business is viewed as a system of interrelated and integrated systems and subsystems, PERT networking technique can serve as one of the necessary catalytic agents.

PERT'S WEAKNESSES

The PERT technique is a logical refinement of planning and control techniques. Its theory is deceivingly simple, and the potential appears unlimited. Experience, however, has shown definite limitations of the technique, particularly in regard to application on large programs. Because of the initial success on military contract applications and the enthusiasm over the technique by the military services, PERT has permeated industry at an accelerated rate. As a result, application of the technique has in some cases resulted in disappointment. This has been a reflection of overenthusiasm, lack of sufficient experience, and the basic weaknesses in the technique when applied to large programs.

PERT'S STRENGTHS

Generally, PERT is a superior system for (a) integration of planning, (b) rapid evaluation of program status, (c) identification of potential trouble spots, and (d) reallocation of resources. In its application to large programs, it is one of the first computer techniques in the management field which not only processes data, but actually helps to make decisions. On small programs, it becomes a highly flexible management tool which does not require computer support.

ITS FUTURE IN MANAGEMENT

Until such time when PERT becomes as common as the bar chart, top management attention is required to coordinate those aspects of PERT which have management and broad technical implications. Experience gained in other companies must be translated in relation to the requirements of each new application, keeping in mind the limitations of applicability, size and accuracy of networks, technical approaches, and cost.

As the technique matures and further experimentation takes place, PERT can be expected to include elements of manpower distribution and cost. The resulting tie-in with operating budgets may bring management a decade closer to the overall control system which it has been seeking.

HOW TO APPLY SAMPLING IN VOUCHER EXAMINATIONS

Benjamin J. Mandel

Although Congress more than one year ago authorized Federal agencies to use statistical sampling procedures in approving vouchers for payment, provided economies or management improvements can be achieved thereby, relatively few agencies to date have taken advantage of this authority. Not unexpectedly to statisticians, Federal agencies have been finding that the task of developing sound sampling applications requires professional statistical knowledge and technical skills of a type not normally included in the training auditors receive to prepare them for their professional careers. Many auditors who would like to take advantage of scientific sampling procedures have been unable to do so simply because they lack the requisite statistical background.

Among the numerous questions auditors and their management superiors have raised regarding the efficient use of voucher sampling procedures are most importantly these five:

1. What size universe is needed to make statistical sampling worthwhile?
2. How does one go about determining whether sampling procedures will result in significant economies or management improvements?
3. Which of the several methods of statistical sampling would be most appropriate for a particular type of vouchers?
4. What size sample should be used?
5. How can a "voucher" be defined to make as many as possible eligible for sample audits within the $100 statutory limitation applicable to sampling procedures in voucher examinations?

These questions fortunately can be answered in terms applicable to all Federal agencies, for the problems agencies encounter in processing vouchers are generally similar. At least experience thus far in operating under the recent congressional statistical-sampling authorization tends to indicate that a general approach to voucher examination is feasible throughout the Federal Government. The following guidance is therefore premised on the concept that agencies can to advantage follow a general approach in making use of the recent sampling authority provided by Congress.

UNIVERSE SIZE

Despite the common belief that only a very large universe will make statistical sampling worthwhile, the universe measured in terms of number of

Article is from Benjamin J. Mandel, *The Federal Accountant*, Vol. 15 (Winter, 1965), pp. 75–87. Used with permission of publisher and author.

vouchers handled is a relatively minor factor in determining whether sampling procedures would be beneficial in any particular agency. Of much greater significance are the:

Current cost of completely auditing the "voucher universe."
Method of sampling.
Sample size.
Projected cost of auditing the universe of vouchers by sampling.

Before these factors can be evaluated, the "universe" of vouchers must be delineated in terms of "reporting units," their locations and time period. From a statistical standpoint, a universe is a collection of related reporting units distinguished by location but having a common time factor. In voucher examinations, because of specific statutory requirements as to evidential criteria and voucher amounts, each different type of voucher—travel, general, commercial and the like—could well be considered a reporting unit of a different universe. Once the specific reporting unit has been determined, in accordance with whatever criteria the agency may apply, the universe of which it is a part must be defined precisely in terms of the total number of reporting units eligible for sample audit.

Inasmuch as the statutory sampling authorization applies only to vouchers of less than $100 in amount, all vouchers of $100 or more must be excluded from the universe eligible for sampling. After this exclusion, the size of the universe still cannot be determined until the time span covered is specified. It should be recognized that the broader the time span over which management is willing to extend the analysis, the larger will be the universe and the greater the likelihood of cost reductions through sampling. In other words, even though vouchers are examined currently, the demonstrable savings likely will be larger if the analysis is extended over a full fiscal year rather than limited to merely one month.

Also to be determined is the location of the universe—that is, the place or places where the audit will be made. Centralized auditing can enlarge the universe and in some cases provide a more economical and more easily coordinated and controlled universe. On the other hand, decentralized auditing may have advantages of speed and facility in communicating with the source on items requiring clarification. The choice between centralized and decentralized auditing is probably best based on the findings of a well planned sampling feasibility study.

FEASIBILITY ANALYSIS

After the universe of interest and its reporting units are determined, the basic question still remains: When is sampling worthwhile? A very practical test of worthwhileness is, of course, the net savings that can be achieved by applying sampling techniques—facts best determined through a careful feasibility study. Feasibility analysis involves gathering data on the characteristics of the universe, the number and magnitude of errors, the causes of errors and costs of auditing. A one-month study, during which a complete voucher audit is made, is usually sufficient to provide guideline data, including:

> Data on the distribution of vouchers, and amounts involved, by dollar size of voucher.
> Data on the number of vouchers found to have errors in amount, with separate totals for "plus" errors and "minus" errors.

The study should also provide data on the nature and causes of these errors and on the time and cost to make a complete audit. This advance-study approach may delay somewhat the actual start of sampling but it has two very substantial advantages:

> *First,* it leads generally to a more efficient sampling plan and therefore to larger savings.
> *Second,* it provides valuable advance experience with sampling techniques.

For purposes of illustrating feasibility study techniques, there is assumed the following hypothetical distribution of 1,000 travel vouchers of less than $100 in amount:

Size of Voucher (amount)	Number of Vouchers	Percent of Total	Amount of Vouchers	Percent of Total
Under $25......	328	32.8	$ 5,700	11.4
$25 - 49........	345	34.5	15,750	31.5
$50 - 74........	222	22.2	17,150	34.3
$75 - 99........	105	10.5	11,400	22.8
Total........	1,000	100.0	$50,000	100.0

Arrangement of the universe into meaningful classes, in this instance by voucher size, is important in feasibility analysis because of the insight this procedure provides into the composition of the universe. A similar tabulation of travel vouchers $100 or more in amount would also be worthwhile, since this will provide data on the additional savings which would accrue to the agency under more comprehensive statutory authority for sampling than that now provided.

Each of the 1,000 vouchers in the universe being studied should be carefully audited in accordance with regular procedures and the various errors discovered should be recorded and tabulated according to voucher grouping and type of error. A summary of the 94 errors assumed discovered in the illustrative audit follows, classified as to overclaims and underclaims:

Size of Voucher	Number of Vouchers in Error			Dollar Magnitude of Errors				
	Total	Over-Claims	Under-Claims	Total	Percentage	Over-Claims	Under-Claims	Net
Under $25..	25	15	10	$13	13.0	$ 6	$ 7	$—1
$25 - 49....	18	9	9	17	17.0	15	2	+13
$50 - 74....	36	14	22	30	30.0	12	18	—6
$75 - 99....	15	8	7	40	40.0	18	22	—4
Total....	94	46	48	$100	100.0	$51	49	$+2

One of the key findings in this analysis is the overall error rate—94 ÷ 1000 or 9.4 percent. This rate signifies that 9.4 percent of all vouchers within the group contain some error in dollar amount. The error rate measured in terms of dollar amount is much smaller—$100 ÷ $50,000 or 0.2 of 1 percent on a gross basis and $2 ÷ $50,000 or 0.004 of 1 percent on a net basis. Since in any feasibility study the errors themselves should be analyzed, the following additional information is assumed with respect to these 94 vouchers found to contain errors:

DISTRIBUTION BY PROBABLE CAUSE OF ERROR

Probable Cause of Error	Number of Vouchers	Percent
Arithmetic	56	60.0
Missing proofs	19	20.0
Procedural misunderstanding	13	13.3
Rules and regulations	6	6.7
Total	94	100.0

DISTRIBUTION BY SIZE OF ERROR

Amount of Error	Number of Vouchers	Percent
Under $1	56	59.6
$1 - 4.99	30	31.9
$5 - 9.99	5	5.3
$10 and over	3	3.2
Total	94	100.0

These varied analyses in combination provide a comprehensive profile both of the travel-voucher universe and of the incidence of errors. From data of this type it is possible to (1) estimate the savings that can be expected from statistical sampling, (2) determine the size of sample to use, and (3) choose an efficient sampling method.

METHOD OF SAMPLING

In statistical sampling a common auditing rule provides excellent guidance: *Invest manpower and resources on those vouchers most prone to money errors and on those with the largest money error amounts, to maximize return on auditing effort.* Far from being novel, this rule is used by many industrial firms which apply statistical quality control and sampling inspection techniques to assure the quality of their products and services. On grounds of efficiency, there is little reason to doubt its general soundness in governmental auditing.

The basic data collected in the feasibility study thus should be analyzed to determine the money concentration points, the largest money error rates, error concentration points and error causes. To yield the largest payoff, the sample audit should be concentrated in these specific areas. In the language of statistical sampling, this audit concentration requires a

587

"stratified," or directed, sampling method based either on the largest-sized vouchers or largest money-error areas.

In the illustrative data, for example, vouchers in the $75-to-$99 class represent only about 10.5 percent of all vouchers eligible for sampling, yet account for 22.8 percent of the claimed reimbursement. It would appear worthwhile to concentrate voucher examination in this voucher class since the coverage is large relative to the investment. On the other hand, it would be a poor investment to examine many vouchers under $25—they constitute about a third of all vouchers eligible for sampling but account for only about one-tenth of the claimed reimbursement.

A similar "investment-type" analysis may be made from the data on gross dollar errors [previously] shown [in the overclaim-underclaim summary—ed.] since 40 percent of the total money error was found among vouchers in the $75-to-$99 class comprising only 10 percent of all eligible vouchers. Another 30 percent of the money errors was found among vouchers in the $50-to-$74 class, which includes 22 percent of all eligible vouchers. Either of these classes thus represents a good examination investment, but the same does not hold for voucher classes below $50.

Still another way of stratifying the vouchers is on the basis of *net* dollar errors, rather than gross dollar errors. This approach requires a policy determination on the use of *net* error amounts in sampling decisions. If the study findings were to prevail throughout the year, it would pay to audit completely all vouchers between $25 and $49 since, on this basis, net loss to the Government would be minimized. The illustrative study data shows that the complete audit of vouchers in this class resulted in the correction of net overclaims amounting to $13. If none of the remaining vouchers were audited, there would be a net gain of $11 to the agency. Should the feasibility findings prevail, this stratification basis would provide almost full assurance that the overpayment error would be zero dollars; actually, study experience would indicate that the agency could expect a net gain of $11 a month from not auditing these remaining vouchers plus an additional gain achieved in the form of reduced auditing cost.

These alternatives illustrate ways of planning a stratified sampling procedure geared to the rule of minimizing auditing costs and the over-payment error rate by maximizing the extent of correction of dollar errors. Other effective approaches can be developed in consultation with management. If individuals preparing vouchers for the first time are not fully acquainted with the rules and regulations of voucher preparation, for example, they may be the primary cause of money errors. A tabulation of vouchers according to the prior travel experience of the claimants would provide a stratification of vouchers whereby the agency could audit mostly vouchers prepared by individuals not fully acquainted with travel regulations and only a small sample of all remaining vouchers.

No reference has thus far been made to an attribute sampling procedure, a form of sampling which in this instance would be directed toward minimizing the error-rate in terms of *number* of vouchers having a money error. Since management interest is likely to focus on the curtailment of overpayments as a percentage of total payments made, this omission was deliberate. There would be relatively little management incentive to concentrate on minimizing the absolute number of voucher errors without regard to overpayments.

SIZE OF SAMPLE

It might be inferred from this discussion that the method of sampling automatically determines the proper or optimum size of sample. Sample size may be clearly indicated when the feasibility study shows definite dollar-error concentration points where the application of auditing manpower would be fruitful. In practice, the size of sample is often determined in part on this basis and in part on the basis of specific management objectives, particularly the level of overpayment errors management is willing to tolerate for purposes of economy. If none of the vouchers in the illustrative case situation had been audited, the gross overpayment error of $100 would have represented only about two-tenths of one percent of all payments made. Management under these circumstances might well conclude that a net saving many times this amount which would result from reduced examination costs, would justify a gross overpayment error-rate of two tenths of one percent. Without an audit, however, there would be no way of knowing whether the findings from the feasibility study still applied in current periods and no controls on a continuing basis would exist. In technical terminology, a zero sample audit provides no assurance and no management controls.

Some auditing is essential, if only for control purposes. An appropriate basis for determining sample size, when the overpayment error rate is within acceptable tolerance, is to include a "reasonable" number of vouchers from the stratum showing error-proneness and a small random sample of remaining vouchers. A sample so constituted will indicate whether the amount of overpayment remains within an acceptable limit on a continuing basis. Thus in the illustrative case, a random sample of from five to ten percent might be selected from the $75-to-$99 voucher class and about two percent from all remaining vouchers. This sampling plan would permit the detection and correction of errors and thus would reduce the overpayment error rate below what it would have been without any audit at all. At the same time management, from estimates derived from the sample, would know the prevailing dollar-error rate.

Should management decide to base sample size on *net* dollar errors, the basic data assembled in the feasibility study on the voucher universe and on errors discovered would be helpful in establishing an appropriate sample size. The illustrative data reflect a net overpayment of $2 or only four one-thousandths of one percent of all payments. Since the dollar errors discovered by audit run in both directions, the *net* dollar error is often likely to be much smaller than the *gross* dollar error. Under these circumstances, stratified sampling should enable the agency to stay close to the *net* overpayment amount while maintaining current controls and, as a practical matter, general judgment can appropriately be employed in determining sample size.

Size determination of the sample is fairly simple when dollar-error rates are small and fruitful auditing locations are clearly evident. If dollar-error rates are large and the feasibility study shows where the errors are concentrated, some form of stratified sampling procedure should be helpful in controlling errors. Sample size may be judgmentally determined, or if desired, a more refined approach may be used to determine sample size in consideration of the following basic elements:

> Overpayment error management is willing to accept for economy reasons
> Extent of variation in the universe of vouchers with dollar errors (measured by the percentage of variation)
> Amount of error management is willing to tolerate in the sample-based estimate of the overpayment error (measured by the relative sampling variation)
> Risk of exceeding the prespecified overpayment error amount (determined by the confidence level)

When sampling is used to estimate overpayment errors, there naturally is some risk of exceeding this acceptable error level but these elements can readily be built into a sample-size formula based on the feasibility study showing the distribution of errors according to error size.

The statistical concepts of "variation in the universe," "tolerable error," "sampling variation" and "risk" are frequently not altogether clear to the auditor and accountant and may warrant explanation. It is generally believed that all money errors will be detected in a complete audit, but this assumption is not always correct and requires verification. When a sample from a universe of vouchers is audited, the total of erroneous payments must be estimated on the basis of sample findings. If $100 in erroneous claims were discovered in a ten percent sample, for example, it might reasonable be concluded that in a complete audit ten times $100 or $1,000 of erroneous claims would have been discovered. The total overpayment error would then be estimated at $900—that is, $1,000 minus the $100 of errors found and corrected on the vouchers in the sample. This estimate, being based on a sample, is subject to sampling variations measurable by appropriate standard-error formulas.

It would be reassuring if the maximum range of sampling variation measured by standard formulas were never exceeded, but this assurance cannot be offered by statistical sampling. There is always some risk that this maximum variation may be exceeded and the sampler therefore must meet the specific level of risk acceptable to management. It should be recognized also that variation in a sample-derived estimate is heavily influenced by the extent of variation in the magnitude of dollar errors from voucher to voucher in the universe of vouchers and that sample size should reflect this element.[1]

MEASURING NET SAVING FROM SAMPLING

A major objective of a sampling feasibility study is to estimate the net savings that the agency would achieve from a sample audit as opposed to a complete audit. The basic formula for this purpose is:

1. Cost of making a complete audit, plus
2. Overpayments made even under a complete audit, less
3. Cost of making a sample audit, less also
4. Overpayments made under a sample audit.

Furnishing reasonably accurate amounts for the four elements in this formula requires careful work. The cost of a complete audit is often not known and therefore has to be developed as part of the feasibility study. If the cost of auditing a voucher in the hypothetical case study is assumed to be one dollar, the total cost of auditing all 1,000 vouchers being studied would be $1,000. The figures for the second factor may be deferred, at least initially, for the only way to measure the magnitude and direction of dollar errors in the voucher universe is to reaudit a sample of the auditors' determinations. While this factor is commonly believed to be zero, perfection cannot reasonably be expected in complex audit situations—even from fully trained auditors. Human errors due to temporary lapses, procedural deviations or misunderstandings do occur, but the effort required to measure these errors is not always warranted so long as it is recognized that the second factor in the savings formula is not necessarily zero. The remaining two factors in the savings formula usually present no particular difficulty.

The cost of auditing a sample of vouchers, rather than all vouchers, is readily determinable from the average cost per voucher applied to the sample number of vouchers to be audited. Since vouchers representing large claims may be more costly to audit on the average than small vouchers, an attempt should be made to use a differential unit cost figure wherever possible. If in the illustrative study all vouchers in the $75-to-$99 class plus 10 percent of all remaining vouchers were to be examined, the cost of auditing would be $195:

105 vouchers in the $75-to-$99 class @ $1 each $105
90 vouchers from the remaining voucher classes @ $1 each 90

Estimated cost of auditing the sample of vouchers. $195

---

[1] A suggested training program in these and other sampling concepts is outlined in "A Course in Statistical Sampling for Accountants, Auditors and Financial Managers," *The Accounting Review* (April, 1963); and in "A Method of Teaching Statistical Sampling to Accountants, Auditors and Financial Managers," *The Internal Auditor* (Summer, 1963).

The overpayment error under the sample audit can be estimated initially from the data compiled during the feasibility study, based on the chosen sampling method and sample size. In the illustrative data, gross dollar errors in the amount of $40 out of the discovered total of $100 presumably would have been found by auditing all vouchers in the $75-to-$99 class. If 10 percent of the remaining vouchers were audited, it may be assumed that 10 percent of the remaining dollar errors (10% of $60, or $6) would have been discovered. Thus, by audit of all vouchers in the $75-to-$99 class and 10 percent of the vouchers in other classes, a total of 195 vouchers would have been audited (105 plus 10% of 895 = 195) and a total of $46 out of the $100 in erroneous payments would have been detected and corrected, leaving undetected errors totaling $54. On this basis, the savings formula previously described would yield the following results:

$$\left(\begin{array}{c} \text{Net} \\ \text{Monthly} \\ \text{Savings} \end{array} \right) = \$1{,}000 + \left(\begin{array}{c} \text{An} \\ \text{Unknown} \\ \text{Amount} \end{array} \right) - \$195 - \$54 = \$751$$

MANAGEMENT PARTICIPATION IMPORTANT

Hopefully, agency management should find these guidelines useful in determining when—and how—to apply statistical sampling techniques to the prepayment audit of reimbursement vouchers. Whatever procedures are followed, high-level management participation is important in developing an effective sampling plan because management cannot avoid its responsibility to determine what error level is tolerable in agency operations. Management also should specify the risk it will accept of exceeding the tolerable amount when one of the more sophisticated sample designs must be used. Other important determinations which fall within the policy purview of management include:

> Whether decentralized audit units should be combined into a central auditing unit.
> Whether the universe of vouchers, for purposes of analysis of final results, should cover a full fiscal year or shorter periods.
> Whether the error-rate should be developed in terms of dollars or in terms of number of vouchers.
> Whether *gross* or *net* dollar results should be used in estimating net savings.

Of primary significance in these determinations is the need to conduct a feasibility study which helps in disclosing the points of concentration of dollar amounts, the rates of dollar error, the causes for error and auditing costs. From the study data, a sampling plan can be developed, based on a stratified grouping of vouchers by dollar amounts or other appropriate characteristics, to minimize dollar voucher errors with the smallest possible sample size. Stratification is in general accord with the sound audit approach of investing available manpower resources on vouchers most prone to the largest dollar errors in order to maximize the results achieved from the investment made.